W9-CCU-849

Fundamentals
of Management

Fundamentals of Management

STEPHEN P. ROBBINS
San Diego State University

MARY COULTER
Southwest Missouri State University

NANCY LANGTON
Sauder School of Business
University of British Columbia

PEARSON
Prentice Hall

Toronto

Library and Archives Canada Cataloguing in Publication

Robbins, Stephen P., 1943–
         Fundamentals of management / Stephen P. Robbins, Mary
Coulter, Nancy Langton.—5th Canadian ed.

Includes index.
Fourth Canadian ed. written by Stephen P. Robbins ... et [al.].

ISBN-13: 978-0-13-198879-8
ISBN-10: 0-13-198879-4

1. Management—Textbooks.   I. Coulter, Mary   II. Langton, Nancy
III. Title.

HD31.R5643 2007   658.4   C2006-904532-1

Copyright © 2008, 2005, 2002, 1999, 1996 Pearson Education Canada, a division of Pearson Canada Inc., Toronto, Ontario.

Pearson Prentice Hall. All rights reserved. This publication is protected by copyright and permission should be obtained from the publisher prior to any prohibited reproduction, storage in a retrieval system, or transmission in any form or by any means, electronic, mechanical, photocopying, recording, or likewise. For information regarding permission, write to the Permissions Department.

Original edition published by Pearson Education, Inc., Upper Saddle River, New Jersey, USA. Copyright © 2005 Pearson Education, Inc. This edition is authorized for sale only in Canada.

ISBN-13: 978-0-13-198879-8
ISBN-10: 0-13-198879-4

Editor-in-Chief: Gary Bennett
Acquisitions Editor: Karen Elliott
Executive Marketing Manager: Cas Shields
Developmental Editors: Su Mei Ku and Kelly Cochrane
Production Editor: Jen Handel
Copy Editor: Claudia Forgas
Proofreader: Kathleen Richards
Production Coordinator: Andrea Falkenberg
Composition: Joan M. Wilson
Photo and Permissions Research: Lisa Brant
Art Direction and Cover Design: Julia Hall
Interior Design: Miguel Acevedo
Cover Image: Stock Illustration Source

For permission to reproduce copyrighted material, the publisher gratefully acknowledges the copyright holders listed on page 439, as well as in the source lines throughout the text, which are considered extensions of this copyright page.

1 2 3 4 5   12 11 10 09 08

Printed and bound in United States of America.

BRIEF CONTENTS

CONTENTS

PART ONE
Defining the Manager's Terrain 2

PART TWO
Planning 66

CHAPTER 3
Planning and Strategic Management 66

CHAPTER 4
Decision Making 98

PART THREE
Organizing   128

CHAPTER 5
Organizational Structure and Design   128

CHAPTER 6
Communication and Information Technology   156

PART FOUR
Leading   220

PART FIVE
Controlling   306

PREFACE

Welcome to the fifth Canadian edition of *Fundamentals of Management*, by Stephen Robbins, Mary Coulter, and Nancy Langton. This edition introduces a new Canadian author to the project, Nancy Langton, and takes a fresh approach to management coverage through

- more relevant examples
- updated theory coverage
- a more pedagogically sound design.

The underlying philosophy in carrying out this revision was to put additional emphasis on the idea that "Management Is for Everyone." Students who are not managers, or who do not envision themselves as managers, do not always understand why studying management is important or relevant. We use examples from a variety of settings and have introduced a new end-of-chapter feature, *Management for You Today*, to help students understand the relevance of studying management for their day-to-day lives.

GENERAL CHANGES TO THE FIFTH CANADIAN EDITION

Our extensive reviews of the text told us that users want short chapters that balance theory and application in a way that makes material more relevant for student learning. In order to accomplish this, the authors have made numerous changes as described below.

Revised Main Chapter Material

- Shortened chapters to allow more focused theoretical and practical discussions
- Added more headings to guide the reader's attention
- NEW! Created new outcomes-based questions at the opening of each chapter to guide student learning. These questions are repeated at the start of each major chapter section to reinforce the learning outcome.
- NEW! *Think About It* questions at the end of the opening vignette for each chapter. These questions give students a chance to put themselves into the shoes of managers in various situations.

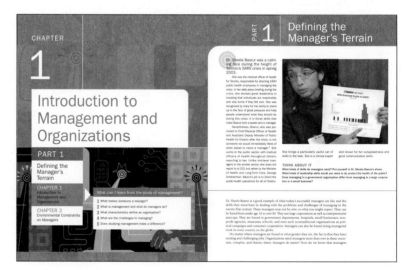

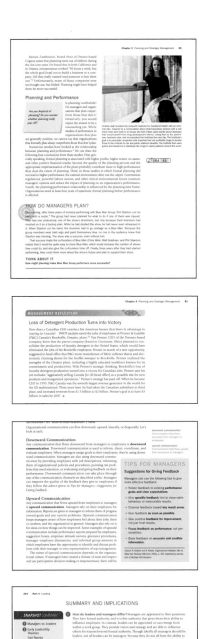

- NEW! Each major section of the chapter is introduced with a short management scenario that extends the opening vignette. Each of these is followed by an additional *Think About It* question.

- NEW! Integrated questions in the form of yellow notes throughout the chapters to help students relate management to their everyday lives

- NEW! Q&A icons throughout the chapters to enhance student learning. This feature anticipates questions that students might have about specific areas of management and refer students to the Q&A section on the enclosed Student CD-ROM.

- NEW! *Management Reflections*. These longer examples at appropriate places within chapters are designed to enhance student learning.

- NEW! *Tips for Managers*. This feature provides "take-aways" from the chapter—things that managers and would-be managers can start to put into action right now, based on what they have learned in the chapter.

- NEW! *Summary and Implications* provides responses to the outcomes-based questions identified at the beginning of each chapter. Accompanying this is a *Snapshot Summary* that provides a quick look at the organization of chapter topics.

- Eliminated all of the "boxiness" found in the design of the fourth Canadian edition. Readers have found these boxes to be distracting.

Introduced More Applications at the End of Each Chapter

We have created a new end-of-chapter section, *Management @ Work*, which includes more applications:

- *Reading for Comprehension*. Students can review their understanding of the chapter content.

- *Linking Concepts to Practice*. Students can see the application of theory to management situations.

- *Management for You Today*. Students can apply material to their daily lives, helping them see that planning, leading, organizing, and controlling are useful in one's day-to-day life too.

- *Self-Assessment Exercise.* Each chapter includes one self-assessment exercise that students can fill out, plus reference to the Student CD-ROM for additional relevant self-assessments.

- *Working Together: Team-Based Exercise.* Students get a chance to work together in groups to solve a management challenge.

- *Ethical Dilemma Exercise.* This feature gives students an opportunity to consider ethical issues that relate to chapter material.

- *Case Application.* This is a decision-focused case that asks students to determine what they would do if they were in the situation described.

- *Developing Your Diagnostic and Analytical Skills.* This feature asks students to apply chapter material to analyze a case.

- *Developing Your Interpersonal Skills.* To reflect the importance being placed on skills, each chapter has this skills-based feature.

- *Managing Workforce Diversity.* This feature appears in some of the chapters and informs students about what can be done to make workplaces more inclusive.

Increased Number of Cases

Our reviews tell us that management courses need more cases. We have responded to this request in a variety of ways.

End-of-Part Case

NEW! A case featuring Markham, Ontario-based CoolBrands appears at the end of each part of the text. The five parts of the case illustrate how the concepts and functions of management can be applied to a real-life corporation. The case can be used in parts, or it can also serve as an integrating case at the end of the term.

End-of-Book Cases

NEW! Two longer cases, "Excel's Tavern," written by Stephen Lynch of the University of Guelph, and "Atlantic Health Centre," written by Shripad Pendse and Kevin Doucette of Saint Mary's University, have been included at the end of the book. These two cases are lengthier and integrate a number of management issues.

Video Cases

Ten video cases appear at the end of the book. A number of these have come from CBC *Venture* programs. The videos generally focus on several management issues within a part. The cases were carefully selected by David Delcorde from the University of Ottawa to provide instructors with audiovisual material to engage their students' attention.

NEW! Main Changes to Content

A number of notable enhancements add to both learning and instruction.

- Greater emphasis on presenting a variety of managers, some in unusual (i.e., not large corporate) settings and some with nontraditional decisions. In the chapter openers, you will meet a public health officer in charge of revamping Ontario's public health system, a school superintendent coping with dress code issues, a company trying to work well with its local Aboriginal community, and the CEO in charge of putting on the Olympics in Vancouver. These examples highlight for students the idea that management takes place in a variety of contexts.

- Significantly increased Canadian content, with an attempt for broader coverage throughout Canada, and examples that cover many different types of organizations: large and small, public and private sector, unionized and non-unionized, privately held and publicly held. Each of these settings provides different challenges for managers, and yet often there are commonalities. The examples help students understand what is the same and what is different.

- Greater emphasis on strategic management

- Greater coverage of ethics, with more examples

CHAPTER-BY-CHAPTER HIGHLIGHT

In addition to major substantive changes within chapters, the chapter order of the fifth Canadian edition is significantly different from that of the fourth Canadian edition. Reviewers have told us that a fundamentals of management text must focus on the fundamentals. In our view, those fundamentals are planning, organizing, leading, and

controlling, and we organize the chapters according to these topics. Chapters can be taught in any order desired, however.

Below, we outline the new chapter order, and highlight the new material that has been added to this edition.

Part 1: Defining the Manager's Terrain

Chapter 1: Introduction to Management and Organizations

- Added a section highlighting the challenges managers face: ethics, social responsibility, diversity, and globalization
- Introduced the topic of ethics, as a precursor to greater coverage in Chapter 4
- Added a lengthy discussion of social responsibility, which includes
  - a section comparing views on social responsibility
  - data on Canadian views toward social responsibility
- Added a supplement, *History of Management Trends*, that covers the important advances in management theory.

NEW! Chapter 2: Environmental Constraints on Managers

Managers do not operate in a vacuum; rather they face constraints and opportunities generated by the environment. We address the environmental constraints of managers in this chapter, including

- a description of the environment, a part of which is the global environment
- Canada's legal environment and how it affects managers
- trade alliances, including NAFTA and the World Trade Organization
- a discussion of how organizations go global
- a discussion of the impact on managers of running Canadian companies that are subsidiaries of US companies
- discussion of global management in today's world, including
  - a discussion on whether globalization is dead
  - a discussion on whether Canada has some advantages over the United States on the globalization front
- a discussion on how to manage stakeholder relationships

Part 2: Planning

Chapter 3: Planning and Strategic Management

- New! How managers plan, including lengthier discussion of goal setting
- Increased the depth and provided greater clarification of the strategic management process, including
  - highlighting the steps of the strategic management process
  - explaining what a mission statement is
- Reorganized the section on corporate-level strategies
- Developed a discussion on types of growth strategies
- New! How to sustain competitive advantage, including Porter's Five Forces

Chapter 4: Decision Making

- Shortened the discussion on bounded rationality
- Shortened the section on structured and unstructured decisions

- New! Discussion on how intuition affects decision making
- New! Discussion of certainty, uncertainty, and risk
- New! Section on bias and decision making
- New! In-depth discussion of ethics, including
  - four views of ethics
  - how to improve ethical behaviour
  - codes of ethics
  - Canada's legal position on ethics and bribery issues

Part 3: Organizing

Chapter 5: Organizational Structure and Design

- Reorganized chapter structure
- Provided greater coverage of boundaryless organizations, including
  - virtual organizations
  - network organizations
  - modular organizations
- Added a discussion on how to introduce organic structure more effectively

Chapter 6: Communication and Information Technology

- New! Section highlighting the function of communication in organizations
- New! What causes distortions in communications?
- New! Effective methods of communicating interpersonally, including greater emphasis on nonverbal communication
- New! Organizational communication networks
- New! Role of email in information overload
- New! How privacy legislation relates to email and voicemail
- New! How to give feedback effectively

Chapter 7: Human Resource Management

- Expanded information on labour unions in Canada
- New! Types of training
- Added more data on sexual harassment
- New! Work–life balance, including a discussion of Linda Duxbury's (Sprott School of Business) research
- Provided a number of new exhibits to clarify the discussion, including "The Human Resource Management Process" and "Selection Devices"

Part 4: Leading

Chapter 8: Leadership

- New! Expanded discussion on charismatic leadership
- New! Managing power
- New! Moral leadership
- New! Online leadership
- Updated statistics on women in leadership positions

Chapter 9: Motivating Employees

- New! Cross-cultural challenges of applying motivation theories
- New! Discussion of money as a motivator
- New! Employee recognition programs
- New! Stock option programs
- New! Suggestions for motivating employees

Chapter 10: Understanding Groups and Teams

- Significantly reorganized the chapter so that the focus is on teams, and how to build more effective teams
- New! Creating effective teams
- New! Are teams always the answer?
- New! Focus on effective group processes: building cohesiveness, managing conflict, and preventing social loafing
- New! Expanded coverage of conflict resolution

Part 5: Controlling

Chapter 11: Foundations of Control

- Completely reorganized chapter, significantly increasing the depth of discussion on control
- New! Organizational culture and how it functions as a control mechanism. Includes
  - strong vs. weak organizational cultures
  - developing organizational culture
  - how employees learn culture
  - how organizational culture affects managers
- New! How managers measure
- New! Financial control measures
  - ratio analysis, budget analysis, EVA, MVA
  - balanced scorecard
  - information control
  - benchmarking best practices
- New! Controlling workplace violence
- New! Corporate governance

Chapter 12: Managing Change

- New! Types of changes in organizations
- New! Ongoing challenge of making change happen successfully
- Mistakes managers make when leading change
- Table on characteristics of change-capable organizations
- New! Communicating effectively when undergoing change
- New! Helping employees accept change

SUPPLEMENTS

With this new edition of *Fundamentals of Management*, we have included a Student CD-ROM that provides students with an assortment of tools to help enrich and expedite learning, including the Self Assessment Library, Version 3.3. Other tools include

- exercises on diversity, ethics, and global management
- an interactive eText
- links to the videos and the Companion Website
- responses to the Q&A feature

Please note: The Q&A icons in the margins of *Fundamentals of Management*, Fifth Canadian Edition, refer to the Q&A questions found in the **Robbins Online Learning System (R.O.L.L.S.)** on the accompanying Student CD-ROM. Because this is a *Fundamentals of Management* textbook, not every Q&A question appears in this text. Thus, questions in the textbook may not appear consecutively, as the numbering corresponds with that in R.O.L.L.S. For example, Chapter 2 in the textbook contains Q&A icons for questions 3.1, 3.2, and 2.9. To find these questions, simply access the Q&A section in R.O.L.L.S. on the Student CD-ROM and refer to questions 3.1, 3.2, and 2.9.

Q&A   3.1

The Companion Website (**www.pearsoned.ca/robbins**) features an online study guide. This interactive tool includes self-tests with feedback, Glossary Flashcards, and more.

For instructors, we have created an outstanding supplements package, all conveniently available on a single CD-ROM. The Instructor's Resource CD-ROM (0-13-241125-3) includes the following:

- Instructor's Resource Manual (includes detailed lecture outlines with teaching tips and strategies and video teaching notes)
- PowerPoint Slides
- PRS Questions
- TestGen
- Links to Videos

These supplements can also be found on the Pearson online catalogue at **http://vig.pearsoned.ca**. The videos are also available in both VHS (0-13-233919-6) and DVD (0-13-233918-8) formats.

ACKNOWLEDGMENTS

A number of people worked hard to give this fifth Canadian edition of *Fundamentals of Management* a new look. Su Mei Ku and Kelly Cochrane shared the role of developmental editor on this project. Together, their wit, good humour, helpfulness, support, and organizational skills made working on this textbook immensely easier.

I received incredible support for this project from a variety of people at Pearson Education Canada. Karen Elliott, Acquisitions Editor, was simply terrific in encouraging a fresh look for this book. Miguel Acevedo translated my thoughts about what this book should look like, creating an exciting new design. I particularly appreciate his responsiveness to suggestions for changes. I appreciated working with Jen Handel again in her role as the Production Editor for this project. Her professionalism, good will, and cheerfulness make the production process a surprisingly enjoyable task. Steve O'Hearn, President of Higher Education, and Gary Bennett, Editor-in-Chief, are extremely supportive on the management side of Pearson Education Canada, and this kind of support makes it much easier for an author to get work done and meet dreams and goals. Lisa Brant once again was very helpful in doing the photo research, and made some incredible finds in her search for photos to highlight management concepts. There are a variety of others at Pearson who also had their hand in making sure that the manuscript would be transformed into this book, and then delivered to your hands. To all of them I extend my thanks for jobs well done. The Pearson sales team is an exceptional group, and I know they will do everything possible to make this book successful. I continue to appreciate and value their support and interaction, particularly that of Cas Shields, Executive Marketing Manager, and Ewan French, my local sales representative.

Claudia Forgas was copyeditor for the project and did an amazing job of making sure everything was in place and written clearly. Kathleen Richards was the proofreader, and was extremely diligent about checking for consistency throughout the text. I enjoyed the opportunity to work with both of them. Their keen eyes helped to make the pages as clean as they are. They also help me remember the necessary qualities of virtual teams.

Finally, I want to acknowledge the many reviewers of this textbook for their detailed and helpful comments:

Doug Beatty, Lambton College

Bruce Bennett, College of New Caledonia

David H. J. Delcorde, University of Ottawa

Vic DeWitt, Red River College

Jane Haddad, Seneca College

Peter J. Holden, Capilano College

Bryan Hunt, Georgian College

Murray Kernaghan, Assiniboine College

Mike Santoro, Niagara College

Jeffrey Young, Mount Saint Vincent University

I dedicate this book to my father, Peter X. Langton. He was a man of many talents, and his understanding of organizations may have been greater than my own. To my family I give silent acknowledgment for everything else.

Nancy Langton
January 2007

ABOUT THE AUTHORS

Stephen P. Robbins received his PhD from the University of Arizona and has taught at the University of Nebraska at Omaha, Concordia University in Montreal, the University of Baltimore, Southern Illinois University at Edwardsville, and San Diego State University. Dr. Robbins' research interests have focused on conflict, power, and politics in organizations, behavioural decision making, and the development of effective interpersonal skills. His articles on these and other topics have appeared in journals such as *Business Horizons*, the *California Management Review*, *Business and Economic Perspectives*, *International Management*, *Management Review*, *Canadian Personnel and Industrial Relations*, and *The Journal of Management Education*.

Dr. Robbins is the world's bestselling textbook author in the areas of management and organizational behaviour. His most recent textbooks include *Organizational Behavior*, 11th ed. (Prentice Hall, 2005), *Essentials of Organizational Behavior*, 8th ed. (Prentice Hall, 2005), *Fundamentals of Management*, 5th ed., with David DeCenzo (Prentice Hall, 2005), and *Supervision Today!*, 4th ed., with David DeCenzo (Prentice Hall, 2004). In addition, Dr. Robbins is the author of the global best-sellers *The Truth About Managing People... and Nothing But the Truth* (Financial Times Press, 2002) and *Decide & Conquer* (Financial Times Press, 2004).

An avid participant in masters' track-and-field competition, Dr. Robbins has set numerous indoor and outdoor age-group world sprint records since turning 50 in 1993. He has won more than a dozen indoor and outdoor US national titles at 60, 100, 200, and 400 meters, and has won seven gold medals at the World Masters Championships.

Mary Coulter received her PhD in Management from the University of Arkansas in Fayetteville. Before completing her graduate work, she held different jobs, including high school teacher, legal assistant, and government program planner. She has taught at Drury University, the University of Arkansas, Trinity University, and since 1983, at Southwest Missouri State University. Dr. Coulter's research interests have focused on competitive strategies for not-for-profit arts organizations and the use of new media in the educational process. Her research on these and other topics has appeared in such journals as *International Journal of Business Disciplines*, *Journal of Business Strategies*, *Journal of Business Research*, *Journal of Nonprofit and Public Sector Marketing*, and *Case Research Journal*. In addition to *Management*, Dr. Coulter has published other books with Prentice Hall including *Strategic Management in Action*, now in its third edition, and *Entrepreneurship in Action*, which is in its second edition. When she is not busy teaching or writing, she enjoys puttering around in her flower gardens, playing the piano, reading different types of books, and enjoying many different activities with her husband Ron and her daughters Sarah and Katie.

Nancy Langton received her PhD from Stanford University. Since completing her graduate studies, Dr. Langton has taught at the University of Oklahoma and the University of British Columbia. Currently a member of the Organizational Behaviour and Human Resources division in the Sauder School of Business, University of British Columbia, and academic director of the Business Families Centre at UBC, she teaches at the undergraduate, MBA and PhD level, and conducts executive programs on family business issues, time management, attracting and retaining employees, as well as women and management issues. Dr. Langton has received several major research grants from the Social Sciences and Humanities Research Council of Canada, and her research interests have focused on human resource issues in the workplace, including pay equity, gender equity, and leadership and communication styles. She is currently conducting longitudinal research with entrepreneurs in the Greater Vancouver Region, trying to understand the relationship

between their human resource practices and the success of their businesses. Her articles on these and other topics have appeared in such journals as *Administrative Science Quarterly, American Sociological Review, Sociological Quarterly, Journal of Management Education, Gender, Work and Organizations,* and *Organization Studies*. She has won Best Paper commendations from both the Academy of Management and the Administrative Sciences Association of Canada, and in 2003 won the Best Women's Entrepreneurship Paper Award given by the Center for Women's Business Research for her work with Jennifer Cliff (University of Alberta) and Howard Aldrich (University of North Carolina). She has also published two textbooks on organizational behaviour with Pearson Education Canada, and this is her fourth textbook on management.

Dr. Langton routinely wins high marks from her students for teaching. She has been nominated many times for the Commerce Undergraduate Society Awards, and has won several honourable mention plaques. She has also won the Sauder School of Business' most prestigious award for teaching innovation, The Talking Stick. The award was given for Dr. Langton's redesign of the undergraduate organizational behaviour course as well as for the many activities that were a spin-off of these efforts. In 2001, she was part of the Sauder School's MBA Core design team that won the national Alan Blizzard award, which recognizes innovation in teaching.

In Dr. Langton's "other life," she teaches the artistry of quiltmaking, and one day hopes to win first prize at *Visions*, the juried show for quilts as works of art. When she is not designing quilts, she is either reading novels (often suggested by a favourite correspondent), or studying cookbooks for new ideas. All of her friends would say that she makes from scratch the best pizza in all of Vancouver.

A Great Way to Learn and Instruct Online

The Pearson Education Canada Companion Website is easy to navigate and is organized to correspond to the chapters in this textbook. Whether you are a student in the classroom or a distance learner you will discover helpful resources for in-depth study and research that empower you in your quest for greater knowledge and maximize your potential for success in the course.

Companion
Website

[www.pearsoned.ca/robbins]

Enter

PEARSON
Prentice
Hall

Jump to...   http://www.pearsoned.ca/robbins   Home | Search | Help | Profile

Companion
Website

Home >

Companion Website

Fundamentals of Management, Fifth Canadian Edition,
by Stephen P. Robbins, Mary Coulter, and Nancy Langton

Student Resources

The modules for each chapter of the text provide students with tools for learning course material. These modules include:
- Learning checklists
- Quizzes
- Short-answer questions
- Glossary Flashcards

Instructor Resources

A link to this book on the Pearson online catalogue (www.pearsoned.ca) provides instructors with additional teaching tools. Downloadable PowerPoint Presentations and an Instructor's Resource Manual are just some of the materials that may be available. The catalogue is password protected. To get a password, simply contact your Pearson Education Canada Representative or call Faculty Sales and Services at 1-800-850-5813.

Introduction to Management and Organizations

What can I learn from the study of management?

1 What makes someone a manager?

2 What is management and what do managers do?

3 What characteristics define an organization?

4 What are the challenges to managing?

5 Does studying management make a difference?

Defining the Manager's Terrain

Dr. Sheela Basrur was a calming face during the height of Toronto's SARS crisis in spring 2003.

She was the medical officer of health for Toronto, responsible for directing 1800 public health employees in managing the crisis. In her daily press briefing during the crisis, she showed great leadership in insisting that individuals act responsibly and stay home if they felt sick. She was recognized by many for her ability to stand up in the face of great pressure and help people understand what they should do during this crisis. It is those skills that make Basrur both a leader and a manager.

Nevertheless, Basrur, who was promoted to Chief Medical Officer of Health and Assistant Deputy Minister of Public Health for Ontario after the crisis, is not someone we would immediately think of when asked to name a manager.[1] She works in the public sector, with medical officers of health throughout Ontario reporting to her. Unlike mid-level managers in the private sector, she does not report to a CEO, but rather to the Minister of Health and Long-Term Care, George Smitherman. Basrur's job is to direct the public-health operations for all of Ontario.

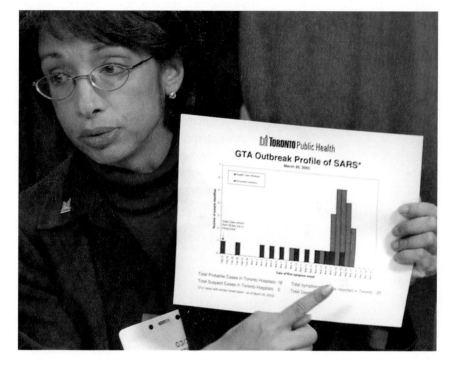

She brings a particularly useful set of skills to the task. She is a clinical expert and known for her outspokenness and good communication skills.

THINK ABOUT IT

What kinds of skills do managers need? Put yourself in Dr. Sheela Basrur's shoes. What kinds of leadership skills would you need to do protect the health of the public? Does managing in a government organization differ from managing in a large corporation or a small business?

Dr. Sheela Basrur is a good example of what today's successful managers are like and the skills they must have in dealing with the problems and challenges of managing in the twenty-first century. These managers may not be who or what you might expect. They can be found from under age 18 to over 80. They run large corporations as well as entrepreneurial start-ups. They are found in government departments, hospitals, small businesses, non-profit agencies, museums, schools, and even such nontraditional organizations as political campaigns and consumer cooperatives. Managers can also be found doing managerial work in every country on the globe.

No matter where managers are found or what gender they are, the fact is that they have exciting and challenging jobs. Organizations need managers more than ever in these uncertain, complex, and chaotic times. *Managers do matter!* How do we know that managers matter to organizations? A Gallup Organization study based on interviews with 2 million employees at 700 companies found that the single most important variable in employee productivity and loyalty was not pay or benefits or workplace environment; it was the quality of the relationship between employees and their direct supervisors.[2] In addition, a recent KPMG/Ipsos Reid study found that many Canadian companies that scored high in great human resource practices also scored high on financial performance and best long-term investment value.[3]

This textbook is about the important managerial work that Sheela Basrur and the millions of other managers like her do. It recognizes the reality facing today's managers—new technologies and new ways of organizing work are altering old approaches. Today's successful managers must be able to blend tried-and-true management approaches with new approaches. Throughout this and subsequent chapters, you will be introduced to a number of managers and the challenging decisions they face through the feature *Management Reflection*. You will also find *Tips for Managers* in many chapters, which presents actions managers can take in specific situations in the workplace.

In this chapter, we introduce you to managers and management by looking at who managers are, what management is, what managers do, and what an organization is. We will wrap up the chapter by discussing the challenges managers face and why it's important to study management.

WHO ARE MANAGERS?

As chief medical officer of health for Ontario, Dr. Sheela Basrur manages the largest public health system in the country. She started her medical career as a general practitioner in Guelph, Ontario, after receiving degrees from the University of Western Ontario and Dalhousie University. Basrur's mother, Parvathi Basrur, said her daughter became interested in public health after a trip to India. "She saw the raw effects of not having sufficient health education."[4]

THINK ABOUT IT

What makes Dr. Sheela Basrur a manager?

---

1 What makes someone a manager?

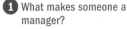

manager
Someone who works with and through other people by coordinating their work activities in order to accomplish organizational goals.

first-line managers
Managers at the lowest level of the organization who manage the work of nonmanagerial employees who are directly or indirectly involved with the production or creation of the organization's products.

It used to be fairly simple to define who managers were: They were the organizational members who told others what to do and how to do it. It was easy to differentiate managers from nonmanagerial employees; nonmanagerial employees were those organizational members who worked directly on a job or task and had no one reporting to them. But it isn't quite that simple anymore, as we can see from the story of Sheela Basrur. The changing nature of organizations and work has, in many organizations, blurred the clear lines of distinction between managers and nonmanagerial employees. Many traditional nonmanagerial jobs now include managerial activities, particularly for employees working in teams.[5]

How do we define who managers are? A **manager** is someone who works with and through other people by coordinating their work activities in order to accomplish organizational goals. A manager's job is not about *personal* achievement—it's about helping *others* do their work and achieve.

Types of Managers

Is there some way to classify managers in organizations? In traditionally structured organizations (often pictured as shaped like a pyramid in which the number of employees is greater at the bottom than at the top), managers are often described as first-line, middle, or top (see Exhibit 1-1). Identifying exactly who the managers are in these organizations isn't difficult, although they may have a variety of titles. **First-line managers** are at the lowest level of management and manage the work of nonmanagerial employees who are directly or indirectly involved with the production or creation of the organization's products.

Exhibit 1-1

Managerial Levels

Top Managers

Middle Managers

First-Line Managers

Nonmanagerial Employees

They are often called *supervisors* but may also be called shift managers, district managers, department managers, office managers, or foremen. **Middle managers** include all levels of management between the first-line level and the top level of the organization. These managers manage the work of first-line managers and may have titles such as regional manager, project leader, plant manager, or division manager. At or near the top of the organization are the **top managers**, who are responsible for making organization-wide decisions and establishing the plans and goals that affect the entire organization. These individuals typically have titles such as executive vice-president, president, managing director, chief operating officer, chief executive officer, or chairman of the board. In the chapter-opening case, Sheela Basrur is a top-level manager for public health in Ontario. She is involved in creating and implementing broad and comprehensive changes that affect the entire organization.

Not all organizations get work done using this traditional pyramidal form, however. Some organizations, for example, are more flexible and loosely structured with work being done by ever-changing teams of employees who move from one project to another as work demands arise. Although it's not as easy to tell who the managers are in these organizations, we do know that someone must fulfill that role—that is, there must be someone who works with and through other people by coordinating their work to accomplish organizational goals.

middle managers
Managers between the first-line level and the top level of the organization who manage the work of first-line managers.

top managers
Managers at or near the top level of the organization who are responsible for making organization-wide decisions and establishing the plans and goals that affect the entire organization.

Donna Rodrigues, principal of the University Park Campus School in Worcester, Massachusetts, has used her management skills to help raise standards among her teachers and students. She improved the curriculum, outlawed swearing and fighting, sent teachers to the homes of students who were absent too often, and promised parents that all their children would go to college. Rodrigues, a middle manager within the school district hierarchy, believes that treating the students like adults helps motivate them to perform at their best.

WHAT IS MANAGEMENT AND WHAT DO MANAGERS DO?

Dr. Sheela Basrur, like all managers, is charged with coordinating the work activities of her department efficiently and effectively.[6] As the Ontario Ministry of Health and Long-Term Care states on its website, "Dr. Basrur will be developing more effective health promotion strategies and programs, to deliver measurable results." She is required to report annually on the state of public health directly to the Ontario legislature.

Managers plan, lead, organize, and control, and Basrur is known for taking strong stands to protect public health. She was instrumental in encouraging Ontario's ban on smoking in public places, which came into effect in June 2006, after leading the effort to ban smoking in bars in Toronto in 2004; she helped establish a pesticide control by-law; she created Toronto's plan to handle bioterrorism; and she initiated the DineSafe program, which requires Toronto's restaurants to post health inspection results in their windows.[7] Management also requires a variety of skills, and Basrur is praised for those she brings to her job. "Sheela Basrur is the kind of civil servant that's really a hero to the people of Toronto," Mayor David Miller said. "The rest of the province will benefit from her wonderful skills."[8]

THINK ABOUT IT

As a manager, Dr. Sheela Basrur needs to plan, lead, organize, and control, and she needs to be efficient and effective. How might Basrur balance the needs of efficiency and effectiveness in her role as the chief medical officer of health for Ontario? What skills are needed for her to plan, lead, organize, and control effectively? What challenges does she face performing these functions while working in the public sector?

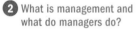 **What is management and what do managers do?**

management
Coordinating work activities so that they are completed efficiently and effectively with and through other people.

efficiency
Getting the most output from the least amount of inputs; referred to as "doing things right."

effectiveness
Completing activities so that organizational goals are achieved; referred to as "doing the right things."

 **Q&A** 1.3

Simply speaking, management is what managers do. But that simple statement does not tell us much, does it? A more thorough explanation is that **management** is coordinating work activities so that they are completed *efficiently* and *effectively* with and through other people. Management researchers have developed three approaches to describe what managers do: functions, roles, and skills. Before we look at each approach in detail, we will consider the challenges of balancing efficiency and effectiveness.

Efficiency and Effectiveness

Efficiency refers to getting the most output from the least amount of inputs, or as management expert Peter Drucker explained, "doing things right."[9] Because managers deal with scarce inputs—including resources such as people, money, and equipment—they are concerned with the efficient use of those resources by getting things done at the least cost.

It's not enough just to be efficient, however. Management is also concerned with being effective, completing activities so that organizational goals are achieved. **Effectiveness** is often described as "doing the right things"—that is, those work activities that will help the organization reach its goals. For instance, hospitals might try to be efficient by reducing the number of days that patients stay in hospital. However, they may not be effective if patients get sick at home shortly after being released.

Whereas efficiency is concerned with the means of getting things done, effectiveness is concerned with the ends, or attaining organizational goals. Management is concerned, then, not only with completing activities to meet organizational goals (effectiveness) but also with doing so as efficiently as possible. In successful organizations, high efficiency and high effectiveness typically go hand in hand. Poor management is most often due to both inefficiency and ineffectiveness or to effectiveness achieved through inefficiency.

Management Functions

According to the functions approach, managers perform certain activities or duties as they efficiently and effectively coordinate the work of others. What are these activities, or functions? In the early part of the twentieth century, French industrialist Henri Fayol first proposed that all managers perform five functions: planning, organizing, commanding,

Think about a manager you have had. To what extent did he or she engage in planning, organizing, leading, and controlling?

coordinating, and controlling.[10] Today, most management textbooks (including this one) are organized around these **management functions**: planning, organizing, leading, and controlling (see Exhibit 1-2). But you do not have to be a manager in order to have a need to plan, organize, lead, and control, so understanding these processes is important for everyone. Let's briefly define what each of these functions encompasses.

management functions
Planning, organizing, leading, controlling

Planning

If you have no particular destination in mind, then you can take any road. However, if you have someplace in particular you want to go, you have got to plan the best way to get there. Because organizations exist to achieve some particular purpose, someone must clearly define that purpose and the means for its achievement. Managers performing the **planning** function define goals, establish an overall strategy for achieving those goals, and develop plans to integrate and coordinate activities. This can be done by the CEO and senior management team for the overall organization. Middle managers often have a planning role within their units. Planning, by the way, is not just for managers. For instance, as a student, you need to plan for exams and your financial needs.

planning
A management function that involves defining goals, establishing a strategy for achieving those goals, and developing plans to integrate and coordinate activities.

Organizing

Managers are also responsible for arranging work to accomplish the organization's goals. We call this function **organizing**. When managers organize, they determine what tasks are to be done, who is to do them, how the tasks are to be grouped, who reports to whom (that is, they define authority relationships), and where decisions are to be made. When you work in a student group, you engage in some of these same organizing activities—deciding on a division of labour, and what tasks will be carried out to get an assignment completed.

organizing
A management function that involves determining what tasks are to be done, who is to do them, how the tasks are to be grouped, who reports to whom, and where decisions are to be made.

Leading

Every organization contains people. Part of a manager's job is to work with and through people to accomplish organizational goals. This is the **leading** function. When managers motivate subordinates, direct the work of individuals or teams, select the most effective communication channel, or resolve employee conflicts, they are leading. Knowing how to manage and lead effectively is an important, and sometimes difficult, skill as it requires the ability to successfully communicate. Leading is not just for managers, however. As a student, you might want to practise leadership skills when working in groups or club activities. You might also want to evaluate whether you need to improve your leadership skills in anticipation of the needs of future jobs.

leading
A management function that involves motivating subordinates, directing the work of individuals or teams, selecting the most effective communication channels, and resolving employee conflicts.

Exhibit 1-2

Management Functions

Planning	Organizing	Leading	Controlling	
Defining goals, establishing strategy, and developing subplans to coordinate activities	Determining what needs to be done, how it will be done, and who is to do it	Directing and motivating all involved parties and resolving conflicts	Monitoring activities to ensure that they are accomplished as planned	*Lead to* → Achieving the organization's stated purpose

controlling
A management function that involves monitoring actual performance, comparing actual to standard, and taking corrective action when necessary.

Controlling

The final management function is **controlling**. After the goals are set (planning), the plans formulated (planning), the structural arrangements determined (organizing), and the people hired, trained, and motivated (leading), there has to be some evaluation of whether things are going as planned (controlling). To ensure that work is going as it should, managers must monitor and evaluate employees' performance. Actual performance must be compared with the previously set goals. If performance of individuals or units does not match the goals set, it's the manager's job to get performance back on track. This process of monitoring, comparing, and correcting is what we mean by the controlling function. Individuals, whether working in groups or alone, also face the responsibility of controlling; that is, they must make sure the goals and actions are achieved and take corrective action when necessary.

Just how well does the functions approach describe what managers do? Do managers always plan, organize, lead, and then control? In reality, what a manager does may not always happen in this logical and sequential order. But that does not negate the importance of the basic functions that managers perform. Regardless of the "order" in which the functions are performed, the fact is that managers do plan, organize, lead, and control as they manage.

The continued popularity of the functions approach is a tribute to its clarity and simplicity. But some have argued that this approach is not appropriate or relevant.[11] So let's look at another perspective.

Management Roles

Henry Mintzberg
www.henrymintzberg.com

Henry Mintzberg, a prominent management researcher at McGill University, has studied actual managers at work. He says that what managers do can best be understood by looking at the roles they play at work. His studies allowed him to conclude that managers perform 10 different but highly interrelated management roles.[12] The term **management roles** refers to specific categories of managerial behaviour. (Think of the different roles you play and the different behaviours you are expected to perform in the roles of student, sibling, employee, volunteer, and so forth.) As shown in Exhibit 1-3, Mintzberg's 10 management roles are grouped around interpersonal relationships, the transfer of information, and decision making.

management roles
Specific categories of managerial behaviour.

interpersonal roles
Management roles that involve working with people or performing duties that are ceremonial and symbolic in nature.

informational roles
Management roles that involve receiving, collecting, and disseminating information.

decisional roles
Management roles that revolve around making choices.

The **interpersonal roles** involve working with people (subordinates and persons outside the organization) or performing duties that are ceremonial and symbolic in nature. The three interpersonal roles include being a figurehead, leader, and liaison. The **informational roles** involve receiving, collecting, and disseminating information. The three informational roles include monitor, disseminator, and spokesperson. Finally, the **decisional roles** revolve around making choices. The four decisional roles include entrepreneur, disturbance handler, resource allocator, and negotiator.

Functions vs. Roles

So which approach to describing what managers do is correct—functions or roles? Each has merit. However, the functions approach still represents the most useful way of conceptualizing the manager's job. "The classical functions provide clear and discrete methods of classifying the thousands of activities that managers carry out and the techniques they use in terms of the functions they perform for the achievement of goals."[13] Many of Mintzberg's roles align well with one or more of the functions. For instance, resource allocation is part of planning, as is the entrepreneurial role, and all three of the interpersonal roles are part of the leading function. Although most of the other roles fit into one or more of the four functions, not all of them do. The difference can be explained by the fact that all managers do some work that is not purely managerial.[14]

Management Skills

As you can see from the preceding discussion, a manager's job is varied and complex. Managers need certain skills to perform the duties and activities associated with being a manager. What types of skills does a manager need? Research by Robert L. Katz found that managers needed three essential skills.[15] **Technical skills** include knowledge of and

technical skills
Knowledge of and expertise in a specialized field.

Exhibit 1-3

Mintzberg's Management Roles

Role	Description	Examples of Identifiable Activities
Interpersonal		
Figurehead	Symbolic head; obliged to perform a number of routine duties of a legal or social nature	Greeting visitors; signing legal documents
Leader	Responsible for the motivation of subordinates; responsible for staffing, training, and associated duties	Performing virtually all activities that involve subordinates
Liaison	Maintains self-developed network of outside contacts and informers who provide favours and information	Acknowledging mail; doing external board work; performing other activities that involve outsiders
Informational		
Monitor	Seeks and receives wide variety of internal and external information to develop thorough understanding of organization and environment	Reading periodicals and reports; maintaining personal contacts
Disseminator	Transmits information received from outsiders or from subordinates to members of the organization	Holding informational meetings; making phone calls to relay information
Spokesperson	Transmits information to outsiders on organization's plans, policies, actions, results, etc.	Holding board meetings; giving information to the media
Decisional		
Entrepreneur	Searches organization and its environment for opportunities and initiates "improvement projects" to bring about changes	Organizing strategy and review sessions to develop new programs
Disturbance handler	Responsible for corrective action when organization faces important, unexpected disturbances	Organizing strategy and review sessions that involve disturbances and crises
Resource allocator	Responsible for the allocation of organizational resources of all kinds—making or approving all significant organizational decisions	Scheduling; requesting authorization; performing any activity that involves budgeting and the programming of subordinates' work
Negotiator	Responsible for representing the organization at major negotiations	Participating in union contract negotiations

Source: H. Mintzberg, *The Nature of Managerial Work* (New York: Harper & Row, 1973), pp. 93–94. Copyright © 1973 by Henry Mintzberg. Reprinted by permission of Harper & Row, Publishers, Inc.

expertise in a certain specialized field, such as engineering, computers, accounting, or manufacturing. These skills are more important at lower levels of management since these managers are dealing directly with employees doing the organization's work. **Human skills** involve the ability to work well with other people both individually and in a group. Because managers deal directly with people, this skill is crucial! Managers with good human skills are able to get the best out of their people. They know how to communicate, motivate, lead, and inspire enthusiasm and trust. These skills are equally important at all levels of management. According to management professor Jin Nam Choi, of McGill University, 40 percent of managers either leave or stop performing within 18 months of starting at an organization "because they have failed to develop relationships with bosses, colleagues or subordinates."[16] Choi's comment underscores the importance of developing human skills. Finally, **conceptual skills** refer to the mental ability to analyze and generate ideas about abstract and complex situations. These skills help managers see the organization as a whole, understand the relationships among various sub-

human skills
The ability to work well with other people both individually and in a group.

conceptual skills
The mental ability to analyze and generate ideas about abstract and complex situations.

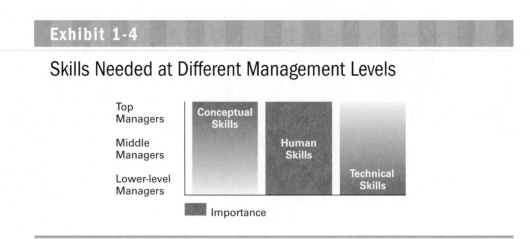

Exhibit 1-4

Skills Needed at Different Management Levels

units, and visualize how the organization fits into its broader environment. These skills are most important at the top manager level. Exhibit 1-4 shows the relationship of the three skills to each level of management. Note that the three skills are important to more than one level.

As you study the management functions in more depth, the exercises in *Developing Your Diagnostic and Analytical Skills* and *Developing Your Interpersonal Skills,* found at the end of most chapters, will give you the opportunity to practise some of the key skills that are part of doing what a manager does. Skill-building exercises cannot make you an instant managerial expert, but they can provide you with a basic understanding of some of the skills you will need to master to become an effective manager. To learn more about becoming a better mentor, see *Developing Your Interpersonal Skills—Mentoring* on pages 25–26, at the end of the chapter.

WHAT IS AN ORGANIZATION?

Dr. Sheela Basrur works for Ontario's Ministry of Health and Long-Term Care. Thus, she works for the government, as a public sector employee. Because she was appointed to her position by the provincial Liberal government, there is concern that she will not have the independent voice she needs to carry out reforms of public health in the province. Still, almost all managers are accountable to someone. Thomas Gauld, president and CEO of Toronto-based Canadian Tire, for example, reports to a board of directors chaired by Gilbert Bennett, who examines Gauld's decisions and actions, and decides whether to continue to support him. The board also determines his compensation, based on his performance. So while Basrur's situation may seem different because she is located in the public sector, she faces many of the same challenges that a manager in the private sector might face.

THINK ABOUT IT

Do managers act differently when they work for large organizations rather than smaller ones? Does working for a government agency change the role of the manager?

---

3 What characteristics define an organization?

organization
A deliberate arrangement of people who act together to accomplish some specific purpose.

Managers work in organizations. But what is an organization? An **organization** is a deliberate arrangement of people who act together to accomplish some specific purpose. Your college or university is an organization; so are fraternities and sororities, government departments, churches, Amazon.ca, your neighbourhood video store, the United Way, the Toronto Raptors basketball team, and the Hudson's Bay Company. These are all organizations because they have three common characteristics, as shown in Exhibit 1-5:

- *Distinct purpose.* This purpose is typically expressed in terms of a goal or a set of goals that the organization hopes to accomplish.

Exhibit 1-5

Characteristics of Organizations

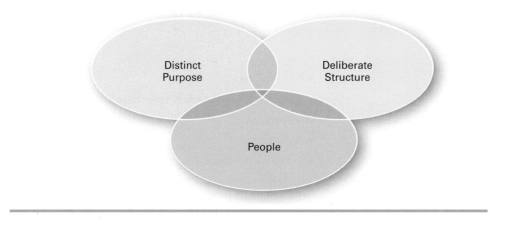

- *People.* One person working alone is not an organization, and it takes people to perform the work that is necessary for the organization to achieve its goals.

- *Deliberate structure.* Whether that structure is open and flexible or traditional and clearly defined, the structure defines members' work relationships. In summary, the term *organization* refers to an entity that has a distinct purpose, includes people or members, and has some type of deliberate structure.

Although these three characteristics are important to our definition of *what* an organization is, the concept of an organization is changing. It's no longer appropriate to assume that all organizations are going to be structured like Air Canada, Petro-Canada, or General Motors, with clearly identifiable divisions, departments, and work units. Just how is the concept of an organization changing? Exhibit 1-6 on page 12 lists some differences between traditional organizations and new organizations. As these lists show, today's organizations are becoming more open, flexible, and responsive to changes.[17]

Does your college or university or an organization in which you have worked represent a "new organization"? Why or why not?

Why are organizations changing? Because the world around them has changed and continues to change. Societal, economic, political, global, and technological changes have created an environment in which successful organizations (those that consistently attain their goals) must embrace new ways of getting work done. As we stated earlier, even though the concept of organizations may be changing, managers and management continue to be important to organizations.

The Size of Organizations

Managers don't just manage in large organizations, which represent only 3 percent of organizations in Canada. Almost 95 percent of the organizations in Canada in 2003 employed fewer than 50 people; and 58 percent employed four or fewer individuals.[18] Big businesses employ just over 40 percent of all employees in Canada, while small businesses employ about 34 percent of all employees.[19] In 2004, on average, about 49 percent of Canadian employees worked for businesses that had fewer than 100 employees. By contrast, about 35 percent of Canadian employees worked for businesses that had 500 employees or more.[20] Organizations of every size need managers. Moreover, in 2004, about 15 percent of the labour force was self-employed, meaning that these people were managing themselves.[21]

Exhibit 1-6

The Changing Organization

Traditional Organization	New Organization
• Stable	• Dynamic
• Inflexible	• Flexible
• Job-focused	• Skills-focused
• Work is defined by job positions	• Work is defined in terms of tasks to be done
• Individual-oriented	• Team-oriented
• Permanent jobs	• Temporary jobs
• Command-oriented	• Involvement-oriented
• Managers always make decisions	• Employees participate in decision making
• Rule-oriented	• Customer-oriented
• Relatively homogeneous workforce	• Diverse workforce
• Workdays defined as 9 to 5	• Workdays have no time boundaries
• Hierarchical relationships	• Lateral and networked relationships
• Work at organizational facility during specific hours	• Work anywhere, anytime

Canada Post
www.canadapost.ca

private sector
The part of the economy that is run by organizations which are free from direct government control.

publicly held organization
A company whose shares are available on the stock exchange for public trading by brokers/dealers.

privately held organization
A company whose shares are not available on the stock exchange but are privately held.

nonprofit sector
The part of the economy that is run by organizations which operate for purposes other than making a profit (that is, providing charity or services).

public sector
The part of the economy that is directly controlled by government.

civil servant
A person who works in a local, provincial, or federal government department.

Crown corporation
A commercial company owned by the government but independently managed.

Managers are also not confined to manufacturing work, as only 13 percent of Canadians work in manufacturing organizations. Most Canadians (around 76 percent) work in the service sector of the economy, with 19 percent working in public sector jobs (those in the local, provincial, or federal government).[22] The government is actually a large employer in Canada. For instance, Canada Post, a Crown corporation, is the fourth largest employer in Canada, employing some 71 000 people, behind only Onex, Loblaws, and Magna.[23]

The Types of Organizations

Managers work in a variety of situations, and thus the people to whom they are held accountable vary considerably. Large organizations in the **private sector** are often **publicly held**, which means that their shares are available on the stock exchange for public trading. Managers of publicly held companies report to a board of directors that is responsible to shareholders (also known as stockholders). There are also numerous **privately held organizations** (whose shares are not available on the stock exchange), both large and small. Privately held organizations can be individually owned, family-owned, or owned by some other group of individuals. A number of managers work in the **nonprofit sector**, where the emphasis is on providing charity or services rather than on making a profit. Examples of such organizations include the SPCA (Society for the Prevention of Cruelty to Animals), the Royal Ontario Museum, and Vancouver's Bard on the Beach Festival. Other organizational forms such as partnerships and cooperatives also require managers.

Many managers work in the **public sector** as **civil servants** for the local, provincial, or federal government. The challenges of managing within government departments can be quite different from the challenges of managing in publicly held organizations. Critics argue that it is less demanding to work for governments because there are few measurable performance objectives, allowing employees to feel less accountable for their actions.

Some managers and employees work for **Crown corporations** such as Canada Post, the CBC, and the Business Development Bank of Canada. Crown corporations are structured like private sector corporations and have boards of directors, CEOs, and so on, but are owned by governments rather than shareholders. Employees in Crown corporations are not civil servants, and managers in Crown corporations are more independent than the senior bureaucrats who manage government departments.

Many of Canada's larger organizations are actually subsidiaries of American parent organizations (e.g., Sears, Safeway, General Motors, and Ford Motor Company). Their managers often report to American top managers, and are not always free to set their own goals and targets. Conflicts can arise when Canadian managers and the American managers to whom they report do not agree on how things should be done.

THE CHALLENGES MANAGERS FACE

As medical officer of health for Toronto, Dr. Sheela Basrur was thrust into the spotlight in Ontario during the SARS crisis in 2003. She, her colleagues, and the city faced a global disease, with little information on how it was transmitted or what its incubation period was. Travellers from Asia landing at Pearson International Airport might have been bringing the disease with them. It was Basrur's job to regularly communicate with the most culturally diverse city in Canada, educating people about the disease and dispelling any misconceptions.

The challenge Basrur faced was magnified by the fact that the city was not prepared for the crisis. There was no computerized system for tracking cases and their contacts. Instead, public health staff used "sticky notes and colour-coded paper files" to keep track of the outbreak. The province sent out email directives in the middle of the night because of the inadequacies of the government Internet system. "Sending such a massive e-mail during the day would have crashed the entire system," reported University Health Network chief executive officer Tom Closson.[24] Basrur managed the crisis well, maintaining a calm and measured presence and clearly communicating the situation despite the systemic limitations in the Ontario health care system.

THINK ABOUT IT

Managing is far more complicated today than it ever was. Managers face technological challenges, multicultural challenges, and the demand for more accountability from customers and clients. How might Dr. Sheela Basrur, or someone like her, prepare to face all of these challenges?

Managers have always had to deal with changes taking place inside and outside their organizations. In today's world, where managers everywhere are dealing with corporate ethics scandals, demands to be more socially responsible, the challenges of managing a diverse workforce, and globalization, change is constant. We briefly describe these challenges below, and then throughout this textbook we will discuss their impact on the way managers plan, organize, lead, and control.

4 What are the challenges to managing?

Ethics

While Canadian corporations were not directly implicated in many of the biggest corporate scandals of recent years, Canada has had its own cases of financial mismanagement, including charges that Conrad Black, the former CEO of Hollinger International (now Sun-Times Media Group), used the company as his personal piggy bank. In 2003, YBM Magnex was ordered by the Ontario Securities Commission to cease operating, and five of its officers and directors were fined. In 2004, some of Toronto-based Atlas Cold Storage's shareholders filed a $358-million class action lawsuit against the company because of losses they suffered from the financial scandal of the refrigerated-warehouse operator. The Liberal sponsorship scandal in the Public Works department showed that even the federal government is not immune to being accused of financial mismanagement.

Ontario Securities Commission
www.osc.gov.on.ca

What do we mean by ethics? The term **ethics** refers to the study of moral values or principles that guide our behaviour, and inform us whether actions are right or wrong.[25] Unfortunately, the ethics of a situation is not always black and white. Consider the following: For some decisions, you can make choices exercising complete freedom of choice, with no regard to others. For other decisions, there is a set of laws that guides your behaviour. In between, there is a set of situations where you might want to consider the impact of your decision on others, even though there are no laws regarding your behaviour. This is the grey area of behaviour. Laws often develop because people did not act responsibly when they had a choice—for instance,

ethics
The study of moral values or principles that guide our behaviour and inform us whether actions are right or wrong.

An internal investigation at Hollinger International concluded that Conrad Black used most of the company's profits between 1997 and 2004 for his own personal gain. The report suggested that Black colluded with others to take more than $400 million from the publishing company.

not that long ago drinking and driving did not have the penalties that it does now. Many people have talked about laws banning cellphones in various situations for much the same reason: Individuals do not think about the impact of their use on others.

What has happened to managerial ethics? This important aspect of managing seems to have been forgotten or ignored in light of recent cases where managers put their self-interest ahead of others. While most managers continue to behave in a highly ethical manner, the ethical abuses that were so widely publicized have indicated a need to "upgrade" ethical standards and accountability. Efforts to improve the ethical behaviour of managers are being made at two levels. First, ethics education is being emphasized in university and college classrooms. Second, organizations themselves are taking a more active role in creating *and using* codes of ethics, providing ethics training, and hiring ethics officers. We want to prepare you to deal with the ethical dilemmas you are likely to face. We cover ethics and decision making in Chapter 4. As well, we have included an *Ethical Dilemma Exercise* at the end of every chapter to help you develop your ethical skills.

Corporate Social Responsibility

corporate social responsibility
A business's obligation, beyond that required by law and economics, to pursue long-term goals that are good for society.

We define **corporate social responsibility** as a business's obligation, beyond that required by law and economics, to pursue long-term goals that are good for society.[26] Note that this definition assumes that a business obeys laws and pursues economic interests. But also note that this definition views business as a moral agent. That is, in its effort to do good for society, it must differentiate between right and wrong. A great deal of attention has been focused on the extent to which organizations and management should act in socially responsible ways. On one side, there's the classical—or purely economic—view, and on the other side is the socio-economic view.

The Classical View

classical view
The view that management's only social responsibility is to maximize profits.

The **classical view** says that management's only social responsibility is to maximize profits. The most outspoken advocate of this approach is the late economist and Nobel laureate Milton Friedman.[27] He argues that managers' primary responsibility is to operate the business in the best interests of the stockholders (the owners of a corporation). What are those interests? Friedman contends that stockholders have a single concern: financial return. He also argues that any time managers decide to spend the organization's resources for "social good," they are adding to the costs of doing business. These costs have to be passed on to consumers either through higher prices or absorbed by stockholders through a smaller profit returned as dividends. Do understand that Friedman isn't saying that organizations should *not* be socially responsible; he thinks they should. But the extent of that responsibility is to maximize organizational profits for stockholders.

Joel Bakan, professor of law at the University of British Columbia, author of *The Corporation*, and co-director of the documentary of the same name, is more critical of organizations than Friedman, though he finds that current laws support corporate behaviour that some might find troubling. Bakan suggests that today's corporations have many of the same characteristics as a psychopathic personality (that is, self-interested, lacking empathy, manipulative, and reckless in one's disregard of others). Bakan notes that even though companies have a tendency to act psychopathically, this is not why they are fixated on profits. Rather,

> *Is it wrong for Canadian companies to employ children to work in factories in countries where child labour is legal?*

though they may have social responsibilities, the only *legal* responsibility corporations have is to maximize organizational profits for stockholders.[28] He suggests that more laws and more restraints need to be put in place if corporations are to behave more socially responsibly, as current laws direct corporations to be responsible to their shareholders, and make little mention of responsibility toward other stakeholders.

The Socio-Economic View

The **socio-economic view** says that management's social responsibility goes beyond making profits to include protecting and improving society's welfare. This position is based on the belief that corporations are *not* independent entities responsible only to stockholders. They also have a responsibility to the larger society that endorses their creation through various laws and regulations and supports them by purchasing their products and services. In addition, proponents of this view believe that business organizations are not mere economic institutions. Society expects and even encourages businesses to become involved in social, political, and legal issues. For example, proponents of the socio-economic view would say that Avon Products was being socially responsible when it initiated its Breast Cancer Crusade to provide women with breast cancer education and early detection screening services, and which, after 14 years, has raised more than $400 million worldwide.[29]

socio-economic view
The view that management's social responsibility goes beyond making profits to include protecting and improving society's welfare.

At Charlottetown, PEI-based APM Group, a construction and property development company, Terry Palmer, APM Group vice-president of finance (left), Tim Banks, president, Duane Lamont, vice-president of construction, and Pam Mullally, director of accounting, think about the bottom line when they review plans for new subdivisions APM might build. However, they also know that corporate social responsibility is a guiding principle for the company. So they also evaluate each project's impact on the environment, focus on design that promotes energy conservation, and strive to create a healthy economic community through the building plan.

Educational programs implemented by Brazilian cosmetics manufacturer Natura Cosmeticos SA in public primary schools in São Paulo to improve children's literacy and decision-making skills are also viewed as socially responsible.[30] Why? Through these programs, the managers are protecting and improving society's welfare. More and more organizations around the world are taking their social responsibilities seriously, especially in Europe, where the view that businesses need to focus on more than just profits has a stronger tradition than in North America.[31] Some even try to measure their "Triple Bottom Line," which takes into account not only financial responsibilities, but social and environmental ones as well.[32]

Comparing the Two Views

The key differences between the two views of corporate social responsibility are easier to understand if we think in terms of the people to whom organizations are responsible. Classicists would say that shareholders, or owners, are the only legitimate concern. Those supporting the socio-economic view would respond that managers should be responsible to any group affected by the organization's decisions and actions—that is, the stakeholders (such as employees and community members).[33] Exhibit 1-7 shows four different approaches that an organization can take toward corporate social responsibility.[34] The defensive approach is consistent with the classical view, while the accommodative and proactive approaches are consistent with the socio-economic view.

obstructionist approach
The avoidance of corporate social responsibility; managers engage in unethical and illegal behaviour that they try to hide from organizational stakeholders and society.

Would you be willing to stop eating your favourite snack if you found out the company did not use environmentally friendly packaging for its products?

Those who avoid corporate social responsibility altogether take an **obstructionist approach**. Obstructionist managers engage in unethical and illegal behaviour, and try to hide their behaviour from organizational stakeholders and society at large.

Those taking the minimal position toward corporate social responsibility use a **defensive approach**. These organizations have a commitment to ethical behaviour, making sure that employees behave legally and no harm is done to others. The claims and interests of shareholders come first with this approach, and little attention is paid to other stakeholders. Managers taking a defensive perspective rely only on legally established rules to guide their behaviour. They do not believe that they should make socially responsible choices that are not spelled out in laws and regulations. For instance, a company that meets pollution control standards established by the federal government or that does not discriminate against employees over the age of 40 in promotion decisions is meeting its social obligation and nothing more because there are laws mandating these actions.

defensive approach
Managers rely only on legally established rules to take the minimal position toward corporate social responsibility.

accommodative approach
Managers make choices that try to balance the interests of shareholders with those of other stakeholders.

Some managers go beyond legal requirements, choosing to support corporate social responsibility in a balanced fashion. These managers take an **accommodative approach**

Exhibit 1-7

Approaches to Corporate Social Responsibility

Obstructionist Approach	Defensive Approach	Accommodative Approach	Proactive Approach
Disregard for social responsibility	Minimal commitment to social responsibility	Moderate commitment to social responsibility	Strong commitment to social responsibility

No Social Responsibility   High Social Responsibility

to corporate social responsibility. Accommodative managers make choices that try to balance the interests of shareholders with those of other stakeholders. For instance, corporate social responsibility goals for suppliers and customers might include fair prices, high-quality products and services, safe products, good supplier relations, and similar actions. Their philosophy is that they can meet their responsibilities to stockholders only by meeting the needs of these other stakeholders.

Finally, some managers take an active interest in corporate social responsibility. These managers take a **proactive approach** to find out about and meet the needs of different stakeholder groups. They promote the interests of shareholders *and* stakeholders, using organizational resources to do so. These managers feel a responsibility to society as a whole. They view their business as a public entity and feel a responsibility to advance the public good, even if such actions may decrease profits. The acceptance of such responsibility means that managers actively promote social justice, preserve the environment, and support social and cultural activities. For instance, Vancouver-based Weyerhaeuser Canada is committed to sustainable forestry practices and has a formal policy for building relationships with Canada's Aboriginal peoples.

proactive approach
Managers go out of their way to actively promote the interests of stockholders *and* stakeholders, using organizational resources to do so.

 **Weyerhaeuser**
www.weyerhaeuser.com

Corporate Social Responsibility and Economic Performance

How do socially responsible activities affect a company's economic performance? Findings from a number of research studies can help us answer this question.[35] The majority of these studies show a positive relationship between social involvement and economic performance. For instance, one study found that firms' corporate social performance was positively associated with both *prior* and *future* financial performance.[36] But we should be cautious about making any compelling assumptions from these findings because of methodological questions associated with trying to measure "corporate social responsibility" and "economic performance."[37] Most of these studies determined a company's social performance by analyzing the content of annual reports, citations of social actions in news articles on the company, or "reputation" indexes based on public perception. Such criteria certainly have drawbacks as reliable measures of corporate social responsibility.

We can also look at what consumers say about corporate social responsibility. A recent survey conducted by GlobeScan, which specializes in corporate issues, found that "83 percent of Canadians believe that corporations should go beyond their traditional economic role; 51 percent say they have punished a socially irresponsible company in the past year."[38] As for naming a socially responsible company, 43 percent of Canadians said they could not do so.

What conclusion can we draw from all of this? Corporate social responsibility is generally good for the bottom line. It matters to consumers and there is little evidence to say that a company's social actions hurt its long-term economic performance. Given political and societal pressures on business to be socially involved, managers would be wise to take social goals into consideration as they plan, organize, lead, and control.

Workforce Diversity

Another challenge managers face is coordinating the work efforts of diverse organizational members in accomplishing organizational goals. Today's organizations are characterized by **workforce diversity**—the mix of people in organizations in terms of gender, race, ethnicity, disability, sexual orientation, and age, and demographic characteristics such as education and socio-economic status. Perhaps the most significant demographic characteristic affecting workforce diversity during the next decade will be the aging of the population.[39]

Canada is a very diverse country, although this might not be apparent to everyone. Based on the 2001 census, on average 13 percent of Canada's population are visible minorities.[40] This varies widely across the country, however. British Columbia has the highest proportion of visible minorities, 22 percent of its population. Ontario is second, with 19 percent of its population being visible minorities. Vancouver and Toronto have much higher rates than their respective provinces. In both of these cities, visible minorities make up about 37 percent of the population. By contrast, in Newfoundland and Labrador and Nunavut only 0.8 percent of the population are visible minorities; in Manitoba this figure is 7.9 percent, and in Alberta it is 11 percent. There are many more women and minorities—

workforce diversity
The mix of people in organizations in terms of gender, race, ethnicity, disability, sexual orientation, and age, and demographic characteristics such as education and socio-economic status.

McDonald's has expanded into India with fast-food menus that bear little resemblance to those served in Canada. Flavoured with Indian spices to cater to local tastes and featuring many vegetarian dishes, the food is also free of beef and beef products in deference to Hindu beliefs. A McDonald's was attacked a few years ago because it was thought to be using beef tallow in its cooking processes.

including people with disabilities and gays and lesbians—in the workforce than ever before, and most experts agree that diversity is steadily increasing.

The challenge for managers is to make organizations more accommodating to diverse groups of people by addressing different lifestyles, family needs, and work styles. Smart managers recognize that diversity can be an asset because it brings a broad range of viewpoints and problem-solving skills to a company, and also helps organizations better understand a diverse customer base. We highlight many diversity-related issues and discuss how companies are responding to them in our *Managing Workforce Diversity* feature in *Management @ Work*.

Globalization

Management is no longer constrained by national borders and has to confront the challenges of operating in a global market.[41] We devote some discussion to globalization in Chapter 2 and integrate discussion of its impact on the various management functions throughout this textbook.

Canada has been slow historically to face the global challenge. The *Fortune* list of the top 500 global companies of 2006 includes only 14 Canadian firms, and none of these appears in the top 200. The majority of the firms listed are American, but there are several entries from Britain, France, Germany, Japan, and China.[42] Managers who make no attempt to learn and adapt to changes in the global environment end up reacting rather than innovating; as a result, their organizations often become uncompetitive and fail.[43]

WHY STUDY MANAGEMENT?

As chief medical officer of health for Ontario, Dr. Sheela Basrur has great ambitions for what she will achieve. "My objective is to build a public health system for Ontario in which the whole is greater than the sum of its parts," she says. "We also need to bring a population health perspective to the health care system so we can prevent premature deaths, diseases and injuries wherever possible."[44] When Basrur was in medical school, studying to be a general practitioner, she may not have thought of being a manager at all. However, she will be more effective in achieving the goals she has set out if she understands the major functions of management: planning, organizing, leading, and controlling.

THINK ABOUT IT

Can knowing about management help, even in nonmanagement situations?

You may be wondering why you need to study management. If you are an accounting major, a marketing major, or any major other than management, you may not understand how studying management is going to help you in your career. We can explain the value of studying management by looking at the universality of management, the reality of work, and how management applies to anyone wanting to be self-employed.

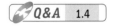

5 Does studying management make a difference?

Q&A 1.4

The Universality of Management

Just how universal is the need for management in organizations? We can say with absolute certainty that management is needed in all types and sizes of organizations, at all organizational levels, in all organizational work areas, and in all organizations, no matter what countries they are located in. This is known as the **universality of management** (see Exhibit 1-8). Managers in all these settings will plan, organize, lead, and control. However, this is not to say that management is done the same way in all settings. The differences in what a supervisor in a software applications–testing facility at Microsoft does versus what the CEO of Microsoft does are a matter of degree and emphasis, not of function. Because both are managers, both will plan, organize, lead, and control, but how they do so will differ.

Since management is universally needed in all organizations, we have a vested interest in improving the way organizations are managed. Why? We interact with organizations every single day of our lives. Are you irritated when none of the salespeople in a department store seems interested in helping you? Do you get annoyed when you call your computer's technical help desk because your CD-ROM drive is no longer working, go through 7 voice menus, and then get put on hold for 15 minutes? These are examples of problems created by poor management. Organizations that are well managed—and we will share many examples of these—develop a loyal customer base, grow, and prosper. Those that are poorly managed find themselves with a declining customer base and reduced revenues. By studying management, you will be able to recognize poor management and work to get it corrected. In addition, you will be able to recognize good management and encourage it, whether it's in an organization with which you are simply interacting or whether it's in an organization in which you are employed.

universality of management
The reality that management is needed in all types and sizes of organizations, at all organizational levels, in all organizational work areas, and in organizations in all countries around the globe.

Exhibit 1-8

Universal Need for Management

The Reality of Work

Another reason for studying management is the reality that most of you, once you graduate and begin your career, will either manage or be managed. For those who plan on management careers, an understanding of the management process forms the foundation upon which to build your management skills. For those of you who don't see yourselves in management positions, you are still likely to have to work with managers. Also, assuming that you will have to work for a living and recognizing that you are very likely to work in an organization, you will probably have some managerial responsibilities even if you are not managers. Our experience tells us that you can gain a great deal of insight into the way your manager behaves and the internal workings of organizations by studying management. Our point is that you don't have to aspire to be a manager to gain something valuable from a course in management.

Self-Employment

You may decide that you want to run your own business rather than work for someone else. This will require that you manage yourself, and may involve managing other people as well. Thus, an understanding of management is equally important, whether you are a manager in someone else's business or running your own business. To find out whether management might be something of interest to you, see *Self-Assessment—How Motivated Am I to Manage?* on pages 22–23, at the end of the chapter.

SUMMARY AND IMPLICATIONS

❶ What makes someone a manager? Managers work with and through other people by coordinating employee work activity in order to accomplish organizational goals. Managers may have personal goals, but management is not about *personal* achievement—it's about helping *others* to achieve for the benefit of the organization as a whole. *As we saw with Dr. Sheela Basrur, though she is quite an accomplished medical specialist, her focus is on improving health care delivery in Ontario, for the benefit of all people.*

❷ What is management and what do managers do? Management is coordinating work activities of people so that they are done efficiently and effectively. Efficiency means "doing things right" and getting things done at the least cost. Effectiveness means "doing the right things" and refers to completing activities that will help achieve the organization's goals. To do their jobs, managers plan, organize, lead, and control. This means they set goals and plan how to achieve those goals; they figure out what tasks need to be done, and who should do them; they motivate individuals to achieve goals, and communicate effectively with others; and they put accountability measures into place to make sure that goals are achieved efficiently and effectively. *In Sheela Basrur's role as chief medical officer of health for Ontario, she sets the goals for health planning in Ontario, working with the various regional medical officers of health. One of the challenges she faces is determining how to best achieve the goal of effective health delivery without getting bogged down with politics.*

❸ What characteristics define an organization? There is no single type of organization. Managers work in a variety of organizations, both large and small. They also work in a variety of industries, including manufacturing and the service sector. The organizations they work for can be publicly held (meaning shares are traded on the stock exchange and managers are responsible to shareholders), privately held (meaning shares are not available to the public), public sector (where the government is the employer), or nonprofit (where the emphasis is on providing charity or services rather than on making a profit). *Sheela Basrur works in the public sector, and she reports to the Ontario Minister of Health and Long-Term Care, George Smitherman. This means that her actions are scrutinized by the government in power, which considers whether her goals are consistent with those of the Ontario provincial government.*

4 **What are the challenges to managing?**   Perhaps one of the greatest challenges of managers is the crisis in ethical responsibility that is damaging confidence in today's organizations. Managers need to ensure organizational members behave ethically in their actions. They also need to consider whether their actions are socially responsible. Managers face the challenge of coordinating the work of a diverse workforce with differing needs. In addition, operating in today's global marketplace presents its own challenges and puts increasing pressure on managers. *Sheela Basrur will likely be concerned with ethical issues—how to report to the government and also do the right thing for public health. Basrur will face health crises that arise because we are interconnected to the rest of the world through air travel, which makes it easier for new diseases to appear in Canada. Her most important challenge may be how to share information rapidly during times of public health crises, something her predecessor was criticized for during the SARS crisis, when information was not shared consistently and openly.*

5 **Does studying management make a difference?**   There are many reasons why students end up in management courses. Some of you are already managers, and are hoping to learn more about the subject. Some of you hope to be managers someday. And some of you might not have ever thought about being managers. Career aspirations are only one reason to study management, however. Any organization you encounter will have managers, and it is often useful to understand their responsibilities, challenges, and experience. Understanding management also helps us improve organizations. *When Sheela Basrur was studying medicine, it is unlikely that she thought that one day she would become a manager, because at that time she was thinking more about how she would work with patients. However, over time her interest in the public health aspects of medicine led her to a more managerial focus in her career.*

CHAPTER 1

Management @ Work

Reading for Comprehension

1. How does a manager's job change with his or her level in the organization?

2. What four common activities compose the functions approach to management? Briefly describe each of them.

3. What are the three categories of management roles proposed by Mintzberg? Provide an example of each.

4. What are the three skills that affect managerial effectiveness?

5. What is an organization? Why are managers important to an organization's success?

6. Contrast the classical and socio-economic views of corporate social responsibility.

7. Discuss the role that stakeholders play in the four approaches to corporate social responsibility.

Linking Concepts to Practice

1. Are effective organizations always efficient? Discuss. If you had to choose between being effective or being efficient, which would you say is more important? Why?

2. In today's economic environment, which is more important to organizations—efficiency or effectiveness? Explain your choice.

3. Contrast planning, organizing, leading, and controlling with Henry Mintzberg's 10 management roles.

4. Is your instructor a manager? Discuss in terms of planning, organizing, leading, and controlling, and of Mintzberg's managerial roles.

5. In what ways would the job activities of an owner of an automotive repair shop that employs two people and

the president of the Ford Motor Company be similar? In what ways would they be different?

6. Some individuals today have the title of project leader. They manage projects of various sizes and durations and must coordinate the talents of many people to accomplish their goals, but none of the employees on their projects reports directly to them. Can these project leaders really be considered managers if they have no employees over whom they have direct authority? Discuss.

7. What does corporate social responsibility mean to you personally? Do you think business organizations should be socially responsible? Explain.

MANAGEMENT FOR YOU TODAY

Think about where you hope to be in your life five years from now (that is, your major goal). What is your competitive advantage for achieving your goal? What do you need to plan, organize, lead, and control to make sure that you reach your goal? Looking over Mintzberg's management roles (Exhibit 1-3), which roles seem comfortable for you? What areas need improvement?

SELF-ASSESSMENT

How Motivated Am I to Manage?

For each of the following statements, circle the level of agreement or disagreement that you personally feel:[45]

> 1 = Strongly Disagree
> 4 = Neither Agree nor Disagree
> 7 = Strongly Agree

1. I have a generally positive attitude toward those holding positions of authority over me.　1 2 3 4 5 6 7

2. I enjoy competition and striving to win for myself and my work group.　1 2 3 4 5 6 7

3. I like to tell others what to do and have no problem with imposing sanctions to enforce my directives.　1 2 3 4 5 6 7

4. I like being active, assertive, and protecting the members of my work group.　1 2 3 4 5 6 7

5. I enjoy the idea of standing out from the group, behaving in a unique manner, and being highly visible.　1 2 3 4 5 6 7

6. I am willing to perform routine, day-to-day administrative tasks and duties.　1 2 3 4 5 6 7

Scoring Key

Add up your responses to the six items.

Analysis and Interpretation

Not everyone is motivated to perform managerial functions. This instrument taps six components that have been found to be related to managerial success, especially in larger organizations. These are a favourable attitude toward authority; a desire to compete; a desire to exercise power; assertiveness; a desire for a distinctive position; and a willingness to engage in repetitive tasks.

Scores on this instrument will range from 6 to 42. Arbitrary cut-offs suggest that scores of 6 to 18 indicate low motivation to manage; 19 to 29 is moderate motivation; and 30 and above is high motivation.

What meaning can you draw from your score? It gives you an idea of how comfortable you would be doing managerial activities. Note, however, that this instrument emphasizes tasks associated with managing in larger and more bureaucratic organizations. A low or moderate score may indicate that you are more suited to managing in a small firm, an organic organization, or in entrepreneurial situations.

More Self-Assessments

To learn more about your skills, abilities, and interests, take the following self-assessments on your enclosed CD-ROM:

- #4—How Well Do I Handle Ambiguity?
- #23—What's My Emotional Intelligence Score?
- #26—Am I Likely to Become an Entrepreneur?
- #49—How Well Do I Respond to Turbulent Change? (This exercise also appears in Chapter 12 on pages 360–362.)

WORKING TOGETHER: TEAM-BASED EXERCISE

A New Beginning

By this time in your life, all of you have had to work with individuals in managerial positions (or maybe you were the manager), either through work experiences or through other organizational experiences (social, hobby/interest, religious, and so forth). What do you think makes some managers better than others? Are there certain characteristics that distinguish good managers? Form small groups of 3 to 4 class members. Discuss your experiences with managers—good and bad. Draw up a list of the characteristics of those individuals you felt were good managers. For each characteristic, indicate which management function (planning, leading, organizing, controlling) you think it falls under. Also identify which of Mintzberg's 10 roles the good managers seemed to fill. Were any of the roles missing from your list of characteristics? What explanation can you give for this? As a group, be prepared to explain the functions and roles that good managers are most likely to fill.

Are Canadian Executives Paid Too Much?

Are we paying executives too much? Is an average salary in 2006 in excess of $9 million justifiable?[46] In any debate, there are two sides to the issue. One fact that supports paying this amount is that CEOs of large organizations have tremendous organizational responsibilities. They not only have to manage the organization in today's environment, but also must keep it moving into the future. Their jobs are not 9-to-5 jobs, but rather 6 to 7 days a week, often 10 to 14 hours a day. If jobs are evaluated on the basis of skills, knowledge, abilities, and responsibilities, executives should be highly paid.[47] Furthermore, there is the issue of motivation and retention. If you want these individuals to succeed and stay with the company, you must provide a compensation package that motivates them to stay. Incentives based on various measures also provide the impetus for them to excel.

Most of the research done on executive salaries questions the link to performance. Even when profits are down, many executives are paid handsomely. In fact, Canadian corporate executives are some of the most highly paid people in the world (although American CEOs are paid more). Additionally, pay does not always seem directly related to performance.[48] If one takes into account company performance when evaluating a CEO's pay, Ian Telfer and Robert McEwen of Vancouver-based Goldcorp together were overpaid $31 510 000 in 2005. Jeffrey Orr and Robert Gratton of Montreal-based Power Financial Corporation together were overpaid $66 241 000, and Gerald Schwartz of Toronto-based Onex was overpaid $21 454 000 for the same year.[49]

Do you believe that Canadian executives are overpaid? Explain your opinion.

Lipschultz Levin & Gray

You might be surprised to find the passionate emphasis placed on people at an accounting firm.[50] Yet at Lipschultz Levin & Gray (**www.thethinkers.com**), self-described "head bean counter" Steven P. Siegel recognizes that his people make the organization. He describes his primary responsibility as assuring that LLG's clients have the best professionals working for them. And the best way to do this, Siegel feels, is by developing the creativity, talent, and diversity of its staff so that new knowledge can be acquired and shared without getting hung up on formal organizational relationships or having employees shut away in corner offices.

The commitment to its people starts with the company's mission, which says,

> LLG's goal is to be the pre-eminent provider of the highest quality accounting, tax and consulting services. LLG accomplishes this goal by leaving no stone unturned in exploring new and superior alternatives of supplying our services, and developing such methods on a global basis. Our environment promotes creativity, individual development, group interchange, diversity, good humor, family and community, all for the purpose of assisting in our clients' growth.

To further demonstrate that commitment, Siegel has implemented several significant changes at LLG. Because he is convinced that people do their best intellectual work in nontraditional settings, every telltale sign of what most people consider boring, dull accounting work has been eliminated. None of the firm's employees or partners has an office or desk to call his or her own. Instead, everyone is part of a nomadic arrangement in which stuff (files, phones, laptops) is wheeled to a new spot every day. Everywhere you look in the company's office, you see versatility, comfort, and individuality. For instance, a miniature golf course is located in the middle of everything. The motivation behind this open office design is to create opportunities for professionals to gather—on purpose or by accident—without walls, cubicles, or offices to get in the way.

Visitors to LLG realize that the firm is different as soon as they walk in the door. A giant, wall-mounted abacus (remember the image of bean counters) decorates the interior. And visitors are greeted by a "Welcome Wall" with a big-screen television that flashes a continuous slide show of one-liners about business, life, and innovation. The setting may be fun and lighthearted, but the LLG team is seriously committed to serving its clients. So serious, in fact, that they state,

> We have one goal. To "Delight" you. Good, even great, is not enough any more. We will "Dazzle" you and we will guarantee it; We will deliver our service with integrity, honesty and openness in everything we do for you and with you; We will absolutely respect the confidentiality of our working relationship; We will return your phone calls, facsimiles and e-mails within 24 hours; We will always provide exceptional service, designed to help you

add significant value to your business; We will meet the deadlines we set together with you; We will communicate with you frequently, building a win-win relationship with you; and You will always know in advance our fee arrangement for any service.

Yesterday, one of Siegel's new employees complained in an email to him that the work environment is too informal and that employees need their own desks. This employee has done well in her first few months on the job. Siegel is meeting with her in an hour. What should he say to her?

DEVELOPING YOUR DIAGNOSTIC AND ANALYTICAL SKILLS

You're Fired!

You're fired! These are two words that no one ever wants to hear. But they quickly became the rage with the television show *The Apprentice,* starring CEO extraordinaire Donald Trump. The premise of the show is simple. Sixteen contestants begin a 15-week journey of difficult tasks, requiring them to demonstrate their intelligence, competency, and competitive edge. Working in a team, contestants are required to deal with business issues in such areas as sales, marketing, finance, and facilities management—concerns that executives face every day in their work. For instance, on one show, teams were required to launch a new product called Trump Ice. Contestants play with real money and real business situations, with teams winning and losing based on their performance. The winning team receives a reward from "The Donald," while the losing team sees one of their team members fired by Mr. Trump. Why do contestants put themselves through this potentially humiliating process? The answer is simple: The winner is awarded an executive position in The Trump Organization, with a starting salary of $250 000 (US) a year.

The show is a success. Ratings are considerably higher than expected. But Trump, who has made a career of taking risks, put his reputation and assets on the line for *The Apprentice.* Some critics felt that the show would put The Trump Organization in a poor light, especially given the backlash that the public has had toward "greed" in corporate America and Trump's image as a publicity seeker. Others felt that the premise of the show could also reveal a cutthroat, status-ridden aspect of business that does not offer a very favourable image of managers. Some, too, felt that the show's emphasis on contestants striving to succeed at all costs was in poor taste and might demoralize many of Trump's current employees, causing them to lose respect and trust for the company's leaders. Trump's response: "I don't worry about them. I pay them a lot of money."

Like so many ventures before, Trump has proven the naysayers wrong. What he has accomplished is something that one may not be able to put a value on—an hour-long, prime-time commercial for Trump himself and The Trump Organization. In fact, other companies are paying upwards of a million dollars just to advertise on the show.

Is Donald Trump a genius? Has he been successful by doing things "outside the box"? Once again it appears so. And both Donald Trump and The Trump Organization are winning.

Questions

1. What management roles does Donald Trump demonstrate in leading his company and in dealing with employees? Cite examples.

2. How does Donald Trump use technical, human, and conceptual skills to encourage his organization to be innovative and creative? Discuss.

3. Do you believe Trump's risk-taking emphasis would work in other organizations? If yes, what type of organization? If no, why not?

DEVELOPING YOUR INTERPERSONAL SKILLS

Mentoring

About the Skill

A mentor is someone in the organization, usually older, more experienced, and in a higher-level position, who sponsors or supports another employee (a protégé) who is in a lower-level position in the organization. A mentor can teach, guide, and encourage. Some organizations have formal mentoring programs, but even if your organization does not, mentoring should be an important skill for you to develop.

Steps in Developing the Skill

You can be more effective at mentoring if you use the following six suggestions as you mentor another person:[51]

1. **Communicate honestly and openly with your protégé.** If your protégé is going to learn from you and benefit from your experience and knowledge, you are going to have to be open and honest as you talk about what you have

done. Bring up the failures as well as the successes. Remember that mentoring is a learning process, and in order for learning to take place you are going to have to be open and honest in "telling it like it is."

2. **Encourage honest and open communication from your protégé.** You need to know as the mentor what your protégé hopes to gain from this relationship. You should encourage the protégé to ask for information and be specific about what he or she wants to gain.

3. **Treat the relationship with the protégé as a learning opportunity.** Do not pretend to have all the answers and all the knowledge, but do share what you have learned through your experiences. In your conversations and interactions with your protégé, you may be able to learn as much from that person as he or she does from you. So be open to listening to what your protégé is saying.

4. **Take the time to get to know your protégé.** As a mentor, you should be willing to take the time to get to know your protégé and his or her interests. If you are not willing to spend that extra time, you should probably not embark on a mentoring relationship.

5. **Remind your protégé that there is no substitute for effective work performance.** In any job, effective work performance is absolutely essential for success. It does not matter how much information you provide as a mentor if the protégé is not willing to strive for effective work performance.

6. **Know when it's time to let go.** Successful mentors know when it's time to let the protégé begin standing on his or her own. If the mentoring relationship has been effective, the protégé will be comfortable and confident in handling new and increasing work responsibilities. Just because the mentoring relationship is over does not mean that you never have contact with your protégé. It just means that the relationship becomes one of equals, not one of teacher and student.

Practising the Skill

Lora Slovinsky has worked for your department in a software design firm longer than any other of your employees. You value her skills and commitment, and you frequently ask for her judgment on difficult issues. Very often, her ideas have been better than yours and you have let her know through both praise and pay increases how much you appreciate her contributions. Recently, though, you have begun to question Lora's judgment. The fundamental problem is in the distinct difference in the ways you both approach your work. Your strengths lie in getting things done on time and under budget. Although Lora is aware of these constraints, her creativity and perfectionism sometimes make her prolong projects, continuously looking for the best approaches. On her most recent assignment, Lora seemed more intent than ever on doing things her way. Despite what you felt were clear guidelines, she was two weeks late in meeting an important customer deadline. While her product quality was high, as always, the software design was far more elaborate than what was needed at this stage of development. Looking over her work in your office, you feel more than a little frustrated and certain that you need to address matters with Lora. What will you say?

History of Management Trends

Walk down almost any street in Vancouver, and you'll spot a number of people carrying paper cups of coffee, picked up from one of the many local coffee shops found on many corners. The per capita coffee consumption in Canada is high, an average of 402 cups of coffee per year, almost 25 percent more than Americans, and 161 percent more than Europeans.[1] Vancouverites do their share to keep the numbers up.

Christine Corkan noticed the coffee drinkers and the coffee shops in Vancouver and realized that there were lots of places where one couldn't easily get a cup of coffee in the city. Trendy coffee shops tend not to be located next door to community parks, for instance, where people play soccer, baseball, and field hockey. From that observation, her business, Java Jazz Mobile Café, was born.

Java Jazz offers coffee, tea, and cold drinks, as well as baked goods, smoothies, and fresh fruit from the side of a cube van outfitted with a small kitchen run on a generator. Corkan aims to fill the niche where other concessions are not available, and can be hired for any private event in the area that wants to have coffee and beverages available onsite.

Corkan started developing her business with $35 000, almost all of it loaned to her by a friend at 5 percent interest. With the money, she had to purchase and furnish the van and buy beverages and serving cups.

In August, two months after starting the business, Corkan feels she is doing well. Her previous job was with Air Canada. "I made more in two days with Java Jazz than I make in a month at the airport," she said. "I have the first payment already saved for my loan and it's not due until November."

It is important for managers such as Corkan to understand how to run a business, a new experience for her, compared with working for Air Canada. Corkan would do well to learn more about different management theories, as they provide a framework for managing one's business, dealing with employees when she brings them on, and understanding the environment of the business. One of the keys to her success will be understanding as much as she can about how management works. Below we review the history of management thought. As you read through it, you may want to identify some of the tips that would help you be a better manager.

INTRODUCTION

Looking at management history can help us understand today's management theory and practice. It can help us see what worked and what didn't work. In this supplement, we'll introduce you to the origins of many contemporary management concepts and show how they have evolved to reflect the changing needs of organizations and society as a whole. Q&A S1.1

Six major management theories have arisen over time: scientific management, general administrative theory, the quantitative approach, organizational behaviour, the systems approach, and the contingency approach (see Exhibit S1-1). Each of the six perspectives contributes to our overall understanding of management. However, each is also a limited view of a particular aspect of management. We begin our journey into management's past by looking at the first major theory of management—scientific management.

SCIENTIFIC MANAGEMENT

If you had to pinpoint the year modern management theory was born, 1911 might be a logical choice. That was the year Frederick Winslow Taylor's *The Principles of Scientific Management* was published. Its contents were widely accepted by managers around the world. The book described the theory of scientific management: the use of scientific methods to define the "one best way" for a job to be done.

Important Contributions

Important contributions to scientific management theory were made by Frederick W. Taylor and Frank and Lillian Gilbreth. Let's look at what they did.

Frederick W. Taylor

Taylor did most of his work at the Midvale and Bethlehem Steel companies in Pennsylvania. As a mechanical engineer with a Quaker and Puritan background, he was continually shocked at how employees performed. He observed that they used vastly different techniques to do the same job and were inclined to "take it easy" on the job. Taylor believed that employee output was only about one-third of what was possible. Virtually no work standards existed. Employees were placed in jobs with little or no concern for matching their abilities and aptitudes with the tasks they were required to do. Taylor set out to correct the situation by applying the scientific method to shop-floor jobs and spent more than two decades passionately pursuing the "one best way" for each job to be done.

Taylor's experiences at Midvale led him to define clear guidelines for improving production efficiency. He argued that four principles of management (see *Tips for Managers—Taylor's Four Principles of Management*) would result in prosperity for both employees and managers.[2] Through his studies

---

Exhibit S1-1

Development of Major Management Theories

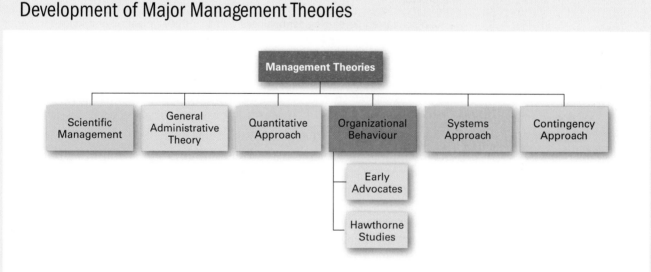

of manual work using scientific principles, Taylor became known as the "father" of scientific management. His ideas spread in the United States, France, Germany, Russia, and Japan, and inspired others to study and develop methods of scientific management. His most prominent followers were Frank and Lillian Gilbreth.

Frank and Lillian Gilbreth

A construction contractor by trade, Frank Gilbreth gave up that career to study scientific management after hearing Taylor speak at a professional meeting. Frank and his wife, Lillian, a psychologist, studied work to eliminate wasteful hand-and-body motions. The Gilbreths also experimented with the design and use of the proper tools and equipment for optimizing work performance.[3]

Frank is probably best known for his experiments in bricklaying. By carefully analyzing the bricklayer's job, he reduced the number of motions in laying exterior brick from 18 to about 5, and on laying interior brick the motions were reduced from 18 to 2. Using Gilbreth's techniques, the bricklayer could be more productive and less fatigued at the end of the day.

The Gilbreths were among the first researchers to use motion pictures to study hand-and-body motions. They invented a device called a micro-chronometer, which recorded an employee's motions and the amount of time spent doing each motion. Wasted motions missed by the naked eye could be identified and eliminated. The Gilbreths also devised a classification scheme to label 17 basic hand motions (such as search, grasp, hold), which they called therbligs ("Gilbreth" spelled backward with the *th* transposed). This scheme allowed the Gilbreths a more precise way of analyzing an employee's exact hand movements.

How Do Today's Managers Use Scientific Management?

The guidelines that Taylor and others devised for improving production efficiency are still used in organizations today.[4] When managers analyze the basic work tasks that must be performed, use time-and-motion study to eliminate wasted motions, hire the best qualified workers for a job, and design incentive systems based on output, they are using the principles of scientific management. But current management practice is not restricted to scientific management. In fact, we can see ideas from the next major approach—general administrative theory—being used as well. **Q&A S1.2**

GENERAL ADMINISTRATIVE THEORY

Another group of writers looked at the subject of management but focused on the entire organization. These general administrative theorists developed more general theories of what managers do and what constitutes good management practice. Let's look at some important contributions that grew out of this perspective.

Important Contributions

The two most prominent theorists behind the general administrative theory were Henri Fayol and Max Weber.

Henri Fayol

We mention Fayol in Chapter 1 because he described management as a universal set of functions that included planning, organizing, commanding, coordinating, and controlling. Because his ideas were important, let's look more closely at what he had to say.[5]

Fayol wrote during the same time period as Taylor. While Taylor was concerned with first-line managers and the scientific method, Fayol's attention was directed at the activities of *all* managers. He wrote from personal experience as he was the managing director of a large French coal-mining firm.

Fayol described the practice of management as something distinct from accounting, finance, production, distribution, and other typical business functions. His belief that management was an activity common to all human endeavours in business, government, and even in the home led him to develop 14 principles of management—fundamental rules of management that could be taught in schools and applied in all organizational situations. These principles are shown in *Tips for Managers—Fayol's 14 Principles of Management.* **Q&A S1.3**

TIPS FOR MANAGERS

Taylor's Four Principles of Management

→ **Develop a science for each element of an individual's work**, which will replace the old rule-of-thumb method.

→ **Scientifically select** and then train, teach, and develop employees.

→ **Heartily cooperate with employees** so as to ensure that all work is done in accordance with the principles of the science that has been developed.

→ **Divide work and responsibility almost equally** between management and employees. Management takes over all work for which it is better fitted than the employees.

Max Weber

Weber (pronounced VAY-ber) was a German sociologist who studied organizational activity. Writing in the early 1900s, he developed a theory of authority structures and relations.[6] Weber described an ideal type of organization that he called a bureaucracy—a form of organization characterized by division of labour, a clearly defined hierarchy, detailed rules and regulations, and impersonal relationships. Weber recognized that this "ideal bureaucracy" did not exist in reality. Instead he intended it as a basis for theorizing about how work could be done in large groups. His theory became the model structural design for many of today's large organizations. The features of Weber's ideal bureaucratic structure are outlined in Exhibit S1-2.

Bureaucracy, as described by Weber, is a lot like scientific management in its ideology. Both emphasize rationality, predictability, impersonality, technical competence, and authoritarianism. Although Weber's writings were less operational than Taylor's, the fact that his "ideal type" still describes many contemporary organizations attests to the importance of his work.

How Do Today's Managers Use General Administrative Theory?

Some of our current management ideas and practices can be traced directly to the contributions of the general administrative theorists. For instance, the functional view of the manager's job can be attributed to Fayol. In addition, his 14 principles serve as a frame of reference from which many current management concepts have evolved.

Weber's bureaucracy was an attempt to formulate an ideal prototype for organizations. Although many characteristics of Weber's bureaucracy are still evident in large organizations, his

TIPS FOR MANAGERS

Fayol's 14 Principles of Management

→ **Division of work.** Specialization increases output by making employees more efficient.

→ **Authority.** Managers must be able to give orders, and authority gives them this right.

→ **Discipline.** Employees must obey and respect the rules that govern the organization.

→ **Unity of command.** Every employee should receive orders from only one superior.

→ **Unity of direction.** The organization should have a single plan of action to guide managers and employees.

→ **Subordination of individual interests to the general interest.** The interests of any one employee or group of employees should not take precedence over the interests of the organization as a whole.

→ **Remuneration.** Employees must be paid a fair wage for their services.

→ **Centralization.** This term refers to the degree to which subordinates are involved in decision making.

→ **Scalar chain.** The line of authority from top management to the lowest ranks is the scalar chain.

→ **Order.** People and materials should be in the right place at the right time.

→ **Equity.** Managers should be kind and fair to their subordinates.

→ **Stability of tenure of personnel.** Management should provide orderly personnel planning and ensure that replacements are available to fill vacancies.

→ **Initiative.** Employees who are allowed to originate and carry out plans will exert high levels of effort.

→ **Esprit de corps.** Promoting team spirit will build harmony and unity within the organization.

model is not as popular today as it was in the twentieth century. Many contemporary managers feel that bureaucracy's emphasis on strict division of labour, adherence to formal rules and regulations, and impersonal application of rules and controls take away the individual employee's creativity and the organization's ability to respond quickly to an increasingly dynamic environment. However, even in highly flexible organizations of talented professionals—such as Calgary-based WestJet Airlines, Toronto-based

ING Bank of Canada, or Ottawa-based Corel—some bureaucratic mechanisms are necessary to ensure that resources are used efficiently and effectively.

THE QUANTITATIVE APPROACH

The quantitative approach involves the use of quantitative techniques to improve decision making. This approach also has been called *operations research* or *management science.*

Exhibit S1-2

Weber's Ideal Bureaucracy

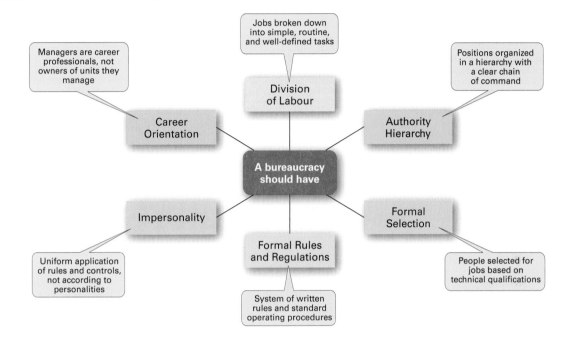

Managers are career professionals, not owners of units they manage

Jobs broken down into simple, routine, and well-defined tasks

Positions organized in a hierarchy with a clear chain of command

Career Orientation

Division of Labour

Authority Hierarchy

A bureaucracy should have

Impersonality

Formal Rules and Regulations

Formal Selection

Uniform application of rules and controls, not according to personalities

System of written rules and standard operating procedures

People selected for jobs based on technical qualifications

Important Contributions

The quantitative approach evolved out of the development of mathematical and statistical solutions to military problems during World War II. After the war was over, many of the techniques that had been used to solve military problems were applied to businesses. One group of military officers, nicknamed the Whiz Kids, joined Ford Motor Company in the mid-1940s and immediately began using statistical methods and quantitative models to improve decision making. Two of these individuals whose names you might recognize are Robert McNamara (who went on to become president of Ford, US Secretary of Defense, head of the World Bank, and was recently featured in the documentary *The Fog of War*) and Charles "Tex" Thornton (who founded Litton Industries).

What exactly does the quantitative approach do? It involves applications of statistics, optimization models, information models, and computer simulations to management activities. Linear programming, for instance, is a technique that managers use to improve resource allocation decisions. Work scheduling can be more efficient as a result of critical-path scheduling analysis. The economic order quantity model helps managers determine optimum inventory levels. Each of these is an example of quantitative techniques being applied to improve managerial decision making.

How Do Today's Managers Use the Quantitative Approach?

The quantitative approach contributes directly to management decision making in the areas of planning and control. For instance, when managers make budgeting, scheduling, quality control, and similar decisions, they typically rely on quantitative techniques. The availability of software programs has made the use of quantitative techniques somewhat less intimidating for managers, although they must still be able to interpret the results.

The quantitative approach has not influenced management practice as much as the next approach we are going to discuss—organizational behaviour—for a number of reasons. These include the fact that many managers are unfamiliar with and intimidated by quantitative tools, behavioural problems are more widespread and visible, and it is easier for most students and managers to relate to real, day-to-day people problems than to the more abstract activity of constructing quantitative models.

Exhibit S1-3

Early Advocates of OB

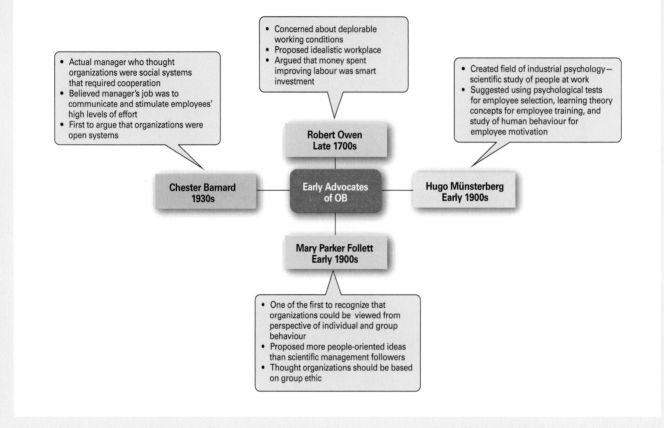

- Actual manager who thought organizations were social systems that required cooperation
- Believed manager's job was to communicate and stimulate employees' high levels of effort
- First to argue that organizations were open systems

- Concerned about deplorable working conditions
- Proposed idealistic workplace
- Argued that money spent improving labour was smart investment

- Created field of industrial psychology—scientific study of people at work
- Suggested using psychological tests for employee selection, learning theory concepts for employee training, and study of human behaviour for employee motivation

Chester Barnard 1930s

Robert Owen Late 1700s

Early Advocates of OB

Hugo Münsterberg Early 1900s

Mary Parker Follett Early 1900s

- One of the first to recognize that organizations could be viewed from perspective of individual and group behaviour
- Proposed more people-oriented ideas than scientific management followers
- Thought organizations should be based on group ethic

ORGANIZATIONAL BEHAVIOUR

As we know, managers get things done by working with people. This explains why some writers have chosen to look at management by focusing on the organization's human resources. The field of study concerned with the actions (behaviour) of people at work is called organizational behaviour (OB). Much of what currently makes up the field of human resource management, as well as contemporary views on motivation, leadership, trust, teamwork, and conflict management, has come out of OB research.

Early Advocates

Although a number of people in the late 1800s and early 1900s recognized the importance of the human factor to an organization's success, four stand out as early advocates of the OB approach: Robert Owen, Hugo Münsterberg, Mary Parker Follett, and Chester Barnard. The contributions of these individuals were varied and distinct, yet they all believed that people were the most important asset of the organization and should be managed accordingly. Their ideas provided the foundation for such management practices as employee selection procedures, employee motivation programs, employee work teams, and organization–environment manage-

ment techniques. Exhibit S1-3 summarizes the most important ideas of the early advocates of OB.

The Hawthorne Studies

Without question, the most important contribution to the developing OB field came out of the Hawthorne Studies, a series of studies conducted at the Western Electric Company Works in Cicero, Illinois. These studies, which started in 1924, were initially designed by Western Electric industrial engineers as a scientific management experiment. They wanted to examine the effect of various illumination levels on employee productivity. As in any good scientific experiment, control and experimental groups were set up with the experimental group's being exposed to various lighting intensities, and the control group working under a constant intensity. If you were the industrial engineers in charge of this experiment, what would you have expected to happen? It's logical to think that individual output in the experimental group would be directly related to the intensity of the light. However, they found that as the level of light was increased in the experimental group, output for both groups increased. Then, much to the surprise of the engineers, as the light level was decreased in the experimental group, productivity continued to increase in both groups. In fact, a productivity decrease was observed in the experimental group *only* when the level of light was reduced to that of a moonlit night. What would explain these unexpected results? The engineers were not sure, but concluded that illumination intensity was not directly related to group productivity, and that something else must have contributed to the results. They were not able to pinpoint what that "something else" was, though.

In 1927, the Western Electric engineers asked Harvard professor Elton Mayo and his associates to join the study as consultants. Thus began a relationship that would last through 1932 and encompass numerous experiments in the redesign of jobs, changes in workday and workweek length, introduction of rest periods, and individual vs. group wage plans.[7] For example, one experiment was designed to evaluate the effect of a group piecework incentive pay system on group productivity. The results indicated that the incentive plan had less effect on an employee's output than did group pressure, acceptance, and security. The researchers concluded that social norms or group standards were the key determinants of individual work behaviour.

Scholars generally agree that the Hawthorne Studies had a dramatic impact on management beliefs about the role of human behaviour in organizations. Mayo concluded that behaviour and attitudes are closely related, that group influences significantly affect individual behaviour, that group standards establish individual worker output, and that money is less a factor in determining output than are group standards, group attitudes, and security. These conclusions led to a new emphasis on the human behaviour factor in the management of organizations and the attainment of goals.

However, these conclusions were criticized. Critics attacked the research procedures, analyses of findings, and conclusions.[8] From a historical standpoint, it's of little importance whether the studies were academically sound or their conclusions justified. What *is* important is that they stimulated an interest in human behaviour in organizations. **Q&A S1.4**

How Do Today's Managers Use the Behavioural Approach?

The behavioural approach has largely shaped today's organizations. From the way managers design motivating jobs to the way they work with employee teams to the way they use open communication, we can see elements of the behavioural approach. Much of what the early OB advocates proposed and the conclusions from the Hawthorne Studies provided the foundation for our current theories of motivation, leadership, group behaviour and development, and numerous other behavioural topics that we address fully in later chapters.

THE SYSTEMS APPROACH

During the 1960s, researchers began to analyze organizations from a systems perspective, a concept taken from the physical sciences. A system is a set of interrelated and interdependent parts arranged in a manner that produces a unified whole. The two basic types of systems are closed and open. Closed systems are not influenced by and do not interact with their environment. This is very much how Air Canada operated when it was a Crown corporation. Because it was in a regulated industry, it did not need to worry about competition. When the Canadian airline industry was deregulated, Air Canada was slow to adapt to the new competitive environment and went into bankruptcy protection in order to restructure its operations and attempt to become a more open system.[9]

Open systems dynamically interact with their environment. Today, when we describe organizations as systems, we mean open systems. Exhibit S1-4 shows a diagram of an organization from an open systems perspective. As you can see, an organization takes in inputs (resources) from the environment and transforms or processes these resources into outputs that are distributed into the environment. The organization is "open" to its environment and interacts with that environment.

The Systems Approach and Managers

How does the systems approach contribute to our understanding of management thinking? Systems researchers envisioned an organization as made up of "interdependent factors, including individuals, groups, attitudes, motives, formal structure, interactions, goals, status, and authority."[10] What this means is that managers coordinate the work activities of the various parts of the organization and ensure that all the interdependent parts of the organization are working together so that the organization's goals can be achieved. For example, the systems approach would recognize that, no

Exhibit S1-4

The Organization as an Open System

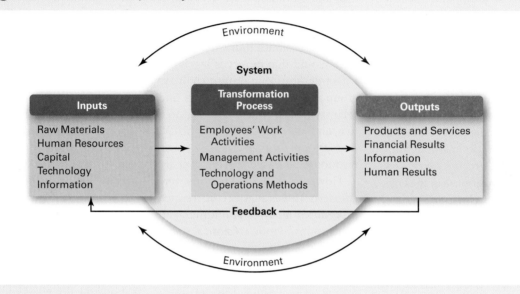

matter how efficient the production department might be, if the marketing department does not anticipate changes in customer tastes and work with the product development department in creating products customers want, the organization's overall performance will suffer. This approach is very different from the "silo" approach in some organizations by which each individual unit operates almost in isolation from other units.

In addition, the systems approach implies that decisions and actions taken in one organizational area will affect others and vice versa. For example, if the purchasing department does not acquire the right quantity and quality of inputs, the production department will not be able to do its job effectively.

Finally, the systems approach recognizes that organizations are not self-contained. They rely on their environments for essential inputs and as sources to absorb their outputs. No organization can survive for long if it ignores government regulations, supplier relations, or the varied external constituencies upon which it depends.

(We cover these external forces in Chapter 2.)

How relevant is the systems approach to management? Quite relevant. Think, for example, of a day-shift manager at a local Harvey's restaurant who every day must coordinate the work of employees filling customer orders at the front counter and the drive-through windows, direct the delivery and unloading of food supplies, and address any customer concerns that come up. This manager "manages" all parts of the "system" so that the restaurant meets its daily sales goals. **Q&A** S1.5

THE CONTINGENCY APPROACH

Early management thinkers such as Taylor, Fayol, and Weber gave us principles of management that they generally assumed to be universally applicable. Later research found exceptions to many of their principles. For example, division of labour is valuable and widely used, but jobs can

become *too* specialized. Bureaucracy is desirable in many situations, but in other circumstances, other structural designs are *more* effective. Management is not (and cannot be) based on simplistic principles to be applied in all situations. Different and changing situations require managers to use different approaches and techniques. The contingency approach (sometimes called the *situational approach*) says that organizations are different, face different situations (contingencies), and require different ways of managing.

The Contingency Approach and Managers

A contingency approach to management is intuitively logical because organizations and even units within the same organization are diverse—in size, goals, work, and the like. It would be surprising to find universally applicable management rules that would work in *all* situations. But, of course, it's one thing to say that the method of managing "depends on the situation" and another to say what

Exhibit S1-5

Popular Contingency Variables

Organization Size. As size increases, so do the problems of coordination. For instance, the type of organization structure appropriate for an organization of 50 000 employees is likely to be inefficient for an organization of 50 employees.

Routineness of Task Technology. To achieve its purpose, an organization uses technology. Routine technologies, such as assembly lines, require organizational structures, leadership styles, and control systems that differ from those required by customized or nonroutine technologies where individuals continually have to make decisions about how their jobs are to be done, such as in the emergency room of a hospital.

Environmental Uncertainty. The degree of uncertainty caused by environmental changes influences the management process. What works best in a stable and predictable environment may be totally inappropriate in a rapidly changing and unpredictable environment.

Individual Differences. Individuals differ in terms of their desire for growth, autonomy, tolerance of ambiguity, and expectations. These and other individual differences are particularly important when managers select motivation techniques, leadership styles, and job designs.

the situation is. Management researchers have been working to identify these "what" variables. Exhibit S1-5 describes four popular contingency variables. The list is by no means comprehensive—more than 100 different "what" variables have been identified—but it represents those most widely used and gives you an idea of what we mean by the term *contingency variable*. As you can see, the contingency variables can have a significant impact on managers. The primary value of the contingency approach is that it stresses there are no simplistic or universal rules for managers to follow. **Q&A S1.6**

SUMMARIZING MANAGEMENT THEORY

It would not be unusual for you to read through this supplement on the history of management theory and wonder whether any of it is relevant to you. Theoretical perspectives and the research that is generated to help examine theories lead us to a more solid understanding of how managers should manage. The theories we present above appear in a historical sequence, but that does not mean that as a new theory was developed, the previous one became irrelevant. Instead, if you carefully consider the theories, you will note that they are somewhat self-contained, each addressing a separate aspect of the various considerations that managers face. Exhibit S1-6 highlights the main emphases of the six theories, so that you can see how each contributes to a better understanding of management as a whole.

Exhibit S1-6

Emphases of Major Management Theories

Management Theories

Scientific Management	General Administrative Theory	Quantitative Approach	Organizational Behaviour	Systems Approach	Contingency Approach
Focuses on jobs	Focuses on entire organization	Focuses on decision making	Focuses on organization's people	Focuses on organization's systems	Focuses on how differences in organizations affect action

CHAPTER

2

Environmental Constraints on Managers

What constraints do managers face?

1 How much control do managers have?

2 What is the external environment for managers?

3 What challenges do managers face in a global environment?

4 How do organizations do business globally?

5 How does the environment affect managers?

Bruce Beairsto wonders how to deal with the fashion sense (or sometimes lack of sense) he sees in secondary students. The Richmond, BC, school board superintendent, in charge of all 51 public schools in the district, is working to change the culture of the schools he oversees.

Some students have been pushing the fashion envelope, showing up for class with revealing tops and low-cut jeans with thongs sticking out. As Beairsto notes, "school is not the mall, not the beach. It's a place of learning."[1]

Beairsto put together a committee of 16 high school students, who together with some parents, teachers, school administrators, and support staff developed clothing guidelines. The guidelines demonstrate "an appropriate respect for the perspectives and sensibilities of others in the school community, recognizing that in a diverse community there will be a wide range of values and beliefs that may relate to clothing."[2]

To signal the importance of dressing appropriately on school grounds, the dress code will be applied to anyone who enters school buildings. The aim is to encourage a culture of respect within schools. "What we are against is clothing that distracts from learning," says Beairsto.[3]

THINK ABOUT IT

What is it like to be the manager of 51 schools in a district, where some people are complaining about what students are wearing? Put yourself in Bruce Beairsto's shoes. What would be the best way to convince teenagers that perhaps they should dress more appropriately at school? How will the school's culture affect Beairsto's ability to introduce a new dress code? How will factors outside the school, such as parental views and the type of clothing available, affect his decisions?

Bruce Beairsto's managerial responsibilities include making sure the climate for learning is a positive one for students in all 51 public schools in the Richmond, BC, school district. He recognizes how important it is to get teachers, students, parents, and the rest of the staff working together. But how much actual impact does a manager like Beairsto have on an organization's success or failure? Can Beairsto's simply impose a dress code? Will students go along readily if he does? Will the parents accept Beairsto's simply imposing a dress code? What if parents feel they cannot afford to buy the recommended clothing? These questions raise the more general questions: Do managers control their environment, or are they controlled by it? Are they affected more by circumstances outside or inside the organization? In this chapter we consider the impact of an organization's external environment on the ability of managers to act. We begin our exploration by considering the degree of control managers have over an organization's performance.

THE MANAGER: HOW MUCH CONTROL?

 1 How much control do managers have?

omnipotent view of management
The view that managers are directly responsible for an organization's success or failure.

 **Q&A** 3.1

symbolic view of management
The view that managers have only a limited effect on substantive organizational outcomes because of the large number of factors outside their control.

 **Q&A** 3.2

The dominant view in management theory and society in general is that managers are directly responsible for an organization's success or failure. We will call this perspective the **omnipotent view of management**. The view of managers as omnipotent is consistent with the stereotypical picture of the take-charge business executive who can overcome any obstacle in carrying out the organization's goals. In the omnipotent view, when organizations perform poorly, someone has to be held accountable regardless of the reasons, and in our society that "someone" is the manager. Of course, when things go well, we need someone to praise. So managers also get the credit—even if they had little to do with achieving positive outcomes.

In contrast, some observers have argued that much of an organization's success or failure is due to external forces outside managers' control. This perspective has been labelled the **symbolic view of management**. The symbolic view says that a manager's ability to affect outcomes is influenced and constrained by external factors.[4] In this view, it's unreasonable to expect managers to significantly affect an organization's performance. Instead, an organization's results are strongly influenced by factors outside the control of managers. These factors include, for example, the economy, customers, government policies, competitors' actions, industry conditions, control over proprietary technology, and decisions made by previous managers.

In reality, managers are neither helpless nor all-powerful. Internal and external constraints that restrict a manager's decision options exist within every organization. Internal constraints arise from the organization's culture (which we discuss in Chapter 11) and external constraints come from the organization's environment, as shown in Exhibit 2-1.

Despite these constraints, managers are not powerless. They can still influence an organization's performance. In the remainder of this chapter, we will discuss how an organization's environment imposes constraints on managers. However, as we will see in other chapters, these constraints don't mean that a manager's hands are tied. As Bruce Beairsto, in our chapter-opening vignette, recognized, managers can and do influence their culture and environment.

When both Home Hardware and Army and Navy closed their stores in downtown Regina, Saskatchewan, Blue Mantle, a thrift store in the same area, faced a loss of customer traffic. Dave Barrett, Blue Mantle's manager worried that his most loyal customers, low-income families and seniors, would be hurt by the other stores' closings.

Exhibit 2-1

Parameters of Managerial Discretion

Organizational Environment ➤ **Managerial Discretion** ◀ Organizational Culture

---

THE EXTERNAL ENVIRONMENT

Schools, just like other organizations, respond to the environment around them. That is why we have heard about some schools banning particular textbooks and others encouraging students to be very active in community affairs. Richmond, BC, where Bruce Beairsto is school board superintendent, is a multicultural community "where two-thirds of the population is made up of immigrant families that have varying ideas about appropriate clothing."[5] It is not only the local environment that affects the schools, however. Teens are influenced by stars such as Lindsay Lohan and Christina Aguilera. Stephanie Ip, 16, says that the media have too much influence on fashion: "There's no more distinction between a pop star or someone who's famous and someone who's a normal 14-year-old girl. She's wearing what Lindsay Lohan could be wearing. There's no distinction any more—and there should be." Beairsto's challenge as a manager is to understand the environment around him, and then adopt a dress code that will convey an appropriate message, without being overbearing or unreasonable. He even acknowledges: "We're not against skin," he says. "Everything they buy seems to have a little bit of skin showing."

THINK ABOUT IT

Bruce Beairsto has to consider how students, teachers, parents, and the local community will respond to his decisions. To what extent does being a school board superintendent reflect the same management challenges as being the CEO of a manufacturing company?

The term **external environment** refers to forces and institutions outside the organization that potentially can affect the organization's performance. The external environment is made up of three components as shown in Exhibit 2-2: the specific environment, the general environment, and the global environment.

Anyone who questions the impact of the external environment on managing should consider the following:

- Surging gas prices in 2006 significantly reduced the demand for gas-guzzling SUVs, leaving auto manufacturers scrambling to meet customer demand for fuel-efficient cars.

- Face-mask manufacturers had to significantly increase production in spring 2003 to meet demand from a nervous public intent on protecting themselves from possible SARS contamination.

As these two examples show, there are forces in the environment that play a major role in shaping managers' actions. In this section, we identify some of the critical environmental forces that affect managers and show how they constrain managerial discretion.

The Specific Environment

The **specific environment** includes those external forces that have a direct and immediate impact on managers' decisions and actions and are directly relevant to the achievement of the organization's goals. Each organization's specific environment is unique and changes with conditions. For instance, Timex and Rolex both make watches, but their

2 What is the external environment for managers?

external environment
Outside forces and institutions that potentially can affect the organization's performance.

specific environment
The part of the external environment that is directly relevant to the achievement of an organization's goals.

Exhibit 2-2

The External Environment

specific environments differ because they operate in distinctly different market niches. What forces make up the specific environment? The main ones are customers, suppliers, competitors, and public pressure groups.

Customers

Organizations exist to meet the needs of customers. It's the customer or client who absorbs the organization's output. This is true even for government organizations and other non-profits.

Customers obviously represent potential uncertainty to an organization. Their tastes can change, or they can become dissatisfied with the organization's products or service. Of course, some organizations face considerably more uncertainty as a result of their customers than do others. For example, what comes to mind when you think of Club Med? Club Med's image was traditionally one of carefree singles having fun in the sun at exotic locales. Club Med found, however, that as their target customers married and had children, these same individuals were looking for family-oriented vacation resorts where they could bring the kids. Although Club Med responded to the changing demands of its customers by offering different types of vacation experiences, including family-oriented ones, the company found it hard to change its image.

Club Med
www.clubmed.com

Suppliers

When you think of an organization's suppliers, you typically think in terms of organizations that provide materials and equipment. For Paramount Canada's Wonderland in Toronto, that includes organizations that sell soft drinks, computers, food, flowers and other nursery stock, concrete, and paper products. But the term *suppliers* also includes providers of financial and labour inputs. Stockholders, banks, insurance companies, pension funds, and other similar organizations are needed to ensure a continuous supply of money. Labour unions, colleges and universities, occupational associations, trade schools, and local labour markets are sources of employees. When the sources of employees dry up, it can constrain managers' decisions and actions. For example, a lack of qualified nurses, a serious problem plaguing the health care industry, is making it difficult for health care providers to meet demand and keep service levels high.

Managers seek to ensure a steady flow of needed inputs at the lowest price available. Because these inputs represent uncertainties—that is, their unavailability or delay can significantly reduce the organization's effectiveness—managers typically go to great lengths to ensure a reliable steady flow. The application of e-business techniques is changing the way that organizations deal with suppliers. For example, Toyota Motor Corporation established electronic links with suppliers to ensure that it has the right materials at the right time and in the right place. Although these links might help managers manage uncertainty, they certainly don't eliminate it.

Competitors

All organizations have one or more competitors. Even though it's a monopoly, Canada Post competes with FedEx, UPS, and other forms of communication such as the telephone, email, and fax. Nike competes against Reebok, Adidas, and Fila, among others. Coca-Cola competes against PepsiCo and other soft drink companies. Nonprofit organizations such as the Royal Ontario Museum and Girl Guides also compete for dollars, volunteers, and customers.

Managers cannot afford to ignore the competition. When they do, they suffer. For instance, until the 1980s, three major US broadcast networks—ABC, CBS, and NBC—virtually controlled what you watched on television. Now, with digital cable, satellite, DVD players, and the web, customers have a much broader choice of what to watch. As technological capabilities continue to expand, the number of viewing options will provide even more competition for the broadcast networks. The Internet is also having an impact on determining an organization's competitors because it has virtually eliminated geographic boundaries. Through the power of Internet marketing, a small maple syrup maker in Montreal can compete with the likes of Pillsbury, Quaker Oats, and Smucker's.

These examples illustrate that competitors—in terms of pricing, new products developed, services offered, and the like—represent an environmental force that managers must monitor and to which they must be prepared to respond.

Public Pressure Groups

Managers must recognize the special-interest groups that attempt to influence the actions of organizations. For instance, both Wal-Mart and Home Depot have had difficulty getting approval to build stores in Vancouver. Neighbourhood activists worry about traffic density brought about by big-box stores, and in the case of both stores there is concern that local businesses will fail if the stores move in. Home Depot's director of real estate called Vancouver city hall's review process "confusing and unfair" and "unlike anything in my experience."[6] Local hardware store owners and resident groups have lobbied against the store to city planners, hoping to keep big-box stores out of the Kitsilano neighbourhood.

As social and political attitudes change, so too does the power of public pressure groups. For example, through their persistent efforts, groups such as MADD (Mothers Against Drunk Driving) and SADD (Students Against Destructive Decisions) have managed to make changes in the alcoholic beverage and restaurant and bar industries, and raised public awareness about the problem of drunk drivers.

The General Environment

The **general environment** includes the broad economic, legal–political, socio-cultural, demographic, and technological conditions that *may* affect the organization. Changes in any of these areas usually do not have as large an impact as changes in the specific environment do, but managers must consider them as they plan, organize, lead, and control.

general environment
Broad external conditions that may affect the organization.

Economic Conditions

Interest rates, inflation, changes in disposable income, stock market fluctuations, and the stage of the general business cycle are some of the economic factors that can affect management practices in Canada. For example, many specialty retailers such as IKEA, Roots, Birks, and Williams-Sonoma are acutely aware of the impact consumer disposable income has on their sales. When interest rates rise, or when consumers' incomes fall or confidence about job security declines, consumers will postpone purchasing anything that is not a necessity. Even charitable organizations such as the United Way and the Heart and Stroke Foundation feel the impact of economic factors. During economic downturns, not only does the demand for their services increase, but also their contributions typically decrease.

Legal–Political Conditions

Federal, provincial, and local governments influence what organizations can and cannot do. Some federal legislation has significant implications. For example, the Canadian Human Rights Act makes it illegal for any employer or provider of service that falls within federal jurisdiction to discriminate on the following grounds: race, national or ethnic origin, colour, religion, age, sex (including pregnancy and childbirth), marital status, family status, mental or physical disability (including previous or present drug or alcohol dependence), pardoned conviction, or sexual orientation. The act covers federal departments and agencies; Crown corporations; chartered banks; national airlines; interprovincial communications and telephone companies; interprovincial transportation companies; and other federally regulated industries, including certain mining operations.

Canada's Employment Equity Act of 1995 protects several categories of employees from employment barriers: Aboriginal peoples (whether First Nation, Inuit, or Metis); persons with disabilities; members of visible minorities (nonCaucasian in race or nonwhite in colour); and women. This legislation aims to ensure that members of these four groups are treated equitably. Employers covered by the Canadian Human Rights Act are also covered by the Employment Equity Act.

Many provinces have their own legislation, including employment equity acts, to cover employers in their provinces. Companies sometimes have difficulty complying with equity acts, as recent audits conducted by the Canadian Human Rights Commission show. In an audit of 180 companies, only Status of Women Canada; Elliot Lake, Ontario-based AJ Bus Lines; the National Parole Board; Canadian Transportation Agency; Les Méchins, Quebec-based Verreault Navigation; and Nortel Networks were compliant on their first try.[7]

 Canadian Human Rights Commission
www.chrc-ccdp.ca

Competition Bureau
www.competition.ic.gc.ca

The Competition Act of 1985 created the Bureau of Competition Policy (now called the Competition Bureau) to maintain and encourage competition in Canada. For example, if two major competing companies consider merging, they will come under scrutiny from the bureau. Heather Reisman and Gerry Schwartz's purchase of Chapters in 2001 needed approval before they could merge Chapters with their Indigo bookstores. Before approving the merger, the bureau imposed a number of conditions, including the sale or closing of 20 stores and a code of conduct for dealing with publishers. The code of conduct was the result of publishers' complaints about the way Chapters had treated them in the past. These rules affected the way Indigo/Chapters could do business until 2006. Beyond that time, the bookseller was allowed to operate without restraint by the Competition Bureau.[8]

To protect farmers, the Canadian government has created marketing boards that regulate the pricing and production of such things as milk and eggs. Those who decide that they want to manufacture small amounts of cheese would have great difficulty starting such a business in Canada because of the difficulties and high cost of buying production quota. Marketing boards restrict imports of some products, but the unintended result is that foreign governments oppose exports from Canada.

Organizations spend a great deal of time and money meeting government regulations, but the effects of these regulations go beyond time and money.[9] They can also reduce managerial discretion by limiting the choices available to managers. In a 2004 COMPAS survey of business leaders, most respondents cited interprovincial trade barriers as a significant hurdle to doing business in this country, calling the barriers "bad economics." One respondent to the survey noted that the federal government fails "to realize that in today's global economy, our real 'competitors' are no longer in the next province (or the next city), not even in the U.S. or Mexico but are the emerging economies of Asia and Europe."[10]

Not all regulations have a negative impact, however, as the following *Management Reflection* shows.

MANAGEMENT REFLECTION

Groupe Savoie Loses Market, Makes a Deal

Can regulations actually improve a company's business? New government regulations that could have put St.-Quentin, New Brunswick-based Groupe Savoie out of business instead turned out to be an opportunity to figure out something else for the company to do.[11] When the provincial government introduced local woodlot marketing boards in 1982 and changed the way buyers were required to purchase wood, Groupe Savoie lost its market, and had 25 000 cords of wood it could not sell. In response, Groupe Savoie made a deal with a local pulp mill that was converting from softwood to hardwood chips and provided a win-win solution for both. Groupe Savoie decided to move into the pallet manufacturing business, and the pulp mill agreed to finance a sawmill that could cut the lumber needed to build the pallets. In return, Groupe Savoie supplied the pulp mill with the hardwood chips it needed. Today Groupe Savoie has three locations and grosses $80 million a year. ■

Other legal–political conditions are the political climate, the general stability of a country where an organization operates, and the attitudes that elected government officials hold toward business. In Canada, for example, organizations have generally operated in a stable political environment. Managers in some other countries do not face such a stable environment, however.

Peter B. Moore, founder, chief executive, and chairman of Barrie, Ontario-based Moore Packaging, which makes corrugated boxes, knows how changes in the general environment can seriously affect one's business. During the first half of 2000, the company experienced double-digit sales growth each year, but he does not expect the rest of the decade to be quite as successful. "The corrugated packaging market is kind of stagnating right now as far as growth is concerned," Mr. Moore says. "Manufacturing companies have shut down and we come and go as they come and go. I used to say everything made goes in a box but I didn't realize it would be going into a box in China."

Socio-cultural Conditions

Frito Lay Canada
www.fritolay.ca

Voortman Cookies
www.voortmancookies.
com

Cambridge, Ontario-based Frito Lay Canada recently announced that it was eliminating trans fatty acids (TFAs) from Doritos, Tostitos, and Sunchips (it had already done so for its Lay's, Ruffles, and Miss Vickie's chips). Marc Guay, president of Frito Lay Canada, explained his decision: "Eliminating trans fat is a major step in Frito Lay Canada's on-going commitment to offer consumers a wide variety of great-tasting snacks made with more healthful oils."[12] Burlington, Ontario-based Voortman Cookies was the first Canadian cookie maker to drop TFAs from its products. President and co-founder Harry Voortman said he dropped the TFAs after his daughter, Lynn, a naturopathic doctor, became concerned enough that she stopped eating her father's cookies altogether.[13]

Why are Frito Lay Canada and Voortman Cookies changing their products? Because health officials and consumers are increasingly anxious about the link between TFAs and heart disease.[14] Managers must adapt their practices to the changing expectations of the societies in which they operate. As societal values, customs, and tastes change, managers also must change. For instance, as employees have begun seeking more balance in their lives, organizations have had to adjust by offering family leave policies, more flexible work hours, and even on-site child care facilities. These trends may pose a potential constraint to managers' decisions and actions. If an organization does business in other countries, managers need to be familiar with those countries' values and cultures and manage in ways that recognize and embrace those specific socio-cultural aspects.

Demographic Conditions

The demographic conditions encompass trends in the physical characteristics of a population such as gender, age, level of education, geographic location, income, family composition, and so forth. Changes in these characteristics may constrain how managers plan, organize, lead, and control.

One population group that we all have heard a lot about is the Baby Boomers, a group that encompasses individuals born between the years 1947 and 1966. The reason you hear so much about Baby Boomers is that there are so many of them. Through every life stage they have entered, they have had an enormous impact because of their sheer numbers. Other age cohorts besides Baby Boomers that have been identified include the Depression group (born 1912–1921), the World War II group (born 1922–1927), the Post-war group (born 1928–1945), Generation X (born 1965–1977), and Generation Y (born 1978–1994). Although each of these groups has its own unique characteristics, this last group is of particular interest because they are thinking, learning, creating, shopping, and playing in fundamentally different ways that are likely to greatly affect managers and organizations.

Technological Conditions

In terms of the general environment, the most rapid changes have occurred in technology. We live in a time of continuous technological change. For instance, the human genetic code has been cracked. Just think of the implications of such an incredible breakthrough! Information gadgets are getting smaller and more powerful. We have automated offices, electronic meetings, robotic manufacturing, lasers, integrated circuits, faster and more powerful microprocessors, synthetic fuels, and entirely new models of doing business in an electronic age. Companies that capitalize on technology, such as Research in Motion (RIM), eBay, and Google, prosper. In addition, many successful retailers such as Wal-Mart use sophisticated information systems to keep on top of current sales trends. Similarly, hospitals, universities, airports, police departments, and even military organizations that adapt to major technological advances have a competitive edge over those that do not. The whole area of technology is radically changing the fundamental ways that organizations are structured and the way that managers manage.

UNDERSTANDING THE GLOBAL ENVIRONMENT

The global environment presents opportunities and challenges for managers. With the entire world as a market and national borders becoming increasingly irrelevant, the potential for organizations to grow expands dramatically. To evaluate your fit for an international position, see *Self-Assessment—Am I Well-Suited for a Career as a Global Manager?* on pages 58–59, at the end of the chapter.

However, even large successful organizations with talented managers face challenges in managing in the global environment. Managers must deal with cultural, economic, and political differences. Meanwhile, new competitors can suddenly appear at any time from any place on the globe. Managers who don't closely monitor changes in their global environment or who don't take the specific characteristics of their location into consideration as they plan, organize, lead, and control are likely to find limited global success. Below, we discuss the issues managers have to face in managing in a global environment.

❸ What challenges do managers face in a global environment?

Global Trade

What is the global environment like? An important feature is global trade. Global trade is not new. Countries and organizations have been trading with each other for centuries. "Trade is central to human health, prosperity, and social welfare."[15] When trade is allowed to flow freely, countries benefit from economic growth and productivity gains because they specialize in producing the goods they are best at and importing goods that are more efficiently produced elsewhere. Global trade is being shaped by two forces: regional trading alliances and the agreements negotiated through the World Trade Organization.

Regional Trading Alliances

The major regional trading alliances are as follows:

- The **European Union (EU)**: A union of European countries (27 in 2007) that forms an economic and political entity. The primary reason these countries joined together was to assert their economic position against the strength of the United States and Japan. Working in separate countries with trade barriers against one another, European industries could not develop the efficiency of American and Japanese businesses. The EU continues to grow, and has become one of the world's richest markets and leading political powers. The EU's population of 456.8 million people is about 150 million more than that of the United States.[16] In 2003, the gross domestic product of the EU was $11 017 billion (US), almost the same that it was for the United States ($11 000 billion [US]).[17]

  European Union (EU)
  A union of 27 European countries that forms an economic and political entity.

- The **North American Free Trade Agreement (NAFTA)**: An agreement reached by the Canadian, American, and Mexican governments that created a vast economic bloc in which barriers to free trade were reduced. Between 1994, when NAFTA went into effect, and 2003 (the most recent year for complete statistics), Canada was the United States' number-one trading partner.[18] In 2003, Canadian exports to the United States were $331 billion, which accounted for almost 83 percent of our total exports.[19] Exports to the United States are equivalent to nearly one-third of Canada's GDP. Free trade did not eliminate all trade problems between Canada and the United States, however, as the ongoing softwood lumber negotiations show.

  North American Free Trade Agreement (NAFTA)
  An agreement among the Canadian, American, and Mexican governments in which barriers to free trade were reduced.

- The **Association of Southeast Asian Nations (ASEAN)**: A trading alliance of 10 Southeast Asian countries. During the years ahead, the Southeast Asian region promises to be one of the fastest-growing economic regions of the world. It will be an increasingly important regional economic and political alliance whose impact eventually could rival that of both NAFTA and the EU.

  Association of Southeast Asian Nations (ASEAN)
  A trading alliance of 10 Southeast Asian countries.

The World Trade Organization

World Trade Organization (WTO)
A global organization of 149
member countries that deals with
the rules of trade among nations.

**World Trade Organization
(WTO)**
www.wto.org

The **World Trade Organization (WTO)** is a global organization that sets rules for international trade and helps countries negotiate trade problems and settle trade disputes.[20]

The WTO was formed in 1995 and evolved from the General Agreement on Tariffs and Trade (GATT), an agreement in effect since the end of World War II. Today, the WTO is the only *global* organization dealing with the rules of trade among nations. Its membership consists of 149 countries (as of November 2006). At its core are the various trade agreements, negotiated and ratified by the vast majority of the world's trading nations. The goal of the WTO is to help businesses conduct trade between countries (importing and exporting) without undesired side effects. Although a number of vocal critics have staged visible protests and criticized the WTO, claiming that it destroys jobs and the natural environment, the WTO appears to play an important role in monitoring and promoting global trade.

The Legal–Political Environment

Canadian managers are accustomed to stable legal and political systems. Changes are slow, and legal and political procedures are well established. The stability of laws governing the actions of individuals and institutions allows for accurate predictions. The same cannot be said for all countries. Managers in a global organization must stay informed of the specific laws in countries where they do business.

Also, some countries have a history of unstable governments. Managers of businesses in these countries face dramatically greater uncertainty as a result of political instability or interference. For instance, the Chinese government controls what organizations do and how they do it. Google has struggled with determining how to manage its website in China. "Figuring out how to deal with China has been a difficult exercise for Google," said Elliot Schrage, vice-president of global communications and public affairs at Google. "The requirements of doing business in China include self-censorship—something that runs counter to Google's most basic values and commitments as a company."[21]

The legal–political environment does not have to be unstable or revolutionary to be a concern to managers. Just the fact that a country's laws and political system differ from those of Canada is important. Managers must recognize these differences to understand the constraints under which they operate and the opportunities that exist.

The Economic Environment

market economy
An economic system in which
resources are primarily owned and
controlled by the private sector.

command economy
An economic system in which all
economic decisions are planned
by a central government.

The global manager must be aware of economic issues when doing business in other countries. First, it's important to have an understanding of the type of economic system under which the country operates. The two major types are a market economy and a command economy. A **market economy** is one in which resources are primarily owned and controlled by the private sector. A **command economy** is one in which all economic decisions are planned by a central government. In actuality, no economy is purely market or command. For instance, Canada and the United States are two countries at the market end of the spectrum but they do have some governmental control. The economies of Vietnam and North Korea, however, would be more command-based. Then there is China, a country that is more command-based, but is moving toward becoming more market-based. Why would managers need to know about a country's economic system? Because it has the potential to constrain decisions and actions. Other economic issues a manager would need to understand include currency exchange rates, inflation rates, and diverse tax policies.

The Cultural Environment

Which is more important to a manager—national culture or organizational culture? For example, is an IBM facility in Germany more likely to reflect German culture or IBM's corporate culture? Research by Geert Hofstede, a professor at Maastricht University in the Netherlands, indicates that national culture has a greater effect on employees than does their

Union leader Yoo Jung Hwan and CEO Kim Seon Joong of Jinro consoled each other after their South Korean company was forced into bankruptcy by a group of foreign creditors. The move was controversial because South Korea has a strong cultural tradition against foreign ownership or control of Korean businesses. (Jinro, a distillery, produces a rice liquor that is popular nationwide.) The court ruling in favour of the creditors is believed to be a first. Following an unsuccessful appeal, Jinro was bought by a consortium led by Hite, Korea's largest beer maker, in 2005.

In what ways do you think culture affects doing business in other countries?

organization's culture.[22] For example, German employees at an IBM facility in Munich will be influenced more by German culture than by IBM's culture. This means that as influential as organizational culture may be on managerial practice, **national culture** is even more influential.

Hofstede surveyed more than 116 000 IBM employees in 40 countries about their work-related values.[23] He found that managers and employees vary on five value dimensions of national culture:

national culture
The values and attitudes shared by individuals from a specific country that shape their behaviour and beliefs about what is important.

- *Power distance.* The degree to which people in a country accept that power in institutions and organizations is distributed unequally. This ranges from relatively equal (low power distance) to extremely unequal (high power distance).

- *Individualism vs. collectivism.* The degree to which people in a country prefer to act as individuals rather than as members of groups.

- *Quantity of life (masculinity) vs. quality of life (femininity).* The degree to which values such as assertiveness, competitiveness, and the desire to acquire money and material goods prevail (quantity of life) vs. the degree to which people value relationships and show sensitivity and concern for the welfare of others (quality of life).[24] Hofstede used the terms *masculinity* and *femininity* for this dimension of culture, but many scholars refer to it as a difference in emphasis in quantity vs. quality of life.

- *Uncertainty avoidance.* The degree to which people in a country prefer structured over unstructured situations. In countries that score high on uncertainty avoidance, people have an increased level of anxiety, which manifests itself in greater nervousness, stress, and aggressiveness.

- *Long-term vs. short-term orientation.* People in cultures with long-term orientations look to the future and value thrift and persistence. A short-term orientation values the past and present and emphasizes respect for tradition and fulfilling social obligations.

Exhibit 2-3 provides a summary of how a number of countries rate on Hofstede's five dimensions. Not surprisingly, most Asian countries are more collectivist than individualistic. On the other hand, the United States ranked highest on individualism among all countries surveyed.

Exhibit 2-3

Examples of National Cultural Values

Country	Power Distance	Individu-alism*	Quantity of Life**	Uncertainty Avoidance	Long-term Orientation***
Canada	Moderate	High	High	Moderate	Low
China	High	Low	Moderate	Moderate	High
France	High	High	Moderate	High	Low
Germany****	Low	High	High	Moderate	Moderate
Hong Kong*****	High	Low	High	Low	High
Indonesia	High	Low	Moderate	Low	Low
Japan	Moderate	Moderate	High	Moderate	Moderate
Mexico	High	Low	High	High	NA
Netherlands	Low	High	Low	Moderate	Moderate
Russia	High	Moderate	Low	High	Low
United States	Low	High	High	Low	Low
West Africa	High	Low	Moderate	Moderate	Low

* A low score is synonymous with collectivism. ** A low score is synonymous with high quality of life. *** A low score is synonymous with a short-term orientation. **** Includes only former West Germany. ***** The former British colony was handed back to the People's Republic of China on July 1, 1997.

Sources: Adapted from G. Hofstede, "Cultural Constraints in Management Theories," *Academy of Management Executive,* February 1993, p. 91; G. Hofstede, "The Cultural Relativity of Organizational Practices and Theories," *Journal of International Business Studies* 14, 1983, pp. 75–89. Mexico's scores were abstracted from G. K. Stephens and C. R. Greer, "Doing Business in Mexico: Understanding Cultural Differences," *Organizational Dynamics,* Special Report, 1998, pp. 43–59.

Hofstede's findings are based on research that is nearly three decades old, and has been subject to some criticism, which he refutes.[25] In addition, he has recently updated his research, and included studies from a variety of disciplines that support his findings.[26] *Developing Your Interpersonal Skills—Becoming More Culturally Aware,* on page 61, encourages you to think about how to become more comfortable when interacting with people from different cultures.

DOING BUSINESS GLOBALLY

It is not only private sector companies that look beyond Canada's borders to conduct business.[27] The Richmond, BC, school district, like other public school systems in Canada, has been recruiting students from a variety of countries (mainly southeast Asia) in recent years as a way of increasing revenues. The school district ran "a structural deficit" for two years (2003–2005). At the start of the 2006–2007 school year, the school district was facing a possible $700 000 shortfall in its budget. "It's not sound financial management, but at the time we were not prepared to make the kind of cuts that we would have had to make as a result of earlier cuts," says school board superintendent Bruce Beairsto. Trying to attract students from around the world, who are willing to pay high tuition fees to attend school in Canada, is one way of helping with these deficits. For instance, Richmond School District's nearly 300 international students brought in $1 million in revenues in 2005.

THINK ABOUT IT

Bruce Beairsto has to balance his budget. To what extent does it make sense for the Richmond school district to look globally for students? What challenges might the district have in finding students overseas? How can these challenges be overcome?

 4 How do organizations do business globally?

Organizations in different industries and from different countries are pursuing global opportunities. In this section, we look at different types of global organizations and how they do business in the global marketplace.

Different Types of Global Organizations

Multinational Corporations

Organizations doing business globally are not anything new. DuPont started doing business in China in 1863. H.J. Heinz Company was manufacturing food products in the United Kingdom in 1905. Ford Motor Company set up its first overseas sales branch in France in 1908. But it was not until the mid-1960s that **multinational corporations (MNCs)** became commonplace. MNCs—which maintain significant operations in multiple countries but are managed from a base in the home country—started the rapid growth in international trade. Some examples of companies that can be considered MNCs include Montreal-based transport manufacturer Bombardier, Montreal-based aluminum producer Alcan, and Tokyo-based consumer electronics firm Sony. Although these companies have considerable global holdings, management decisions with company-wide implications are made from headquarters in the home countries.

multinational corporation (MNC)
A company that maintains significant operations in multiple countries but manages them from a base in the home country.

Transnational Corporations

Another type of global organization is the **transnational corporation (TNC)**—a company that maintains significant operations in more than one country but decentralizes management to the local country. This type of organization does not attempt to manage foreign operations from its home country. Instead, local employees typically are hired to manage the business, and marketing strategies are tailored to that country's unique characteristics. For example, Frito-Lay, a division of PepsiCo, sells a Doritos chip in the British market that differs in both taste and texture from the Canadian and US versions. Many consumer companies manage their global businesses as TNCs because they must adapt their products and services to meet the needs of the local markets.

transnational corporation (TNC)
A company that maintains significant operations in more than one country but decentralizes management to the local country.

Borderless Organizations

Many companies are globalizing by eliminating structural divisions that impose artificial geographical barriers. This type of global organization is called a **borderless organization**. For example, IBM dropped its organizational structure based on country and reorganized into industry groups such as software, IT services, and financing. Borderless management is an attempt by organizations to increase efficiency and effectiveness in a competitive global marketplace.[28]

borderless organization
A type of global organization in which artificial geographical barriers are eliminated.

How Organizations Go Global

Organizations have different ways of going global (see Exhibit 2-4). The choice depends on the level of investment and risk managers want to take.

Exhibit 2-4

How Organizations Go Global

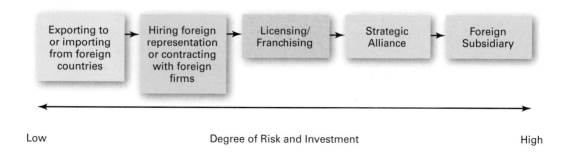

Low   Degree of Risk and Investment   High

Importing and Exporting

exporting
An approach to going global that involves making products at home and selling them overseas.

importing
An approach to going global that involves selling products at home that are made overseas.

If a company wants to do business in other countries, what choices does it have?

An organization can go global by **exporting** its products—that is, by making products at home and selling them overseas. In addition, an organization can go global by **importing** products—that is, by selling products at home that are made overseas. Both exporting and importing are small steps toward being a global business and involve minimal investment and minimal risk. Many organizations enter the global marketplace through importing or exporting, with some building multimillion-dollar businesses. For instance, that is what Montreal-based Mega Brands (formerly Mega Bloks), Canada's largest toy company, has done. The company, with sales in more than 100 countries, has 30 percent of the Canadian toy market share, 20 percent of the US toy market share, and 7 percent of the global toy market share.[29] Mega Brands is only one example of Canada's increasing reliance on export business. The value of merchandise exported from Canada totalled $435 billion in 2005.[30] Transportation equipment manufacturing, primary metal manufacturing, and paper manufacturing account for the largest volume of Canadian exports.[31]

Internal Sales or Manufacturing

Managers can make an overt commitment to sell products in foreign countries or have their products made in foreign factories, but still with no physical presence of company employees outside the home country. Instead, what managers typically do on the sales side is send domestic employees on regular business trips to meet foreign customers or to hire foreign agents or brokers to represent the organization's product line. Or, on the manufacturing side, managers will contract with a foreign firm to produce the organization's products.

Licensing/Franchising

licensing
An approach to going global in which a manufacturer gives another organization the right to use its brand name, technology, or product specifications.

franchising
An approach to going global in which a service organization gives a person or group the right to sell a product, using specific business methods and practices that are standardized.

Managers can give another firm the right to use their organization's brand name, technology, or product specifications in return for a lump-sum payment or a fee usually based on sales through licensing or franchising. **Licensing** is a business arrangement in which a manufacturer gives another organization the right to use its brand name, technology, or product specifications. For instance, Anheuser-Busch licenses the right to brew and market Budweiser beer to other brewers, such as Labatt in Canada, Modelo in Mexico, and Kirin in Japan. **Franchising** is a business arrangement in which a service organization gives a person or group the right to sell a product, using specific business methods and practices that are standardized. For example, Russian consumers can enjoy McDonald's hamburgers that are similar to the hamburgers found in Canada because McDonald's Canada opened the first Russian franchise in Moscow. Franchises have also made it possible for Mexicans to dine on Richmond, BC-based Boston Pizza and Koreans to consume frozen yogourt from Markham, Ontario-based Coolbrands' Yogen Früz. Licensing and franchising involve more investment and risk than exporting and importing because the company's brand is more at stake.

Strategic Alliance

strategic alliance
An approach to going global that involves a partnership between a domestic and a foreign company in which both share resources and knowledge in developing new products or building production facilities.

A **strategic alliance** is a partnership between a domestic and a foreign company in which both share resources and knowledge in developing new products or building production facilities. The partners also share the risks and rewards of this alliance. It is not always easy to find a partner, however. When Starbucks decided to open coffee shops in France, it was turned down by four major French food companies it approached as joint venture partners. Jean-Paul Brayer, former head of one of the food companies Starbucks approached, commented, "Their contract was way too expensive. It was a win-win situation—but only for Starbucks."[32] Starbucks ended up partnering with a Spanish firm, Grupo VIPS, and together they opened the first Parisian Starbucks in January 2004.

 Starbucks Canada
www.starbucks.ca

Victor Sassoon, pictured here at The Coffee Bean & Tea Leaf store on one of Singapore's most popular streets, hopes to rival Starbucks some day with his US-based chain of coffee shops. With over 300 outlets in 15 countries, Coffee Bean is making headway, and future plans include opening new outlets in the United States, Spain, Germany, and Japan. For now, Sassoon is using a combination of business ownership models. The parent company owns all the American locations and franchises those outside the United States.

A specific type of strategic alliance in which the partners agree to form a separate, independent organization for some business purpose is called a **joint venture**. For example, Hewlett-Packard has had numerous joint ventures with various suppliers around the globe to develop different components for its computer equipment, such as Tokyo-based Hitachi, which supplies hard drives for HP. These partnerships provide a faster and more inexpensive way for companies to compete globally than doing it on their own.

joint venture
An approach to going global in which the partners agree to form a separate, independent organization for some business purpose; it is a type of strategic alliance.

Foreign Subsidiary

Managers can make a direct investment in a foreign country by setting up a **foreign subsidiary**, a separate and independent production facility or office. This subsidiary can be managed as an MNC (domestic control), a TNC (foreign control), or as a borderless organization (global control). As you can probably guess, this arrangement involves the greatest commitment of resources and poses the greatest amount of risk. Many of the larger companies operating in Canada are actually subsidiaries of US corporations, including GM Canada, Procter & Gamble Canada, and McDonald's Canada. Canadian subsidiaries manage their operations and set their own targets and goals, but they also report to head office in the United States.

foreign subsidiary
An approach to going global that involves a direct investment in a foreign country by setting up a separate and independent production facility or office.

HOW THE ENVIRONMENT AFFECTS MANAGERS

School board superintendent Bruce Beairsto, of the Richmond, BC, school district supported the school board's recommendation to recruit students from overseas.[33] Not everyone is happy about that decision, however. Al Klassen, president of the Richmond Teachers Association, objects to the idea of running a school like a business. "Our main issue with this is that district staff are being forced to focus on revenue generation which undermines the public nature of a public school system." Teachers are also concerned about the welfare of international students, many of whom are in Canada without their parents. They generally stay with local families through homestay programs, although some of the teens end up living on their own, which can be a challenge for someone still in secondary school. Some parents and other taxpayers worry that the growth in the number of ESL students in the classroom can negatively affect the educational environment for English-speaking students.

THINK ABOUT IT

Bruce Beairsto has to consider how his stakeholders (students, teachers, parents, and the local community) will react to the school board's decision to continue and perhaps increase the number of students that will be recruited internationally. What steps can he take to manage stakeholder relations while expanding global opportunities?

5 How does the environment affect managers?

Knowing *what* the various components of the environment are is important to managers. However, understanding *how* the environment affects managers is equally important. The environment affects managers through the degree of environmental uncertainty that is present; through the various stakeholder relationships that exist between the organization and its external constituencies; and through the challenges of managing in a global environment.

Assessing Environmental Uncertainty

environmental uncertainty
The degree of change and degree of complexity in an organization's environment.

Not all environments are the same. They differ by what we call their degree of **environmental uncertainty**, which is the degree of change and degree of complexity in an organization's environment (see Exhibit 2-5).

The first of these dimensions is the degree of change. If the components in an organization's environment change frequently, we call it a *dynamic* environment. If change is minimal, we call it a *stable* one. A stable environment might be one in which there are no new competitors, few technological breakthroughs by current competitors, little activity by pressure groups to influence the organization, and so forth. For instance, Zippo Canada, best known for its Zippo lighters, faces a relatively stable environment. There are few competitors and there is little technological change. Probably the main environmental concern for the company is the declining trend in tobacco smokers, although the company's lighters have other uses and global markets remain attractive.

 Zippo Canada
www.zippo.ca

In contrast, the recorded music industry faces a highly uncertain and unpredictable environment. Digital formats like MP3, music-swapping Internet services, and the ability to buy individual tunes from companies like iTunes and Puretracks have turned the indus-

---

Exhibit 2-5

Environmental Uncertainty Matrix

		Degree of Change	
		Stable	**Dynamic**
Degree of Complexity	**Simple**	**Cell 1** Stable and predictable environment Few components in environment Components are somewhat similar and remain basically the same Minimal need for sophisticated knowledge of components	**Cell 2** Dynamic and unpredictable environment Few components in environment Components are somewhat similar but are in continual process of change Minimal need for sophisticated knowledge of components
	Complex	**Cell 3** Stable and predictable environment Many components in environment Components are not similar to one another and remain basically the same High need for sophisticated knowledge of components	**Cell 4** Dynamic and unpredictable environment Many components in environment Components are not similar to one another and are in continual process of change High need for sophisticated knowledge of components

try upside down. Although music companies traditionally earned revenues by selling physical products such as LP records, cassettes, and CDs, the digital future represents chaos and uncertainty. This environment can definitely be described as dynamic.

What about rapid change that is predictable? Is that considered a dynamic environment? Bricks-and-mortar retail department stores provide a good example. They typically make one-quarter to one-third of their sales in December. The drop-off from December to January is significant. However, because the change is predictable, we don't consider the environment to be dynamic. When we talk about degree of change, we mean change that is unpredictable. If change can be accurately anticipated, it's not an uncertainty that managers must confront.

The other dimension of uncertainty describes the degree of **environmental complexity**. The degree of complexity refers to the number of components in an organization's environment and the extent of the knowledge that the organization has about those components. For example, Hasbro, the second-largest toy manufacturer (behind Mattel) has simplified its environment by acquiring many of its competitors such as Tiger Electronics, Wizards of the Coast, Kenner Toys, Parker Brothers, and Tonka Toys. The fewer competitors, customers, suppliers, government agencies, and so forth that an organization must deal with, the less complexity and, therefore, the less uncertainty there is in its environment.

Complexity is also measured in terms of the knowledge an organization needs to have about its environment. For instance, managers at the online brokerage E*TRADE must know a great deal about their Internet service provider's operations if they want to ensure that their website is available, reliable, and secure for their stock-trading customers. On the other hand, managers of grocery stores have a minimal need for sophisticated knowledge about their suppliers.

How does the concept of environmental uncertainty influence managers? Looking again at Exhibit 2-5, each of the four cells represents different combinations of degree of complexity and degree of change. Cell 1 (an environment that is stable and simple) represents the lowest level of environmental uncertainty. Cell 4 (an environment that is dynamic and complex) represents the highest. Not surprisingly, managers' influence on organizational outcomes is greatest in cell 1 and least in cell 4.

Because uncertainty is a threat to an organization's effectiveness, managers try to minimize it. Given a choice, managers would prefer to operate in environments such as those in cell 1. However, they rarely have full control over that choice. In addition, most industries today are facing more dynamic change, making their environments more uncertain. Thus, managers, as planners, need to consider the environment they currently face, as well as thinking ahead about possible changes in the environment, and act accordingly. In a simple, stable environment, a manager may decide to continue doing things in the usual way. In a dynamic, complex environment, a manager may want to develop plans for how to beat competitors, or develop new niches in which to operate.

Managing Stakeholder Relationships

Managers are also affected by the nature of the relationships they have with external stakeholders. The more obvious and secure these relationships become, the more influence managers will have over organizational outcomes.

Who are **stakeholders**? We define them as groups in the organization's external environment that are affected by and/or have an effect on the organization's decisions and actions. These groups have a stake in or are significantly influenced by what the organization does. In turn, these groups can influence the organization. For example, think of the groups that might be affected by the decisions and actions of Starbucks' managers—coffee bean farmers, employees, specialty coffee competitors, local communities, and so forth. Some of these stakeholders also may affect decisions and actions of Starbucks' managers. For example, recently Starbucks changed the way it purchased coffee beans after activists pressured the company to stop buying from plantations that treated their workers poorly. The idea that organizations have stakeholders is now widely accepted by both management academics and practising managers.[34] *Stakeholders* should not be confused with *shareholders,* although shareholders are also stakeholders in an organization. **Shareholders** (also known as stockholders) own one or more shares of stock in a company.

environmental complexity
The number of components in an organization's environment and the extent of the organization's knowledge about those components.

 Hasbro
www.hasbro.com

stakeholders
Any constituencies in the organization's external environment that are affected by the organization's decisions and actions.

 **Q&A** 2.9

shareholders
Individuals or companies that own stocks in a business.

Protestors in the Mexican colonial city of Oaxaca believed having a McDonald's in the city's historic central square would change the atmosphere of the square and destroy local heritage. McDonald's tried to appease the stakeholders by saying that it wanted "to be another option for the consuming public and thus form part of their community." In the end, McDonald's was not able to reach consensus with all stakeholders and gave up on opening a store there. However, not everyone in Oaxaca is happy that McDonald's will not be one of the city's employers.

With what types of stakeholders might an organization have to deal? Exhibit 2-6 identifies some of the most common. Note that these stakeholders include internal and external groups. Why? Because both can affect what an organization does and how it operates. However, in this chapter we are primarily interested in the external groups and their impact on managers' discretion in planning, organizing, leading, and controlling. This does not mean that internal stakeholders are not important; we address internal stakeholders, primarily employees, throughout the rest of the textbook.

Why is stakeholder-relationship management important? Why should managers care about stakeholders?[35] One reason is that it can lead to organizational outcomes such as improved predictability of environmental changes, more successful innovations, a greater degree of trust among stakeholders, and greater organizational flexibility to reduce the impact of change. But does it affect organizational performance? The answer is yes!

Exhibit 2-6

Organizational Stakeholders

Management researchers who have looked at this issue are finding that managers of high-performing companies tend to consider the interests of all major stakeholder groups as they make decisions.[36]

Another reason given for managing external stakeholder relationships is that it's the "right" thing to do. What does this mean? It means that an organization depends on these external groups as sources of inputs (resources) and as outlets for outputs (goods and services), and managers should consider their interests as they make decisions and take actions. We addressed the idea of corporate social responsibility in Chapter 1.

How can external stakeholder relationships be managed? There are four steps:

- *Identify the organization's stakeholders.* Which of the various groups might be affected by decisions that managers make and which groups might influence those decisions? Those groups that are likely to be influenced by and have influence on organizational decisions are the organization's stakeholders.

- *Determine what particular interests or concerns the stakeholders might have.* These interests or concerns could be product quality, financial issues, safe working conditions, environmental protection, and so forth.

- *Decide how critical each stakeholder is to the organization's decisions and actions.* Some stakeholders are more critical to the organization's decisions and actions than others. For instance, a critical stakeholder of the University of Saskatchewan would be the province's legislature since it controls how much budget money the university gets each year. On the other hand, the university's computer hardware and software suppliers are important but not critical.

- *Determine how to manage the different stakeholder relationships.* This decision depends on how critical the stakeholder is to the organization and how uncertain the environment is.[37]

The more critical the stakeholder and the more uncertain the environment, the more managers need to rely on establishing explicit stakeholder partnerships rather than just acknowledging their existence.

The Challenge of Global Management

What is your attitude toward globalization? Is it favourable or unfavourable?

Doing business globally today is not easy! Advocates praise the economic and social benefits that come from globalization. Yet that very globalization has created challenges because of the openness that is necessary for it to work. One challenge is the economic interdependence of trading countries. If one country's economy falters, it could have a domino effect on the other countries with which it does business. So far, however, that has not happened. The world economy has proven to be quite resilient. And there are mechanisms in place, such as the World Trade Organization, to isolate and address potential problems.

Some have predicted that globalization is dead, including philosopher John Ralston Saul. However, Joel Bakan, a University of British Columbia law professor who wrote *The Corporation* and co-produced the documentary of the same name, claims, "It's overly optimistic to say globalization is dead."[38] In support of Bakan's view, consulting firm A.T. Kearney concluded, based on a 2002 survey of the situation, that, overall, globalization remains a strong force, even if there has been some slowdown.[39] The survey concluded that the aftermath of the September 11, 2001, terrorist attacks continues to slow the global movement of money and goods because of travel restrictions and greater security. Economic links grew weaker in 2002, with levels lower than those recorded in 1998. However, information technology and travel still keep people and countries connected.

Successfully managing in today's global environment will require incredible sensitivity and understanding. Bear in mind that although globalization has long been praised for its economic benefits, there are those who think that it is simply a euphemism for "Americanization"—that is, the way US cultural values and US business philosophy are said to be slowly taking over the world.[40] Critics claim that this attitude of the "almighty American dollar wanting to spread the American way to every single country" has created many problems.[41]

Because Canada is not seen as a country that wants to spread Canadian values and culture, Canadian managers may have some advantages over their American counterparts in doing business internationally. However, managers still need to be aware of how their decisions and actions will be viewed globally, not only by those who may agree, but, more importantly, by those who may disagree. They will need to adjust their leadership styles and management approaches to accommodate these diverse views. They will need to do this while still being as efficient and effective as possible in reaching the organization's goals.

SUMMARY AND IMPLICATIONS

❶ How much control do managers have? The omnipotent view of management suggests that managers are directly responsible for an organization's success or failure. While this is the dominant view of managers, there is another perspective. The symbolic view of management argues that much of an organization's success or failure is due to external forces outside managers' control. The reality is probably somewhere in between these two views, with managers often able to exert control, but also facing situations over which they have no control. *Bruce Beairsto, the Richmond, BC, school board superintendent, shows the importance of being aware of how little control one often has. While he could have imposed a dress code on his own, it likely would have met a lot of resistance. By involving many others, he has a better chance of the code's being accepted.*

❷ What is the external environment for managers? The external environment plays a major role in shaping managers' actions. In the specific environment, managers have to be responsive to customers and suppliers while being aware of competitors and public pressure groups. As well, economic, legal–political, sociocultural, demographic, and technological conditions in the general environment affect the issues managers face in doing their job. *Bruce Beairsto, in trying to determine an appropriate dress code for students, had to acknowledge the concerns of students, parents, and teachers. He was also aware that teens are very much influenced by external factors, including the media and what retailers are selling. Thus, his dress code policy had to work within those constraints.*

❸ What challenges do managers face in a global environment? Global trade is affected by two forces: regional trading alliances and the agreements negotiated through the World Trade Organization (WTO). The most prominent regional trading alliances are the European Union (EU), the North American Free Trade Agreement (NAFTA), and the Association of Southeast Asian Nations (ASEAN). These regional alliances specify how trade is conducted between countries. The goal of the WTO is to help businesses conduct trade between countries (importing and exporting) through various trade agreements, negotiated and ratified by the vast majority of the world's trading nations. When managers do business in other countries, they face the legal–political and economic environments of those countries. Some governments are very restrictive in how foreign companies are able to conduct business in their countries. Additionally, managers must be aware of the culture of the countries in which they do business.

4 **How do organizations do business globally?** Organizations can take on a variety of structures when they go global, including multinational corporations (MNCs), transnational corporations (TNCs), or borderless organizations. An organization can take a lower-risk and lower-investment strategy for going global through importing or exporting, hiring foreign representation, or contracting with foreign manufacturers. It can also increase its presence in another country by joining with another business to form a strategic alliance or joint venture. Or it can set up a foreign subsidiary in order to have a full presence in the country. *The Richmond public school district has chosen a strategy of importing students from other countries in order to increase revenues.*

5 **How does the environment affect managers?** Because environments can change, sometimes even unexpectedly, managers have to be aware of the degree of environmental uncertainty they face. They also have to be aware of the complexity of the environment that they face. Managers need to manage relationships with their stakeholders, individuals who are influenced by and have an influence on the organization's decisions and actions. Successfully managing in today's global environment requires incredible sensitivity and understanding. Canadian managers may have some advantages over their American counterparts in doing business internationally, because American companies are sometimes viewed as trying to impose American culture on foreign countries. *School board superintendent Bruce Beairsto has to manage his stakeholders as the Richmond public school district increases the number of international students it enrolls. Some teachers, parents, and taxpayers have concerns about the impact of international students on the learning environment of Canadian students. As well, parents of international students may want assurances that their offspring are well served in the Canadian school environment, and that they are receiving good value for the high tuition they pay.*

CHAPTER 2

Management @ Work

Reading for Comprehension

1. Describe the components of the specific and general environments.

2. Describe the role of the World Trade Organization.

3. Contrast multinational corporations, transnational corporations, and borderless organizations.

4. Define exporting, importing, licensing, and franchising.

5. Define global strategic alliances, joint ventures, and foreign subsidiaries.

6. Discuss the two dimensions of environmental uncertainty.

7. Identify the most common organizational stakeholders.

8. Explain the four steps in managing external stakeholder relationships.

Linking Concepts to Practice

1. Why is it important for managers to understand the external forces that act on them and their organizations?

2. "Businesses are built on relationships." What do you think this statement means? What are the implications for managing the external environment?

3. What would be the drawbacks in *not* managing stakeholder relationships?

4. What are the managerial implications of a borderless organization?

5. Compare the advantages and disadvantages of the various approaches to going global.

6. What challenges might confront a Mexican manager transferred to Canada to manage a manufacturing plant in Winnipeg? Will these be the same for a Canadian manager transferred to Guadalajara, Mexico? Explain.

MANAGEMENT FOR YOU TODAY

You are considering organizing an event to raise funds for a special cause (children living in poverty, breast cancer research, illiteracy, or another cause of your choice). Think about who you might invite to this event (that is, your "customers"—those who will buy tickets to the event). What type of event might appeal to them? What suppliers might you approach for help in organizing the event? What legal issues might you face in setting up this event? After considering all these specific environmental forces, describe the challenges you could face in holding this event.

SELF-ASSESSMENT

Am I Well-Suited for a Career as a Global Manager?

For each of the following statements, circle the level of agreement or disagreement with how well the statement describes you:[42]

> 1 = Very Strongly Disagree
> 4 = Neither Agree nor Disagree
> 7 = Very Strongly Agree

1. When working with people from other cultures, I work hard to understand their perspectives. 1 2 3 4 5 6 7

2. I have a solid understanding of my organization's products and services. 1 2 3 4 5 6 7

3. I am willing to take a stand on issues.   1 2 3 4 5 6 7

4. I have a special talent for dealing with people.   1 2 3 4 5 6 7

5. I can be depended on to tell the truth regardless of circumstances.   1 2 3 4 5 6 7

6. I am good at identifying the most important part of a complex problem or issue.   1 2 3 4 5 6 7

7. I clearly demonstrate commitment to seeing the organization succeed.   1 2 3 4 5 6 7

8. I take personal as well as business risks.   1 2 3 4 5 6 7

9. I have changed as a result of feedback from others.   1 2 3 4 5 6 7

10. I enjoy the challenge of working in countries other than my own.   1 2 3 4 5 6 7

11. I take advantage of opportunities to do new things.   1 2 3 4 5 6 7

12. I find criticism hard to take.   1 2 3 4 5 6 7

13. I seek feedback even when others are reluctant to give it.   1 2 3 4 5 6 7

14. I don't get so invested in things that I cannot change when something does not work.   1 2 3 4 5 6 7

Scoring Key

Reverse your scoring for item 12 (that is, 1 = 7, 2 = 6, 3 = 5, etc.), and then add up your total score.

Analysis and Interpretation

Your total score will range from 14 to 98. The higher your score, the greater your potential for success as an international manager.

In today's global economy, being a manager often means being a global manager. But unfortunately, not all managers are able to transfer their skills smoothly from domestic environments to global ones. Your results here can help you assess whether your skills align with those needed to succeed as an international manager.

WORKING TOGETHER: TEAM-BASED EXERCISE

Assessing Employees' Global Aptitudes

Moving to a foreign country is not easy, no matter how many times you have done it or how receptive you are to new experiences. Successful global organizations are able to identify the best candidates for global assignments, and one of the ways they do this is through individual assessments prior to assigning people to global facilities. Form groups of 3 to 5 individuals. Your newly formed team, the Global Assignment Task Force, has been given the responsibility for developing a global aptitude assessment form for Zara, the successful European clothing retailer.[43] Although the company is not well known in North America, Zara's managers have positioned the company for continued global success. That success is based on a simple principle—in fashion, nothing is as important as time to market.

Zara's store managers (more than 600 worldwide) offer suggestions every day on cuts, fabrics, and even new lines. After reviewing the ideas, a team at headquarters in La Coruna,

Spain, decides what to make. Designers draw up the ideas and send them over the company's intranet to nearby factories. Within days, the cutting, dyeing, sewing, and assembling start. In three weeks, the clothes will be in stores from Barcelona to Berlin to Buenos Aires. That's 12 times faster than its rivals. Zara has a twice-a-week delivery schedule that restocks old styles and brings in new designs. Rivals tend to get new designs once or twice a season.

Because Zara is expanding its global operations significantly, it wants to make sure that it's sending the best possible people to the various global locations. Your team's assignment is to come up with a rough draft of a form to assess people's global aptitudes. Think about the characteristics, skills, attitudes, and so on, that you think a successful global employee would need. Your team's draft should be at least a half page but not longer than 1 page. Be prepared to present your ideas to your classmates and instructor.

Alcan Goes to India

Montreal-based Alcan is the world's largest primary aluminum producer.[44] The company has some 65 000 employees and 430 facilities in 59 countries; it posted a profit of $129 million in 2005. The company plans to develop a $1.8-billion strip mine and refinery in Orissa state, 1200 kilometres southeast of New Delhi, India.

The company has only recently been given permission to begin developing the mine. For a number of years, local people have expressed concern that the mining activities will uproot the Adivasis, some of India's indigenous tribes. Several years ago the protests against developing the mine grew violent when state police fired guns at the Adivasis, killing three protesters. Alcan's plans were put on hold while government officials conducted an inquiry into the deaths. The government concluded that tribal areas "cannot afford to remain backward for the sake of so-called environmental protection."

Bhagawan Majhi serves as sarpanch (chief) of Kucheipadar village, where the violence took place. He has led the opposition to the mines since he was a teen, and says, "Our fight will continue until the government revokes its agreement with the company."

Alcan insists on carrying through with the mine, even though one of its partners in the project, Norway-based Norsk Hydro, decided to quit the project after three of its employees were kidnapped by tribe members.

Alcan spokespeople claim that the mine can actually improve the life of the Adivasis. The company promises to create more than 1000 jobs, and each tribal family will be given at least one. Employees will get a health clinic that others in the area can use. Majhi does not believe that the Adivasis will be better off with the mine. For one thing, the Baphlimali Hill, which is sacred to their tribe, will be ruined. He also says that land is more important than jobs. "What will we do with the money? We don't know how to do business," he notes. He also talks about how the lives of villagers who accepted money from Alcan in exchange for drilling rights have been ruined: "They spent it on alcohol, they married two or three women, they bought wristwatches and motorcycles," Majhi says.

Alcan's CEO, Travis Engen, was given notice two weeks before the annual general meeting that several shareholders would protest the company's plans to develop the mine on Adivasis land. He knows that he must respond to their complaints at the meeting. Does it make sense to simply abandon the mining plans in the face of protests? What should he tell shareholders at the meeting about Alcan's future plans for the region?

National Basketball Association

Using an exceptionally well-executed game plan, the National Basketball Association (NBA) has emerged as the first truly global sports league.[45] During the 2005–2006 season, viewers in 215 countries watched NBA basketball games broadcast in 43 different languages by 164 different television partners.[46] The game was invented in 1891 by Canadian James Naismith, from Almonte, Ontario, and the Toronto Raptors and Vancouver Grizzlies were the first non-US cities to join the league, during the 1995–1996 season.

The desire to transform the once-faltering domestic sport into a global commercial success reflects a keen understanding of managing in a global environment. Much of the credit should go to NBA commissioner David Stern, who has been consciously building the NBA into a global brand.

Professional basketball sparked the interest of fans and players around the globe in the mid-1990s. At one time, if you had asked someone in China what the most popular basketball team was, the answer would have been the "Red Oxen" from Chicago (the Bulls). Today, the NBA's centre of attention comes from China. Yao Ming, the 2.2-metre-tall centerpiece of the Houston Rockets, has a personality that appeals to fans around the world. But he is not the only foreign player in the league. Others include Andrea Bargnani of the Toronto Raptors (from Italy); Dirk Nowitzki of the Dallas Mavericks (from Germany); Pau Gasol of the Memphis Grizzlies (from Spain); Tony Parker of the San Antonio Spurs (from France); Nene Hilario of the Denver Nuggets (from Brazil); and Gordan Giricek of the Utah Jazz (from Croatia). What started as a trickle in the 1980s with occasional foreign stars like Hakeem Olajuwon (Nigeria) and the late Drazen Petrovic (Croatia), has turned into a flood. A record 82 players from 38 countries and territories outside the United States were playing in the NBA as of March 2006. These include Canadian players Jamaal Magloire of the Portland Trail Blazers and Steve Nash of the Phoenix Suns, who won the 2005–2006 Most Valuable Player award. Seventeen Canadian basketball players have played in the NBA over the years. The NBA wants to prove that one day there can be affiliated teams throughout the world.

What strategies can Stern use to increase consumer familiarity with basketball both domestically and globally? How can he develop a greater basketball presence in Canada?

Becoming More Culturally Aware

About the Skill

"Understanding and managing people who are similar to us are challenges—but understanding and managing those who are dissimilar from us and from each other can be even tougher." Workplaces around the world are becoming increasingly diverse. Thus, managers need to recognize that not all employees want the same thing, act in the same manner, and can be managed in the same way. What is a diverse workforce? It's one that is heterogeneous in terms of gender, race, ethnicity, age, and other characteristics that reflect differences. Valuing diversity and helping a diverse workforce achieve its maximum potential are becoming indispensable skills for more and more managers.

Steps in Developing the Skill

The diversity issues an individual manager might face are many. They might include communicating with employees whose familiarity with the language might be limited; creating career development programs that fit the skills, needs, and values of a variety of employees; helping a diverse team cope with a conflict over goals or work assignments; or learning which rewards are valued by different groups of employees. You can improve your handling of diversity issues by following these eight behaviours:[47]

1. **Fully accept diversity.** Successfully valuing diversity starts with each individual's accepting the principle of multiculturalism. Accept the value of diversity for its own sake—not simply because you have to. Accepting and valuing diversity is important because it's the right thing to do. And it's important that you reflect your acceptance in all you say and do.

2. **Recruit broadly.** When you have job openings, work to get a diverse applicant pool. Although referrals from current employees can be a good source of applicants, they tend to produce candidates similar to the current workforce.

3. **Select fairly.** Make sure that the selection process does not discriminate. One suggestion is to use job-specific tests rather than general aptitude or knowledge tests. Such tests measure specific skills, not subjective characteristics.

4. **Provide orientation and training for minorities.** Making the transition from outsider to insider can be particularly difficult for a diverse employee. Provide support either through a group or through a mentoring arrangement.

5. **Sensitize nonminorities.** Not only do you personally need to accept and value diversity, but as a manager you need to encourage all your employees to do so. Many organizations do this through diversity training programs, where employees examine the cultural norms of different groups.

The most important thing a manager can do is show by his or her actions that diversity is valued.

6. **Strive to be flexible.** Part of valuing diversity is recognizing that different groups have different needs and values. Be flexible in accommodating employees' requests.

7. **Seek to motivate individually.** Motivating employees is an important skill for any manager; motivating a diverse workforce has its own special challenges. Managers must be more in tune with the background, cultures, and values of employees. What motivates a single mother with two young children and who is working full time to support her family is likely to be different from the needs of a young, single, part-time employee or an older employee who is working to supplement his or her retirement income.

8. **Reinforce employee differences.** Encourage individuals to embrace and value diverse views. Create traditions and ceremonies that promote diversity. Celebrate diversity by accentuating its positive aspects. However, also be prepared to deal with the challenges of diversity such as mistrust, miscommunication, lack of cohesiveness, attitudinal differences, and stress.

Practising the Skill

Read the descriptions of the following employees who work for the same organization. After reading each description, write a short paragraph describing what you think the goals and priorities of each employee might be. With what types of employee issues might the manager of each employee have to deal? How could these managers exhibit the value of diversity?

Lester is 57 years old, a college graduate, and a vice-president of the firm. His two children are married, and he is a grandparent of three beautiful grandchildren. He lives in a condo with his wife who does volunteer work and is active in their church. Marvin is healthy and likes to stay active, both physically and mentally.

Sanjyot is a 30-year-old clerical worker who came to Canada from Indonesia 10 years ago. She completed high school after moving to Canada and has begun to attend evening classes at a local college. Sanjyot is a single parent with two children under the age of eight. Although her health is excellent, one of her children suffers from a severe learning disability.

Yuri is a recent immigrant from one of the former Soviet republics. He is 42 years old and his English communication skills are quite limited. He has an engineering degree from his country but since he is not licensed to practise in Canada, he works as a parts clerk. He is unmarried and has no children but feels an obligation to his relatives back in his home country. He sends much of his paycheque to them.

CoolBrands A: Frozen Yogurt Comes to Canada

It's 1997, and Michael Serruya, co-founder and president of Markham, Ontario-based Yogen Früz World-Wide, is studying the company's balance sheets and considering expansion possibilities. The company has faced considerable growth since it started in 1986, including development of a substantial international presence. Serruya is not sure that international conditions support moving into additional countries. He thinks perhaps he should start pulling out of the ones he's already in. He also wonders whether Yogen Früz has taken on too many different products. He realizes he needs a plan.

Yogen Früz's Beginnings

Yogen Früz started in August 1986 with one outlet in the Promenade Mall in Thornhill, Ontario. Brothers Michael and Aaron Serruya, who grew up in Thornhill, came up with the idea while holidaying in Florida. Frozen yogurt was very popular there, and the brothers had seen no such product in Canada. They believed frozen yogurt had unlimited potential in their home country and were eager to open such a store to prove themselves right.

Michael had always wanted to be a businessman. "I knew that I wanted to be a business owner from having been exposed to it through my dad," he says. The boys' father, Samuel, had moved the family to Canada from Morocco in 1966 and eventually founded his own business, Computer Composition of Canada, a typesetting company.

Michael, then 21, and his brother Aaron, then 18, were sure they wanted to get into the frozen yogurt business together. They had worked together since Michael was 12, selling T-shirts and managing their paper routes. "Who better than your brother?" says Aaron.

They turned to their father for help in starting their business. They needed a substantial loan to lease the space for their shop in Promenade Mall. Samuel lent them $100 000, but the loan came with a string attached: The two brothers would have to work for their father if their company failed.

In less than a year, Michael and Aaron were hooked on running their business and wanted to expand. Their first concern was how to raise the capital to do so. They decided to start a franchise operation, after seeing all the difficulties their father had faced in raising capital. They would lease the space and the equipment to each franchise owner, thus reducing their own capital risks. All but one location, the original store in Thornhill, are owned by the franchisees.

Locating space in malls for their stores was their next challenge. The brothers were young, and landlords worried they didn't have the experience or the resources to manage their business. The landlords also knew that frozen yogurt was an impulse item; people don't usually travel to the mall just to buy frozen yogurt. But the brothers were hardworking, putting in 80-hour weeks to make the company grow.

The hard work and decision to create a franchise operation paid off. By 1991, the Serruya brothers had 64 Yogen Früz outlets in Canada, almost all in shopping malls.

Undertaking Growth, 1986–1997

The early success of Yogen Früz encouraged the brothers to continue growing their business. The critical changes included the following:

- *June 1991:* The company established its first international franchise, granting a regional franchise to Latin America. The company also acquired its largest competitor in Canada, Yogurty's Yogurt Discovery.
- *Late 1991:* The company formed a strategic alliance with Ontario-based Country Style Donuts, putting 139 Yogen Früz mini-counters into the doughnut shops. The company followed with strategic alliances with Mrs. Fields Cookies, Amigos Restaurants, and Taco Time Restaurants in the United States; Pizza Pizza in Ontario; and Dunkin Donuts, Kentucky Fried Chicken, and Esso internationally.
- *July 1995:* The company acquired Bresler's Industries, a US franchisor of ice cream and frozen yogurt outlets.
- *March 1996:* The company acquired I Can't Believe It's Yogurt, the second-largest franchisor of ice cream and frozen yogurt in the United States, with a significant presence outside North America.

Exhibit 1

Yogen Früz Corporate Chart, 1997[a]

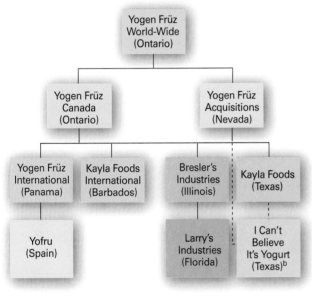

[a] Includes all of the principal wholly-owned subsidiaries and entities of the company and their jurisdictions of incorporation.
[b] Yogen Früz Acquisitions (Nevada) has 100% General Partnership Interest; Kayla Foods (Texas) has 100% Limited Partnership Interest.

Source: Yogen Früz World-Wide, *Prospectus,* June 11, 1997.

The Company's Businesses

In 1997, Yogen Früz was the world's largest franchisor of frozen yogurt outlets, with approximately 3100 outlets in 79 countries under the names of Yogen Früz, I Can't Believe It's Yogurt, and Bresler's. The company also operated 216 gourmet coffee outlets in 15 countries under the name Java Coast Fine Coffees. Here is a brief description of each of these businesses.[1]

Yogen Früz

Status   Yogen Früz is the largest chain of frozen yogurt outlets in Canada. The company had 701 franchised outlets as of February 28, 1997: 343 of these were in Canada and the rest were distributed across 48 other countries.

Products   The outlets sell vanilla and chocolate frozen yogurt, which is blended with fresh frozen fruit when the customer places an order. Outlets sell other products, including frozen yogurt shakes, cakes, pies, fresh juices, and hot and cold nonalcoholic beverages. "The Yogen Früz concept is simple, easy to operate, and can be implemented in a variety of different formats: mini-counters located as part of other larger establishments, carts, small kiosks, and in-line and traditional stores."

How the Business Operates   The company contracts with manufacturers around the world to produce yogurt for its franchisees. The company buys the yogurt from the manufacturers, and resells it at a mark-up through distributors.

I Can't Believe It's Yogurt

Status   The I Can't Believe It's Yogurt chain was the second-largest frozen yogurt chain in the United States and was a significant chain outside North America. As of February 28, 1997, there were 1210 I Can't Believe It's Yogurt outlets in the United States and 756 I Can't Believe It's Yogurt outlets in 33 other countries.

Products   I Can't Believe It's Yogurt outlets sell several flavours of soft-serve and hard-packed "scooped" frozen yogurt. The outlets' menu also includes frozen yogurt shakes, sorbets, cakes, pies, and hot and cold nonalcoholic beverages. Some of the outlets also serve a limited selection of Bresler's ice cream. In addition, approximately 59 outlets in the United States have a Java Coast Fine Coffees mini-counter.

How the Business Operates   I Can't Believe It's Yogurt manufactures frozen yogurt, ice cream, and other frozen dessert products and ingredients at its production facility in Carrollton, Texas. Outside the United States, there are four manufacturers who produce I Can't Believe It's Yogurt frozen yogurt products for distribution through local distributors.

Bresler's

Status   As of February 28, 1997, there were 432 Bresler's outlets in the United States as well as 34 outlets in 26 other countries.

Products   The Bresler's chain serves premium ice creams, frozen yogurts, sherbets, sorbets, ices, soda fountain products, ice cream specialty items, and nonalcoholic beverages.

Exhibit 2

Yogen Früz, Revenue by Region

(For the year ended August 31, 1996)

Region	Yogen Früz Business	I Can't Believe It's Yogurt Business[a]	Bresler's Business	Java Coast Fine Coffees Business	Company[a]
Canada	$4 525 301 (54.2%)	—	—	—	$4 525 301 (15.1%)
United States	$197 351 (2.4%)	$8 228 775 (81.7%)	$9 978 748 (86.8%)	$117 907 (100%)	$18 522 781 (61.7%)
Central and South America	$912 110 (10.9%)	$409 150 (4.1%)	$187 134 (1.6%)	—	$1 508 394 (5.0%)
Middle and Far East	$1 890 198 (22.6%)	$745 259 (7.4%)	$1 300 752 (11.3%)	—	$3 936 209 (13.1%)
Europe	$829 218 (9.9%)	$693 372 (6.8%)	$23 348 (0.3%)	—	$1 545 938 (5.1%)
TOTAL	$8 354 178	$10 076 556	$11 489 982	$117 907	$30 038 623

[a] I Can't Believe It's Yogurt was acquired on March 8, 1996. Accordingly, these figures reflect only the results of operations of I Can't Believe It's Yogurt for the period between March 8, 1996, and August 30, 1996.

Source: Yogen Früz World-Wide, *Prospectus,* June 11, 1997.

How the Business Operates

All of Bresler's soft-serve ice cream is produced at I Can't Believe It's Yogurt's Carrollton, Texas, manufacturing facility. The facility also produces much of Bresler's hard-packed ice cream for its US outlets. Third-party manufacturers in the United States and Mexico produce the rest.

Java Coast Fine Coffees

Status The Java Coast Fine Coffees business was acquired at the same time that the company acquired I Can't Believe It's Yogurt. In the United States, Java Coast Fine Coffees mini-outlets are add-ons to existing I Can't Believe It's Yogurt outlets or to convenience stores and gas station food marts. By contrast, internationally, the company operates larger full-menu coffee shops. As of February 28, 1997, there were 177 licensed Java Coast Fine Coffee outlets in the United States. There were 39 franchised outlets in 14 other countries.

Products The Java Coast Fine Coffees menu includes espresso-based beverages, granita, exotic juices, gourmet coffees, and iced/hot teas.

How the Business Operates All Java Coast coffees are made from 100 percent pure Arabica beans. The coffee is produced by Superior Coffee and Foods, which jointly markets and supports Java Coast Fine Coffees locations across the United States with Yogen Früz.

Sources of Revenue

The company's revenues come from the following sources:[2]

- *Revenues from franchise, licence, and other fees.* The company charges its franchisees and some of its licensees an initial fee for the franchise or licence, and sometimes a renewal fee. Sometimes there are also fees for support, marketing, and other services.

- *Revenues from product manufacturing and sales.* The company earns revenues on products that franchisees and licensees are required to purchase, such as "frozen yogurt, ice cream and other menu items, outlet supplies such as cups, napkins, uniforms, etc., and required machinery and equipment." Some of these products are also sold at convenience stores, service stations, fast food chains, and food outlets in universities, public stadiums, hospitals, and similar businesses.

- *Revenues from royalties.* The company earns royalties from Yogen Früz and Bresler's franchisees on the basis of their gross sales.

- *Revenues from corporate stores.* The company owns and operates five Yogen Früz stores in Canada and five Bresler's stores and two ice cream stores under the name Larry's Ice Cream & Yogurt Parlours in the United States.

- *Rental revenues.* The company sublets locations to some of US Bresler's franchisees, often at a mark-up. The com-

Exhibit 3

Yogen Früz, Percentage of Revenue by Source

(For the year ended August 31, 1996)

Revenue Source	Yogen Früz Business	I Can't Believe It's Yogurt Business[a]	Bresler's Business	Java Coast Fine Coffees Business	Company[a]
Franchise, licence, and other fees	24%	2%	10%	—	11%
Product manufacturing and sales	47%	97%	31%	100%	58%
Royalties	9%	1%	18%	—	10%
Corporate stores	10%	—	12%	—	7%
Rent	—	—	27%	—	10%
Turnkey sales and construction-related services	10%	—	2%	—	4%

[a] I Can't Believe It's Yogurt was acquired on March 8, 1996. Accordingly, these figures reflect only the results of operations of I Can't Believe It's Yogurt for the period between March 8, 1996, and August 30, 1996.

Source: Yogen Früz World-Wide, *Prospectus,* June 11, 1997.

pany assists Yogen Früz Canada franchisees in obtaining leases for a one-time flat fee.

- *Revenues from turnkey sales and construction-related services.* The company occasionally builds outlets on a turnkey basis for Yogen Früz franchisees in Canada and provides other services to US Bresler's franchisees in connection with the design, layout, and construction of Bresler's shops. The company charges fees for those services.

The Decision

The company's objective from its beginnings was to become "the world's largest franchisor and licensor of frozen yogurt outlets." The company achieved that objective in 1997. Michael Serruya wonders what his next objectives might be. To find out,

he needs to better understand the political, legal, and economic environments where his companies operate. He also needs to determine whether there are any demographic considerations that might affect the consumption of frozen yogurt and ice cream products in the years ahead. How much uncertainty is in his environment? He wonders whether the different organizational cultures of his operations need to be considered as part of determining his next objectives. He also wonders whether he should consider any other corporate strategies for continuing his global expansion.

Sources: Yogen Früz World-Wide, *Prospectus,* June 11, 1997; S. Kirshner, "Frozen Yogurt Kings Bask in Their Success," *Canadian Jewish News,* August 2, 2001, p. 40; L. Wright, "This Thornhill Duo Has the Business World Licked," *Toronto Star,* August 16, 1988, p. N18; T. Tillson, "Mister Freeze: Now That Yogen Früz's Meltdown Is Over, Michael Serruya Is Out Shopping for New Treats," *Report on Business Magazine,* February 2002, pp. 16–18.

Planning and Strategic Management

How do I make plans to carry out decisions?

1 What does planning involve?

2 How do managers set goals and develop plans?

3 What are the steps in strategic management?

4 What kinds of strategies can managers use?

5 How can quality be a competitive advantage?

Blue Man Group is one of the hottest performance groups today.[1]

Its theatrical productions have appeared in New York City, Boston, Chicago, and Las Vegas for years. The group opened a production in Berlin in 2004, one in Toronto in June 2005, one in London in December 2005, and then one in Amsterdam in December 2006. Blue Man performances are a mix of mime, percussion music, and splashing paint.

The group was founded in 1988 by three guys who decided it was time to stage a funeral for the 1980s. They put on bald wigs, painted themselves blue, and carried a coffin filled with items representing the worst of the decade (such as yuppies and Rambo) into New York City's Central Park. MTV recorded the ceremony.

Encouraged by their friends, the trio (Chris Wink, Matt Goldman, and Phil Stanton) started giving small performances around the city. None of the three had formal training in music or acting. They really had not planned to become performers. Three years later, they had performed on national TV, spitting paint on *The Tonight Show* and *Live with Regis and Kathie Lee.* They also had an off-Broadway show called *Tubes.*

Wink, Goldman, and Stanton were also starting to burn out. They were working six days a week, had gone three years without a break, and performed 1200

consecutive shows. Once success started, the three just kept going, not giving thought to how to manage the show or their time. They did not have time to create new material, so they were just performing the same show over and over. They had a small crew who had "never worked in theater and [did not] have a clue, just like us," says Wink. They spent 90 minutes each night making themselves up before a performance. Then they were part of the cleanup crew. They were so tired that they did not have time for a personal life. How did they get into this situation? "We've never planned ahead," explained Wink.

THINK ABOUT IT

How much planning should organizations do? Put yourself in Blue Man Group's shoes. How can it make sure that the show goes on should one of its members become ill or get injured?

Managers everywhere need to plan. In this chapter we present the basics of planning: what it is, why managers plan, and how they plan. We will also discuss the importance of strategic management and choosing effective strategies to develop a competitive advantage.

Blue Man Group
www.blueman.com

WHAT IS PLANNING?

 What does planning involve?

planning
A management function that involves defining goals, establishing a strategy for achieving those goals, and developing plans to integrate and coordinate activities.

As we stated in Chapter 1, **planning** involves defining goals, establishing an overall strategy for achieving those goals, and developing a comprehensive set of plans to integrate and coordinate the work needed to achieve the goals. It is concerned with both ends (what is to be done) and means (how it is to be done). For instance, you and your classmates may want to organize a large graduation dinner dance. To do so, you would consider the goals, the strategy, the plans, and assign committees to get the work done.

Planning can either be formal or informal. In informal planning, nothing is written down, and there is little or no sharing of goals with others. Informal planning is general and lacks continuity. Although it's more common in smaller organizations, where the owner-manager has a vision of where he or she wants the business to go and how to get there, informal planning does exist in some large organizations as well. At the same time, some small businesses may have very sophisticated planning processes and formal plans. For a look at your response to planning, see *Self-Assessment—How Good Am I at Personal Planning?* on pages 94–95, at the end of the chapter.

When we use the term *planning* in this book, we mean *formal* planning. In formal planning, specific goals covering a period of years are defined. These goals are written and shared with organization members. Then a specific action program for the achievement of these goals is developed; that is, managers clearly define the path they want to take to get the organization and the various work units from where they are to where they want them to be.

Setting goals, establishing a strategy to achieve those goals, and developing a set of plans to integrate and coordinate activities seem pretty complicated. So why would managers want to plan? Does planning affect performance? We address these issues next.

 Q&A 6.1

Purposes of Planning

We can identify at least four reasons for planning:

Are you a planner or a doer? Do you prefer to make plans or just act?

- *Planning provides direction to managers and nonmanagers alike.* When employees know where the organization or work unit is going and what they must contribute to reach goals, they can coordinate their activities, cooperate with each other, and do what it takes to accomplish those goals. Without planning, departments and individuals might work at cross purposes, preventing the organization from moving efficiently toward its goals. This would also be true if you and your friends were planning your grad party— if you did not coordinate and cooperate, you might not actually get the party organized in time.

- *Planning reduces uncertainty by forcing managers to look ahead, anticipate change, consider the impact of change, and develop appropriate responses.* Even though planning cannot eliminate change or uncertainty, managers plan in order to anticipate change and develop the most effective response to it. Similarly, by planning a grad party ahead of time, you can make sure that it's held at a desired location, rather than at the only one that was left because you waited until the last minute.

- *Planning reduces overlapping and wasteful activities.* When work activities are coordinated around established plans, redundancy can be minimized. Furthermore, when means and ends are made clear through planning, inefficiencies become obvious and can be corrected or eliminated.

- *Planning establishes the goals or standards that are used in controlling.* If we are unsure of what we are trying to accomplish, how can we determine whether we have actually achieved it? In planning, we develop the goals and the plans. Then, through controlling, we compare actual performance against the goals, identify any significant deviations, and take any necessary corrective action. Without planning, there would be no way to control outcomes.

Renato Zambonini, board chair of Ottawa-based Cognos notes that planning went out of fashion during the dot-com years. He found that in both California and in Ottawa, entrepreneurs worked "90 hours a week, but the whole goal [was] not to build a business or a company. [All they really wanted was] someone to buy them out."[2] Unfortunately, many of those companies were not bought out, but folded. Planning might have helped them be more successful.

Planning and Performance

Are you skeptical of planning? Do you wonder whether planning really pays off?

Is planning worthwhile? Do managers and organizations that plan outperform those that don't? Intuitively, you would expect the answer to be a resounding yes. While studies of performance in organizations that plan are generally positive, we cannot say that organizations that formally plan *always* outperform those that don't plan.

Numerous studies have looked at the relationship between planning and performance.[3] We can draw the following four conclusions from these studies. First, generally speaking, formal planning is associated with higher profits, higher return on assets, and other positive financial results. Second, the quality of the planning process and the appropriate implementation of the plans probably contribute more to high performance than does the extent of planning. Third, in those studies in which formal planning did not lead to higher performance, the external environment often was the culprit. Government regulations, powerful labour unions, and other critical environmental forces constrain managers' options and reduce the impact of planning on an organization's performance. Fourth, the planning/performance relationship is influenced by the planning time frame. Organizations need at least four years of systematic formal planning before performance is affected.

Victoria Hale founded the nonprofit Institute for OneWorld Health with an informal plan. Inspired by a conversation about pharmaceutical science with a cab driver, Hale went back to an essay she had written years earlier about diseases that would benefit from drug development efforts. Using that as her preliminary business plan, she incorporated the Institute the next day. The Institute's goal is to persuade companies with important but not profitable drugs to donate those to the Institute for tax and public relations benefits. The Institute then uses grants and donations to distribute the drugs to needy patients around the world.

Q&A 6.2

HOW DO MANAGERS PLAN?

One evening, after three years of nonstop performing with Blue Man Group, Phil Stanton cut his hand with a router.[4] The group had never planned for what to do if one of them was injured. They had one understudy, one of the show's drummers, but only because their investors had insisted on it as a backup plan. While he had studied the show, he had never even rehearsed in it. When Stanton cut his hand, the drummer had to go onstage as a Blue Man. Because the group members wear bald wigs and paint themselves blue, no one in the audience knew that Stanton was missing. The show was a success, even without him.

That success made the co-founders of Blue Man (Chris Wink, Matt Goldman, and Phil Stanton) realize that it would be quite easy to clone Blue Man, which would increase the number of shows they could do, and also give the co-founders time off. Finally, three years after they had started performing, they could think more about the show's future and plan to expand their show.

THINK ABOUT IT

How might planning make Blue Man Group performers more successful?

② How do managers set goals
and develop plans?

goals
Desired outcomes for individuals,
groups, or entire organizations.

plans
Documents that outline how goals
are going to be met and describe
resource allocations, schedules,
and other necessary actions to
accomplish the goals.

Planning is often called the primary management function because it establishes the basis for all the other functions that managers perform. Without planning, managers would not know what to organize, lead, or control. In fact, without plans, there would not be anything to organize, lead, or control! So how do managers plan?

Planning involves two important elements: goals and plans. **Goals** are the desired outcomes for individuals, groups, or entire organizations.[5] Goals are objectives, and we use the two terms interchangeably. They provide the direction for all management decisions and form the criteria against which actual work accomplishments can be measured. That is why they are often called the foundation of planning. You have to know the desired target or outcome before you can establish plans for reaching it. **Plans** are documents that outline how goals are going to be met and that typically describe resource allocations, schedules, and other necessary actions to accomplish the goals. As managers plan, they are developing both goals and plans.

In the next section we consider how to establish goals.

Approaches to Establishing Goals

Goals provide the direction for all management decisions and actions and form the criteria against which actual accomplishments are measured. Everything organizational members do should be oriented toward helping their work units and the organization achieve its goals. Goals can be established through a process of traditional goal setting or management by objectives.

Traditional Goal Setting

traditional goal setting
An approach to setting goals in
which goals are set at the top of the
organization and then broken into
subgoals for each organizational
level.

In **traditional goal setting**, goals are set at the top of the organization and then broken into subgoals for each organizational level. This traditional perspective assumes that top managers know what is best because they see "the big picture." Thus, the goals that are established and passed down to each succeeding level serve to direct and guide, and in some ways constrain, individual employees' work behaviours. Employees work to meet the goals that have been assigned in their areas of responsibility.

In traditional goal setting, if top management wants to increase sales by 10 percent for the year, the marketing and sales departments need to develop action plans that will yield

Goals are the outcomes we desire.
At the Bronx Zoo, where Patrick
Thomas, curator of mammals,
recently gazed into the eyes of
Siberian tiger "Taurus" through a
sheet of inch-thick glass, "Our goal
is to have animals engaged in normal behaviors." Thomas goes on to
say of the new tiger habitat, "You
want the exhibit to inspire visitors
to care about saving tigers." The
goal of the 3-acre Tiger Mountain is
particularly important; its 6 residents represent the mere 5000
tigers left in the wild.

these results. The manufacturing department needs to develop plans for how to produce more product. An individual salesperson may need to make more calls to new clients, or convince current clients that they need more product. Thus, each of the lower levels (individual employee, sales, marketing, production) becomes a means to achieving the corporate end of increasing sales.

Management by Objectives

Instead of traditional goal setting, many organizations use **management by objectives (MBO)**, an approach in which specific performance goals are jointly determined by employees and their managers, progress toward accomplishing these goals is periodically reviewed, and rewards are allocated on the basis of this progress. Rather than using goals only as controls, MBO uses them to motivate employees as well. Employees will be more committed to goals that they help set.

Management by objectives consists of four elements: goal specificity, participative decision making, an explicit time period, and performance feedback.[6] Its appeal lies in its focus on the accomplishment of participatively set objectives as the reason for and motivation behind individuals' work efforts. Exhibit 3-1 lists the steps in a typical MBO program.

> *Have you occasionally failed at your goals? How can you develop more achievable goals?*

Do MBO programs work? Studies of actual MBO programs confirm that MBO increases employee performance and organizational productivity. A review of 70 programs, for example, found organizational productivity gains in 68 of them.[7] This same review also identified top management commitment and involvement as important conditions for MBO to succeed.

management by objectives (MBO)
An approach to goal setting in which specific measurable goals are jointly set by managers and employees, progress on goals is periodically reviewed, and rewards are allocated on the basis of this progress.

Characteristics of Well-Designed Goals

Goals are not all created equal. Some goals are better than others. How can you tell the difference? What makes a "well-designed" goal?[8] Exhibit 3-2 on page 72 outlines the characteristics of well-designed goals.

Exhibit 3-1

Steps in a Typical MBO Program

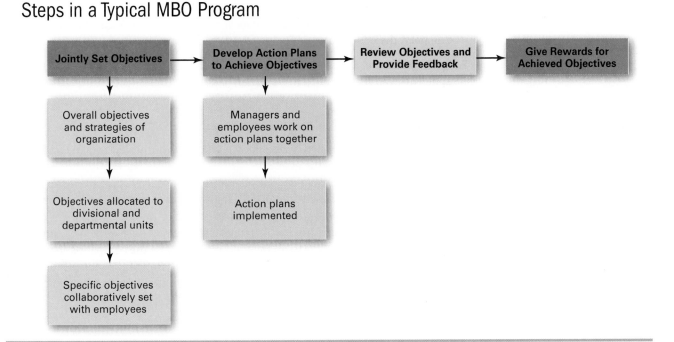

Exhibit 3-2

Characteristics of Well-Designed Goals

- Written in terms of outcomes rather than actions

- Measurable and quantifiable

- Clear time frame

- Communicated to all necessary organizational members

- Challenging yet attainable

- Written down

Steps in Goal Setting

What steps should managers follow in setting goals? The goal-setting process consists of five steps.

mission
The purpose of an organization.

1. *Review the organization's mission.* The **mission** is the purpose of an organization. The broad statement of what the organization's purpose is and what it hopes to accomplish provides an overall guide to what organizational members think is important. It's important to review these statements before writing goals because the goals should reflect what the mission statement says.

2. *Evaluate available resources.* You don't want to set goals that are impossible to achieve given your available resources. Even though goals should be challenging, they should be realistic. After all, if the resources you have to work with will not allow you to achieve a goal no matter how hard you try or how much effort is exerted, that goal should not be set. That would be like the person with a $50 000 annual income and no other financial resources setting a goal of building an investment portfolio worth $1 million in three years. No matter how hard he or she works at it, it's not going to happen.

3. *Determine the goals individually or with input from others.* The goals reflect desired outcomes and should be consistent with the organization's mission and goals in other organizational areas. These goals should be measurable, specific, and include a time frame for accomplishment.

4. *Write down the goals and communicate them to all who need to know.* We have already explained the benefit of writing down and communicating goals.

5. *Review results and whether goals are being met.* Make changes, as needed. For any plan to be effective, reviews need to be done.

Developing Plans

Once goals have been established, written down, and communicated, a manager is ready to develop plans for pursuing the goals.

What are the advantages of specifying the plans to achieve goals? Jean-Marc Eustache, president and CEO of Montreal-based Transat A.T., knows he cannot relax just because he has one of the largest international travel and tourism companies in the world. He recently told shareholders that he plans "to double [Transat's] revenues during the next three-and-a-half years."[9] To do this, he plans to do the following: increase the company's share of the leisure travel business into and out of Ontario; increase the company's share of the leisure travel business in France; increase flights between Canada and the United Kingdom; move into the United States and offer flights to Mexico and the Caribbean; and increase the company's ownership and management of hotels in the Caribbean and Mexico. By specifying the plans to achieve his goal to double revenues, Eustache let Transat employees know where to focus attention when helping people make their travel plans.

Types of Plans

The most popular ways to describe an organization's plans are by their breadth (strategic vs. operational), time frame (short term vs. long term), specificity (directional vs. specific), and frequency of use (single use vs. standing). These planning classifications are not independent. As Exhibit 3-3 illustrates, strategic plans are long-term, directional, and single-use. Operational plans are short-term, specific, and standing. Let's examine each of these types of plans.

Strategic plans are plans that apply to the entire organization, establish the organization's overall goals, and seek to position the organization in terms of its environment. Plans that specify the details of how the overall goals are to be achieved are called **operational plans**. How do the two types of plans differ? Strategic plans tend to cover a longer time frame and a broader view of the organization. Strategic plans also include the formulation of goals, whereas operational plans define ways to achieve the goals. Also, operational plans tend to cover short time periods—monthly, weekly, and day-to-day.

strategic plans
Plans that apply to the entire organization, establish the organization's overall goals, and seek to position the organization in terms of its environment.

operational plans
Plans that specify the details of how the overall goals are to be achieved.

Exhibit 3-3

Types of Plans

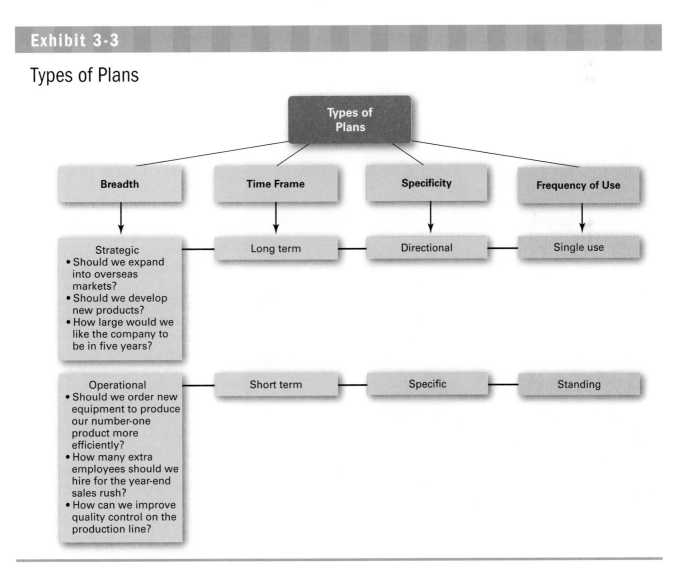

long-term plans
Plans with a time frame beyond three years.

short-term plans
Plans with a time frame of one year or less.

specific plans
Plans that are clearly defined and leave no room for interpretation.

directional plans
Plans that are flexible and that set out general guidelines.

single-use plan
A one-time plan specifically designed to meet the needs of a unique situation.

standing plans
Plans that are ongoing and provide guidance for activities performed repeatedly.

The difference in years between short term and long term has shortened considerably. It used to be that long term meant anything more than seven years. Try to imagine what you would like to be doing in seven years, and you can begin to appreciate how difficult it was for managers to establish plans that far in the future. As organizational environments have become more uncertain, the definition of *long term* has changed. We define **long-term plans** as those with a time frame beyond three years.[10] For instance, an organization may develop a five-year plan for increasing its sales in Asia. We define **short-term plans** as those with a time frame of one year or less. For instance, a company may decide that it will increase sales by 10 percent over the next year. The *intermediate term* is any time period in between. Although these time classifications are fairly common, an organization can designate any time frame it wants for planning purposes.

Intuitively, it would seem that specific plans would be preferable to directional, or loosely guided, plans. **Specific plans** are plans that are clearly defined and that leave no room for interpretation. They have clearly defined objectives. There is no ambiguity and no problem with misunderstanding. For example, a manager who seeks to increase his or her unit's work output by 8 percent over a given 12-month period might establish specific procedures, budget allocations, and schedules of activities to reach that goal. The drawbacks of specific plans are that they require clarity and a sense of predictability that often do not exist. This clarity and predictability worked well for Blue Man Group, however, because they wanted to create a very uniform product.

When uncertainty is high and managers must be flexible in order to respond to unexpected changes, directional plans are preferable. **Directional plans** are flexible plans that set out general guidelines. They provide focus but don't lock managers into specific goals or courses of action. (Exhibit 3-4 illustrates how specific and directional plans differ, with the directional plan indicating only the *intent* to get from "A" to "B" and the specific plan *identifying the exact route* that one would take to get from "A" to "B.") Instead of detailing a specific plan to cut costs by 4 percent and increase revenues by 6 percent in the next six months, managers might formulate a directional plan for improving profits by 5 to 10 percent over the next six months. The flexibility inherent in directional plans must be weighed against the loss of clarity provided by specific plans.

Some plans that managers develop are ongoing, while others are used only once. A **single-use plan** is a one-time plan specifically designed to meet the needs of a unique situation. For instance, when Charles Schwab introduced its online discount stock-brokerage service, top-level executives used a single-use plan to guide the creation and implementation of the new service. In contrast, **standing plans** are ongoing and provide guidance for activities performed repeatedly. Standing plans include policies, rules, and procedures, which we define in Chapter 4. An example of a standing plan would be the discrimination and harassment policy developed by the University of

Planning is definitely not just for managers. When families in the *Vancouver Sun*'s distribution area were asked to take the newspaper's "car free challenge" for a month, they learned that planning became a much greater part of their lives. The three families pictured above took the challenge and found that figuring out how long a journey took and the best way to get there required being more aware of their schedules than when they could just grab their car keys and drive off.

Exhibit 3-4

Specific vs. Directional Plans

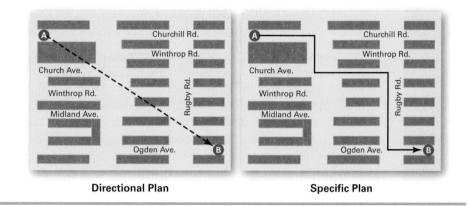

Directional Plan   **Specific Plan**

British Columbia. It provides guidance to university administrators, faculty, and staff as they perform their job duties.

Q&A 6.5

Contingency Factors in Planning

What kinds of plans are needed in a given situation? Will strategic or operational plans be needed? How about specific or directional plans? In some situations, long-term plans make sense; in others they do not. What are these situations? The process of developing plans is influenced by two contingency factors—the degree of environmental uncertainty and the length of future commitments—and by the planning approach followed.[11]

When environmental uncertainty is high, plans should be specific, but flexible. Managers must be prepared to amend plans as they are implemented. At times, managers may even have to abandon their plans.[12] For example, as CEO of Continental Airlines, Gordon M. Bethune, together with his management team, established the specific goal of focusing on a key concern of customers—on-time flights—to help the company become more competitive in the highly uncertain airline industry. Because of the high level of uncertainty, the management team identified a "destination, but not a flight plan," and changed plans as necessary to achieve that goal of on-time service. Also, it's important for managers to continue formal planning efforts through periods of environmental uncertainty because studies have shown that it takes at least four years of such efforts before any positive impact on organizational performance is seen.[13]

Continental Airlines
www.continental.com

The second contingency factor that affects planning is the time frame of plans. The more that current plans affect future commitments, the longer the time frame for which managers should plan. This means that plans should extend far enough to meet those future commitments made when the plans were developed. Planning for too long or too short a time period is inefficient and ineffective.

Criticisms of Planning

Formalized organizational planning became popular in the 1960s and, for the most part, it is still popular today. It makes sense for an organization to establish some direction. But critics have challenged some of the basic assumptions underlying planning. What are the primary criticisms directed at formal planning?

What if you really don't like to make plans?

- *Planning may create rigidity.*[14] Formal planning efforts can lock an organization into specific goals to be achieved within specific timetables. When these goals

Terri Williamson put her backgrounds in chemistry and professional branding to good use when she decided to create a line of cosmetics under the brand name "Glow." She planned carefully, checking the Internet to be sure the product name was available, creating a distinctive look and feel for the packaging of her product line, hand-picking the Hollywood location of her store, and mixing and remixing essential oils and other ingredients in her home to come up with a distinctive sandalwood scent. Williamson's plans were coming to fruition in 2001 and 2002, with steadily rising sales among her celebrity clients, when everything changed. Jennifer Lopez unveiled her own new fragrance called "Glow by J.Lo," and Williamson's Glow Industries began a trademark infringement suit. The suit has since been settled out of court between the two parties.

are set, the assumption may be that the environment will not change during the time period the goals cover. If that assumption is faulty, managers who follow a plan may face trouble. Rather than remaining flexible—and possibly throwing out the plan—managers who continue to do the things required to achieve the original goals may not be able to cope with the changed environment. Forcing a course of action when the environment is fluid can be a recipe for disaster.

- *Plans cannot be developed for a dynamic environment.*[15] Most organizations today face dynamic environments. If a basic assumption of making plans—that the environment will not change—is faulty, then how can you make plans at all? Today's business environment is often chaotic at best. By definition, that means random and unpredictable. Managing under those conditions requires flexibility, and that may mean not being tied to formal plans.

- *Formal plans cannot replace intuition and creativity.*[16] Successful organizations are typically the result of someone's innovative vision. But visions have a tendency to become formalized as they evolve. Formal planning efforts typically involve a thorough investigation of the organization's capabilities and opportunities and a mechanical analysis that reduces the vision to some type of programmed routine. That approach can spell disaster for an organization. Apple Computer learned this the hard way. In the late 1970s and throughout the 1980s Apple's success was attributed, in part, to the innovative and creative approaches of co-founder Steve Jobs. Eventually, Jobs was forced to leave, and with his departure came increased organizational formality, including detailed planning—the same things that Jobs despised so much because he felt that they hampered creativity. During the 1990s, the situation at Apple became so bad that Jobs was brought back as CEO to get Apple back on track. The company's renewed focus on innovation led to the debut of the iMac in 1998, the iPod in 2001, a radically new look for the iMac in 2002, and an online music store in 2003.

- *Planning focuses managers' attention on today's competition, not on tomorrow's survival.*[17] Formal planning has a tendency to focus on how to capitalize on existing business opportunities within an industry. It often does not allow managers to consider creating or reinventing an industry. Consequently, formal plans may result in costly blunders and high catch-up costs when other competitors take the lead. On the other hand, companies such as Intel, General Electric, Nokia, and Sony have found success by forging into uncharted waters, spawning new industries as they go.

- *Formal planning reinforces success, which may lead to failure.*[18] It's hard to change or discard previously successful plans—to leave the comfort of what works for the anxiety of the unknown. Successful plans, however, may provide a false sense of security, generating more confidence in the formal plans than is warranted. Many managers will not face the unknown until they are forced to do so by environmental changes. By then, it may be too late!

How valid are these criticisms? Should managers forget about planning? No! Although the criticisms have merit when directed at rigid, inflexible planning, today's managers can be effective planners if they understand the need to be flexible in responding to environmental change.

 *Q&A* 6.6

ORGANIZATIONAL STRATEGY: CHOOSING A NICHE

Shortly after they became successful, Blue Man Group faced opportunities from various partners, including product endorsements.[19] For example, Disney approached the group with proposals for a movie and a related theme ride. The group rejected most of these opportunities, for fear that quick payoffs on their Blue Man character could lead to quick failure of the character. Chris Wink, Matt Goldman, and Phil Stanton wanted the Blue Man character to grow over decades, and worried that a steep growth curve could bring the group crashing down just as quickly. Wink explained the group's cautious strategy: "It's funny, when you try to get something off the ground, you can't even get a door, and...[t]hen you finally get there and all the doors open—and it's about not going through them."

THINK ABOUT IT
How could a focus on controlled growth work to Blue Man Group's advantage?

To begin to understand why organizational strategy matters, you need look no further than at what has happened in the discount retail industry in Canada. The industry's two largest competitors—Wal-Mart and Zellers—have battled for market dominance since Wal-Mart entered Canada in 1992. The two chains have some striking similarities: store atmosphere, markets served, and organizational purpose. Yet Wal-Mart's performance (financial and otherwise) has taken market share from Zellers every single year. Wal-Mart is the world's largest and most successful retailer, and Zellers is the second-largest discount retailer in Canada. Why the difference in performance? Organizations vary in how well they perform because of differences in their strategies and differences in competitive abilities.[20] Wal-Mart excels at strategic management, while Zellers struggles to find the right niche.

Strategic management is that set of managerial decisions and actions that determines the long-run performance of an organization.[21] It is an important task of managers and involves all of the basic management functions.

The **strategic management process**, as illustrated in Exhibit 3-5, is a six-step process that encompasses strategic planning, implementation, and evaluation. Although the first four steps describe the planning that must take place, implementation and evaluation are just as important. Even the best strategies can fail if management does not implement or evaluate them properly. Let's examine the six steps in detail.

3 What are the steps in strategic management?

strategic management
That set of managerial decisions and actions that determines the long-run performance of an organization.

strategic management process
A six-step process that encompasses strategic planning, implementation, and evaluation.

Exhibit 3-5

The Strategic Management Process

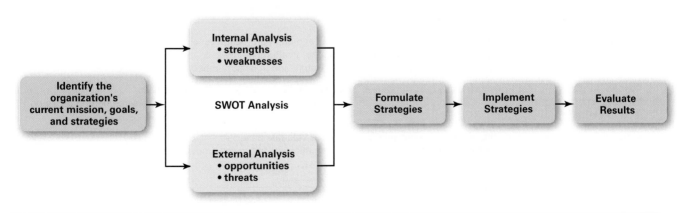

Step 1: Identify the Organization's Current Mission, Goals, and Strategies

How would you develop a strategic plan for the next five or ten years of your life? What would be your mission, goals, and strategies?

Every organization needs a mission—a statement of the purpose of an organization. The mission answers the question What is our reason for being in business? Defining the organization's mission forces managers to carefully identify the scope of their products or services. For example, CanWest Global Communications' mission statement is "to inform, enlighten and entertain people everywhere so as to improve the quality of their lives." The mission of the Workers' Compensation Board (WCB) of British Columbia is "promoting workplace health and safety for the workers and employers of [the] province." The mission of eBay is "to build an online marketplace that enables practically anyone to trade practically anything almost anywhere in the world." These statements provide clues to what these organizations see as their reason for being in business. Exhibit 3-6 describes the typical components of a mission statement.

Q&A 7.2

Exhibit 3-6

Components of a Mission Statement

Customers: Who are the organization's customers?
We believe our first responsibility is to the doctors, nurses, and patients, to mothers and all others who use our products and services. (Johnson & Johnson)

Products or services: What are the organization's major products or services?
To enrich the lives of everyone in WestJet's world by providing safe, friendly, affordable air travel. (WestJet Airlines)

Markets: Where does the organization compete geographically?
To invoke the senses, evoke the imagination and provoke the emotions of people around the world! (Cirque du Soleil)

Technology: How technologically current is the organization?
Pushing the limits of what technology can accomplish: Pushing the limits means focusing more of our resources and attention on what we do not know rather than on controlling what we already know. The fact that something has not worked in the past does not mean that it cannot be made to work in the future; and the fact that something did work in the past doesn't mean that it can't be improved upon. (Syncrude)

Concern for survival, growth, and profitability: Is the organization committed to growth and financial stability?
We expand our thinking and grow faster than the industry average, and we enjoy being seen as a young aggressive company. We believe that we do not have to compromise our integrity to be profit driven. (G.A.P Adventures)

Philosophy: What are the organization's basic beliefs, values, aspirations, and ethical priorities?
Ducks Unlimited Canada (DUC) envisions Canada as a nation that can sustain use by people and wildlife without endangering the amount or functions of natural lands. DUC leads wetland conservation for waterfowl, other wildlife and people in North America. (Ducks Unlimited Canada)

Self-concept: What are the organization's major competitive advantage and core competencies?
CBC Television, as Canada's national public television broadcaster, has a cultural mandate to tell compelling, original, audacious and entertaining Canadian stories in a way that Canadians want to watch, and in large numbers. (CBC Television)

Concern for public image: How responsive is the organization to societal and environmental concerns?
As a vital measure of integrity, we will ensure the health and safety of our communities, and protect the environment in all we do. (Dow Chemical)

Concern for employees: Does the organization consider employees a valuable asset?
At IBM, we recognize individual differences and appreciate how these differences provide a powerful competitive advantage and a source of great pride and opportunity in the workplace and marketplace. (IBM Canada)

Sources: Based on company websites; and F. David, *Strategic Management,* 8th ed. (Upper Saddle River, NJ: Prentice Hall, 2001), pp. 65–68.

It's also important for managers to identify goals and strategies consistent with the mission being pursued. For instance, based on its mission statement, the WCB established the following goals:[22]

- Creation of workplaces that are safe and secure from injury and disease

- Successful rehabilitation and return-to-work of injured workers

- Fair compensation for workers suffering injury or illness on the job

- Sound financial management to ensure a viable WCB system

- Protection of the public interest

Step 2: Internal Analysis

What are your strengths and weaknesses for developing a successful career?

The internal analysis should lead to a clear assessment of the organization's resources (such as financial capital, technical expertise, skilled employees, experienced managers, and so forth) and capabilities in performing the different functional activities (such as marketing, manufacturing, information systems, human resource management, and so forth). Any activities the organization does well or any unique resources that it has are called **strengths**. **Weaknesses** are activities the organization does not do well or resources it needs but does not possess. This step forces managers to recognize that every organization, no matter how large or successful, is constrained by the resources and capabilities it has available.

The internal analysis provides important information about an organization's specific resources and capabilities. If any of these organizational capabilities or resources are exceptional or unique, they are called the organization's **core competencies**. The core competencies are the organization's major value-creating skills, capabilities, and resources that determine its competitive advantage.[23] Mississauga, Ontario-based Contract Pharmaceuticals' core competencies are in manufacturing and packaging prescription and over-the-counter drugs, rather than in researching and developing them. Multinational drug companies, whose competitive advantage is research and development of new products and then marketing these products, find it makes more sense to outsource production to companies like Contract Pharmaceuticals, so that they can focus on their core competencies.[24]

strengths
Any activities the organization does well or any unique resources that it has.

weaknesses
Activities the organization does not do well or resources it needs but does not possess.

core competencies
The organization's major value-creating skills, capabilities, and resources that determine its competitive advantage.

Step 3: External Analysis

What changes in the world are happening that might affect how your career might unfold over time? How might this affect your strategic plan?

In Chapter 2, we described the external environment as an important constraint on a manager's actions. Analyzing that environment is a critical step in the strategic management process. Managers in every organization need to do an external analysis. They need to know, for instance, what the competition is doing, what pending legislation might affect the organization, or what the labour supply is like in locations where it operates. In analyzing the external environment, managers should examine both the specific and general environments to see what trends and changes are occurring.

After analyzing the environment, managers need to assess what they have learned in terms of opportunities that the organization can exploit, and threats that it must counteract. **Opportunities** are positive trends in external environmental factors; **threats** are negative trends. For CanWest managers, one opportunity is the increased use of the Internet, and managers have looked for ways to get more revenue from this medium. Threats to CanWest include the decrease in newspaper readership and increasing competition by alternative sources of radio and television programs.

opportunities
Positive trends in external environmental factors.

threats
Negative trends in external environmental factors.

Managers of the New Horizons seniors' residence at Bloor and Dufferin streets in Toronto know how to recognize a good opportunity. In 2003, the nonprofit home was losing a lot of money, and half of its rooms were empty. The double-cohort was about to hit Toronto post-secondary schools, and New Horizons had rooms and rents that would appeal to student budgets. So New Horizons decided to open the residence to college and university students. Both seniors and students feel they benefit from the situation, and New Horizons is on a better financial footing these days.

One last thing to understand about external analysis is that the same environment can present opportunities to one organization and pose threats to another in the same industry because of their different resources and capabilities. For example, WestJet Airlines has prospered in a turbulent industry, while Air Canada has struggled.

The combined external and internal analyses are called the **SWOT analysis** because it's an analysis of the organization's *s*trengths, *w*eaknesses, *o*pportunities, and *t*hreats. Based on the SWOT analysis, managers can identify a strategic niche that the organization might exploit (see Exhibit 3-7). For example, owner Leonard Lee started Ottawa-based Lee Valley Tools in 1982 to help individual woodworkers, and later gardeners, find just the right tools for their tasks. This niche strategy enabled Lee to grow Lee Valley into one of North America's leading garden and woodworking catalogue companies for over 25 years.

SWOT analysis was very effective in keeping jobs at Proctor & Gamble Canada's Brockville, Ontario, plant, as the following *Management Reflection* shows.

SWOT analysis

An analysis of the organization's *s*trengths, *w*eaknesses, *o*pportunities, and *t*hreats.

Exhibit 3-7

Identifying the Organization's Opportunities

Organization's
Resources/Capabilities

Organization's
Opportunities

Opportunities in
the Environment

Loss of Detergent Production Turns into Victory

How does a Canadian CEO convince his American bosses that there is advantage to staying in Canada?   SWOT analysis saved the jobs of employees at Proctor & Gamble (P&G) Canada's Brockville, Ontario, plant.[25] Tim Penner, CEO of the Toronto-based company, knew that the parent company (based in Cincinnati, Ohio) planned to consolidate the production of laundry detergent in the United States, which would have eliminated the jobs of the Brockville employees. Penner, in search of a new opportunity, suggested to head office that P&G move manufacture of fabric softener sheets and electrostatic cleaning sheets for the Swiffer sweeper to Brockville. Penner outlined the strengths of the Ontario plant, including a highly educated workforce known for its commitment and productivity. With Penner's strategic thinking, Brockville's loss of laundry detergent production turned into a victory for Canadian jobs. Penner says his job includes "aggressively selling Canada [to US head office] as a possible site for new products and reorganized operations." Penner's strategy has paid off. When he became CEO in 1999, P&G Canada was the seventh-largest revenue generator in the world for the US multinational. Three years later, he had taken the Canadian subsidiary to third place, and increased revenues from $1.5 billion to $2 billion. Penner's goal is to have $3 billion in sales by 2007. ■

Step 4: Formulate Strategies

Once the SWOT analysis is complete, managers need to develop and evaluate strategic alternatives and then select strategies that capitalize on the organization's strengths and exploit environmental opportunities or that correct the organization's weaknesses and buffer it against threats. Strategies need to be established for the corporate, business, and functional levels of the organization, which we will describe shortly. This step is complete when managers have developed a set of strategies that gives the organization a relative advantage over its rivals. Professor Henry Mintzberg of McGill Business School notes that strategies often emerge from actions that organizations take rather than simply reflect the original strategic intent of the organization.[26]

Step 5: Implement Strategies

After strategies are formulated, they must be implemented. No matter how effectively an organization has planned its strategies, it cannot succeed if the strategies are not implemented properly. Involving all members of the organization in strategic planning is also important.

Step 6: Evaluate Results

The final step in the strategic management process is evaluating results. How effective have the strategies been? What adjustments, if any, are necessary? We discuss this step in our coverage of the control process in Chapter 11.

TYPES OF ORGANIZATIONAL STRATEGIES

After Blue Man Group's co-founders discovered they could clone their performances, they were able to grow their business, opening new venues in other parts of the world.[27] Blue Man Group's strategy of emphasizing consistency in its shows, along with its strong creative edge, has helped it stand out among other performing groups. The group has been remarkably successful in New York City (where a show has been running at the Astor since 1991), Chicago, Las Vegas, Boston, London, and Berlin. They recently had to close their show in Toronto after 18 months there, "the only place where this funky spoof of performance art has ever closed." But they opened a new production in Amsterdam in December 2006, which suggests Blue Man Group has a solid strategy for growth.

THINK ABOUT IT
What strategies did Blue Man Group use in order to expand from its first venue in New York City?

---

4 What kinds of strategies can managers use?

Organizational strategies include strategies at the corporate level, the business level, and the functional level (see Exhibit 3-8). Managers at the top level of the organization typically are responsible for corporate-level strategies. Managers at the middle level typically are responsible for business-level strategies. Departmental managers are typically responsible for functional-level strategies.

Corporate-Level Strategy

grand strategies
The four primary types of corporate-level strategy: growth, stability, retrenchment, and combination.

> If you were to develop your own company, what business would it be in? Why?

A company's **grand strategy** seeks to determine what businesses a company should be in or wants to be in. It reflects the direction the organization is going and the roles that each business unit in the organization will play in pursuing that direction. There are four main grand strategies: growth, stability, retrenchment, and combination.

Growth

growth strategy
A corporate-level strategy that seeks to increase the organization's operations by expanding the number of products offered or markets served.

The **growth strategy** is a corporate-level strategy that seeks to increase the organization's business by expanding the number of products offered or markets served. By pursuing a growth strategy, the organization may increase sales revenues, number of employees, market share, or other quantitative measures. How can organizations grow? Through concentration, vertical integration, horizontal integration, or diversification.

Concentration   Growth through *concentration* is achieved when an organization concentrates on its primary line of business and increases the number of products offered or markets served in this primary business. No other firms are acquired or merged with; instead, the company chooses to grow by increasing its own business operations. For instance, Oakville, Ontario-based Tim Hortons opens about 200 new stores a year, and

---

Exhibit 3-8

Levels of Organizational Strategy

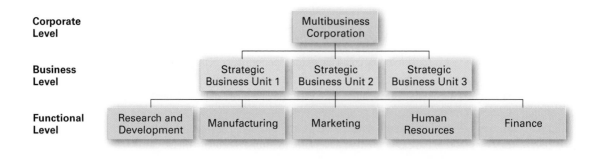

has been recently focusing most of its new openings in small-town western Canada, Quebec, and the United States (where it had 297 stores in 2006).[28] Blue Man Group also follows a concentration strategy in expanding the number of performance sites it has throughout the world.

Vertical Integration   A company also might choose to grow by *vertical integration*, which is an attempt to gain control of inputs (backward vertical integration), outputs (forward vertical integration), or both. In backward vertical integration, the organization attempts to gain control of its inputs by becoming its own supplier. For instance, French hospitality giant Accor, which owns Motel 6, Red Roof Inns, and numerous other lodging properties, also owns a majority of Carlson Wagonlit Travel, one of the world's largest travel agencies. In forward vertical integration, the organization gains control of its outputs (products or services) by becoming its own distributor. For example, The Body Shop controls the distribution of its products by selling them in its own retail stores.

Horizontal Integration   In *horizontal integration*, a company grows by combining with other organizations in the same industry—that is, combining operations with competitors. Interbrew SA of Belgium, which owns Labatt Breweries, is now the number-two brewer in the world, and is a dominant player in Canada, Britain, and parts of Asia and Africa because of its acquisition of local breweries. Horizontal integration has been suggested frequently in the banking industry in recent years.

When Stewart Gilliland took over as CEO of Labatt Breweries in January 2004, he discovered that with its concentration strategy, the company had been more of a follower than a leader. He vowed to change that immediately be putting a "fresh emphasis on quality, brewing process and taste among his company's many products, including its flagship Blue brand."

Both vertical and horizontal integration may involve mergers or acquisitions of other companies. A **merger** occurs when two companies of about the same size combine to form a new company. An **acquisition** occurs when a larger company buys a smaller company and integrates that company and its resources into its own.

Because combining with competitors might decrease the amount of competition in an industry, the Competition Bureau assesses the impact of such proposed growth actions and must approve any proposed horizontal integration strategy. Other countries have similar restrictions. For instance, the US Federal Trade Commission examines horizontal integration in the States. Even though their companies are based in the United States, managers at AOL and Time Warner had to make certain concessions before the European Commission, the "watchdog" for the European Union, allowed that merger to go through.

merger
When two companies of relatively similar size combine resources to form a new company.

acquisition
When a larger company buys a smaller company and integrates it into the larger company.

Diversification   Finally, an organization can grow through *diversification*, either related or unrelated. In **related diversification** a company grows by merging with or acquiring firms in different, but related, industries. In **unrelated diversification** a company grows by merging with or acquiring firms in different and unrelated industries. Toronto-based Brookfield Asset Management (formerly Brascan) is one of the few Canadian conglomerates that pursues a diversified strategy. Under CEO Bruce Flatt, the company has focused its development in three areas: real estate (Brookfield Properties), financial services (Brookfield Asset Management), and power generation (Brookfield Power).[29] The company also owns 43 percent of three other Toronto-based organizations: Noranda, a mining subsidiary; Norbord, a paperboard company; and Fraser Papers, a leading manufacturer of specialized printing, publishing, and converting papers.

Many companies use a combination of these approaches to grow. However, unrelated diversification has fallen out of favour in recent years. Too much diversification can cause managers to lose control of their organizations' core business and, as a result, decrease rather than increase the companies' value.[30]

related diversification
When a company grows by merging with or acquiring firms in different, but related, industries.

unrelated diversification
When a company grows by merging with or acquiring firms in different and unrelated industries.

Stability

stability strategy
A corporate-level strategy
characterized by an absence of
significant change.

A **stability strategy** is a corporate-level strategy characterized by an absence of significant change. Examples of this strategy include continuing to serve the same clients by offering the same product or service, maintaining market share, and sustaining the organization's return-on-investment results.

Although it may seem strange that an organization might not want to grow, there are times when its resources, capabilities, and core competencies are stretched to their limits, and expanding operations further might jeopardize its future success. When might managers decide that the stability strategy is the most appropriate choice? One situation might be periods during which an industry is in a period of rapid upheaval with external forces drastically changing and making the future uncertain. At times like these, managers might decide that the prudent course of action is to sit tight and wait to see what happens.

Another situation for which the stability strategy might be appropriate is if the industry is facing slow- or no-growth opportunities. In this instance, managers might decide to keep the organization operating at its current levels before making any strategic moves. This period of stability would allow them time to analyze their strategic options.

Finally, owners and managers of small businesses, such as small neighbourhood grocers, often purposefully choose to follow a stability strategy. Why? They may feel that their business is successful enough just as it is, that it adequately meets their personal goals, and that they don't want the hassles of a growing business.

Retrenchment

retrenchment strategy
A corporate-level strategy designed
to address organizational weaknesses that are leading to a
decline in performance.

The popular business periodicals frequently report stories of organizations that are not meeting their goals or whose performance is declining. When an organization is in trouble, something needs to be done. Managers need to develop strategies that address organizational weaknesses that are leading to performance declines. A **retrenchment strategy** reduces the company's activities or operations. Retrenchment strategies include cost reductions, layoffs, closing underperforming units, or closing entire product lines or services.[31] There is no shortage of companies that have pursued a retrenchment strategy, including Procter & Gamble, Sears Canada, Corel, and Nortel Networks. When an organization is facing minor performance setbacks, a retrenchment strategy helps it stabilize operations, revitalize organizational resources and capabilities, and prepare to compete once again.

Combination

combination strategy
The simultaneous pursuit by an
organization of two or more of
growth, stability, and retrenchment
strategies.

A **combination strategy** is the simultaneous pursuit of two or more of the strategies described above. That is, one part of the organization may be pursuing a growth strategy while another is retrenching. That is precisely what happened when Procter & Gamble sold off its Jif and Crisco brands in 2002. By selling these brands to The J.M. Smucker Company (of jam and jelly fame), Procter & Gamble was better able to pursue a concentration strategy for its consumer brands.[32]

Business-Level Strategy

What might be the competitive advantage of a business you would like to create?

The selection of a grand strategy sets the direction for the entire organization. Subsequently, each unit within the organization has to translate this grand strategy into a set of business-level strategies that will give the organization a competitive advantage. **Competitive advantage** is what sets an organization apart: that is, its distinct edge. That distinct edge comes from the organization's core competencies—what the organization does that others cannot do or does better than others can do.

competitive advantage What sets
an organization apart: its distinct
edge.

Competitive Strategies

Many important ideas in strategic management have come from the work of Michael Porter.[33] His competitive strategies framework identifies three generic strategies from which managers can choose. Success depends on selecting the right strategy—one that fits the competitive strengths (resources and capabilities) of the organization and the industry it's in. Porter's major contribution has been to explain how managers can create and sustain a competitive advantage that will give a company above-average profitability. An important element in doing this is an industry analysis.

Porter proposes that some industries are inherently more profitable (and, therefore, more attractive to enter and remain in) than others. For example, the pharmaceutical industry is one with historically high profit margins, and the airline industry is one with notoriously low ones. But a company can still make a lot of money in a "dull" industry and lose money in a "glamorous" industry. The key is to exploit a competitive advantage.

In any industry, five competitive forces dictate the rules of competition. Together, these five forces (see Exhibit 3-9 on page 86) determine industry attractiveness and profitability. Managers assess an industry's attractiveness using these forces:

- *Threat of new entrants.* Factors such as economies of scale, brand loyalty, and capital requirements determine how easy or hard it is for new competitors to enter an industry.

- *Threat of substitutes.* Factors such as switching costs and buyer loyalty determine the degree to which customers are likely to buy a substitute product.

- *Bargaining power of buyers.* Factors such as number of customers in the market, customer information, and the availability of substitutes determine the amount of influence that buyers have in an industry.

- *Bargaining power of suppliers.* Factors such as the degree of supplier concentration and availability of substitute inputs determine the amount of power that suppliers have over firms in the industry.

- *Current rivalry.* Factors such as industry growth rate, increasing or falling demand, and product differences determine how intense the competitive rivalry will be among firms currently in the industry.

In trying to find a niche for his bread-making company, Dokse Perklin, founder of Mississauga, Ontario-based Le Bon Croissant, realized that he could do something that grocery stores and restaurants couldn't: ensure high-quality bakery products while controlling costs. "Hotels, grocery chains, restaurant chains [and] institutions just can't afford to bake on premises anymore," Perklin says. "They can't find the staff, they can't effectively control overheads, they can't ensure consistent quality." So Perklin filled that need, and has created a bread-baking business that ships frozen unbaked and baked goods throughout Canada, the United States, the Caribbean, Hong Kong, and Great Britain.

Exhibit 3-9

Forces in an Industry Analysis

Source: Based on M. E. Porter, *Competitive Strategy: Techniques for Analyzing Industries and Competitors* (New York: Free Press, 1980).

Once managers have assessed the five forces and determined what threats and opportunities exist, they are ready to select an appropriate competitive strategy. According to Porter, no firm can be successful by trying to be all things to all people. He proposes that managers select a strategy that will give the organization a competitive advantage, which he says arises out of either having lower costs than all other industry competitors or by being significantly different from competitors. On that basis, managers can choose one of three strategies: cost leadership, differentiation, or focus. Which one managers select depends on the organization's strengths and core competencies and its competitors' weaknesses (see Exhibit 3-10).

cost leadership strategy
A business-level strategy in which the organization sets out to be the lowest-cost producer in its industry.

Cost Leadership Strategy   When an organization sets out to be the lowest-cost producer in its industry, it's following a **cost leadership strategy**. A low-cost leader aggressively searches out efficiencies in production, marketing, and other areas of operation. Overhead is kept to a minimum, and the firm does everything it can to cut costs. You will not find expensive art or interior décor at offices of low-cost leaders. For example, at Wal-Mart's headquarters in Bentonville, Arkansas, office furnishings are sparse and drab but functional.

Although low-cost leaders don't place a lot of emphasis on "frills," the product or service being sold must be perceived as comparable in quality to that offered by rivals or at least be acceptable to buyers. Examples of companies that have used the low-cost leader strategy include Zellers, Hyundai, and WestJet Airlines.

differentiation strategy
A business-level strategy in which a company seeks to offer unique products that are widely valued by customers.

Differentiation Strategy   The company that seeks to offer unique products that are widely valued by customers is following a **differentiation strategy**. Sources of differentiation might be exceptionally high quality, extraordinary service, innovative design, technological capability, or an unusually positive brand image. The key to this competitive strategy is that whatever product or service attribute is chosen for differentiating must set the firm

Exhibit 3-10

Requirements for Successfully Pursuing Porter's Competitive Strategies

Generic Strategy	Commonly Required Skills and Resources	Common Organizational Requirements
Cost Leadership	Sustained capital investment and access to capital Process engineering skills Intense supervision of labour Products designed for ease in manufacture Low-cost distribution system	Tight cost control Frequent, detailed control reports Structured organization and responsibilities Incentives based on meeting strict quantitative targets
Differentiation	Strong marketing abilities Product engineering Creative flair Strong capability in basic research Corporate reputation for quality or technological leadership Long tradition in the industry or unique combination of skills drawn from other businesses Strong cooperation from channels	Strong coordination among functions in R&D, product development, and marketing Subjective measurement and incentives instead of quantitative measures Amenities to attract highly skilled labour, scientists, or creative people
Focus	Combination of the foregoing skills and resources directed at the particular strategic target	Combination of the foregoing organizational requirements directed at the particular strategic target

Source: Reprinted from M. E. Porter, *Competitive Strategy: Techniques for Analyzing Industries and Competitors* (New York: Free Press, 1980), pp. 40–41.

apart from its competitors and be significant enough to justify a price premium that exceeds the cost of differentiating. For instance, St. Stephen, New Brunswick-based Ganong Bros., a small chocolate maker, differentiates itself from bigger boxed-chocolate makers by focusing on the assorted chocolates market. This enables it to rank second in Canada in that market. Its Fruitfull brand, made with real fruit puree and packaged like chocolates, had a 43 percent share of fruit jelly sales in 2003.[34] Blue Man Group differentiates itself from competitors by maintaining the same quality standards for its show, whether it is performed in a US city, or in London, Amsterdam, or Berlin. Vancouver-based Vancouver City Savings Credit Union differentiates itself from competitors through a focus on the community and the customer, as the following *Management Reflection* shows.

MANAGEMENT REFLECTION

Vancity Champions the Underdog

How does a small bank compete against the larger ones? Vancouver City Savings Credit Union (Vancity) does not hope to be like the country's Big Five banks.[35] It is much smaller, for one thing. Profit is not the bank's only goal. Even so, the bank made record profits last year, but returned 30 percent of the profits to its members and the community. Says CEO Dave Mowat, "What we completely understand is that if we ever just focus on the profit end, maybe a $9-billion organization isn't big enough to be a financial institution. And you just lost your differential. That's where all the community service and advocacy comes in."

Vancity is sometimes mocked for its "left coast ways," but it is not afraid to be clear about its mission: The bank is committed to the community, corporate social responsibility, and the environment. This is also what makes the bank unique. "Every day of our lives we're trading on our differentiation," Mowat says. "We have to do it a little bit different, a little bit better to give value-added to draw people to our organization. There isn't an end point where we can win on scale." What they can win on is customer service. As Mowat explains, "We're always looking to provide that extra bit of customization."

While Vancity has many wealthy clients, it likes to work with the less fortunate. Mowat believes these clients can be just as trustworthy when you take the time to get to know them. To that end, in 2004, Vancity helped set up Pigeon Park Savings, a joint venture with The Portland Hotel Society. Pigeon Park provides banking services to Canada's poorest neighbourhood, East Vancouver, using Vancity's banking network. Vancity also provides technical support, administrative services, training, and ongoing security and fraud support for Pigeon Park Savings.[36] Vancity is so dedicated to customer service that its customer satisfaction rating is at 85 percent, compared with 60 percent for the big banks. ■

By looking at successful consumer products or services, a company's differentiation strategy is often clear: Calgary-based WestJet Airlines—customer service; Ottawa-based Research In Motion, the maker of the BlackBerry—quality and innovative design; Vancouver-based Martha Sturdy—sleek furniture design and brand image; and Ottawa-based Lee Valley Tools—quality product design.

How can a Canadian company compete against imports from low-labour-cost countries like China? Mississauga, Ontario-based Dahl Brothers Canada, which makes valves and fittings for plumbing and hot-water heating systems, found a way. "Where we compete is on design, quality, response time and choice," president Jannike Godfrey says. "By doing that, we can hold our own against imports."

Focus Strategy   The first two of Porter's competitive strategies seek a competitive advantage in the broad marketplace. However, the **focus strategy** involves a cost advantage (cost leadership focus) or a differentiation advantage (differentiation focus) in a narrow market segment. That is, managers select a market segment in an industry and tailor their strategy to serve it rather than the broad market. Segments can be based on product variety, type of end buyer, distribution channel, or geographical location of buyers. For example, at Compania Chilena de Fosforos SA, a large Chilean wood products manufacturer, Vice-Chair Gustavo Romero Zapata devised a focus strategy to sell chopsticks in Japan. Competitors, and even other company managers, thought he was crazy. However, by focusing on this segment, Romero's strategy managed to create more demand for his company's chopsticks than it had mature trees with which to make the products. Whether a focus strategy is feasible depends on the size of the segment and whether the organization can support the additional cost of focusing. Research suggests that the focus strategy may be the most effective choice for small businesses because they typically do not have the economies of scale or internal resources to successfully pursue one of the other two strategies.[37]

focus strategy
A business-level strategy in which a company pursues a cost or differentiation advantage in a narrow market segment.

Stuck in the Middle   What happens if an organization is unable to develop a competitive advantage through either cost or differentiation? Porter uses the term **stuck in the middle** to describe those organizations that find it very difficult to achieve long-term success. He goes on to note that successful organizations frequently get into trouble by reaching beyond their competitive advantage and end up stuck in the middle. The Hudson's Bay Company department store in recent years seems to have had this strategy, avoiding the low-cost strategy of its sister store, Zellers, and avoiding the strategies of higher end fashion boutiques like Holt Renfrew.

stuck in the middle
A situation in which an organization is unable to develop a competitive advantage through cost or differentiation.

We now realize organizations *can* achieve competitive advantage by pursuing a cost-leadership and a differentiation strategy at the same time. Studies have shown that such a dual emphasis can result in high performance.[38] However, an organization must be strongly committed to quality products or services, and consumers of those products or services must value quality. By providing high-quality products or services, an organization differentiates itself from its rivals. Consumers who value high quality will purchase more of the organization's products, and the increased demand will lead to economies of scale and lower per-unit costs. For example, companies such as Molson, Toyota, Intel, and Coca-Cola differentiate their products while at the same time maintaining low-cost operations.

Functional-Level Strategy

Functional-level strategies support the business-level strategy. For organizations that have traditional functional departments such as manufacturing, marketing, human resources, research and development, and finance, these strategies must support the business-level strategy. Problems arise when employees and customers don't understand a company's strategy. For instance, Air Canada did not articulate a clear strategy in creating Tango and Zip to operate alongside the parent airline. By spring 2004, Tango had become a fare category rather than a brand, and it was announced that Zip would no longer operate as a separate carrier. By contrast, WestJet Airlines communicates a very clear strategy to its employees: enjoyable flights and an affordable experience for travellers. Employees are to ensure these while keeping costs down and improving turnaround time. Aware of the strategy, all WestJet employees know what is expected of them in a crisis, and all employees help in whatever ways are necessary to meet this strategy.

functional-level strategy
An organizational strategy that supports the business-level strategy.

QUALITY AS A COMPETITIVE ADVANTAGE

Blue Man Group found that after it opened a second venue, in Boston, it became more difficult to maintain a quality show.[39] Co-founders Chris Wink, Matt Goldman, and Phil Stanton split their time between their New York City venue and Boston, but it meant that they were less "hands on" at their shows. Quality started to slip. They finally realized they needed to communicate the standards of the show to the 38 new performers they were bringing on board. They locked themselves in an apartment and talked through their creative vision in great detail. The result? A 132-page operating manual that tells the story of the Blue Man show and enables it to be reproduced by others. Ironically, by writing the manual, though it is a somewhat unorthodox one, the co-founders were able to express artistic ideals that had been understood among them but never stated before. Today, the former drummer who was their first understudy trains new Blue Man performers. Wink, Goldman, and Stanton make only occasional appearances onstage. The show, delivered in a number of cities, maintains the same quality as it first did when only Wink, Goldman, and Stanton were the performers.

THINK ABOUT IT

How can attention to quality make a difference for Blue Man Group?

---

5 How can quality be a competitive advantage?

quality management
A philosophy of management driven by continual improvement and responding to customer needs and expectations.

A quality revolution swept through both the business and public sectors during the 1980s and 1990s.[40] The generic term used to describe this revolution was *total quality management,* or *TQM.*

Quality management describes management's commitment to constantly improving the quality of products and services and responding to customer needs and expectations (see Exhibit 3-11). The term *customer* generally includes anyone who interacts with the organization's product or services internally or externally, such as employees, suppliers, and the people who purchase the organization's goods or services.

If implemented properly, quality can be a way for an organization to create a sustainable competitive advantage.[41] That is why many organizations apply quality management concepts to their operations in an attempt to set themselves apart from competitors. Constant improvement in the quality and reliability of an organization's products or services may result in a competitive advantage that cannot be taken away.[42] Kerry Shapansky, president of Toronto-based Pareto, a marketing services company, emphasizes the value of quality as a competitive advantage. "You can do 984 things right and just one thing wrong for it all to come apart," he says. "Nobody remembers the 984 things you did right; all focus is on that one thing you did wrong."

How Can Benchmarking Help Promote Quality?

benchmarking
The search for the best practices among competitors or noncompetitors that lead to their superior performance.

Benchmarking involves the search for the best practices among competitors or noncompetitors that lead to their superior performance.[43] The basic idea underlying benchmarking is that management can improve quality by analyzing and then copying the methods of the leaders in various fields.

Exhibit 3-11

Characteristics of Quality Management

1. Intense focus on the *customer.*

2. Concern for *continual improvement.*

3. Attention to the *work process.*

4. Improvement in the *quality of everything* the organization does.

5. *Accurate measurement* of all critical variables in the organization's operations.

6. *Empowered employees.*

To illustrate benchmarking in practice, let's look at an application at Ford Motor Company. Ford used benchmarking in early 2000 to develop its highly promising Range Rover line. The company compiled a lengthy list of features that its customers said were the most important and then set about finding vehicles with the best of each. Then it tried to match or top the best of the competition in an effort to produce the world's best sport utility vehicle.[44]

What Is the ISO 9000 Series?

During the 1980s, there was an increasing push among global corporations to improve their quality. They knew that to compete in the global village they had to offer some assurances to purchasers of their products and services that what they were buying was of the quality they expected. To address this concern, the International Organization for Standardization, based in Geneva, Switzerland, designed the **ISO 9000 series** in 1987.[45] The ISO standards reflect a process whereby independent auditors attest that a company's factory, laboratory, or office has met quality management requirements.[46] These standards, once met, assure customers that a company uses specific steps to test the products it sells; continuously trains its employees to ensure they have up-to-date skills, knowledge, and abilities; maintains satisfactory records of its operations; and corrects problems when they occur. Some of the multinational and transnational companies that have met these standards are British Airways; Shanghai Foxboro Company; Braas Company; Betz Laboratories; Hong Kong Mass Transit Railway Corporation; BP Chemicals International; Borg Warner Automotive; Standard Aero Alliance; Taiwan Synthetic Rubber Corporation; and Weyerhaeuser.[47]

Achieving ISO certification is far from cost free. Most organizations that want certification spend nearly one year and incur several hundreds of thousands of dollars in costs to achieve that goal. This type of certification is quickly becoming a necessity for exporting goods to organizations in the nations that support the ISO 9000 series standards.[48]

> **ISO 9000 series**
> Designed by the International Organization for Standardization, these standards reflect a process whereby independent auditors attest that a company's factory, laboratory, or office has met quality management standards.

How Can Attaining Six Sigma Signify Quality?

Wander around organizations like London, Ontario-based 3M Canada, Morristown, New Jersey-based Honeywell, and Toronto-based Maple Leaf Foods, and you are likely to find green and black belts. Karate classes? Hardly. These green and black belts signify individuals trained in six sigma processes.[49]

Six sigma is a philosophy and measurement process developed in the 1980s at Motorola.[50] The premise behind six sigma is to design, measure, analyze, and control the input side of a production process to achieve the goal of no more than 3.4 defects per million parts or procedures.[51] That is, rather than measuring the quality of a product after it is produced, six sigma attempts to design quality in as the product is being made (see Exhibit 3-12 on page 92 for the six sigma process steps). It is a process that uses statistical models, coupled with specific quality tools, high levels of rigor, and know-how when improving processes.[52] How effective is six sigma at ensuring quality? Let's answer that by posing a question. In your opinion, is 99.9 percent effective enough? Consider this: At 99.9 percent effectiveness, 12 babies would be given to the wrong parents each day; 22 000 cheques would be deducted from the incorrect chequing accounts each hour, and 2 planes a day would fail to land safely at Chicago's O'Hare International Airport.[53]

Six sigma applications can also be useful on the service side of the business—especially in identifying cost savings. For example, at General Electric, the company spent more than $125 million (US) in an effort to find more than $2.5 billion in cost-cutting savings. These savings came from reduced personnel, reduced inventories, and increased procurement and sales activities. General Electric also assisted two of its customers—Wal-Mart and Dell—by lending these organizations its six sigma expertise in an effort to eliminate more than $1 billion in inefficiencies in the two organizations.[54]

> **six sigma**
> A philosophy and measurement process that attempts to have no more than 3.4 defects per million parts or procedures.

Exhibit 3-12

Six Sigma Process Steps

- Select the critical-to-quality characteristics.

- Define the required performance standards.

- Validate measurement system, methods, and procedures.

- Establish the current processes' capability.

- Define upper and lower performance limits.

- Identify sources of variation.

- Screen potential causes of variation to identify the vital few variables needing control.

- Discover variation relationship for the vital variables.

- Establish operating tolerances on each of the vital variables.

- Validate the measurement system's ability to produce repeatable data.

- Determine the capability of the process to control the vital variables.

- Implement statistical process control on the vital variables.

Source: Cited in D. Harold and F. J. Bartos, "Optimize Existing Processes to Achieve Six Sigma Capability," reprinted from *Control Engineering Practice,* © 1998, p. 87.

SUMMARY AND IMPLICATIONS

❶ **What does planning involve?** Planning is the process of defining goals and assessing how those goals can best be achieved. The goals are written and shared with organizational members. Once the goals are agreed upon, specific action plans are created to achieve the goals. Planning's purpose is to provide direction, reduce uncertainty, reduce overlapping and wasteful activities, and establish the goals or standards used in controlling. Without planning, managers would not know what to organize, lead, or control. *In Blue Man Group's case, lack of planning in the early years led to exhaustion and near burnout. The co-founders claimed they did not have time to plan.*

❷ **How do managers set goals and develop plans?** Planning involves two important elements: goals and plans. Goals are the desired outcomes for individuals, groups, or entire organizations. They provide the direction for all management decisions and form the criteria against which actual work accomplishments can be measured. Goals can be set at the top of the organization, or through management by objectives (MBO), where employees and managers jointly develop goals. Once goals have been established, managers develop plans to achieve them, either on their own, or with the help of employees. Plans outline how goals are going to be met. They typically describe resource allocations, schedules, and other necessary actions to accomplish the goals. Planning can lock people into a particular way of behaving, which might not be appropriate at a later point. Therefore, plans need to be somewhat flexible so that managers can respond to environmental changes. *Blue Man Group developed a very elaborate plan for their shows, enabling "clones" of the co-founders to deliver the same quality show wherever they performed.*

③ What are the steps in strategic management? The strategic management process is a six-step process that encompasses strategic planning, implementation, and evaluation. The first four steps involve planning: identifying the organization's current mission, goals, and strategies; analyzing the internal environment; analyzing the external environment; and formulating strategies. The fifth step is implementing strategies, and the sixth step is evaluating the results. Even the best strategies can fail if management does not implement or evaluate them properly. *Shortly after they became successful, Blue Man Group faced opportunities from various partners, including product endorsements. The group turned down most opportunities. They wanted to grow the Blue Man character over a number of years and make sure that their growth strategy was manageable.*

④ What kinds of strategies can managers use? There are corporate-level strategies, business-level strategies, and functional-level strategies. They describe the strategies developed at specific levels of the organization. The corporate level develops growth, stability, or retrenchment strategies for the organization. The business level has to translate the corporate-level direction into strategies that will help the organization sustain or develop its competitive advantage in the marketplace: through cost leadership, differentiation, or focus. Functional-level strategies support the corporate- and business-level strategies. *Blue Man Group has a growth strategy, achieved by developing a performance manual, to make it easier to deliver shows based on quality in New York City, Chicago, Las Vegas, Amsterdam, Berlin, and London. Blue Man Group took a differentiation strategy by emphasizing consistency in the product that they delivered to audiences, while maintaining their creative edge.*

⑤ How can quality be a competitive advantage? To the degree that an organization can satisfy customers' needs for quality, it can differentiate itself from competitors and attract a loyal customer base. Moreover, constant improvement in the quality and reliability of an organization's products or services is something that other organizations cannot necessarily copy. Three ways of managing quality are identified in this chapter: benchmarking, by which management improves quality by analyzing best practices of the leaders in various fields; meeting ISO 9000 series standards for quality management; and using six sigma to achieve the goal of no more than 3.4 defects per million parts or procedures. *The co-founders of Blue Man Group found that writing a 132-page operating manual that told the story of the Blue Man show has enabled the show to be reproduced by other Blue Man performers. Today, the former drummer who was the group's first understudy trains new performers. The co-founders make only occasional appearances onstage, and the show maintains the same quality that it had when it first opened.*

Management @ Work

Reading for Comprehension

1. Contrast formal with informal planning.

2. Under what circumstances are short-term plans preferred? Under what circumstances are specific plans preferred?

3. Describe the differences between (a) strategic and operational plans, (b) short- and long-term plans, and (c) specific and directional plans.

4. If planning is so crucial, why do some managers choose not to do it? What would you advise these managers about planning?

5. Will planning become more or less important to managers in the future? Why?

6. Compare an organization's mission with its goals.

7. Describe the six-step strategic management process.

8. What is a SWOT analysis?

9. How can quality provide a competitive advantage? Give an example.

Linking Concepts to Practice

1. "Organizations that fail to plan are planning to fail." Do you agree or disagree with this statement? Explain your position.

2. Under what circumstances do you believe management by objectives and traditional goal setting would be most useful? Discuss.

3. Using Michael Porter's generic strategies (cost leadership, differentiation, and focus), describe the strategy used by each of the following companies to develop a competitive advantage in its industry: Wal-Mart, Home Depot, Holt Renfrew, and WestJet Airlines. Provide specific examples.

4. How might planning in a nonprofit organization such as the Canadian Cancer Society differ from planning in a for-profit organization such as Molson?

5. "The primary means of sustaining a competitive advantage is to adjust faster to the environment than your competitors do." Do you agree or disagree with this statement? Explain your position.

6. "Benchmarking, six sigma, and ISO 9000 series all have the effect of assisting a company to develop a competitive advantage." Do you agree? Why or why not? Cite specific examples.

MANAGEMENT FOR YOU TODAY

Think ahead to five years from now, to consider what it is that you might like to be doing with your life. Develop your own vision and mission statements. Establish a set of goals that will help you achieve your vision and mission. Develop a SWOT analysis for considering what you want to be doing in five years. What are your strengths and weaknesses? What are the opportunities and threats in carrying out this plan? Develop a five-year plan that maps out the steps you need to take in order to get to where you want to be with your life at that time.

SELF-ASSESSMENT

How Good Am I at Personal Planning?

Indicate how much you agree or disagree with each of the six statements as they relate to your school and personal life. Use the following scale to record your answers:[55]

1 = Strongly Disagree	4 = Agree
2 = Disagree	5 = Strongly Agree
3 = Neither Agree nor Disagree	

1. I am proactive rather than reactive.   1 2 3 4 5

2. I set aside enough time and resources to study and complete projects.   1 2 3 4 5

3. I am able to budget money to buy the things I really want without going broke.   1 2 3 4 5

4. I have thought through what I want to do in school.   1 2 3 4 5

5. I have a plan for completing my major.   1 2 3 4 5

6. My goals for the future are realistic.   1 2 3 4 5

Scoring Key

A score of 5 on any item means that you are doing well in planning and goal setting in that area. The authors of this instrument suggest that scores of 3 or less on any item indicate you need to gain a better understanding of the importance of goal setting and what is involved in the process.

Analysis and Interpretation

Successful people have goals and establish plans to help them achieve those goals. This exercise is designed to get you to think about goal setting as it relates to your school and personal life.

If your performance on this instrument was less than you desire, consider practising skills related to goal setting and time management. Toward that end, you might want to read one or more of the following books: D. K. Smith, *Make Success Measurable! A Mindbook-Workbook for Setting Goals and Taking Action* (New York: Wiley, 1999); G. R. Blair, *Goal Setting 101: How to Set and Achieve a Goal!* (Syracuse, NY: GoalsGuy Learning, 2000); and M. Leboeuf, *Working Smart: How to*

Accomplish More in Half the Time (New York: Warner Books, Inc., 1993).

More Self-Assessments

To learn more about your own skills, abilities, and interests, take the following self-assessments on your enclosed CD-ROM:

- #24—What Time of Day Am I Most Productive?
- #49—How Well Do I Respond to Turbulent Change? (This exercise also appears in Chapter 12 on pages 360–362.)

WORKING TOGETHER: TEAM-BASED EXERCISE

Your College or University's Mission

You might not pay much attention to the goals and objectives of your college or university because you are focusing on your studies. But your college or university had to carve out its niche in an effort to provide something of value to its students, and it must continue to monitor its performance.

For this exercise, break up into small groups. The task of each small group is to prepare responses to the following questions and present its findings to the class.

1. What is your college or university's mission? What resources does your college or university have that support its mission?

2. How would you describe your college or university's environment in terms of technology and government regulations?

3. What do you believe are the strengths and weaknesses of your college or university? Its opportunities and threats?

4. Which grand strategy is your college or university following? How does this relate to its strengths, weaknesses, opportunities, and threats?

5. Which of Porter's generic strategies is evident at your college or university?

6. What do you believe is your college or university's competitive advantage? What do you think your college or university should do to sustain its competitive advantage?

Manipulating Sales Numbers

Some lower- and mid-level managers go to great lengths to achieve their goals rather than disrupt the means–ends chain that supports the accomplishment of higher-level goals. But how far is too far? Coca-Cola has admitted that some employees acted improperly when they took steps to manipulate the results of a product test at Burger King restaurants in Richmond, Virginia. If the test succeeded, the product—Frozen Coke—would have been introduced in more Burger King outlets. In turn, the prospect of higher sales was a milestone toward meeting Coca-Cola's overall revenue and profit goals.

Burger King executives and franchisees were not pleased when they found out about the manipulated test results. Coca-Cola's president sent a written apology to Burger King, noting:

"These actions were wrong and inconsistent with the values of the Coca-Cola Company. Our relationships with Burger King and all our customers are of the utmost importance to us and should be firmly grounded in only the highest-integrity actions."[56] Did Coca-Cola managers feel too much pressure to deliver results?

Imagine that you are a district manager with Coca-Cola and you are being promoted to a new position at the end of the month. Your area's sales are an important component of the corporation's provincial and national sales goals. However, this month's sales are running below the planned level. Should you ask area supermarkets to double their current monthly order and promise that any unsold Coca-Cola products can be returned during the following month?

Lend Lease Corporation

"Every project we take on starts with a question: How can we do what's never been done before?"[57] That's the guiding philosophy of Australia's Lend Lease Corporation (**www.lendlease.com**). And it has done some pretty spectacular projects, including building the foundations for the Sydney Opera House, the Newington Olympic Village for the 2000 Summer Olympics, and soundstages for *The Matrix* and *Mission: Impossible 2.* But building is not the company's only business. It's also a market leader in terms of being a global, integrated real estate business with expertise in real estate investment, project management and construction, and property development. It currently manages more than $10 billion in global real estate assets.

Lend Lease is an Australian business success story and is seen as one of the most exciting companies to work for in Australia. Recently, two Lend Lease executives—Chair Stuart Hornery and Director of Special Projects Malcolm Latham—stood at the edge of an abandoned limestone quarry about 32 kilometres outside London, surveying the barren landscape. Instead of seeing what most people would—an industrial wasteland—they envisioned a dramatic and unique civic space that would be a community gathering place in addition to a popular retail shopping centre. They made the decision to purchase the site from Blue Circle Industries, a British cement company that had been trying to develop it for more than eight years. Upon signing the deal, Lend Lease got a pre-approved development plan that was in place for the site. However, company executives chose to abandon everything in this plan but the project's name: Bluewater.

Less than three weeks after that initial visit to the site, a team of Lend Lease employees, including Hornery, Latham, and six of the company's best retail, property, and project-management experts, met with Eric Kuhne, a well-respected US architect. The team's goal was to bring to life Hornery and Latham's vision for the Bluewater site. What they developed was an innovative, break-the-mold plan, simply titled The Bluewater Factors. The team's plan outlined a shopping complex featuring a glowing white roofscape; more than 148 644 square metres of retail space; a 13 000-car parking garage; and more than 20 hectares of parks, 7 lakes, and more than 1 million trees and shrubs. The project's scale would be an enormous undertaking.

Managing Director and CEO Greg Clarke recognizes that effective managerial planning plays an important role in developing successful projects. He is considering using a project-control group (PCG) to help advise Hornery, Latham, and Kuhne on the project. Members of the PCG would not work on the project day-to-day, but would be accountable for it. Clarke has heard that PCGs can include as few as three or as many as 15 members who are chosen with consideration for the diverse mix of skills, intuition, and experiences they bring from both inside *and* outside the company. Members meet every six or seven weeks during a project's duration. Clarke thinks that having a PCG could be a good idea, but also worries that if the group becomes too seriously involved in giving advice and cannot reach agreement on what should be done, the company might have to pull the plug on Bluewater and move on.

Clarke is trying to decide whether to put together a PCG for this project, and has come to you for advice. Would this level of planning help the project? What kind of team should he consider putting together for the PCG and why? What might be the downsides of using a PCG?

DEVELOPING YOUR DIAGNOSTIC AND ANALYTICAL SKILLS

XXL No More!

For more than a decade, McDonald's was the leader in pioneering what it thought customers wanted—larger and larger portions. Although its menu had remained relatively stable, McDonald's management was always looking for ways to improve sales and fend off strong competition from the likes of Wendy's and Burger King. It would also periodically add items to its menu to address small changes in people's fast-food desires, but these items often met with additional competition from other fast-food restaurants such as Taco Bell or even Subway. The one thing that McDonald's did to boost sales and create a marketing coup was the addition of the Supersized Meal. Starting in the early 1990s, customers at McDonald's could add to their meal an extra large soda and an extra large order of french fries by simply saying "supersize it." Nearly 1 in 10 customers took advantage of the company's offer to "supersize" their meal for just 39 cents (US).[58]

But since this expanded offering hit stores, McDonald's has come under fire. Public concern with the fattening of America was often focused on McDonald's. The company's primary products were high in fat content, high in calories, and high in carbohydrates. Public pressure was mounting to the point that individuals sued McDonald's for causing their physical ailments brought about by obesity. Likened to the nicotine controversy surrounding cigarette smoking, lawyers were trying to make the connection that eating McDonald's food was addictive and a primary cause of obesity—especially among young people. Criticism reached its height early in 2004, when the effects of eating McDonald's food was the subject of the award-winning documentary *Supersize Me*. In it, producer Morgan Spurlock chronicled his 30-day effects of eating only McDonald's food for all of his meals. At the end of the month-long experiment, Spurlock spoke of his deteriorating health due solely to eating this fast food—and the 24 pounds he gained during that period.

Changes in public health consciousness and competitive pressures, along with this documentary film, led McDonald's to announce in March 2004 that it would eliminate all supersized offerings. McDonald's management claims that such action was warranted to simplify its menu offering and to promote efficiency in the organization. Additionally, McDonald's has also begun altering its menu offerings. It now offers salads as an entrée meal, has reduced the fat content of its milk from 2 to 1 percent, and is attempting to promote itself as more health conscious.

McDonald's action was largely driven by the reality that its sales had plummeted, as had its stock price. Competition from "health-friendly" alternatives was having a major effect on the company's revenues. McDonald's was losing market share and something had to be done. The company's announcement of the elimination of the supersized option and the addition of healthier substitutes is being viewed as a move that is entirely responsive to the changing market environment—something that executives at Burger King and Wendy's are watching very closely.

Questions

1. Explain how the external environment has affected McDonald's plans to discontinue offering supersized meals.

2. Describe how McDonald's can use the decision to stop selling supersized meals as a competitive advantage.

3. Would you classify this action by McDonald's as a growth strategy, a stability strategy, or a retrenchment strategy? Defend your choice.

4. Do you believe McDonald's was socially responsive in its actions to discontinue supersizing? Why or why not?

Decision Making

How do I make good decisions?

1 What are the steps in the decision-making process?

2 What factors affect how decisions are made?

3 What is ethics, and how can ethical behaviour be encouraged?

Peter Brown, chair and CEO of Vancouver-based Canaccord Capital faced a very big decision in spring 2004.[1]

At the time, Canaccord was Canada's largest independent investment firm, with a specialty in small-, mid-, and large-size capitalization companies. Brown wondered whether the company should file for an initial public offering (IPO) in June. An IPO would allow Canaccord to raise money by letting people purchase shares in the company. Firms often raise between $20 million and $40 million in an IPO. Brown had weighed the issue for quite some time, and had originally decided that 2005 would be a better time to file for an IPO. But recent gains in North American stock markets led him to reconsider the decision.

Brown's decision was complicated by his feelings about Canaccord: "We enjoy being a private company now and I hate the thought of being public. But having said that, the landscape has changed."[2] By selling its shares on the stock market, Canaccord would become a public company and be put under greater media spotlight, something Brown does not really look forward to. Three of Canaccord's competitors in Toronto—Griffiths McBurney, First Associates, and Dundee—had gone public recently, fuelling speculation that Canaccord would follow suit. "Canaccord has reached a size now where going public would be an expected development," says Tony Hepburn, president of Vancouver-based Odlum Brown. "It has been talked about before and I have definitely had the impression that this was something on their calendar."[3]

THINK ABOUT IT

How do CEOs make important decisions? Put yourself in Peter Brown's shoes. What steps would you take to determine whether Canaccord should go public or remain a private corporation? How could he evaluate the effectiveness of a decision to go public? What decision criteria might he use?

Peter Brown needs to make good decisions. Making good decisions is something that every manager strives to do, since the overall quality of managerial decisions has a major influence on organizational success or failure. In this chapter, we examine the concept of decision making and how managers can make ethical decisions.

Canaccord Capital
www.canaccord.com

THE DECISION-MAKING PROCESS

While watching a sports competition, have you ever felt that you could make better decisions than the coaches on the field or court? Soccer fans outside Helsinki, Finland, get to do just that, as the following *Management Reflection* shows.

1 What are the steps in the decision-making process?

Fans Help Soccer Coach Make Decisions

Can you really coach a team by getting input from 300 fans?   In the Helsinki suburb of Pukinmaki, the fans of PK-35, an amateur soccer team, get that chance![4] The coach does not make decisions about what to do on the field by himself, but instead relies on 300 fans who text message their instructions via their cellphones. Each week, the coach posts between 3 and 10 questions about training, team selection, and game tactics to the fans. They have three minutes to respond via cellphone text messaging, and they receive immediate feedback on what others think.

Does shared decision making work? During the first season of the experiment, the team won first place in its division and was promoted to the next higher division. Although we are unlikely to see this type of wireless interactive decision making any time soon in organizations, it does illustrate that decisions, and maybe even how they are made, play a role in performance. ■

decision
A choice from two or more alternatives.

Individuals must continually make **decisions**. Although decision making is typically described as "choosing among alternatives," that view is simplistic. Why? Because decision making is a comprehensive process, not just a simple act of choosing among alternatives.[5] Even for something as straightforward as deciding where to go for lunch, you do more than just choose burgers or pizza. You may consider various restaurants, how you will get there, who might go with you. Granted, you may not spend a lot of time contemplating a lunch decision, but you still go through a process when making that decision. What *does* the decision-making process involve?

decision-making process
A set of eight steps that includes identifying a problem, selecting an alternative, and evaluating the decision's effectiveness.

Exhibit 4-1 illustrates the **decision-making process**, a set of eight steps that begins with identifying a problem, the decision criteria, and the weights for those criteria; moves to developing, analyzing, and selecting an alternative that can resolve the problem; then moves to implementing the alternative; and concludes with evaluating the decision's effectiveness. This process is as relevant to your personal decision about what movie to see on a Friday night as it is to a corporate action such as a decision to use technology in managing client relationships. The process also can be used to describe both individual and group decisions. Let's take a closer look at the process in order to understand what each step involves. We will use an example—deciding what is the best franchise to purchase—to illustrate.

Step 1: Identify a Problem

problem
A discrepancy between an existing and a desired state of affairs.

The decision-making process begins with the existence of a **problem** or, more specifically, a discrepancy between an existing and a desired state of affairs.[6] Take Joan, a laid-off sales manager who has been out of work for six months. She has decided she wants to become an entrepreneur rather than return to a corporate job. For simplicity's sake, assume that Joan does not want to purchase an existing small business and instead has decided to look at possible franchises to purchase. Now we have a problem. There is a disparity between where Joan is now (unemployed) and where she wants to be (an entrepreneur and franchise owner). She has a decision to make about the best franchise to purchase.

Step 2: Identify Decision Criteria

decision criteria
Criteria that define what is relevant in making a decision.

Once a manager has identified a problem, the **decision criteria** important to resolving the problem must be identified. That is, managers must determine what is relevant in making a decision. Whether explicitly stated or not, every decision maker has criteria that guide his or her decisions. These criteria are generally determined by one's objectives. For instance, when you buy a car, your objective might be to have a car that shouts "status symbol." Or you might want a car that is low maintenance. With your objective in mind, you might consider speed, fuel efficiency, colour, manufacturer, size, and so on as criteria on which to evaluate which car to buy. In our franchise purchase example, Joan has to assess what fac-

Exhibit 4-1

The Decision-Making Process

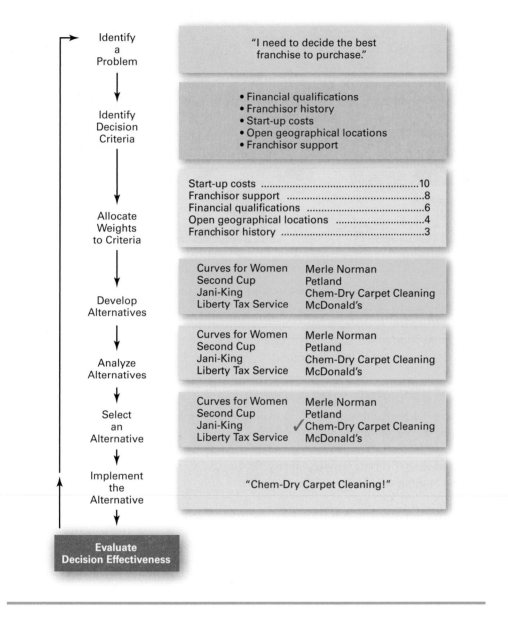

Identify a Problem

"I need to decide the best franchise to purchase."

Identify Decision Criteria

- Financial qualifications
- Franchisor history
- Start-up costs
- Open geographical locations
- Franchisor support

Allocate Weights to Criteria

Start-up costs 10
Franchisor support 8
Financial qualifications 6
Open geographical locations 4
Franchisor history 3

Develop Alternatives

Curves for Women   Merle Norman
Second Cup   Petland
Jani-King   Chem-Dry Carpet Cleaning
Liberty Tax Service McDonald's

Analyze Alternatives

Curves for Women   Merle Norman
Second Cup   Petland
Jani-King   Chem-Dry Carpet Cleaning
Liberty Tax Service McDonald's

Select an Alternative

Curves for Women   Merle Norman
Second Cup   Petland
Jani-King   ✓ Chem-Dry Carpet Cleaning
Liberty Tax Service McDonald's

Implement the Alternative

"Chem-Dry Carpet Cleaning!"

Evaluate Decision Effectiveness

tors are relevant to her decision. These might include criteria such as start-up costs, financing availability, failure rate, growth potential, open geographical locations, franchisor history, financial qualifications, and franchisor support. After careful consideration, Joan decides that start-up costs, financial qualifications, franchisor history, open geographical locations, and franchisor support are the relevant criteria in her decision.

Step 3: Allocate Weights to Criteria

If the criteria identified in Step 2 are not equally important, the decision maker must weight the items in order to give them the correct priority in the decision. How do you weight criteria? A simple approach is to give the most important criterion a weight of 10 and then assign weights to the rest against that standard. Thus, a criterion with a weight of 10 would be twice as important as one given a 5. Of course, you could use 100 or 1000 or

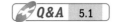
Q&A 5.1

For Russell Ziegler, pictured here with his family, the decision to delay a family move to Singapore, where he is to oversee his company's regional office for two years, hinged on criteria that included the progress of the SARS outbreak in Asia, its possible risk to the family's health, and the willingness of his employer, Macromedia, to allow him to wait a few weeks to see whether the disease would escalate. In the interim, Ziegler travelled to Singapore alone for a two-week trip during which he was impressed by the government's efforts to contain SARS. He returned home more confident and prepared to make the move with his wife and two children.

any number you select as the highest weight. The idea is to prioritize the criteria you identified in Step 2 by assigning a weight to each.

Exhibit 4-2 lists the criteria and weights that Joan developed for her franchise purchase decision. As you can see, start-up costs are the most important criteria in her decision, and franchisor history is the least important.

Step 4: Develop Alternatives

The fourth step requires the decision maker to list viable alternatives that could resolve the problem. No attempt is made to evaluate the alternatives, only to list them. Joan identified eight potential franchises as viable choices including Curves for Women, Second Cup, Jani-King Cleaning Service, Liberty Tax Service, Merle Norman, Petland, Chem-Dry Carpet Cleaning, and McDonald's.

Step 5: Analyze Alternatives

Once the alternatives have been identified, a decision maker must analyze each one. How? By appraising each against the criteria established in Steps 2 and 3. From this comparison, the strengths and weaknesses of each alternative become evident. Exhibit 4-3 shows the assessed values that Joan gave each of her eight alternatives after extensively studying the franchise opportunities and reading the latest information from business magazines.

Exhibit 4-2

Criteria and Weights for Franchise Decision

Criterion	Weight
Start-up costs	10
Franchisor support	8
Financial qualifications	6
Open geographical locations	4
Franchisor history	3

Exhibit 4-3

Assessed Values of Franchise Opportunities Using Decision Criteria

Franchise	Start-up Costs	Franchisor Support	Financial Qualifications	Open Locations	Franchisor History
Curves for Women	10	3	10	8	5
Second Cup	8	7	7	8	7
Jani-King	8	5	7	10	10
Liberty Tax Service	8	7	7	8	7
Merle Norman	7	8	7	8	7
Petland	8	3	6	10	8
Chem-Dry Carpet Cleaning	10	7	8	6	7
McDonald's	4	10	4	8	10

Keep in mind that the ratings given the eight franchises are based on the personal assessment made by Joan. Some assessments can be done objectively. For instance, the start-up costs reflect the total investment required by each franchisor, and financial qualifications are the amounts set by each franchisor. However, the assessment of franchisor support is more a personal judgment. The point is that most decisions by managers involve judgments—the criteria chosen in Step 2, the weights given to the criteria in Step 3, and the analysis of alternatives in Step 5. This explains why two franchise buyers with the same amount of money may look at two totally different sets of alternatives or even rate the same alternatives differently.

Exhibit 4-3 represents only an assessment of the eight alternatives against the decision criteria. It does not reflect the weighting done in Step 3. If you multiply each alternative's assessed value (Exhibit 4-3) by its weight (Exhibit 4-2), you get the scores presented in Exhibit 4-4. The sum of these scores represents an evaluation of each alternative against both the established criteria and weights. At times a decision maker might not have to take this step. If one choice had scored 10 on every criterion, you would not need to consider the weights. Similarly, if the weights were all equal, you could evaluate each alternative merely by summing up the appropriate lines in Exhibit 4-3. In this instance, the score for Curves for Women would be 36 and the score for Petland would be 35.

Step 6: Select an Alternative

Step 6 is choosing the best alternative from among those considered. Once all the pertinent criteria in the decision have been weighted and viable alternatives analyzed, we simply choose the alternative that generated the highest total in Step 5. In our example (see Exhibit 4-4, p. 104), Joan would choose Chem-Dry Carpet Cleaning since it scored highest on the basis of the criteria identified, the weights given to the criteria, and her assessment of each franchise's ranking on the criteria. It's the "best" alternative and the one she should choose.

What does it mean if the "best" alternative does not feel right to you after going through the decision-making steps?

Step 7: Implement the Alternative

Step 7 is concerned with putting the decision into action. This involves conveying the decision to those affected by it and getting their commitment to it. Managers often fail to get buy-in from those around them before making a decision, even though successful implementation requires participation. One study found that managers used participation in only 20 percent of decisions, even though broad participation in decisions led to successful implementation

Exhibit 4-4

Evaluation of Franchise Alternatives Against Weighted Criteria

Franchises	Start-up Costs	Franchisor Support	Financial Qualifications	Open Locations	Franchisor History	Total
Curves for Women	100	24	60	32	15	231
Second Cup	80	56	42	32	21	231
Jani-King	80	40	42	40	30	232
Liberty Tax Service	80	56	42	32	21	231
Merle Norman	70	64	42	32	21	229
Petland	80	24	36	40	24	204
Chem-Dry Carpet Cleaning	100	56	48	24	21	249
McDonald's	40	80	24	32	30	206

 **Q&A**   5.2

 **Q&A**   5.3

80 percent of the time. The same study found that managers most commonly tried to implement decisions through power or persuasion (used in 60 percent of decisions). These tactics were successful in only one of three decisions, however.[7] If the people who must carry out a decision participate in the process, they are more likely to enthusiastically support the outcome than if you just tell them what to do. Parts 3, 4, and 5 of this book discuss how decisions are implemented by effective organizing, leading, and controlling.

Step 8: Evaluate Decision Effectiveness

The last step in the decision-making process involves evaluating the outcome of the decision to see if the problem has been resolved. Did the alternative chosen in Step 6 and implemented in Step 7 accomplish the desired result? In Part 5 of this book, in which we look at the controlling function, we will see how to evaluate the results of decisions.

What if the evaluation shows the problem still exists? The manager would need to assess what went wrong. Was the problem incorrectly defined? Were errors made in the evaluation of the various alternatives? Was the right alternative selected but poorly implemented? Answers to questions like these might send the manager back to one of the earlier steps. It might even require re-doing the whole decision process. To learn more about creativity and decision making, see *Developing Your Interpersonal Skills—Solving Problems Creatively* on page 124, at the end of the chapter.

THE MANAGER AS DECISION MAKER

As chair and CEO Peter Brown considered whether or not to take Canaccord Capital public, he weighed the pros and cons. Going public would provide greater liquidity, giving the company money to make more acquisitions. The downside was the media scrutiny, making the affairs of the company less private. There were other negatives as well.

Said Brown, "There'd be things like reporting costs and filing costs and road shows. It's very expensive to be public and it's very overregulated to be public. It's very public to be public. The mood of our partners is probably split on what we should do."[8]

THINK ABOUT IT

What biases might enter into Peter Brown's decision making, and how might he overcome these? How can Brown improve his decision making, given that he is dealing with uncertainty and risk? How might escalation of commitment affect his decision?

Everyone in an organization makes decisions, but decision making is particularly important in a manager's job. As Exhibit 4-5 shows, decision making is part of all four managerial functions. That's why managers—when they plan, organize, lead, and control—are frequently called *decision makers.*

The decision making process described in Exhibit 4-1 on page 101 suggests that individuals make rational, carefully scripted decisions. But, is *rational* the best word to describe the decision making process and the person who actually makes the decisions? We look at these issues in this section. We start by looking at three perspectives on how decisions are made.

2 What factors affect how decisions are made?

Making Decisions: Rationality, Bounded Rationality, and Intuition

Our model of the decision-making process implies that individuals engage in **rational decision making**. By that we mean that people make consistent, value-maximizing choices within specified constraints.[9] What are the underlying assumptions of rationality, and how valid are those assumptions?

rational decision making
Making decisions that are consistent and value-maximizing within specified constraints.

Assumptions of Rationality

Would you say you make decisions rationally or do you rely on gut instinct?

A decision maker who was perfectly rational would be fully objective and logical. He or she would carefully define a problem and would have a clear and specific goal. Moreover, making decisions using rationality would consistently lead to selecting the alternative that maximizes the likelihood of achieving that goal. Exhibit 4-6 on page 106 summarizes the assumptions of rationality.

The assumptions of rationality apply to any decision—personal or managerial. However, because we are concerned with managerial decision making, we need to add one further assumption. Rational managerial decision making assumes that decisions are made in the best interests of the organization. That is, the decision maker is assumed to be maximizing the organization's interests, not his or her own interests.

How realistic are these assumptions? Not all problems are simple with clear goals and limited alternatives. Often there are time pressures involved in decision making. There can be high costs in seeking out and evaluating alternatives. For these reasons, most decisions that managers face in the real world don't meet the assumptions of rationality.[10] So how are most decisions in organizations usually made? The concept of bounded rationality can help answer that question.

Exhibit 4-5

Decisions in the Management Functions

Planning
- What are the organization's long-term objectives?
- What strategies will best achieve those objectives?
- What should the organization's short-term objectives be?
- How difficult should individual goals be?

Leading
- How do I handle employees who appear to be low in motivation?
- What is the most effective leadership style in a given situation?
- How will a specific change affect worker productivity?
- When is the right time to stimulate conflict?

Organizing
- How many employees should I have report directly to me?
- How much centralization should there be in the organization?
- How should jobs be designed?
- When should the organization implement a different structure?

Controlling
- What activities in the organization need to be controlled?
- How should those activities be controlled?
- When is a performance deviation significant?
- What type of management information system should the organization have?

Exhibit 4-6

Assumptions of Rationality

Lead to

- The problem is clear and unambiguous.
- A single, well-defined goal is to be achieved.
- All alternatives and consequences are known.
- Preferences are clear.
- Preferences are constant and stable.
- No time or cost constraints exist.
- Final choice will maximize payoff.

Rational Decision Making

Bounded Rationality

bounded rationality
Limitations on a person's ability to interpret, process, and act on information.

satisfice
To accept solutions that are "good enough."

Q&A   5.4

Q&A   5.5

Managers tend to operate under assumptions of **bounded rationality**; that is, they make decisions rationally, but are limited (bounded) by their ability to process information.[11] Because they cannot possibly analyze all information on all alternatives, managers **satisfice**, rather than maximize. That is, they accept solutions that are "good enough." They are being rational within the limits (bounds) of their information-processing ability.

Let's look at an example. Suppose that you are a finance major and upon graduation you want a job, preferably as a personal financial planner, with a minimum salary of $50 000 and within 100 kilometres of your hometown. You are in a hurry to get a job, so you accept a job offer as a business credit analyst—not exactly a personal financial planner but still in the finance field—at a bank 50 kilometres from your hometown at a starting salary of $55 000. A more comprehensive job search would have revealed a job in personal financial planning at a trust company only 25 kilometres from your hometown and starting at a salary of $57 000. Because the first job offer was satisfactory (or "good enough"), you behaved in a boundedly rational manner by accepting it, although according to the assumptions of perfect rationality you did not maximize your decision by searching all possible alternatives and then choosing the best.

Intuition

Do you prefer to make decisions intuitively? Are these good decisions?

Rod Aissa, vice-president for talent and development and casting at MTV, says, "One day I was home with strep throat and I saw a rerun of MTV's *Cribs* that featured the Osbournes' house. They were such a dynamic family. I thought, 'They would make great TV.' So I set up a dinner with Sharon Osbourne, the kids, and two MTV executives. We just wanted to watch them interact.... All of it hit us in the gut so strongly. We never tested the show. We just knew it would make great TV."[12] Like Rod Aissa, managers regularly use their intuition and it may actually help improve their decision making.[13]

intuitive decision making
Making decisions on the basis of experience, feelings, and accumulated judgment.

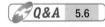
Q&A   5.6

What is **intuitive decision making**? It's making decisions on the basis of experience, feelings, and accumulated judgment. Researchers studying managers' use of intuitive decision making identified five different aspects of intuition, which are described in Exhibit 4-7.

Making a decision on intuition or "gut feeling" does not necessarily happen independently of rational analysis; rather, the two complement each other. A manager who has had experience with a particular, or even similar, type of problem or situation often can act quickly with what appears to be limited information. Such a manager does not rely on a systematic and thorough analysis of the problem or identification and evaluation of alternatives but instead uses his or her experience and judgment to make a decision.

How common is intuitive decision making? One survey of managers and other organizational employees revealed that almost one-third of them emphasized "gut feeling" over

Exhibit 4-7

What Is Intuition?

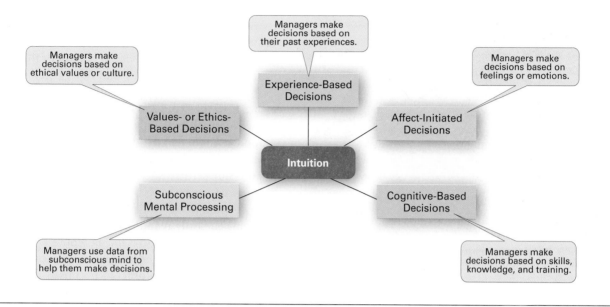

Source: Based on L. A. Burke and M. K. Miller, "Taking the Mystery Out of Intuitive Decision Making." *Academy of Management Executive,* October 1999, pp. 91–99.

cognitive problem solving and decision making.[14] To discover your own intuitive abilities, see *Self-Assessment—How Intuitive Am I?* on pages 120–121, at the end of the chapter.

Types of Problems and Decisions

Managers at eating establishments in Whitehorse, Yukon, make decisions weekly about purchasing food supplies and scheduling employee work shifts. It is something they have done numerous times. But in 2004 they faced a different kind of decision—one they had never encountered—how to adapt to a newly enacted no-smoking ordinance. And this situation is not all that unusual. Managers in all kinds of organizations will face different types of problems and decisions as they do their jobs. Depending on the nature of the problem, a manager can use different types of decisions.

Structured Problems and Programmed Decisions

Some problems are straightforward. The goal of the decision maker is clear, the problem is familiar, and information about the problem is easily defined and complete. Examples of these types of problems could include what to do when a customer returns a purchase to a store, a supplier delivers an important product late, a news team wants to respond to a fast-breaking event, or a student wants to drop a class. Such situations are called **structured problems** because they are straightforward, familiar, and easily defined problems. When situations are structured, there is probably some standardized routine for handling problems that may arise. For example, when a restaurant server spills a drink on a customer's coat, the manager offers to have the coat cleaned at the restaurant's expense. This is what we call a **programmed decision**, a repetitive decision that can be handled by a routine approach. Because the problem is structured, the manager does not have to go to the trouble and expense of following an involved decision process. Programmed decisions can have negative consequences, however, particularly when decision makers deal with diverse populations/clients/customers. For instance, it may be difficult to have one's coat

structured problems
Straightforward, familiar, and easily defined problems.

programmed decision
A repetitive decision that can be handled by a routine approach.

Intuition played a strong part in Barbara Choi's decision to locate her firm, a cosmetics and personal care products manufacturer, in Valley Springs Industrial Center in Los Angeles. In Chinese, the numbers of the building's address signify continued growth.

procedure
A series of interrelated sequential steps that a decision maker can use to respond to a structured problem.

rule
An explicit statement that tells a decision maker what he or she can or cannot do.

policy
A guideline for making a decision.

Q&A 5.7

unstructured problems
Problems that are new or unusual and for which information is ambiguous or incomplete.

nonprogrammed decisions
Decisions that are unique and nonrecurring and require custom-made solutions.

cleaned immediately if one is away from home on a business trip in the middle of winter. Employees of Ottawa-based JDS Uniphase were not happy with the programmed decision they received from the Canada Revenue Agency about hefty taxes they were asked to pay on their company stock options. When JDS stock was trading for $300, employees were saddled with tax bills of several hundred thousand dollars for their stock options, even though they had not cashed in their options. When employees asked the Canada Revenue Agency how they could be expected to pay such big tax bills when they earned only $50 000 per year, the agency responded unsympathetically that they had to pay up.[15]

Managers make programmed decisions by falling back on procedures, rules, and policies.

A **procedure** is a series of interrelated sequential steps that a decision maker can use to respond to a structured problem. The only real difficulty is in identifying the problem. Once it's clear, so is the procedure. For instance, when bad weather grounds airplanes, airlines have procedures for helping customers who miss their flights. Customers may request that they be put up in a hotel for the night. The customer service agent knows how to make this decision—follow the established airline procedure for dealing with customers when flights are grounded.

A **rule** is an explicit statement that tells a decision maker what he or she can or cannot do. Rules are frequently used because they are simple to follow and ensure consistency. For example, rules about lateness and absenteeism permit supervisors to make disciplinary decisions rapidly and fairly.

A **policy** is a guideline for making a decision. In contrast to a rule, a policy establishes general parameters for the decision maker rather than specifically stating what should or should not be done. Policies typically contain an ambiguous term that leaves interpretation up to the decision maker. "The customer always comes first and should always be *satisfied*" is an example of a policy statement. While ambiguity of policies is often intended to allow more flexibility in action, not all employees and customers are comfortable with flexibly determined policies.

Unstructured Problems and Nonprogrammed Decisions

Many organizational situations involve **unstructured problems**, which are problems that are new or unusual and for which information is ambiguous or incomplete. Whether to build a new manufacturing facility in Beijing is an example of an unstructured problem.

Nonprogrammed decisions are unique and nonrecurring and require custom-made solutions. For instance, after the collapse of the World Trade Center on September 11, 2001, CEOs with businesses in the buildings had to decide when and how to start operating again, and what to do for family members of employees who had died. When a manager confronts an unstructured problem, there is no cut-and-dried solution. It requires a custom-made response through nonprogrammed decision making.

Few managerial decisions in the real world are either fully programmed or nonprogrammed. These are extremes, and most decisions fall somewhere in between. Few programmed decisions are designed to eliminate individual judgment completely. At the other extreme, even a unique situation requiring a nonprogrammed decision can be helped by programmed routines. It's best to think of decisions as *mainly* programmed or *mainly* nonprogrammed, rather than as completely one or the other.

One of the more challenging tasks facing managers as they make decisions is analyzing decision alternatives (Step 5 in the decision-making process). In the next section, we look at analyzing alternatives under different conditions.

Matthew Jay's innovative ski trail maps, printed on plastic and attached to the safety bars of chair lifts, presented the USDA Forest Service with a nonprogrammed decision. The Aspen Skiing Company's four resorts had agreed to try the maps, but the USDA Forest Service has jurisdiction over Colorado's White River National Forest, in which the resorts operate and in which outdoor advertising is banned. The USDA Forest Service ordered the maps removed at once, but Jay lobbied for another chance, and the agency granted time to come up with a compromise.

Decision-Making Conditions

When managers make decisions, they face three conditions: certainty, risk, and uncertainty. What are the characteristics of each?

Certainty

The ideal condition for making decisions is one of **certainty**, that is, a condition in which a decision maker can make accurate decisions because the outcome of every alternative is known. For example, when Alberta's finance minister is deciding in which bank to deposit excess provincial funds, he knows the exact interest rate being offered by each bank and the amount that will be earned on the funds. He is certain about the outcomes of each alternative. As you might expect, most managerial decisions are not like this.

> How much do uncertainty and risk affect your decisions?

certainty
A condition in which a decision maker can make accurate decisions because the outcome of every alternative is known.

Risk

A far more common condition is one of **risk**, a condition in which a decision maker is able to estimate the likelihood of certain outcomes. The ability to assign probabilities to outcomes may be the result of personal experiences or secondary information. With risk, managers have historical data that let them assign probabilities to different alternatives. Let's work through an example.

Suppose that you manage a ski resort in Whistler, BC. You are thinking about adding another lift to your current facility. Obviously, your decision will be influenced by the additional revenue that the new lift would generate, and additional revenue will depend on snowfall. The decision is made somewhat clearer because you have fairly reliable weather data from the past 10 years on snowfall levels in your area—three years of heavy snowfall, five years of normal snowfall, and two years of light snowfall. Can you use this information to help you make your decision about adding the new lift? If you have good information on the amount of revenues generated during each level of snow, the answer is yes.

You can calculate expected value—the expected return from each possible outcome—by multiplying expected revenues by snowfall probabilities. The result is the average revenue you can expect over time if the given probabilities hold. As Exhibit 4-8 shows on page 110, the expected revenue from adding a new ski lift is $687 500. Of course, whether that justifies a decision to build or not depends on the costs involved in generating that revenue—

risk
A condition in which a decision maker is able to estimate the likelihood of certain outcomes.

Exhibit 4-8

Expected Value for Revenues from the Addition of One Ski Lift

Event	Expected Revenues	× Probability	= Expected Value of Each Alternative
Heavy snowfall	$850 000	0.3	$255 000
Normal snowfall	725 000	0.5	362 500
Light snowfall	350 000	0.2	70 000
			$687 500

such as the cost to build the lift, the additional annual operating expenses for the lift, the interest rate for borrowing money, and so forth.

Uncertainty

uncertainty

A condition in which a decision maker is not certain about the outcomes and cannot even make reasonable probability estimates.

What happens if you have a decision where you are not certain about the outcomes and cannot even make reasonable probability estimates? We call such a condition **uncertainty**. Managers do face decision-making situations of uncertainty. Under these conditions, the choice of alternative is influenced by the limited amount of information available to the decision maker and by the psychological orientation of the decision maker. The optimistic manager will follow a *maximax* choice (maximizing the maximum possible payoff) in order to get the largest possible gain. The pessimist will follow a *maximin* choice (maximizing the minimum possible payoff) to make the best of a situation should the worst possible outcome occur. The manager who desires to minimize his maximum "regret" will opt for a *minimax* choice, to avoid having big regrets after decisions play out.

Decision-Making Styles

Suppose that you are a new manager at Sony or at the local YMCA. How would you make decisions? Decision-making styles differ along two dimensions.[16] The first dimension is an individual's *way of thinking*. Some of us are more rational and logical in the way we process information. A rational type processes information in order and makes sure that it's logical and consistent before making a decision. Others tend to be creative and intuitive. An intuitive type does not have to process information in a certain order and is comfortable looking at it as a whole.

The other dimension is an individual's *tolerance for ambiguity*. Some of us have a low tolerance for ambiguity. These types need consistency and order in the way they structure information so that ambiguity is minimized. On the other hand, some of us can tolerate high levels of ambiguity and are able to process many thoughts at the same time. When we diagram these two dimensions, four decision-making styles are evident: directive, analytic, conceptual, and behavioural (see Exhibit 4-9). Let's look more closely at each style.

directive style

A decision-making style characterized by a rational way of thinking and a low tolerance for ambiguity.

- *Directive style.* Individuals with a **directive style** have low tolerance for ambiguity and are rational in their way of thinking. They are efficient and logical. Directive types make fast decisions and focus on the short run. Their efficiency and speed in making decisions often result in decisions that are made with minimal information and assessment of few alternatives.

analytic style

A decision-making style characterized by a rational way of thinking and a high tolerance for ambiguity.

- *Analytic style.* Individuals with an **analytic style** have much greater tolerance for ambiguity than do directive types. They want more information before making a decision and consider more alternatives than directive-style decision makers do. Analytic-style decision makers are characterized as careful decision makers with the ability to adapt to or cope with unique situations.

Exhibit 4-9

Decision-Making Styles

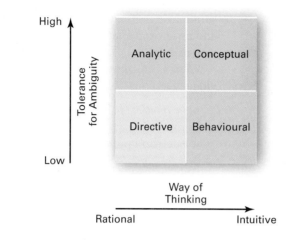

Source: S. P. Robbins and D. A. DeCenzo, *Supervision Today*, 2nd ed. (Upper Saddle River, NJ: Prentice Hall, 1998), p. 166.

- *Conceptual style.* Individuals with a **conceptual style** tend to be very broad in their outlook and consider many alternatives. They are intuitive, focus on the long run, and are very good at finding creative solutions to problems.

- *Behavioural style.* Individuals with a **behavioural style** have a low tolerance for ambiguity and an intuitive way of thinking. They work well with others, are concerned about the achievements of those around them, and are receptive to suggestions from others. They often use meetings to communicate, although they try to avoid conflict. Acceptance by others is important in this decision-making style.

Although these four decision-making styles are distinct, most managers have characteristics of more than one style. It's probably more realistic to think of a manager's dominant style and his or her alternative styles. Although some managers will rely almost exclusively on their dominant style, others are more flexible and can shift their style depending on the situation.

Managers should also recognize that their employees may use different decision-making styles. Some employees may take their time, carefully weighing alternatives and considering riskier options (analytic style), while other employees may be more concerned about getting suggestions from others before making decisions (behavioural style). This does not make one approach better than the other. It just means that their decision-making styles are different. For a look at the issues associated with diversity and making decisions, see *Managing Workforce Diversity—The Value of Diversity in Decision Making* on page 125, at the end of the chapter.

conceptual style
A decision-making style characterized by an intuitive way of thinking and a high tolerance for ambiguity.

behavioural style
A decision-making style characterized by an intuitive way of thinking and a low tolerance for ambiguity.

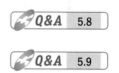 **Q&A** 5.8

Q&A 5.9

Group Decision Making

Do you think individuals or groups make better decisions?

Many organizational decisions are made by groups. It's a rare organization that does not at some time use committees, task forces, review panels, study teams, or similar groups to make decisions. In addition, studies show that managers may spend up to 30 hours a week in group meetings.[17] Undoubtedly, a large portion of that time is

The choice of an advertising agency is often made by those with a conceptual approach to decision making. Marketing executives from Virgin Atlantic Airways saw presentations from five ad agencies before choosing Crispin Porter & Bogusky, a small firm whose inventive proposal showed how efficiently the airline's $19 million ad budget could be spent. The marketing team from Virgin allowed 10 weeks to make a decision; it took four days. The winning team is pictured here with the paper airplanes that played a part in their pitch.

spent identifying problems, developing solutions, and determining how to implement the solutions. It's possible, in fact, for groups to be assigned any of the eight steps in the decision-making process. In this section, we look at the advantages and disadvantages of group decision making, discuss when groups would be preferred, and review some techniques for improving group decision making.

What advantages do group decisions have over individual decisions?

- *More complete information and knowledge.* A group brings a diversity of experience and perspectives to the decision process that an individual cannot.

- *More diverse alternatives.* Because groups have a greater amount and diversity of information, they can identify more diverse alternatives than an individual.

- *Increased acceptance of a solution.* Group members are reluctant to fight or undermine a decision they have helped develop.

- *Increased legitimacy.* Decisions made by groups may be perceived as more legitimate than decisions made unilaterally by one person.

If groups are so good at making decisions, how did the phrase "A camel is a horse put together by a committee" become so popular? The answer, of course, is that group decisions also have disadvantages:

- *Increased time to reach a solution.* Groups almost always take more time to reach a solution than it would take an individual.

- *Opportunity for minority domination.* The inequality of group members creates the opportunity for one or more members to dominate others. A dominant and vocal minority frequently can have an excessive influence on the final decision.

- *Ambiguous responsibility.* Group members share responsibility, but the responsibility of any single member is diluted.

- *Pressures to conform.* There can be pressures to conform in groups. This pressure undermines critical thinking in the group and eventually harms the quality of the final decision.[18]

Groupthink

groupthink

The withholding by group members of different views in order to appear to be in agreement.

The pressure to conform is what Irving Janis called the "groupthink" phenomenon. For instance, have you ever been in a situation in which several people were sitting around discussing a particular item and you had something to say that ran contrary to the consensus views of the group, but you remained silent? Were you surprised to learn later that others shared your views and also had remained silent? What you experienced is what Janis termed **groupthink**.[19] This is a form of conformity in which group members withhold deviant, minority, or unpopular views in order to give the appearance of agreement. As a result, groupthink undermines critical thinking in the group and eventually harms the quality of the final decision.

Groupthink applies to a situation in which a group's ability to appraise alternatives objectively and arrive at a quality decision is jeopardized. Because of pressures for conformity, groups often deter individuals from critically appraising unusual, minority, or unpopular views. Consequently, an individual's mental efficiency, reality testing, and moral judgment deteriorate.

How does groupthink occur? The following are examples of situations in which group-think is evident:

- Group members rationalize any resistance to the assumptions they have made.

- Members apply direct pressure on those who momentarily express doubts about any of the group's shared views or who question the validity of arguments favoured by the majority.

- Those members who have doubts or hold differing points of view seek to avoid going against what appears to be group consensus.

- There is an illusion of unanimity. If someone does not speak, it is assumed that he or she is in full agreement.

Does groupthink really hinder decision making? Yes. Several research studies have found that groupthink symptoms were associated with poorer quality decision outcomes. But groupthink can be minimized if the group is cohesive, fosters open discussion, and has an impartial leader who seeks input from all members.[20]

Individual vs. Group Decision Making

Determining whether a group or an individual will be more effective in making a particular decision depends on the criteria you use to assess effectiveness.[21] Exhibit 4-10 summarizes when groups and individuals are most effective.

Keep in mind, however, that the effectiveness of group decision making is also influenced by the size of the group. Although a larger group provides greater opportunity for diverse representation, it also requires more coordination and more time for members to contribute their ideas. So groups probably should not be too large. Evidence indicates, in fact, that groups of five, and to a lesser extent, seven, are the most effective.[22] Having an odd number in the group helps avoid decision deadlocks. Also, these groups are large enough for members to shift roles and withdraw from unfavourable positions but still small enough for quieter members to participate actively in discussions.

Decision-Making Biases and Errors

When managers make decisions, not only do they use their own particular style, but many use "rules of thumb," or **heuristics**, to simplify their decision making. Rules of thumb can be useful to decision makers because they help make sense of complex, uncertain, and ambiguous information.[23] Even though managers may use rules of thumb, that does not mean those rules are reliable. Why? Because they may lead to errors and biases in processing and evaluating information. Exhibit 4-11 identifies seven common decision-making biases and errors. Let's take a quick look at each.[24]

heuristics
Rules of thumb that managers use to simplify decision making.

Exhibit 4-10

Group vs. Individual Decision Making

Criteria of Effectiveness	Groups	Individuals
Accuracy	✔	
Speed		✔
Creativity	✔	
Degree of acceptance	✔	
Efficiency		✔

Exhibit 4-11

Common Decision-Making Biases and Errors

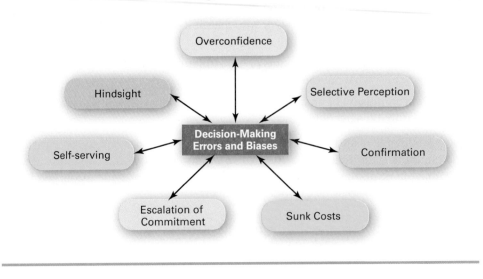

- *Overconfidence bias.* Decision makers tend to think they know more than they do or hold unrealistically positive views of themselves and their performance. For instance, a sales manager brags that his presentation was so good that there is no doubt the sale will be his. Later he learns that he lost the sale because the client found him obnoxious.

- *Selective perception bias.* Decision makers selectively organize and interpret events based on their biased perceptions. This influences the information they pay attention to, the problems they identify, and the alternatives they develop. For instance, before John meets with two job candidates, he learns that one went to his alma mater. He does not seriously consider the other job candidate because he believes that graduating from the same university as he did makes the candidate superior.

- *Confirmation bias.* Decision makers seek out information that reaffirms their past choices and discount information that contradicts past judgments. These people tend to accept at face value information that confirms their preconceived views and are critical and skeptical of information that challenges these views. For instance, Pierre continues to give business to the same supplier, even though the supplier has been late on several deliveries. Pierre thinks the supplier is a nice person, and the supplier keeps promising to deliver on time.

- *Sunk costs error.* Decision makers forget that current choices cannot correct the past. They incorrectly fixate on past expenditures of time, money, or effort in assessing choices rather than on future consequences. For instance, Hakan has spent thousands of dollars and several months introducing new procedures for handling customer complaints. Both customers and employees are complaining about the new procedures. Hakan does not want to consider the possibility that the procedures are needlessly complicated because of the investment in time and money he has already made.

- *Escalation of commitment error.* Decisions can also be influenced by a phenomenon called **escalation of commitment**, which is an increased commitment to a previous decision despite evidence that it might have been wrong.[25] For example, studies of the events leading up to the space shuttle *Columbia* disaster in 2003 point to an escalation of commitment by decision makers to ignore the possible damage

escalation of commitment
An increased commitment to a previous decision despite negative information.

that foam striking the shuttle at takeoff might have had, even though the decision was questioned by some individuals. Why would decision makers want to escalate commitment to a bad decision? Because they don't want to admit that their initial decision might have been flawed. Rather than search for new alternatives, they simply increase their commitment to the original solution.

- *Self-serving bias.* Decision makers take credit for their successes and blame failure on outside factors. For instance, Jesse dismisses his team's efforts when he wins a contract, although he blames them for the small error that was in the final report.

- *Hindsight bias.* Decision makers falsely believe that they would have accurately predicted the outcome of an event once that outcome is actually known. For instance, after a client cancelled a contract that had been drawn up, Cindy tells her manager she knew ahead of time that was going to happen, even though she'd had no such thoughts before the contract was cancelled. After the fact, some outcomes seem more obvious than they did beforehand.

How can managers avoid the negative effects of these decision errors and biases? The main thing is being aware of them and then trying not to exhibit them. Beyond that, managers also should pay attention to "how" they make decisions and try to identify the heuristics they typically use and critically evaluate how appropriate those are. Finally, managers might want to ask those around them to help identify weaknesses in their decision-making style and try to improve on them.

ETHICS AND DECISION MAKING

One of Canaccord Capital's goals is to "enhance the quality of life" of the communities it serves.[26] Employees engage in volunteer work, and the company contributed more than $860 000 in fiscal 2006 to a variety of programs and organizations. For instance, Cannacord is the title sponsor for the Big Brothers Whistler Golf Classic. This charitable golf tournament raises more than $400 000 each year in support of Big Brothers of Greater Vancouver. Canaccord is also committed to helping Canadian culture and arts reach the world stage. To that end, Canaccord made a substantial donation toward the construction of a new teaching facility for the National Ballet School of Canada.

Canaccord has a code of ethics that governs its employees. Employees are not to engage in any "personal conflict of interest," which is defined as happening "when an individual's private interest improperly interferes with the interests of the firm." Employees are reminded that they should not engage in actions that might help themselves or family members get a personal benefit, such as loans or guarantees of obligations.

THINK ABOUT IT

How would you expect a code of ethics to be related to a company's corporate social responsibility decisions? What considerations would you include in a code of ethics?

When you see top managers like those formerly at Enron, WorldCom, Tyco International, and ImClone being greedy and using financial manipulations, lying, and group pressure to deceive others, you might conclude that corporations have no ethics. Although that is by no means true, what *is* true is that managers—at all levels, in all areas, and in all kinds of organizations—will face ethical issues and dilemmas. As managers plan, organize, lead, and control, they must consider ethical dimensions.

What do we mean by ethics? The term **ethics** refers to the study of moral values or principles that guide our behaviour, and inform us whether actions are right or wrong.[27] In this section, we examine the ethical dimensions of managerial decisions. Many decisions that managers make require them to consider who may be affected—in terms of the result as well as the process.[28] To better understand the complicated issues involved in managerial ethics, we will look at four different views of ethics and the factors that influence a person's ethics, and offer some suggestions for what organizations can do to improve the ethical behaviour of employees.

3 What is ethics, and how can ethical behaviour be encouraged?

Q&A 4.4

ethics
The study of moral values or principles that guide our behaviour and inform us whether actions are right or wrong.

Four Views of Ethics

There are four views of ethics: the utilitarian view, the rights view, the theory of justice view, and the integrative social contracts theory.[29]

The Utilitarian View of Ethics

utilitarian view of ethics
A view of ethics that says that ethical decisions are made solely on the basis of their outcomes or consequences.

The **utilitarian view of ethics** says that ethical decisions are made solely on the basis of their outcomes or consequences. Utilitarian theory uses a quantitative method for making ethical decisions by looking at how to provide the greatest good for the greatest number. Following the utilitarian view, a manager might conclude that laying off 20 percent of the workforce in her plant is justified because it will increase the plant's profitability, improve job security for the remaining 80 percent, and be in the best interest of stockholders. Utilitarianism encourages efficiency and productivity and is consistent with the goal of profit maximization. However, it can result in biased allocations of resources, especially when some of those affected by the decision lack representation or a voice in the decision. Utilitarianism can also result in the rights of some stakeholders being ignored.

The Rights View of Ethics

rights view of ethics
A view of ethics that is concerned with respecting and protecting individual liberties and privileges.

The **rights view of ethics** is concerned with respecting and protecting individual liberties and privileges such as the rights to privacy, freedom of conscience, free speech, life and safety, and due process. This would include, for example, protecting the free speech rights of employees who report legal violations by their employers. The positive side of the rights perspective is that it protects individuals' basic rights, but the drawback is that it can hinder productivity and efficiency by creating a work climate that is more concerned with protecting individuals' rights than with getting the job done.

The Theory of Justice View of Ethics

theory of justice view of ethics
A view of ethics in which managers impose and enforce rules fairly and impartially and do so by following all legal rules and regulations.

According to the **theory of justice view of ethics**, managers impose and enforce rules fairly and impartially and do so by following all legal rules and regulations. A manager following this view would decide to provide the same rate of pay to individuals who are similar in their levels of skills, performance, or responsibility and not base that decision on arbitrary differences such as gender, personality, race, or personal favourites. Using standards of justice also has pluses and minuses. It protects the interests of those stakeholders who may be underrepresented or lack power, but it can encourage a sense of entitlement that might make employees reduce risk-taking, innovation, and productivity.

The Integrative Social Contracts Theory

integrative social contracts theory
A view of ethics that proposes that ethical decisions be based on existing ethical norms in industries and communities in order to determine what constitutes right and wrong.

The **integrative social contracts theory** proposes that ethical decisions be based on existing ethical norms in industries and communities in order to determine what constitutes right and wrong. This view of ethics is based on the integration of two "contracts": the general social contract that allows businesses to operate and defines the acceptable ground rules and a more specific contract among members of a community that addresses acceptable ways of behaving. For instance, in deciding what wage to pay employees in a new factory in Ciudad Juarez, Mexico, Canadian managers following the integrative social contracts theory would base the decision on existing wage levels in the community. Although this theory focuses on looking at existing practices, the problem is that some of these practices may be unethical.[30]

Which approach to ethics do most businesspeople follow? Not surprisingly, most follow the utilitarian approach.[31] Why? It's consistent with such business goals as efficiency, productivity, and profits. However, that perspective needs to change because of the changing world facing managers. Trends toward individual rights, social justice, and community standards mean that managers need ethical standards based on nonutilitarian criteria. This is an obvious challenge for managers because making decisions on such criteria involves far more ambiguities than using utilitarian criteria such as efficiency and profits. The result, of course, is that managers increasingly find themselves struggling with the question of the right thing to do.

Improving Ethical Behaviour

Managers can do a number of things if they are serious about reducing unethical behaviour in their organizations. They can seek to hire individuals with high ethical standards, establish codes of ethics and decision rules, lead by example, delineate job goals and performance appraisal mechanisms, provide ethics training, conduct independent social audits, and provide support to individuals facing ethical dilemmas. Taken individually, these actions will probably not have much impact. But when all or most of them are implemented as part of a comprehensive ethics program, they have the potential to significantly improve an organization's ethical climate. The key term here, however, is *potential*. There are no guarantees that a well-designed ethics program will lead to the desired outcome.

Sometimes corporate ethics programs can be little more than public relations gestures, having minimal influence on managers and employees. For instance, retailer Sears has a long history of encouraging ethical business practices and, in fact, has a corporate Office of Compliance and Ethics. However, the company's ethics programs did not stop managers from illegally trying to collect payments from bankrupt charge-account holders or from routinely deceiving automotive–service centre customers in California into thinking they needed unnecessary repairs. Even Enron's 2000 annual report outlined values that most would consider ethical—communication, respect, integrity, and excellence—yet the way top managers behaved did not reflect those values at all.[32]

Codes of Ethics and Decision Rules

Toronto-based Royal Bank of Canada has had a corporate code of conduct for more than 20 years. Christina Donely, the bank's senior adviser on employee relations and policy governance, says that the code "focuses on outlining behaviours that support honesty and integrity . . . and covers environmental [and] social issues."[33] However, that is not the way it is in all organizations. The US government passed the Sarbanes–Oxley Act in 2002 to crack down on business wrongdoing in publicly traded companies. Following the American example, the Canadian Securities Administrators' rules came into effect in March 2004, although these are not as tough as the American rules.[34] As well, the securities regulators of all 10 provinces and 3 territories have proposed that all public companies adopt written codes of ethics and conduct, or explain why they do not have them.[35] But the proposal carries no enforcement requirements or mechanisms.

Royal Bank of Canada
www.royalbank.com

Ambiguity about what is and is not ethical can be a problem for employees. A **code of ethics**, a formal statement of an organization's primary values and the ethical rules it expects its employees to follow, is a popular choice for reducing that ambiguity. About 60 percent of Canada's 650 largest corporations have some sort of ethics code.[36] Codes of ethics are also becoming more popular globally. A survey of business organizations in 22 countries found that 78 percent have formally stated ethics standards and codes of ethics.[37]

code of ethics
A formal statement of an organization's primary values and the ethical rules it expects its employees to follow.

What should a code of ethics look like? It has been suggested that codes should be specific enough to show employees the spirit in which they are supposed to do things yet loose enough to allow for freedom of judgment.[38] A survey of companies' codes of ethics found their content tended to fall into three categories: (1) Be a dependable organizational citizen; (2) don't do anything unlawful or improper that will harm the organization; and (3) be good to customers.[39]

How well do codes of ethics work? The reality is they are not always effective in encouraging ethical behaviour in organizations. While no comparable Canadian data are available, a survey of employees in US businesses with ethics codes found that 75 percent of those surveyed had observed ethical or legal violations in the previous 12 months, including such things as deceptive sales practices, unsafe working conditions, sexual harassment, conflicts of interest, and environmental violations.[40] Companies with codes of ethics may not do enough monitoring. For instance, David Nitkin, president of Toronto-based EthicScan Canada, an ethics consultancy, notes that "only about 15% of [larger Canadian corporations with codes of ethics] have designated an ethics officer or ombudsman" or provide an ethics hotline, and that less than 10 percent offer whistle-blower protection.[41] Does this mean that codes of ethics should not be developed? No. But there are some suggestions managers can

EthicScan Canada
www.ethicscan.ca

Exhibit 4-12

12 Questions for Examining the Ethics of a Business Decision

1. Have you defined the problem accurately?

2. How would you define the problem if you stood on the other side of the fence?

3. How did this situation occur in the first place?

4. To whom and to what do you give your loyalty as a person and as a member of the corporation?

5. What is your intention in making this decision?

6. How does this intention compare with the probable results?

7. Whom could your decision or action injure?

8. Can you discuss the problem with the affected parties before you make the decision?

9. Are you confident that your position will be as valid over a long period of time as it seems now?

10. Could you disclose without qualm your decision or action to your boss, your chief executive officer, the board of directors, your family, society as a whole?

11. What is the symbolic potential of your action if understood? If misunderstood?

12. Under what conditions would you allow exceptions to your stand?

Source: Reprinted by permission of *Harvard Business Review*. An exhibit from "Ethics Without the Sermon" by L. L. Nash. November–December 1981, p. 81. Copyright © 1981 by the President and Fellows of Harvard College. All rights reserved.

follow. First, ethics codes should be developed and then communicated regularly to employees. Second, all levels of management should continually reaffirm the importance of the ethics code and the organization's commitment to it, and consistently discipline those who break it. When managers consider the code of ethics important, regularly affirm its content, and publicly reprimand rule breakers, ethics codes can supply a strong foundation for an effective corporate ethics program.[42] Finally, an organization's code of ethics might be designed around the 12 questions listed in Exhibit 4-12, which can be used as decision rules in guiding managers as they handle ethical dilemmas in decision making.[43]

SUMMARY AND IMPLICATIONS

SNAPSHOT SUMMARY

1 The Decision-Making Process

Step 1: Identify a Problem

Step 2: Identify Decision Criteria

Step 3: Allocate Weights to Criteria

Step 4: Develop Alternatives

Step 5: Analyze Alternatives

▶

1 What are the steps in the decision-making process? The steps include identifying a problem and the decision criteria; allocating weights to those criteria; developing, analyzing, and selecting an alternative that can resolve the problem; implementing the alternative; and evaluating the decision's effectiveness. *While Peter Brown, Canaccord Capital's chair and CEO, could determine the criteria and the weights for the criteria to make a decision about taking Canaccord public, it will be some time before he will actually be able to evaluate the effectiveness of his decision.*

2 What factors affect how decisions are made? It is often assumed that managers make decisions that follow the steps of the rational decision-making process. However, not all decisions follow that process for a variety of reasons. Often managers work within bounded rationality, because they are not able to collect and process all the information on all possible alternatives. Or they might make a satisficing decision—one that is "good enough," rather than the "best." Managers sometimes use intuition to enhance their decision-making process. Managers are affected by a variety of biases and errors: overconfidence bias, selective perception bias, confirmation bias, sunk costs error, escalation of commitment error, self-serving bias, and hindsight bias. Managers also need to decide whether they should make decisions themselves or encourage a team to help make the decision. A team can make better decisions in many cases, but generally it takes more time to do so than an individual. *Peter Brown was aware of a variety of positives and negatives in the decision to take Canaccord public, and it was also important for him to recognize that his own preference for privacy might affect how he made his decision.*

3 **What is ethics, and how can ethical behaviour be encouraged?** Ethics refers to rules and principles that define right and wrong conduct. There are four views of ethics: the utilitarian view, the rights view, the theory of justice view, and the integrative social contracts theory. The utilitarian view of ethics says that ethical decisions are made solely on the basis of their outcomes or consequences. The rights view of ethics is concerned with respecting and protecting individual liberties and privileges. According to the theory of justice view of ethics, managers impose and enforce rules fairly and impartially, following all legal rules and regulations. The integrative social contracts theory proposes that ethical decisions be based on existing ethical norms in industries and communities.

To improve ethical behaviour, managers can hire individuals with high ethical standards, design and implement a code of ethics, lead by example, undertake performance appraisals, provide ethics training, conduct independent social audits, and provide formal protective mechanisms for employees who face ethical dilemmas. *Canaccord employees are governed by the company's code of ethics. The code reminds them that they should not engage in actions that may help themselves or family members get personal benefits, such as loans or guarantees of obligations. Canaccord also has a corporate social responsibility program. Employees are encouraged to engage in volunteer work, and the company contributes money to a variety of programs and organizations.*

Management @ Work

Reading for Comprehension

1. Why is decision making often described as the essence of a manager's job?

2. How is implementation important to the decision-making process?

3. What is a satisficing decision? How does it differ from a maximizing decision?

4. How do certainty, risk, and uncertainty affect decision making?

5. What is groupthink? How does it affect decision making?

6. Describe the decision-making biases and errors managers may exhibit.

7. How does escalation of commitment affect decision making? Why would managers make this type of error?

8. Define the four views of ethics.

Linking Concepts to Practice

1. Describe a decision you have made that closely aligns with the assumptions of perfect rationality. Compare this with the process you used to select your major. Is there a departure from the rational model in your choice of major? Explain.

2. Is the order in which alternatives are considered more critical under assumptions of perfect rationality or bounded rationality? Why?

3. Explain how a manager might deal with making decisions under conditions of uncertainty.

4. "With more and more managers using computers, they'll be able to make more rational decisions." Do you agree or disagree with the statement? Why?

5. Why do you think organizations have increased the use of groups for making decisions during the past 20 years? When would you recommend using groups to make decisions?

6. Do you think it's difficult to make ethical decisions when a company focuses primarily on the bottom line?

MANAGEMENT FOR YOU TODAY

Suppose your uncle said that he would help you open your own business. You are not sure whether you really want to run your own business, or work for a large consulting firm. However, you have always been interested in running a restaurant. How would you go about making a decision on what kind of restaurant you might open? How would you decide whether you should take him up on his offer?

SELF-ASSESSMENT

How Intuitive Am I?

For each of the following questions, select the response that first appeals to you:[44]

1. When working on a project, I prefer to
   a. be told what the problem is, but left free to decide how to solve it.
   b. get very clear instructions about how to go about solving the problem before I start.

2. When working on a project, I prefer to work with colleagues who are
   a. realistic.
   b. imaginative.

3. I most admire people who are   a. creative.   b. careful.

4. The friends I choose tend to be   a. serious and hard-working.   b. exciting and often emotional.

5. When I ask a colleague for advice on a problem I have, I   a. seldom or never get upset if he/she questions my basic assumptions.   b. often get upset if he/she questions my basic assumptions.

6. When I start my day, I   a. seldom make or follow a specific plan.   b. usually make a plan first to follow.

7. When working with numbers, I find that I   a. seldom or never make factual errors.   b. often make factual errors.

8. I find that I   a. seldom daydream during the day and really don't enjoy doing so when I do it.   b. frequently daydream during the day and enjoy doing so.

9. When working on a problem, I   a. prefer to follow the instructions or rules when they are given to me.   b. often enjoy circumventing the instructions or rules when they are given to me.

10. When I try to put something together, I prefer to have   a. step-by-step written instructions on how to assemble the item.   b. a picture of how the item is supposed to look once assembled.

11. I find that the person who irritates me the most is the one who appears to be   a. disorganized.   b. organized.

12. When an unexpected crisis comes up that I have to deal with, I   a. feel anxious about the situation.   b. feel excited by the challenge of the situation.

Scoring Key

For items 1, 3, 5, 6, and 11, score as follows: a = 1, b = 0.
For items 2, 4, 7, 8, 9, 10, and 12, score as follows: a = 0, b = 1.
Your total score will range between 0 and 12.

Analysis and Interpretation

Decision making isn't all systematic logic. Good decision makers also have developed, through experience, an intuitive ability that complements rational analysis. This ability is particularly valuable when decision makers face high levels of uncertainty, when facts are limited, when there is little previous precedent, when time is pressing, or when there are multiple plausible alternatives to choose among and there are good arguments for each.

If you have an intuitive score greater than 8, you prefer situations where there is a lack of structure and rules. You can handle uncertainty, spontaneity, and openness. Whether this ability is a plus in your job depends to a great extent on the culture of your organization. Where rationality is highly valued, reliance on intuition is likely to be seen as a negative quality. In open and creative-type cultures, intuitive ability is more likely to be valued.

More Self-Assessments

To learn more about your skills, abilities, and interests, take the following self-assessments on your enclosed CD-ROM:

- #4—How Well Do I Handle Ambiguity?
- #22—How Do My Ethics Rate?
- #20—What's My Decision-Making Style?
- #49—How Well Do I Respond to Turbulent Change? (This exercise also appears in Chapter 12 on pages 360–362.)

Individual vs. Group Decisions

Objective To contrast individual and group decision making.
Time 15 minutes.

Step 1 You have 5 minutes to read the following story and individually respond to each of the 11 statements as either true, false, or unknown.

The Story

A salesclerk had just turned off the lights in the store when a man appeared and demanded money. The owner opened a cash register. The contents of the cash register were scooped up, and the man sped away. A member of the police force was notified promptly.

Statements About the Story

1. A man appeared after the owner had turned off his store lights. True, false, or unknown?

2. The robber was a man. True, false, or unknown?

3. The man did not demand money. True, false, or unknown?

4. The man who opened the cash register was the owner. True, false, or unknown?

5. The store owner scooped up the contents of the cash register and ran away. True, false, or unknown?

6. Someone opened a cash register. True, false, or unknown?

7. After the man who demanded the money scooped up the contents of the cash register, he ran away. True, false, or unknown?

8. The cash register contained money, but the story does not state how much. True, false, or unknown?

9. The robber demanded money of the owner. True, false, or unknown?

10. The story concerns a series of events in which only three persons are referred to: the owner of the store, a man who demanded money, and a member of the police force. True, false, or unknown?

11. The following events in the story are true: Someone demanded money; a cash register was opened; its contents were scooped up; a man dashed out of the store. True, false, or unknown?

Step 2 After you have answered the 11 questions individually, form groups of 4 or 5 members each. The groups have 10 minutes to discuss their answers and agree on the correct answers to each of the 11 statements.

Step 3 Your instructor will give you the actual correct answers. How many correct answers did you get at the conclusion of Step 1? How many did your group achieve at the conclusion of Step 2? Did the group outperform the average individual? The best individual? Discuss the implications of these results.

Stem Cell Research

Advanced Cell Technology is embarking on a major activity—"to produce the world's first-ever cloned human embryo . . . a microscopic version of an already living person."[45] Michael West, chair, president, and chief scientific officer, and Robert Lanza, vice-president of research and scientific development, have begun implementation of this goal by interviewing women to serve as egg donors. Combining these eggs with a human cell produces an embryo that permits scientists at Advanced Cell to capture stem cells. As the stem cells are captured, the embryo is destroyed. Stem cells are believed to be able to develop into human tissue that could help cure a variety of diseases or even repair a severed spinal cord.

Advanced Cell Technology's goal, of course, is facing a major debate. People supporting both sides of the issue have strongly voiced their opinions. On one hand, if such research is proven effective, many diseases as we know them today—like Parkinson's disease and muscular dystrophy—could be eliminated. That could be both a major scientific breakthrough in our world and clearly a major financial coup for Advanced Cell. Moreover, similar research is being conducted in other parts of the globe, such as Europe, where it has received support. And to assist in these endeavours in an attempt to ensure that the highest ethics enter into all decisions made, Michael West has formed an ethical board of advisers consisting of scientists and professors of religion.

But critics see such research differently. They view stem cell research as the next step toward cloning humans—and, at times, liken it to creating a "great society." Religious groups, too, have voiced this concern over Advanced Cell's decisions, claiming that it is working in an area that it should not be. They also say that making decisions regarding such research raises significant ethical issues, particularly as to how far this research can go. The Canadian federal government has also entered into the stem cell discussion, with the Canadian Institutes of

Health Research setting specific regulations on what kind of stem cell research is to be funded by government. At Advanced Cell, even a few ethics board members have resigned, complaining that Advanced Cell is more interested in "obtaining patents in the field and using the board as a rubber stamp."

Do you believe that a company like Advanced Cell Technology can make ethical decisions in this arena when so much is at stake? Should public opinion keep a company from doing something simply because it is unpopular—even though it is legal? What's your opinion?

CASE APPLICATION

C. F. Martin Guitar Company

The C. F. Martin Guitar Company (**www.mguitar.com**) has been producing acoustic instruments since 1833.[46] A Martin guitar is among the best that money can buy. Current CEO Christian Frederick Martin IV—better known as Chris—continues to be committed to the guitar maker's craft. During 2002, the company sold about 77 000 instruments and hit a record $77 million in revenue. Despite this success, Chris is facing some serious issues.

Martin Guitar is an interesting blend of old and new. Although the equipment and tools may have changed over the years, employees remain true to the principle of high standards of musical excellence. Building a guitar to meet these standards requires considerable attention and patience. In a 1904 catalogue, a family member explained, "How to build a guitar to give this tone is not a secret. It takes care and patience." Now well over a century later, this statement is still an accurate reflection of the company's philosophy.

From the very beginning, quality has played an important role in everything that Martin Guitar does. Part of that quality approach includes a long-standing ecological policy. The company depends on natural-wood products to make its guitars, but a lot of the wood supply is vanishing. Chris has long embraced the responsible use of traditional wood materials, going so far as to encourage suppliers to find alternative species. Based on thorough customer research, Martin Guitar introduced guitars that used structurally sound woods with natural cosmetic defects that were once considered unacceptable. In addition, Martin Guitar follows the directives of CITES, the Convention on International Trade in Endangered Species of Wild Fauna and Flora (**www.cites.org**), even though it has the potential to affect Martin Guitar's ability to produce the type of quality products it has in the past. This treaty barred the export of the much-desired Brazilian rosewood, which is considered endangered. A guitar built from the remaining supply of this popular wood has a hefty price tag—more than $9500. Similar prices may be in line for the leading alternative, Honduras mahogany. Chris says, "All of us who use wood for the tone [it makes] are scrambling. Options are limited."

Although the company is rooted in its past, Chris is wondering whether he should go in new directions. For instance, he could try selling guitars in the under-$800 segment, a segment that accounts for 65 percent of the acoustic guitar industry's sales. A less expensive guitar would not look, smell, or feel like the company's pricier models. But Chris thinks that it would sound better than guitars in that price range made by other companies. Chris explains, "My fear is that if we don't look at alternatives, we'll be the company making guitars for doctors and lawyers. If Martin just worships its past without trying anything new, there won't be a Martin left to worship."

What should Chris do? Why?

DEVELOPING YOUR DIAGNOSTIC AND ANALYTICAL SKILLS

Some Solutions Create More Problems

With sentences handed down to executives involved in the Enron scandal, the conviction of Martha Stewart in March 2004 for lying to federal investigators during a stock-scandal investigation, and the investigation of Conrad Black for using most of Hollinger International's profits between 1997 and 2004 for his own personal gain, being a CEO appears to be losing some of its lustre. Why these individuals did what they did and why they made such decisions that are now proving to be so wrong is difficult to say. You just have to wonder what under-lies the CEO decision-making process. Take the case of Robert Milton, CEO of Montreal-based Air Canada.[47]

Air Canada has been struggling financially for a number of years. As the company went into bankruptcy in the early 2000s, Milton pleaded with the union leaders representing the company's 25 000 employees to consider accepting significant pay and benefits cuts. Milton built the case that this was a last resort and without the employees' acceptance of the cuts, the company was doomed.

The company emerged from bankruptcy in late 2004, but employees have not seen pay raises in a while. Milton informed employees in spring 2006 that Air Canada will find it "hard" to increase wages in labour contract talks later in the year because other carriers have reduced pay. He added that expecting pay raises was not realistic, "given that in most places around North America wages are going down very, very significantly."

Meanwhile, the company distributed $266 million to its shareholders, leading union members to conclude that the company was doing better than the CEO was acknowledging. That money, had it been distributed to employees, would have resulted in a $10 000 bonus for each one. Employees were furious, and demanded that Milton step down. However, Milton explained his logic for not giving that money to employees: "By providing a return of capital to our shareholders, ACE is rewarding investors for their confidence while maintaining a firm foundation for future prosperity."

Questions

1. How do you think poor decision making contributed to the failures of Martha Stewart and Robert Milton? Discuss.

2. How could the eight-step decision-making process have helped Milton make a better decision? Explain.

3. What role, if any, did escalation of commitment play in Milton's decision? Defend your opinion.

Solving Problems Creatively

Creativity is a frame of mind. You need to expand your mind's capabilities—that is, open up your mind to new ideas. Every individual has the ability to improve his or her creativity, but many people simply don't try to develop that ability. In a global business environment, where changes are fast and furious, organizations desperately need creative people. The uniqueness and variety of problems that managers face demand that they be able to solve problems creatively.

Steps in Developing the Skill

You can be more effective at solving problems creatively if you use the following 10 suggestions:[48]

1. **Think of yourself as creative.** Although this may be a simple suggestion, research shows that if you think you cannot be creative, you won't be. Believing in your ability to be creative is the first step in becoming more creative.

2. **Pay attention to your intuition.** Every individual has a subconscious mind that works well. Sometimes answers will come to you when you least expect them. Listen to that "inner voice." In fact, most creative people keep notepads near their beds and write down ideas when the thoughts come to them. That way they don't forget them.

3. **Move away from your comfort zone.** Every individual has a comfort zone in which certainty exists. But creativity and the known often do not mix. To be creative, you need to move away from the status quo and focus your mind on something new.

4. **Determine what you want to do.** This includes taking time to understand a problem before beginning to try to resolve it, getting all the facts in mind, and trying to identify the most important facts.

5. **Look for ways to tackle the problem.** This can be accomplished by setting aside a block of time to focus on it; working out a plan for attacking it; establishing subgoals; imagining or actually using analogies wherever possible (for example, could you approach your problem like a fish out of water and look at what the fish does to cope? Or can you use the things you have to do to find your way when it's foggy to help you solve your problem?); using different problem-solving strategies such as verbal, visual, mathematical, theatrical (for instance, you might draw a diagram of the decision or problem to help you visualize it better or you might talk to yourself out loud about the problem, telling it as you would tell a story to someone); trusting your intuition; and playing with possible ideas and approaches (for example, look at your problem from a different perspective or ask yourself what someone else, like your grandmother, might do if faced with the same situation).

6. **Look for ways to do things better.** This may involve trying consciously to be original, not worrying about looking foolish, eliminating cultural taboos (such as gender stereotypes) that might influence your possible solutions, keeping an open mind, being alert to odd or puzzling facts, thinking of unconventional ways to use objects and the environment (for instance, thinking about how you could use newspaper or magazine headlines to help you be a better problem solver), discarding usual or habitual ways of doing things, and striving for objectivity by being as critical of your own ideas as you would be of those of someone else.

7. **Find several right answers.** Being creative means continuing to look for other solutions even when you think you have solved the problem. A better, more creative solution just might be found.

8. **Believe in finding a workable solution.** Like believing in yourself, you also need to believe in your ideas. If you don't think you can find a solution, you probably won't.

9. **Brainstorm with others.** Creativity is not an isolated activity. Bouncing ideas off others creates synergy.

10. **Turn creative ideas into action.** Coming up with creative ideas is only part of the process. Once the ideas are generated, they must be implemented. Keeping great ideas in your mind, or on papers that no one will read, does little to expand your creative abilities.

Practising the Skill

How many words can you make using the letters in the word *brainstorm*? (There are at least 95.)

MANAGING WORKFORCE DIVERSITY

The Value of Diversity in Decision Making

Have you decided what your major is going to be? How did you decide? Do you feel your decision is a good one? Is there anything you could have done differently to make sure that your decision was the best one?[49]

Making good decisions is tough! Managers are continuously making decisions—for instance, developing new products, establishing weekly or monthly goals, implementing advertising campaigns, reassigning employees to different work groups, resolving customers' complaints, or purchasing new laptops for sales representatives. One important suggestion for making better decisions is to tap into the diversity of the work group. Drawing upon the ideas of diverse employees can prove valuable to a manager's decision making. Why? Diverse employees can provide fresh perspectives on issues. They can offer differing interpretations on how a problem is defined and may be more open to trying new ways of doing things. Diverse employees usually are more creative in generating alternatives and more flexible in resolving issues. And getting input from diverse sources increases the likelihood of finding creative and unique solutions.

Even though diversity in decision making can be valuable, there are drawbacks. The lack of a common perspective usually means that more time is spent discussing the issues. Communication may be a problem, particularly if language barriers are present. In addition, seeking out diverse opinions can make the decision-making process more complex, confusing, and ambiguous. In addition, with multiple perspectives on the decision, it may be difficult to reach a single agreement or to agree on specific actions. Although these drawbacks are valid concerns, the value of diversity in decision making outweighs the potential disadvantages.

When you have worked in teams, what advantages and disadvantages arose because of the diversity (or lack of diversity) in the group? What measures could be taken to make sure that diversity is an asset for a team, rather than something that causes problems?

CoolBrands B:
Evaluating the Strategic Plan

By 2004, CoolBrands was third internationally in the consumer products and franchising segments of the frozen dessert industry. Things were looking good for the company. Then a key licensing agreement, responsible for a big part of the company's revenues, fell through. Michael Serruya, co-chair of CoolBrands with responsibility for setting strategy, needs to determine how the company should respond to this loss of revenue.

Operations

Yogen Früz, started in 1986, rapidly expanded its areas of operation. By 1997, the company was the largest franchisor of frozen yogurt outlets, with approximately 3100 outlets in 79 countries. It had a number of other products and a manufacturing facility. In recent years, the company grew as follows:

- *January 1998:* Yogen Früz acquired US-based Ice Cream Churn, which operated outlets in Wal-Mart stores.
- *March 1998:* Yogen Früz acquired Integrated Brands, which included a number of highly recognizable brands such as Godiva ice cream, Atkins Endulge ice cream products, Tropicana frozen desserts, and Yoplait frozen desserts. Because of this merger, Yogen Früz's name was changed to CoolBrands.
- *Late 2000:* CoolBrands acquired Eskimo Pie, creator of the frozen novelty industry in 1921 with the Eskimo Pie ice cream bar.
- *2001:* Michael Serruya stepped down as CEO and became co-chair of the board of directors, with responsibility for setting strategy.
- *2003:* The company gained the rights to Dreyer's Dreamery Ice Cream, Whole Fruit Sorbet, and Godiva ice cream brands.

By the start of 2004, CoolBrands had four major operations consisting of four distinct segments:

- *Prepackaged consumer products business* involves manufacturing, selling, and distributing prepackaged frozen dessert products under a variety of names, including Eskimo Pie, Dreamery, Godiva, Tropicana, and Weight Watchers Smart Ones.

- *Franchising and licensing business* includes operations under the Yogen Früz, I Can't Believe It's Yogurt, Bresler's, and Swensen's banners, among others.
- *Foodservice business* involves manufacturing soft-serve yogurt and ice cream mixes that are sold to foodservice distributors, yogurt shops, and other foodservice establishments.
- *Dairy components business* involves manufacturing flavours, ingredients, and packaging that are sold to frozen novelty manufacturers and the dairy industry.

New Threats

In July 2004, CoolBrands announced disturbing news to its shareholders. Weight Watchers International would not be renewing its licensing agreement, a contract that was expected to bring in $113-million in sales for 2004 (about 18 percent of CoolBrand's sales) and 32 percent of CoolBrand's profits. Under the termination agreement, CoolBrands would have the right to make and sell the Weight Watchers Smart Ones products until September 2005. After that, CoolBrands would need to use a different name and packaging on the Smart Ones product. The loss of Weight Watchers' business will cut 4 percent from the company's revenues and 10 percent from its earnings in 2006.

Michael Serruya recognizes that the company will have to replace these sales. The strength of the Weight Watchers brand required "far less marketing than many other brands because it is not considered an impulse item." One strategy would be for the company to identify another company with which they could market a line of "low fat and fat-free 'better for you' frozen desserts." CoolBrands was in first place with a 26 percent market share of these "better for you" desserts at the time of the Weight Watchers announcement.

One concern in finding a new diet product, however, is that CoolBrands already has a licensing agreement with Atkins Nutritionals, the marketing operation behind the Atkins diet revolution, to manufacture and market a low-carb frozen treats line called Endulge. Some have already speculated that Weight Watchers was not happy that CoolBrands also had licensing arrangements with Atkins. Serruya has to consider the possibility that Atkins could object to brand competition as well.

New Opportunities

Dogsters sells "ice cream-style" frozen treats for dogs including special-occasion cakes and two flavours of ice cream cups. These products are available in the northeastern United States and are marketed as a "better for you" treat for dogs, providing dog lovers with healthier treats for their pets. Serruya wonders if it would be worth acquiring the licensing rights to Dogsters, so that it can expand sales in the United States and bring the product to Canada. The licensing rights would include manufacturing, marketing, and distributing the frozen snack treats.

The Decision

What are the strengths, weaknesses, opportunities, and threats of the current CoolBrands operations? What might the company consider doing next? Does it make sense to enter the dog treat market?

Sources: CoolBrands International, "Annual Information Form," January 13, 2004; D. Berman, "CoolBrands Reels on Lost Deal," *Financial Post,* July 29, 2004, p. FP1; D. Berman, "CoolBrands Gets Cold Shoulder, Stock Plunges $4.90," *Financial Post,* July 30, 2004, p. IN1; R. Bloom, "CoolBrands Moves to Reassure Investors," *Globe and Mail,* July 30, 2004, p. B4; K. Howlett and R. Bloom, "CoolBrands Trading Frenzy Cancelled," *Globe and Mail,* July 29, 2004, p. B1; "CoolBrands Makes Money, Ices 'Pet Project,'" *Refrigerated Transporter,* July 2004, p. 12; "CoolBrands Helps Share Ice Cream with Man's Best Friend," *Dairy Foods,* May 2004, p. 18; M. DaCruz, "Subject: CoolBrands International Inc.," *National Post,* Oct 1, 2004, p. 28.

Exhibit 1

CoolBrands, Revenue by Industry Segments and Classes of Products and Services

(For the year ended August 31, 2003, in thousands of dollars)

Revenue Source	Prepackaged Consumer Products	Franchising and Licensing	Foodservice	Dairy Components	Corporate
United States	275 446	13 400	26 234	41 594	—
Canada	947	3996	—	—	214
International	741	3494	—	—	—
Inter-segment revenues	(5389)	—	(991)	(2943)	(214)
Other revenues	575	126	—	—	43
Total consolidated revenues	272 320	21 016	25 243	38 651	43

Source: CoolBrands International, "Annual Information Form," January 13, 2004.

Exhibit 2

CoolBrands, Balance Sheet Data

(For the year ended August 31, 2003, in thousands of dollars)

	2003	2002	2001	2000	1999
Working capital	85 734	57 354	43 408	30 053	36 109
Total assets	313 850	283 662	225 876	142 300	172 686
Total long-term liabilities	50 345	38 469	42 710	1158	4244
Shareholders' equity	187 851	170 708	132 637	114 091	140 174

Source: CoolBrands International, "Annual Information Form," January 13, 2004.

Organizational Structure and Design

What kind of organizational structure do I need?

1 What are the major elements of organizational structure?

2 What factors affect organizational structure?

3 Beyond traditional organizational designs, how else can organizations be structured?

Richard A. Peddie is the president and CEO of Maple Leaf Sports & Entertainment (MLSE), which owns the NHL's Toronto Maple Leafs and the NBA's Toronto Raptors, Leafs TV, Raptors NBA TV, as well as Air Canada Centre, where both teams play their home games.

Peddie's job is complex—he is responsible for the business affairs of both teams. This includes "team operations, sales, marketing, finance, administration, event operations, broadcast, communications, and community development."[1] He is also responsible for the operation of Air Canada Centre and guided its planning and development, bringing the project in on time and on budget.

To perform his job, Peddie needs a variety of people and departments to help him. One of his jobs, then, is to create an organizational structure for MLSE that supports operations of both teams and the Centre. He has a great deal of flexibility in determining some parts of the structure, and less flexibility in determining others. For instance, the number of athletes that can fill positions on a hockey team is determined by the NHL. Through the draft and trades, Peddie and his coaches have some ability to choose the particular players who fill these positions, however.

Other operations that Peddie oversees include ticket sales for both the Raptors and the Maple Leafs. In determining how to

manage ticket sales, Peddie can consider whether there should be separate ticket sales departments for each team, whether marketing should be included with or separate from ticket sales, and whether ticket salespeople should be subdivided into specialties: corporate sales, season tickets, playoff tickets, etc.

THINK ABOUT IT

How do you run two sports teams and a sports facility? Put yourself in Richard Peddie's shoes. He wants to continue to make MLSE successful. What can he do so that MLSE continues to adapt and change? What organizational structure can best ensure his goal?

Richard Peddie's desire to make Maple Leaf Sports & Entertainment successful illustrates how important it is for managers to design an organizational structure that helps accomplish organizational goals and objectives. In this chapter, we present information about designing appropriate organizational structures. We look at the various elements of organizational structure and the factors that influence their design. We also look at some traditional and contemporary organizational designs.

DEFINING ORGANIZATIONAL STRUCTURE

 What are the major elements of organizational structure?

organizing
A management function that involves determining what tasks are to be done, who is to do them, how the tasks are to be grouped, who reports to whom, and where decisions are to be made.

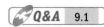 **9.1**

organizational structure
How job tasks are formally divided, grouped, and coordinated within an organization.

organizational design
The process of developing or changing an organization's structure.

work specialization
The degree to which tasks in the organization are subdivided into separate jobs; also known as *division of labour*.

 **9.2**

No other topic in management has undergone as much change in the past few years as that of organizing and organizational structure. Traditional approaches to organizing work are being questioned and re-evaluated as managers search out organizational structures that will best support and facilitate employees' doing the organization's work—ones that can achieve efficiency but also have the flexibility that is necessary for success in today's dynamic environment. Recall from Chapter 1 that **organizing** is defined as the process of creating an organization's structure. That process is important and serves many purposes (see Exhibit 5-1). The challenge for managers is to design an organizational structure that allows employees to do their work effectively and efficiently.

Just what is **organizational structure**? It's how job tasks are formally divided, grouped, and coordinated within an organization. When managers develop or change the structure, they are engaged in **organizational design**, a process that involves decisions about six key elements: work specialization, departmentalization, chain of command, span of control, centralization and decentralization, and formalization.[2]

Work Specialization

When you are working in a team on a course project, does it make sense to specialize tasks? What are the advantages and disadvantages?

Adam Smith first identified division of labour and concluded that it contributed to increased employee productivity. Early in the twentieth century, Henry Ford applied this concept in an assembly line where every Ford employee was assigned a specific, repetitive task.

Today we use the term **work specialization** to describe the degree to which tasks in the organization are subdivided into separate jobs. The essence of work specialization is that an entire job is not done by one individual but instead is broken down into steps, and each step is completed by a different person. Individual employees specialize in doing part of an activity rather than the entire activity.

During the first half of the twentieth century, managers viewed work specialization as an unending source of increased productivity. And for a time it was! Because it was not widely used, when work specialization *was* implemented, employee productivity rose. By the 1960s, however, it had become evident that a good thing could be carried too far. The point had been reached in some jobs where human diseconomies from work specialization—boredom, fatigue, stress, poor quality, increased absenteeism, and higher turnover—more than offset the economic advantages.

Most managers today see work specialization as an important organizing mechanism but not as a source of ever-increasing productivity. They recognize the economies it provides in certain types of jobs, but they also recognize the problems it creates when it's carried to extremes, including job dissatisfaction, poor mental health, and a low sense of accomplishment.[3] McDonald's uses high work specialization to efficiently make and sell its prod-

Exhibit 5-1

Purposes of Organizing

- Divides work to be done into specific jobs and departments.
- Assigns tasks and responsibilities associated with individual jobs.
- Coordinates diverse organizational tasks.
- Clusters jobs into units.
- Establishes relationships among individuals, groups, and departments.
- Establishes formal lines of authority.
- Allocates and deploys organizational resources.

ucts, and most employees in health care organizations are specialized. However, other organizations, such as Bolton, Ontario-based Husky Injection Molding Systems, and Ford Australia have successfully broadened the scope of jobs and reduced work specialization. Still, specialization has its place in some organizations. No hockey team has anyone play both goalie and centre positions. Rather, players tend to specialize in their positions.

Departmentalization

Does your college or university have an office of student affairs? A financial aid or student housing department? Once jobs have been divided up through work specialization, they have to be grouped back together so that common tasks can be coordinated. The basis on which jobs are grouped together is called **departmentalization**. Every organization will have its own specific way of classifying and grouping work activities. Exhibit 5-2 on page 132 shows the five common forms of departmentalization.

Functional departmentalization groups jobs by functions performed. This approach can be used in all types of organizations, although the functions change to reflect the organization's purpose and work. **Product departmentalization** groups jobs by product line. In this approach, each major product area is placed under the authority of a manager who is responsible for everything

Work specialization might make the job of answering phone calls all day monotonous to some, but not to Graciela Barreña (in front in picture), who works for the Argentine call centre Indicom, in Buenos Aires. Her six-hour shift follows a pattern, with pager messages and calls about highway toll cards arriving in the early morning, and responses to free raffles and other toll-free calling services her employer offers filling much of the rest of the day. In between, Barreña provides customer service for a cheese factory and a diaper manufacturer.

having to do with that product line. For instance, Estée Lauder sells lipsticks, eyeshadow, blush, and a variety of other cosmetics, represented by different product lines. The company's lines include Clinique, Prescriptives, and Origins, in addition to Canadian-created MAC Cosmetics and its own original line of Estée Lauder products, each of which operates as a distinct company. Similarly, while Richard Peddie is the president and CEO of both the Raptors and the Maple Leafs, each team is treated as a separate product line in terms of the rest of its management and operations, with each team being led by its own general manager.

Geographical departmentalization groups jobs on the basis of territory or geography such as the East Coast, western Canada, or central Ontario, or maybe by US, European, Latin American, and Asia–Pacific regions. **Process departmentalization** groups jobs on the basis of product or customer flow. In this approach, work activities follow a natural processing flow of products or even of customers. For instance, many beauty salons have separate employees for shampooing, colouring, and cutting hair, all different processes for having one's hair styled. Finally, **customer departmentalization** groups jobs on the basis of customers who have common needs or problems that can best be met by having specialists for each. There are advantages to matching departmentalization to customer needs, as the following *Management Reflection* shows.

departmentalization
The basis on which jobs are grouped together.

functional departmentalization
Groups jobs by functions performed.

product departmentalization
Groups jobs by product line.

geographical departmentalization
Groups jobs on the basis of territory or geography.

process departmentalization
Groups jobs on the basis of product or customer flow.

customer departmentalization
Groups jobs on the basis of customers who have common needs or problems.

MANAGEMENT REFLECTION

RBC Financial Group Moves from Geographic to Product Organization

Why would a bank change its departmentalization? When Toronto-based RBC Financial Group moved from geographic to product organization, Gordon Nixon, president and CEO, explained that the change would help services and products be delivered more efficiently. Each client deals with just one employee, who is accountable for overseeing all of the financial products Royal Bank delivers to that client.

Exhibit 5-2

The Five Common Forms of Departmentalization

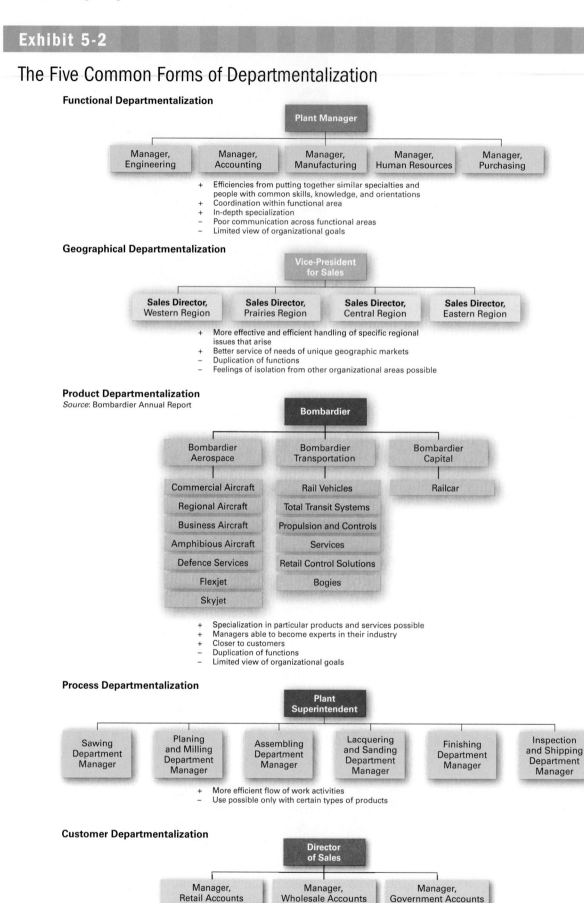

Functional Departmentalization

Plant Manager
- Manager, Engineering
- Manager, Accounting
- Manager, Manufacturing
- Manager, Human Resources
- Manager, Purchasing

+ Efficiencies from putting together similar specialties and people with common skills, knowledge, and orientations
+ Coordination within functional area
+ In-depth specialization
− Poor communication across functional areas
− Limited view of organizational goals

Geographical Departmentalization

Vice-President for Sales
- Sales Director, Western Region
- Sales Director, Prairies Region
- Sales Director, Central Region
- Sales Director, Eastern Region

+ More effective and efficient handling of specific regional issues that arise
+ Better service of needs of unique geographic markets
− Duplication of functions
− Feelings of isolation from other organizational areas possible

Product Departmentalization
Source: Bombardier Annual Report

Bombardier
- Bombardier Aerospace
  - Commercial Aircraft
  - Regional Aircraft
  - Business Aircraft
  - Amphibious Aircraft
  - Defence Services
  - Flexjet
  - Skyjet
- Bombardier Transportation
  - Rail Vehicles
  - Total Transit Systems
  - Propulsion and Controls
  - Services
  - Retail Control Solutions
  - Bogies
- Bombardier Capital
  - Railcar

+ Specialization in particular products and services possible
+ Managers able to become experts in their industry
+ Closer to customers
− Duplication of functions
− Limited view of organizational goals

Process Departmentalization

Plant Superintendent
- Sawing Department Manager
- Planing and Milling Department Manager
- Assembling Department Manager
- Lacquering and Sanding Department Manager
- Finishing Department Manager
- Inspection and Shipping Department Manager

+ More efficient flow of work activities
− Use possible only with certain types of products

Customer Departmentalization

Director of Sales
- Manager, Retail Accounts
- Manager, Wholesale Accounts
- Manager, Government Accounts

+ Specialists able to meet customers' needs and problems
− Duplication of functions
− Limited view of organizational goals

Royal Bank also created a global banking division to better integrate banking services.[4] Previously, clients were contacted by both a corporate banker (to determine whether they wanted to become a customer of the bank and to understand their debt needs) and an investment banker (for their investment business). The new structure means that one relationship officer is responsible for debt, equity, and advisory services. Relationship officers are assigned to one of eight industry groups: communications and technology, diversified industries, energy, financial institutions, mining, forest products, real estate, and the public sector.

The advantage to this restructuring is that corporate clients have industry specialists serving their needs rather than bankers from geographic regions. This restructuring provides more personalized service to customers. It also puts less stress on bankers, who were forced to understand the various needs of clients from different industries. Thus, the change from a geographic to a market structure makes it easier for the sales force to serve Royal Bank's customers. There is one downside to this approach, though Royal Bank has not found it to be a problem with its own clients. In the geographic organization, specialists understood the specific economic environments of their regions, which helped them advise clients better about the pressures of different regional markets. ■

Royal Bank of Canada
www.royalbank.com

Large organizations often combine forms of departmentalization. For example, a major Japanese electronics firm organizes each of its divisions along functional lines: its manufacturing units around processes, its sales units around seven geographic regions, and sales regions into four customer groupings.

Two popular trends in departmentalization are the increasing use of customer departmentalization and the use of cross-functional teams. Managers use customer departmentalization to monitor customers' needs and to respond to changes in those needs. For example, Toronto-based Dell Canada is organized around four customer-oriented business units: home and home office; small business; medium and large business; and government, education, and health care. Burnaby, BC-based TELUS is organized around six customer-oriented business units: personal (focused on households and individuals), consumer solutions (focused on small- to medium-sized businesses), advanced business solutions (focused on large businesses), service providers (focused on Canadian and global companies), TELUS Mobility (focused on people and businesses on the go), and TELUS Québec (a TELUS company for the Quebec marketplace). Customer-oriented structures enable companies to better understand their customers and to respond faster to their needs.

Dell Canada
www.dell.ca

Managers use **cross-functional teams**—teams made up groups of individuals who are experts in various specialties and who work together—to increase knowledge and understanding for some organizational task. For instance, Scarborough, Ontario-based Aviva Canada, a leading property and casualty insurance group, puts together catastrophe teams to more quickly help policyholders when a crisis occurs. The cross-functional teams, with trained representatives from all relevant departments, are called upon to provide services in the event of a crisis. During the BC wildfires of summer 2003, the catastrophe team worked on both local and corporate issues, including managing information technology, internal and external communication, tracking, resourcing, and vendors. This made it easier to meet the needs of policyholders as quickly as possible.[5] We discuss the use of cross-functional teams more fully in Chapter 10.

TELUS
www.telus.com

cross-functional team
A group of employees at about the same hierarchical level, but from different work areas, who come together to accomplish a task.

Aviva Canada
www.avivacanada.com

Chain of Command

Have you ever worked in an organization where the chain of command was not clear? What effect did this have on employees?

For many years, the chain-of-command concept was a cornerstone of organizational design. As you will see, it has far less importance today. But contemporary managers still need to consider its implications when deciding how best to structure their organizations.

The **chain of command** is the continuous line of authority that extends from upper organizational levels to the lowest levels and clarifies who reports to whom. It helps employees answer questions such as "Who do I go to if I have a problem?" or "To whom am I responsible?"

chain of command
The continuous line of authority that extends from the top of the organization to the lowest level and clarifies who reports to whom.

You cannot discuss the chain of command without discussing these other concepts: authority, responsibility, accountability, unity of command, and delegation. **Authority** refers to the rights inherent in a managerial position to tell people what to do and to expect them to do it.[6] To facilitate decision making and coordination, an organization's managers are part of the chain of command and are granted a certain degree of authority to meet their responsibilities. Some senior managers and CEOs are better at granting authority than others. For instance, when Richard Peddie hired Rob Babcock to be the general manager of the Raptors in 2004, some sports writers raised concerns over whether Babcock would have enough autonomy to do his job. It was noted that Peddie "has a reputation for meddling with basketball operations."[7] When Babcock was fired in 2006, sports writers observed that many of his decisions were actually made by senior management.[8]

As managers coordinate and integrate the work of employees, those employees assume an obligation to perform any assigned duties. This obligation or expectation to perform is known as **responsibility**. Responsibility brings with it **accountability**, which is the need to report and justify work to a manager's superiors. When Brian Burke was dismissed as general manager of the Vancouver Canucks in 2004, team owners were signalling that they held Burke accountable for the inability of the Canucks to get further in the playoffs in recent years.

The **unity of command** principle (one of Fayol's 14 principles of management discussed in the supplement *History of Management Trends* on page 29) helps preserve the concept of a continuous line of authority. It states that every employee should receive orders from only one superior. Without unity of command, conflicting demands and priorities from multiple managers can create problems.

Because managers have limited time and knowledge, they may delegate some of their responsibilities to other employees. **Delegation** is the assignment of authority to another person to carry out specific duties, allowing the employee to make some of the decisions. Delegation is an important part of a manager's job, as it can ensure that the right people are part of the decision-making process. To learn more about being an effective delegator, see *Developing Your Interpersonal Skills—Delegating,* on pages 153–154, at the end of the chapter.

Line and Staff Authority

In many organizations there is a distinction between line and staff authority. Line managers are responsible for the essential activities of the organization, including production and sales. Line managers have the authority to issue orders to those in the chain of command. The president, the production manager, and the sales manager are examples of line managers. Staff managers have advisory authority, and cannot issue orders to those in the chain of command (except those in their own department). The vice-president of accounting, the human resource manager, and the marketing research manager are examples of staff managers. For instance, Mardi Walker, senior vice-president, People, for Maple Leafs Sports & Entertainment, may have recommendations about how the Raptors might win more games, but cannot expect that such recommendations to current General Manager Bryan Colangelo will be followed. However, as senior vice-president, People, Walker can give advice about managing employee benefits.

Span of Control

How many employees can a manager efficiently and effectively manage? This question of **span of control** is important because, to a large degree, it determines the number of levels and managers an organization has. All things being equal, the wider or larger the span, the more efficient the organization. An example can show why.

Assume that we have two organizations, both of which have almost 4100 employees. As Exhibit 5-3 shows, if one organization has a uniform span of four and the other a span of eight, the wider span will have two fewer levels and approximately 800 fewer managers. If the average manager made $42 000 a year, the organization with the wider span would save more than $33 million a year in management salaries alone! Obviously, wider spans are more efficient in terms of cost. However, at some point, wider spans reduce *effectiveness*. When the span becomes too large, employee performance suffers because managers no longer have the time to provide the necessary leadership and support.

authority
The rights inherent in a managerial position to tell people what to do and to expect them to do it.

responsibility
The obligation or expectation to perform any assigned duties.

accountability
The need to report and justify work to a manager's superiors.

unity of command
The management principle that states every employee should receive orders from only one superior.

delegation
The assignment of authority to another person to carry out specific duties, allowing the employee to make some of the decisions.

span of control
The number of employees a manager can efficiently and effectively manage.

Exhibit 5-3

Contrasting Spans of Control

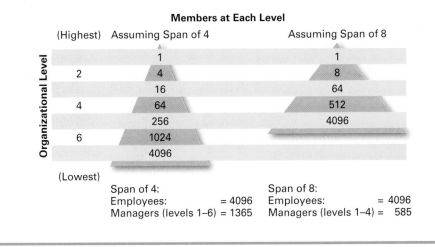

Members at Each Level

	(Highest)	Assuming Span of 4	Assuming Span of 8
		1	1
2		4	8
		16	64
4		64	512
		256	4096
6		1024	
		4096	

(Lowest)

Span of 4:
Employees: = 4096
Managers (levels 1–6) = 1365

Span of 8:
Employees: = 4096
Managers (levels 1–4) =   585

The contemporary view of span of control recognizes that many factors influence the appropriate number of employees a manager can efficiently *and* effectively manage. These factors include the skills and abilities of the manager and the employees, and characteristics of the work being done. For instance, the more training and experience employees have, the less direct supervision they need. Therefore, managers with well-trained and experienced employees can function quite well with a wider span. Other contingency variables that determine the appropriate span include similarity of employee tasks, the complexity of those tasks, the physical proximity of subordinates, the degree to which standardized procedures are in place, the sophistication of the organization's information system, the strength of the organization's culture, and the preferred style of the manager.[9] Wider spans of control are also possible due to technology—it is easier for managers and their subordinates to communicate with each other, and there is often more information readily available to help employees perform their jobs.

The trend in recent years has been toward larger spans of control, which are consistent with managers' efforts to reduce costs, speed up decision making, increase flexibility, get closer to customers, and empower employees. However, to ensure that performance does not suffer because of these wider spans, organizations are investing heavily in employee training. Managers recognize that they can handle a wider span when employees know their jobs well or can turn to co-workers if they have questions.

Centralization and Decentralization

In some organizations, top managers make all the decisions and lower-level managers and employees simply carry out their orders. At the other extreme are organizations in which decision making is pushed down to the managers who are closest to the action. The former organizations are centralized, and the latter are decentralized.

Centralization describes the degree to which decision making is concentrated at a single point in the organization. If top managers make the organization's key decisions with little or no input from below, then the organization is centralized. We noted above that Richard Peddie tends to be closely involved in decisions regarding the Raptors. In contrast, the more that lower-level employees provide input or actually make decisions, the more **decentralization** there is. Keep in mind that the concept of centralization/decentralization is relative, not absolute—that is, an organization is never completely centralized or decentralized. Few organizations could function effectively if all decisions were made by only a select group of top managers; nor could they function if all decisions were delegated to employees at the lowest levels.

centralization
The degree to which decision making is concentrated at a single point in the organization.

decentralization
The degree to which lower-level employees provide input or actually make decisions.

Many employees are asked to work in teams to get things done. These Xerox employees are a self-managed team. They make decisions about managing and scheduling production, and they monitor the quality of their output.

As organizations become more flexible and responsive, there is a distinct trend toward decentralizing decision making. In large companies especially, lower-level managers are "closer to the action" and typically have more detailed knowledge about problems and how best to solve them than do top managers. For instance, the Bank of Montreal's some 1000 branches are organized into "communities"—a group of branches within a limited geographical area. Each community is led by a community area manager, who typically works within a 20-minute drive of the other branches. This area manager can respond faster and more intelligently to problems in his or her community than could some senior executive in Toronto. The following *Management Reflection* considers the case of Cascades, a pulp-and-paper company, which illustrates a few of the reasons for having a decentralized structure.

MANAGEMENT REFLECTION

Brothers Decentralize to Increase Entrepreneurial Management

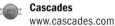
Cascades
www.cascades.com

Does decentralization lead to better management?   Kingsey Falls, Quebec-based Cascades, Canada's second-largest pulp-and-paper company, has around 160 operating units located in Canada, the United States, Mexico, France, England, Germany and Sweden.[10] Alain Lemaire is president and CEO, and his two brothers, Bernard and Laurent, are also a part of the business.

Five autonomous units form Cascades: the Boxboard Group, the Containerboard Group, the Specialty Products Group, the Tissue Group, and the Fine Papers Group. The companies produce coated boxboard and folding cartons, container-board packaging, specialty paper products, tissues, and fine papers. Boralex, a company affiliated with Cascades, produces energy and is headed by Bernard Lemaire. The companies are treated as separate entities, based on product, and operate like a federation of small and medium-sized businesses. Each mill within a subsidiary operates as a separate business unit and is accountable for its own bottom line.

The company motivates its employees through profit sharing, although employees share only in the profits generated by their own mill. Because each mill is evaluated separately, managers have to be both more responsible and more accountable for their operations, and encourage employees to take more ownership of their job performance. The Lemaires' emphasis on decentralized, entrepreneurial management has been copied by other Canadian forest products companies, such as Domtar. ■

Another term for increased decentralization is **employee empowerment**, which is increasing the decision-making discretion of employees.

What determines whether an organization will move toward more centralization or decentralization? Exhibit 5-4 lists some of the factors that influence the amount of centralization or decentralization an organization uses.[11]

employee empowerment
Giving employees responsibility for what they do.

Formalization

Formalization refers to the degree to which jobs within the organization are standardized and the extent to which employee behaviour is guided by rules and procedures. If a job is highly formalized, then the person doing that job has little discretion as to what is to be done, when it's to be done, and how he or she does it. Employees can be expected to handle the same input in exactly the same way, resulting in consistent and uniform output. In organizations with high formalization, there are explicit job descriptions, numerous organizational rules, and clearly defined procedures covering work processes. On the other hand, where formalization is low, job behaviours are relatively unstructured and employees have a great deal of freedom in how they do their work.

The degree of formalization varies widely between organizations and even within organizations. For instance, at a newspaper, news reporters often have a great deal of discretion in their jobs. They may pick their news topics, find their own stories, research them the way they want, and write them up, usually within minimal guidelines. On the other hand, employees who lay out the newspaper pages don't have that type of freedom. They have constraints—both time and space—that standardize how they do their work.

formalization
The degree to which jobs within the organization are standardized and the extent to which employee behaviour is guided by rules and procedures.

Q&A 9.6

Exhibit 5-4

Factors That Influence the Amount of Centralization and Decentralization

More Centralization	More Decentralization
• Environment is stable.	• Environment is complex, uncertain.
• Lower-level managers are not as capable or experienced at making decisions as upper-level managers.	• Lower-level managers are capable and experienced at making decisions.
• Lower-level managers do not want to have a say in decisions.	• Lower-level managers want a voice in decisions.
• Decisions are significant.	• Decisions are relatively minor.
• Organization is facing a crisis or the risk of company failure.	• Corporate culture is open to allowing managers have a say in what happens.
• Company is large.	• Company is geographically dispersed.
• Effective implementation of company strategies depends on managers' retaining say over what happens.	• Effective implementation of company strategies depends on managers' having involvement and flexibility to make decisions.

ORGANIZATIONAL DESIGN DECISIONS

2 What factors affect organizational structure?

Organizations don't have the same structures. A company with 30 employees is not going to look like one with 30 000 employees. But even organizations of comparable size don't necessarily have similar structures. What works for one organization may not work for another. How do managers decide what organizational structure to use? Organizational design decisions depend upon certain contingency factors. In this section, we look at two generic models of organizational design and then at the contingency factors that favour each.

Mechanistic and Organic Organizations

Dining in Vancouver can get you two very different experiences. At McDonald's, you will find a limited selection of menu items, most available daily. Employees are not expected to be decision makers. Rather, they are closely supervised and follow well-defined rules and standard operating procedures. Only one employee helps each customer. At Blue Water Café in downtown Vancouver, by contrast, there is no division of labour, and management does not dictate what the kitchen serves. Instead, the chef on duty creates a meal of his choice while you sit at the sushi bar and watch. The chef chooses the meal from the fresh fish of the day that he bought at the market earlier, so each day's menu can be quite original. Waiters work collaboratively, helping each other serve all customers, rather than being assigned to specific tables.

mechanistic organization
An organizational design that is rigid and tightly controlled.

Exhibit 5-5 describes two organizational forms.[12] A **mechanistic organization** is a rigid and tightly controlled structure, much like McDonald's. It's characterized by high specialization, rigid departmentalization, a limited information network (mostly downward communication), narrow spans of control, little participation in decision making by lower-level employees, and high formalization.

Mechanistic organizational structures tend to be efficiency machines and rely heavily on rules, regulations, standardized tasks, and similar controls. This organizational structure tries to minimize the impact of differing personalities, judgments, and ambiguity because these human traits are seen as inefficient and inconsistent. Although there is no totally mechanistic organization, almost all large corporations and government agencies have some of these mechanistic characteristics.

organic organization
An organizational design that is highly adaptive and flexible.

In direct contrast to the mechanistic form of organization is the **organic organization**, which is as highly adaptive and flexible a structure as the mechanistic organization is rigid and stable. This characterizes Vancouver's Blue Water Café. Rather than having standardized jobs and regulations, the organic organization is flexible, which allows it to change rapidly as needs require. Organic organizations have a division of labour, but the jobs

Exhibit 5-5

Mechanistic vs. Organic Organization

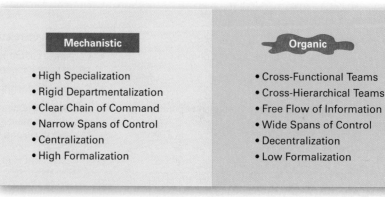

Mechanistic	Organic
• High Specialization	• Cross-Functional Teams
• Rigid Departmentalization	• Cross-Hierarchical Teams
• Clear Chain of Command	• Free Flow of Information
• Narrow Spans of Control	• Wide Spans of Control
• Centralization	• Decentralization
• High Formalization	• Low Formalization

people do are not standardized. Employees are highly trained and empowered to handle diverse job activities and problems, and these organizations frequently use cross-functional and cross-hierarchical teams. Employees in organic-type organizations require minimal formal rules and little direct supervision; instead, they rely on a free flow of information and a wide span of control. Their high levels of skills and training and the support provided by other team members make formalization and tight managerial controls unnecessary.

When is a mechanistic structure preferable, and when is an organic one more appropriate? Let's look at the main contingency factors that influence the decision.

Contingency Factors

Top managers of most organizations typically put a great deal of thought into designing an appropriate structure. What that appropriate structure is depends on four contingency variables: the organization's strategy, size, technology, and degree of environmental uncertainty. It is important to remember that because these variables can change over the life cycle of the organization, managers should consider from time to time whether the current organizational structure is best suited for what the organization is facing.

Strategy and Structure

An organization's structure should facilitate the achievement of goals. Because goals are influenced by the organization's strategies, it's only logical that strategy and structure should be closely linked. More specifically, structure should follow strategy. If managers significantly change the organization's strategy, they need to modify the structure to accommodate and support the change.

Most current strategy frameworks tend to focus on three dimensions:

- *Innovation.* This dimension reflects the organization's pursuit of meaningful and unique innovations.

- *Cost minimization.* This dimension reflects the organization's pursuit of tightly controlled costs.

- *Imitation.* This dimension reflects an organization's attempt to minimize risk and maximize profit opportunities by copying the market leaders.

What organizational structure works best with each?[13] Innovators need the flexibility and free-flowing information of the organic structure, whereas cost minimizers seek the efficiency, stability, and tight controls of the mechanistic structure. Imitators use structural characteristics of both—the mechanistic structure to maintain tight controls and low costs and the organic structure to mimic the industry's innovative directions.

Size and Structure

There's considerable evidence that an organization's size significantly affects its structure.[14] For instance, large organizations—those with 2000 or more employees—tend to have more specialization, departmentalization, centralization, and rules and regulations than do small organizations. However, the relationship is not linear. Rather, beyond a certain point, size becomes a less important influence on structure as an organization grows. Why? Essentially, once an organization has around 2000 employees, it's already fairly mechanistic. Adding 500 employees to an organization with 2000 employees will not have much of an impact. On the other hand, adding 500 employees to an organization that has only 300 members is likely to result in a shift toward a more mechanistic structure.

When Heather Reisman, CEO of Indigo Books & Music, pictured here with former South African President Nelson Mandela, took over Chapters, she had a difficult challenge on her hands. The relatively simple structure of Indigo, which had only 14 stores, was not complex enough to accommodate 90 Chapters stores and the nationwide chain of 210 Coles and SmithBooks stores, as well as Chapters online.

Technology and Structure

Every organization has at least one form of technology to convert its inputs into outputs. For instance, employees at GM Canada's Oshawa, Ontario-based plant build Chevrolet Impala, Chevrolet Monte Carlo, Buick Allure, and Pontiac Grand Prix cars on a standardized assembly line. Employees at FedEx Kinko's produce custom print jobs for individual customers. And employees at Bayer AG make aspirin and other pharmaceutical products using a continuous-flow production line. Each of these organizations uses a different type of technology.

The initial interest in technology as a determinant of structure can be traced to the work of British scholar Joan Woodward.[15] She studied several small manufacturing firms in southern England to determine the extent to which organizational design elements were related to organizational success. Woodward was unable to find any consistent pattern until she segmented the firms into three categories based on the size of their production runs. The three categories, representing three distinct technologies, have increasing levels of complexity and sophistication. The first category, **unit production**, describes the production of items in units or small batches. The second category, **mass production**, describes large-batch manufacturing. Finally, the third and most technically complex group, **process production**, describes the production of items in continuous processes. A summary of her findings is shown in Exhibit 5-6.

Since Woodward's initial work, numerous studies have been done on the technology–structure relationship. These studies generally demonstrate that organizations adapt their structures to their technology.[16] The processes or methods that transform an organization's inputs into outputs differ by their degree of routineness or standardization. In general, the more routine the technology, the more mechanistic the structure can be. Organizations with more nonroutine technology, such as custom furniture building or online education, are more likely to have organic structures because the product delivery cannot be standardized.[17]

Environmental Uncertainty and Structure

In Chapter 2 we discussed the organization's environment and the amount of uncertainty in that environment as constraints on managerial discretion. Why should an organization's structure be affected by its environment? Because of environmental uncertainty! Some organizations face relatively stable and simple environments; others face dynamic and complex environments. Because uncertainty threatens an organization's effectiveness, man-

unit production
The production of items in units or small batches.

mass production
The production of items in large batches.

process production
The production of items in continuous processes.

Exhibit 5-6

Woodward's Findings on Technology, Structure, and Effectiveness

	Unit Production	Mass Production	Process Production
Structural Characteristics	• Low vertical differentiation • Low horizontal differentiation • Low formalization	• Moderate vertical differentiation • High horizontal differentiation • High formalization	• High vertical differentiation • Low horizontal differentiation • Low formalization
Most Effective Structure	• Organic	• Mechanistic	• Organic

Source: Based on J. Woodward, *Industrial Organization: Theory and Practice* (London: Oxford University Press, 1965).

agers will try to minimize it. One way to reduce environmental uncertainty is through adjustments in the organization's structure.[18] The greater the uncertainty, the more an organization needs the flexibility offered by an organic structure. On the other hand, in a stable, simple environment, a mechanistic structure tends to be most effective.

The evidence on the environment–structure relationship helps explain why so many managers today are restructuring their organizations to be lean, fast, and flexible. Global competition, accelerated product innovation by competitors, and increased demands from customers for high quality and faster deliveries are examples of dynamic environmental forces. Mechanistic organizations are not equipped to respond to rapid environmental change and environmental uncertainty. As a result, we are seeing a greater number of organizations designed to be more organic. However, a purely organic organization may not be ideal. One study found that organic structures may work more effectively if managers establish semistructures that govern "the pace, timing, and rhythm of organizational activities and processes." Thus, introducing a bit of structure while keeping most of the flexibility of the organic structure may reduce operating costs.[19]

> **Q&A** 9.9

COMMON ORGANIZATIONAL DESIGNS

Maple Leaf Sports & Entertainment (MLSE) is divided into three operating units: MLSE, Toronto Raptors, and Toronto Maple Leafs. Richard Peddie is the president and CEO for all three units. The Raptors and the Maple Leafs each have separate general managers who manage the day-to-day operations of the team, develop recruiting plans, and oversee training. The general managers report to the CEO, and each general manager has a number of management personnel who report to him. MLSE has a divisional structure, whereby the Raptors, the Maple Leafs, and the Air Canada Centre each operate separately, on a day-to-day basis.

THINK ABOUT IT

Why do organizations vary in the types of structures they have? How do organizations choose their structures? Why does Maple Leaf Sports & Entertainment have the structure it does?

What types of organizational designs exist in small businesses or in big companies such as Ford Canada, Corel, McCain Foods, Procter & Gamble, and eBay? When making organizational design decisions, managers can choose from traditional organizational designs and contemporary organizational designs.

3 Beyond traditional organizational designs, how else can organizations be structured?

Traditional Organizational Designs

In designing a structure to support the efficient and effective accomplishment of organizational goals, managers may choose to follow more traditional organizational designs. These designs— the simple structure, functional structure, and divisional structure—tend to be more mechanistic. Exhibit 5-7 on page 142 summarizes the strengths and weaknesses of each design.

Simple Structure

Most organizations start as entrepreneurial ventures with a simple structure consisting of owners and employees. A **simple structure** is an organizational structure with low departmentalization, wide spans of control, authority centralized in a single person, and little formalization.[20] This structure is most commonly used by small businesses in which the owner and manager are one and the same.

simple structure
An organizational structure with low departmentalization, wide spans of control, authority centralized in a single person, and little formalization.

Most organizations do not remain simple structures. As an organization grows, it generally reaches a point where it has to add employees. As the number of employees rises, the structure tends to become more specialized and formalized. Rules and regulations are introduced, work becomes specialized, departments are created, levels of management are added, and the organization becomes increasingly bureaucratic. At this point, a manager might choose to organize around a functional structure or a divisional structure.

> **Q&A** 9.10

Exhibit 5-7

Strengths and Weaknesses of Common Traditional Organizational Designs

Structure	Strengths	Weaknesses
Simple Structure	Fast; flexible; inexpensive to maintain; clear accountability.	Not appropriate as organization grows; reliance on one person is risky.
Functional Structure	Cost-saving advantages from specialization (economies of scale, minimal duplication of people and equipment) and employees are grouped with others who have similar tasks.	Pursuit of functional goals can cause managers to lose sight of what's best for overall organization; functional specialists become insulated and have little understanding of what other units are doing.
Divisional Structure	Focuses on results—division managers are responsible for what happens to their products and services.	Duplication of activities and resources increases costs and reduces efficiency.

functional structure
An organizational structure that groups similar or related occupational specialties together.

Functional Structure

A **functional structure** is an organizational structure that groups similar or related occupational specialties together. It's the functional approach to departmentalization applied to the entire organization. For instance, Revlon is organized around the functions of operations, finance, human resources, and product research and development.

divisional structure
An organizational structure that consists of separate business units or divisions.

Divisional Structure

The **divisional structure** is an organizational structure that consists of separate business units or divisions.[21] In this structure, each unit or division has relatively limited autonomy, with a division manager responsible for performance and with strategic and operational authority over his or her unit. In divisional structures, however, the parent corporation typically acts as an external overseer to coordinate and control the various divisions, and it often provides support services such as financial and legal. As we noted earlier, Maple Leaf Sports & Entertainment has three divisions, including the two sports teams the Raptors and the Maple Leafs.

Contemporary Organizational Designs

Managers in some contemporary organizations are finding that these traditional hierarchical designs often are not appropriate for the increasingly dynamic and complex environments they face. In response to marketplace demands for being lean, flexible, and innovative, managers are finding creative ways to structure and organize work and to make their organizations more responsive to the needs of customers, employees, and other organizational constituents.[22] For instance, at the Canada Revenue Agency the workforce is spread out, and employees rely on shared workspaces, mobile computing, and virtual private networks to get work done. Nevertheless, work gets done effectively and efficiently.[23] Now, we want to introduce you to some of the newest concepts in organizational design. Exhibit 5-8 summarizes these contemporary organizational designs.

team structure
An organizational structure in which the entire organization is made up of work groups or teams.

Team Structure

In a **team structure**, the entire organization is made up of work groups or teams that perform the organization's work.[24] Needless to say, employee empowerment is crucial in a team structure because there is no line of managerial authority from top to bottom. Rather, employee teams are free to design work in the way they think is best. However, the teams

Exhibit 5-8

Contemporary Organizational Designs

Structure	Description	Advantages	Disadvantages
Team	A structure in which the entire organization is made up of work groups or teams.	Employees are more involved and empowered. Reduced barriers among functional areas.	No clear chain of command. Pressure on teams to perform.
Matrix–Project	Matrix is a structure that assigns specialists from different functional areas to work on projects but who return to their areas when the project is completed. Project is a structure in which employees continuously work on projects. As one project is completed, employees move on to the next project.	Fluid and flexible design that can respond to environmental changes. Faster decision making.	Complexity of assigning people to projects. Task and personality conflicts.
Boundaryless	A structure that is not defined by or limited to artificial horizontal, vertical, or external boundaries; includes virtual, networked, and modular types of organizations.	Highly flexible and responsive. Draws on talent wherever it's found.	Lack of control. Communication difficulties.
Learning Organization	A structure that supports an organization's capacity to continuously adapt and change.	Employees are continuously sharing and applying knowledge. Ability to learn can be a source of sustainable competitive advantage.	Getting employees to share what they know can be difficult. Collaboration conflicts can arise.

are also held responsible for all work and performance results in their respective areas. Let's look at some examples of organizations that are organized around teams.

Whole Foods Market, the largest natural-foods grocer in the United States, opened its first Canadian outlet in Toronto in 2002, its second in North Vancouver in 2004, and its third in Oakville, Ontario, in 2005. The stores are structured around teams.[25] Each Whole Foods store is an autonomous profit centre composed of an average of 10 self-managed teams, each with a designated team leader. The team leaders in each store are a team; store leaders in each region are a team; and the company's six regional presidents are a team. At the Sun Life Assurance Company of Canada (US) office in Wellesley Hills, Massachusetts, customer representatives work in eight-person teams trained to expedite all customer requests. When customers call in, they are not switched from one specialist to another, but to one of the teams who takes care of every aspect of the customer's request.

In large organizations, the team structure complements what is typically a functional or divisional structure. This enables the organization to have the efficiency of a bureaucracy while providing the flexibility that teams provide. To improve productivity at the operating level, for instance, companies such as Toyota's CAPTIN plant (based in Delta, BC), Motorola, and Xerox extensively use self-managed teams. At Saturn and Hewlett-Packard, cross-functional teams are used to design new products or coordinate major projects. Scarborough, Ontario-based Aviva Canada, a property and casualty insurance group, uses a cross-functional team for handling BC wildfire catastrophes. The Cat (which stands for "Catastrophe") team includes specialists in information technology, internal and external communication, tracking, resourcing, and vendor management. Together, team members work to make resolving insurance difficulties after a disaster go much smoother.[26]

Q&A 9.11

Whole Foods Market
www.wholefoodsmarket.com

Acxiom, of Little Rock, Arkansas, needed a new organizational design in order to stay at the cutting edge of its field (data mining). So the company abandoned its old hierarchical structure and adopted a streamlined culture that focuses on teams, such as the Global Data Development team shown here, which meets twice each month. Lee Parrish, leader of another Acxiom team, compared the firm's team structure to the hierarchy at his previous employer: "You had a job title.... Here, you have a role. Instead of a lot of wasted motion, you can reach out to people and spend your time working on proactive solutions to problems."

Matrix and Project Structures

matrix structure
An organizational structure that assigns specialists from different functional departments to work on one or more projects.

Have you ever had to work for two managers at the same time? Was this a positive or negative experience?

Q&A 9.12

Other popular contemporary designs are the matrix and project structures. The **matrix structure** is an organizational structure that assigns specialists from different functional departments to work on one or more projects being led by project managers. Once a project is completed, the specialists return to their functional departments. Exhibit 5-9 shows an example of the matrix structure used in an aerospace firm. Along the top are the familiar organizational functions. The specific projects the firm is currently working on are listed along the left-hand side. Each project is managed by an individual who staffs his or her project with people from each of the functional departments. The addition of this vertical dimension to the traditional horizontal functional departments in effect "weaves together" elements of functional and product departmentalization, creating a matrix arrangement. One other unique aspect of this design is that it creates a *dual chain of command*. It explicitly violates the classical organizing principle of unity of command. How does a matrix structure work in reality?

Employees in a matrix organization have two managers: their functional department manager and their product or project manager, who share authority. The project managers have authority over the functional members who are part of their project team in areas relative to the project's goals. However, decisions such as promotions, salary recommendations, and annual reviews remain the functional manager's responsibility. To work effectively, project and functional managers have to communicate regularly, coordinate work demands on employees, and resolve conflicts together.

Although the matrix structure continues to be an effective organizational structure choice for some organizations, many are using a more "advanced" type of **project structure**, in which employees continuously work on projects. Unlike the matrix structure, a project structure has no formal departments that employees return to at the completion of a project. Instead, employees take their specific skills, abilities, and experiences to other projects. In addition, all work in project structures is performed by teams of employees who become part of a project team because they have the appropriate work skills and abilities. For instance, at Oticon A/S, a Danish hearing-aid manufacturer, there are no departments or employee job titles. All work is project-based, and these project teams form, disband, and form again as the work requires. Employees "join" project teams because they bring needed skills and abilities to that project. Once the project is completed, they move on to the next one.[27]

project structure
An organizational structure in which employees continuously work on projects.

Exhibit 5-9

A Matrix Organization in an Aerospace Firm

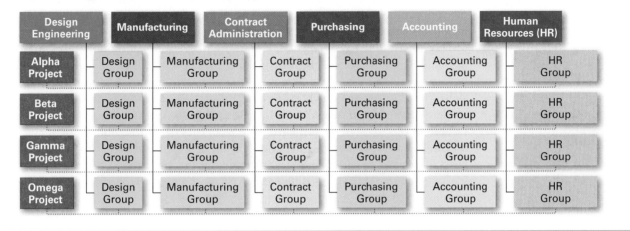

	Design Engineering	Manufacturing	Contract Administration	Purchasing	Accounting	Human Resources (HR)
Alpha Project	Design Group	Manufacturing Group	Contract Group	Purchasing Group	Accounting Group	HR Group
Beta Project	Design Group	Manufacturing Group	Contract Group	Purchasing Group	Accounting Group	HR Group
Gamma Project	Design Group	Manufacturing Group	Contract Group	Purchasing Group	Accounting Group	HR Group
Omega Project	Design Group	Manufacturing Group	Contract Group	Purchasing Group	Accounting Group	HR Group

Project structures tend to be fluid and flexible organizational designs. There is no departmentalization or rigid organizational hierarchy to slow down decision making or taking actions. In this type of structure, managers serve as facilitators, mentors, and coaches. They "serve" the project teams by eliminating or minimizing organizational obstacles and by ensuring that the teams have the resources they need to effectively and efficiently complete their work.

Boundaryless Organizations

Another approach to contemporary organizational design is the concept of a **boundaryless organization**—an organization whose design is not defined by a chain of command, places no limits on spans of control, and replaces departments with empowered teams.[28] The term was coined by Jack Welch, former chair of General Electric (GE), who wanted to eliminate vertical and horizontal boundaries within GE and break down external barriers between the company and its customers and suppliers. This idea may sound odd, yet many successful organizations are finding that they can operate more effectively in today's environment by remaining flexible and *un*structured: that the ideal structure for them is *not* having a rigid, predefined structure. Instead, the boundaryless organization seeks to eliminate the chain of command, to have limitless spans of control, and to replace departments with empowered teams.[29]

What do we mean by "boundaries"? In a typical organization there are internal boundaries—horizontal boundaries imposed by work specialization and departmentalization, and vertical boundaries that separate employees into organizational levels and hierarchies. Then there are external boundaries that separate the organization from its customers, suppliers, and other stakeholders. To minimize or eliminate these boundaries, managers might use virtual, network, or modular organizational structures.

So how does a boundaryless organization operate in practice? GE is made up of a large number of companies including GE Consumer Finance, which provides financial services to consumers and retailers; GE Insurance Solutions, which offers a full range of insurance and investment products; GE Energy, which supplies technology to the energy industry; and NBC Universal Studios, a leading media and entertainment company. One way that the boundaryless organization functions for employees is that anyone working in any division of GE can learn about opportunities available in the other business units, and how to move into those units, if so desired. Outside the company, the boundaryless structure means that some GE customers can send information to the factories to increase inventory when the customer needs more product. Thus, the customer makes a decision about inventory that was once made inside the organization. GE also encourages customers and suppliers to evaluate its service levels, giving direct and immediate feedback to employees.

boundaryless organization
An organization that is not defined by a chain of command, places no limits on spans of control, and replaces departments with empowered teams.

Q&A 9.13

virtual organization
A continually evolving network of independent companies—suppliers, customers, even competitors—linked together to share skills, costs, and access to one another's markets.

iGEN Knowledge Solutions
www.igen.ca

network organization
A small core organization that outsources major business functions.

Virtual Organizations   A **virtual organization** is an organization that consists of a small core of full-time employees that temporarily hires outside specialists to work on opportunities that arise.[30] An example of a virtual organization is StrawberryFrog, an international advertising agency based in Amsterdam. The small administrative staff accesses a network of more than 100 people around the globe to complete advertising projects. By relying on this web of freelancers around the globe, the company enjoys a network of talent without all the overhead and structural complexity of a more traditional organization. The inspiration for this structural approach comes from the film industry. If you look at the film industry, people are essentially "free agents" who move from project to project applying their skills—directing, talent search, costuming, makeup, set design—as needed.

New Westminster, BC-based iGEN Knowledge Solutions uses its virtual form to bring technical solutions to its business clients. iGEN associates work from home offices, connected by wireless technologies, to solve client problems collaboratively. This structure allows faster idea implementation, product development, and service delivery. The company finds it easy to set up operations in different regions of the country without large overhead costs because of its virtual structure.

Network Organizations   Another structural option for managers wanting to minimize or eliminate organizational boundaries is the **network organization**, which is a small core organization that outsources major business functions.[31] This approach allows organizations to concentrate on what they do best and contract out other activities to companies that can do those activities best. Many large organizations use the network structure to outsource manufacturing. Companies like Cisco Systems, Nike, Ericsson, L.L. Bean, and Reebok have found that they can do hundreds of millions of dollars of business without owning manufacturing facilities. For instance, San Jose, California-based Cisco Systems is essentially a research and development company that uses outside suppliers and independent manufacturers to assemble the Internet routers its engineers design. Beaverton, Oregon-based Nike is essentially a product development and marketing company that contracts with outside organizations to manufacture its athletic footwear. Stockholm, Sweden-based Ericsson contracts its manufacturing and even some of its research and development to more cost-effective contractors in New Delhi, Singapore, California, and other global locations.[32]

While many companies use outsourcing, not all are successful at it. Managers should be aware of some of the problems involved in outsourcing, such as the following:

- Choosing the wrong activities to outsource
- Choosing the wrong vendor
- Writing a poor contract
- Failing to consider personnel issues
- Losing control over the activity
- Ignoring the hidden costs
- Failing to develop an exit strategy (for either moving to another vendor or deciding to bring the activity back in-house)

A review of 91 outsourcing activities found that the most likely reasons for an outsourcing venture to fail were writing a poor contract and losing control of the activity.[33] Canadian managers say they are reluctant to outsource.[34] In a 2004 survey of 603 Canadian companies by Ipsos Reid, 60 percent were not eager to ship software development overseas. While a number of managers said

The Rolling Stones is a global business with budgets, profit and loss statements, and a virtual organization of accountants, bankers, lawyers, promoters, and others who manage its various revenue streams from ticket sales, album sales, royalties, merchandise, sponsorships, and other activities. All this is masterminded by Prince Rupert Zu Loewenstein, who has been the band's chief business adviser for more than 30 years. Speaking of the band's legendary leader, Keith Richards told *Fortune* magazine, "Mick likes to run a pretty tight ship."

they were concerned with controlling costs (36 percent), almost the same number said they preferred to keep jobs in Canada (32 percent), and one third were also concerned about losing control of projects that went overseas.

Modular Organizations   The final boundaryless option for managers is similar to the network organization. It's a **modular organization**, which is a manufacturing organization that uses outside suppliers to provide product components or modules that are then assembled into final products.[35] An easy way to understand the modular structure is by using the analogy of building a home.[36] Just like a traditional organizational structure with its fairly stable boundaries, a traditional home is a solid, stable object that takes a long time to build. It's built where it will remain and once it is built, it takes major effort to modify or add to it. On the other hand, the pieces of a modular home are assembled in an off-site location, broken apart, and reassembled on location to meet the owner's needs. Just like that modular home, a modular organization can quickly be redesigned as needed. Automobile manufacturers are leaders in this type of modular organizing. For instance, General Motors (GM) has a modular factory in Brazil where outside suppliers provide engineering and production of entire sections of the cars. The modules are delivered right to the assembly line where a small number of GM employees put them together into finished automobiles.[37]

modular organization
A manufacturing organization that uses outside suppliers to provide product components or modules that are then assembled into final products.

Learning Organizations

The concept of a learning organization does not involve a specific organizational design per se, but instead describes an organizational mindset or philosophy that has significant design implications. What is a **learning organization**? It's an organization that has developed the capacity to continuously learn, adapt, and change.[38] In a learning organization, employees practise knowledge management by continuously acquiring and sharing new knowledge, and by applying that knowledge to making decisions or performing their work. Some organizational theorists go so far as to say that an organization's ability to do this— that is, to learn and to apply that learning—may be the only sustainable source of competitive advantage.[39]

Q&A 9.14

learning organization
An organization that has developed the capacity to continuously learn, adapt, and change.

What does a learning organization look like? As you can see in Exhibit 5-10, the characteristics of a learning organization revolve around organizational design, information sharing, leadership, and organizational culture.

Q&A 9.15

Exhibit 5-10

Characteristics of a Learning Organization

Sources: Based on P. M. Senge, *The Fifth Discipline: The Art and Practice of Learning Organizations* (New York: Doubleday, 1990); and R. M. Hodgetts, F. Luthans, and S. M. Lee, "New Paradigm Organizations: From Total Quality to Learning to World Class," *Organizational Dynamics*, Winter 1994, pp. 4–19.

In a learning organization, it's critical for members to share information and collaborate on work activities throughout the entire organization—across different functional specialties and even at different organizational levels. This can be done by minimizing or eliminating the existing structural and physical boundaries. In this boundaryless environment, employees are free to work together and collaborate in doing the organization's work the best way they can and to learn from each other. Because of this need to collaborate, teams also tend to be an important feature of a learning organization's structural design. Employees work in teams on whatever activities need to be done, and these employee teams are empowered to make decisions regarding their work or resolving issues. With empowered employees and teams, there is little need for managers to direct and control. Instead, managers serve as facilitators, supporters, and advocates for employee teams.

Learning cannot take place without information. For an organization to "learn," information must be shared among members. This means sharing information openly, in a timely manner, and in as accurate a form as possible. Because there are few structural and physical barriers in a learning organization, the environment is conducive to open communication and extensive information sharing.

Leadership also plays an important role as an organization becomes a learning organization. What should leaders in a learning organization do? One of their most important functions is facilitating the creation of a shared vision for the organization's future and then keeping organizational members working toward that vision. In addition, leaders should support and encourage the collaborative environment that is critical to learning. Without strong and committed leadership throughout the organization, it would be extremely difficult to be a learning organization.

Finally, the organizational culture is an important characteristic of a learning organization. In a learning organization, the culture is one in which everyone agrees on a shared vision and everyone recognizes the inherent interrelationships among the organization's processes, activities, functions, and external environment. There is a strong sense of community, caring for each other, and trust. In a learning organization, employees feel free to openly communicate, share, experiment, and learn without fear of criticism or punishment.

A Final Thought

No matter what structural design managers choose for their organization, it should help employees work in the most efficient and effective way possible to meet the organization's goals. After all, the structure is simply a means to an end. To understand your reaction to organizational structure, see *Self-Assessment—What Type of Organizational Structure Do I Prefer?* on pages 150–151, at the end of the chapter.

SUMMARY AND IMPLICATIONS

SNAPSHOT SUMMARY

1 Defining Organizational Structure
Work Specialization
Departmentalization
Chain of Command
Span of Control
Centralization and Decentralization
Formalization

➤

1 **What are the major elements of organizational structure?** Organizational structure is the formal arrangement of jobs within an organization. Organizational structures are determined by six key elements: work specialization, departmentalization, chain of command, span of control, centralization and decentralization, and formalization. Decisions made about these elements define how work is organized; how many employees managers supervise; where in the organization decisions are made; and whether employees follow standardized operating procedures or have greater flexibility in how they do their work. *For Maple Leafs Sports & Entertainment, it makes sense to separate the operation of the two sports teams because of the work specialization involved: The manager of the Raptors would not necessarily make good decisions about what Maple Leafs players should do to improve their game.*

2 **What factors affect organizational structure?** There is no one best organizational structure. The appropriate structure depends on the organization's strategy (innovation, cost minimization, imitation), its size, the technology it uses (unit production, mass production, or process production), and the degree of environmental uncertainty the organization faces. *For Maple Leaf Sports & Entertainment, because hockey and basketball are in two different "industries" with different types of players, it makes sense to organize the teams by industry. However, the teams have more of a mechanistic structure than an organic one. Each team would have a similar organizational structure because size, technology, and environmental uncertainty would not differ significantly for the two teams.*

3 **Beyond traditional organizational designs, how else can organizations be structured?** The traditional structures of organizations are simple, functional, and divisional. More contemporary organizational designs include team structure, matrix and project structures, boundaryless organizations, and learning organizations. *Maple Leaf Sports & Entertainment maintains a traditional structure for its sport teams. It has the opportunity to consider other structures for running the Air Canada Centre, such as a project structure or a boundaryless organization, because events and ticket management can be handled in a variety of different ways.*

Management @ Work

Reading for Comprehension

1. Describe what is meant by the term *organizational design*.

2. In what ways can management departmentalize? When should one approach be considered over the others?

3. What is the difference between a mechanistic and an organic organization?

4. Why is the simple structure inadequate in large organizations?

5. Describe the characteristics of a boundaryless organization structure.

6. Describe the characteristics of a learning organization. What are its advantages?

Linking Concepts to Practice

1. Which do you think is more efficient—a wide or a narrow span of control? Support your decision.

2. "An organization can have no structure." Do you agree or disagree with this statement? Explain.

3. Show how both the functional and matrix structures might create conflict within an organization.

4. Do you think the concept of organizational structure, as described in this chapter, is appropriate for charitable organizations? If yes, which organizational design do you believe to be most appropriate? If no, why not? Explain your position.

5. What effects do you think the characteristics of the boundaryless organization have on employees in today's contemporary organizations?

MANAGEMENT FOR YOU TODAY

Choose an organization for which you have worked. How did the structure of your job and the organization affect your job satisfaction? Did the tasks within your job make sense? In what ways could they be better organized? What structural changes would you make to this organization? Would you consider making this a taller or flatter organization? How would the changes you have proposed improve responsiveness to customers and your job satisfaction?

SELF-ASSESSMENT

What Type of Organizational Structure Do I Prefer?

For each of the following statements, circle your level of agreement or disagreement:[40]

> 1 = Strongly Disagree
> 3 = Neither Agree nor Disagree
> 5 = Strongly Agree

I prefer to work in an organization where:

1. Goals are defined by those at higher levels.   1   2   3   4   5

2. Clear job descriptions exist for every job.   1   2   3   4   5

3. Top management makes important decisions.   1   2   3   4   5

4. Promotions and pay increases are based as much on length of service as on level of performance. 1 2 3 4 5

5. Clear lines of authority and responsibility are established. 1 2 3 4 5

6. My career is pretty well laid out for me. 1 2 3 4 5

7. I have a great deal of job security. 1 2 3 4 5

8. I can specialize. 1 2 3 4 5

9. My boss is readily available. 1 2 3 4 5

10. Organization rules and regulations are clearly specified. 1 2 3 4 5

11. Information rigidly follows the chain of command. 1 2 3 4 5

12. There is a minimal number of new tasks for me to learn. 1 2 3 4 5

13. Work groups incur little turnover in members. 1 2 3 4 5

14. People accept the authority of a leader's position. 1 2 3 4 5

15. I am part of a group whose training and skills are similar to mine. 1 2 3 4 5

Scoring Key

Add up the numbers for each of your responses to get your total score.

Analysis and Interpretation

This instrument measures your preference for working in a mechanistic or an organic organizational structure.

Scores above 60 suggest that you prefer a mechanistic structure. Scores below 45 indicate a preference for an organic structure. Scores between 45 and 60 suggest no clear preference.

Because the trend in recent years has been toward more organic structures, you are more likely to find a good organizational match if you score low on this instrument. However, there are few, if any, pure organic structures. Therefore, very low scores may also mean that you are likely to be frustrated by what you perceive as overly rigid structures of rules, regulations, and boss-centred leadership. In general, however, low scores indicate that you prefer small, innovative, flexible, team-oriented organizations. High scores indicate a preference for stable, rule-oriented, more bureaucratic organizations.

More Self-Assessments

To learn more about your skills, abilities, and interests, take the following self-assessments on your enclosed CD-ROM:

- #4—How Well Do I Handle Ambiguity?
- #35—How Power-Oriented Am I?
- #42—How Willing Am I to Delegate?

WORKING TOGETHER: TEAM-BASED EXERCISE

How Is Your School Organized?

Every university or college displays a specific type of organization structure. For example, if you are a business major, your classes are often housed in a department, school, or faculty of business. But have you ever asked why? Or is it something you just take for granted?

In Chapter 3 you had an opportunity to assess your college or university's strengths, weaknesses, and competitive advantage and see how these fit into its strategy. Now, in this chapter we have argued that structure follows strategy.

Given your analysis in Chapter 3 (if you have not done so, you may want to refer to page 95 for the strategy part of this exercise), analyze your college or university's overall structure in terms of its degree of formalization, centralization/decentralization, and complexity. Furthermore, look at the departmentalization that exists. Is your college or university more organic or mechanistic? Now analyze how well your college or university's structure fits with its strategy. Do the same thing for your college or university's size, technology, and environment. That is, assess its size, degree of technological routineness, and environmental uncertainty. Based on these assessments, what kind of structure would you predict your college or university to have? Does it have this structure now? Compare your findings with those of other classmates. Are there similarities in how each viewed the college or university? Differences? To what do you attribute these findings?

ETHICAL DILEMMA EXERCISE

Orders from the Top

Is a manager acting unethically by simply following orders within the chain of command? One recent survey of human resource managers found that 52 percent of the respondents felt some pressure to bend ethical rules, often because of orders from above or to achieve ambitious goals. This might happen in any organization. At WorldCom, for example, Betty Vinson was a senior manager when she and others received orders, through the chain of command, to slash expenses through improper accounting. She argued against the move. Her manager said he had also objected and was told this was a one-time "fix" to make WorldCom's finances look better. Vinson reluctantly agreed, but she felt guilty and told her manager she wanted to resign. A senior executive persuaded her to stay, and she continued following orders to fudge the accounting.

Soon Vinson realized that the figures would need fudging for some time. After investigators started to probe WorldCom's finances, she and others cooperated with regulators and prosecutors. Ultimately, the company was forced into bankruptcy. Some managers were indicted; some (including Vinson) pleaded guilty to conspiracy and fraud.[41]

Imagine that you are a salesperson for a high-tech company. Your manager invites you to an expensive restaurant where she is entertaining several colleagues and their spouses. The manager orders you to put the meal on your expense account as a customer dinner. She says she will approve the expense so you are reimbursed, and higher-level managers will not know that managers and their spouses were in attendance. What would you do? (Review this chapter's Chain of Command section, on pages 133–134, as you consider your decision.)

CASE APPLICATION

Indigo Books & Music

Before 2001 there were two big-box bookstore chains in Canada—Chapters and Indigo.[42] Indigo was formed in 1996 by Heather Reisman, who left her job as president of Cott, the beverage supplier, to found Indigo. It was the first book retail chain to add music, gifts, and licensed cafés to store locations. By 2000, the chain had expanded to 14 locations across Canada. The other large chain, Chapters, was formed in 1995 with the merger of Canada's then two largest bookstore chains—Coles and SmithBooks. In 2001, Reisman pulled a shocking coup when her company took over the much bigger Chapters chain. Chapters' losses were crippling the company, and its shareholders quickly approved the takeover bid.

What followed for Reisman was the task of merging the two organizations into one. Indigo and Chapters both had similar organizational structures—a functional-based design. Indigo's corporate structure, for instance, consisted of departments such as marketing, human resources, and retail. However, the new organization suddenly had 90 big-box stores and close to 7000 employees. Moreover, with the takeover,

Indigo gained control of the nationwide chain of 210 Coles and SmithBooks stores, as well as a new Internet division, Chapters online. The structure of the newly merged organization had to change in order to incorporate these new businesses.

The combined company, Indigo Books & Music, is now Canada's top bookseller. It has 250 stores spread throughout the country's provinces that sell books, magazines, CDs, and other items. Making the combined organization run efficiently has been a major challenge for Reisman. Indigo lost approximately $48 million in 2002 even as the number of employees grew by 26 percent. But results three years later (2005) showed significant improvements, with the company posting $25.3 million in net earnings.

Reisman must continue to address the issue of keeping the company profitable in a challenging retail climate. She wonders whether there were other, perhaps better, ways to have combined Indigo and Chapters than what she did. What advice might you give her concerning her questions?

A Learning Organization at Svenska

Svenska Handelsbanken, Sweden's premier bank, is one of the largest banks in the Nordic region. Pär Boman, Svenska's president and group chief executive, oversees a business that is organized around a decentralized structure. This structure has a network consisting of hundreds of branches in Sweden, Denmark, Finland, Norway, and Great Britain, as well as those located in 14 nonEuropean countries such as China, Poland, and Russia.[43] Boman believes that the bank's 30-plus years of developing its branch network have allowed it to consistently grow market share and achieve a return on equity that has been above the average of its competitors. Now these competitors are starting to copy Svenska's structure in an attempt to model the bank's success. But Boman believes the bank's competitive advantage is not simply from having more branches. Rather, he believes it comes from the degree of autonomy that branch managers have.

Svenska's branch managers can choose their customers and product offerings. They can also set staffing numbers and decide salary levels at their branch. All customers, private and corporate, no matter what their size, are the sole responsibility of the branch. That means, for example, that even a large global corporation like Volvo is managed by a branch bank operation. Yet, to better facilitate customer service, each branch office can buy specialized services it may need in serving such a large customer. Each branch manager is also responsible for branch performance, which is measured by a ratio of costs divided by revenues. At Svenska, this measure is used to benchmark every branch against each other. If a branch starts underperforming, the regional office will offer consultative services about what other branches are doing successfully. To stop predatory competition among its own branches, the company has set up strict geographical boundaries. Svenska's number of centralized staff is a relatively small percentage of what its competitors have, and guidelines from headquarters are few and seldom issued. The bank's flat management structure and emphasis on personal responsibility and consensus approach are well suited to the Swedish culture.

Boman wants to continue to build the learning organization the bank has started. He wants to improve its capacity to continuously learn, adapt, and change. That's an interesting goal for a 130-year-old bank that has proven to be successful in the industry.

Questions

1. What do you see as the advantages and disadvantages of Svenska Handelsbanken's structure?

2. Do you believe such a structure could work effectively in other cultures, such as that of the United States, in which there is less emphasis placed on consensus-building?

3. What do you believe Pär Boman could do to enhance the learning organization concept at Svenska?

Delegating

About the Skill

Managers get things done through other people. Because there are limits to any manager's time and knowledge, effective managers need to understand how to delegate. *Delegation* is the assignment of authority to another person to carry out specific duties. It allows an employee to make some of the decisions. Delegation should not be confused with participation. In participative decision making, there is a sharing of authority. In delegation, employees make decisions on their own.

Steps in Developing the Skill

A number of actions differentiate the effective delegator from the ineffective delegator. You can be more effective at delegating if you use the following five suggestions:[44]

1. **Clarify the assignment.** Determine what is to be delegated and to whom. You need to identify the person who is most capable of doing the task and then determine whether or not he or she has the time and motivation to do the task. If you have a willing and able employee, it's

your responsibility to provide clear information on what is being delegated, the results you expect, and any time or performance expectations you may have. Unless there is an overriding need to adhere to specific methods, you should delegate only the results expected. Get agreement on what is to be done and the results expected, but let the employee decide the best way to complete the task.

2. **Specify the employee's range of discretion.** Every situation of delegation comes with constraints. Although you are delegating to an employee the authority to perform some task or tasks, you are not delegating unlimited authority. You are delegating authority to act on certain issues within certain parameters. You need to specify what those parameters are so that employees know, without any doubt, the range of their discretion.

3. **Allow the employee to participate.** One of the best ways to decide how much authority will be necessary to accomplish a task is to allow the employee who will be held accountable for that task to participate in that decision. Be aware, however, that allowing employees to participate can present its own set of potential problems as a result of employees' self-interests and biases in evaluating their own abilities.

4. **Inform others about the delegation.** Delegation should not take place behind the scenes. Not only do the manager and employee need to know specifically what has been delegated and how much authority has been given, but so does anyone else who is likely to be affected by the employee's decisions and actions. This includes people inside and outside the organization. Essentially, you need to communicate what has been delegated (the task and amount of authority) and to whom.

5. **Establish feedback channels.** To delegate without establishing feedback controls is to invite problems. The establishment of controls to monitor the employee's performance increases the likelihood that important problems will be identified and that the task will be completed on time and to the desired specifications. Ideally, these controls should be determined at the time of the initial assignment. Agree on a specific time for the completion of the task and then set progress dates when the employee will report back on how well he or she is doing and any major problems that may have arisen. These controls can be supplemented with periodic checks to ensure that authority guidelines are not being abused, organizational policies are being followed, proper procedures are being met, and the like.

Practising the Skill

Ricky Lee is the manager of the contracts group of a large regional office-supply distributor. His manager, Anne Zumwalt, has asked him to prepare by the end of the month the department's new procedures manual that will outline the steps followed in negotiating contracts with office products manufacturers who supply the organization's products. Because Ricky has another major project he is working on, he went to Anne and asked her if it would be possible to assign the rewriting of the procedures manual to Bill Harmon, one of his employees who has worked in the contracts group for about three years. Anne said she had no problems with Ricky reassigning the project as long as Bill knew the parameters and the expectations for the completion of the project. Ricky is preparing for his meeting in the morning with Bill regarding this assignment. Prepare an outline of what Ricky should discuss with Bill to ensure the new procedures manual meets expectations.

CHAPTER

6

Communication and Information Technology

How do I communicate effectively?

1. What are the functions of communication?
2. Why does communication break down?
3. How does communication flow in organizations?
4. How does information technology affect organizations?

Communication is an important part of Rick Thomas' job with the City of Richmond, BC.

As manager, People & Organization Development, Thomas is responsible for encouraging the city's employees to sign up for training and development courses that will help them further their careers. Because all of the employees work within a relatively limited geographical area, Thomas has more flexibility in how he communicates his training messages. Prior to working for the City of Richmond, Thomas worked for a province-wide operation where he could not often meet with managers face-to-face to discuss training opportunities. This made his job more challenging.

Thomas understands that communicating is not always an obvious and straightforward task. He notes that one of the major barriers to effective communication for the City of Richmond is that it is a multi-cultured organization; each work group (e.g., fire, RCMP, public works, parks board, and professional staff) has its own workplace culture and norms. This means that different strategies need to be used in communicating with these different groups. "It's important for leaders and managers to look at how we communicate," Thomas says, "and learn more about each other's perspectives and perceptions so that we can communicate more effectively."

THINK ABOUT IT

What makes communication work and why does it fail? Put yourself in Rick Thomas' shoes. How can he be sure to communicate effectively with the different work groups of the City of Richmond?

Communication between managers and employees provides the information necessary to get work done effectively and efficiently in organizations. As such, there is no doubt that communication is fundamentally linked to managerial performance.[1] In this chapter, we present basic concepts in managerial communication. We describe the interpersonal communication process, distortions that can happen in interpersonal communication, the channels of communication, as well as the barriers to effective interpersonal communication and ways to overcome those barriers. We also look at how communication flows in organizations, communication networks, and the effects of information technology on organizational communication.

UNDERSTANDING COMMUNICATION

If you have not studied communication before, you might think it's a pretty normal process, and that almost anyone can communicate effectively without much thought. So many

1 What are the functions of communication?

things can go wrong with communication, though, that it's clear not everyone thinks about how to communicate effectively. For instance, unlike the character Bill Murray plays in *Groundhog Day*, Neal L. Patterson, chair and CEO of Cerner, a health care software development company based in Kansas City, probably wishes he *could* do over one particular day. Upset with the fact that employees did not seem to be putting in enough hours, he sent an angry and emotional email to about 400 company managers that said, in part:

> We are getting less than 40 hours of work from a large number of our K.C.-based EMPLOYEES. The parking lot is sparsely used at 8 a.m.; likewise at 5 p.m. As managers, you either do not know what your EMPLOYEES are doing, or you do not CARE. You have created expectations on the work effort which allowed this to happen inside Cerner, creating a very unhealthy environment. In either case, you have a problem and you will fix it or I will replace you ....I will hold you accountable. You have allowed things to get to this state. You have two weeks. Tick, tock.[2]

Patterson had a message, and he wanted to get it out to his managers. Although the email was meant only for the company's managers, it was leaked and posted on a Yahoo! discussion site. The tone of the email surprised industry analysts, investors, and, of course, Cerner's managers and employees. The company's stock price dropped 22 percent over the next 3 days. Patterson apologized to his employees and acknowledged, "I lit a match and started a firestorm." This is a good example of why it's important for individuals to understand the impact of communication.

The importance of effective communication for managers cannot be overemphasized for one specific reason: Everything a manager does involves communicating. Not *some* things, but everything! A manager cannot make a decision without information. That information has to be communicated. Once a decision is made, communication must again take place. Otherwise, no one would know that a decision was made. The best idea, the most creative suggestion, the best plan, or the most effective job redesign cannot take shape without communication. Managers need effective communication skills. We are not suggesting that good communication skills alone make a successful manager. We can say, however, that ineffective communication skills can lead to a continuous stream of problems for a manager.

What Is Communication?

Communication is the transfer and understanding of meaning. The first thing to note about this definition is the emphasis on the *transfer* of meaning. This means that if no information or ideas have been conveyed, communication has not taken place. The speaker who is not heard or the writer who is not read has not communicated.

More importantly, however, communication involves the *understanding* of meaning. For communication to be successful, the meaning must be imparted and understood. A letter written in Portuguese addressed to a person who does not read Portuguese cannot be considered communication until it's translated into a language the person does read and understand. Perfect communication, if such a thing existed, would be the receiver's understanding a transmitted thought or idea exactly as it was intended by the sender.

Another point to keep in mind is that *good* communication is often erroneously defined by the communicator as *agreement* with the message instead of clearly *understanding* the message.[3] If someone disagrees with us, many of us assume that the person just did not fully understand our position. In other words, many of us define good communication as having someone accept our views. But I can clearly understand what you mean and just *not* agree with what you say. In fact, many times when a conflict has gone on for a long time, people will say it's because the parties are not communicating effectively. That assumption reflects the tendency to think that effective communication equals agreement.

The final point we want to make about communication is that it encompasses both **interpersonal communication**—communication between two or more people—and **organizational communication**—all the patterns, networks, and systems of communication within an organization. Both these types of communication are important to managers in organizations.

Cerner Corporation
www.cerner.com

communication
The transfer and understanding of meaning.

Q&A 10.1

interpersonal communication
Communication between two or more people.

organizational communication
All the patterns, networks, and systems of communication within an organization.

Functions of Communication

Why is communication important to managers and organizations? It serves four major functions: control, motivation, emotional expression, and information.[4]

Communication acts to *control* member behaviour in several ways. As we know from Chapter 5, organizations have authority hierarchies and formal guidelines that employees are required to follow. For instance, when employees are required to communicate any job-related grievance first to their immediate manager, or to follow their job description, or to comply with company policies, communication is being used to control. But informal communication also controls behaviour. When work groups tease or harass a member who is working too hard or producing too much (making the rest of the group look bad), they are informally controlling the member's behaviour.

Communication encourages *motivation* by clarifying to employees what is to be done, how well they are doing, and what can be done to improve performance if it's not up to par. As employees set specific goals, work toward those goals, and receive feedback on their progress, communication is required. Managers motivate more effectively if they show support for the employee when communicating constructive feedback, rather than mere criticism.

For many employees, their work group is a primary source of social interaction. The communication that takes place within the group is a fundamental mechanism by which members share frustrations and feelings of satisfaction. Communication, therefore, provides a release for *emotional expression* of feelings and for fulfillment of social needs.

If you have ever had a bad haircut, you have probably never forgotten the experience. And you might never have returned to the stylist again. Dorys Belanger, owner of Montreal-based Au Premier Spa Urbain, says that a bad haircut should not be blamed on the stylist alone. Good communication is "50 percent up to the hairdresser, 50 percent up to the client," she says.

Finally, individuals and groups need information to get things done in organizations. Communication provides that *information.*

No one of these four functions is more important than the others. For groups to work effectively, they need to maintain some form of control over members, motivate members to perform, provide a means for emotional expression, and make decisions. You can assume that almost every communication interaction that takes place in a group or organization is fulfilling one or more of these four functions.

INTERPERSONAL COMMUNICATION

In his job with the City of Richmond, Rick Thomas thinks a lot about how best to deliver messages to the people with whom he works. His preferred way of dealing with most communication issues is to face, particularly when he has a difficult message to convey. He also likes to give congratulatory messages face to face, but will use the telephone if necessary. He avoids email for messages that he feels should be given personally, relying on email more when there is need for a physical record of the communication. He remarks that "email has become a communication vehicle, although that wasn't why it was developed initially."

Thomas also notes that he tries to be aware that people prefer different styles of communication. Some people are far more comfortable with electronic communication than others, for instance. He also tries to remember that people with different backgrounds don't always hear messages the same way, so he sometimes adjusts the way he communicates to fit the needs of his audience.

THINK ABOUT IT
When is face-to-face communication more effective than email? Is Rick Thomas wise to emphasize face-to-face communication?

2 Why does communication break down?

message
A purpose to be conveyed.

encoding
Converting a message into symbols.

channel
The medium a message travels along.

decoding
A receiver's translation of a sender's message.

communication process
The seven elements involved in transferring meaning from one person to another.

noise
Disturbances that interfere with the transmission, receipt, or feedback of a message.

Before communication can take place, a purpose, expressed as a **message** to be conveyed, must exist. It passes between a source (the sender) and a receiver. The message is converted into symbols (called **encoding**) and passed by way of some medium (**channel**) to the receiver, who translates the sender's message (called **decoding**). The result is the transfer of meaning from one person to another.[5] Exhibit 6-1 illustrates the seven elements of the interpersonal **communication process**: the sender, the message, encoding, the channel, the receiver, decoding, and feedback. In addition, note that **noise**—disturbances that interfere with the transmission, receipt, or feedback of a message—can affect the entire process. Typical examples of noise include external factors such as illegible print, phone static, or background sounds of machinery or co-workers. However, noise can be the result of internal factors such as inattention of the receiver, as well as perceptions and personality traits of the receiver. Remember that anything that interferes with understanding can be noise, and noise can create distortion at any point in the communication process.

How Distortions Can Happen in Interpersonal Communication

Distortions can happen with the sender, the message, the channel, the receiver, or the feedback loop. Let's look at each.

Sender

A *sender* initiates a message by *encoding* a thought. Four conditions influence the effectiveness of that encoded message: the skills, attitudes, and knowledge of the sender, and the social–cultural system. How? We will use ourselves, as your textbook authors, as an example. If we don't have the required skills, our message won't reach you, the reader, in the form desired. Our success in communicating to you depends on our writing skills. In addition, any preexisting ideas (attitudes) that we may have about numerous topics will affect how we communicate. For instance, our attitudes about managerial ethics or the importance of managers to organizations influence our writing. Next, the amount of knowledge we have about a subject affects the message(s) we are transferring. We cannot communicate what we don't know; and if our knowledge is too extensive, it's possible that our writing won't be understood by the readers. Finally, the socio-cultural system in which we live influences us as communication senders. Our beliefs and values (all part of culture) act to influence what and how we communicate.

Exhibit 6-1

The Interpersonal Communication Process

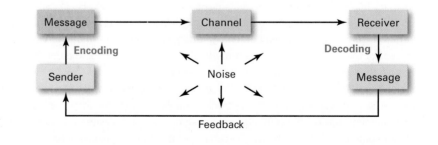

Message

The *message* itself can distort the communication process, regardless of the kinds of supporting tools or technologies used to convey it. A message is the actual physical product encoded by the source. It can be a written document, a speech, or even the gestures and facial expressions we make. The message is affected by the symbols used to transfer meaning (words, pictures, numbers, etc.), the content of the message itself, and the decisions that the sender makes in selecting and arranging both the symbols and the content. Noise can distort the communication process in any of these areas.

Channel

Your instructor chooses to interact with all students via email, rather than hold office hours. How effective do you think email is as the channel of communication in this context?

The *channel* chosen to communicate the message also has the potential to be affected by noise. Whether it's a face-to-face conversation, an email message, or a company-wide memo, distortions can, and do, occur. Managers need to recognize that certain channels are more appropriate for certain messages. (Think back to how Cerner's CEO chose to communicate his frustration with his managers by email and whether that was an appropriate choice.) Obviously, if the office is on fire, a memo to convey the fact is inappropriate. And if something is important, such as an employee's performance appraisal, a manager might want to use multiple channels—perhaps an oral review followed by a written letter summarizing the points. Using multiple channels to communicate a message decreases the potential for distortion. In general, the type of channel chosen will affect the extent to which accurate emotional expression can be communicated. For instance, Individuals often make stronger negative statements when using email than they would in holding a face-to-face conversation.[6] Additionally, individuals often give little thought to how their emails might be interpreted, and assume that their intent will be readily apparent to the recipient, even though this is not always the case.[7]

Receiver

The *receiver* is the individual to whom the message is directed. Before the message can be received, however, the symbols in it must be translated into a form that the receiver can understand. This is the *decoding* of the message. Just as the sender was limited by his or her skills, attitudes, knowledge, and socio-cultural system, so is the receiver. And just as the

Communication channels have multiplied with the spread of new technologies such as Wi-Fi, which provides wireless high-speed Internet access. At the more than 160 warehouse-type stores operated by BJ's Wholesale Club, for instance, managers have saved time and money by switching to Wi-Fi for their internal communications. The devices mean that managers like John Barrows can talk to customers, suppliers, or even his manager without having to hike across the aisles to the store's front-office telephone.

sender must be skillful in writing or speaking, so the receiver must be skillful in reading or listening. A person's knowledge influences his or her ability to receive. Moreover, the receiver's attitudes and socio-cultural background can distort the message. *Managing Workforce Diversity—The Communication Styles of Men and Women* considers how men and women might hear messages differently, on page 184, at the end of the chapter.

Feedback Loop

The final link in the communication process is a *feedback loop.* Feedback returns the message to the sender and provides a check on whether understanding has been achieved. Because feedback can be transmitted along the same types of channels as the original message, it faces the same potential for distortion. Many receivers forget that there is a responsibility involved in communication: to give feedback. For instance, if you sit in a boring lecture but never discuss with the instructor ways that the delivery could be improved, you have not engaged in communication with your instructor.

When either the sender or the receiver fails to engage in the feedback process, the communication is effectively one-way communication. Two-way communication involves both talking and listening. Many managers communicate badly because they fail to use two-way communication.[8]

Channels for Communicating Interpersonally

Q&A 10.2

Are there any guidelines on which communication channel is best for a given circumstance?

Managers have a wide variety of communication channels from which to choose. These include face-to-face, telephone, group meetings, formal presentations, memos, postal (snail) mail, fax machines, employee publications, bulletin boards, other company publications, audio- and videotapes, hot lines, email, computer conferences, voice mail, teleconferences, and videoconferences. All of these communication channels include oral or written symbols, or both. How do you know which to use? Managers can use 12 questions to help them evaluate appropriate communication channels for different circumstances.[9]

1. *Feedback.* How quickly can the receiver respond to the message?

2. *Complexity capacity.* Can the method effectively process complex messages?

3. *Breadth potential.* How many different messages can be transmitted using this method?

4. *Confidentiality.* Can communicators be reasonably sure their messages are received only by those for whom they are intended?

5. *Encoding ease.* Can the sender easily and quickly use this channel?

6. *Decoding ease.* Can the receiver easily and quickly decode messages?

7. *Time–space constraint.* Do senders and receivers need to communicate at the same time and in the same space?

8. *Cost.* How much does it cost to use this method?

9. *Interpersonal warmth.* How well does this method convey interpersonal warmth?

10. *Formality.* Does this method have the needed amount of formality?

11. *Scanability.* Does this method allow the message to be easily browsed or scanned for relevant information?

12. *Time of consumption.* Does the sender or receiver exercise the most control over when the message is dealt with?

Exhibit 6-2 provides a comparison of the various communication channels based on these 12 criteria. Which channel a manager ultimately chooses should reflect the needs of the

Exhibit 6-2

Comparison of Communication Channels

Criteria

Channel	Feedback Potential	Complexity Capacity	Breadth Potential	Confiden-tiality	Encoding Ease	Decoding Ease	Time-Space Constraint	Cost	Interpersonal Warmth	Formality	Scan-ability	Consumption Time
Face-to-face	1	1	1	1	1	1	1	2	1	4	4	S/R
Telephone	1	4	2	2	1	1	3	3	2	4	4	S/R
Group meetings	2	2	2	4	2	2	1	1	2	3	4	S/R
Formal presentations	4	2	2	4	3	2	1	1	3	3	5	Sender
Memos	4	4	2	3	4	3	5	3	5	2	1	Receiver
Postal mail	5	3	3	2	4	3	5	3	4	1	1	Receiver
Fax	3	4	2	4	3	3	5	3	3	3	1	Receiver
Publications	5	4	2	5	5	3	5	2	4	1	1	Receiver
Bulletin boards	4	5	1	5	3	2	2	4	5	3	1	Receiver
Audio-/videotapes	4	4	3	5	4	2	3	2	3	3	5	Receiver
Hot lines	2	5	2	2	3	1	4	2	3	3	4	Receiver
Email	3	4	1	2	3	2	4	2	4	3	4	Receiver
Computer conference	1	2	2	4	3	2	3	2	3	3	4	S/R
Voice mail	2	4	2	1	2	1	5	3	2	4	4	Receiver
Teleconference	2	3	2	5	2	2	2	2	3	3	5	S/R
Videoconference	3	3	2	4	2	2	2	1	2	3	5	S/R

Note: Ratings are on a 1–5 scale where 1 = high and 5 = low. Consumption time refers to who controls the reception of communication. S/R means the sender and receiver share control.

Source: P. G. Clampitt, *Communicating for Managerial Effectiveness* (Newbury Park, CA: Sage Publications, 1991), p. 136.

sender, the attributes of the message, the attributes of the channel, and the needs of the receiver. For instance, if you need to communicate to an employee the changes being made in her job, face-to-face communication would be a better choice than a memo since you want to be able to address immediately any questions and concerns that she might have. To find out more about face-to-face communication, see *Self-Assessment—What's My Face-to-Face Communication Style?* on pages 178–180, at the end of the chapter.

We cannot leave the topic of interpersonal communication without looking at the role of **nonverbal communication**—that is, communication transmitted without words. Some of the most meaningful communications are neither spoken nor written. A loud siren or a red light at an intersection tells you something without words. When an instructor is teaching a class, she does not need words to tell her that her students are bored when their eyes are glazed over or they begin to read the school newspaper in the middle of class. Similarly, when students start putting their papers, notebooks, and books away, the message is clear: Class time is about over. The size of a person's office or the clothes he or she wears also convey messages to others. These are all forms of nonverbal communication. The best-known types of nonverbal communication are body language and verbal intonation.

nonverbal communication
Communication transmitted without words.

body language
Gestures, facial expressions, and other body movements that convey meaning.

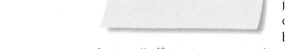
Does body language really affect how communication is received?

Body language refers to gestures, facial expressions, and other body movements that convey meaning. A person frowning "says" something different from one who is smiling. Hand motions, facial expressions, and other gestures can communicate emotions or temperaments such as aggression, fear, shyness, arrogance, joy, and anger. Knowing the meaning behind someone's body moves and learning how to put forth your best body language can help you personally and professionally.[10] For instance, studies indicate that those who maintain eye contact while speaking are viewed with more credibility than those whose eyes wander. People who make eye contact are also deemed more competent than those who do not.

Be aware that what is communicated nonverbally may be quite different from what is communicated verbally. A manager may say it's a good time to discuss a raise, but then keep looking at the clock. This nonverbal signal may indicate that the manager has other things to do right now. Thus actions can speak louder (and more accurately) than words.

A variety of popular books have been written to help one interpret body language. However, do use some care when interpreting their messages. For instance, while it is often thought that crossing one's arms in front of one's chest shows resistance to a message, it might also mean the person is feeling cold.

verbal intonation
An emphasis given to words or phrases that conveys meaning.

Verbal intonation (more appropriately called *paralinguistics*) refers to the emphasis someone gives to words or phrases that convey meaning. To illustrate how intonations can change the meaning of a message, consider the student who asks the instructor a question. The instructor replies, "What do you mean by that?" The student's reaction will vary, depending on the tone of the instructor's response. A soft, smooth vocal tone conveys interest and creates a different meaning from one that is abrasive and puts a strong emphasis on saying the last word. Most of us would view the first intonation as coming from someone sincerely interested in clarifying the student's concern, whereas the second suggests that the person is defensive or aggressive.

The fact that every oral communication also has a nonverbal message cannot be overemphasized. Why? Because the nonverbal component usually carries the greatest impact. "It's not *what* you said, but *how* you said it." People respond to *how* something is said as well as *what* is said. Managers should remember this as they communicate.

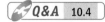
Q&A 10.3

Barriers to Effective Interpersonal Communication

In addition to the general distortions identified in the communication process, managers face other barriers to effective interpersonal communication.

Q&A 10.4

Filtering

Filtering is the deliberate manipulation of information to make it appear more favourable to the receiver. For example, when a person tells his or her manager what the manager wants to hear, that individual is filtering information. Does this happen much in organizations? Yes, it does! As information is communicated up through organizational levels, it's condensed and synthesized by senders so those on top don't become overloaded with information. Those doing the condensing filter communications through their personal interests and their perceptions of what is important.

The extent of filtering tends to be a function of the number of vertical levels in the organization and the organizational culture. The more vertical levels there are in an organization, the more opportunities there are for filtering. As organizations become less dependent on strict hierarchical arrangements and instead use more collaborative, cooperative work arrangements, information filtering may become less of a problem. In addition, the ever-increasing use of email to communicate in organizations reduces filtering because communication is more direct as intermediaries are bypassed. Finally, the organizational culture encourages or discourages filtering by the type of behaviour it rewards. The more that organizational rewards emphasize style and appearance, the more managers will be motivated to filter communications in their favour.

Filtering, or shaping information to make it look good to the receiver, might not always be intentional. For John Seral, vice-president and chief information officer of GE Aviation and GE Energy, the problem was that "when the CEO asked how the quarter was looking, he got a different answer depending on whom he asked." Seral solved the problem by building a continuously updated database of the company's most important financial information that gives not just the CEO but also 300 company managers instant access to sales and operating figures on their PCs and BlackBerrys. Instead of dozens of analysts compiling the information, the new system requires only six.

Emotions

How a receiver feels when a message is received influences how he or she interprets it. You will often interpret the same message differently, depending on whether you are happy or upset. Extreme emotions are most likely to hinder effective communication. In such instances, we often disregard our rational and objective thinking processes and substitute emotional judgments. It's best to avoid reacting to a message when you are upset because you are not likely to be thinking clearly.

filtering
The deliberate manipulation of information to make it appear more favourable to the receiver.

Information Overload

A marketing manager goes on a week-long trip to Spain and does not have access to his email. On his return, he is faced with 1000 email messages. It's not possible to fully read and respond to each and every one of those messages without facing **information overload**—when the information we have to work with exceeds our processing capacity. Today's typical executive frequently complains of information overload. Email has added considerably to the number of hours worked per week, according to a recent study by Christina Cavanagh, professor of management communications at the University of Western Ontario's Richard Ivey School of Business.[11] Researchers calculate that 141 billion email messages circulate the globe each day. Five years ago, that number was 5.1 billion email messages.[12] One researcher suggests that knowledge workers devote about 28 percent of their days to email.[13] The demands of keeping up with email, phone calls, faxes, meetings, and professional reading create an onslaught of data that is nearly impossible to process and assimilate. What happens when individuals have more information than they can sort and use? They tend to select out, ignore, pass over, or forget information. Or they may put off further processing until the overload situation is over. Regardless, the result is lost information and less effective communication.

information overload
When the information we have to work with exceeds our processing capacity.

 **Christina Cavanagh**
www.christinacavanagh.com

 **Q&A** 10.5

Selective Perception

Individuals don't see reality; rather, they interpret what they see and call it "reality." These interpretations are based on an individual's needs, motivations, experience, background, and other personal characteristics. Individuals also project their interests and expectations when they are listening to others. For example, the employment interviewer who believes that young people spend too much time on leisure and social activities will have a hard time believing that young job applicants will work long hours.

Defensiveness

When people feel that they are being threatened, they tend to react in ways that reduce their ability to achieve mutual understanding. That is, they become defensive—engaging in behaviours such as verbally attacking others, making sarcastic remarks, being overly judgmental, and questioning others' motives.[14] When individuals interpret another's message as threatening, they often respond in ways that hinder effective communication.

Language

Words mean different things to different people. Age, education, and cultural background are three of the more obvious variables that influence the language a person uses and the definitions he or she gives to words. News anchor Peter Mansbridge and rap artist Nelly both speak English, but the language each uses is vastly different.

In an organization, employees typically come from diverse backgrounds and have different patterns of speech. Even employees who work for the same organization but in different departments often have different **jargon**—specialized terminology or technical language that members of a group use to communicate among themselves. Keep in mind that while we may speak the same language, our use of that language is far from uniform. Senders tend to assume that the words and phrases they use mean the same to the receiver as they do to them. This, of course, is incorrect and creates communication barriers. Knowing how each of us modifies the language would help minimize those barriers.

jargon
Specialized terminology or technical language that members of a group use to communicate among themselves.

National Culture

Communication differences can also arise from the different languages that individuals use to communicate and the national cultures they are part of. Interpersonal communication is not conducted the same way around the world. For example, let's compare countries that place a higher value on individualism (such as Canada) with countries in which the emphasis is on collectivism (such as Japan).[15]

In Canada, communication patterns tend to be oriented to the individual and clearly spelled out. Canadian managers rely heavily on memos, announcements, position papers, and other formal forms of communication to state their positions on issues. Supervisors may hoard information in an attempt to make themselves look good and as a way of persuading their employees to accept decisions and plans. For their own protection, lower-level employees often engage in this practice as well.

In collectivist countries, such as Japan, there is more interaction for its own sake. The Japanese manager, in contrast to the Canadian manager, engages in extensive verbal consultation with subordinates over an issue first and draws up a formal document later to outline the agreement that was made. The Japanese value decisions by consensus, and open communication is an inherent part of the work setting. Also, face-to-face communication is encouraged.

Cultural differences can affect the way a manager chooses to communicate. These differences undoubtedly can be a barrier to effective communication if not recognized and taken into consideration.

Overcoming the Barriers

What can we do to overcome barriers to communication? The following suggestions should help make your interpersonal communication more effective.

Use Feedback

Many communication problems can be directly attributed to misunderstanding and inaccuracies. These problems are less likely to occur if individuals use the feedback loop in the communication process, either verbally or nonverbally.

If a speaker asks a receiver, "Did you understand what I said?" the response represents feedback. Good feedback should include more than yes-and-no answers. The speaker can ask a set of questions about a message to determine whether or not the message was received and understood as intended. Better yet, the speaker can ask the receiver to restate the message in his or her own words. If the speaker hears what was intended, understanding and accuracy should improve. Feedback includes subtler methods than directly asking questions or having the receiver summarize the message. General comments can give the speaker a sense of the receiver's reaction to a message. To learn more about giving feedback, see *Self-Assessment—How Good Am I at Giving Performance Feedback?* on page 214, in Chapter 7.

Of course, feedback does not have to be conveyed in words. Actions *can* speak louder than words. A sales manager sends an email to his or her staff describing a new monthly sales report that all sales representatives will need to complete. If some of them don't turn in the new report, the sales manager has received feedback. This feedback suggests that the sales manager needs to clarify further the initial communication. Similarly, when you are talking to people, you watch their eyes and look for other nonverbal clues to tell whether they are getting your message or not.

Simplify Language

Because language can be a barrier, managers should choose words and structure their messages in ways that will make those messages clear and understandable to the receiver. Remember, effective communication is achieved when a message is both received and *understood.* Understanding is improved by simplifying the language used in relation to the audience intended. This means, for example, that a hospital administrator should always try to communicate in clear, easily understood terms. The language used in messages to the emergency room staff should be purposefully different from that used with office employees. Jargon can facilitate understanding when it's used within a group of those who know what it means, but it can cause many problems when used outside that group.

Listen Actively

Do you know the difference between hearing and listening? When someone talks, we hear. But too often we don't listen. Listening is an active search for meaning, whereas hearing is passive. In listening, two people are engaged in thinking: the sender *and* the receiver.

Many of us are poor listeners. Why? Because it's difficult and usually more satisfying to be on the offensive. Listening, in fact, is often more tiring than talking. It demands intellectual effort. Unlike hearing, **active listening**, which is listening for full meaning without making premature judgments or interpretations, demands total concentration. The average person normally speaks at a rate of about 125 to 200 words per minute. However, the average listener can comprehend up to 400 words per minute.[16] The difference obviously leaves lots of idle time for the brain and opportunities for the mind to wander.

Active listening is enhanced by developing empathy with the sender—that is, by placing yourself in the sender's position. Because senders differ in attitudes, interests, needs, and expectations, empathy makes it easier to understand the actual content of a message. An empathetic listener reserves judgment on the message's content and carefully listens to what is being said. The goal is to improve your ability to receive the full meaning of a communication without having it distorted by premature judgments or interpretations. Other specific behaviours that active listeners demonstrate are listed in Exhibit 6-3 on page 168. To learn more about being an effective listener, see *Developing Your Interpersonal Skills—Active Listening* on page 183, at the end of the chapter.

active listening
Listening for full meaning without making premature judgments or interpretations.

Exhibit 6-3

Active Listening Behaviours

Source: Based on P. L. Hunsaker, *Training in Management Skills* (Upper Saddle River, NJ: Prentice Hall, 2001).

Constrain Emotions

It would be naive to assume that managers always communicate in a rational manner. We know that emotions can severely cloud and distort the transference of meaning. A manager who is emotionally upset over an issue is more likely to misconstrue incoming messages and fail to communicate clearly and accurately. What can the manager do? The simplest answer is to refrain from communicating until he or she has regained composure.

Watch Nonverbal Cues

If actions speak louder than words, then it's important to watch your actions to make sure they align with and reinforce the words that go along with them. The effective communicator watches his or her nonverbal cues to ensure that they convey the desired message.

ORGANIZATIONAL COMMUNICATION

At the City of Richmond, the primary channel for communicating with employees is email, which covers about 80 percent of the messages delivered to employees. Not everyone is connected via email, however, so managers are responsible for passing on important messages to all staff. The organization also places posters of important announcements near elevators and other publicly visible locations to spread information.

Rick Thomas notes that one of the challenges of his job is spreading the word that training and education are an important part of career development at the City of Richmond. He wants to develop a quarterly newsletter that makes all City of Richmond staff more aware of training and development opportunities.

THINK ABOUT IT

What are the different ways that organizations can use to communicate to employees? Are some ways of communicating more effective than others? Should Rick Thomas develop an employee newsletter?

An understanding of managerial communication is not possible without looking at the fundamentals of organizational communication. In this section, we look at several important aspects of organizational communication including formal vs. informal communication, the direction of communication flow, and organizational communication networks.

3 How does communication flow in organizations?

Formal vs. Informal Communication

Communication within an organization is often described as formal or informal. **Formal communication** refers to communication that follows the official chain of command or is part of the communication required to do one's job. For example, when a manager asks an employee to complete a task, he or she is communicating formally. So is the employee who brings a problem to the attention of his or her manager. Any communication that takes place within prescribed organizational work arrangements would be classified as formal.

Informal communication is communication that is not defined by the organization's structural hierarchy. When employees talk with each other in the lunch room, as they pass in hallways, or as they are working out at the company exercise facility, that is informal communication. Employees form friendships and communicate with each other. The informal communication system fulfills two purposes in organizations: (1) it permits employees to satisfy their need for social interaction and (2) it can improve an organization's performance by creating alternative, and frequently faster and more efficient, channels of communication.

formal communication
Communication that follows the official chain of command or is part of the communication required to do one's job.

informal communication
Communication that is not defined by the organization's structural hierarchy.

Direction of Communication Flow

Organizational communication can flow downward, upward, laterally, or diagonally. Let's look at each.

downward communication
Communication that flows downward from managers to employees.

upward communication
Communication that flows upward from employees to managers.

Downward Communication

Any communication that flows downward from managers to employees is **downward communication**. Downward communication is used to inform, direct, coordinate, and evaluate employees. When managers assign goals to their employees, they're using downward communication. Managers are also using downward communication by providing employees with job descriptions, informing them of organizational policies and procedures, pointing out problems that need attention, or evaluating and giving feedback on their performance. Downward communication can take place through any of the communication channels we described earlier. Managers can improve the quality of the feedback they give to employees if they follow the advice given in *Tips for Managers—Suggestions for Giving Feedback*.

Upward Communication

Any communication that flows upward from employees to managers is **upward communication**. Managers rely on their employees for information. Reports are given to managers to inform them of progress toward goals and any current problems. Upward communication keeps managers aware of how employees feel about their jobs, their co-workers, and the organization in general. Managers also rely on it for ideas on how things can be improved. Some examples of upward communication include performance reports prepared by employees, suggestion boxes, employee attitude surveys, grievance procedures, manager–employee discussions, and informal group sessions in which employees have the opportunity to identify and discuss problems with their manager or even representatives of top management.

The extent of upward communication depends on the organizational culture. If managers have created a climate of trust and respect and use participative decision making or empowerment, there will be

TIPS FOR MANAGERS

Suggestions for Giving Feedback

Managers can use the following tips to give more effective feedback:

→ Relate feedback to existing **performance goals and clear expectations**.

→ Give **specific feedback** tied to observable behaviour or measurable results.

→ Channel feedback toward **key result areas**.

→ Give feedback **as soon as possible**.

→ Give positive **feedback for improvement**, not just final results.

→ **Focus feedback on performance**, not personalities.

→ Base feedback on **accurate and credible information**.

Source: R. Kreitner and A. Kinicki, *Organizational Behavior*, 6th ed. (New York: McGraw-Hill/Irwin, 2004), p. 335. Reprinted by permission of McGraw Hill Education.

When Paul and Peter Centenari pulled their cardboard box–manufacturing company, Atlas Container, back from the brink of bankruptcy, they had a revelation. They decided that one key aspect of their new start would be opening the financial books of the firm to all 150 employees and discussing their significance at monthly meetings attended by the entire staff. Employees like Ranard Austin (pictured here) have been trained to understand Atlas's financial statements and now participate in decisions about everything from company policy to production-line improvements. For open-book management like this to work, the flow of downward communication has to be steady.

considerable upward communication as employees provide input to decisions. For instance, Ernst & Young encourages employees to evaluate the principals, partners, and directors on how well they create a positive work climate. A partner in the Montreal office was surprised to learn that people in her office found her a poor role model, and she took care to explain her actions more as a result.[17] In a highly structured and authoritarian environment, upward communication still takes place, but is limited in both style and content.

Lateral Communication

lateral communication
Communication that takes place among employees on the same organizational level.

Communication that takes place among employees on the same organizational level is called **lateral communication**. In today's often chaotic and rapidly changing environment, horizontal communication is frequently needed to save time and facilitate coordination. Cross-functional teams, for instance, rely heavily on this form of communication. However, it can create conflicts if employees don't keep their managers informed about decisions they have made or actions they have taken.

Diagonal Communication

diagonal communication
Communication that cuts across both work areas and organizational levels.

Communication that cuts across both work areas *and* organizational levels is **diagonal communication**. When an analyst in the credit department communicates directly with a regional marketing manager—note the different department and different organizational level—about a customer problem, that is diagonal communication. In the interest of efficiency and speed, diagonal communication can be beneficial. Email facilitates diagonal communication. In many organizations, any employee can communicate by email with any other employee, regardless of organizational work area or level. However, just as with lateral communication, diagonal communication has the potential to create problems if employees don't keep their managers informed.

Organizational Communication Networks

communication networks
The variety of patterns of vertical and horizontal flows of organizational communication.

The vertical and horizontal flows of organizational communication can be combined into a variety of patterns called **communication networks**. Exhibit 6-4 illustrates three common communication networks.

Types of Communication Networks

In the *chain* network, communication flows according to the formal chain of command, both downward and upward. The *wheel* network represents communication flowing between a

Exhibit 6-4

Three Common Organizational Communication Networks and How They Rate on Effectiveness Criteria

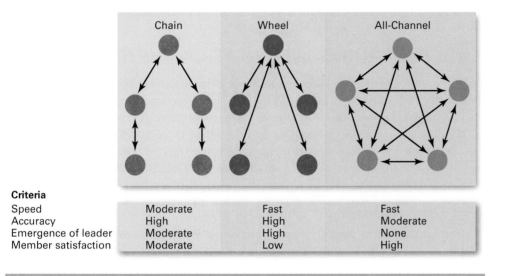

Criteria	Chain	Wheel	All-Channel
Speed	Moderate	Fast	Fast
Accuracy	High	High	Moderate
Emergence of leader	Moderate	High	None
Member satisfaction	Moderate	Low	High

clearly identifiable and strong leader and others in a work group or team. The leader serves as the hub through whom all communication passes. Finally, in the *all-channel* network, communication flows freely among all members of a work team.

As a manager, which network should you use? The answer depends on your goal. Exhibit 6-4 also summarizes the effectiveness of the various networks according to four criteria: speed, accuracy, the probability that a leader will emerge, and the importance of member satisfaction. One observation is immediately apparent: No single network is best for all situations. If you are concerned with high member satisfaction, the all-channel network is best; if having a strong and identifiable leader is important, the wheel facilitates this; and if accuracy is most important, the chain and wheel networks work best.

The Grapevine

We cannot leave our discussion of communication networks without discussing the **grapevine**—the informal organizational communication network. The grapevine is active in almost every organization. Is it an important source of information? You bet! One survey reported that 75 percent of employees hear about matters first through rumours on the grapevine.[18]

What are the implications for managers? Certainly, the grapevine is an important part of any group or organization communication network and well worth understanding.[19] It identifies for managers those bewildering issues that employees consider important and anxiety-producing. It acts as both a filter and a feedback mechanism, picking up on the issues employees consider relevant. More importantly, from a managerial point of view, it *is* possible to analyze what is happening on the grapevine—what information is being passed, how information seems to flow along the grapevine, and which individuals seem to be key conduits of information on the grapevine. By being aware of the grapevine's flow and patterns, managers can stay on top of issues that concern employees and, in turn, can use the grapevine to disseminate important information. Since the grapevine cannot be eliminated, managers should "manage" it as an important information network.

Rumours that flow along the grapevine also can never be eliminated entirely. Managers can minimize the negative consequences of rumours by limiting their range and impact. How? By communicating openly, fully, and honestly with employees, particularly in situ-

grapevine The informal organizational communication network.

Q&A   10.8

ations where employees may not like proposed or actual managerial decisions or actions. Open and honest communication with employees can affect the organization in various ways. A study of employee attitudes by Watson Wyatt Worldwide concluded that open communication had a significant positive impact on employee attitudes, but only one out of three employees surveyed rated their company as favourable in this area. But for those companies that scored high on communication, total returns to shareholders were three times higher than at companies that had poor communication.[20]

UNDERSTANDING INFORMATION TECHNOLOGY

The City of Richmond tries to keep all employees informed of what the organization is doing through its intranet site. When employees log on to the computers at the start of their day, they are automatically taken to the "What's News" page, where "items for the day" are displayed.

Many managers in the City of Richmond use a BlackBerry to check on their email while in meetings. While Rick Thomas finds this can be disruptive in meetings (he does not carry a BlackBerry because he "doesn't want to be glued to it"), he also notes that the culture of the organization is to be very responsive to customers. Thus, employees are caught between being responsive to whatever is happening in a meeting and trying to make sure that there is not a customer service request that must be attended to immediately.

Thomas notes that he turns off his work cellphone at night and on weekends. He believes this action is consistent with being a dedicated employee. "I'm available for true emergencies during off hours, but it's important that I signal to staff that they should be trying to achieve a balance between work and the rest of their lives, especially in this day and age where oftentimes our out-of-work responsibilities rival those within our professional capacities."

THINK ABOUT IT

What are the benefits of turning off one's cellphone after work hours? Is it appropriate that Rick Thomas does so? Would you be able to tell if you have become a slave to communication technology?

---

4 How does information technology affect organizations?

Information technology has changed the way we live and work. Take the following four examples: Japanese employees, managers, housewives, and teens use wireless interactive web phones to send email, surf the web, swap photos, and play computer games. Service technicians at Ajax, Ontario-based Pitney Bowes Canada use instant messaging rather than pagers, because "it's cheaper and it's two-way"; also, the company can know when messages are received.[21] IBM's 320 000 employees regularly use instant messaging software for both communicating and workplace collaboration.[22]

The world of communication is not what it used to be. Managers are challenged to keep their organizations functioning smoothly while continually improving work operations *and* staying competitive even though both the organization and the environment are changing rapidly. Although changing technology has been a significant source of the environmental uncertainty facing organizations, these same technological advances have enabled managers to coordinate the work efforts of employees in ways that can lead to increased efficiency and effectiveness. Information technology now touches every aspect of almost every company's business. The implications for the ways individuals communicate are profound.

 Q&A   10.9

How Information Technology Affects Communication

Information technology has radically changed the way organizational members communicate. For example, it has

- significantly improved a manager's ability to monitor individual or team performance

- allowed employees to have more complete information to make faster decisions

- provided employees with more opportunities to collaborate and share information

- made it possible for employees to be fully accessible, any time, regardless of where they are.

Two developments in information technology seem to be having the most significant impact on current managerial communication: networked computer systems and wireless capabilities.

Networked Computer Systems

Have you ever emailed or instant-messaged someone who was just in the next office? Does the reliance on technology make it harder or easier to communicate effectively with people?

In a networked computer system, an organization links its computers to create an organizational network. Organizational members can then communicate with each other and tap into information whether they are down the hall, across town, or halfway across the world. Although we will not get into the mechanics of how a network system works, we will address some of its communication applications including email, instant messaging, voice mail, fax, electronic data interchange, teleconferencing, videoconferencing, intranets, and extranets.

Q&A 10.10

Email   Email is a quick and convenient way for organizational members to share information and communicate. Many people complain about email overload, and it is not always used effectively, however. A recent study found that opening nasty messages from your boss can harm your health over time.[23] While negative email messages from anyone had health consequences, those from superiors showed the most significant increase in a person's blood pressure.

To construct more effective emails, you might want to consider the following tips for writing and sending email offered by Professor Christina Cavanagh of the University of Western Ontario's Richard Ivey School of Business:[24]

- Don't send emails without a subject line.

- Be careful in your use of emoticons and acronyms for business communication.

- Write your message clearly and briefly.

- Copy emails to others only if they really need the information.

- Sleep on angry emails before sending to be sure you are sending the right message.

Email is not necessarily private communication, and organizations often take the position that they have the right to read your email.

Instant Messaging   Instant messaging (IM) first became popular among teens and preteens who wanted to communicate online immediately with their friends. Now, it has moved to the workplace. There were 11.4 billion IMs sent worldwide each day in 2004, and this figure is expected to increase to more than 45.8 billion by 2008.[25] However, there are a couple of drawbacks to IM. Unlike email, it requires users to be logged on to the organization's computer network in order to communicate with one another. This leaves the network open to security breaches, and some organizations have limited which employees can use IM in the workplace as a result.

Voice Mail and Fax   Voice mail allows information to be transmitted even though a receiver may not be physically present to take the information. Receivers can choose to save the message for future use, delete it, or route it to other parties. Fax machines allow the transmission of documents containing both text and graphics over ordinary telephone lines. Faxes allow information that is best viewed in printed form to be easily and quickly shared by organizational members.

electronic data interchange (EDI)
A way for organizations to exchange standard business transaction documents using direct computer-to-computer networks.

teleconferencing
A communication system that allows a group of people to confer simultaneously using the telephone.

videoconferencing
A communication system that allows a group of people to confer simultaneously while seeing each other on video screens.

web conferencing
The use of the Internet to allow a group of people to confer simultaneously online in real time.

intranet
An organizational communication network that uses Internet technology and is accessible only by employees.

extranet
An organizational communication network that uses Internet technology and allows authorized users inside the organization to communicate with certain outsiders.

Electronic Data Interchange **Electronic data interchange (EDI)** is a way for organizations to exchange standard business transaction documents, such as invoices or purchase orders, using direct computer-to-computer networks. Organizations often use EDI with vendors, suppliers, and customers because it saves time and money. How? Information on transactions is transmitted from one organization's computer system to another through a telecommunications network. The printing and handling of paper documents at one organization are eliminated as is the inputting of data at the other organization.

Teleconferencing, Videoconferencing, and Web Conferencing Meetings—one-on-one, team, divisional, or organization-wide—have always been one way to share information. The limitations of technology used to dictate that meetings take place among people in the same physical location, but that is no longer the case. **Teleconferencing** allows a group of people to confer simultaneously using the telephone. If meeting participants can see each other on video screens, the simultaneous conference is called **videoconferencing**. **Web conferencing** uses the Internet to enable a group of people to hold a meeting or make a presentation online in real time. Work groups, large and small, that might be in different locations, can use these communication network tools to collaborate and share information. During the SARS virus outbreak in 2003, several companies used videoconferencing to communicate with customers and employees. Although videoconferencing allows communication to continue, it still lacks a personal touch, and it's not a perfect substitute for face-to-face meetings.

Intranets and Extranets Networked computer systems have allowed the development of organizational intranets and extranets. An **intranet** is an organizational communication network that uses Internet technology and is accessible only by employees. Many organizations are using intranets as ways for employees to share information and collaborate on documents and projects from different locations. For example, BMO Financial Group used to wait almost half a month for the previous month's financial results to be available in paper format. This delay slowed their ability to find out how they were doing. Through the bank's Web Monthly Progress Monitor (WebMPM), financial results are available to all employees across Canada through the company's intranet.[26] An **extranet** is an organizational communication network that uses Internet technology and allows authorized users inside the organization to communicate with certain outsiders such as customers or vendors. For instance, Whitby, Ontario-based Sklar Peppler Furniture has developed an extranet that allows faster and more convenient communications between customers and sales representatives. Major retailers such as Leon's and The Brick can place orders, and then check their status online. An added benefit to Sklar Peppler is that the number of telephone calls to its customer service department dropped dramatically.[27]

Wireless Capabilities

At Seattle-based Starbucks, 600 district managers have been outfitted with mobile technology, allowing them to spend more time in the company's stores. Anne Saunders, vice-president of Starbucks Interactive, says, "These are the most important people in the company. Each has between 8 and 10 stores that he or she services. While their primary job is outside of the office—and in those stores—they still need to be connected."[28] While the communication possibilities for a manager in a networked world are exciting, the real potential is just beginning! Networked computer systems require organizations (and employees) to be connected by wires. Wireless communication depends on signals sent through air or space without any physical connection, using things such as microwave signals, satellites, radio waves, radio antennas, or infrared light rays. The latest twist in wireless capability is Internet access made possible by "hot spots," which are simply locations where users gain wireless access to the Internet.

In 2003, 31 percent of large Canadian corporations and 18 percent of medium-size companies provided wireless access to their networks. In addition, the number of "hot spots" in Canada continues to increase, with a number of cities examining the possibility

Technology need not always reduce face-to-face communication. To make contact easier between employees at its call centre and in its information systems department, ASB, a New Zealand bank, adopted an open layout encompassing five areas on three different floors. There is a landscaped park area in the centre, a café, a minigolf green, a TV room, and a barbecue area, all of which help bring people together. Since moving into the new design, bank managers have noted that the volume of interdepartmental emails has dropped, indicating that people are communicating in person more.

of providing such service to residents. Since 1.5 million Canadian employees are on the move on any given day, wireless smart phones, notebook computers, and other pocket communication devices have spawned a whole new way for managers to "keep in touch." The number of worldwide mobile users keeps increasing. In the Asia–Pacific region alone, there were more than 206 million mobile users in 2001.[29] Employees don't have to be at their desks with their phones or computers wired in and turned on to communicate with others in the organization. As technology continues to improve in this area, we will see more and more organizational members using wireless communication as a way to collaborate and share information.

How Information Technology Affects Organizations

Employees—working in teams or as individuals—need information to make decisions and do their work. After describing the communications capabilities managers have at their disposal, it's clear that technology *can* significantly affect the way that organizational members communicate, share information, and do their work. Information technology also creates opportunities for organizations. For instance, colleges and universities now have the capability of offering online courses and degrees, which could, over time, decrease the number of students taught in face-to-face settings, while increasing the overall number of students who can be reached because of online methods of teaching.

The following *Management Reflection* explores how one Canadian firm reduced cost and improved service for customers using Voice over Internet Protocol (VoIP) technology.

MANAGEMENT REFLECTION

VoIP Improves Communication and Customer Service

Can saving money increase service?   Johnson, a St. John's, Newfoundland-based national insurance company, founded in 1880, recently introduced the latest in long-distance telephone technology: Voice over Internet Protocol (VoIP).[30] The technology, purchased from Cisco Systems, treats long distance calls as if they were local ones. With appropriate hardware, subscribers can use the same cable that connects their computer to the Internet to connect their telephone to make calls. It is not just a cost-saving measure, though. C. C. Huang, Johnson's president and CEO says, "We really believe in Voice over IP [Internet protocol]. It's helping us provide better customer service, improve our productivity—and outperform the industry." The IP infrastructure allows voice, video, and data to be transferred on a single network.

When customers call in, the network can direct calls to staff members who have the appropriate skills and are available to handle the call. The network is also able to link a caller's phone number to his or her electronic file, making it immediately available to the employee handling the phone call. Employees are able to see their voice mail, email, and faxes on their telephone screens. Huang is enthusiastic about the system because "we're actually spending less money—and doing more than we have before." ■

Communication and the exchange of information among organizational members are no longer constrained by geography or time. Collaborative work efforts among widely dispersed individuals and teams, information sharing, and the integration of decisions and work throughout an entire organization have the potential to increase organizational efficiency and effectiveness. While the economic benefits of information technology are obvious, managers must not forget to address the psychological drawbacks.[31] For instance, what is the psychological cost of an employee's always being accessible? Will there be increased pressure for employees to "check in" even during their off hours? How important is it for employees to separate their work lives and their personal lives? While there are no easy answers to these questions, these are issues that managers will have to face.

The widespread use of voice mail and email at work has led to some ethical concerns as well. These forms of communication are not necessarily private, because employers have access to them. The federal Privacy Act (which protects the privacy of individuals and provides individuals with a right to access personal information about themselves) and the Access to Information Act (which allows individuals to access government information) apply to all federal government departments, most federal agencies, and some federal Crown corporations. However, many private sector employees are not covered by privacy legislation. Only Quebec's privacy act applies to the entire private sector. Managers need to clearly convey to employees the extent to which their communications will be monitored, and policies on such things as personal Internet and email use.

SUMMARY AND IMPLICATIONS

① **What are the functions of communication?** Communication serves four major functions: control, motivation, emotional expression, and information. In the control function, communication sets out the guidelines for behaviour. Communication motivates by clarifying to employees what is to be done, how well they are doing, and what can be done to improve performance if it's not up to par. Communication provides an opportunity to express feelings and also fulfills social needs. Finally, communication also provides the information to get things done in organizations. *As manager, People & Organization Development, for the City of Richmond, BC, Rick Thomas communicates to let people know about training activities and to tell people when they have done a good job.*

② **Why does communication break down?** When a message passes between a sender and a receiver, it needs to be converted into symbols (called encoding) and passed to the receiver by some channel. The receiver translates (decodes) the sender's message. At any point in this process, communication can be distorted by noise. A variety of other factors can also affect whether the message is interpreted correctly, including the degree of filtering, the sender's or receiver's emotional state, and whether too much information is being sent (information overload). *Rick*

Thomas finds that he must consider the needs of the different subcultures within the organization when he plans to communicate with employees.

(3) How does communication flow in organizations? Communication can be of the formal or informal variety. Formal communication follows the official chain of command or is part of the communication required to do one's job. Informal communication is not defined by the organization's structural hierarchy. Communication can flow downward, upward, laterally to those at the same organizational level, or diagonally, which means that the communication cuts across both work areas and organizational levels. Communication can also flow through networks and through the grapevine. *One of Rick Thomas's challenges is to get information to those employees who are not connected via email.*

(4) How does information technology affect organizations? Information technology allows managers and employees more access to each other and to customers and clients. It provides more opportunities for monitoring, as well as a greater ability to share information. Information technology also increases flexibility and responsiveness. *At the City of Richmond, many managers use a BlackBerry to stay connected. However, this technology can blur the boundary between work life and home life.*

Management @ Work

Reading for Comprehension

1. What are the four functions of communication?

2. What steps can you take to make interpersonal communication more effective?

3. What can managers do to help them determine which communication channel to use in a given circumstance?

4. Describe the barriers to effective interpersonal communication. How can they be overcome?

5. Which do you think is more important for a manager: speaking accurately or listening actively? Why?

6. Identify four types of channels and when they might be best used.

7. How has information technology enhanced a manager's communication effectiveness?

Linking Concepts to Practice

1. "Ineffective communication is the fault of the sender." Do you agree or disagree with this statement? Explain your position.

2. Describe why effective communication is not synonymous with agreement between the communicating parties.

3. "As technology improves, employees will be working more, be more accessible to employers, and be suffering from information overload." Do you agree or disagree with this statement? Explain your position.

4. How might a manager use the grapevine to his or her advantage? Support your response.

5. Using what you have learned about active listening in this chapter, would you describe yourself as a good listener? Are there any areas in which you are deficient? If so, how could you improve your listening skills?

MANAGEMENT FOR YOU TODAY

Consider a person with whom you have had difficulty communicating. Using the barriers to effective communication as a start, analyze what has gone wrong with the communication process with that person. What can be done to improve communication? To what extent did sender and receiver problems contribute to the communication breakdown?

SELF-ASSESSMENT

What's My Face-to-Face Communication Style?

For each of the following statements, circle the level of agreement or disagreement that you personally feel:[32]

> 1 = Strongly Disagree
> 3 = Neither Agree nor Disagree
> 5 = Strongly Agree

1. I am comfortable with all varieties of people.	1	2	3	4	5
2. I laugh easily.	1	2	3	4	5
3. I readily express admiration for others.	1	2	3	4	5
4. What I say usually leaves an impression on people.	1	2	3	4	5

5. I leave people with an impression of me which they definitely tend to remember.   1 2 3 4 5

6. To be friendly, I habitually acknowledge verbally others' contributions.   1 2 3 4 5

7. I have some nervous mannerisms in my speech.   1 2 3 4 5

8. I am a very relaxed communicator.   1 2 3 4 5

9. When I disagree with somebody, I am very quick to challenge them.   1 2 3 4 5

10. I can always repeat back to a person exactly what was meant.   1 2 3 4 5

11. The sound of my voice is very easy to recognize.   1 2 3 4 5

12. I leave a definite impression on people.   1 2 3 4 5

13. The rhythm or flow of my speech is sometimes affected by nervousness.   1 2 3 4 5

14. Under pressure I come across as a relaxed speaker.   1 2 3 4 5

15. My eyes reflect exactly what I am feeling when I communicate.   1 2 3 4 5

16. I dramatize a lot.   1 2 3 4 5

17. Usually, I deliberately react in such a way that people know that I am listening to them.   1 2 3 4 5

18. Usually, I do not tell people much about myself until I get to know them well.   1 2 3 4 5

19. Regularly I tell jokes, anecdotes, and stories when I communicate.   1 2 3 4 5

20. I tend to gesture constantly when I communicate.   1 2 3 4 5

21. I am an extremely open communicator.   1 2 3 4 5

22. I am vocally a loud communicator.   1 2 3 4 5

23. In arguments I insist upon very precise definitions.   1 2 3 4 5

24. In most social situations I generally speak very frequently.   1 2 3 4 5

25. I like to be strictly accurate when I communicate.   1 2 3 4 5

26. Because I have a loud voice, I can easily break into a conversation.   1 2 3 4 5

27. Often I physically and vocally act out when I want to communicate.   1 2 3 4 5

28. I have an assertive voice.   1 2 3 4 5

29. I readily reveal personal things about myself.   1 2 3 4 5

30. I am dominant in social situations.   1 2 3 4 5

31. I am very argumentative.   1 2 3 4 5

32. Once I get wound up in a heated discussion, I have a hard time stopping myself.   1 2 3 4 5

33. I am always an extremely friendly communicator.   1 2 3 4 5

34. I really like to listen very carefully to people.   1 2 3 4 5

35. Very often I insist that other people document or present some kind of proof for what they are arguing.   1 2 3 4 5

36. I try to take charge of things when I am with people.   1 2 3 4 5

37. It bothers me to drop an argument that is not resolved.   1 2 3 4 5

38. In most social situations I tend to come on strong.   1 2 3 4 5

39. I am very expressive nonverbally in social situations.   1 2 3 4 5

40. The way I say something usually leaves an impression on people.   1 2 3 4 5

41. Whenever I communicate, I tend to be very encouraging to people.   1 2 3 4 5

42. I actively use a lot of facial expressions when I communicate.   1 2 3 4 5

43. I very frequently exaggerate verbally to emphasize a point.   1 2 3 4 5

44. I am an extremely attentive communicator.   1 2 3 4 5

45. As a rule, I openly express my feelings and emotions.   1 2 3 4 5

Scoring Key

Step 1: Reverse the score on items 4, 17, and 26 (1 = 5, 2 = 4, 3 = 3, etc.).

Step 2: Add together the scores on the following items to get a final total for each dimension.

1. 5, 7, 9, 20, 44   = _____ (Dominant)
2. 22, 28, 30, 32, 39 = _____ (Dramatic)
3. 2, 10, 13, 37, 41   = _____ (Contentious)
4. 6, 21, 24, 34, 42   = _____ (Animated)
5. 11, 14, 18, 31, 40 = _____ (Impression-leaving)
6. 4, 12, 16, 17, 36   = _____ (Relaxed)
7. 15, 23, 27, 29, 45 = _____ (Attentive)
8. 1, 25, 26, 33, 38   = _____ (Open)
9. 3, 8, 19, 35, 43   = _____ (Friendly)

Analysis and Interpretation

This scale measures the following dimensions of communication style:

Dominant—Tends to take charge of social interactions.

Dramatic—Manipulates and exaggerates stories and uses other stylistic devices to highlight content.

Contentious—Is argumentative.

Animated—Uses frequent and sustained eye contact and many facial expressions and gestures often.

Impression-leaving—Is remembered because of the communicative stimuli that are projected.

Relaxed—Is relaxed and void of nervousness.

Attentive—Makes sure that the other person knows that he or she is being listened to.

Open—Is conversational, expansive, affable, convivial, gregarious, unreserved, somewhat frank, definitely extroverted, and obviously approachable.

Friendly—Ranges from being unhostile to showing deep intimacy.

For each dimension, your score will range from 5 to 25. The higher your score for any dimension, the more that dimension characterizes your communication style. When you review your results, consider to what degree your scores aid or hinder your communication effectiveness. High scores for being attentive and open would almost always be positive qualities. A high score for contentiousness, on the other hand, could be a negative in many situations.

More Self-Assessments

To learn more about your skills, abilities, and interests, take the following self-assessments on your enclosed CD-ROM:

- #28—How Good Are My Listening Skills?
- #43—How Good Am I at Giving Performance Feedback? (This exercise also appears in Chapter 7 on page 214.)

WORKING TOGETHER: TEAM-BASED EXERCISE

Choosing the Right Communication Channel

Purpose

To reinforce the idea that some channels are more appropriate for certain communications than others.

Time Required

Approximately 20 minutes.

Procedure

Form groups of 5 or 6 individuals. Evaluate the most appropriate channel to use to deliver the following information to employees. Justify your choices.

1. The company has just been acquired by a large competitor, and 15 percent of the employees will be laid off within the next 3 months.

2. A customer has complained about an employee via email. You have investigated and found the complaint justified. How do you convey this to the employee?

3. The founder of the company, who is well liked, died of a heart attack last night.

4. Bonus decisions have been made. Not all individuals will receive a bonus.

5. An employee has gone above and beyond in meeting a customer's request. You want to acknowledge the employee's efforts.

ETHICAL DILEMMA EXERCISE

Distorting Information Purposely

The issue of withholding information is always a concern for supervisors. Because it's so closely intertwined with interpersonal communication, this might be a good time to think about ethical dilemmas that supervisors face relating to the intentional distortion of information. Read through the following incidents.[33]

- **Incident 1:** You are an accountant with a large accounting firm. One of your clients is the CFO of a large energy conglomerate. The CFO has just seen a report on the losses from activities the company is involved in. Rather than show the losses on the corporate income statement, the CFO would like you to verify that these losses rightfully belong to a subsidiary company. In doing so, the company's stock prices will not be affected. What do you do?

- **Incident 2:** As a sales manager, you just received your department's sales report for last month. Sales are down considerably. Your boss, who works 2000 kilometres away in another city, is unlikely to see last month's sales figures. You are optimistic that sales will pick up this month and next so that your overall quarterly numbers will be right on target. You also know that your boss is the type of person who hates to hear bad news. You are having a phone conversation today with your boss. He happens to ask in passing how last month's sales went. What do you tell him?

- **Incident 3:** You represent a high-profile individual who is a friend of a CEO of a company. Your client has invested money in that company. One day you are advised to sell the stocks before news about the company that will drastically reduce the company's stock price becomes public. Your client says the timing was coincidental. You believe otherwise. What do you tell your securities regulator when it contacts you about the incident?

- **Incident 4:** An employee asks you about a rumour she has heard that your department and all its employees will be transferred from Ottawa to Fredericton. You know the rumour is true, but you would rather not let the information out just yet. You are fearful that it could hurt departmental morale and lead to premature resignations. What do you say to your employee?

These four incidents illustrate potential dilemmas that supervisors face relating to evading the truth, distorting facts, or lying to others. There is something else that makes the dilemmas even more problematic: It might not always be in the best interest of a supervisor or those in his or her department to provide full and complete information. Keeping communications fuzzy can cut down on questions, permit faster decision making, minimize objections, reduce opposition, make it easier to deny one's earlier statements, preserve the freedom to change one's mind, permit one to say "no" diplomatically, help avoid confrontation and anxiety, and provide other benefits that work to the advantage of the manager.

Is it unethical to purposely distort communications to get a favourable outcome? What about "little white lies" that really don't hurt anybody? Are these ethical? What guidelines could you suggest for managers who want guidance in deciding whether distorting information is ethical or unethical?

Voyant Technologies

After a chance meeting in a headquarters hallway with his chief engineer, Bill Ernstrom, CEO of Voyant Technologies (a company that makes teleconferencing equipment), decided to have his engineers add streaming media to the company's flagship product.[34] Four months and $200 000 later, Ernstrom wishes he had never had that conversation. Last week, one of his product managers, who only recently learned of the project, produced a marketing report that showed most customers had little interest in streaming anything.

Ernstrom realizes that he has been ignoring a communication challenge for too long: The top engineers are not listening to the product managers—and vice versa. Ernstrom says, "We got a long way down the road, built the code, got the engineers excited. Then we found out that we'd sell about 10 units."

Ernstrom recognizes that there may be communication barriers in high-tech organizations between engineers and product managers. He notes that cultural and language gaps between computer "geeks" and the more market/business-oriented colleagues happen time and time again.

Ernstrom's not sure what to do. Usually, in a high-tech organization, the early stages of a new project belong to the engineers. It is crucial to get the technology right, but what they produce is "often elegant technology that has no market, is too complicated, or doesn't match customers' expectations." Ernstrom's challenge is to get the two competing groups to collaborate. What steps can he take to make this happen?

English-Only Rules

Canada is a multicultural country. "One in six Canadians in their 20s are immigrants, and one in five are the children of at least one immigrant parent."[35] In 2001, 44 percent of Metropolitan Toronto's population, 38 percent of Vancouver's, and 18.6 percent of Montreal's were made up of immigrants.[36]

The 2001 census found that 38 percent of Vancouver's population over age five spoke neither of the country's two official languages as their first language.[37] The largest number of people who don't speak either English or French, speak Chinese (mainly Mandarin or Cantonese). The other dominant language in Vancouver is Punjabi but many other languages are represented as well. Very few Vancouverites speak French, however.

Can an organization in BC require its employees to speak only English on the job?[38] There are many sides to this issue. On the one hand, employers have identified the need to have a common language spoken in the workplace. Employers must be able to communicate effectively with all employees, especially when safety or productive efficiency matters are at stake. This, they claim, is a business necessity. Consequently, if it is a valid requirement of the job, the practice could be permitted. Furthermore, an employer's desire to have one language also stems from the fact that some employees may use bilingual capabilities to harass and insult other employees in a language they cannot understand. With today's increasing concern with protecting employees, especially women, from hostile environments, English-only rules serve as one means of reasonable care.

A counterpoint to this English-only rule firmly rests with the workforce diversity issue. Employees in today's organizations come from all nationalities and speak different languages. What about these individuals' desire to speak their languages, to communicate effectively with their peers, and to maintain their cultural heritages? To them, English-only rules are discriminatory in terms of national origin in that they have an adverse impact on nonEnglish-speaking individuals. Moreover, promoting the languages of employees might be one way for organizations to avert marketing disasters. For example, marketing campaigns by Kentucky Fried Chicken and Coors have caused some embarrassment when these campaigns are translated in the global arena. Specifically, while Kentucky Fried Chicken's "Finger Licking Good" implies great-tasting fried chicken in North America, those same words in Chinese translate into "Eat Your Fingers Off." Likewise, Coors's marketing adage to "Turn It Loose," in Spanish means "Drink Coors and Get Diarrhea." Probably not the images the companies had in mind.

Questions

1. Should employers be permitted to require that only English be spoken in the workplace? Defend your position.

2. What suggestions for communication effectiveness, if any, would you give to organizations that market goods globally? Explain.

Active Listening

About the Skill

The ability to be an effective listener is often taken for granted. Hearing is often confused with listening, but hearing is merely recognizing sound vibrations. Listening is making sense of what we hear and requires paying attention, interpreting, and remembering. Effective listening is active rather than passive. Active listening is hard work and requires you to "get inside" the speaker's head in order to understand the communication from his or her point of view.

Steps in Developing the Skill

You can be more effective at active listening if you use the following eight suggestions:[39]

1. **Make eye contact.** Making eye contact with the speaker focuses your attention, reduces the likelihood that you will be distracted, and encourages the speaker.

2. **Exhibit affirmative nods and appropriate facial expressions.** The effective active listener shows interest in what is being said through nonverbal signals. Affirmative nods and appropriate facial expressions that signal interest in what is being said, when added to eye contact, convey to the speaker that you are really listening.

3. **Avoid distracting actions or gestures.** The other side of showing interest is avoiding actions that suggest your mind is elsewhere. When listening, don't look at your watch, shuffle papers, play with your pencil, or engage in similar distractions.

4. **Ask questions.** The serious active listener analyzes what he or she hears and asks questions. This behaviour provides clarification, ensures understanding, and assures the speaker you are really listening.

5. **Paraphrase.** Restate in your own words what the speaker has said. The effective active listener uses phrases such as "What I hear you saying is . . ." or "Do you mean . . . ?" Paraphrasing is an excellent control device to check whether or not you are listening carefully and it is also a control for accuracy of understanding.

6. **Avoid interrupting the speaker.** Let the speaker complete his or her thoughts before you try to respond. Don't try to second-guess where the speaker's thoughts are going. When the speaker is finished, you will know it.

7. **Don't overtalk.** Most of us would rather speak our own ideas than listen to what others say. While talking might be more fun and silence might be uncomfortable, you cannot talk and listen at the same time. The good active listener recognizes this fact and does not overtalk.

8. **Make smooth transitions between the roles of speaker and listener.** In most work situations, you are continually shifting back and forth between the roles of speaker and listener. The effective active listener makes transitions smoothly from speaker to listener and back to speaker.

Practising the Skill

Ben Lummis has always been one of the most reliable technicians at the car stereo shop you manage. Even on days when the frantic pace stressed most other employees, Ben was calm and finished his work efficiently and effectively. You don't know much about his personal life except that he likes to read books about model railroading during his lunch break and he has asked to listen to his favourite light jazz station on the shop radio for part of the day. Because his work has always been top-notch, you were happy to let him maintain his somewhat aloof attitude. But over the past month, you have wished you knew Ben better. He has been averaging about an absence a week, and he no longer spends his lunch break reading in the break room. When he returns from wherever it is he goes, he seems even more remote than when he left. You strongly suspect that something is wrong. Even his normally reliable work has changed. Several irate customers have returned with sound systems he installed improperly. At the time of these complaints, you reviewed each problem with him carefully, and each time he promised to be more careful. In addition, you checked the company's work absence records and found that Ben has enough time saved up to take seven more sick days this year. But things don't seem to be improving. Just this week Ben took another suspicious sick day, and another angry customer has demanded that his improperly installed sound system be fixed. How would you discuss the matter with Ben?

The Communication Styles of Men and Women

"You don't understand what I'm saying, and you never listen!" "You're making a big deal out of nothing." Have you said (or heard) these statements or ones like them made to friends of the opposite sex? Most of us probably have! Research shows us that men and women tend to have different communication styles.[40] Let's look more closely at these differing styles and the problems that can arise, and try to suggest ways to minimize the barriers.

Deborah Tannen has studied the ways that men and women communicate, and reports some interesting differences. The essence of her research is that men use talk to emphasize status, while women use it to create connection. She states that communication between the sexes can be a continual balancing act of juggling our conflicting needs for intimacy, which emphasizes closeness and commonality, and independence, which emphasizes separateness and differences. It's no wonder, then, that communication problems arise! Women hear and speak a language of connection and intimacy. Men hear and speak a language of status and independence. For many men, conversations are merely a way to preserve independence and maintain status in a hierarchical social order. Yet for many women, conversations are negotiations for closeness and seeking out support and confirmation. Let's look at a few examples of what Tannen has described.

Men frequently complain that women talk on and on about their problems. Women, however, criticize men for not listening. What is happening is that when a man hears a woman talking about a problem, he frequently asserts his desire for independence and control by offering solutions. Many women, in contrast, view conversing about a problem as a way to promote closeness. The woman talks about a problem to gain support and connection, not to get the male's advice.

Here is another example: Men are often more direct than women in conversation. A man might say, "I think you're wrong on that point." A woman might say, "Have you looked at the marketing department's research report on that issue?" The implication in the woman's comment is that the report will point out the error. Men frequently misread women's indirectness as "covert" or "sneaky," but women are not as concerned as men with the status and one-upmanship that directness often creates.

Finally, men often criticize women for seeming to apologize all the time. Men tend to see the phrase "I'm sorry" as a sign of weakness because they interpret the phrase to mean the woman is accepting blame, when he may know she's not to blame. The woman also knows she is not at fault. Yet she is typically using "I'm sorry" to express regret: "I know you must feel bad about this and I do, too."

What differences do you see in men's and women's communication styles? Have these differences ever gotten in the way of working together? Describe some of the issues you have encountered.

Human Resource Management

How do I make sure that I have the right employees
to carry out my mission?

1 What factors affect human resource planning?

2 How do organizations assess their human resource needs?

3 How do organizations identify and select competent employees?

4 How do organizations help employees adapt and stay up-to-date?

5 What can organizations do to help employees achieve high performance throughout their careers?

6 How do compensation and benefits motivate employees?

7 How are careers managed?

8 What are some current issues in human resource management?

Toronto-based Bank of Nova Scotia (also called Scotiabank), Canada's second-largest bank, provides retail, corporate, and investment banking services worldwide.

Scotiabank has more than 950 domestic branches and offices in 50 countries, including Mexico, Ireland, and China.[1] In fiscal year 2005, the bank had total assets of almost $314 billion, making it the number two bank by market capitalization. From 1993 to the end of 2003, Scotiabank grew earnings per share at a compound annual rate of 12.1 percent, while dividends increased 11.6 percent annually. Scotiabank has more than 50 000 employees, but President and CEO Rick Waugh worries that too many will be leaving within the next 5 to 10 years. He expects about half of the bank's senior management—vice-presidents and those at higher levels—will retire during that time.

Managing human resources so that an organization has the right people in place at the right time is often thought of as a key role of human resource managers. Waugh thinks that is not enough, however. "Responsibility for leadership development must begin at the very top. HR can and does play an important role facilitating the process, but it must be owned and executed by current leaders," Waugh told attendees at a recent Conference Board of Canada National Leadership Summit.

Waugh also wants to make sure that Scotiabank taps the full potential of its workforce. For instance, while women represent about 50 percent of Scotiabank's management-level employees, they have much less representation at the executive level. Waugh will be working with senior managers to make sure that more qualified women get opportunities in senior management.

THINK ABOUT IT

How do companies manage their human resources to achieve strong organizational performance? Put yourself in Rick Waugh's shoes. What policies and practices can he adopt to ensure that the bank has a high quality workforce? What might he do to make sure that Scotiabank will have enough people to fill important roles as Baby Boomers retire?

Rick Waugh is faced with the challenge of making sure that Scotiabank recruits and retains high quality employees. This type of human resource management challenge is just one of many facing today's managers. If an organization does not take its human resource–management responsibilities seriously, work performance and goal accomplishment may suffer. The quality of an organization is, to a large degree, merely the sum of the quality of people it hires and keeps. Getting and keeping competent employees are critical to the success of every organization, whether the organization is just starting out or has been in business for years. Therefore, part of every manager's job in the organizing function is human resource management.

Scotiabank
www.scotiabank.com

Q&A 11.1

Exhibit 7-1

The Human Resource Management Process

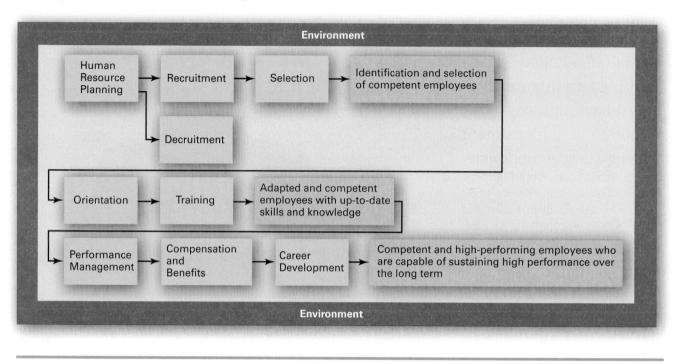

THE HUMAN RESOURCE MANAGEMENT (HRM) PROCESS

What factors affect human resource planning?

"Our people are our most important asset." Many organizations use this phrase, or something close to it, to acknowledge the important role that employees play in organizational success. These organizations also recognize that *all* managers must engage in some human resource management (HRM) activities—even in large ones that have a separate HRM department. These managers interview job candidates, orient new employees, and evaluate their employees' work performance. Because human resources also involves appropriate ways for treating co-workers, even nonmanagers must be aware of basic HR principles and practices.

Can HRM be an important strategic tool? *Can* it help establish an organization's sustainable competitive advantage? The answer to these questions seems to be yes. Various studies have concluded that an organization's human resources can be a significant source of competitive advantage.[2] And that's true for organizations around the world, not just Canadian firms. The Human Capital Index, a comprehensive global study of more than 2000 firms conducted by consulting firm Watson Wyatt Worldwide, concluded that a people-oriented approach to human resources can be a true source of competitive advantage.[3]

Exhibit 7-1 introduces the key components of an organization's **human resource management (HRM) process**, which consists of eight activities for staffing the organization and sustaining high employee performance. The first three activities ensure that competent employees are identified and selected; the next two activities involve providing employees with up-to-date knowledge and skills; and the final three activities entail making sure that the organization retains competent and high-performing employees who are capable of sustaining high performance.

human resource management (HRM) process
Activities necessary for staffing the organization and sustaining high employee performance.

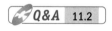

Environmental Factors Affecting HRM

Notice in Exhibit 7-1 that the entire HRM process is influenced by the external environment. Whatever effect the external environment has on the organization ultimately affects the organization's employees. We elaborated on the constraints that the environment puts on managers in Chapter 2. The environmental factors that most directly influence the HRM process are economic conditions, labour unions, and government legislation.

Economic Conditions

The ability of employers to recruit is dependent upon local (and national) unemployment rates, competition in regional and local labour markets, and industry-specific labour market conditions. For instance, BC is facing a shortage in skilled labour in the leadup to the 2010 Olympics because of the increasing number of jobs available, the decreasing number of people available because of demographic issues, such as the oldest Baby Boomers nearing the age of retirement, and Alberta's higher wage rates. Similarly, hospitals across the country are facing a shortage of nurses, so provinces compete with each other to recruit and retain nurses. When the unemployment rate is high, employers have more potential employees to choose from.

Labour Unions

The Canada Labour Code covers employment by the federal government and Crown corporations and establishes the right of employees to join labour unions if they desire. The provinces and territories have similar legislation to cover workplaces within their areas. This legislation provides a general framework for fair negotiations between management and labour unions and also provides guidelines to make sure that labour disputes do not unduly inconvenience the public.

A **labour union** is an organization that represents employees and seeks to protect their interests through collective bargaining. Labour unions try to improve pay and benefits and working conditions for members. They also try to have greater control over the rules and procedures covering issues such as promotions, layoffs, transfers, and outsourcing.

In unionized organizations, many HRM decisions are regulated by the terms of collective agreements. These agreements usually define such things as recruitment sources; criteria for hiring, promotions, and layoffs; training eligibility; and disciplinary practices. About 31 percent of Canadian employees belong to labour unions, a figure that has been consistent for the past 20 years.[4] Individuals join a labour union for any number of reasons.[5] Wages, working conditions, lack of respect by managers, unfair working hours, job security, and the desire for safer workplaces all contribute to unionization. For example, students working at Montreal's downtown Indigo Books, Music & Café were unhappy with their working conditions and voted to join the Confédération des syndicats nationaux in February 2003.[6]

labour union
An organization that represents employees and seeks to protect their interests through collective bargaining.

Q&A 11.3

Government Legislation

The federal government has greatly expanded its influence over HRM by enacting a number of laws and regulations including the Canada Labour Code, employment standards legislation, the Charter of Rights and Freedoms, and the Canadian Human Rights Act. The provincial governments also have their own labour legislation that governs the workplace.

Legislation Affecting Workplace Conditions As noted above, the Canada Labour Code establishes the right of employees to join labour unions if they desire. Part II of this legislation outlines the health and safety obligations of federal employers to prevent accidents and injury to their employees.

Each province and territory has health and safety regulations that cover most nonfederal workplaces in its region. This legislation is typically called the Occupational Health and Safety Act, or something similar. The act generally does not cover work done in private homes or work done in farming operations (unless separate regulations have been added). There is separate legislation covering workplace hazards: the Workplace Hazardous Materials Information System (WHMIS). This is a comprehensive plan for providing information on the safe use of potentially hazardous materials in the workplace.

Employment standards legislation sets minimum employment standards in the private sector in Canada. It covers such things as the minimum age of employees, hours of work and overtime pay, minimum wages, equal pay, general holidays and annual vacations with pay, parental leave, and termination of employment.

Anti-Discrimination Legislation   The Charter of Rights and Freedoms and the Canadian Human Rights Act require employers to ensure that equal employment opportunities exist for job applicants and current employees. Decisions regarding who will be hired, for instance, or which employees will be chosen for a management training program must be made without regard to race, sex, religion, age, colour, national origin, or disability.

Trying to balance the "shoulds and should-nots" of these laws often falls within the realm of employment equity. The Employment Equity Act creates four "protected categories"—women, Aboriginal peoples, people with disabilities, and visible minorities. These groups must not be discriminated against by federally regulated employers and all employers who receive federal contracts worth more than $200 000. Employment equity is intended to ensure that all citizens have an equal opportunity to obtain employment regardless of gender, race or ethnicity, or disabilities.

The intent of the Canada Labour Code, Occupational Health and Safety Act, employment standards legislation, the Charter of Rights and Freedoms, and the Canadian Human Rights Act is to ensure that all employees have a safe work environment, that they are not asked to work too many hours, that they have reasonable opportunities to be considered for jobs, and that pay for jobs is not discriminatory. Because an increasing number of workplace lawsuits are targeting supervisors, as well as their organizations, managers need to be aware of what they can and cannot do by law.[7]

Q&A 11.4

HUMAN RESOURCE PLANNING

As president and CEO of Scotiabank, Rick Waugh recognizes that providing good service means having good employees.[8] Scotiabank needs to recruit more employees to replace those who move into senior management positions in the next few years.

THINK ABOUT IT

How will changes in the age of the population affect the way organizations hire people? How can Scotiabank and other organizations respond successfully?

---

2 How do organizations assess their human resource needs?

Canada will experience a shortage of 1 million skilled workers over the next 20 years, according to The Conference Board of Canada.[9] Aware of these predictions, managers at many companies are developing plans to ensure that they will have enough qualified people to fulfill their human resource needs.

human resource planning
The process by which managers ensure that they have the right number and kinds of people in the right places, and at the right times, who are capable of effectively and efficiently performing assigned tasks.

Through **human resource planning** managers ensure that they have the right number and kinds of people in the right places, and at the right times, who are capable of effectively and efficiently performing assigned tasks. Through planning, organizations can avoid sudden talent shortages and surpluses.[10] Human resource planning can be condensed into two steps: (1) assessing current human resources and (2) assessing future human resource needs and developing a program to meet those future needs.

Assessing Current Human Resources

Managers begin human resource planning by reviewing the organization's current human resource status, usually through a *human resource inventory*. This information is taken from forms filled out by employees, and includes things such as name, education, training, prior employment, languages spoken, special capabilities, and specialized skills. Many firms have introduced HR management information systems (HRMIS) to track employee information for policy and strategic needs. For instance, these systems can be used for salary and benefits administration. They can also be used to track absenteeism, turnover, and health and safety data. More strategically, HRMIS can be used to keep track of employee skills and education, and match these to ongoing needs of the organization.

Another part of the current assessment is the **job analysis**, which is an assessment that defines jobs and the behaviours necessary to perform them. Information for a job analysis can be gathered by directly observing or videotaping individuals on the job, interviewing employees individually or in a group, having employees complete a structured questionnaire, having job "experts" (usually managers) identify a job's specific characteristics, or having employees record their daily activities in a diary or notebook.

With information from the job analysis, managers develop or revise job descriptions and job specifications. A **job description** is a written statement of what a jobholder does, how it is done, and why it is done. It typically describes job content, environment, and conditions of employment. A **job specification** states the minimum qualifications that a person must possess to perform a given job successfully. It identifies the human traits, knowledge, skills, and attitudes needed to do the job effectively. The job description and the job specification are both important documents that aid managers in recruiting and selecting employees.

job analysis
An assessment that defines jobs and the behaviours necessary to perform them.

job description
A written statement of what a jobholder does, how it is done, and why it is done.

job specification
A statement of the minimum qualifications that a person must possess to perform a given job successfully.

Meeting Future Human Resource Needs

Future human resource needs are determined by the organization's mission, goals, and strategies. Demand for employees is a result of demand for the organization's products or services. On the basis of its estimate of total revenue, managers can attempt to establish the number and mix of employees needed to reach that revenue. In some cases, however, that situation may be reversed. When particular skills are necessary but in short supply, the availability of appropriate human resources determines revenues.

After they have assessed both current capabilities and future needs, managers are able to estimate human resource shortages—both in number and in type—and to highlight areas in which the organization will be overstaffed. Managers can then develop replacement charts for managerial positions, which outline what employees are available to fill future managerial needs, and can indicate who might be ready for promotion, and who might need more training to move into upper-level positions. With all of this information, managers are ready to proceed to the next step in the HRM process.

STAFFING THE ORGANIZATION

To deal with recruiting issues, Scotiabank has developed a Careers webpage to target young graduates and encourage them to think about working for the bank.[11] "We looked at our audience and their primary medium is the Internet. We're matching the channels with the audience we're trying to attract," says Arlene Russell, vice-president of HR. The site gives corporate information, and users can do job searches and read about what makes Scotiabank a good employer.

Russell notes that e-recruiting is not the only way that the bank seeks job applicants. Scotiabank also uses print advertising and recruitment fairs, for instance. "There are still strengths in all mediums and I think to really attract job seekers, you have to deliver on all the channels people want," says Russell. "The bottom line is you need to understand who you're speaking to and speak to them in the medium they're comfortable with."

THINK ABOUT IT
What kinds of selection techniques can Scotiabank use to choose suitable employees?

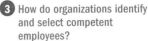 **3** How do organizations identify and select competent employees?

recruitment
The process of locating, identifying, and attracting capable applicants.

decruitment
Techniques for reducing the organization's workforce.

Once managers know their current human resource status and their future needs, they can begin to do something about any shortages or excesses. If one or more vacancies exist, they can use the information gathered through job analysis to guide them in **recruitment**—that is, the process of locating, identifying, and attracting capable applicants.[12] On the other hand, if human resource planning shows a surplus of employees, management may want to reduce the organization's workforce through **decruitment**.[13]

Exhibit 7-2

Major Sources of Potential Job Candidates

Source	Advantages	Disadvantages
Internet	Reaches large numbers of people; can get immediate feedback	Generates many unqualified candidates
Employee Referrals	Knowledge about the organization provided by current employee; can generate strong candidates because a good referral reflects on the recommender	May not increase the diversity and mix of employees
Company Website	Wide distribution; can be targeted to specific groups	Generates many unqualified candidates
College/University Recruiting	Large centralized body of candidates	Limited to entry-level positions
Professional Recruiting Organizations	Good knowledge of industry challenges and requirements	Little commitment to specific organization

Recruitment

How would you go about recruiting team members to work on a course project?

At a career fair and expo at Edmonton City Centre mall, police tried to convince high school students that they should consider a career with the police force. To show that there are many different opportunities in police service, they brought their vehicles, including police motorcycles and dirt bikes. Explains spokesperson Dean Parthenis, "People may have thought that once you become a police officer, you stay in that position on patrol for the rest of your life. You can if you like. But there's lots of opportunity to move around once you become a police officer."[14] Potential job candidates can be found through several sources, as Exhibit 7-2 shows.[15]

Web-based recruiting, or e-recruiting, has become a popular choice for organizations and applicants. For instance, when Yum! Brands needed job applicants for management positions at its restaurants (Taco Bell, KFC, A&W, and Pizza Hut), they turned to online recruiter FlipDog.com. The results were so positive that they expanded their use of it.[16] Although e-recruiting allows organizations to identify applicants cheaply and quickly, the quality of those applicants may not be as good as other sources. Burnaby, BC-based Electronic Arts Canada, following the lead of some other Canadian companies, decided to recruit at universities in recent years to win "the best and the brightest" from computer science programs.[17] Pat York, director of human resources, is pleased with the results, as the interviews have led to hires more than a third of the time.

Despite the popularity of new recruiting techniques, the majority of studies have found that employee referrals generally produce the best candidates.[18]

 Electronic Arts Canada
http://eacanada.ea.com

Decruitment

The other approach to controlling labour supply is through decruitment, which is not a pleasant task for any manager. The decruitment options are shown in Exhibit 7-3. Obviously people can be fired, but other choices may be more beneficial to the organization. Keep in mind that, regardless of the method used to reduce the number of employees in the organization, there is no easy way to do it, even though it may be absolutely necessary.

Exhibit 7-3

Decruitment Options

Option	Description
Firing	Permanent involuntary termination
Layoffs	Temporary involuntary termination; may last only a few days or extend to years
Attrition	Not filling openings created by voluntary resignations or normal retirements
Transfers	Moving employees either laterally or downward; usually does not reduce costs but can reduce intraorganizational supply–demand imbalances
Reduced Workweeks	Having employees work fewer hours per week, share jobs, or perform their jobs on a part-time basis
Early Retirements	Providing incentives to older and more senior employees for retiring before their normal retirement dates
Job Sharing	Having employees share one full-time position

Selection

Once the recruiting effort has developed a pool of candidates, the next step in the HRM process is to determine who is best qualified for the job. This step is called the **selection process**, the process of screening job applicants to ensure that the most appropriate candidates are hired. Errors in hiring can have far-reaching implications. Hiring the right people pays off, however, as the following *Management Reflection* shows.

selection process
The process of screening job applicants to ensure that the most appropriate candidates are hired.

Karen Flavelle, president of Vancouver-based Purdy's Chocolates, agonizes over new hires because she really wants them to fit in with the company's culture. A search for a new personnel director took three years, until she could find someone who would support "the company's practice of rotating store clerks and plant workers into challenging projects to test their suitability for supervisory and management posts." Most managers at Purdy's are promoted from within.

Hiring for Passion Decreases Turnover

How closely should companies look for "fit" in prospective employees? Earl Brewer, CEO of Greenarm, believes company fit makes a big difference. He makes sure Greenarm hires people who put people first.[19] "We don't want people working excessively and neglecting their families," he says of the Fredericton, New Brunswick-based developer and property management firm. Brewer says the low turnover at the firm is because they hire the right people: "They have to have passion for the job."

A *Progress* magazine survey of the employees found them raving about working for the company. The employees appreciate that senior management leads by example, and emphasize the importance of balancing work and family life. As one employee explains, "I tell people that my company expects hard, good quality work, but also expects me and others to have a family life and to be happy."

Greenarm, named by *Progress* magazine as a Best Company to Work for in Atlantic Canada, turns its hiring success into business success. The company is New Brunswick's largest private-sector property management company. ∎

What Is Selection?

Selection is an exercise in prediction. It seeks to predict which applicants will be successful if hired. *Successful* in this case means performing well on the criteria the organization uses to evaluate employees. In filling a sales position, for example, the selection process should be able to predict which applicants will generate a high volume of sales; for a position as a network administrator, it should predict which applicants will be able to effectively oversee and manage the organization's computer network.

Consider, for a moment, that any selection decision can result in four possible outcomes. As shown in Exhibit 7-4, two of these outcomes would be correct, and two would indicate errors.

A decision is correct when the applicant was predicted to be successful and proved to be successful on the job, or when the applicant was predicted to be unsuccessful and would have been so if hired. In the first case, we have successfully accepted; in the second case, we have successfully rejected.

Problems arise when errors are made in rejecting candidates who would have performed successfully on the job (reject errors) or accepting those who ultimately perform poorly

---

Exhibit 7-4

Selection Decision Outcomes

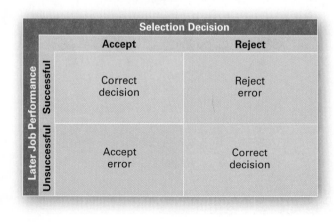

(accept errors). These problems can be significant. Given today's human resource laws and regulations, reject errors can cost more than the additional screening needed to find acceptable candidates. They can expose the organization to charges of discrimination, especially if applicants from protected groups are disproportionately rejected. The costs of accept errors include the cost of training the employee, the profits lost because of the employee's incompetence, the cost of severance, and the subsequent costs of further recruiting and screening. The major thrust of any selection activity should be to reduce the probability of making reject errors or accept errors while increasing the probability of making correct decisions. How do managers do this? By using selection procedures that are both valid and reliable.

Validity and Reliability

Any selection device that a manager uses should demonstrate **validity**, a proven relationship between the selection device and some relevant job criterion. For example, the law prohibits managers from using a test score as a selection device unless there is clear evidence that, once on the job, individuals with high scores on the test outperform individuals with low test scores. The burden is on managers to show that any selection device they use to differentiate between applicants is related to job performance.

validity
The proven relationship that exists between the selection device and some relevant job criterion.

In addition to being valid, a selection device must also demonstrate **reliability**, which indicates whether the device measures the same thing consistently. For example, if a test is reliable, any single individual's score should remain fairly consistent over time, assuming that the characteristics being measured are also stable. No selection device can be effective if it's low in reliability. Using such a device would be like weighing yourself every day on an erratic scale. If the scale is unreliable—randomly fluctuating, say, 4 to 7 kilos every time you step on it—the results will not mean much. To be effective predictors, selection devices must possess an acceptable level of consistency.

reliability
The ability of a selection device to measure the same thing consistently.

Types of Selection Devices

Managers can use a number of selection devices to reduce accept and reject errors. The best-known include application forms, written tests, performance-simulation tests, interviews, background investigations, and, in some cases, physical examinations. Let's briefly review each of these devices. Exhibit 7-5 on page 196 lists the strengths and weaknesses of each of these devices.[20] We review these devices below.

Application Forms Almost all organizations require job candidates to fill out an application. The form might include space in which the candidate can write his or her name, address, and telephone number. Or it might be a comprehensive personal-history profile that details the candidate's activities, skills, and accomplishments.

Written Tests Typical written tests include tests of intelligence, aptitude, ability, and interest. Such tests have been used for years, although their popularity tends to run in cycles. Today, personality, behavioural, and aptitude assessment tests are popular among businesses. Managers need to be careful regarding their use, however, since legal challenges against such tests have been successful when the tests are not job related or when they elicit information concerning sex, race, age, or other areas protected by the Employment Equity Act.

Managers know that poor hiring decisions are costly and that properly designed tests can reduce the likelihood of poor decisions. In addition, the cost of developing and validating a set of written tests for a specific job has decreased significantly.

A review of the evidence finds that tests of intellectual ability, spatial and mechanical ability, perceptual accuracy, and motor ability are moderately valid predictors for many semi-skilled and unskilled operative jobs in manufacturing.[21] However, an enduring criticism of written tests is that intelligence and other tested characteristics can be somewhat removed from the actual performance of the job itself.[22] For example, a high score on an intelligence test is not necessarily a good indicator that the applicant will perform well as a computer programmer. This criticism has led to an increased use of performance-simulation tests.

Exhibit 7-5

Selection Devices

Selection Device	Strengths	Weaknesses
Application Forms	Relevant biographical data and facts that can be verified have been shown to be valid performance measures for some jobs. When items on the form have been weighted to reflect job relatedness, this device has proved to be a valid predictor for diverse groups.	Usually only a couple of items on the form prove to be valid predictors of job performance and then only for a specific job. Weighted-item applications are difficult and expensive to create and maintain.
Written Tests	Tests of intellectual ability, spatial and mechanical ability, perceptual accuracy, and motor ability are moderately valid predictors for many semi-skilled and unskilled lower-level jobs in manufacturing. Intelligence tests are reasonably good predictors for supervisory positions.	Intelligence and other tested characteristics can be somewhat removed from actual job performance, thus reducing their validity.
Performance-Simulation Tests	Tests are based on job analysis data and easily meet the requirement of job relatedness. Tests have proven to be valid predictors of job performance.	They are expensive to create and administer.
Interviews	Interviews must be structured and well organized to be effective predictors. Interviewers must use common questions to be effective predictors.	Interviewers must be aware of the legality of certain questions. Interviews are subject to potential biases, especially if they are not well structured and standardized.
Background Investigations	Verifications of background data are valuable sources of information.	Reference checks are essentially worthless as a selection tool.
Physical Examinations	Physical exams have some validity for jobs with certain physical requirements.	Managers must be sure that physical requirements are job related and do not discriminate.

work sampling
A selection device in which applicants for a job are asked to perform a representative set of tasks that are central to it.

assessment centres
Places in which job candidates undergo performance-simulation tests to evaluate managerial potential.

Performance-Simulation Tests What better way is there to find out whether an applicant for a technical writing position at Matsushita can write technical manuals than by having him or her do it? Performance-simulation tests are made up of actual job behaviours. The best-known performance-simulation tests are **work sampling** (a miniature model of a job) and **assessment centres** (simulating real problems one may face on the job).

The advantage of performance simulation over traditional testing methods should be obvious. Because content is essentially identical to job content, performance simulation should be a better predictor of short-term job performance and should minimize potential employment discrimination allegations. Additionally, because of the nature of their content and the methods used to determine content, well-constructed performance-simulation tests are valid predictors.

Interviews The interview, like the application form, is an almost universal selection device.[23] Not many of us have ever been hired without one or more interviews. Because there are so many variables that can influence interviewer judgment, the value of the interview as a selection device has been of considerable debate.[24] Managers can make interviews more valid and reliable by following the approach presented in *Tips for Managers—Some Suggestions for Interviewing*. See also *Developing Your Interpersonal Skills—Interviewing*, on page 217, at the end of the chapter.

Another important factor in interviewing job candidates is the legality of certain interview questions. Employment law attorneys warn managers to be extremely cautious in the types of questions they ask candidates. Questions about age, marital status, and childbearing plans, for instance, are not appropriate.

A new approach that some companies are using is *situational interviews* in which candidates role play in mock scenarios. For instance, at a Bay Street bank in Toronto, a prospective account representative might be asked to role-play dealing with a customer who has an account discrepancy. The interviewers watch the candidate's reaction: how he or she processes the information, how he or she interacts with the "client," his or her body language, and which words he or she chooses.[25] Some companies also use group interviews, in which job candidates are interviewed by multiple people at once. In some settings, the interviews are conducted by different people across the organization, to assess whether the candidate fits in with the organizational culture. In other settings, the work team in which the candidate will work conducts the interview, to determine whether the candidate will fit into the work team. Candidates may even be asked to perform tasks with the team, to better assess how the candidate works with the team members.

Background Investigations If managers at Lucent Technologies had done a thorough background check, they might have discovered that the individual who eventually became director of recruitment (who is no longer with the company) was imprisoned for stealing money from student funds while a principal at a California high school and had lied about earning a doctorate at Stanford.[26]

Background investigations are of two types: verifications of application data and reference checks. The first type has proved to be a valuable source of selection information and can lower turnover, which saves the company the headaches and additional costs of continually hiring.[27] The second type can be worthless as a selection tool because applicants' references tend to be almost universally positive. Employers should consider contacting the previous employer to get further information, although employers have become reluctant to reveal negative information in recent years.

Physical Examinations This selection device would be useful for only a small number of jobs that have certain physical requirements.

What Works Best and When?

Many selection devices are of limited value to managers in making selection decisions. Exhibit 7-6 on page 198 summarizes the validity of these devices for particular types of jobs. Managers should use those devices that effectively predict success for a given job.

In addition, managers who treat the recruiting and hiring of employees as if the applicants must be sold on the job and exposed only to an organization's positive characteristics are likely to have a workforce that is dissatisfied and has higher turnover.[28] During the hiring process, every job applicant develops a set of expectations about the company and about the job for which he or she is interviewing. When the information an applicant receives is excessively inflated, a number of things happen that have potentially negative effects on the company. First, mismatched applicants are less likely to withdraw from the selection process. Second, because inflated information builds unrealistic expectations, new employees are likely to

Q&A 11.5

Q&A 11.6

TIPS FOR MANAGERS

Some Suggestions for Interviewing

→ Structure a **fixed set of questions** for all applicants.

→ Have **detailed information about the job** for which applicants are interviewing.

→ **Minimize any prior knowledge** of applicants' backgrounds, experience, interests, test scores, or other characteristics.

→ **Ask behavioural questions** that require applicants to give detailed accounts of actual job behaviours.

→ Use a **standardized evaluation form**.

→ **Take notes** during the interview.

→ **Avoid short interviews** that encourage premature decision making.

Source: Based on D. A. DeCenzo and S. P. Robbins, *Human Resource Management*, 7th ed. (New York: Wiley, 2002), p. 200.

Exhibit 7-6

Quality of Selection Devices as Predictors

Selection Device	Position			
	Senior Management	Middle and Lower Management	Complex Nonmanagerial	Routine Work
Application Forms	2	2	2	2
Written Tests	1	1	2	3
Work Sampling	—	—	4	4
Assessment Centres	5	5	—	—
Interviews	4	3	2	2
Verification of Application Data	3	3	3	3
Reference Checks	1	1	1	1
Physical Exams	1	1	1	2

Note: Validity is measured on a scale from 5 (highest) to 1 (lowest). A dash means "not applicable."

become quickly dissatisfied and leave the organization. Third, new hires are likely to become disillusioned and less committed to the organization when they face the unexpected harsh realities of the job. In many cases, these individuals may feel that they were misled during the hiring process and may become problem employees.

To increase job satisfaction among employees and reduce turnover, you should consider providing a **realistic job preview (RJP)**. An RJP includes both positive and negative information about the job and the company. For instance, in addition to the positive comments typically expressed during an interview, the job applicant might be told that there are limited opportunities to talk to co-workers during work hours, that promotional advancement is slim, or that work hours fluctuate so erratically that employees may be required to work during what are usually off hours (nights and weekends). Research indicates that applicants who have been given a realistic job preview hold lower and more realistic job expectations for the jobs they will be performing and are better able to cope with the frustrating elements of the job than are applicants who have been given only positive information.

realistic job preview (RJP)
A preview of a job that includes both positive and negative information about the job and the company.

ORIENTATION AND SKILL DEVELOPMENT

Thirty-year-old Roxann Linton is enthusiastic about her career at Scotiabank.[29] "Working with an international and diverse organization like Scotiabank, there are so many opportunities," says Linton. The young woman was chosen for Leading Edge, Scotiabank's fast-track leadership program. In the application process, she had to prepare a challenging business case analysis, go through psychometric testing, and be interviewed twice by a total of eight executives. The Leading Edge program prepares employees for senior management positions by rotating them through a series of assignments.

Linton worked for the bank for about five years in the bank's internal audit department in Kingston, Jamaica. She then transferred to Halifax and worked in commercial banking. During the first 15 months of the Leading Edge program, Linton managed more than 100 people in the electronic banking contact centre. Her next assignment was as director of special projects at Scotia Cassels Investment Counsel, part of the bank's wealth management division. She launched a new corporate bond fund during her first three months in that assignment. She will have one more 12-to-18-month assignment in another part of the bank, and then she can start applying for vice-president positions.

Organizations have to introduce new members to the work they will do and the organization. They do this through their orientation programs. As time goes by, employees may need to increase their skills. This is handled through training. We review the strategies that organizations use for orientation and training below.

4 How do organizations help employees adapt and stay up-to-date?

Orientation

Did you participate in some type of organized "introduction to campus life" when you started school? If so, you might have been told about your school's rules and regulations, the procedures for activities such as applying for financial aid, cashing a cheque, or registering for classes, and you were probably introduced to some of the campus administrators. A person starting a new job needs the same type of introduction to his or her job and the organization. This introduction is called **orientation**.

There are two types of orientation. *Work unit orientation* familiarizes the employee with the goals of the work unit, clarifies how his or her job contributes to the unit's goals, and includes an introduction to his or her new co-workers. *Organization orientation* informs the new employee about the organization's objectives, history, philosophy, procedures, and rules. This should include relevant human resource policies and benefits such as work hours, pay procedures, overtime requirements, and fringe benefits. In addition, a tour of the organization's work facilities is often part of the organization orientation.

orientation
Introduction of a new employee to his or her job and the organization.

Managers have an obligation to make the integration of the new employee into the organization as smooth and as free of anxiety as possible. They need to openly discuss employee beliefs regarding mutual obligations of the organization and the employee.[30] It's in the best interests of the organization and the new employee to get the person up and running in the job as soon as possible. Successful orientation, whether formal or informal, results in an outsider–insider transition that makes the new member feel comfortable and fairly well adjusted, lowers the likelihood of poor work performance, and reduces the probability of a surprise resignation by the new employee only a week or two into the job.

Training

Employee training is an important HRM activity. As job demands change, employee skills have to be altered and updated. It's been estimated that US business firms spend more than $54 billion on workforce development.[31] Canadian companies spend far less than American firms on training and development; Canadian companies spent $914 per employee in 2004, while American companies spent $1135 per employee in 2003 (the latest years for which figures are available).[32] Managers, of course, are responsible for deciding what type of training employees need, when they need it, and what form that training should take.

Toronto-based Labatt Breweries is putting its more than 3200 employees through more than beer school over the next few years. Beer "professors" at Labatt's beer school teach employees how to pour the perfect glass of beer and how to match food with certain beers.

Types of Training

When organizations invest in employee training, what are they offering? Exhibit 7-7 describes the major types of training that organizations provide.[33] Interpersonal skills training is a high priority for many organizations. For example, Shannon Washbrook, director of training and development for Vancouver-based Boston Pizza International, says, "Our people know the Boston Pizza concept; they have all the hard skills. It's the soft skills they lack." To address that, Washbrook launched Boston Pizza College, a training initiative that uses hands-on, scenario-based learning about many interpersonal skills topics.[34] SaskPower, like Scotiabank, uses training to develop leadership potential, as the following *Management Reflection* shows.

MANAGEMENT REFLECTION

SaskPower Sends Its Leaders to Leadership School

Are leaders made or born? Managers at Regina-based SaskPower believe that leaders are developed, not born.[35] The company has developed a leadership program that is similar to a mini-MBA. It introduces participants to leadership skills and other areas of business. The company selects employees for the program based on leadership potential. Individuals can nominate themselves for the leadership-training program by persuading management with examples of why they would make great managers.

The program works better than the way managers were chosen previously at SaskPower. "It was unorganized, and the 'old boys network' was still at work," said Bill Hyde, former vice-president of human resources. The program also ensures that SaskPower continues to have a skilled workforce and trained managers for the future, when Baby Boomers start retiring in large numbers. ■

Exhibit 7-7

Types of Training

Type	Includes:
Interpersonal Skills	Leadership, coaching, communication skills, conflict resolution, team building, customer service, diversity and cultural awareness, other interpersonal skills
Technical	Product training and knowledge, sales process, information technology, computer applications, other technical skills necessary to do a particular job
Business	Finance, marketing, lean manufacturing, quality, strategic planning, organizational culture
Mandatory	Safety, health, sexual harassment, and other legal compliance
Performance Management	Any training to help an individual employee improve his or her work performance
Problem Solving/Decision Making	Defining problems, assessing causation, creativity in developing alternatives, analyzing alternatives, selecting solution
Personal	Career planning, time management, wellness, personal finance or money management, public speaking

Training Methods

Is college or university education enough for the workplace, or do you need more training?

Employee training can be delivered in traditional ways including on-the-job training, job rotation, mentoring and coaching, experiential exercises, workbooks and manuals, classroom lectures or videos. Toronto-based Labatt Breweries has created its own beer school at an on-site pub at company headquarters to learn about the qualities of beer.[36] It might seem obvious that those in sales should know the product, but even accountants and human resource specialists from head office learn how to change a keg and clean the lines. They learn that "Keith's is a fast-pouring beer, that Stella Artois is best served in a glass with a stem and that foam bubbles should be sliced from the heads of some beers because 'large CO_2 bubbles will bloat us.'" Bruce Elliot, president of Labatt's Canadian operations, explains why everyone goes through Labatt's beer school. "It doesn't matter whether you work in the sales office or on the shop floor, all of our employees need to be beer experts . . . we'd like all of our people to be salespeople."

Labatt Breweries
www.labatt.com

Many organizations are relying more on technology-based training methods because of their accessibility, lower cost, and ability to deliver information. For instance, a computer-based simulation called Virtual Leader by SimuLearn provides trainees with realistic leadership scenarios, including the following:

> "Be in the boardroom in 10 minutes," reads the email from Senior Vice President Alan Young. The CEO is out on his boat, and a storm has knocked out all communication. Worse, there has been a massive fire in the call centre in South America. "We could lose billions," Young says. The board has given senior staff emergency powers. You're a top manager who has been called in to help. What do you do?[37]

Exhibit 7-8 provides a description of the various traditional and technology-based employee training methods that managers might use. Although web-based or online train-

---

Exhibit 7-8

Employee Training Methods

Traditional Training Methods

- *On-the-job*—Employees learn how to do tasks simply by performing them, usually after an initial introduction to the task.

- *Job rotation*—Employees work at different jobs in a particular area, getting exposure to a variety of tasks.

- *Mentoring and coaching*—Employees work with an experienced worker who provides information, support, and encouragement; also called an apprentice in certain industries.

- *Experiential exercises*—Employees participate in role playing, simulations, or other face-to-face types of training.

- *Workbooks/manuals*—Employees refer to training workbooks and manuals for information.

- *Classroom lectures*—Employees attend lectures designed to convey specific information.

Technology-Based Training Methods

- *CD-ROM/DVD/videotapes/audiotapes*—Employees listen to or watch selected media that convey information or demonstrate certain techniques.

- *Videoconferencing/teleconferencing/satellite TV*—Employees listen to or participate as information is conveyed or techniques demonstrated.

- *E-learning*—Internet-based learning where employees participate in multimedia simulations or other interactive modules.

ing had been predicted just a few years ago to become the most popular method of training, it simply has not lived up to expectations, Julie Kaufman, an industry analyst with IDC Canada, told attendees at a training and development conference in March 2004. Most organizations have not yet figured out how to make use of this type of training.[38]

MANAGING AND REWARDING PERFORMANCE

5 What can organizations do to help employees achieve high performance throughout their careers?

Managers need to know whether their employees are performing their jobs efficiently and effectively or whether there is need for improvement. Employees are often compensated based on those evaluations. For more on giving evaluations, see *Self-Assessment—How Good Am I at Giving Performance Feedback?* on page 214, at the end of the chapter.

Performance Management

performance management system
A process of establishing performance standards and evaluating performance in order to arrive at objective human resource decisions as well as to provide documentation to support those decisions.

What techniques might you want to use if you had to evaluate the members of your student project group?

Evaluating employee performance is part of a **performance management system**, which is a process of establishing performance standards and appraising employee performance in order to arrive at objective human resource decisions as well as to provide documentation to support those decisions. Performance appraisal is a critical part of a performance management system. Some companies invest far more effort in it than others.

Performance appraisal is not easy to do, and many managers do it poorly. Both managers and employees often dread the appraisal process. A recent survey found that 41 percent of employees report having had a least one incident of being demotivated after feedback from their managers.[39] Let's look at some different methods of doing performance appraisal. Performance appraisal can also be subject to politics, not unlike the 2002 Olympic Winter Games ice skating controversy in which the French judge was accused of manipulating her scores to enable the Russian skaters to win the gold over Canadians Jamie Salé and David Pelletier.

Performance Appraisal Methods

Managers can choose from seven major performance appraisal methods. The advantages and disadvantages of each of these methods are shown in Exhibit 7-9.

Exhibit 7-9

Advantages and Disadvantages of Performance Appraisal Methods

Method	Advantage	Disadvantage
Written Essays	Simple to use	More a measure of evaluator's writing ability than of employee's actual performance
Critical Incidents	Rich examples; behaviourally based	Time-consuming; lack quantification
Graphic Rating Scales	Provide quantitative data; less time-consuming than others	Do not provide depth of job behaviour assessed
BARS	Focus on specific and measurable behaviours	Time-consuming; difficult to develop job behaviours
Multiperson Comparisons	Compare employees with one another	Unwieldy with large number of employees; legal concerns
MBO	Focuses on end goals; results oriented	Time-consuming
360-Degree Feedback	Thorough	Time-consuming

Written Essays The **written essay** is a performance appraisal method in which the evaluator writes out a description of an employee's strengths and weaknesses, past performance, and potential. The evaluator also makes suggestions for improvement.

Critical Incidents The use of **critical incidents** focuses the evaluator's attention on critical or key behaviours that separate effective from ineffective job performance. The evaluator writes down anecdotes that describe what an employee did that was especially effective or ineffective. The key here is that only specific behaviours, not vaguely defined personality traits, are cited.

Graphic Rating Scales One of the most popular performance appraisal methods is **graphic rating scales**. This method lists a set of performance factors such as quantity and quality of work, job knowledge, cooperation, loyalty, attendance, honesty, and initiative. The evaluator then goes down the list and rates the employee on each factor using an incremental scale, which usually specifies five points. For instance, a factor such as job knowledge might be rated from 1 ("poorly informed about work duties") to 5 ("has complete mastery of all phases of the job").

Behaviourally Anchored Rating Scales Another popular performance appraisal method is **behaviourally anchored rating scales (BARS)**. These scales combine major elements from the critical incident and graphic rating scale approaches. The evaluator rates an employee according to items along a numeric scale, but the items are examples of actual job behaviours rather than general descriptions or traits.

Multiperson Comparisons **Multiperson comparisons** compare one individual's performance with that of others. This performance appraisal method has received a lot of attention recently.[40] Made popular by former General Electric (GE) CEO Jack Welch, employees were rated as top performers (20 percent), middle performers (70 percent), or bottom performers (10 percent). For instance, when Ford Motor Company used this performance appraisal method, it evaluated managers in groups of 30 to 50. In each group, 10 percent had to get an A score, 80 percent a B score, and 10 percent a C score. Although Ford no longer uses this ranking system, more than a third of companies do.[41]

Management by Objectives We previously introduced management by objectives (MBO) when we discussed planning in Chapter 3. MBO is also a mechanism for appraising performance. In fact, it's often used for assessing managers and professional employees.[42] With MBO, employees are evaluated according to how well they accomplish specific goals that have been established by them and their managers.

360-Degree Feedback **360-degree feedback** is a performance appraisal method that uses feedback from supervisors, employees, and co-workers. In other words, this appraisal uses information from the full circle of people with whom the manager interacts. Of the 101 large Canadian organizations surveyed by professors Mehrdad Debrayen and Stephane Brutus of the John Molson School of Business at Concordia University, 43 percent used 360-degree feedback.[43] Toronto-based Hill & Knowlton Canada, a public relations firm, uses 360-degree feedback to help employees learn what they need to get to the next level of the organization. The feedback has had the added benefit of reducing turnover to 18 percent.[44]

Users caution that, although it's effective for career coaching and helping a manager recognize his or her strengths and weaknesses, this method is not appropriate for determining pay, promotions, or terminations. Managers using 360-degree feedback also have to carefully consider the pros and cons of using anonymous evaluations.[45]

Not all organizations conduct performance evaluations; in particular, smaller organizations often do not. Consequently, it can be useful as an employee to ask your manager for an annual appraisal, if you do not routinely receive one. The feedback will allow you to determine your goals for the following year, and identify anything for which you need improvement or training.

written essay
A performance appraisal method in which the evaluator writes out a description of an employee's strengths and weaknesses, past performance, and potential.

critical incidents
A performance appraisal method in which the evaluator focuses on the critical behaviours that separate effective from ineffective job performance.

graphic rating scales
A performance appraisal method in which the evaluator rates an employee on a set of performance factors.

behaviourally anchored rating scales (BARS)
A performance appraisal method in which the evaluator rates an employee on examples of actual job behaviours.

multiperson comparisons
A performance appraisal method by which one individual's performance is compared with that of others.

360-degree feedback
A performance appraisal method that uses feedback from supervisors, employees, and co-workers.

What Happens When Performance Falls Short?

So far, our discussion has focused on the performance management system. But what if an employee is not performing in a satisfactory manner? What can you do?

If, for some reason, an employee is not meeting his or her performance goals, a manager needs to find out why. If it is because the employee is mismatched for the job (a hiring error) or because he or she does not have adequate training, something relatively simple can be done: The manager can either reassign the individual to a job that better matches his or her skills or train the employee to do the job more effectively. If the problem is associated not with the employee's abilities but with his or her desire to do the job, it becomes a **discipline** problem. In that case, a manager can try counselling and, if necessary, can take disciplinary action such as oral and written warnings, suspensions, and even termination.

Employee counselling is a process designed to help employees overcome performance-related problems. Rather than viewing the performance problem as something that needs to be punished (discipline), employee counselling attempts to uncover why employees have lost their desire or ability to work productively. More important, it is designed to find ways to fix the problem. In many cases, employees don't go from being productive one day to being unproductive the next. Rather, the change happens gradually and may be a function of what is occurring in their personal lives. Employee counselling attempts to assist employees in getting help to resolve whatever is bothering them.

COMPENSATION AND BENEFITS

discipline
Actions taken by a manager to enforce an organization's standards and regulations.

employee counselling
A process designed to help employees overcome performance-related problems.

6 How do compensation and benefits motivate employees?

How would you know whether your employer was paying you fairly?

Q&A　11.7

Most of us expect to receive appropriate compensation from our employers. Therefore, developing an effective and appropriate compensation system is an important part of the HRM process.[46] Why? Because it helps attract and retain competent and talented individuals who help the organization accomplish its mission and goals. In addition, an organization's compensation system has been shown to have an impact on its strategic performance.[47]

Managers must develop a compensation system that reflects the changing nature of work and the workplace in order to keep people motivated. Organizational compensation can include many different types of rewards and benefits such as base wages and salaries, wage and salary add-ons, incentive payments, as well as other benefits and services, including dental, eye care, and short- and long-term disability coverage.

How do managers determine who gets paid $9 an hour and who gets $350 000 a year? Several factors influence the differences in compensation and benefit packages for different employees. Exhibit 7-10 summarizes these factors, which are both job-based and business- or industry-based.

Many organizations use an alternative approach to determining compensation called **skill-based pay**, which rewards employees for the job skills and competencies they demonstrate. In a skill-based pay system, an employee's job title does not define his or her pay category; skills do.[48] Skill-based pay systems seem to mesh nicely with the changing nature of jobs and today's work environment. As one expert noted, "Slowly, but surely, we're becoming a skill-based society where your market value is tied to what you can do and what your skill set is. In this new world where skills and knowledge are what really count, it doesn't make sense to treat people as jobholders. It makes sense to treat them as people with specific skills and to pay them for these skills."[49]

Although many factors influence the design of an organization's compensation system, flexibility is a key consideration. The traditional approach to paying people reflected a time of job stability when an employee's pay was largely determined by seniority and job level. Given the dynamic environments that many organizations face in which the skills that are absolutely critical to organizational success can change in a matter of months, the trend is to make pay systems more flexible and to reduce the number of pay levels. However, whatever approach managers take, they must establish a fair, equitable, and motivating compensation system that allows the organization to recruit and keep a productive workforce.

skill-based pay
Pay based on the job skills and competencies employees demonstrate.

Exhibit 7-10

Factors That Influence Compensation and Benefits

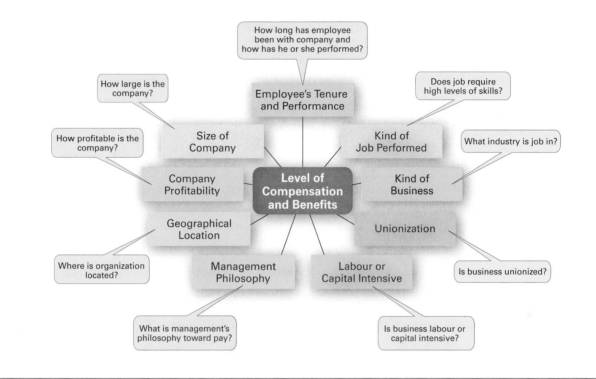

Sources: Based on R. I. Henderson, *Compensation Management,* 6th ed. (Upper Saddle River, NJ: Prentice Hall, 1994), pp. 3–24; and A. Murray, "Mom, Apple Pie, and Small Business," *Wall Street Journal,* August 15, 1994, p. A1.

CAREER DEVELOPMENT

The term *career* has several meanings. In popular usage, it can mean advancement ("she is on a management career track"), a profession ("he has chosen a career in accounting"), or a lifelong sequence of jobs ("his career has included 12 jobs in 6 organizations"). For our purposes, we define a **career** as the sequence of positions held by a person during his or her lifetime.[50] Using this definition, it's apparent that we all have, or will have, a career. Moreover, the concept is as relevant to unskilled labourers as it is to software designers or physicians.

Managing One's Career

Downsizing, restructuring, and other organizational adjustments have brought us to one significant conclusion about career development: The individual—not the organization—is responsible for his or her own career!

Individuals need to assume primary responsibility for career planning, career goal setting, and education and training.[51]

One of the first career decisions you have to make is career choice. The optimum career choice is one that offers the best match between what you want out of life and your interests, abilities, and market opportunities. Good career choice outcomes should result in a series of positions that give you an opportunity to be a good performer, make you want to maintain your commitment to your career, lead to highly satisfying work, and give you the proper balance between work and personal life. A good career match, then, is one in which you are able to develop a positive self-concept, to do work that you think is impor-

7 How are careers managed?

career
A sequence of positions held by a person during his or her lifetime.

Q&A 11.8

Exhibit 7-11

Top 10 Important Job Factors for College Graduates

(Ranked in order of importance)

1. Enjoying what they do
2. Opportunity to use skills and abilities
3. Opportunity for personal development
4. Feeling what they do matters
5. Benefits

6. Recognition for good performance
7. Friendly co-workers
8. Job location
9. Lots of money
10. Working on teams

Source: Based on V. Frazee, "What's Important to College Grads in Their First Jobs?" *Personnel Journal,* July 1996, p. 21.

tant, and to lead the kind of life you desire.[52] Exhibit 7-11 provides the results of a survey of American college graduates regarding what is important to them in their first jobs. How would you have ranked these items?

Once you have identified a career choice, it's time to initiate the job search. We are not going to get into the specifics of job hunting, writing a résumé, or interviewing successfully, although those career actions are important. Let's fast forward through all that and assume that your job search was successful. It's time to go to work! How do you survive and excel in your career? See *Tips for Managers—Some Suggestions for a Successful Management Career.*[53] By taking an active role in managing your career, your work life can be more exciting, enjoyable, and satisfying.

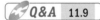 **Q&A 11.9**

CURRENT ISSUES IN HUMAN RESOURCE MANAGEMENT

Scotiabank prides itself on its work with the Aboriginal community.[54] The bank sponsors scholarships, events, and programs for community members, and also supports Aboriginal business initiatives.

The bank actively recruits from the Aboriginal community. Scotiabank's recruiting strategy is based "on the medicine wheel and the teachings of the medicine wheel, in terms of all the components's [of the medicine wheel] need to exist in balance together," says Michele Baptiste, national manager of Aboriginal relations with Scotiabank. The bank has also approached the Aboriginal Human Resource Development Council of Canada to assist "in recruitment and retention of Aboriginal people across the country," according to Baptiste.

THINK ABOUT IT

How are companies managing diversity in their workplaces? To what extent are they addressing issues such as work–life balance? Should they be doing so?

 What are some current issues in human resource management?

We conclude this chapter by looking at some contemporary human resource issues facing today's managers—workforce diversity, sexual harassment, work–life balance, and layoff-survivor sickness.

Workforce Diversity

We have discussed the changing makeup of the workforce in several places throughout this textbook and provided insights in our *Managing Workforce Diversity* feature in several chapters. In this section, we discuss how workforce diversity is directly affected by basic HRM activities including recruitment, selection, and orientation and training.

Recruitment

To improve workforce diversity, managers need to widen their recruiting net. For example, the popular practice of relying on employee referrals as a source of job applicants tends to produce candidates who are similar to present employees. However, some organizations, such as Toronto-based TELUS Mobility, have recruited and hired diverse individuals by relying on referrals from their current employees. But not every organization has the employee resources needed to achieve workforce diversity through employee referrals. So managers may have to look for job applicants in places where they might not have looked before. To increase diversity, managers from such companies as Calgary-based Suncor Energy, Saskatoon, Saskatchewan-based Cameco, and Toronto-based Scotiabank and TELUS Mobility are increasingly turning to nontraditional recruitment sources such as women's job networks, over-50 clubs, urban job banks, disabled people's training centres, ethnic newspapers, and gay rights organizations. This type of outreach should enable the organization to broaden its pool of diverse applicants. When IKEA went to Seville, Spain, it followed an alternative recruiting strategy, as the following *Management Reflection* shows.

> ## TIPS FOR MANAGERS
>
> ### Some Suggestions for a Successful Management Career
>
> → Develop a **network**.
> → Continue **upgrading** your skills.
> → Consider **lateral career moves**.
> → Stay **mobile**.
> → Support your **boss**.
> → Find a **mentor**.
> → **Don't stay too long** in your first job.
> → Stay **visible**.
> → Gain control of **organizational resources**.
> → Learn the **power structure**.
> → Present **the right image**.
> → Do **good work**.
> → Select your **first job carefully**.

MANAGEMENT REFLECTION

IKEA Taps into New Labour Force

Should you hire people with no previous experience? When Swedish-based IKEA opened up a store in Seville, its fifth location in Spain, the company decided to search for a different type of employee.[55] The company advertised for "single mothers, students, people with disabilities and long-term unemployed." They did not even require working experience. Andalusia, the region where the store was opening, has an 18.5 percent unemployment rate, and 30 000 applicants responded to IKEA's ads.

Employers in Spain had never recruited from these categories of workers before. IKEA's model for employment is unique: It targets people who really need jobs. The company provides training to its employees to help them overcome any initial hurdles from lack of experience. People with disabilities were hired for customer service, administration, and logistics. Juvencio Maeztu, the store manager, explained the store's hiring policy: "We were more interested in finding people with the right motivation than with the right college degrees."

IKEA's strategy of hiring the previously "unhirable" may well pay off in Spain. With high unemployment rates and IKEA's plan to open 22 new stores, those in Spain looking for jobs have renewed hope they will be able to find work. ■

Selection

Once a diverse set of applicants exists, efforts must be made to ensure that the selection process does not discriminate. Moreover, applicants need to be made comfortable with the organization's culture and be made aware of management's desire to accommodate their needs. For instance, at TD Canada Trust, managers are trained to respond positively to requests by employees who need a prayer room or whose religion requires them to stop working by sundown.[56]

Orientation and Training

The outsider–insider transition is often more challenging for women and minorities than for white males. Many organizations provide special workshops to raise diversity awareness issues. However, some organizations pursue diversity efforts only after being hit with legal claims. For instance, Denny's was hit with a series of legal claims in the early 1990s. It responded with aggressive minority hiring and a supplier-diversity effort. The company was ranked in the top 3 of *Fortune* magazine's "America's 50 Best Companies for Minorities" survey from 2000 to 2003, suggesting its diversity efforts had paid off. Coca-Cola, which settled a class-action suit by black employees for more than $250 million (US) in November 2000, has made strides in its diversity efforts, including launching a formal mentoring program and required diversity training for employees.[57]

Sexual Harassment

Sexual harassment is a serious issue in both public and private sector organizations. A recent survey by York University found that 48 percent of working women in Canada reported they had experienced some form of "gender harassment" in the year before they were surveyed.[58] A 1996 RCMP survey found that 6 out of every 10 female Mounties said they had experienced sexual harassment.[59] Barbara Orser, a research affiliate with The Conference Board of Canada, notes that "sexual harassment is more likely to occur in workplace environments that tolerate bullying, intimidation, yelling, innuendo and other forms of discourteous behaviour."[60] Sexual harassment is not a problem just in Canada. Data indicate that almost all *Fortune* 500 companies in the United States have had complaints lodged by employees, and about a third of them have been sued.[61] Sexual harassment is a global issue: Charges have been filed against employers in such countries as Japan, Australia, the Netherlands, Belgium, New Zealand, Sweden, Ireland, and Mexico.[62]

 Q&A 11.10

Even though discussions of sexual harassment cases often focus on the large awards granted by a court, there are other concerns for employers. Sexual harassment creates an unpleasant work environment and undermines employees' ability to perform their jobs.

Sexual harassment is defined by the Supreme Court of Canada as unwelcome behaviour of a sexual nature in the workplace that negatively affects the work environment or leads to adverse job-related consequences for the employee.[63] Sexual harassment can occur between members of the opposite sex or of the same sex. Although such activity is generally covered under employment discrimination laws, in recent years this problem has gained more recognition. By most accounts, prior to the mid-1980s this problem was generally viewed as an isolated incident, with the individual at fault being solely responsible (if at all) for his or her actions.

sexual harassment
Any unwelcome behaviour of a sexual nature in the workplace that negatively affects the work environment or leads to adverse job-related consequences for the employee.

Many problems associated with sexual harassment involve interpreting the Supreme Court's definition to determine exactly what constitutes illegal behaviour. For many organizations, conveying what an offensive or hostile environment looks like is not completely black and white. For instance, while it is relatively easy to focus on problems of an individual employee's being harassed, this may not address more systemic problems in the workplace. Other employees can also be negatively affected when they witness offensive conduct.[64] Thus managers need to be attuned to what makes fellow employees uncomfortable—and if they don't know, they should ask.[65]

What can an organization do to protect itself against sexual harassment claims?[66] The courts want to know two things: Did the organization know about, or should it have known about, the alleged behaviour? and What did management do to stop it? With the number and dollar amounts of the awards against organizations increasing, organizations should develop sexual harassment policies, educate all employees on sexual harassment matters, and have mechanisms available to monitor employees and deal with complaints, should they arise.

Work–Life Balance

What kinds of work–life balance issues are affecting your life right now?

Professors Linda Duxbury of the Sprott School of Business at Carleton University and Chris Higgins of the University of Western Ontario are the leading Canadian researchers on the issue of work–life balance. Their research shows that employees are working long hours, and are also increasingly being asked to work a number of unpaid hours a week. This affects employees' abilities to manage their family lives.

What kinds of work–life balance issues can arise that might affect an employee's job performance? Here are some examples:

- Is it okay for someone to bring his baby to work because of an emergency crisis with normal child care arrangements?

- Is it okay to expect an employee to work 60 or more hours a week?

- Should an employee be given the day off to watch her child perform in a school event?

In the 1980s, organizations began to recognize that employees don't leave their families and personal lives behind when they walk into work. An organization hires a person who has a personal life outside the office, personal problems, and family commitments. Although managers cannot be sympathetic to every detail of an employee's family life, we *are* seeing organizations more aware of the fact that employees have sick children, elderly parents who need special care, and other family issues that may require special arrangements. In response, most major organizations have taken actions to make their workplaces more family-friendly by offering **family-friendly benefits**, which include a wide range of work and family programs to help employees.[67] They have introduced programs such as on-site child care, summer day camps, flextime, job sharing, leaves for school functions, telecommuting, and part-time employment. Work–life conflicts are as relevant to male employees with children and female employees without children as they are to female employees with children. Heavy workloads and increased travel demands, for instance, are making it increasingly hard for many employees, male and female, to meet both work and personal responsibilities.

family-friendly benefits
Benefits that accommodate employees' needs for work–life balance.

Today's progressive workplace is becoming more accommodating to the varied needs of a diverse workforce. It provides a wide range of scheduling options and benefits that give employees more flexibility at work and allow employees to better balance or integrate their work and personal lives. Despite these organizational efforts, work–life programs have room for improvement. Workplace surveys still show high levels of employee stress stemming from work–life conflicts. And large groups of women and minority employees remain unemployed or underemployed because of family responsibilities and bias in the workplace.[68] So what can managers do?

Recent research on work–life conflicts has provided new insights. For instance, evidence indicates that time pressures are not the primary problem underlying the conflicts.[69] It's the psychological intrusion of work into the family domain and vice versa. People are worrying about personal problems at work and thinking about work problems at home. So Dad may physically make it home in time for dinner but his mind is elsewhere while he is at the dinner table. This suggests that organizations

Does being rigid about not offering flextime harm employers? Surrey, BC, mom Sheila Whitehead thinks so. She quit her job as a marketing manager for a pharmaceuticals company when she could not get the flextime she needed to spend more time with her four-year-old-daughter Abigail and her other two young children. She says that employers are "missing out on incredibly talented people who simply don't want the rigid nine-to-five hours." She has created a website, Beyond9to5.com, to help match employers with employees who want to have more flexible work hours.

should devote less effort to helping employees with time-management issues and more effort to helping them clearly segment their lives. Keeping workloads reasonable, reducing work-related travel, and offering on-site quality child care are examples of human resource practices that can help. Also, not surprisingly, people have been found to differ in their preferences for scheduling options and benefits.[70] Some people prefer organizational initiatives that better separate work from their personal lives. Others prefer programs that facilitate integration. For instance, flextime separates because it allows employees to schedule work hours that are less likely to conflict with personal responsibilities. On the other hand, on-site child care integrates by blurring the boundaries between work and family responsibilities. People who prefer segmentation are more likely to be satisfied and committed to their jobs when offered options such as flextime, job sharing, and part-time hours. People who prefer integration are more likely to respond positively to options such as on-site child care, gym facilities, and company-sponsored family picnics.

Helping Survivors Respond to Layoffs

downsizing
The planned elimination of jobs in an organization.

Downsizing is the planned elimination of jobs in an organization. When an organization has too many employees—which can happen when it needs to cut costs, is faced with declining market share, or has grown too aggressively—one option for shoring up profits is by eliminating some of those surplus employees. Well-known companies such as Air Canada, Nortel, Shaw Communications, Domtar, BCE, and others have had to downsize in recent years.[71] How can managers best manage a downsized workplace? Expect disruptions in the workplace and in employees' personal lives. Stress, frustration, anxiety, and anger are typical reactions of both individuals being laid off and the job survivors. But are there things managers can do to lessen the pain? Yes.[72]

Open and honest communication is critical. Individuals who are being let go need to be informed as soon as possible. In providing assistance to employees being downsized, the law requires some form of severance pay in lieu of proper notice. Benefit extensions to help employees while they find new plans must also be covered for a specified period of time. Managers want to be sure to follow any laws that might affect the length of time that pay and benefits must be offered. In addition, many organizations provide job search assistance.

layoff-survivor sickness
A set of attitudes, perceptions, and behaviours of employees who remain after involuntary employee reductions; it includes insecurity, guilt, depression, stress, fear, loss of loyalty, and reduced effort.

It may surprise you to learn that both victims and survivors experience feelings of frustration, anxiety, and loss.[73] But layoff victims get to start over with a clean slate and a clear conscience. Survivors don't. A new syndrome seems to be popping up in more and more organizations: **layoff-survivor sickness**, a set of attitudes, perceptions, and behaviours of employees who survive involuntary staff reductions.[74] Symptoms include job insecurity, perceptions of unfairness, guilt, depression, stress from increased workload, fear of change, loss of loyalty and commitment, reduced effort, and an unwillingness to do anything beyond the required minimum.

To address this survivor syndrome, managers may want to provide opportunities for employees to talk to counsellors about their guilt, anger, and anxiety.[75] Group discussions can also provide an opportunity for the survivors to vent their feelings. Some organizations have used downsizing as the spark to implement increased employee participation programs such as empowerment and self-managed work teams. In short, to keep morale and productivity high, every attempt should be made to ensure that those individuals who are still working in the organization know that they are valuable and much-needed resources.

Michele Baptiste, national manager of Aboriginal relations with Scotiabank, created the bank's Aboriginal employment strategy. It is based on the teachings of the medicine wheel (an example of which is shown here). The idea behind the medicine wheel is that the four major components of an individual (mental, spiritual, emotional, physical) have to be in balance. Baptiste emphasizes that Scotiabank takes a holistic approach to Aboriginal relations, bringing together employment, business, and community involvement.

SUMMARY AND IMPLICATIONS

1 **What factors affect human resource planning?** The human resource management (HRM) process consists of eight activities for staffing the organization and sustaining high employee performance. These include making sure that competent employees are identified and selected; trained appropriately; and motivated to stay with the organization and perform at a high level. The entire HRM process is influenced by the external environment, particularly economic conditions, labour unions, and government legislation. When managers hire employees, they must follow laws that have been written to protect employees and the workplace, including the Canada Labour Code, employment standards legislation, the Charter of Rights and Freedoms, and the Canadian Human Rights Act. Therefore, managers are not completely free to choose whom they hire, promote, or fire. *Practically speaking, managers such as Rick Waugh of Scotiabank cannot simply hire their friends, or decide to exclude from hire a particular ethnic group. While Scotiabank's employees are not unionized, managers within a unionized environment are obligated to uphold the collective agreement negotiated with the labour union.*

2 **How do organizations assess their human resource needs?** Human resource managers do a human resource inventory to discover what skills and capabilities current employees have. They map that inventory against what might be needed in the future, based on the organization's mission, goals, and strategies. *Because President and CEO Rick Waugh would like to see more women in senior management positions, Scotiabank needs to assess which of its female employees have the skills and leadership qualities to move into senior management.*

3 **How do organizations identify and select competent employees?** Organizations first need to assess their current and future needs for employees, to make sure they have enough of the right people to accomplish the organization's goals. When selecting new employees, organizations need to determine whether potential employees will be successful once they are on the job. To do this, managers use application forms, written tests, performance-simulation tests, interviews, background investigations, and, in some cases, physical examinations to screen employees. Managers also need to make sure that they do not engage in discrimination in the hiring process. *One way that Scotiabank identifies potential employees is through applications that come in through its Careers webpage, which targets young graduates and encourages them to think about working for the bank.*

4 **How do organizations help employees adapt and stay up-to-date?** Organizations, particularly larger ones, have orientation programs for new employees. The orientation introduces the new employee to his or her job, and also to the organization. As job demands change, employees may need to have their skills updated through training programs. Companies use a variety of training methods, from on-the-job training to classroom work to technology-based training. *Among other programs, Scotiabank has Leading Edge, the bank's fast-track leadership program.*

5 **What can organizations do to help employees achieve high performance throughout their careers?** Organizations should develop performance standards for employees, and then evaluate employees on a regular basis. Through performance appraisal, employees learn whether they are performing effectively, or whether they need help to improve, including getting additional training.

How do compensation and benefits motivate employees? Organizations develop compensation and benefit programs that will motivate employees to achieve high performance. Many organizations have implemented skill-based pay systems, which reward employees for the job skills and competencies they can demonstrate.

7 **How are careers managed?** A career is the sequence of positions held by a person during his or her lifetime. Employees are encouraged to create their own development programs, in addition to whatever their companies provide, because often employees work for multiple organizations during their careers.

8 **What are some current issues in human resource management?** The major current issues in human resource management include workforce diversity, sexual harassment, work–life balance, and layoff-survivor sickness. *Scotiabank prides itself on its work with the Aboriginal community, sponsoring scholarships, events, and programs for community members and also supporting Aboriginal business initiatives. The bank also permits flex hours, flex days, job sharing, and telecommuting so that employees can find the right "work life" to match their personal needs.*

CHAPTER 7

Management @ Work

Reading for Comprehension

1. Describe the environmental factors that most directly influence the human resource management process.

2. Contrast reject errors and accept errors. Which are more likely to open an employer to charges of discrimination? Why?

3. What is the relationship among job analysis, recruitment, and selection?

4. What are the major problems of the interview as a selection device?

5. What are the benefits and drawbacks of realistic job previews? (Consider this question from the perspective of both the organization and the employee.)

6. How are orientation and employee training alike? How are they different?

7. Describe three performance appraisal methods as well as the advantages and disadvantages of each.

8. What is skill-based pay?

9. How do recruitment, selection, orientation, and training directly affect workforce diversity?

Linking Concepts to Practice

1. Should an employer have the right to choose employees without government interference in the hiring process? Explain your position.

2. Do you think there are moral limits on how far a prospective employer should delve into an applicant's life by means of interviews, tests, and background investigations? Explain your position.

3. Studies show that women's salaries still lag behind men's, and even with equal opportunity laws and regulations women are paid about 73 percent of what men are paid. How would you design a compensation system that would address this issue?

4. What in your view constitutes sexual harassment? Describe how companies can minimize sexual harassment in the workplace.

5. Why should managers be concerned with diversity in the workplace? What special human resource management issues does diversity raise?

6. "Victims of downsizing are not those employees who were let go. Rather, the victims are the ones who have kept their jobs." Do you agree or disagree with this statement? Defend your position.

MANAGEMENT FOR YOU TODAY

Your instructor has asked class members to form teams to work on a major class project. You have worked on teams before, and have not always been pleased with the results. This time you are determined to have a good team experience. You have reason to believe that how people are recruited to and selected for teams might make a differ-ence. You also know that evaluating performance and giving feedback are important. You have also heard that training can make a difference. With all of this in mind, write up a plan that indicates how you might recruit an excellent set of team members, and make sure that they perform well throughout.

How Good Am I at Giving Performance Feedback?

For each of the following pairs, identify the statement that most closely matches what you normally do when you give feedback to someone else.[76]

1. a. Describe the behaviour.   **b.** Evaluate the behaviour.

2. a. Focus on the feelings that the behaviour evokes.   **b.** Tell the person what he or she should be doing differently.

3. a. Give specific instances of the behaviour.   **b.** Generalize.

4. a. Deal only with behaviour that the person can control.   **b.** Sometimes focus on something the person can do nothing about.

5. a. Tell the person as soon as possible after the behaviour.   **b.** Sometimes wait too long.

6. a. Focus on the effect the behaviour has on me.   **b.** Try to figure out why the individual did what he or she did.

7. a. Balance negative feedback with positive feedback.   **b.** Sometimes focus only on the negative.

8. a. Do some soul searching to make sure that the reason I am giving the feedback is to help the other person or to strengthen our relationship.   **b.** Sometimes give feedback to punish, win, or dominate the other person.

Scoring Key

Total the number of "a" responses, and then total the number of "b" responses, and then form an a/b ratio. For instance, if you have 6 "a" responses and 2 "b" responses, your a/b ratio would be 6/2.

Analysis and Interpretation

Along with listening skills, feedback skills comprise the other primary component of effective communication. This instrument is designed to assess how good you are at providing feedback.

In this assessment instrument, the "a" responses are your self-perceived strengths and the "b" responses are your self-perceived weaknesses. By looking at the proportion of your "a" and "b" responses, you will be able to see how effective you feel you are when giving feedback and determine where your strengths and weaknesses lie. For instance, an a/b ratio of 8/0, 7/1, or 6/2 suggests relatively strong feedback skills. In contrast, ratios of 3/5, 2/6, 1/7, or 0/8 indicate significant self-perceived weaknesses that can be

improved upon. To work on improving your feedback skills, see M. London, *Job Feedback: Giving, Seeking, and Using Feedback for Performance Improvement* (Lawrence Erlbaum, 2003).

More Self-Assessments

To learn more about your skills, abilities, and interests, take the following self-assessments on your enclosed CD-ROM:

- #8—How Satisfied Am I with My Job?
- #46—Am I Experiencing Work/Family Conflict?

Laying Off Workers

Every manager, at some point in his or her career, is likely to be faced with the difficult task of laying off employees. Assume that you are the manager in the internal auditing department of a 4500-member corporation. You have been notified by top management that you must permanently reduce your staff of five by two. Following are some data about your five employees.

Emma Liu: Chinese Canadian female, age 32. Emma has been employed with your company for five years in the accounting department. Her evaluations over the past three years have been above average and outstanding. Emma has an MBA from a top business school. She has been on maternity leave for the past few weeks because of the birth of her second child and is expected to return to work in 20 weeks.

Ron Johnson: White male, age 49. Ron has been with you for four months and has 11 years of experience in the company in payroll. He has a B.Comm. and an MBA, and he specialized in accounting during both degree programs. He is also a CGA. Ron's evaluations over the past three years in payroll have been average, but he did save the company $150 000 on a suggestion he made regarding the use of electronic time sheets.

Satish Patel: Indo-Canadian male, age 31. Satish has been with the company for almost four years. His evaluations over the past three years in your department have been outstanding. He is committed to getting the job done and doing whatever it takes. He has also shown initiative by taking job assignments that no one else wanted, and he has recovered a number of overdue and uncollected accounts that you had simply thought should be written off as a loss.

Julie Sapp: White female, age 35. Julie has been with your company for seven years. Four years ago, Julie was in an automobile accident while travelling on business to a customer's location. As a result of the accident, she was disabled and is wheelchair-bound. Rumours have it that she is about to receive several million dollars from the insurance company of the driver who hit her. Her performance during the past two years has been above average. She has a B.Comm. in accounting and has developed considerable expertise in computer information systems.

Bobby Hayden: African Canadian male, age 43. Bobby just completed his double master's degree in taxation and law and recently passed the bar exam. He has been with your department for four years. His evaluations have been good to above average. Five years ago, Bobby won a lawsuit against your company for discriminating against him in a promotion to a supervisory position. Rumours have it that now, with his new degree, Bobby is actively pursuing another job outside the company.

In a group of three to five students, seek consensus on the questions that follow. Given the five brief descriptions above, which two employees should be laid off? Are there any other options that can be used to meet the requirement of downsizing by two employees without resorting to layoffs? What will you do to assist the two individuals who have been let go and to assist the remaining three employees? Be prepared to defend your actions.

ETHICAL DILEMMA EXERCISE

But I Deserve an "A"!

Everybody wants an A ranking; nobody wants a C ranking. Yet the multiperson ranking system used by Goodyear Tire & Rubber Company forced managers to rank 10 percent of the workforce as A performers, 80 percent as B performers, and 10 percent as C performers. Those ranked as A performers were rewarded with promotions; those ranked as C performers were told they could be demoted or fired for a second C rating. Goodyear abandoned its 10-80-10 system just before some C employees who had been fired filed a lawsuit claiming age discrimination. "It is very unfair to start with the assumption that a certain percentage of your employees are unsatisfactory," said one of the plaintiffs. "It was very subjective and designed to weed out the older people."

Like Goodyear, a growing number of companies have followed the lead of General Electric in regularly ranking employees. Many companies give poor performers an opportunity to improve before taking action. However, critics say the ranking system forces managers to penalize employees on poorly performing teams. They also say the ranking system can lead to age, gender, or race discrimination. In response, companies are training managers to use more objective measures for appraisals, such as monitoring progress toward preset goals.[77]

Imagine that you must rank 20 percent of your subordinate managers as top performers, 70 percent as average, and 10 percent as needing improvement. Retaining incompetent or unmotivated managers is unfair to the rest of the staff and sends mixed signals. On the other hand, even if all your managers are competent, you must put 10 percent into the bottom category. Now it's appraisal time and you do not feel that any of your employees deserve to be in the bottom category. What should you do? (Review Exhibit 7-9 on page 202 as you consider this ethical challenge.)

CASE APPLICATION

Mitsubishi Motors North America

When Rich Gilligan took over as plant manager at Mitsubishi Motors North America's (MMNA) manufacturing facility in Normal, Illinois, in 1998 the plant had two notorious distinctions: It was one of the most automated yet least productive plants in the industry, and it was known as the place sued by the US government for the sexual harassment of its female employees.[78] That lawsuit was what most people knew about Mitsubishi Motors.

The high-profile case told the story of a dismal workplace: "sexual graffiti written on fenders about to pass female line employees; pornographic pictures taped on walls; male employees taunting women with wrenches and air compressors; women asked by male employees to bare their breasts; other women fondled; and women who complained of being fired or passed over for promotion." Almost from the beginning, the plant had a bad reputation regarding the employment of women. People in the local community looked with suspicion at plant employees. One of the shift managers said, "We had guys who had no bad marks asked to stop coaching girls' softball teams just because they worked at that plant." After numerous employee complaints, the Equal Employment Opportunity Commission (EEOC) entered the picture and filed suit on behalf of 500 female employees, charging the company with sexual harassment. The case dragged on for three years, further draining employee morale and damaging an already distant relationship between American employees and Japanese managers. That is the environment that Gilligan inherited.

Right before Gilligan was hired, MMNA settled the EEOC lawsuit for more than $44 million (US)—still the largest sexual harassment settlement in US history. The money was distributed to more than 400 women, many of whom still work at the plant. The EEOC settlement also dictated a makeover of the work environment.

Gilligan needs to change the culture of the plant, and improve productivity and quality. He knows that Mitsubishi's mission statement is "We are a spirited, diverse workforce. We are a culture that looks for, and rewards, hard work and dedication. We are winners." Although each member of the Mitsubishi Group is independent, they are supposed to share the guiding principles of the Sankoryo, first announced in the 1930s by founder Mr. Koyata Iwasaki and revised to reflect today's realities:

- *Shoki Hoko:* Strive to enrich society, both materially and spiritually, while contributing toward the preservation of the environment.

- *Shoji Komei:* Maintain principles of transparency and openness, conducting business with integrity and fairness.

- *Ritsugyo Boeki:* Expand business, based on an all-encompassing global perspective.

Conduct like this was not happening at MMNA as Gilligan took over. What should he do to improve the culture and increase productivity?

DEVELOPING YOUR DIAGNOSTIC AND ANALYTICAL SKILLS

The Benefits of Benefits

Can the benefits offered to employees be a factor in encouraging individuals to apply for and accept jobs in an organization? Would your response to a job viewed as less than desirable, in which the work hours are long and the pay is low, be the same if it had benefits? For some people, benefits are critical to whether they take and keep a job. Take the case of Patsy Sechrest.

Patsy Sechrest is among a growing number of contemporary employees who cannot afford to retire. She is in her twenty-eighth year as an employee at a family restaurant in BC. She works more than 50 hours a week, earning $9.00 per hour and arriving to work at 4:05 a.m. each day. Sechrest, like many others more than 50 years old, continues to work simply because she needs the money and the extended health benefits (eye care, dental care, prescription drugs, massage, and physiotherapy) that working provides. Compounding this issue is the fact that Sechrest and her husband live in a depressed area that was hit hard by the closing of a local pulp-and-paper mill.

Sechrest is also dealing with health ailments that have created a financial burden for her family. Making just over $20 000 annually, she is one of the more fortunate ones. Her employer provides generous extended health benefits. Without it, she would be financially devastated and in physical pain. Due to arthritis she needs to see a massage therapist and a physiotherapist regularly. Her health insurance pays most of the costs. Without the health insurance coverage, she simply could not have afforded the alternative medical treatments she receives.

For Patsy Sechrest, work and therapist visits have become a way of life. She is not bitter at the hand she has been dealt, but rather she is thankful for what her employer has provided—a paying job and extended health benefits. She expects to hang on to both for as long as she can!

Questions

1. How do benefits, such as those that the family restaurant provides, assist organizations in competing for and retaining employees?

2. Do you believe employee benefits should be membership-based (you get them simply because you work for the company) or performance-based (you earn them)? Defend your position.

3. Do you believe providing extended health care benefits for employees is a competitive necessity or a socially responsible action by the organization? Defend your position.

Interviewing

About the Skill

The interview is used almost universally as part of the employee selection process. Not many of us have ever been hired without having gone through one or more interviews. Interviews can be valid and reliable selection tools, but they need to be structured and well organized.

Steps in Developing the Skill

You can be an effective interviewer by using the following seven suggestions for interviewing job candidates:[79]

1. **Review the job description and job specification.** Be sure that prior to the interview you have reviewed pertinent information about the job. Why? Because this will provide you with valuable information on which to assess the job candidate. Furthermore, knowing the relevant job requirements will help eliminate interview bias.

2. **Prepare a structured set of questions you want to ask all job applicants.** By having a set of prepared questions, you ensure that you will get the information you want. Furthermore, by asking similar questions, you are able to better compare all candidates' answers against a common base.

3. **Before meeting a candidate, review his or her application form and résumé.** By doing this, you will be able to create a complete picture of the candidate in terms of what is represented on the résumé or application and what the job requires. You can also begin to identify areas to explore during the interview; that is, areas that are not clearly defined on the résumé or application but that are essential to the job can become a focal point in your discussion with the candidate.

4. **Open the interview by putting the applicant at ease and by providing a brief preview of the topics to be discussed.** Interviews are stressful for job candidates. Opening the discussion with small talk, such as the weather, can give the candidate time to adjust to the interview setting. By providing a preview of topics to come, you are giving the candidate an agenda. This helps the candidate begin framing what he or she will say in response to your questions.

5. **Ask your questions and listen carefully to the candidate's answers.** Select follow-up questions that flow naturally from the answers given. Focus on the candidate's responses as they relate to information you need to ensure that the person meets your job requirements. If you are still uncertain, use a follow-up question to probe further for information.

6. **Close the interview by telling the applicant what is going to happen next.** Applicants are anxious about the status of your hiring decision. Be upfront with candidates regarding others who will be interviewed and the remaining steps in the hiring process. Let the person know your time frame for making a decision. In addition, tell the applicant how you will notify him or her about your decision.

7. **Write your evaluation of the applicant while the interview is still fresh in your mind.** Don't wait until the end of the day, after interviewing several people, to write your analysis of each person. Memory can (and often will) fail you! The sooner you write your impressions after an interview, the better chance you have of accurately noting what occurred in the interview and your perceptions of the candidate.

Practising the Skill

Review and update your résumé. Then have several friends critique it who are employed in management-level positions or in management training programs. Ask them to explain their comments and make any changes to your résumé that they think will improve it.

Now inventory your interpersonal and technical skills and any practical experiences that do not show up in your résumé. Draft a set of leading questions you would like to be asked in an interview that would give you a chance to discuss the unique qualities and attributes you could bring to the job.

CoolBrands C: Thoughts of Restructuring

Michael Serruya, co-chair of CoolBrands, is responsible for setting strategy. He studies the complexities of the company's organizational structure. There is concern that some products may be getting to the end of their natural product life cycle (such as frozen yogurt), while others may simply be riding the current diet fad (such as the Atkins Endulge line). The company needs to stay on top of the changing environment. Serruya wants to make sure the organizational structure is flexible enough to rapidly respond to change. He considers the following factors that affect CoolBrands' structure.

Operations

CoolBrands has four major operations:

- *Prepackaged consumer products business* involves manufacturing, selling, and distributing prepackaged frozen dessert products under a variety of names, including Eskimo Pie, Dreamery, Godiva, Tropicana, and Weight Watchers Smart Ones.
- *Franchising and licensing business* includes operations under the Yogen Früz, I Can't Believe It's Yogurt, Bresler's, and Swensen's banners, among others.
- *Foodservice business* involves manufacturing soft-serve yogurt and ice cream mixes that are sold to foodservice distributors, yogurt shops, and other foodservice establishments.
- *Dairy components business* involves manufacturing flavours, ingredients, and packaging that are sold to frozen novelty manufacturers and the dairy industry.

Franchising

In order to manage its brand, CoolBrands engages in two types of franchise agreements:

- *Retail franchises.* These are sold to individuals who manage larger locations (traditional stores or kiosks) that offer a full range of products.
- *Master franchises.* These are sold to individuals who manage specific regions, countries, or other geographical areas. The master franchisor can then sell franchises or grant licences in his or her territory.

Exhibits 1 and 2 indicate the complicated nature of how these franchises are distributed, using just four of CoolBrands' many brands for illustration purposes.

Product Lines

While the company's different franchises sell most of the company's products, CoolBrands also distributes products to grocers. The company makes a variety of frozen products, including ice cream, yogurt, and frozen bars. These products can be further subdivided along snack foods, health and diet lines, and gourmet treats.

The company markets a broad range of ice cream, frozen novelties, and frozen dessert products under the Atkins, Godiva, Tropicana, Welch's, Weight Watchers Smart Ones, Betty Crocker, Trix, Yoplait, Dreamery Ice Cream, Whole Fruit Sorbet, Eskimo Pie, Chipwich, and Fruit-A-Freeze brand names. CoolBrands also distributes ice cream and frozen dessert products for other ice cream brands, including Nestlé, Dreyer's, Edy's, Häagen-Dazs, Friendly's, and Carvel.

Exhibit 1

Franchise Reporting Arrangements

Source: Based on Yogen Früz World-Wide, *Prospectus*, June 11, 1997.

Geographical Dispersion

While CoolBrands' largest sales market is the United States, followed by Canada, CoolBrands' products are sold throughout the world. Canada's franchising and licensing sales are about 25 percent of US sales. Total international sales are slightly less than Canada's.

Serruya understands the importance of identifying differences across markets. "You have to adapt yourself to the local market to be accepted," he says. CoolBrands' research and development team visits countries before opening franchises, studying the culture and trying to understand food preferences. In Thailand, Yogen Früz sells lichee- and mango-flavoured yogurts. In North America, the favourite yogurt is strawberry, but in Thailand, lichee outsells strawberry three to one.

Serruya wonders whether international sales might rise if there was even more focus on developing specialized products. He also considers whether creating specific divisions based on geography might increase international sales.

The Decision

Serruya has heard about functional, product, geographical structure, process, and customer departmentalization. Currently, CoolBrands has a mix of regional and product units responsible for franchise operations. He would like to see the operations run efficiently, while remaining responsive to regional differences. At the same time, he needs a structure that will encourage innovation. Serruya must also resolve how to keep all the different franchisors and master franchisors informed about new product lines and directions. With everyone spread throughout the world, this has become increasingly complicated.

Sources: CoolBrands International, *Annual Report,* 2003; R. Kang, "Wordly Flavor," *Profit,* December 1, 2000, p. 15.

Exhibit 2

Franchise Responsibilities

Company	Franchise Responsibilities
Yogen Früz Canada	• Yogen Früz franchisor for all of Canada, except BC and Quebec • Franchisor for master franchises for BC and Quebec
Yogen Früz USA	• Yogen Früz franchisor for all of United States, except Florida • Franchisor for master franchises for Florida
Yogen Früz International	• Yogen Früz franchisor for Yogen Früz Latin America (an arm's-length company that holds the master franchises for Latin America)
Kayla Foods International	• Yogen Früz franchisor for part of Europe and franchisor for Yogen Früz Europe (an arm's-length company that holds the master franchises for most of western Europe and Morocco) • Yogen Früz franchisor for Asia, South Pacific, Middle East, and Africa (except Morocco) • I Can't Believe It's Yogurt franchisor for all of United States • Franchisor for all I Can't Believe It's Yogurt master franchises (regions include Europe; Asia; North, Central, and South America; the Caribbean; Africa; and the Middle East) • Java Coast Fine Coffees franchisor for all Java Coast master franchises (regions include North, Central and South America; Europe; the Middle East; and Asia)
Bresler's Industries	• Bresler's franchisor for all of United States • Franchisor for Bresler's master franchises (regions include Central and South America, Europe, the Middle East, Africa, and Asia)
Yofru	• Yogen Früz franchisor for all of Spain

Source: Based on Yogen Früz World-Wide, *Prospectus,* June 11, 1997.

Leadership

What does it take to be a good leader?

1 How do leaders and managers differ?

2 What do trait and behavioural theories tell us about leadership?

3 How do contingency theories of leadership improve our understanding of leadership?

4 What are some contemporary approaches to leadership?

5 What are some current issues in leadership?

Calgary-based Shell Canada is one of the country's largest integrated oil companies.

Linda Cook was named Shell Canada's president and CEO in August 2003.[1] Growing up, she never imagined she might be the first woman president and CEO of a major Canadian petroleum company. In fact, she was somewhat of a failure at her first job. At 16, she pumped gas at one of her father's retail outlets. "My objectives weren't really professional," she admits. "I wanted to be outdoors and to meet cute guys with cool cars. It didn't work, and I only lasted about a month."

At Shell Canada, Cook headed a company in a male-dominated industry. The Calgary Petroleum Club did not allow women members until 1989. Today it has 55 female members, out of 1500.

To do her job, Cook emphasizes three priorities: "One is the strategy, given the competitive environment. Number two is delivering results, setting challenging targets and then delivering against them. And the third is the people in the organization, making sure there is talent in the pipeline and making sure we are developing the leaders of tomorrow."

THINK ABOUT IT

What does it mean to be a leader for today's organizations? Put yourself in Linda Cook's shoes: What kinds of challenges does she face as a leader in the oil industry? What can she do to encourage support for her leadership style from both men and women?

Linda Cook faced a major leadership challenge when she became head of Shell Canada. It was important that she be seen as an effective leader. Why is leadership so important? Because it's the leaders in organizations who make things happen.

If leadership is so important, it's only natural to ask: What differentiates leaders from non-leaders? What is the most appropriate style of leadership? And what can you do if you want to be seen as a leader? In this chapter, we try to answer these and other questions about what it means to be a leader.

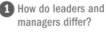

Shell Canada
www.shell.ca

MANAGERS VS. LEADERS

Let's begin by clarifying the distinction between managers and leaders. *Leadership* and *management* are two terms that are often confused. What is the difference between them?

Professor Rabindra Kanungo at McGill University finds that management scholars are beginning to reach a consensus that leadership and supervision/management are different.[2] Exhibit 8-1 on page 222 illustrates the distinctions Kanungo sees between managership and

1 How do leaders and managers differ?

Exhibit 8-1

Distinguishing Management from Leadership

Management	Leadership
1. Engages in day-to-day caretaker activities: Maintains and allocates resources	Formulates long-term objectives for reforming the system: Plans strategy and tactics
2. Exhibits supervisory behaviour: Acts to make others maintain standard job behaviour	Exhibits leading behaviour: Acts to bring about change in others congruent with long-term objectives
3. Administers subsystems within organizations	Innovates for the entire organization
4. Asks how and when to engage in standard practice	Asks what and why to change standard practice
5. Acts within established culture of the organization	Creates vision and meaning for the organization
6. Uses transactional influence: Induces compliance in manifest behaviour using rewards, sanctions, and formal authority	Uses transformational influence: Induces change in values, attitudes, and behaviour using personal examples and expertise
7. Relies on control strategies to get things done by subordinates	Uses empowering strategies to make followers internalize values
8. Status quo supporter and stabilizer	Status quo challenger and change creator

Source: R. N. Kanungo, "Leadership in Organizations: Looking Ahead to the 21st Century," *Canadian Psychology* 39, nos. 1–2 (1998), p. 77.

leader
Someone who can influence others and provide vision and strategy to the organization.

leadership
The process of influencing a group toward the achievement of goals.

leadership. **Leaders** provide vision and strategy to the organization; managers implement that vision and strategy, coordinate and staff the organization, and handle day-to-day problems. **Leadership** is the process of influencing a group toward the achievement of goals.

Can managers be leaders? Should leaders be managers? Because no one yet has shown that leadership ability is a handicap to a manager, we believe that all managers should ideally be leaders. However, not all leaders have the capabilities or skills of effective managers, and thus not all leaders should be managers. The fact that an individual can set vision and strategy does not mean that he or she can also plan, organize, and control.

EARLY LEADERSHIP THEORIES

Linda Cook describes herself as competitive.[3] "I've been 'the only' or 'the first' for 20 years at Shell," Cook said in 2000. "It can be a bit lonely at times. One of the reasons I am where I am today is because I'm fiercely competitive. It's not a powder-puff derby." Cook says that she was never the smartest engineer at Shell Canada, but says she is "commercially minded, and good at strategic thinking." She always did what she could "to deliver against the targets that were set."

Even though she is competitive, she considers herself a team player. "I like in the end to move forward as a team with important decisions we have made and expect people to stand behind them. I have high standards and expectations in terms of performance and delivery against targets, including for myself."

THINK ABOUT IT

A president and CEO of any company has to manage people effectively. What skills and traits does Linda Cook have to do so? Are there specific traits or behaviours that leaders should have?

 What do trait and behavioural theories tell us about leadership?

Leadership has been of interest since the early days of people gathering together in groups to accomplish goals. However, it was not until the early part of the twentieth century that researchers began to study leadership. These early leadership theories focused on the *leader* (trait theories) and how the *leader interacted* with his or her group members (behavioural theories).

Trait Theories

Think about some of the managers you have encountered. How did their traits affect whether they were good or bad managers?

Leadership research in the 1920s and 1930s focused on leader traits—characteristics that might be used to differentiate leaders from nonleaders. The intent was to isolate traits that leaders possessed and nonleaders did not. Some of the traits studied included physical stature, appearance, social class, emotional stability, fluency of speech, and sociability. Despite the best efforts of researchers, it proved to be impossible to identify a set of traits that would *always* differentiate leaders (the person) from nonleaders. Maybe it was a bit optimistic to think that there could be consistent and unique traits that would apply universally to all effective leaders, whether they were in charge of Toyota Motor Corporation, the Moscow Ballet, Ted's Outfitters Shop, or Queen's University. However, more recent attempts to identify traits consistently associated with leadership (the process, not the person) have been more successful. Seven traits associated with effective leadership include drive, the desire to lead, honesty and integrity, self-confidence, intelligence, job-relevant knowledge, and extraversion.[4] These traits are briefly described in Exhibit 8-2.

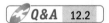 Q&A 12.1

Researchers have begun organizing traits around the Big Five personality framework.[5] They have found that most of the dozens of traits that emerged in various leadership reviews fall under one of the Big Five personality traits (extraversion, agreeableness, conscientiousness, emotional stability, and openness to experience). This approach has resulted in consistent and strong support for traits as predictors of leadership.

Q&A 12.2

Researchers agreed that traits alone were not sufficient for explaining effective leadership because explanations based solely on traits ignored the interactions of leaders and their group members as well as situational factors. Possessing the appropriate traits only made it more likely that an individual would be an effective leader. Therefore, leadership research from the late 1940s to the mid-1960s concentrated on the preferred behavioural styles that leaders demonstrated. Researchers wondered whether there was something unique in what effective leaders *did*—in other words, in their *behaviour*.

Exhibit 8-2

Seven Traits Associated With Leadership

1. **Drive.** Leaders exhibit a high effort level. They have a relatively high desire for achievement; they are ambitious; they have a lot of energy; they are tirelessly persistent in their activities; and they show initiative.

2. **Desire to lead.** Leaders have a strong desire to influence and lead others. They demonstrate the willingness to take responsibility.

3. **Honesty and integrity.** Leaders build trusting relationships between themselves and followers by being truthful or nondeceitful and by showing high consistency between word and deed.

4. **Self-confidence.** Followers look to leaders for an absence of self-doubt. Leaders, therefore, need to show self-confidence in order to convince followers of the rightness of their goals and decisions.

5. **Intelligence.** Leaders need to be intelligent enough to gather, synthesize, and interpret large amounts of information, and they need to be able to create visions, solve problems, and make correct decisions.

6. **Job-relevant knowledge.** Effective leaders have a high degree of knowledge about the company, industry, and technical matters. In-depth knowledge allows leaders to make well-informed decisions and to understand the implications of those decisions.

7. **Extraversion.** Leaders are energetic, lively people. They are sociable, assertive, and rarely silent or withdrawn.

Sources: S. A. Kirkpatrick and E. A. Locke, "Leadership: Do Traits Really Matter?" *Academy of Management Executive*, May 1991, pp. 48–60; and T. A. Judge, J. E. Bono, R. Ilies, and M. Werner, "Personality and Leadership: A Qualitative and Quantitative Review," *Journal of Applied Psychology*, August 2002, pp. 765–780.

Conservative MP Steven Fletcher (Charleswood–St. James–Assiniboia, Manitoba) is driven to be a leader. A car accident left him quadriplegic when he was 23, and this inspired him to take charge of his life. He won his first political campaign to become president of the University of Manitoba Students Union. He later became president of the Progressive Conservative Party of Manitoba. When he was elected MP, he defeated his riding's incumbent Liberal candidate. He says many of his constituents are not aware that he is quadriplegic until they meet him.

Behavioural Theories

Rick Waugh, president and CEO of Scotiabank, has very little in common with his predecessors who led the bank before him. Both Cedric Ritchie, CEO in the 1970s and 1980s, and Peter Godsoe, who succeeded Ritchie, are described as "autocratic, undemocratic and one-man army" when others reflect on their leadership styles.[6] Waugh, who was appointed president and CEO in 2003, is seen as kinder and gentler. "He is always open to discussion," says Laurent Lemaire, executive vice-chairman of pulp-and-paper manufacturer Cascades and a member of Scotiabank's executive and risk committee and human resources committee. "He will listen to you bring ideas."[7] Scotiabank has been quite successful under different leaders, and moved from the number five to the number two bank in Canada under Godsoe. But this example shows that leaders can behave in very different ways, even when working for the same organization. What do we know about leader behaviour, and how can it help us in our understanding of what an effective leader is?

Behavioural theories of leadership identify behaviours that differentiate effective leaders from ineffective leaders. Researchers hoped that the behavioural theories approach would provide more definitive answers about the nature of leadership than did the trait theories. There are four main leader behaviour studies we need to examine. (Exhibit 8-3 provides a summary of the major leader behavioural dimensions and the conclusions of each of the studies.)

University of Iowa Studies

The University of Iowa studies (conducted by Kurt Lewin and his associates) explored three leadership styles.[8] The **autocratic style** describes a leader who tends to centralize authority, dictate work methods, make unilateral decisions, and limit employee participation. The **democratic style** describes a leader who tends to involve employees in decision making, delegate authority, encourage participation in deciding work methods and goals, and use feedback as an opportunity for coaching employees. Finally, the **laissez-faire-style** describes a leader who generally gives the group complete freedom to make decisions and complete the work in whatever way it sees fit.

behavioural theories
Leadership theories that identify behaviours that differentiate effective leaders from ineffective leaders.

autocratic style
A leadership style where the leader tends to centralize authority, dictate work methods, make unilateral decisions, and limit employee participation.

democratic style
A leadership style where the leader tends to involve employees in decision making, delegate authority, encourage participation in deciding work methods and goals, and use feedback as an opportunity for coaching employees.

laissez-faire style
A leadership style where the leader tends to give the group complete freedom to make decisions and complete the work in whatever way it sees fit.

Exhibit 8-3

Behavioural Theories of Leadership

	Behavioural Dimension	Conclusion
University of Iowa	*Democratic style:* involving subordinates, delegating authority, and encouraging participation	Democratic style of leadership was most effective, although later studies showed mixed results.
	Autocratic style: dictating work methods, centralizing decision making, and limiting participation	
	Laissez-faire style: giving group freedom to make decisions and complete work	
Ohio State	*Consideration:* being considerate of followers' ideas and feelings	High-high leader (high in consideration and high in initiating structure) achieved high subordinate performance and satisfaction, but not in all situations.
	Initiating structure: structuring work and work relationships to meet job goals	
University of Michigan	*Employee oriented:* emphasizes interpersonal relationships and taking care of employees' needs	Employee-oriented leaders were associated with high group productivity and higher job satisfaction.
	Production oriented: emphasized technical or task aspects of job	
Managerial Grid	*Concern for people:* measures leader's concern for subordinates on a scale of 1 to 9 (low to high)	Leaders performed best with a 9,9 style (high concern for production and high concern for people).
	Concern for production: measures leader's concern for getting job done on a scale of 1 to 9 (low to high)	

Lewin and his associates researched which one of the three leadership styles was most effective. Their results seemed to indicate that the democratic style contributed to both good quantity and quality of work. Had the answer to the question of the most effective leadership style been found? Unfortunately, it was not that simple. Later studies of the autocratic and democratic styles showed mixed results. For instance, the democratic style sometimes produced higher performance levels than the autocratic style, but at other times it produced lower or equal performance levels. More consistent results were found, however, when a measure of subordinate satisfaction was used. Group members' satisfaction levels were generally higher under a democratic leader than under an autocratic one.[9] To learn more about your leadership style, see *Self-Assessment—What's My Leadership Style?* on pages 245–247, at the end of the chapter.

Q&A 12.3

Now leaders faced a dilemma! Should they focus on achieving higher performance or on achieving higher member satisfaction? This recognition of the dual nature of a leader's behaviour—that is, focusing on the task and on the people—was also a key characteristic of the other behavioural studies.

Ohio State Studies

The Ohio State studies identified two important dimensions of leader behaviour.[10] Beginning with more than 1000 behavioural dimensions, the researchers eventually narrowed the list down to just two categories that accounted for most of the leadership behaviour described by individuals: initiating structure and consideration.

Initiating structure refers to the extent to which a leader is likely to define and structure his or her role and the roles of group members in the search for goal attainment. It includes behaviour that attempts to organize work, work relationships, and goals. **Consideration** refers to the extent to which a leader has job relationships characterized by mutual trust and respect for group members' ideas and feelings. A leader who is high in con-

initiating structure
The extent to which a leader is likely to define and structure his or her role and the roles of group members in the search for goal attainment.

consideration
The extent to which a leader has job relationships characterized by mutual trust and respect for group members' ideas and feelings.

sideration helps group members with personal problems, is friendly and approachable, and treats all group members as equals. He or she shows concern for (is considerate of) his or her followers' comfort, well-being, status, and satisfaction.

Were these behavioural dimensions adequate descriptions of leader behaviour? Research found that a leader who is high in both initiating structure and consideration behaviours (a **high-high leader**) achieved high group task performance and satisfaction more frequently than one who is low on either dimension or both. However, the high-high style did not always yield positive results. Enough exceptions were found to indicate that perhaps situational factors needed to be integrated into leadership theory.

high-high leader
A leader high in both initiating structure and consideration behaviours.

University of Michigan Studies

Leadership studies conducted at the University of Michigan's Survey Research Center at about the same time as those being done at Ohio State had a similar research objective: Identify behavioural characteristics of leaders that are related to performance effectiveness. The Michigan group also came up with two dimensions of leadership behaviour, which they labelled employee oriented and production oriented.[11] *Employee-oriented* leaders tend to emphasize interpersonal relationships; they take a personal interest in the needs of their followers and accept individual differences among group members. In contrast, *production-oriented* leaders tend to emphasize the technical or task aspects of the job; they are concerned mainly with accomplishing their group's tasks and regard group members as a means to that end. The conclusions of the Michigan researchers strongly favoured leaders who are employee oriented, as they were associated with high group productivity and high job satisfaction.

The Managerial Grid

managerial grid
A two-dimensional view of leadership style that is based on concern for people vs. concern for production.

The behavioural dimensions from these early leadership studies provided the basis for the development of a two-dimensional grid for assessing leadership styles. This **managerial grid**, developed by R. R. Blake and Jane S. Mouton, uses the behavioural dimensions "concern for people" and "concern for production" and evaluates a leader's use of these behaviours, ranking them on a scale from 1 (low) to 9 (high).[12] Although the grid (shown in Exhibit 8-4) has 81 different categories into which a leader's behavioural style might fall, emphasis has been placed on five: impoverished management (1,1), task management (9,1), middle-of-the-road management (5,5), country club management (1,9), and team management (9,9). Of these five styles, Blake and Mouton concluded that managers performed best when using a 9,9 style. Unfortunately, the grid offers no answers to the question of what makes a manager an effective leader; it only provides a framework for conceptualizing leadership style. In fact, there has been little substantive evidence to support the conclusion that a 9,9 style is most effective in all situations.[13]

A lengthy review of the results of behavioural studies supports the idea that people-oriented behaviours are related to follower satisfaction, motivation, and leader effectiveness while production-oriented behaviours are slightly more strongly related to performance by the leader, the group, and the organization.[14]

CONTINGENCY THEORIES OF LEADERSHIP

3 How do contingency theories of leadership improve our understanding of leadership?

Do you know what your leadership style is? What impact might your style have on how you lead?

Contingency theories of leadership developed after it became clear that identifying traits or key behaviours was not enough to understand what made good leaders. Contingency researchers considered whether different situations required different styles of leadership. To illustrate how situations might affect the ability to lead, consider the fate of some of the Americans who have been recruited to run Canadian companies. Hudson's Bay Company hired American Bill Fields and Zellers hired American Millard Barron to replicate their US retail successes in Canada. Neither was able to do so. Successful Texas oilman J. P. Bryan was given two chances to restore profitability at Canadian companies—Gulf Canada Resources

Exhibit 8-4

The Managerial Grid

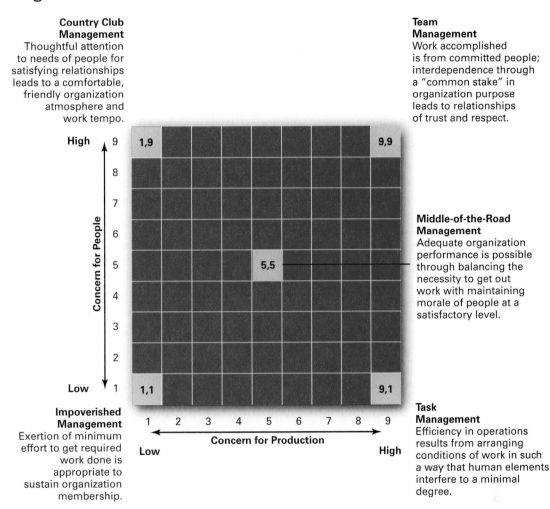

Country Club Management
Thoughtful attention to needs of people for satisfying relationships leads to a comfortable, friendly organization atmosphere and work tempo.

Team Management
Work accomplished is from committed people; interdependence through a "common stake" in organization purpose leads to relationships of trust and respect.

Middle-of-the-Road Management
Adequate organization performance is possible through balancing the necessity to get out work with maintaining morale of people at a satisfactory level.

Impoverished Management
Exertion of minimum effort to get required work done is appropriate to sustain organization membership.

Task Management
Efficiency in operations results from arranging conditions of work in such a way that human elements interfere to a minimal degree.

Source: Reprinted by permission of *Harvard Business Review*. An exhibit from R. R. Blake, J. S. Mouton, L. B. Barnes, and L. E. Greiner, "Breakthrough in Organization Development," *Harvard Business Review*, November–December 1964, p. 136. Copyright © 1964 by the President and Fellows of Harvard College. All rights reserved.

(now ConocoPhillips) and Canadian 88 Energy (which later became Esprit Exploration)—and failed in both attempts.[15] These examples suggest that one's leadership style may need to be adjusted for different companies and employees, and perhaps even for different countries. This is consistent with research findings that not all leaders can lead in any situation.[16]

In this section we examine four contingency theories of leadership—Fiedler contingency model, Hersey and Blanchard's Situational Leadership®, leader participation model, and path-goal theory. All of these theories focus on the relationship of the leader to followers, and there is broad support for the idea that this relationship is important.[17] Each theory attempts to answer *if-then* contingencies (that is, *if* this is the situation, *then* this is the best leadership style to use).

Fiedler Contingency Model

The first comprehensive contingency model for leadership was developed by Fred Fiedler.[18] The **Fiedler contingency model** proposes that effective group performance depends on the proper match between the leader's style of interacting with his or her followers and the

Fiedler contingency model
A leadership theory that proposes effective group performance depends on the proper match between the leader's style of interacting with followers and the degree to which the situation gives the leader control and influence.

degree to which the situation gives the leader control and influence. The model was based on the premise that a certain leadership style would be most effective in specific types of situations. The key was to define different leadership styles and types of situations and then determine the combinations of style and situation that were well matched.

Fiedler proposed that an important factor in leadership success is an individual's basic leadership style, which is either task oriented or relationship oriented. To measure a leader's orientation, Fiedler developed the **least-preferred co-worker (LPC) questionnaire**.

Leaders who describe the least-preferred co-worker in relatively positive terms are primarily interested in good personal relations with co-workers (that is, they are *relationship oriented*). Leaders who describe the least-preferred co-worker in relatively unfavourable terms (a low LPC score), are primarily interested in productivity and getting the job done (that is, they are *task oriented*). Fiedler did acknowledge that there was a small group of people who fell in between these two extremes and who did not have a cut-and-dried leadership style. It's important to point out that Fiedler assumed a person's leadership style was always the same (fixed), regardless of the situation. In other words, a relationship-oriented leader would always be one, and the same was true for a task-oriented leader.

Fiedler identified three contingency dimensions that together define the situation a leader faces:

- *Leader–member relations.* The degree of confidence, trust, and respect employees have for their leader; rated as either good or poor.
- *Task structure.* The degree to which job assignments are formalized and procedurized; rated as either high or low.
- *Position power.* The degree of influence a leader has over power-based activities such as hiring, firing, discipline, promotions, and salary increases; rated as either strong or weak.

Fiedler evaluated leadership situations in terms of these three contingency variables, and concluded that there are eight possible situations in which a leader could find himself or herself (see the bottom of the chart in Exhibit 8-5). Each of these situations was described in terms of its favourableness (or situational control) for the leader. Situations I, II, and III

least-preferred co-worker (LPC) questionnaire
A questionnaire that measures whether a leader is task oriented or relationship oriented.

Q&A 12.4

Exhibit 8-5

Findings of the Fiedler Contingency Model

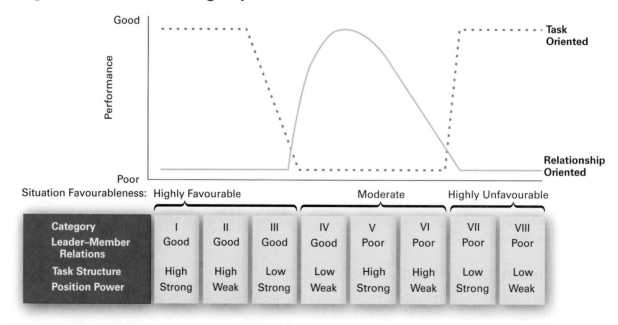

Category	I	II	III	IV	V	VI	VII	VIII
Leader–Member Relations	Good	Good	Good	Good	Poor	Poor	Poor	Poor
Task Structure	High	High	Low	Low	High	High	Low	Low
Position Power	Strong	Weak	Strong	Weak	Strong	Weak	Strong	Weak

were classified as very favourable for the leader. Situations IV, V, and VI were moderately favourable for the leader. Situations VII and VIII were very unfavourable for the leader.

Fiedler concluded that task-oriented leaders performed better in either very favourable situations or very unfavourable situations. (See the top of Exhibit 8-5 where performance is shown on the vertical axis and situation favourableness is shown on the horizontal axis.) In a high control situation, a leader can "get away" with task-orientation, because the relationships are good, and followers are easily influenced.[19] In a low control situation (which is characterized by poor relations, ill-defined task, and low influence), task orientation may be the only thing that makes it possible to get something done. On the other hand, relationship-oriented leaders performed better in moderately favourable situations. In a moderate control situation, being relationship oriented may smooth the way to getting things done.

Since Fiedler treated an individual's leadership style as fixed, there were only two ways to improve leader effectiveness. First, you could bring in a new leader whose style better fit the situation. For instance, if the group situation was rated as highly unfavourable but was led by a relationship-oriented leader, the group's performance could be improved by replacing that person with a task-oriented leader. The second alternative was to change the situation to fit the leader. This could be done by restructuring tasks or increasing or decreasing the power that the leader had over factors such as salary increases, promotions, and disciplinary actions.

Reviews of the major studies undertaken to test the overall validity of Fiedler's model have shown considerable evidence to support the model.[20] However, this theory was not without criticism. For instance, additional variables are probably needed to fill in some gaps in the model. Moreover, there were problems with the LPC, and the practicality of it needed to be addressed. In addition, it's probably unrealistic to assume that a person cannot change his or her leadership style to fit the situation. Effective leaders can, and do, change their styles to meet the needs of a particular situation. Finally, the contingency variables were difficult for practitioners to assess.[21] Despite its shortcomings, the Fiedler contingency model showed that effective leadership style needed to reflect situational factors.

Hersey and Blanchard's Situational Leadership®

Paul Hersey and Ken Blanchard developed a leadership theory that has gained a strong following among management development specialists.[22] This contingency theory of leadership, called **Situational Leadership® (SL)**, focuses on followers' readiness. Hersey and Blanchard argue that successful leadership is achieved by selecting the right leadership style, which is contingent upon the level of the followers' readiness. Before we proceed, there are two points we need to clarify: Why a leadership theory focuses on the followers, and what is meant by the term *readiness*.

The emphasis on the followers in leadership effectiveness reflects the reality that it is the followers who accept or reject the leader. Regardless of what the leader does, effectiveness depends on the actions of his or her followers. This is an important dimension that has been overlooked or underemphasized in most leadership theories. **Readiness**, as defined by Hersey and Blanchard, refers to the extent to which people have the ability and willingness to accomplish a specific task.

SL uses the same two leadership dimensions that Fiedler identified: task and relationship behaviours. However, Hersey and Blanchard go a step further by considering each as either high or low and then combining them into four specific leadership styles (see Exhibit 8-6 on page 230), described as follows:

- *Telling* (high task–low relationship): The leader defines roles and tells people what, how, when, and where to do various tasks.

- *Selling* (high task–high relationship): The leader provides both directive and supportive behaviour.

Situational Leadership® (SL)
A leadership theory that focuses on the readiness of followers.

Q&A 12.5

readiness
The extent to which people have the ability and willingness to accomplish a specific task.

Exhibit 8-6

Hersey and Blanchard's Situational Leadership® Theory

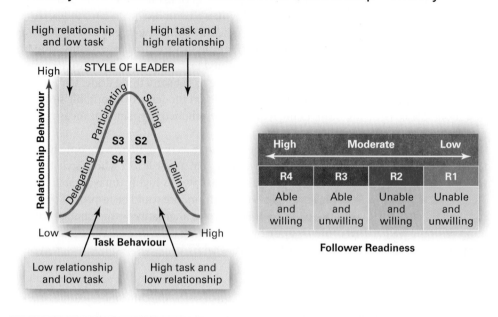

Source: Reprinted with permission from the Center for Leadership Studies. Situational Leadership is a registered trademark of the Center for Leadership Studies, Escondido, California. All rights reserved.

- *Participating* (low task–high relationship): The leader and follower share in decision making; the main role of the leader is facilitating and communicating.

- *Delegating* (low task–low relationship): The leader provides little direction or support.

The final component in the theory is the four stages of follower readiness:

- *R1:* People are both *unable* and *unwilling* to take responsibility for doing something. They are neither competent nor confident.

- *R2:* People are *unable* but *willing* to do the necessary job tasks. They are motivated but currently lack the appropriate skills.

- *R3:* People are *able* but *unwilling* to do what the leader wants.

- *R4:* People are both *able* and *willing* to do what is asked of them.

SL essentially views the leader–follower relationship as similar to that of a parent and a child. Just as a parent needs to give up control as a child becomes more mature and responsible, so, too, should a leader. As followers reach high levels of readiness, the leader responds not only by continuing to decrease control over their activities, but also by continuing to decrease relationship behaviour. SL says if followers are *unable* and *unwilling* to do a task, the leader needs to give clear and specific directions; if followers are *unable* and *willing*, the leader needs to display high task orientation to compensate for the followers' lack of ability and high relationship orientation to get followers to "buy into" the leader's desires; if followers are *able* and *unwilling*, the leader needs to use a supportive and participative style; and if employees are both *able* and *willing*, the leader does not need to do much.

SL has intuitive appeal. It acknowledges the importance of followers and builds on the logic that leaders can compensate for ability and motivational limitations in their followers. Yet research efforts to test and support the theory generally have been disappointing.[23] Why? Possible explanations include internal inconsistencies in the model itself as well as problems with research methodology. So despite its appeal and wide popularity, any endorsement should be made with caution.

Many leaders in Vancouver have had to change their management style because of changes in the economic environment in recent years. With many large construction projects under way because of the upcoming 2010 Olympics, organizations are struggling to hire qualified employees. There are more jobs than employees, or that is what many managers believe when they cannot find someone to hire. Because of the boom in business, managers have to work hard to keep their best employees from accepting better offers from competing firms.

Leader Participation Model

Another early contingency theory of leadership, developed by Victor Vroom and Phillip Yetton, is the **leader participation model**, which relates leadership behaviour and participation to decision making.[24] Developed in the early 1970s, the model argued that leader behaviour must adjust to reflect the task structure—whether it is routine, nonroutine, or in between. Vroom and Yetton's model is what we call *normative*. That is, it provides a sequential set of rules (norms) to follow in determining the form and amount of participation a leader should exercise in decision making in different types of situations.

The leader participation model has changed as research continues to provide additional insights into effective leadership style.[25] The current model reflects *how* and *with whom* decisions are made and uses variations of the same five leadership styles identified in the original model:[26]

leader participation model
A leadership theory that relates leadership behaviour and participation to decision making.

- *Decide.* Leader makes the decision alone and either announces or sells it to the group.

- *Consult individually.* Leader presents the problem to group members individually, gets their suggestions, and then makes the decision.

- *Consult group.* Leader presents the problem to group members in a meeting, gets their suggestions, and then makes the decision.

- *Facilitate.* Leader presents the problem to the group in a meeting and, acting as facilitator, defines the problem and the boundaries within which a decision must be made.

- *Delegate.* Leader permits the group to make the decision within prescribed limits.

The contingencies that affect the leadership style chosen are decision significance, importance of commitment, leader expertise, likelihood of commitment, group support, group expertise, and team competence.[27]

Path-Goal Theory

path-goal theory

A leadership theory that says it's the leader's job to assist his or her followers in attaining their goals and to provide the necessary direction and/or support to ensure that their goals are compatible with the overall objectives of the group or organization.

Currently, one of the most respected approaches to understanding leadership is **path-goal theory**, which states that it's the leader's job to assist his or her followers in attaining their goals and to provide the necessary direction and/or support to ensure that their goals are compatible with the overall objectives of the group or organization. Developed by University of Toronto Professor Martin Evans in the late 1960s, it was subsequently expanded upon by Robert House (formerly at the University of Toronto, and now at the Wharton School of Business). Path-goal theory is a contingency model of leadership that takes key elements from the expectancy theory of motivation (see Chapter 9, pages 263–264).[28] The term *path-goal* is derived from the belief that effective leaders clarify the path to help their followers get from where they are to the achievement of their work goals and make the journey along the path easier by reducing roadblocks and pitfalls.

Path-goal theory identifies four leadership behaviours:

- *Directive leader.* Leader lets subordinates know what is expected of them, schedules work to be done, and gives specific guidance on how to accomplish tasks.

- *Supportive leader.* Leader is friendly and shows concern for the needs of followers.

- *Participative leader.* Leader consults with group members and uses their suggestions before making a decision.

- *Achievement-oriented leader.* Leader sets challenging goals and expects followers to perform at their highest level.

In contrast to Fiedler's view that a leader could not change his or her behaviour, House assumed that leaders are flexible. In other words, path-goal theory assumes that the same leader can display any or all of these leadership styles, depending on the situation.

As Exhibit 8-7 illustrates, path-goal theory proposes two situational or contingency variables that moderate the leadership behaviour–outcome relationship: *environmental* factors that are outside the control of the follower (including task structure, formal authority system, and the work group) and factors that are part of the personal characteristics of the *follower* (including locus of control, experience, and perceived ability). Environmental factors determine the type of leader behaviour required if subordinate outcomes are to be maximized; per-

Exhibit 8-7

Path-Goal Theory

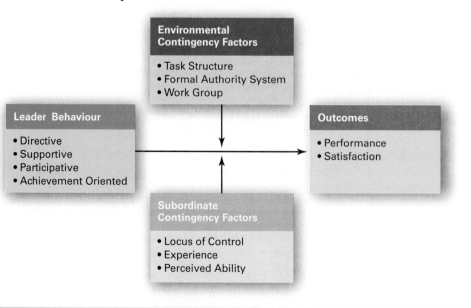

sonal characteristics of the follower determine how the environment and leader behaviour are interpreted. The theory proposes that leader behaviour will be ineffective when it's redundant with sources of environmental structure or incongruent with follower characteristics.

Research on the path-goal theory is generally encouraging. Although not every study has found support, the majority of the evidence supports the logic underlying the theory.[29] In summary, employee performance and satisfaction are likely to be positively influenced when the leader compensates for shortcomings in either the employee or the work setting. However, if the leader spends time explaining tasks that are already clear or when the employee has the ability and experience to handle them without interference, the employee is likely to see such directive behaviour as redundant or even insulting.

CONTEMPORARY APPROACHES TO LEADERSHIP

In this section, we look at three contemporary approaches to leadership including transformational-transactional leadership, charismatic-visionary leadership, and team leadership.

4 What are some contemporary approaches to leadership?

Transformational-Transactional Leadership

Most of the leadership theories presented so far in this chapter have described **transactional leaders**; that is, leaders who guide or motivate their followers in the direction of established goals by clarifying role and task requirements. But there is another type of leader who inspires followers to go beyond their own self-interests for the good of the organization, and who is capable of having a profound and extraordinary effect on his or her followers. **Transformational leaders** include such individuals as Matthew Barrett, chairman of Barclays PLC, Britain's second-largest bank, and former CEO of Bank of Montreal; Frank Stronach, chairman of Toronto-based Magna International; and Mogens Smed, CEO of Calgary-based DIRTT (Doing It Right This Time) and former CEO of SMED International. They pay attention to the concerns and developmental needs of individual followers; they change followers' awareness of issues by helping those followers look at old problems in new ways; and they are able to excite, arouse, and inspire followers to put out extra effort to achieve group goals.[30]

Transactional and transformational leadership should not be viewed as opposing approaches to getting things done.[31] Transformational leadership is built on top of transactional leadership. Transformational leadership produces levels of employee effort and performance that go beyond what would occur with a transactional approach alone. Moreover, transformational leadership is more than charisma, since the transformational leader attempts to instill in followers the ability to question not only established views but those views held by the leader.[32]

The evidence supporting the superiority of transformational leadership over transactional leadership is overwhelmingly impressive. For instance, studies that looked at managers in different settings, including the military and business, found that transformational leaders were evaluated as more effective, higher performers, and more promotable than their transactional counterparts.[33] In addition, evidence indicates that transformational leadership is strongly correlated with lower turnover rates, higher productivity, and higher employee satisfaction.[34] Subordinates of transformational leaders may trust their leaders and their organizations more and feel that they are being fairly treated, which in turn may positively influence their work motivation (see Chapter 9).[35] Finally, an increasing body of research shows that people working for charismatic leaders are motivated to exert extra work effort and, because they like their leaders, they express greater satisfaction.[36]

transactional leaders
Leaders who guide or motivate their followers in the direction of established goals by clarifying role and task requirements.

transformational leaders
Leaders who inspire followers to transcend their own self-interests for the good of the organization, and who have a profound and extraordinary effect on their followers.

Charismatic-Visionary Leadership

Have you ever encountered a charismatic leader? What was this person like?

Jeff Bezos, founder and CEO of Amazon.com, is a person who exudes energy, enthusiasm, and drive.[37] He is fun-loving (his legendary laugh has been described as a flock of Canada geese on nitrous oxide), but has pursued his vision for Amazon with serious intensity and has demonstrated an ability to inspire his employees through the ups and downs of a rapidly growing company. Bezos is what we

charismatic leader
An enthusiastic, self-confident leader whose personality and actions influence people to behave in certain ways.

call a **charismatic leader**—that is, an enthusiastic, self-confident leader whose personality and actions influence people to behave in certain ways.

Characteristics of Charismatic Leaders

Several authors have attempted to identify the personal characteristics of charismatic leaders.[38] The most comprehensive analysis identified five such characteristics that differentiate charismatic leaders from noncharismatic ones: They have a vision, are able to articulate that vision, are willing to take risks to achieve that vision, are sensitive to both environmental constraints and follower needs, and exhibit behaviours that are out of the ordinary.[39]

Effects of Charismatic Leadership

What can we say about the charismatic leader's effect on his or her followers? There is an increasing body of evidence that shows impressive correlations between charismatic leadership and high performance and satisfaction among followers.[40] Research shows that people who work for charismatic leaders are motivated to exert extra work effort and express greater satisfaction, because they like their leaders.[41] One of the most cited studies of the effects of charismatic leadership was done at the University of British Columbia in the early 1980s by Jane Howell (now at the University of Western Ontario) and Peter Frost.[42] They found that those who worked under a charismatic leader generated more ideas, produced better results, reported higher job satisfaction, and showed stronger bonds of loyalty. Howell concludes, "Charismatic leaders know how to inspire people to think in new directions."[43]

Charismatic leadership also affects overall company performance. Robert House and colleagues studied 63 American and 49 Canadian companies (including Nortel Networks, Molson, Gulf Canada, and Manulife Financial) and found that "between 15 and 25 percent of the variation in profitability among the companies was accounted for by the leadership qualities of their CEO."[44] Charismatic leaders led more profitable companies.

Charismatic leadership may have a downside, however, as we see from the recent accounting scandals and high-profile bankruptcies of North American companies. WorldCom's Bernard Ebbers and Enron's Kenneth Lay "seemed almost a breed apart, blessed with unique visionary powers" when their companies were increasing stock prices at phenomenal rates in the 1990s.[45] After the scandals, however, there was some agreement that CEOs with less vision and more ethical and corporate responsibility might be more desirable.

Becoming Charismatic

Can people learn to be charismatic leaders? Or are charismatic leaders born with their qualities? Although a small number of experts still think that charisma cannot be learned, most believe that individuals can be trained to exhibit charismatic behaviours.[46] For example, researchers have succeeded in teaching undergraduate students to "be" charismatic. How? They were taught to articulate a sweeping goal, communicate high performance expectations, exhibit confidence in the ability of subordinates to meet those expectations, and empathize with the needs of their subordinates; they learned to project a powerful, confident, and dynamic presence; and they practised using a captivating and engaging voice tone. The researchers also trained the student leaders to use charismatic nonverbal behaviours including leaning toward the follower when communicating, maintaining direct eye contact, and having a relaxed posture and animated facial expressions. In groups with these "trained" charismatic leaders, members had higher task performance, higher task adjustment, and better adjustment to the leader and to the group than did group members who worked in groups led by noncharismatic leaders.

One last thing we need to say about charismatic leadership is that it may not always be needed to achieve high levels of employee performance. It may be most appropriate when the follower's task has an ideological purpose or when the environment involves a high degree of stress and uncertainty.[47] This may explain why, when charismatic leaders surface, it's more likely to be in the arenas of politics, religion, or war; or when a business firm is starting up or facing a survival crisis. For example, Martin Luther King Jr. used his charisma to bring about social equality through nonviolent means; and Steve Jobs achieved unwavering loyalty and commitment from Apple Computer's technical staff in the early 1980s by articulating a vision of personal computers that would dramatically change the way people lived. Finally, transformational leadership should be used with some caution in non-North American contexts because its effectiveness may be affected by cultural values concerning leadership.[48]

Visionary Leadership

Although the term *vision* is often linked with charismatic leadership, **visionary leadership** goes beyond charisma since it's the ability to create and articulate a realistic, credible, and attractive vision of the future that improves upon the present situation.[49] This vision, if properly selected and implemented, is so energizing that it "in effect jump-starts the future by calling forth the skills, talents, and resources to make it happen."[50]

visionary leadership
The ability to create and articulate a realistic, credible, and attractive vision of the future that improves upon the present situation.

A vision should offer clear and compelling imagery that taps into people's emotions and inspires enthusiasm to pursue the organization's goals. It should be able to generate possibilities that are inspirational and unique and offer new ways of doing things that are clearly better for the organization and its members. Visions that are clearly articulated and have powerful imagery are easily grasped and accepted. For instance, Michael Dell (of Dell Computer) created a vision of a business that sells and delivers a finished PC directly to a customer in less than a week. The late Mary Kay Ash's vision of women as entrepreneurs selling products that improved their self-image guided her cosmetics company, Mary Kay Cosmetics.

What skills do visionary leaders have? Once the vision is identified, these leaders appear to have three skills that are related to effectiveness in their visionary roles.[51] First is the *ability to explain the vision to others* by making the vision clear in terms of required goals and actions through clear oral and written communication. The second skill is the *ability to express the vision not just verbally but through behaviour*, which requires behaving in ways that continuously convey and reinforce the vision. The third skill is the *ability to extend or apply the vision to different leadership contexts*. For instance, the vision has to be as meaningful to the people in accounting as it is to those in production, and to employees in Halifax as it is to those in Toronto.

Team Leadership

Since leadership is increasingly taking place within a team context and more organizations are using work teams, the role of the leader in guiding team members has become increasingly important. The role of team leader *is* different from the traditional leadership role. Many leaders are not equipped to handle the change to employee teams. As one consultant noted, "Even the most capable managers have trouble making the transition because all the command-and-control type things they were encouraged to do before are no longer appropriate. There's no reason to have any skill or sense of this."[52] This same consultant estimated that "probably 15 percent of managers are natural team leaders; another 15 percent could never lead a team because it runs counter to their personality—that is, they're unable to sublimate their dominating style for the good of the team. Then there's that huge group in the middle: Team leadership doesn't come naturally to them, but they can learn it."[53]

The challenge for many managers is learning how to become an effective team leader. They have to learn skills such as having the patience to share information, being able to trust others and to give up authority, and understanding when to intervene. Effective team leaders have mastered the difficult balancing act of knowing when to leave their teams alone and when to get involved. New team leaders may try to retain too much control at a time when team members need more autonomy, or they may abandon their teams at times when team members need support and help.[54] To learn more about team leadership, see *Self-Assessment— How Good Am I at Building and Leading a Team?* on pages 298–299, in Chapter 10.

Q&A 12.9

Paul Okalik (left) was the first sitting premier of Nunavut and has been chosen to serve a second term. Okalik heads a nonpartisan government run by consensus built from the principles of parliamentary democracy and Aboriginal values. Okalik's leadership skills include team building. He was the key negotiator in the settlement that led to the creation of Nunavut, and in his role as premier he must balance the needs of the Inuit and qallunaat (nonInuit) residents in Nunavut.

What has been your biggest challenge when trying to lead team members?

One study of organizations that had reorganized themselves around employee teams found certain common responsibilities of all leaders. These included coaching, facilitating, handling disciplinary problems, reviewing team and individual performance, training, and communication.[55] However, a more meaningful way to describe the team leader's job is to focus on two priorities: (1) managing the team's external boundary and (2) facilitating the team process.[56] These priorities entail four specific leadership roles (see Exhibit 8-8).

Team leaders are *liaisons with external constituencies*. These may include upper management, other organizational work teams, customers, or suppliers. The leader represents the team to other constituencies, secures needed resources, clarifies others' expectations of the team, gathers information from the outside, and shares that information with team members.

Team leaders are *troubleshooters*. When the team has problems and asks for assistance, team leaders sit in on meetings and try to help resolve the problems. Troubleshooting rarely

Exhibit 8-8

Specific Team Leadership Roles

```
            Coach              Liaison With
                               External
                               Constituencies

  Conflict        Team Leader
  Manager           Roles          Troubleshooter
```

involves technical or operational issues because the team members typically know more about the tasks being done than does the leader. The leader is most likely to contribute by asking penetrating questions, helping the team talk through problems, and getting needed resources to tackle problems.

Team leaders are *conflict managers*. They help identify issues such as the source of the conflict, who is involved, the issues, the resolution options available, and the advantages and disadvantages of each. By getting team members to address questions such as these, the leader minimizes the disruptive aspects of intrateam conflicts.

Finally, team leaders are *coaches*. They clarify expectations and roles, teach, offer support, and do whatever else is necessary to help team members keep their work performance high. Team leaders are required in a variety of situations, as the following *Management Reflection* shows.

MANAGEMENT REFLECTION

Derek Jeter Inspires the New York Yankees

Can a shortstop really lead the team?   Leaders come in a variety of forms and contexts. New York Yankees shortstop Derek Jeter is team captain and definitely his team's leader.[57] Jeter is known as a player who adjusts to any situation—his only goal is to win.

Yankees' owner George Steinbrenner refers to Jeter as "an inspiration for all of our nation's youth." Jeter's very bruised face appeared in sports sections across North America in July 2004 after a crucial catch in the twelfth inning to help the Yankees win a big game against the Boston Red Sox. As Jeter ran to catch the ball, he had to make a split decision: catch the ball, but crash into the stands and injure himself, or let the ball fall, and hope no one scored.

Jeter caught the ball, cut his chin, and bruised his right cheek and right shoulder. He was immediately taken to hospital to get seven stitches. Meanwhile, his teammates, two runs down but inspired by his heroics, came back to win the game. "The team would have been devastated to lose the game after Jeter's selflessness," says Yankees General Manager Brian Cashman.

Jeter's a leader on and off the field. In the clubhouse and the dugout he checks up on the other players and lets them know he's available to talk with them. Paul Quantrill, the former Toronto Blue Jays pitcher who was Jeter's teammate in 2004–2005, says Jeter "will do what it takes for the team to win, to beat you, so you'd better be careful." His entire team looks up to him. "It's the real deal," Quantrill says. "He carries himself the right way ....He's very approachable, he's one of the guys, but he's a rock star." ■

CURRENT ISSUES IN LEADERSHIP

When Linda Cook first started working as a petroleum engineer, it was very unusual to see a woman in that position.[58] She was often treated poorly by her male peers in those early days. Foremen at the drilling sites often enforced "men only" policies, and she had to convince them she belonged there. She also had to convince her superiors that women could be managers of field operations. "I spent a lot of [energy] just trying to change people's perceptions of what women were capable of," she says. "You delivered. You did every job you got the best you possibly could, and you proved women are capable of holding these positions, and that there isn't a gender difference in the capacity to do well, to lead. It was just a matter of one job at a time."

Cook notes that there are few women in senior positions in the oil industry. "The oil and gas sector has largely been led by engineers and scientists in most companies and there were so few women in technical positions 20 to 30 years ago, certainly when I was in university," she said. "The industry has a reputation for being a bit tough or a bit dirty and also there was a lack of female role models in the sector." Cook faced her most difficult experience when she had just graduated and started a six-month assignment on a drilling rig. One man refused to work with women and had to be reassigned. Women are somewhat more welcome in the oil patch these days. Shell aims to have women fill 20 percent of its senior executive positions by 2008.

In August 2004, Cook became managing director of Netherlands-based Royal Dutch Petroleum Company (Shell Canada's parent organization), as well as group managing director and CEO for Shell Gas & Power. The company had faced several scandals in the previous year, and wanted to put a fresh face on the company's leadership. Martin Molyneaux, an oilpatch analyst with Calgary-based FirstEnergy Capital, says of Cook's new position: "It's certainly sending a message that they're bringing home their best and their brightest to take on front-line worldwide roles."

THINK ABOUT IT

Do men and women lead differently? Do men and women face different challenges in moving to the top of an organization? What factors might have affected Linda Cook's rise in leadership?

---

5 What are some current issues in leadership?

In this section, we look at some of the issues that face leaders today, including managing power, developing trust, providing moral leadership, providing online leadership, and understanding gender differences in leadership.

Managing Power

Where do leaders get their power—that is, their capacity to influence work actions or decisions? Five sources of leader power have been identified: legitimate, coercive, reward, expert, and referent.[59]

legitimate power
The power a leader has as a result of his or her position in the organization.

Legitimate power and authority are the same. Legitimate power represents the power a leader has as a result of his or her position in the organization. People in positions of authority are also likely to have reward and coercive power, but legitimate power is broader than the power to coerce and reward.

coercive power
The power a leader has through his or her ability to punish or control.

Coercive power is the power that rests on the leader's ability to punish or control. Followers react to this power out of fear of the negative results that might occur if they did not comply. As a manager, you typically have some coercive power, such as being able to suspend or demote employees or to assign them work they find unpleasant or undesirable.

reward power
The power a leader has to give benefits or rewards.

Reward power is the power to give benefits or rewards. These rewards can be anything that another person values. In an organizational context, that might include money, favourable performance appraisals, promotions, interesting work assignments, friendly colleagues, and preferred work shifts or sales territories.

expert power
The power a leader has based on his or her expertise, special skills, or knowledge.

Expert power is influence that is based on expertise, special skills, or knowledge. As jobs have become more specialized, managers have become increasingly dependent on staff "experts" to achieve the organization's goals. If an employee has skills, knowledge, or expertise that is critical to the operation of a work group, that person's expert power is enhanced.

referent power
The power a leader has based on his or her desirable resources or personal traits.

Finally, **referent power** is the power that arises because of a person's desirable resources or personal traits. If I admire and identify with you, you can exercise power over me because I want to please you. Referent power develops out of admiration of another and a desire to be like that person. If you admire someone to the point of modelling your behaviour and attitudes after him or her, that person has referent power over you.

Most effective leaders rely on several different forms of power to affect the behaviour and performance of their followers. For example, Lieutenant Commander Geoffrey Wadley, commanding officer of one of Australia's state-of-the-art submarines, the HMAS *Sheean*, employs different types of power in managing his crew and equipment. He gives orders to the crew (legitimate), praises them (reward), and disciplines those who commit infractions (coercive). As an effective leader, he also strives to have expert power (based on his expertise and knowledge) and referent power (based on his being admired) to influence his crew.[60] To learn more about acquiring and using power, see *Developing Your Interpersonal Skills—Acquiring Power* on pages 250–251, at the end of the chapter.

Developing Trust

After union members reluctantly agreed to $850 million a year in concessions that they believed were necessary to keep their company from bankruptcy, Air Canada's employees were stunned at President and CEO Robert Milton's after-the-fact disclosure of lucrative compensation policies and pension protections designed to retain key executives. Milton and his chief restructuring officer, Calin Rovinescu, were to receive 1 percent of the airline's shares, potentially worth an estimated $21 million, if the proposed takeover by Victor Li was successful. Any trust that employees had in Milton's ability to lead the airline into the future was eroded. In the end, the deal with Li collapsed when union members could not agree to further concessions relating to their pension plans.[61]

Milton's behaviour illustrates how fragile leader trust can be. In today's uncertain environment, an important consideration for leaders is building trust and credibility. Before we can discuss ways leaders can build trust and credibility, we have to know what trust and credibility are and why they are so important.

The main component of credibility is honesty. Surveys show that honesty is consistently singled out as the number-one characteristic of admired leaders. "Honesty is absolutely essential to leadership. If people are going to follow someone willingly, whether it be into battle or into the boardroom, they first want to assure themselves that the person is worthy of their trust." In addition to being honest, credible leaders are competent and inspiring.[62] They are personally able to communicate effectively their confidence and enthusiasm. Thus, followers judge a leader's **credibility** in terms of his or her honesty, competence, and ability to inspire.

credibility
The degree to which someone is perceived as honest, competent, and able to inspire.

Trust is closely entwined with the concept of credibility, and, in fact, the terms are often used interchangeably. **Trust** is defined as the belief in the integrity, character, and ability of a person. Followers who trust a leader are willing to be vulnerable to the leader's actions because they are confident that their rights and interests will not be abused.[63] Research has identified five dimensions that make up the concept of trust:[64]

trust
The belief in the integrity, character, and ability of a person.

- *Integrity:* Honesty and truthfulness

- *Competence:* Technical and interpersonal knowledge and skills

- *Consistency:* Reliability, predictability, and good judgment in handling situations

- *Loyalty:* Willingness to protect a person, physically and emotionally

- *Openness:* Willingness to share ideas and information freely

Of these five dimensions, integrity seems to be the most critical when someone assesses another's trustworthiness.[65] However, both integrity and competence were seen in our earlier discussion of leadership traits as consistently associated with leadership.

Workplace changes have reinforced why such leadership qualities are so important. For instance, the trend toward empowerment and self-managed work teams has reduced or eliminated many of the traditional control mechanisms used to monitor employees. If a work team is free to schedule its own work, evaluate its own performance, and even make its own hiring decisions, trust becomes critical. Employees have to trust managers to treat them fairly, and managers have to trust employees to conscientiously fulfill their responsibilities.

Also, leaders have to increasingly lead others who may not be in their immediate work group—members of cross-functional teams, individuals who work for suppliers or customers, and perhaps even people who represent other organizations through strategic alliances.

TIPS FOR MANAGERS

Suggestions for Building Trust

→ Practise **openness**.

→ Be **fair**.

→ Speak your **feelings**.

→ Tell the **truth**.

→ Show **consistency**.

→ Fulfill your **promises**.

→ Maintain **confidences**.

→ Demonstrate **competence**.

These situations don't allow leaders the luxury of falling back on their formal positions for influence. Many of these relationships, in fact, are fluid and fleeting. So the ability to develop trust quickly is crucial to the success of the relationship.

Why is it important that followers trust their leaders? Research has shown that trust in leadership is significantly related to positive job outcomes, including job performance, organizational citizenship behaviour, job satisfaction, and organizational commitment.[66] Given the importance of trust in effective leadership, how should leaders build trust? See *Tips for Managers—Suggestions for Building Trust* on page 239.[67]

Providing Moral Leadership

The topic of leadership and ethics has received surprisingly little attention. Only recently have ethics and leadership researchers begun to consider the ethical implications of leadership.[68] Visit your local bookstore and you will find quite a few books on ethics and leadership. Why now? One reason is a growing general interest in ethics throughout the field of management. Another, without a doubt, is the recent corporate and government financial scandals that have increased the public's and politicians' concerns about ethical standards.

Ethics is part of leadership in a number of ways. For instance, transformational leaders have been described as fostering moral virtue when they try to change the attitudes and behaviours of followers.[69] We can also see an ethical component to charisma. Unethical leaders may use their charisma to enhance their power over followers and use that power for self-serving purposes. On the other hand, ethical leaders may use their charisma in more socially constructive ways to serve others.[70] We also see a lack of ethics when leaders abuse their power and give themselves large salaries and bonuses while, at the same time, they seek to cut costs by laying off employees. And of course, trust, which is important to ethical behaviour, explicitly deals with the leadership traits of honesty and integrity.

As we have seen recently, leadership is not value-free. Providing moral leadership involves addressing the *means* that a leader uses in trying to achieve goals as well as the content of those goals. As a recent study concluded, ethical leadership is more than being ethical; it's reinforcing ethics through organizational mechanisms such as communication and the reward system.[71] Thus, before we judge any leader to be effective, we should consider both the moral content of his or her goals *and* the means used to achieve those goals.

Linda Cook, former president and CEO of Shell Canada, will have to confront some moral leadership issues in her new position at Royal Dutch Petroleum Company.[72] In 2004 it was discovered that Royal Dutch's top management had considerably overestimated the oil reserves the company had and, as a result, executives including the chair, the head of exploration, and the chief financial officer were forced to resign. Cook acknowledged that the scandal "impacts all of us [in the company], when there's a hit on your reputation like that, and knowing it will take years now to restore our reputation to the place that we think it should be."

Providing Online Leadership

Would you expect your job as a leader to be more difficult if employees are working from home, connected by computer?

How do you lead people who are physically separated from you and where interactions are basically reduced to written online communications? Pat O'Day, manager of a five-person virtual team at KPMG International, understands the challenges of providing online leadership. To help his team be more effective, O'Day says, "We communicate through email and conference calls and meet in person four times a year."[73]

What little research has been done in online leadership has focused on managing virtual teams.[74] This research suggests that there are three fundamental challenges in providing online leadership: communication, performance management, and trust.

Communication

In a virtual setting, leaders may need to learn new communication skills in order to be seen as effective. To effectively convey online leadership, managers must realize that they have choices in words, structure, tone, and style of their online communications and be alert to expressions of emotions. For instance, in face-to-face communications, harsh *words* can be softened by nonverbal action. A smile and comforting gestures, for instance, can lessen the blow behind words like *disappointed, unsatisfactory, inadequate,* or *below expectations.* In online interactions, that nonverbal aspect does not exist.

The *structure* of words in online communication has the power to motivate or demotivate the receiver. Is the message made up of full sentences or just phrases? The latter, for instance, is likely to be seen as curt and more threatening. Similarly, a message in ALL CAPS is the equivalent of shouting.

Leaders also need to be sure the *tone* of their message correctly conveys the emotions they want to send. Is the message formal or informal? Does it convey the appropriate level of importance or urgency? Also, is the leader's writing style consistent with his or her oral style? For instance, if a leader's written communication is more formal than his or her oral style, it will likely create confusion for employees and hinder the effectiveness of the message.

Online leaders must also choose a *style.* Do they use emoticons, abbreviations, jargon, and the like? Do they adapt their style to their audience? Observation suggests that some managers are having difficulty adjusting to computer-based communications. For instance, they use the same style with their bosses that they use with their staff. Or they selectively use online communication to "hide" when delivering bad news. Finally, online leaders need to develop the skills of "reading between the lines" in the messages they receive so they can decipher the emotional components.

Online leadership encompasses many new tasks, even for managers in firms that have already established themselves in the brick-and-mortar world as Costco has. Costco's eight-year-old Internet company, Costco.com, offers shoppers only a fraction of the products they can find in one of its warehouse stores. Susan Castillo, vice-president of e-commerce, has made the site a success with unexpected items like computers and diamond jewellery instead of "safe" items like books and CDs. Castillo likes relying on the Internet to control performance. "We know immediately whether something is successful simply by how many people order it," she says. "That's the joy of the Internet. You can see minute by minute what members are ordering."

Performance Management

Another challenge of online leadership is managing performance. How? By defining, facilitating, and encouraging it.[75] As leaders *define* performance, it's important to ensure that all members of a virtual team understand the team's goals, their responsibilities in achieving those goals, and how goal achievement is going to be assessed. There should be no surprises or uncertainties about performance expectations. Although these are important managerial responsibilities in all situations, they are particularly critical in virtual work environments as there are no face-to-face interactions to convey expectations or address performance problems.

Online leaders also have a responsibility to *facilitate* performance. This means reducing or eliminating obstacles to successful performance and providing adequate resources to get the job done. This can be particularly challenging, especially if the virtual team is global, since the physical distance separating the leader and the team means it's not easy to get team members the resources they may need.

Finally, online leaders are responsible for *encouraging* performance by providing sufficient rewards that virtual employees really value. As we will see in Chapter 9, motivating employees can be difficult, even in work settings where there is face-to-face interaction. In a virtual setting, the motivational challenge can be even greater because the leader is not there in person to encourage, support, and guide. So what can online leaders do? They can ask virtual employees what rewards are most important to them—pay, benefits, technology upgrades, opportunities for professional development, or whatever. Then, they can make sure the rewards are provided in a timely manner after major work goals have been achieved. Finally, any rewards program must be perceived as fair. This expectation is not any different from that of leaders in nonvirtual settings—employees want and expect rewards to be distributed fairly.

Trust

Cypress Semiconductor
www.cypress.com

The final challenge of providing online leadership is the trust issue. In a virtual setting, there are numerous opportunities to violate trust. One possible trust issue is whether the system is being used to monitor and evaluate employees. The technology is there to do so, but leaders must consider whether that is really the best way to influence employee behaviour. For instance, T. J. Rodgers, founder and CEO of Cypress Semiconductor, found out the hard way that it might not be.[76] He built an in-house system that tracked goals and deadlines. If a department missed its target, the software shut down its computers and cancelled the manager's next paycheque. After realizing the system encouraged dishonesty, Rodgers ditched it. The experience made him understand that it was more important to create a culture where trust among all participants is expected and required. In fact, the five dimensions of trust we described earlier—integrity, competence, consistency, loyalty, and openness—would be vital to the development of such a culture.

Understanding Gender Differences and Leadership

There was a time when the question "Do males and females lead differently?" could be accurately characterized as a purely academic issue—interesting, but not very relevant. That time has certainly passed! Many women now hold management positions, and many more around the world will continue to join the management ranks. For instance, women fill 32 percent of managerial roles in Canada, although only 14 percent of the senior management roles, and 6.7 percent of the highest corporate titles—CEO, chief financial officer, or chief operating officer.[77] They are highly involved in smaller companies, however. Industry Canada reports that in 2000, 45 percent of all small- to medium-sized enterprises had some degree of female ownership.[78] Moreover, women start almost half of all small businesses in Canada today and, among young people, women start almost 80 percent of small businesses.[79]

In other economically developed countries, the percentage of female managerial/administrative employees is as follows: Australia—24 percent; France—10 percent; Germany—19 percent; Japan—9 percent; Poland—66 percent; and Sweden—59 percent.[80] Misconceptions about the relationship between leadership and gender can adversely affect hiring, performance evaluation, promotion, and other human resource decisions for both men and women. For instance, evidence indicates that a "good" manager is still perceived as predominantly masculine.[81] A warning before we proceed: This topic is controversial. If male and female styles differ, is one inferior? If there is a difference, is one gender more effective in leading than the other? These are important questions and we will address them shortly.

A number of studies focusing on gender and leadership style have been conducted in recent years.[82] Their general conclusion is that males and females *do* use different styles. Specifically, women tend to adopt a more democratic or participative style. Women are more likely to encourage participation, share power and information, and attempt to enhance followers' self-worth. They lead through inclusion and rely on their charisma, expertise, contacts, and interpersonal skills to influence others. Women tend to use transformational leadership, motivating others by transforming their self-interest into organizational goals. Men are more likely to use a directive, command-and-control style. They rely on formal position authority for their influence. Men use transactional leadership, handing

Exhibit 8-9

Where Female Managers Do Better: A Scorecard

None of the five studies set out to find gender differences. They stumbled on them while compiling and analyzing performance evaluations.

Skill (Each check mark denotes which group scored higher on the respective studies.)	MEN	WOMEN
Motivating Others		✓ ✓ ✓ ✓ ✓
Fostering Communication		✓ ✓ ✓ ✓ *
Producing High-Quality Work		✓ ✓ ✓ ✓ ✓
Strategic Planning	✓ ✓	✓ ✓ *
Listening to Others		✓ ✓ ✓ ✓ ✓
Analyzing Issues	✓ ✓	✓ ✓ *

* In one study, women's and men's scores in these categories were statistically even.

Data: Hagberg Consulting Group, Management Research Group, Lawrence A. Pfaff, Personnel Decisions International Inc., Advanced Teamware Inc.

Source: R. Sharpe, "As Leaders, Women Rule," *BusinessWeek*, November 20, 2000, p. 75.

out rewards for good work and punishment for bad.[83] There is an interesting qualifier to the above findings. The tendency of female leaders to be more democratic than males declines when women are in male-dominated jobs. In such jobs, apparently, group norms and male stereotypes influence women, and they are likely to act more autocratically.[84]

Although it's interesting to see how male and female leadership styles differ, a more important question is whether they differ in effectiveness. Although some researchers have shown that males and females tend to be equally effective as leaders,[85] an increasing number of studies have shown that women executives, when rated by their peers, employees, and bosses, score higher than their male counterparts on a wide variety of measures, including getting extra effort from subordinates and overall effectiveness in leading. Subordinates also reported more satisfaction with the leadership given by women.[86] See Exhibit 8-9 for a scorecard on where female managers do better, based on a summary of five studies. Why these differences? One possible explanation is that in today's organizations, flexibility, teamwork and partnering, trust, and information sharing are rapidly replacing rigid structures, competitive individualism, control, and secrecy. In these types of workplaces, effective managers must use more social and interpersonal behaviours. They listen, motivate, and provide support to their people. They inspire and influence rather than control. And women seem to do those things better than men.[87]

Although women seem to rate highly on those leadership skills needed to succeed in today's dynamic global environment, we don't want to fall into the same trap as the early leadership researchers who tried to find the "one best leadership style" for all situations. We know that there is no one *best* style for all situations. Instead, which leadership style is effective will depend on the situation. So even if men and women differ in their leadership styles, we should not assume that one is always preferable to the other.

SUMMARY AND IMPLICATIONS

1 **How do leaders and managers differ?** Managers are appointed to their positions. They have formal authority, and it is this authority that gives them their ability to influence employees. In contrast, leaders can be appointed or can emerge from within a work group. They provide vision and strategy and are able to influence others for reasons beyond formal authority. Though ideally all managers should be leaders, not all leaders can be managers, because they do not all have the ability to plan, organize, and control. *Linda Cook has demonstrated the ability to both lead and manage in her many roles at Shell.*

2 **What do trait and behavioural theories tell us about leadership?** Researchers agree that traits alone are not sufficient for explaining effective leadership. Possessing the appropriate traits only makes it more likely that an individual would be an effective leader. In general, behavioural theories have identified useful behaviours that managers should have, but the research could not identify when these behaviours were most useful. *Linda Cook notes that one of her most useful leadership traits is being good at strategic thinking.*

3 **How do contingency theories of leadership improve our understanding of leadership?** Contingency theories acknowledge that different situations require different leadership styles. The theories suggest that leaders may need to adjust their style to the needs of different organizations and employees, and perhaps different countries. *Linda Cook has demonstrated an ability to use different leadership styles at different times, suggesting that she has an understanding of a contingency approach to leadership.*

4 **What are some contemporary approaches to leadership?** The cutting-edge approaches to leadership are transformational-transactional leadership, charismatic-visionary leadership, and team leadership. While most leaders are transactional, guiding followers to achieve goals by clarifying role and task requirements, transformational leaders inspire their followers. Although transformational leadership is not always necessary, it can have very positive results. Charismatic-visionary leaders are a particular type of transformational leader. They are known for having and articulating a vision, and being willing to take risks to achieve that vision. Team leadership is becoming increasingly important in today's workplace. It is sometimes a difficult form of leadership, as it requires more collaboration, and some leaders have "command and control" tendencies. *Linda Cook, however, emphasizes that she considers herself a team player and that is how she likes to lead.*

5 **What are some current issues in leadership?** The major leadership issues today include managing power, developing trust, providing moral leadership, providing online leadership, and understanding gender differences and leadership. *Linda Cook's career at Shell demonstrates some of the differences men and women face in the workplace. She had to convince her superiors that women could be managers of field operations, something her male superiors had not considered before.*

CHAPTER 8

Management @ Work

Reading for Comprehension

1. Discuss the strengths and weaknesses of the trait theory of leadership.

2. What is the managerial grid? Contrast this approach to leadership with that developed by the Ohio State and Michigan groups.

3. How is a least-preferred co-worker (LPC) determined? What is the importance of one's LPC for the Fiedler contingency model for leadership?

4. What are the two contingency variables of the path-goal theory of leadership?

5. What similarities, if any, can you find among Fiedler's model contingency model, Hersey and Blanchard's Situational Leadership®, and path-goal theory?

6. What sources of power are available to leaders? Which ones are most effective?

7. What are the five dimensions of trust?

Linking Concepts to Practice

1. "All managers should be leaders, but not all leaders should be managers." Do you agree or disagree with that statement? Support your position.

2. If you ask people why a given individual is a leader, they tend to describe the person in terms such as competent, consistent, self-assured, inspiring a shared vision, and enthusiastic. How do these descriptions fit with leadership concepts presented in the chapter?

3. Do you think that most managers in real life use a contingency approach to increase their leadership effectiveness? Discuss.

4. Do you think trust evolves out of an individual's personal characteristics or out of specific situations? Explain.

5. "Charismatic leadership is always appropriate in organizations." Do you agree or disagree? Support your position.

6. What kinds of campus activities could a full-time student do that might lead to the perception that he or she is a charismatic leader? In pursuing those activities, what might the student do to enhance this perception of being charismatic?

MANAGEMENT FOR YOU TODAY

Your school is developing a one-day orientation program for new students majoring in business. You have been asked to consider leading the group of students who will design and implement the orientation program. Develop a 2- to 3-page "handout" that shows whether the position is a natural fit for you. To do this, (1) identify your strengths and weaknesses in the sources of power you can bring to the project; and (2) discuss whether you would be a transactional or transformational leader and why. Provide a strong concluding statement about whether or not you would be the best leader for this task.

SELF-ASSESSMENT

What's My Leadership Style?

The following items describe aspects of leadership behaviour. Respond to each item according to the way you would be most likely to act if you were the leader of a work group. Use this scale for your responses:[88]

A = Always	S = Seldom
F = Frequently	N = Never
O = Occasionally	

1. I would most likely act as the spokesperson of the group.   A   F   O   S   N

2. I would encourage overtime work.   A   F   O   S   N

3. I would allow group members complete freedom in their work.   A   F   O   S   N

4. I would encourage the use of uniform procedures.   A   F   O   S   N

5. I would permit group members to use their own judgment in solving problems.   A   F   O   S   N

6. I would stress being ahead of competing groups.   A   F   O   S   N

7. I would speak as a representative of the group.   A   F   O   S   N

8. I would needle group members for greater effort.   A   F   O   S   N

9. I would try out my ideas in the group.   A   F   O   S   N

10. I would let group members do their work the way they think best.   A   F   O   S   N

11. I would be working hard for a promotion.   A   F   O   S   N

12. I would be able to tolerate postponement and uncertainty.   A   F   O   S   N

13. I would speak for the group when visitors were present.   A   F   O   S   N

14. I would keep the work moving at a rapid pace.   A   F   O   S   N

15. I would turn group members loose on a job and let them go to it.   A   F   O   S   N

16. I would settle conflicts when they occur in the group.   A   F   O   S   N

17. I would get swamped by details.   A   F   O   S   N

18. I would represent the group at outside meetings.   A   F   O   S   N

19. I would be reluctant to allow group members any freedom of action.   A   F   O   S   N

20. I would decide what shall be done and how it shall be done.   A   F   O   S   N

21. I would push for increased production.   A   F   O   S   N

22. I would let some group members have authority that I should keep.   A   F   O   S   N

23. Things would usually turn out as I predicted.   A   F   O   S   N

24. I would allow the group a high degree of initiative.   A   F   O   S   N

25. I would assign group members to particular tasks.   A   F   O   S   N

26. I would be willing to make changes.   A   F   O   S   N

27. I would ask group members to work harder.   A   F   O   S   N

28. I would trust group members to exercise good judgment.   A   F   O   S   N

29. I would schedule the work to be done.   A   F   O   S   N

30. I would refuse to explain my actions.   A   F   O   S   N

31. I would persuade group members that my ideas are to their advantage.   A   F   O   S   N

32. I would permit the group to set its own pace.   A   F   O   S   N

33. I would urge the group to beat its previous record.   A   F   O   S   N

34. I would act without consulting the group.   A   F   O   S   N

35. I would ask that group members follow standard rules and regulations.   A   F   O   S   N

Scoring Key

1. Circle the numbers 8, 12, 17, 18, 19, 30, 34, and 35.

2. Write a 1 in front of the circled number if you responded Seldom or Never.

3. Also write a 1 in front of any remaining (uncircled) items if you responded Always or Frequently to these.

4. Circle the 1s that you have written in front of the following questions: 3, 5, 8, 10, 15, 18, 19, 22, 24, 26, 28, 30, 32, 34, and 35.

5. Count the circled 1s. This is your score for "Concern for People."

6. Count the uncircled 1s. This is your score for "Task."

Analysis and Interpretation

This leadership instrument taps the degree to which you are task or people oriented. Task orientation is concerned with getting the job done, whereas people orientation focuses on group interactions and the needs of individual members.

The cutoff scores separating high and low scores are approximately as follows. For task orientation, high is a score above 10; low is below 10. For people orientation, high is a score above 7; low is below 7.

The best leaders are ones who can balance their task/people orientation to various situations. A high score on both would indicate this balance. If you are too task oriented, you tend to be autocratic. You get the job done but at a high emotional cost. If you are too people oriented, your leadership style may be overly laissez-faire. People are likely to be happy in their work but sometimes at the expense of productivity.

Your score should also help you to put yourself in situations that increase your likelihood of success. So, for instance, evidence indicates that when employees are experienced and know their jobs well, they tend to perform best with a people-oriented leader. If you are people oriented, then this is a favourable situation for you. But if you are task oriented, you might want to pass on this situation.

More Self-Assessments

To learn more about your skills, abilities, and interests, take the following self-assessments on your enclosed CD-ROM:

- #30—How Charismatic Am I?
- #32—Do Others See Me as Trustworthy?
- #34—How Good Am I at Building and Leading a Team? (This exercise also appears in Chapter 10 on pages 298–299.)

WORKING TOGETHER: TEAM-BASED EXERCISE

The Pre–Post Leadership Assessment

Objective

To compare characteristics intuitively related to leadership with leadership characteristics found in leadership theory.

Procedure

Identify 3 people (for example, friends, relatives, previous boss, public figures) whom you consider outstanding leaders. List why you feel each individual is a good leader. Compare your lists of the 3 people. Which traits, if any, are common to all 3? Your instructor will lead the class in a discussion of leadership characteristics based on your lists. Students will call out what they identified, and your instructor will write the traits on the chalkboard. When all students have shared their lists, class discussion will focus on the following:

- What characteristics consistently appeared on students' lists?
- Were these characteristics more trait oriented or behaviour oriented?
- In what situations were these characteristics useful?
- What, if anything, does this exercise suggest about leadership attributes?

Is an Eye for an Eye Fair Play?

What happens when a charismatic leader's relentless pursuit of a vision encourages extreme or even ethically questionable behaviour? Consider the CEO of a company that hired an investigator to dive into other firms' dumpsters for information about their dealings with a major competitor. The same CEO's company has used precisely timed news releases as strategic weapons against particular rivals. And the same CEO's company once announced a hostile takeover bid for a direct competitor with the stated intention of not actively selling its products but acquiring its best customers and employees. This CEO, described by the *Wall Street Journal* as "a swashbuckling figure in Silicon Valley," is Larry Ellison of Oracle.

Ellison's charismatic leadership has built Oracle into a software powerhouse. Although it is locked in fierce competition with Microsoft and other giants, it does not ignore smaller rivals such as i2 Technologies. Oracle once issued a news release belittling i2's attempt to develop a certain type of software only minutes before i2's CEO was to meet with influential analysts. Such hardball tactics are hardly random or spontaneous. "We definitely sit down with a calendar and work out

which week we're going to pick on Siebel and which week we're going to pick on i2," says Oracle's chief marketing officer. When Oracle pursued an unwelcome acquisition bid for rival PeopleSoft, the two CEOs traded barbed quotes for weeks as the companies battled in courtrooms and in the media. PeopleSoft's CEO, a former Oracle executive, described the situation as "enormously bad behavior from a company that's had a history of it."[89] Nevertheless, Oracle finally bought PeopleSoft in 2005.

Imagine that you are the CEO of i2 Technologies, which makes inventory and supply tracking systems that compete with Oracle's large-scale business software suites. In five minutes, you will be meeting with a roomful of financial analysts who make buy or sell recommendations to investors. Your goal is to showcase your company's accomplishments, outline your vision for its future, and encourage a positive recommendation so your stock price will go even higher. You just heard about Oracle's news release belittling your product in development—and you suspect the analysts also know about it. How will you handle the news release?

Dale Earnhardt

Stock car racing is one of the fastest-growing spectator sports in the United States and attracts fans from all different demographics.[90] One of the most popular NASCAR (National Association for Stock Car Auto Racing) drivers was the late Dale Earnhardt, who died in an accident at the Daytona International racetrack on February 18, 2001. After his death, there were questions about the future of his racing empire, Dale Earnhardt, Inc. (DEI), an organization with annual revenues of over $26 million (US). However, Earnhardt's widow, Teresa, was determined not to let anything happen to the organization Dale had worked so hard to build. She went from a behind-the-scenes negotiator for Dale Earnhardt merchandising to the CEO of a multimillion-dollar organization with four race teams and an assortment of other business ventures. In so doing, she had to take on a leader's role.

Teresa Earnhardt is not a flashy person and does not enjoy being the centre of attention. She tends to be more emotionally guarded by nature, and she is not comfortable with having to engage in small talk. She says, "I'm not an entertainer. However, I'll do what I need to do." She prefers

staying in the background. For instance, on race weekends, while other NASCAR owners make the rounds of the garage area, Teresa negotiates business deals, reads through contracts, and deals with employee issues. She approaches decisions differently from her late husband as well. While Dale was more adamant, spontaneous, and headstrong—after all, his racing nickname was "The Intimidator"—Teresa makes more calculated decisions. She uses her quiet demeanour and strong determination and character to make DEI even more successful.

DEI's female CEO may be quiet and subdued, but she is no pushover. Soon after assuming control of the company's business decisions, Teresa eliminated some excessive corporate expenses, one of which was Dale's helicopter, a luxury she felt was no longer necessary. Michael Waltrip, one of the drivers for DEI, says, "When it's the gloomiest and the darkest and other people say there's no way, that's when she really shines. She comes in with her style and takes control and fixes things." At the end of the 2002 Winston Cup season DEI finished eleventh and fourteenth in the point totals standings. Several high-ranking company executives were in a room discussing the pluses and minuses of the season when Teresa said, "How do I tell you guys you did a good job but your results stink?" It was a "subtle reminder that the season wasn't up to the standards she and Dale were used to."

Teresa's leadership style has had to evolve to meet the demands of running a successful business in an industry that is very much male dominated. NASCAR president Mike Helton has talked to her about becoming more visible—something he thinks is important for her team and for the sport in which there are few women in positions of power. Teresa recognizes that there are times when, as the organization's CEO, she needs to be out in front as the company's spokesperson. For instance, in January 2003, Teresa helped Dale Earnhardt Jr. unveil the logo for the shop of his new Busch series team. She continues her work behind the scenes as well. Teresa helped sign her other well-known driver, Michael Waltrip, and his primary sponsor, NAPA Auto Parts, to a new contract.

Teresa is working on improving her leadership style so that she can more effectively replace her well-known husband. She wonders whether being a woman in a male-dominated organization might make it difficult to continue signing successful drivers and sponsors. What can Teresa do to continue the sccess of DEI?

DEVELOPING YOUR DIAGNOSTIC AND ANALYTICAL SKILLS

Reverse Mentoring at Grafik Marketing

When more seasoned employees take less experienced employees under their wings, we call this mentoring. The wisdom and guidance of these seasoned individuals serve to assist the less experienced employees in obtaining the necessary skills and socialization to succeed in the organization. It is also helpful in facilitating an individual's career progress. Technology, however, is starting to change some of this traditional mentoring process in terms of who does the mentoring. For Judy Kirpich, for example, technological advances have resulted in significant increases in mentoring in her organization, Grafik Marketing Communications. However, the company's senior managers are the ones being mentored! They are getting technology information from younger employees who have grown up on computers, resulting in what is called reverse mentoring.[91]

Actually, reverse mentoring started years ago at General Electric. Then CEO Jack Welch recognized that his senior managers needed to become more proficient with using technology—especially the Internet. Accordingly, Welch had several hundred senior managers partner with younger employees in the organization. Not only were these managers able to learn about the Internet, but reverse mentoring also enhanced intergenerational understanding and gave senior decision makers a new perspective on younger consumer products and service needs. It also helped the organization in brainstorming for new and creative ideas.

Reverse mentoring, however, is not without drawbacks. For these younger employees to mentor properly, they must be trained. They must understand how to be patient with those individuals who may have a technology phobia. These reverse mentors need to recognize their mentoring is limited to offering advice solely on relevant technology topics. They must also understand and acknowledge the need for confidentiality because many senior managers may be reluctant to have this mentoring relationship widely known. Furthermore, when reverse mentors exist, organizational members must be made aware that problems arising out of favouritism are a reality. As a result of these concerns, many reverse mentoring relationships are built on external mentors; that is, reverse mentors who come from outside the organization.

Despite these potential drawbacks, Kirpich has moved reverse mentoring forward. Through her organization's formal program, she and other senior managers get the latest software and technology systems information that will enhance their productivity. In the end, Grafik Marketing Communications has found that the program helps with design ideas and technical innovation. It has helped the organization be more effective and efficient, which is something Kirpich desires.

Questions

1. What role does mentoring play in leadership?

2. Does reverse mentoring alter the leader–follower relationship? Explain your position.

3. Do you believe individuals serving as coaches to senior managers should be external to the organization? Discuss.

Acquiring Power

About the Skill

The exercise of power is a natural process in any group or organization, and to perform their jobs effectively managers need to know how to acquire and use power—the capacity of a leader to influence work actions or decisions. We discussed the concept of power earlier in the chapter and identified five different sources of power for leaders, including legitimate, coercive, reward, expert, and referent. Why is having power important? Because power makes you less dependent on others. When a manager has power, he or she is not as dependent on others for critical resources. If the resources a manager controls are important, scarce, and nonsubstitutable, her power will increase because others will be more dependent on her for those resources.

Steps in Developing the Skill

You can be more effective at acquiring and using power if you accept the following eight suggestions:[92]

1. **Frame arguments in terms of organizational goals.** To be effective at acquiring power means camouflaging your self-interests. Discussions over who controls what resources should be framed in terms of the benefits that will accrue to the organization; do not point out how you personally will benefit.

2. **Develop the right image.** If you know your organization's culture, you already understand what the organization wants and values from its employees in terms of dress, associates to cultivate and those to avoid, whether to appear risk taking or risk aversive, the preferred leadership style, the importance placed on getting along well with others, and so forth. With this knowledge, you are equipped to project the appropriate image. Because the assessment of your performance is not always a fully objective process, you need to pay attention to style as well as substance.

3. **Gain control of organizational resources.** Controlling organizational resources that are scarce and important is a source of power. Knowledge and expertise are particularly effective resources to control. They make you more valuable to the organization and, therefore, more likely to have job security, chances for advancement, and a receptive audience for your ideas.

4. **Make yourself appear indispensable.** Because we are dealing with appearances rather than objective facts, you can enhance your power by appearing to be indispensable. You don't really have to be indispensable as long as key people in the organization believe that you are.

5. **Be visible.** If you have a job that brings your accomplishments to the attention of others, that is great. However, if you don't have such a job, you will want to find ways to let others in the organization know what you are doing by highlighting successes in routine reports, having satisfied customers relay their appreciation to senior executives, being seen at social functions, being active in your professional associations, and developing powerful allies who speak positively about your accomplishments. Of course, you will want to be on the lookout for those projects that will increase your visibility.

6. **Develop powerful allies.** To get power, it helps to have powerful people on your side. Cultivate contacts with potentially influential people above you, at your own level, and at lower organizational levels. These allies often can provide you with information that is otherwise not readily available. In addition, having allies can provide you with a coalition of support if and when you need it.

7. **Avoid "tainted" members.** In almost every organization, there are fringe members whose status is questionable. Their performance and/or loyalty may be suspect. Keep your distance from such individuals.

8. **Support your manager.** Your immediate future is in the hands of your current manager. Because he or she evaluates your performance, you will typically want to do whatever is necessary to have your manager on your side. You should make every effort to help your manager succeed, make her look good, support her if she is under siege, and spend the time to find out the criteria she will use to assess your effectiveness. Don't undermine your manager. And don't speak negatively of her to others.

Practising the Skill

You used to be the star marketing manager for Hilton Electronics. But for the past year, you have been outpaced again and again by Conor, a new manager in the design department, who has been accomplishing everything expected of her and more. Meanwhile, your best efforts to do your job well have been sabotaged and undercut by Leonila—your and Conor's manager. For example, before last year's international consumer electronics show, Leonila moved $30 000 from your budget to Conor's. Despite your best efforts, your marketing team could not complete all the marketing materials normally developed to showcase all of your organization's new products at this important industry show. Leonila has chipped away at your staff and budget ever since. Although you have been able to meet most of your goals with fewer staff and less budget, Leonila has continued to slice away resources of your group. Just last week, she eliminated two positions in your team of eight marketing specialists to make room for a new designer and some extra equipment for Conor. Leonila is clearly taking away your resources while giving Conor whatever she wants and more. You think it's time to do something or soon you will not have any team or resources left. How should you approach the problem?

Motivating Employees

How do I motivate people to accomplish organizational goals?

1 What is motivation?

2 How can needs help one be motivated?

3 What are the contemporary theories of motivation?

4 What are some current issues in motivation?

5 What can managers learn from motivation theories?

How do you motivate employees in an industry where absenteeism rates average 5 percent of all working hours, but can be as high as 10 percent in urban areas?[1]

What do you do when the turnover rate of managers averages 20 percent, and the turnover rate of nonmanagerial employees averages 30 percent?

Sir Terry Leahy, CEO of UK-based Tesco, faces these problems daily. The company has almost 2500 supermarkets, hypermarkets, and convenience stores in the United Kingdom, Ireland, Central Europe, and Asia. Once a discount supermarket, Tesco has built itself as a dressier, mid-market retailer while becoming the number-one food retailer in the United Kingdom.

The company is trying to keep its Generation-Y employees (Generation Y includes those born between 1979 and 1994) motivated, while also trying to accommodate the needs of other groups of employees, including ethnic minorities and mothers returning to the workplace. Not all of the jobs are interesting, and many can be quite repetitive, like stocking shelves, or running groceries past scanners for hours on end.

Leahy believes in starting with the basics in dealing with employees. "We've built Tesco around sound values and principles," he says. Therefore, he makes sure that employees are treated with respect. But he is also concerned about performance: "If that's bad and there's no good reason, I get cross."

THINK ABOUT IT

What are the different motivation tools that managers use? Put yourself in Sir Terry Leahy's shoes. How should he motivate his managers so that he will have lower turnover? What can he do to keep his shelf-stockers and cashiers motivated?

Motivating and rewarding employees is one of the most important, and one of the most challenging, activities that managers perform. Successful managers, like Sir Terry Leahy, understand that what motivates them personally may have little or no effect on others. Just because *you* are motivated by being part of a cohesive work team, don't assume everyone is. Or the fact that you are motivated by challenging work does not mean everyone is. Effective managers who want their employees to put forth maximum effort recognize that they need to know how and why employees are motivated and to tailor their motivational practices to satisfy the needs and wants of those employees.

In this chapter, we first look at some early motivation theories and then at the contemporary theories. We finish by looking at some current motivation issues and some practical suggestions that managers can use in motivating employees.

 **Tesco**
www.tesco.com

WHAT IS MOTIVATION?

All managers need to be able to motivate their employees, and that requires an understanding of what motivation is. Many people incorrectly view motivation as a personal trait—that is, a trait that some people have and others don't. Our knowledge of motivation tells us that we cannot label people that way. What we *do* know is that motivation is the result of the interaction between a person and a situation. Certainly, individuals differ in motivational drive but, overall, motivation varies from situation to situation. For instance, your

1 What is motivation?

Exhibit 9-1

The Motivation Process

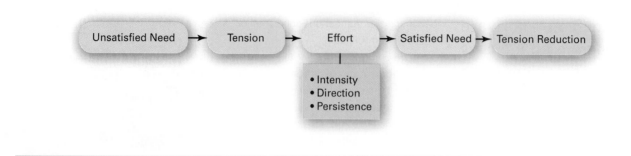

level of motivation probably differs among the various courses you take each term. As we analyze the concept of motivation, keep in mind that the level of motivation varies both between individuals and within individuals at different times.

motivation
An individual's willingness to exert high levels of effort to reach organizational goals, conditioned by the degree to which that effort satisfies some individual need.

Motivation refers to an individual's willingness to exert high levels of effort to reach organizational goals, conditioned by the effort's ability to satisfy some individual need. Although, in general, motivation refers to effort exerted toward any goal, here it refers to organizational goals because our focus is on work-related behaviour.

The three key elements in the definition of motivation are effort, organizational goals, and need. The *effort* element is a measure of intensity or drive.[2] A motivated person tries hard. But high levels of effort are unlikely to lead to favourable job performance unless the effort is channelled in a direction that benefits the organization.[3] Therefore we must consider the quality of the effort as well as its intensity. Effort that is directed toward, and consistent with, *organizational goals* is the kind of effort that we should be seeking. Finally, we will treat motivation as a *need-satisfying* process, as shown in Exhibit 9-1.

need
An internal state that makes certain outcomes appear attractive.

A **need** is an internal state that makes certain outcomes appear attractive. An unsatisfied need creates tension, which an individual reduces by exerting effort. Because we are interested in work behaviour, this tension-reduction effort must be directed toward organizational goals. Therefore, inherent in our definition of motivation is the requirement that the individual's needs be compatible with the organization's goals. When the two don't match, individuals may exert high levels of effort that run counter to the interests of the organization. Incidentally, this is not all that unusual. Some employees regularly spend a lot of time talking with friends at work to satisfy their social need. There is a high level of effort, but little if any is being directed toward work.

What motivates you?

Finding ways to motivate employees to achieve high levels of performance is an important organizational problem, and managers keep looking for a solution. A recent Canadian Policy Research Network survey found that only 40 percent of Canadians are very satisfied with their jobs. By comparison, 47 percent of American workers are happy with their work, and 54 percent of Danish workers report high satisfaction.[4] In light of these results, it's no wonder that both academic researchers and practising managers want to understand and explain employee motivation.

EARLY THEORIES OF MOTIVATION

Management at Tesco was interested in discovering what concerns their employees had and how these might be addressed.[5] They conducted research on their employees and found that many of their staff were single and worked mainly to have the money to travel overseas and participate in leisure activities. Their research also found that these employees "were unlikely to take much pride in their work, would lack commitment and would have little hesitation about going to work elsewhere if the pay were better."

THINK ABOUT IT
What kinds of needs do employees have? How can they be addressed?

We begin by looking at needs theories of motivation, which are probably the most widely known approaches to employee motivation. Below, we briefly review Maslow's hierarchy of needs, McGregor's Theory X and Theory Y, Herzberg's motivation-hygiene theory, and McClelland's theory of needs.

Maslow's Hierarchy of Needs Theory

The best-known theory of motivation is probably Abraham Maslow's **hierarchy of needs theory**.[6] Maslow was a psychologist who proposed that within every person is a hierarchy of five needs:

1. *Physiological needs*. Food, drink, shelter, sexual satisfaction, and other physical requirements.

2. *Safety needs*. Security and protection from physical and emotional harm, as well as assurance that physical needs will continue to be met.

3. *Social needs*. Affection, belongingness, acceptance, and friendship.

4. *Esteem needs*. Internal esteem factors such as self-respect, autonomy, and achievement, and external esteem factors such as status, recognition, and attention.

5. *Self-actualization needs*. Growth, achieving one's potential, and self-fulfillment; the drive to become what one is capable of becoming.

Maslow argued that each level in the needs hierarchy must be substantially satisfied before the next is activated and that once a need is substantially satisfied, it no longer motivates behaviour. In other words, as each need is substantially satisfied, the next need becomes dominant. In terms of Exhibit 9-2, an individual moves up the needs hierarchy. From the standpoint of motivation, Maslow's theory proposed that, although no need is ever fully satisfied, a substantially satisfied need will no longer motivate an individual.

2 How can needs help one be motivated?

 **Q&A** 13.1

hierarchy of needs theory
Maslow's theory that there is a hierarchy of five human needs: physiological, safety, social, esteem, and self-actualization; as each need becomes satisfied, the next need becomes dominant.

physiological needs
A person's need for food, drink, shelter, sexual satisfaction, and other physical requirements.

safety needs
A person's need for security and protection from physical and emotional harm; as well as assurance that physical needs will continue to be met.

social needs
A person's need for affection, belongingness, acceptance, and friendship.

esteem needs
A person's need for internal esteem factors such as self-respect, autonomy, and achievement, and external esteem factors such as status, recognition, and attention.

self-actualization needs
A person's need to grow and become what he or she is capable of becoming.

Exhibit 9-2

Maslow's Hierarchy of Needs

Therefore, according to Maslow, if you want to motivate someone, you need to understand what level that person is on in the hierarchy and focus on satisfying needs at or above that level.

The practical significance of Maslow's theory is widely accepted.[7] However, Maslow provided no empirical support for his theory, and several studies that sought to validate it could not.[8]

McGregor's Theory X and Theory Y

Do you need to be rewarded by others or are you a self-motivator?

Are individuals intrinsically or extrinsically motivated? Douglas McGregor tried to uncover the answer to this question through his discussion of Theory X and Theory Y.[9] **Extrinsic motivation** comes from outside the person and includes such things as pay, bonuses, and other tangible rewards. **Intrinsic motivation** reflects an individual's internal desire to do something, with motivation coming from interest, challenge, and personal satisfaction. Individuals show intrinsic motivation when they deeply care about their work, look for ways to improve the work, and are fulfilled by doing it well.[10]

McGregor's **Theory X** offers an essentially negative view of people. It assumes that employees have little ambition, dislike work, want to avoid responsibility, and need to be closely controlled to work effectively. It suggests that people are almost exclusively driven by extrinsic motivators. **Theory Y** offers a positive view. It assumes that employees can exercise self-direction, accept and actually seek out responsibility, and consider work a natural activity. It suggests that people are more intrinsically motivated. McGregor believed that Theory Y assumptions best captured the true nature of employees and should guide management practice.

What did McGregor's analysis imply about motivation? The answer is best expressed in the framework presented by Maslow. Theory X assumed that lower-order needs dominated individuals, and Theory Y assumed that higher-order needs dominated individuals. McGregor himself held to the belief that the assumptions of Theory Y were more valid than those of Theory X. Therefore, he proposed that participation in decision making, responsible and challenging jobs, and good group relations would maximize employee motivation.

Our knowledge of motivation tells us that neither theory alone fully accounts for employee behaviour. What we know is that motivation is the result of the interaction of the individual and the situation. Individuals differ in their basic motivational drive. As well, while you may find completing a homework assignment boring, you might enthusiastically plan a surprise party for a friend. These points underscore that the level of motivation varies both *between* individuals and *within* individuals at different times. They also suggest that managers should try to make sure that situations are motivating for employees.

Herzberg's Motivation-Hygiene Theory

Frederick Herzberg's **motivation-hygiene theory** proposes that intrinsic factors are related to job satisfaction and motivation, whereas extrinsic factors are related to job dissatisfaction.[11] Believing that individuals' attitudes toward work determined success or failure, Herzberg investigated the question "What do people want from their jobs?" He asked people for detailed descriptions of situations in which they felt exceptionally good or bad about their jobs. These findings are shown in Exhibit 9-3.

Herzberg concluded from his analysis that the replies people gave when they felt good about their jobs were significantly different from the replies they gave when they felt bad. Certain characteristics were consistently related to job satisfaction (factors on the left side of the exhibit), and others to job dissatisfaction (factors on the right side). Those factors associated with job satisfaction were intrinsic and included things such as achievement, recognition, and responsibility. When people felt good about their work, they tended to attribute these characteristics to themselves. On the other hand, when they were dissatisfied with their

---

extrinsic motivation
Motivation that comes from outside the person and includes such things as pay, bonuses, and other tangible rewards.

intrinsic motivation
Motivation that comes from the person's internal desire to do something, due to such things as interest, challenge, and personal satisfaction.

Theory X
The assumption that employees have little ambition, dislike work, want to avoid responsibility, and must be closely controlled to perform.

Theory Y
The assumption that employees can exercise self-direction, accept and seek out responsibility, and consider work a natural activity.

Q&A 13.2

motivation-hygiene theory
Herzberg's theory that intrinsic factors are related to job satisfaction and motivation, whereas extrinsic factors are related to job dissatisfaction.

Exhibit 9-3

Herzberg's Motivation-Hygiene Theory

Motivators	Hygiene Factors
• Achievement	• Supervision
• Recognition	• Company Policy
• Work Itself	• Relationship With
• Responsibility	Supervisor
• Advancement	• Working Conditions
• Growth	• Salary
	• Relationship With Peers
	• Personal Life
	• Relationship With
	Subordinates
	• Status
	• Security

Extremely Satisfied	Neutral	Extremely Dissatisfied

work, they tended to cite extrinsic factors such as supervision, company policy, interpersonal relationships, and working conditions.

In addition, Herzberg believed that the data suggested that the opposite of satisfaction was not dissatisfaction, as traditionally had been believed. Removing dissatisfying characteristics from a job would not necessarily make that job more satisfying (or motivating). As shown in Exhibit 9-4, Herzberg proposed that his findings indicated the existence of a dual continuum: The opposite of "satisfaction" is "no satisfaction," and the opposite of "dissatisfaction" is "no dissatisfaction."

According to Herzberg, the factors that led to job satisfaction were separate and distinct from those that led to job dissatisfaction. Therefore, managers who sought to eliminate factors that created job dissatisfaction could bring about workplace harmony but not necessarily motivation. The extrinsic factors that create job dissatisfaction were called **hygiene factors**. When these factors are adequate, people won't be dissatisfied, but they won't be satisfied (or motivated) either. To motivate people in their jobs, Herzberg suggested emphasizing **motivators**, the intrinsic factors that increase job satisfaction.

Herzberg's theory enjoyed wide popularity from the mid-1960s to the early 1980s, but criticisms arose concerning his procedures and methodology. Although today we say the theory is simplistic, it has had a strong influence on how we currently design jobs, as the following *Management Reflection* shows.

hygiene factors
Factors that eliminate job dissatisfaction, but don't motivate.

motivators
Factors that increase job satisfaction and motivation.

Exhibit 9-4

Contrasting Views of Satisfaction–Dissatisfaction

Machine Shop Cleans Up Its Act

Can the design of a machine shop affect employee morale?   Langley, BC-based Pazmac Enterprises uses insights from Herzberg's theory to organize its workplace.[12] The employees at the machine shop enjoy perks often associated with employees in the high-tech industry. Owner Steve Scarlett provides opportunities for his employees to be involved in decision making. "I believe business needs to be planned diplomatically— we talk things out," says Scarlett. He ensures good relationships among employees, and he also shows concern about employees' hygiene needs, reflecting Herzberg. Usually machine shops are noisy and messy, the floors are covered with oil, and employees wear dirty overalls. Pazmac, however, is spotlessly clean. The lunch room is tastefully designed, and the men's washroom is plush, with potpourri bowls and paintings on the walls.

Scarlett believes that employees should be treated the way he himself would like to be treated, which explains why he provides an on-site swimming pool, personal trainers, weekly yoga classes, and professional counselling services for employees. Scarlett clearly considers both hygiene factors and motivator factors in dealing with his employees. His strategy has paid off. The company has had very little employee turnover in recent years, and a number of employees have worked there for more than 15 years.[13] ∎

McClelland's Theory of Needs

theory of needs
McClelland's theory that the needs for achievement, power, and affiliation are major motives in work.

need for achievement (nAch)
The drive to excel, to achieve in relation to a set of standards, and to strive to succeed.

need for power (nPow)
The need to make others behave in a way that they would not have behaved otherwise.

need for affiliation (nAff)
The desire for friendly and close interpersonal relationships.

David McClelland and his associates proposed the **theory of needs**, which says there are three acquired (not innate) needs that motivate work performance.[14] These three needs are the **need for achievement (nAch)**, which is the drive to excel, to achieve in relation to a set of standards, and to strive to succeed; the **need for power (nPow)**, which is the need to make others behave in a way that they would not have behaved otherwise; and the **need for affiliation (nAff)**, which is the desire for friendly and close interpersonal relationships. Of these three needs, the need for achievement has been researched the most. What does this research show?

People with a high need for achievement are striving for personal achievement rather than for the trappings and rewards of success. They have a desire to do something better or more efficiently than it's been done before.[15] They prefer jobs that offer personal responsibility for finding solutions to problems, in which they can receive rapid and unambiguous feedback on their performance in order to tell whether they are improving, and in which they can set moderately challenging goals.

While needs theories give us some insights into motivating employees, they don't provide a complete picture of motivation. Moreover, additional needs seem to motivate some employees. For example, employees are increasingly feeling the need for work–life balance. They need time to take care of their loved ones while managing their workloads. Having some time during the day when one can at least see nature may be another important need. Recent research suggests that being exposed to nature (even just being able to see some trees from your office window) has many beneficial effects. A lack of such exposure can actually impair well-being and performance.[16]

CONTEMPORARY THEORIES OF MOTIVATION

One of the challenges of motivating employees is linking productivity to rewards. Compounding this challenge for Tesco is that some jobs are very boring.[17] Clare Chapman, Tesco's director of human resources, says, "We're trying to take the routine out of the workplace, and build in more interest." The company eliminated the boring task of unloading soft drinks by ordering merchandising units that come fully stocked, ready to be wheeled into the store.

Tesco also encourages employees to buy shares of the company, so that staff can "share in the success they helped to create," says reward manager Helen O'Keefe. To help employees understand the potential benefits of shares, the annual benefit report includes share price graphs and a reward statement for staff. The benefit report helps employees see how the share price performs over the longer term and in comparison with the shares of other companies.

Sir Terry Leahy says he wants his employees to take four things from the job: "They find it interesting, they're treated with respect, they have the chance to get on, and they find their boss is helpful and not their biggest problem." All of these rewards make it easier for employees to perform well.

THINK ABOUT IT
How can you link productivity to rewards so that employees feel motivated? What other things can be done at Tesco to ensure that employees feel motivated?

The theories we discuss in this section represent contemporary explanations of employee motivation. Although they may not be as well known as some of the theories we just discussed, they do have reasonable degrees of valid research support.[18] What are the contemporary theories of motivation? We look at four: reinforcement theory, job characteristics model, equity theory, and expectancy theory.

> **3** What are the contemporary theories of motivation?

Reinforcement Theory

Reinforcement theory says that behaviour is influenced by consequences. Reinforcement theory argues that behaviour is externally caused by **reinforcers**, which are consequences that, when given immediately following a behaviour, increase the probability that the behaviour will be repeated.

Reinforcement theory focuses solely on what happens to a person when he or she takes some action. According to B. F. Skinner, reinforcement theory can be explained as follows: People will most likely engage in desired behaviours if they are rewarded for doing so; these rewards are most effective if they immediately follow a desired behaviour, and behaviour that is not rewarded, or is punished, is less likely to be repeated.[19]

In keeping with reinforcement theory, managers can influence employees' behaviour by reinforcing actions they deem desirable. However, the emphasis is on positive reinforcement, which means managers should ignore, not punish, unfavourable behaviour. Even though punishment eliminates undesired behaviour faster than nonreinforcement does, its effect is often only temporary and may result in workplace conflicts, absenteeism, and turnover. Research has shown that reinforcement is an important influence on employee behaviour, but it is not the only explanation for differences in employee motivation.[20]

reinforcement theory
The theory that behaviour is influenced by consequences.

reinforcers
Consequences that, when given immediately following a behaviour, increase the probability that the behaviour will be repeated.

Job Characteristics Model

Have you ever had a job that was really motivating? What were its characteristics?

Because managers are primarily interested in how to motivate individuals on the job, we need to look at ways to design motivating jobs. The **job characteristics model (JCM)** provides a conceptual framework for analyzing jobs and for guiding managers in designing motivating jobs.[21] It identifies five core job dimensions, their interrelationships, and their impact on employee productivity, motivation, and satisfaction.

According to the JCM, any job can be described in terms of the following five core dimensions:

Q&A 13.3

job characteristics model (JCM)
A framework for analyzing jobs and designing motivating jobs that identifies five core job dimensions, their interrelationships, and their impact on employees.

skill variety
The degree to which the job requires a variety of activities so the employee can use a number of different skills and talents.

task identity
The degree to which the job requires completion of a whole and identifiable piece of work.

1. **Skill variety.** The degree to which the job requires a variety of activities so the employee can use a number of different skills and talents.

2. **Task identity.** The degree to which the job requires completion of a whole and identifiable piece of work.

Exhibit 9-5

Job Characteristics Model

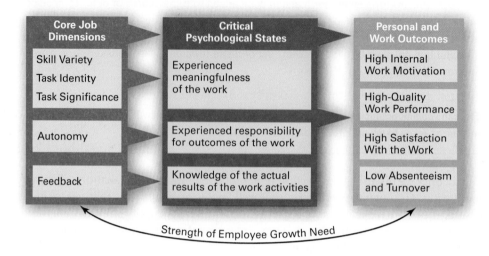

Core Job Dimensions	Critical Psychological States	Personal and Work Outcomes
Skill Variety Task Identity Task Significance	Experienced meaningfulness of the work	High Internal Work Motivation
Autonomy	Experienced responsibility for outcomes of the work	High-Quality Work Performance
Feedback	Knowledge of the actual results of the work activities	High Satisfaction With the Work Low Absenteeism and Turnover

Strength of Employee Growth Need

Source: J. R. Hackman and J. L. Suttle, eds., *Improving Life at Work* (Glenview, IL: Scott, Foresman, 1977). With permission of the authors.

task significance
The degree to which the job affects the lives or work of other people.

autonomy
The degree to which the job provides substantial freedom, independence, and discretion to the individual in scheduling the work and determining the procedures to be used in carrying it out.

feedback
The degree to which carrying out the work activities required by the job results in the individual's obtaining direct and clear information about the effectiveness of his or her performance.

3. **Task significance**. The degree to which the job affects the lives or work of other people.

4. **Autonomy**. The degree to which the job provides substantial freedom, independence, and discretion to the individual in scheduling the work and determining the procedures to be used in carrying it out.

5. **Feedback**. The degree to which carrying out the work activities required by the job results in the individual's obtaining direct and clear information about the effectiveness of his or her performance.

Exhibit 9-5 presents the model. Notice how the first three dimensions—skill variety, task identity, and task significance—combine to create meaningful work. What we mean is that if these three characteristics exist in a job, we can predict that the person will view his or her job as important, valuable, and worthwhile. Notice, too, that jobs that possess autonomy give the job incumbent a feeling of personal responsibility for the results, and that if a job provides feedback the employee will know how effectively he or she is performing.

From a motivational standpoint, the JCM suggests that internal rewards are obtained when an employee *learns* (knowledge of results through feedback) that he or she *personally* (experienced responsibility through autonomy of work) has performed well on a task that he or she *cares about* (experienced meaningfulness through skill variety, task identity, and/or task significance).[22]

It is easy to identify the task that Manuela Frank and Erika Seres perform at Audi's headquarters in Ingolstadt, Germany. Their job is to ensure that new cars have no unappealing odours. "You can't smell more than six specimens at a time," says Seres (right), "because after that, you are not discerning. Like wine tasters, we have rules."

Exhibit 9-6

Guidelines for Job Redesign

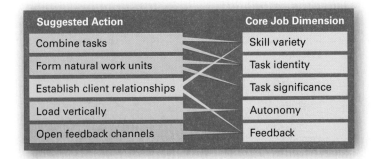

Source: J. R. Hackman and J. L. Suttle, eds., *Improving Life at Work* (Glenview, IL: Scott, Foresman, 1977). With permission of the authors.

The more these three conditions characterize a job, the greater the employee's motivation, performance, and satisfaction and the lower his or her absenteeism and likelihood of resigning. As the model shows, the links between the job dimensions and the outcomes are moderated by the strength of the individual's growth need (the person's desire for self-esteem and self-actualization). This means that individuals with a high growth need are more likely to experience the critical psychological states and respond positively when their jobs include the core dimensions than are individuals with a low growth need. This may explain the mixed results with job enrichment: Individuals with low growth need don't tend to achieve high performance or satisfaction by having their jobs enriched. For further insights into motivating employees, see *Developing Your Interpersonal Skills—Maximizing Employee Effort* on pages 279–280, at the end of the chapter.

The JCM provides specific guidance to managers for job redesign. These guidelines are shown in Exhibit 9-6, which specifies the types of changes in jobs that are most likely to lead to improvement in each of the five core job dimensions.

Equity Theory

Have you ever thought someone else's pay was unfair compared with yours?

After graduating from the University of New Brunswick, Mike Wilson worked in Northern Alberta as a civil engineer. He liked his job, but he became frustrated with his employer. "If you did a great job you were treated just the same as if you did a poor job," he says.[23] Wilson decided to return home to work in the business his father had started in 1965—Dorchester, New Brunswick-based Atlantic Industries, which designs, fabricates, and builds corrugated steel structures. At Atlantic Industries, Wilson's hard work has paid off: He received the 2005 Ernst & Young Entrepreneur of the Year Award for the Atlantic Region.

Wilson's decision to leave his job in Northern Alberta can be explained by equity theory. The term *equity* is related to the concept of fairness and equal treatment compared with others who behave in similar ways. There is considerable evidence that employees compare their job inputs and outcomes relative to others' and that inequities influence the degree of effort that employees exert.[24]

Q&A 13.4

Exhibit 9-7

Equity Theory

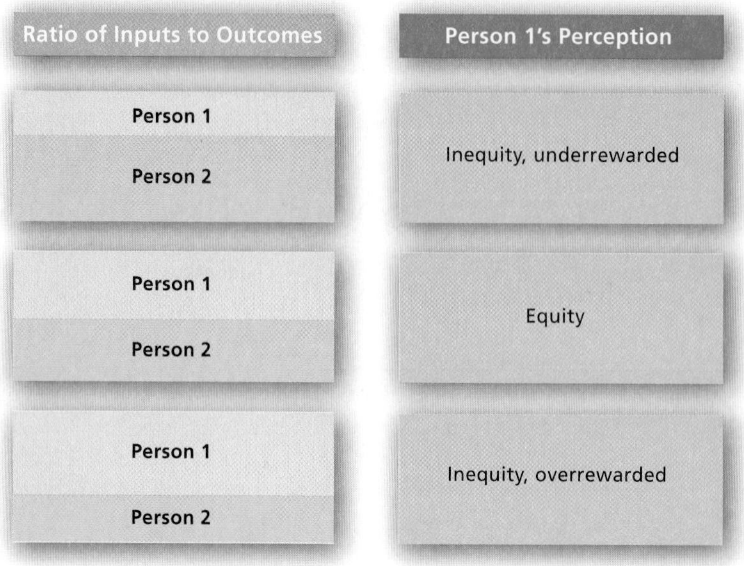

Ratio of Inputs to Outcomes	Person 1's Perception
Person 1 / Person 2	Inequity, underrewarded
Person 1 / Person 2	Equity
Person 1 / Person 2	Inequity, overrewarded

equity theory

The theory that an employee compares his or her job's inputs–outcomes ratio with that of relevant others and then responds to correct any inequity.

Equity theory, developed by J. Stacey Adams, proposes that employees perceive what they get from a job situation (outcomes) in relation to what they put into it (inputs) and then compare their inputs–outcomes ratio with the inputs–outcomes ratio of relevant others (see Exhibit 9-7). If an employee perceives her ratio as equal to those of relevant others, a state of equity exists. In other words, she perceives that her situation is fair—that justice prevails. However, if the ratio is perceived as unequal, inequity exists and she views herself as underrewarded or overrewarded. Not all inequity (or equity) is real. It is important to underscore that it is the individual's *perception* that determines the equity of the situation.

What will employees do when they perceive an inequity? Equity theory proposes that employees might (1) distort either their own or others' inputs or outcomes, (2) behave in some way to induce others to change their inputs or outcomes, (3) behave in some way to change their own inputs or outcomes, (4) choose a different comparison person, or (5) quit their jobs. These types of employee reactions have generally proved to be accurate.[25] A review of the research consistently confirms the equity thesis: Whenever employees perceive inequity, they will act to correct the situation.[26] The result might be lower or higher productivity, improved or reduced quality of output, increased absenteeism, or voluntary resignation.

When Greater Vancouver Regional District directors faced inequity in their pay, they responded by voting themselves a raise, as the following *Management Reflection* shows.

MANAGEMENT REFLECTION

Directors End "Inequitable" Pay

What is fair pay for a director in government?   Greater Vancouver Regional District directors voted themselves a 60-percent pay raise in June 2003, at the same time that government services were being cut across the province of BC.[27] On a percentage basis, the pay raise seems extraordinary. Other government employees might have considered this outrageous.

But what should a municipal councillor be paid? In 2003, Members of Parliament earned annual salaries of $139 200, and members of the BC legislature earned $68 500, plus expenses. Councillors earned about $40 000 a year, on average. Despite working at different levels of government—federal, provincial, and local—all of these officials make complex decisions, and need many of the same skills. Many of them could make more money working in the private sector.

When the BC municipal councillors voted themselves a pay raise, they were not comparing themselves to government employees whose wages had been cut recently. Instead, they were responding to the idea that they were underpaid compared to other government decision makers who performed duties similar to their own. ■

The **referent** against which individuals compare themselves is an important variable in equity theory.[28] Three referent categories have been defined: other, system, and self. The *other* category includes other individuals with similar jobs in the same organization but also includes friends, neighbours, or professional associates. On the basis of what they hear at work or read about in newspapers or trade journals, employees compare their pay with that of others. The *system* category includes organizational pay policies and procedures and the administration of the system. Whatever precedents have been established by the organization regarding pay allocation are major elements of this category. The *self* category refers to the inputs–outcomes ratios that are unique to the individual. It reflects personal experiences and contacts and is influenced by criteria such as previous jobs or family commitments. The choice of a particular set of referents is related to the information available about the referents as well as to their perceived relevance.

In conclusion, equity theory shows that, for most employees, motivation is influenced significantly by relative rewards as well as by absolute rewards, but some key issues are still unclear.[29] For instance, how do employees define inputs and outcomes? How do they combine and weigh their inputs and outcomes to arrive at totals? When and how do the factors change over time? How do people choose referents? Despite these issues, equity theory does have an impressive amount of research support and offers us some important insights into employee motivation.

referents
Those things individuals compare themselves against in order to assess equity.

Expectancy Theory

The most comprehensive and widely accepted explanation of employee motivation to date is Victor Vroom's expectancy theory.[30] Although the theory has its critics,[31] most research evidence supports it.[32]

Expectancy theory states that an individual tends to act in a certain way based on the expectation that the act will be followed by a given outcome and on the attractiveness of that outcome to the individual. It includes three variables or relationships (see Exhibit 9-8 on page 264):

- *Expectancy or effort–performance linkage.* The probability perceived by the individual that exerting a given amount of effort will lead to a certain level of performance.

- *Instrumentality or performance–reward linkage.* The degree to which the individual believes that performing at a particular level is instrumental in attaining the desired outcome.

- *Valence or attractiveness of reward.* The importance that the individual places on the potential outcome or reward that can be achieved on the job. Valence considers both the goals and needs of the individual. (See also *Self-Assessment—What Rewards Do I Value Most?* on page 276, at the end of the chapter.)

expectancy theory
The theory that an individual tends to act in a certain way based on the expectation that the act will be followed by a given outcome and on the attractiveness of that outcome to the individual.

This explanation of motivation might sound complex, but it really isn't. It can be summed up in these questions: How hard do I have to work to achieve a certain level of performance, and can I actually achieve that level? What reward will I get for working at that level of performance? How attractive is the reward to me, and does it help me achieve my goals? Whether you are motivated to put forth effort (that is, to work) at any given time depends on your particular goals and your perception of whether a certain level of performance is necessary to attain those goals.

Exhibit 9-8

Simplified Expectancy Model

A = Effort–performance linkage
B = Performance–reward linkage
C = Attractiveness of reward

The key to expectancy theory is understanding an individual's goal and the link between effort and performance, between performance and rewards, and finally, between rewards and individual goal satisfaction. Expectancy theory recognizes that there is no universal principle for explaining what motivates individuals and thus stresses that managers need to understand why employees view certain outcomes as attractive or unattractive. After all, we want to reward individuals with those things they value as positive. Also, expectancy theory emphasizes expected behaviours. Do employees know what is expected of them and how they will be evaluated? Finally, the theory is concerned with perceptions. Reality is irrelevant. An individual's own perceptions of performance, reward, and goal outcomes, not the outcomes themselves, will determine his or her motivation (level of effort). Exhibit 9-9 suggests how managers might increase employee motivation, using expectancy theory.

Q&A 13.5

Integrating Contemporary Theories of Motivation

We have presented four contemporary motivation theories. You might be tempted to view them independently, but doing so would be a mistake. Many of the ideas underlying the theories are complementary, and you will better understand how to motivate people if you see how the theories fit together.[33]

Expectancy theory predicts that an employee will exert a high level of effort if he or she perceives that there is a strong relationship between effort and performance, performance and rewards, and rewards and satisfaction of personal goals. Each of these relationships is, in turn, influenced by certain factors. The level of individual performance is determined not only by the level of individual effort but also by the individual's ability to perform and

Exhibit 9-9

Steps to Increasing Motivation, Using Expectancy Theory

Improving Expectancy	Improving Instrumentality	Improving Valence
Improve the ability of the individual to perform.	**Increase the individual's belief that performance will lead to reward.**	**Make sure that the reward is meaningful to the individual.**
• Make sure employees have skills for the task. • Provide training. • Assign reasonable tasks and goals.	• Observe and recognize performance. • Deliver rewards as promised. • Indicate to employees how previous good performance led to greater rewards.	• Ask employees what rewards they value. • Give rewards that are valued.

by whether the organization has a fair and objective performance evaluation system. The performance–reward relationship will be strong if the individual perceives that it is performance (rather than seniority, personal favourites, or some other criterion) that is rewarded. The final link in expectancy theory is the rewards–goal relationship. Needs theories come into play at this point. Motivation is high to the degree that the rewards an individual received for his or her high performance satisfy the dominant needs consistent with his or her individual goals.

Rewards also play a key part in equity theory. Individuals will compare the rewards (outcomes) they have received from the inputs or efforts they made with the inputs–outcomes ratio of relevant others. Any inequities may influence the effort expended.

The JCM suggests that task characteristics (job design) influence job motivation at two places. First, jobs that are designed around the five core dimensions are likely to lead to higher actual job performance because the individual's motivation will be stimulated by the job itself—that is, he or she will increase the link between effort and performance. Second, jobs that are designed around the five core dimensions also increase an employee's control over key elements in his or her work. Therefore, jobs that offer autonomy, feedback, and similar task characteristics help satisfy the individual goals of employees who desire greater control over their work.

Reinforcement theory says that behaviour is influenced by consequences, which is consistent with expectancy theory. The theory argues that when consequences are given immediately following a behaviour, the behaviour is more likely to be repeated. Thus, much like expectancy theory, the emphasis is on linking rewards (consequences) directly to performance.

CURRENT ISSUES IN MOTIVATION

One of the challenges managers at Tesco faced was how to motivate its many different employee groups: students, new graduates, mothers returning to the workplace, and ethnic minorities.[34] In a survey of its employees, the company found that older female employees wanted flexible hours and stimulating work, but they were not looking to be promoted. Young college graduates working in head office wanted a challenging, well-paid career and time to pursue personal interests and family life.

Tesco has come up with a variety of practices to meet employee needs, including career breaks of up to eight months, discounts on family holidays, driving lessons, and magazine subscriptions. Tesco has a website that offers career and financial advice and discounts on meals, cinema tickets, and travel for its 16- to 24-year-old employees who are in school or have recently left school. Clare Chapman, Tesco's director of human resources, says the company has not limited specific rewards for specific groups. "It's more a question of being mindful of the needs of all staff instead of catering for one or two types of attitude."

THINK ABOUT IT

What factors need to be considered when motivating employees who have very different needs? Is there anything else Tesco can do to motivate young people?

So far, we have covered a lot of the theoretical bases of employee motivation. Understanding and predicting employee motivation continues to be one of the most popular areas in management research. However, even current studies of employee motivation are influenced by several significant workplace issues—issues such as motivating a diverse workforce, designing effective rewards programs, and improving work–life balance. Let's take a closer look at each of these issues.

4 What are some current issues in motivation?

Motivating a Diverse Workforce

Motivating employees has never been easy. Employees come into organizations with very different needs, personalities, skills, abilities, interests, and aptitudes. They have different expectations of their employers and different views of what they think their employer's have a right to expect of them. And they vary widely in what they want from their jobs. Baby Boomers may need more flextime as they manage the needs of their children and their aging parents. Gen-Xers want employers to add to their experience so they develop portable skills. Meanwhile, Gen-Yers want more opportunities, and the ability to work in teams.[35] The differences in needs across the generations makes it difficult for employers to motivate individuals with a one-size-fits-all approach to rewards.

To maximize motivation in today's workforce, managers need to think in terms of *flexibility*. For instance, studies tell us that men place more importance on having autonomy in their jobs than do women. In contrast, the opportunity to learn, convenient and flexible work hours, and good interpersonal relations are more important to women.[36] Managers need to recognize that what motivates a single mother with two dependent children who is working full time to support her family may be very different from the needs of a single part-time employee or an older employee who is working only to supplement his or her retirement income. A diverse array of rewards is needed to motivate employees with such diverse needs.

Motivating Employees from Diverse Cultures

In today's global business environment, managers cannot automatically assume that motivational programs that work in one location are going to work in others. Most current motivation theories were developed in the United States by Americans about Americans.[37] Maybe the most blatant pro-American characteristic in these theories is the strong emphasis on individualism and quantity-of-life cultural characteristics. For instance, both goal-setting and expectancy theories emphasize goal accomplishment as well as rational and individual thought. Let's look at several theories to see if there is any cross-cultural transferability.

Maslow's hierarchy of needs proposes that people start at the physiological level and then move progressively up the hierarchy in order. This hierarchy, if it has any application at all, aligns with American culture. In countries like Japan, Greece, and Mexico, where uncertainty-avoidance characteristics are strong (that is, individuals prefer structured situations), security needs would be on the top of the needs hierarchy. Countries that score high on quality-of-life characteristics (that is, individuals value relationships and are concerned with the welfare of others)—Denmark, Sweden, Norway, the Netherlands, and Finland—would have social needs on top.[38] We would predict, for instance, that group work will motivate employees more when a country's culture scores high on quality-of-life characteristics.

In countries like the Netherlands, where the needs identified in Maslow's famous hierarchy are ranked differently than they are in North America, quality of life is probably more important to employees like these. Thus, they may be more motivated by group work because it meets their social needs to gather and cooperate.

Equity theory has a relatively strong following in the United States. That is not surprising given that US-style reward systems are based on the assumption that employees are highly sensitive to equity in reward allocations. And in the United States, equity is meant to closely tie pay to performance. However, recent evidence suggests that even in collectivist cultures (where individuals expect that others will look after and protect them), especially in the former socialist countries of Central and Eastern Europe, employees expect rewards to reflect their individual needs as well as their performance.[39] Moreover, consistent with a legacy of communism and centrally planned economies, employees exhibited a greater "entitlement" attitude—that is, they expected outcomes to be greater than their inputs.[40] These findings suggest that US-style pay practices may need modification, especially in Russia and former communist countries, in order to be perceived as fair by employees.

Despite these cross-cultural differences in motivation, don't assume there are no cross-cultural consistencies. For instance, the desire for interesting work seems important to almost all employees, regardless of their national culture. In a study of seven countries, employees in Belgium, Britain, Israel, and the United States ranked "interesting work" number one among 11 work goals. And this factor was ranked either second or third in Japan, the Netherlands, and Germany.[41] Similarly, in a study comparing job-preference outcomes among graduate students in the United States, Canada, Australia, and Singapore, growth, achievement, and responsibility were rated the top three and had identical rankings.[42] Both of these studies suggest some universality to the importance of intrinsic factors identified by Herzberg in his motivation-hygiene theory. For a discussion of diversity initiatives in the workplace, see *Managing Workforce Diversity—Developing Employee Potential: The Bottom Line of Diversity* on pages 280–281, at the end of the chapter.

Motivating Minimum-Wage Employees

Suppose that in your first managerial position after graduating, you are responsible for managing a work group composed of minimum-wage employees. Offering more pay to these employees for high levels of performance is out of the question: Your company just cannot afford it.[43] In addition, these employees have limited education and skills. What are your motivational options at this point? One of the toughest motivational challenges facing many managers today is how to achieve high performance levels from minimum-wage employees.

Q&A 13.7

One trap we often fall into is thinking that people are motivated only by money. Although money is important as a motivator, it's not the only reward that people seek and that managers can use. What are some other types of rewards? Many companies use employee recognition programs such as employee of the month, quarterly employee performance award ceremonies, or other celebrations of employee accomplishment. For instance, at many fast-food restaurants such as McDonald's and Wendy's, you will often see plaques hanging in prominent places that feature the "Crew Member of the Month." These types of programs highlight employees whose performance has been of the type and level the organization wants to encourage. Many managers also recognize the power of praise, but you need to be sure that these "pats on the back" are sincere and done for the right reasons; otherwise, employees can interpret such actions as manipulative.

We know from the motivation theories presented earlier that rewards are only part of the motivation equation. We need to look at other elements such as empowerment and career development assistance. We can look to job

Nancy Gray-Starkebaum, director of human resources at Vancouver-based Electronic Arts Canada, finds that companies have to pay attention to employee needs in order to motivate them. The cafeteria at Electronic Arts is well stocked with employee favourites, and employees can purchase takeout dinners at good prices for their families if they do not have time to cook dinner.

design and expectancy theories for these insights. In service industries such as travel and hospitality, retail sales, child care, and maintenance, where pay for front-line employees generally does not get much higher than the minimum-wage level, successful companies are empowering these front-line employees with more authority to address customers' problems. If we use the JCM to examine this change, we can see that this type of job redesign provides enhanced motivating potential because employees now experience increased skill variety, task identity, task significance, autonomy, and feedback. Also, employees facing this situation often want to better themselves professionally. They need guidance, assistance in self-assessment, and training. By providing these to minimum-wage employees, you are preparing them for the future—one that ideally promises better pay. For many, this is a strong motivator![44]

Motivating Professional and Technical Employees

In contrast to a generation ago, the typical employee today is more likely to be a highly trained professional with a post-secondary degree than a blue-collar factory worker. What special concerns should managers be aware of when trying to motivate a team of engineers at Inco, software designers at ATI Technologies, or a group of consultants at Accenture?

Professionals are typically different from nonprofessionals.[45] They have a strong and long-term commitment to their field of expertise. Their loyalty is more often to their profession than to their employer. To keep current in their field, they need to regularly update their knowledge, and because of their commitment to their profession they rarely define their workweek as 8:00 a.m. to 5:00 p.m., five days a week.

What motivates professionals? Money and promotions typically are low on their priority list. Why? They tend to be well paid and enjoy what they do. In contrast, job challenge tends to be ranked high. They like to tackle problems and find solutions. Their chief reward in their jobs is the work itself. Professionals also value support. They want others to think that what they are working on is important.[46] That may be true for all employees, but professionals tend to be focused on their work as their central life interest, whereas nonprofessionals typically have other interests outside work that can compensate for needs not met on the job. The preceding points imply that managers should provide professional and technical employees with new assignments and challenging projects. Give them autonomy to follow their interests and allow them to structure their work in ways they find productive. Reward them with educational opportunities—training, workshops, conferences—that allow them to keep current in their field and to network with their peers. Also reward them with recognition. Managers should ask questions and engage in other actions that demonstrate to their professional and technical employees that they are sincerely interested in what they are doing.

Designing Effective Rewards Programs

Employee rewards programs play a powerful role in motivating for appropriate employee behaviour. In this section, we look at how managers can design effective rewards programs by using employee recognition programs, pay-for-performance programs, and stock option programs. First, though, we should examine the issue of the extent to which money motivates.

The Role of Money

The most commonly used reward in organizations is money. As one author notes, "Money is probably the most emotionally meaningful object in contemporary life: only food and sex are its close competitors as common carriers of such strong and diverse feelings, significance, and strivings."[47]

Little research attention has been given to individual differences in people's feelings about money, although some studies indicate that money is not employees' top priority.[48] A survey of 2500 Canadians discovered that relationships in the workplace mattered more than pay or benefits when it came to employee satisfaction.[49] One respondent explained, "Of course money is important, but that's not what's going to make you jump out of bed in the morning." Another noted, "Everyone here would take more money and more time off—that's a given. But some of the things that really make the job a good or bad one are your relations with your boss."

A number of studies suggest that an individual's attitude toward money is correlated with personality traits and demographic factors.[50] People who value money score higher on "attributes like sensation seeking, competitiveness, materialism, and control." People who desire money score higher on self-esteem, need for achievement, and Type A personality measures. Men seem to value money more than women. These studies suggest that individuals who value money will be more motivated by it than individuals who value other things.

What these findings suggest is that when organizations develop reward programs, they need to consider very carefully what individuals value.

Employee Recognition Programs

Employee recognition programs provide managers with opportunities to give employees personal attention and express interest, approval, and appreciation for a job well done.[51] These programs can take many forms. For instance, you can personally congratulate an employee in private for a good job. You can send a handwritten note or an email message acknowledging something positive that the employee has done. For employees with a strong need for social acceptance, you can publicly recognize accomplishments. To enhance group cohesiveness and motivation, you can celebrate team successes. For instance, you can throw a pizza party to celebrate a team's accomplishments.

A survey of Canadian firms in 2006 by Hewitt Associates found that 35 percent of companies recognized individual or group achievements with cash or merchandise.[52] Do employees think employee recognition programs are important? You bet! One of the consistent themes that has emerged in the six years that Hewitt Associates has studied the 50 Best Companies to work for in Canada is the importance of recognition. A large number of the winning companies show appreciation for their employees frequently and visibly.[53]

> **employee recognition programs**
> Reward programs that provide managers with opportunities to give employees personal attention and express interest, approval, and appreciation for a job well done.

Pay-for-Performance Programs

What's in it for me? That is a question every person consciously or unconsciously asks before engaging in any form of behaviour. Our knowledge of motivation tells us that people act in order to satisfy some need. Before they do anything, therefore, they look for a payoff or reward. Although many different rewards may be offered by organizations, most of us are concerned with earning an amount of money that allows us to satisfy our needs and wants. In fact, a large body of research suggests that pay is far more motivational than some motivation theorists such as Maslow and Herzberg suggest.[54] Because pay is an important variable in motivation, we need to look at how we can use pay to motivate high levels of employee performance. This concern explains the logic behind pay-for-performance programs.

> **pay-for-performance programs**
> Variable compensation plans that pay employees on the basis of some performance measure.

Pay-for-performance programs are variable compensation plans that pay employees on the basis of some performance measure.[55] Piece-rate pay plans, wage-incentive plans, profit-sharing, and lump-sum bonuses are examples. What differentiates these forms of pay from more traditional compensation plans is that instead of paying a person for time on the job, pay is adjusted to reflect some performance measure. These performance measures might include such things as individual productivity, team or work-group productivity, departmental productivity, or the overall organization's profit performance.

Pay-for-performance is probably most compatible with expectancy theory. Specifically, individuals should perceive a strong relationship between their performance and the rewards they receive if motivation is to be maximized. If

Employee recognition plays an important role in motivating the employees at Nichols Foods in Merseyside, England, where the average wage is only a little above the norm. The main hallway in the production department is hung with "bragging boards" on which the accomplishments of employee teams are noted. Monthly awards are presented to employees recognized for their efforts by their peers, and plant-floor supervisors make presentations about their results at every annual meeting. "To deliver really great customer service," says operations manager Martin Lee, "you need really great, motivated people."

rewards are allocated only on nonperformance factors—such as seniority, job title, or across-the-board pay raises—then employees are likely to reduce their efforts.

Pay-for-performance programs are popular. The number of employees affected by variable-pay plans has been rising in Canada. A 2006 survey of 465 firms by Hewitt Associates found that 83 percent of respondents have variable-pay programs in place, compared with 43 percent in 1994.[56] Pay-for-performance programs are more common for non-unionized employees than unionized ones, although more than 30 percent of unionized companies had such plans in 2002.[57] Prem Benimadhu, an analyst with The Conference Board of Canada, notes, "Canadian unions have been very allergic to variable compensation."[58] In addition to wage uncertainty, employees may object to pay for performance if they feel that factors out of their control might affect the extent to which bonuses are possible.

Do pay-for-performance programs work? The evidence is mixed, at best.[59] One recent study that followed the careers of 1000 top economists found that they put in more effort early in their careers, at a time when productivity-related incentives had a larger impact.[60] A recent study of Finnish white-collar employees found that higher levels of payment and more frequent payments positively affected productivity, while lower levels of payment did not improve productivity.[61] A recent study in Canada looked at both unionized and non-unionized workplaces, and found that variable pay plans result in "increased productivity, a safer work environment, a better understanding of the business by employees, and little risk of employees losing base pay," according to Prem Benimadhu.[62] But there are studies that question effectiveness of pay-for-performance approaches, suggesting they can lead to less group cohesiveness in the workplace.[63]

If the organization uses work teams, managers should consider group-based performance incentives that will reinforce team effort and commitment. But whether these programs are individual based or team based, managers do need to ensure that they are specific about the relationship between an individual's pay and his or her expected level of appropriate performance. Employees must clearly understand exactly how performance—theirs and the organization's—translates into dollars on their paycheques.[64] Ottawa-based Lee Valley Tools uses quarterly newsletters to employees to let them know how much profit is forecast. This helps employees understand how hard work will pay off for them. Robin Lee, the company's president, says that "sharing information and profits promotes an atmosphere in which hard work, innovation and efficiency pay off for everybody."[65] The sometimes weak link between pay and performance is nowhere more evident than in the final type of rewards program we are going to look at—employee stock options.

Q&A 13.8

Stock Option Programs

Saputo
www.saputo.com

Biovail
www.biovail.com

During 2003, Lino Saputo, chair of Montreal-based Saputo, one of the largest cheese producers in North America, received a salary of $600 000, bonuses of $330 000, and no stock options. Eugene Melnyk, chair of Mississauga, Ontario-based Biovail, a pharmaceutical company, received a salary of $830 463, no bonus, and $56.4 million in long-term incentives. Total compensation for the two men over the period 2000–2003 was quite different: Saputo received $2.43 million, just a little more than 10 percent of the $202 million Melnyk received. Yet by March 2004, Biovail's shares had declined 74 percent from their high in December 2001, while Saputo's share price was similar to what it was at its high in early 2002.[66] These results mirror a 2006 study of the largest Canadian public companies by the Teachers Pension Plan, which found little evidence that the amount paid to Canada's top executives was related to the performance of their companies.[67]

Executive bonus and stock option programs have come under fire because they seem to fly in the face of the belief that executive pay aligns with the organization's performance. What are stock option programs and what are they designed to do?

stock options
A financial incentive that gives employees the right to purchase shares of company stock, at some time in the future, at a set price.

Stock options are a financial incentive that gives employees the right to purchase shares of company stock, at some time in the future, at a set price. The original idea behind stock options was to turn employees into owners and give them strong motivation to work hard to make the company successful.[68] If the company was successful, the value of the stock went up, making the stock options valuable. In other words, there was a link between performance and reward. The popularity of stock options as a motivational and compensation tool skyrocketed during the dot-com boom in the late 1990s. Because many dot-coms could not afford to pay employees the going market-rate salaries, stock options were offered as performance incentives. However, the shakeout among dot-com stocks in 2000 and 2001 illustrated one of the inherent risks of offering stock options. As long as the market was rising, employees were willing to give up large salaries in exchange for stock options. However, when stock prices tanked, many individuals who joined and stayed with a dot-com for the opportunity to get rich through stock options found those stock options had become worthless. The declining stock market became a powerful demotivator.

Despite the risk of potential lost value and the widespread abuse of stock options, managers might want to consider them as part of their overall motivational program. An appropriately designed stock option program can be a powerful motivational tool for the entire workforce.[69]

Improving Work–Life Balance

While many employees continue to work an eight-hour day, five days a week with fixed start and end times, organizations have started to implement programs to help employees manage their lives outside work. Many of the work–life balance programs that organizations have implemented are a response to the varied needs of a diverse workforce. At Electronic Arts Canada, employees are given help with their family and personal needs, as the following *Management Reflection* shows.

MANAGEMENT REFLECTION

Electronic Arts Canada Meets Family Needs

Can your workplace really make life easier?　It is not always easy to make sure that employees working in the computer game–designing industry do not decide to take a job elsewhere.[70] Nancy Gray-Starkebaum's job as director of human resources at Vancouver-based Electronic Arts Canada (EA), the world's leading game developer, is to make sure that the employees do not think about looking for jobs elsewhere.

"Demographics are shifting and companies have learned they need to pay attention to employees' needs across the demographic scale," says Gray-Starkebaum. During the 1990s, it became commonplace for high-tech firms to offer free beverages, including lattes, and other perks that suited 20-something employees. EA has found that different perks are needed now that these same employees have moved into their thirties and beyond.

One emphasis at EA is having more family-friendly policies in the workplace. During spring break, children accompany their parents to work, and there are high chairs in the company cafeteria. New parents get generous leave time. Employees can even take dinner home to their families. Gray-Starkebaum says she was able to buy a chicken and rice dish and spareribs and found it "a comparative bargain at $18 to feed her family." The cafeteria offers breakfast, lunch, dinner, and snacks, and even provides Atkins, HeartSmart, and vegetarian meals.

The firm tries to make it easier for its employees to balance work life with family life. It takes care of many of the errands people might have to do at night or on weekends by providing drop-off dry cleaning services, a hairdresser and a barber who regularly show up to give haircuts, and a seamstress who does alterations. On Fridays, employees can have their cars washed.

EA also has a gym, with Pilates classes and a personal trainer, and a massage therapist is on site several days a week. ■

In addition to helping with errands and meals, contemporary companies are looking at a variety of scheduling options, including flextime, job sharing, and telecommuting to help employees balance work and personal life.

Flexible Work Schedules

Many organizations have developed flexible working schedules that recognize different needs. For instance, a **compressed workweek** is a workweek in which employees work longer hours per day but fewer days per week. The most common form is four 10-hour days (a 4-40 program). However, organizations could design whatever schedules they wanted to fit employees' needs. Another alternative is **flexible work hours** (also popularly known as **flextime**), a scheduling option in which employees are required to work a specific number of hours per week but are free to vary those hours within certain limits. In a flextime schedule, there are certain common core hours when all employees are required to be on the job, but starting, ending, and lunch-hour times are flexible. Flextime is one of the most desired benefits among employees.[71] Employers have responded; a survey shows that 55 percent of Canadian employers were offering flexible work options in 2003, although this was down from 64 percent in 2002.[72]

Job Sharing

Another scheduling option that can be effective in motivating a diverse workforce is **job sharing**—the practice of having two or more people split a full-time job. This type of job schedule might be attractive to individuals who want to work but do not want the demands and hassles of a full-time position.

Telecommuting

Another alternative made possible by information technology is **telecommuting**, in which employees work at home and are linked to the workplace by computer and other technology. Since many jobs are computer- and Internet-oriented, this job arrangement might be considered ideal for some people as there is no commuting, the hours are flexible, there is freedom to dress as you please, and there are few or no interruptions from colleagues. However, keep in mind that not all employees embrace the idea of telecommuting. A number of employees enjoy the informal interactions at work that satisfy their social needs and provide a source of new ideas.

compressed workweek
A workweek in which employees work longer hours per day but fewer days per week.

flexible work hours (flextime)
A scheduling option in which employees are required to work a specific number of hours per week but are free to vary those hours within certain limits.

job sharing
The practice of having two or more people split a full-time job.

telecommuting
A job arrangement in which employees work at home and are linked to the workplace by computer and other technology.

 **Q&A 13.6**

FROM THEORY TO PRACTICE: SUGGESTIONS FOR MOTIVATING EMPLOYEES

5 What can managers learn from motivation theories?

We have covered a lot of information about motivation in this chapter. If you are a manager concerned with motivating your employees, what specific recommendations can you draw from the theories and issues discussed so far? Although there is no simple, all-encompassing set of guidelines, the following suggestions draw on what we know about motivating employees:

- *Recognize individual differences.* Almost every contemporary motivation theory recognizes that employees are not identical. They have different needs, attitudes, personalities, and other important individual variables. Managers may not be giving enough consideration to what employees really want in terms of pay and benefits from the workplace. A recent survey of 75 Canadian employers by N. Winter Consulting found that most employers focus on compensation for their employees.[73] By contrast, only 25 percent of respondents had plans to introduce flexible hours, on-site child care, or subsidized fitness to their workplace in the next two years. Meanwhile, a recent Statistics Canada survey found that employees want "challenging work, continuous learning, flexible work arrangements and better communication with their employers."[74] Employers in Winter's survey said they were having difficulty attracting and retaining employees. Employers may need to pay more attention to what their employees say they want. Winter found that only 48 percent of the companies in the survey found out their employees' needs, wants, and values.

- *Match people to jobs.* There is a great deal of evidence showing the motivational benefits of carefully matching people to jobs. For example, high achievers should have jobs that let them participate in setting moderately challenging goals and give them autonomy and feedback. Also, keep in mind that not everybody is motivated by jobs that are high in autonomy, variety, and responsibility.

- *Individualize rewards.* Because employees have different needs, what acts as a reinforcer for one may not for another. Managers should use their knowledge of employee differences to individualize the rewards they control, such as pay, promotions, recognition, desirable work assignments, autonomy, and participation.

- *Link rewards to performance.* Managers need to make rewards contingent on performance. Rewarding factors other than performance will only reinforce those other factors. Important rewards such as pay increases and promotions should be given for the attainment of specific goals. Managers should also look for ways to increase the visibility of rewards, making them potentially more motivating.

- *Check the system for equity.* Employees should perceive that rewards or outcomes are equal to the inputs. On a simple level, experience, ability, effort, and other obvious inputs should explain differences in pay, responsibility, and other obvious outcomes. And remember that one person's equity is another's inequity, so an ideal reward system should probably weigh inputs differently in arriving at the proper rewards for each job.

Andrew Robinson, who runs an information security company in Portland, ME, has taken the idea of matching people to jobs a step further than most by matching future employees to potential jobs. Robinson runs a free after-school program to teach students like these about "ethical hacking," or the fine art of protecting computer systems by hacking them first. Of the 50 students in the program, Robinson says, "They have all the skills that they need to cause trouble, and some of them may have even started doing some of those things just for fun." His point to the students is "Here's how you can do this legally, within a moral and ethical framework, and make a good amount of money doing it."

- *Use recognition.* Recognize the power of recognition. In a stagnant economy where cost-cutting is widespread (as it was from 2001 to 2003), using recognition is a low-cost means to reward employees. And it's a reward that most employees consider valuable.

- *Don't ignore money.* It's easy to get so caught up in setting goals, creating interesting jobs, and providing opportunities for participation that you forget that money is a major reason why most people work. Some studies indicate that money is not the top priority of employees. Professor Graham Lowe at the University of Alberta and a colleague found that relationships in the workplace are more important than pay or benefits in determining job satisfaction.[75] Nevertheless, the allocation of performance-based wage increases, piecework bonuses, and other pay incentives is important in determining employee motivation. We are not saying that managers should focus solely on money as a motivational tool. Rather, we are simply stating the obvious—that is, if money is removed as an incentive, people are not going to show up for work. The same cannot be said for removing performance goals, enriched work, or participation.

SUMMARY AND IMPLICATIONS

1 **What is motivation?** Motivation refers to an individual's willingness to exert high levels of effort to reach organizational goals, conditioned by the effort's ability to satisfy some individual need. *At Tesco, one challenge was to motivate employees so that there would be less turnover.*

2 **How can needs help one be motivated?** Needs theories point out that individuals have needs that, when fulfilled, will motivate individuals to perform well. While the theories do not account for all aspects of motivation, they do inform managers that individuals have different needs that should be considered when developing reward plans. *Managers at Tesco discovered that different employee groups, such as students and mothers returning to the workplace, had different needs, and tried to address these needs to keep employees motivated.*

3 **What are the contemporary theories of motivation?** Equity theory proposes that employees compare their rewards and their productivity with others, and then determine whether they have been treated fairly. Individuals who perceive that they are underrewarded will try to adjust their behaviour to correct this imbalance. Expectancy theory explores the link between people's belief in whether they can do the work assigned, their belief in whether they will get the rewards promised, and the extent to which the reward is something they value. Most research evidence supports expectancy theory. *Tesco encourages employees to buy shares of the company, so that they can "share in the success they helped to create" and see the link between performance and reward.*

4 **What are some current issues in motivation?** Current issues in motivation include motivating a diverse workforce, designing effective rewards programs, and improving work–life balance. *One of Tesco's challenges was motivating employees who had somewhat repetitive jobs.*

5 **What can managers learn from motivation theories?** Managers can motivate employees by recognizing individual differences, matching people to jobs, individualizing rewards, linking rewards to performance, checking the system for equity, using recognition, and not ignoring that money is a major reason why most people work. *Tesco has worked hard to recognize the different needs of students and mothers returning to the workplace. The company also uses recognition to motivate employees and reduce turnover.*

CHAPTER 9

Management @ Work

Reading for Comprehension

1. How do needs affect motivation?

2. Contrast lower-order and higher-order needs in Maslow's needs hierarchy.

3. Describe the three needs in McClelland's theory of needs.

4. Define the five core dimensions of the job characteristics model.

5. What are some of the possible consequences of employees's perceiving an inequity between their inputs and outcomes and those of others?

6. What are some advantages of using pay-for-performance programs to motivate employee performance? Are there drawbacks? Explain.

7. What are the advantages of flextime from an employee's perspective? From management's perspective?

8. What can organizations do to create more motivating environments for their employees?

Linking Concepts to Practice

1. Most of us have to work for a living, and a job is a central part of our lives. So why do managers have to worry so much about employee motivation issues?

2. What role would money play in (1) the hierarchy of needs theory, (2) motivation-hygiene theory, (3) equity theory, and (4) expectancy theory?

3. If you accept Theory Y assumptions, how would you be likely to motivate employees? What would you do if you accept Theory X assumptions?

4. What difficulties do you think workforce diversity causes for managers who are trying to use equity theory?

5. Describe a task you have done recently for which you exerted a high level of effort. Explain your behaviour

using the following motivation approaches: (1) the hierarchy of needs theory, (2) motivation-hygiene theory, (3) equity theory, and (4) expectancy theory.

6. Describe several means that you might use to motivate (1) minimum-wage employees working for a small company that makes tortillas or (2) professional and technical employees working for a software design firm. Which of your suggestions do you think is best? Support your position.

7. Many job design experts who have studied the changing nature of work say that people do their best work when they are motivated by a sense of purpose rather than by the pursuit of money. Do you agree? Explain your position.

MANAGEMENT FOR YOU TODAY

You are in a team with six other management students, and you have a major case analysis due in four weeks. The case project will count for 25 percent of the course mark. You are the team's leader. Several team members are having diffi-

culty getting motivated to get started on the project. Identify ways you could motivate your team members, using needs theories, expectancy theory, and equity theory. How will you motivate yourself?

What Rewards Do I Value Most?

Below are 10 work-related rewards.[76] For each, identify the number that best describes the value that a particular reward has for you personally. Use the following scale to express your feelings:

> 1 = No Value at All
> 2 = Slight Value
> 3 = Moderate Value
> 4 = Great Value
> 5 = Extremely Great Value

1. Good pay	1	2	3	4	5		**6.** Interesting work	1	2	3	4	5
2. Prestigious title	1	2	3	4	5		**7.** Pleasant conditions	1	2	3	4	5
3. Vacation time	1	2	3	4	5		**8.** Chances to advance	1	2	3	4	5
4. Job security	1	2	3	4	5		**9.** Flexible schedule	1	2	3	4	5
5. Recognition	1	2	3	4	5		**10.** Friendly co-workers	1	2	3	4	5

Scoring Key

To assess your responses, prioritize them into groups. Put all the rewards you gave a 5 together. Do the same for your other responses. The rewards you gave 5s or 4s are the ones that you most desire and that your employer should emphasize with you.

Analysis and Interpretation

What motivates you does not necessarily motivate me. So employers that want to maximize employee motivation should determine what rewards each employee individually values. This instrument can help you understand which work-related rewards have the greatest value to you.

Compare the rewards that your employer offers with your scores. The greater the disparity, the more you might want to consider looking for opportunities at another organization with a reward structure that better matches your preferences.

More Self-Assessments

To learn more about your skills, abilities, and interests, take the following self-assessments on your enclosed CD-ROM:

- #10—What Motivates Me?
- #13—What's My View on the Nature of People?
- #17—How Sensitive Am I to Equity Differences?

How Can You Motivate Others?

This exercise is designed to help increase your awareness of how and why you motivate others and to help focus on the needs of those you are attempting to motivate.

Step 1

Break into groups of 5 to 7 people. Each group member is to respond individually to the following:

Situation 1: You are the owner and president of a 50-employee organization that provides call-centre services to a number of local businesses. There are 2 major units. *Customer care* answers questions from customers about malfunctioning technology (computers, cellphones, and home networks). *Sales and marketing* makes telemarketing calls to people's homes. Employees who work in sales and marketing phone

people and try to sell them cellphone plans and/or Internet access at reduced prices. They also conduct market research via phone, calling people to ask them to answer survey questions. Employees who work in customer care often receive calls from irate customers who are having technical difficulties. Employees who work in sales and marketing often encounter irate people when they phone to sell them something or conduct a survey, particularly at dinner time. Your goal is to motivate all 50 employees to their highest level of effort.

Task 1: On a separate piece of paper, list the factors you would use to motivate your employees. Avoid general statements such as "give them a raise." Rather, be as specific as possible, such as "give them a 5-percent raise."

Task 2: Rank (from most important to least important) all the factors listed in Task 1.

Situation 2: Consider now that you are 1 of the 50 employees who have been given insight into what motivates you.

Task 3: As an employee, list those factors that would motivate you most effectively. Again, be as specific as possible.

Task 4: Rank (from most important to least important) all the factors listed in Task 3.

Step 2

Each member should share his or her prioritized lists (the lists from Tasks 2 and 4) with the other members of the group.

Step 3

After each member has presented his or her lists, the group should respond to the following questions:

1. Are each individual's lists (Task 2 and Task 4) similar or dissimilar to the others? What do the differences or similarities suggest to you?

2. What have you learned about how and why to motivate others, and how can you apply these data?

ETHICAL DILEMMA EXERCISE

Are Some Employees More Deserving Than Others?

Employees who feel unfairly forced into accepting deep cuts in salary and benefits may not be the most motivated employees. This is the situation facing many major North American airlines as they struggle for survival. To stay in business, management at Air Canada and other carriers have pressured unionized pilots, mechanics, and flight attendants for concessions on pay and work rules again and again.

Still, many North American airline employees are resentful that their compensation will not return to previous levels until the end of 2008—at the earliest. Air Canada employees are not even sure there will be an airline in 2008. Moreover, there is concern that cuts in management's compensation will not last as long as those for unionized employees. Many employees are bitter about what they see as inequitable treatment. "We know we had to help the airline," says one flight attendant. "But we think they took more than they needed from us." This sense of

inequity could dampen motivation and affect the way employees work together and deal with customers.[77]

Imagine that you were just promoted and now manage one of your airline's mechanical maintenance facilities at a regional airport. Your manager just told you that the airline has lost many managers to jobs outside the industry. To stop defections and retain good managers, your company has decided to return managers to full pay and benefits within 12 months. However, employees must wait much longer. You sympathize with your employees' gripes about compensation cuts, and you know they have little hope of getting maintenance jobs at other airlines. Although you like your new job and would welcome full pay, you could easily move to another industry. What, if anything, would you do about the nonmanagerial employees who will continue working with the pay cuts? (Look back at this chapter's discussion of equity theory as you consider this ethical challenge.)

CASE APPLICATION

Motive

"We're not warm and fuzzy, there's not a lot of cheerleading, and we don't give back rubs on Friday."[78] Such is the motivational philosophy of Scott Harmon, CEO and co-founder of Motive, a software development company. Founded in 1997, Motive provides customer service software that enables com-

panies to offer and manage a variety of services. Some of its customers include such well-known global corporations as Bell, British Telecom, AT&T, and Verizon Online. The company's mission is this: "To enable companies to compete and win with superior service. We believe that service is more than just an obligation, or a necessary expense. Service is our singular focus. From the beginning, Motive has helped its customers revolutionize the way they deliver services to improve profitability and reduce costs."

Although the company is passionate about serving customers, Harmon does not believe in coddling employees. Steven Semelsberger, who oversees the company's business partnerships, says, "If you need a lot of pats on the back, this place is not for you." Claire Campbell-Seeger, Motive's public relations director, says that during her five years at Motive, she has received only three emails from Harmon praising her work. Employees who need more visible and vocal praise and recognition tend to leave the company. Those who stay and succeed tend to be athletes or sports fans who thrive on competition and winning. As the company says on the Careers page of its website, "Our culture attracts employees who are results-oriented, fueled by technology and above all, driven to succeed."

Harmon's philosophy of people management was shaped by *Atlas Shrugged,* the 1957 novel by Ayn Rand, in which a person's main source of strength is described as thinking and reason. This philosophy can be seen, as well, in the way business decisions are made at Motive. The process is no-nonsense, and to keep emotions from influencing decisions, executives debate an issue and then wait a day to make the final decision. At meetings, employees better be prepared with the facts. One company story tells of a meeting in which an account representative described a customer as "pleasantly content." Harmon shot back, "Did you just make that up? If we aren't measuring it, how do you really know?"

One of Harmon's managers sent him an email yesterday, saying she was having difficulty hiring two software developers for her team. Everyone she interviewed said they did not like Motive's philosophy on rewards. Harmon is meeting with her this morning. What should he tell her?

Motivation at Classic Hospitality

The reality of service work in a hotel is that a substantial portion of your work involves days of boredom punctuated by hours of tedium. You basically spend your time in isolation, often doing work that will make the quality of a guest's stay better. You are typically low paid and advancement is often lacking. But that is not necessarily the case at Hotel Lombardy, a hotel that is part of the Classic Hospitality Consortium. If you are like Charles Hegeman, what you thought was a quick job to make a few extra bucks to travel across North America has turned into a career with Classic that has lasted more than five years.[79]

The hospitality industry in general has a terrible record of employee loyalty. Because the jobs are often viewed as low-paying service jobs, turnover is unbelievably high. In fact, most companies in the hospitality industry experience turnover rates of around 160 percent annually. That means that they have an entirely new set of employees every eight months. Continuity of quality service, as you can imagine, can be extremely difficult under such circumstances.

But Classic Hospitality views jobs at its hotels differently. It has made a corporate commitment to attract good employees and to encourage the best employees to stay. Although company officials recognize there is a lot of competition for these employees, they believe that they can find a way to motivate this group of individuals and keep them longer. For instance, because of the excellent work Hegeman did as a front office clerk, he was promoted to front office manager. After a period of time in that job with outstanding per-

formance, Hegeman notified hotel management that he was ready for a promotion. Working with him to match his skills and abilities to hotel needs, management promoted him to sales manager at another of Classic's properties.

In addition to internal advancement, Classic Hospitality offers employees bonuses, recognition, and even transportation assistance. For example, the cleaning staff has a checklist that they must complete when cleaning a guest room. Periodically a supervisor will evaluate how well the staff performed their jobs. If over a six-month period a staff member has achieved a 95-percent-or-greater effectiveness rating, that individual is given an extra week's pay. And on those really busy nights when hotel occupancy exceeds 80 percent, which makes the employees' jobs just that much harder, each hotel staff member is given a $100 bonus. Needless to say, employees are very happy when the hotel is full!

No discussion of employee life at Classic Hospitality would be complete without mentioning the company's focus on family. Each year the organization holds an annual holiday party, inviting employees, their spouses, and children to attend as a way of saying thanks for the hard work they have done. Management knows that the work hours often take employees away from their families. The holiday party is just one added means of letting employees and their loved ones know that they matter to Classic.

Is this form of motivation effective? By most accounts it is, considering, as we mentioned previously, that the turnover rate in the hospitality industry typically is around 160 percent

annually. Turnover at Classic Hospitality is less than 25 percent. That is a tremendous saving for the corporation—something that company officials appear to share with their loyal employees.

Questions

1. If you were interested in working in the hospitality industry, would you consider a job at Classic Hospitality? Why or why not?

2. How many activities in this Case Application can you tie into specific motivation theories? List the activities, the motivation theory, and how the activities apply.

3. Do you believe that bonus programs, such as an extra week's pay if at least 95 percent effectiveness of a job is achieved, transportation assistance, and the like, would work in other types of jobs? If so, which ones, and why? If not, why not?

DEVELOPING YOUR INTERPERSONAL SKILLS

Maximizing Employee Effort

About the Skill

There is no simple, all-encompassing set of motivational guidelines, but the following suggestions draw on the essence of what we know about motivating employees.[80]

Steps in Developing the Skill

You can be more effective at maximizing employee effort if you apply the following eight suggestions:

1. **Recognize individual differences.** Almost every contemporary motivation theory recognizes that employees are not homogeneous. They have different needs. They also differ in terms of attitudes, personality, and other important individual variables.

2. **Match people to jobs.** There is a great deal of evidence showing the motivational benefits of carefully matching people to jobs. People who lack the necessary skills to perform successfully will be disadvantaged.

3. **Use goals.** You should ensure that employees have hard, specific goals and feedback on how well they are doing in pursuit of those goals. In many cases, these goals should be participatively set.

4. **Ensure that goals are perceived as attainable.** Regardless of whether goals are actually attainable, employees who see goals as unattainable will reduce their effort. Be sure, therefore, that employees feel confident that increased efforts can lead to achieving performance goals.

5. **Individualize rewards.** Because employees have different needs, what acts as a reinforcer for one may not do so for another. Use your knowledge of employee differences to individualize the rewards over which you have control. Some of the more obvious rewards that you can allocate include pay, promotions, autonomy, and the opportunity to participate in goal setting and decision making.

6. **Link rewards to performance.** You need to make rewards contingent on performance. Rewarding factors other than performance will only reinforce the importance of those other factors. Key rewards such as pay increases and promotions should be given for the attainment of employees' specific goals.

7. **Check the system for equity.** Employees should perceive that rewards or outcomes are equal to the inputs given. On a simplistic level, experience, ability, effort, and other obvious inputs should explain differences in pay, responsibility, and other obvious outcomes.

8. **Don't ignore money.** It's easy to get so caught up in setting goals, creating interesting jobs, and providing opportunities for participation that you forget that money is a major reason why most people work. Thus, the allocation of performance-based wage increases, piecework bonuses, employee stock ownership plans, and other pay incentives are important in determining employee motivation.

Practising the Skill

Employees at Radialpoint in Montreal can get their laundry washed, dried, and folded for them at work. At trucking company Groupe Robert, based in Rougemont, Quebec, employees are entered into monthly draws for concerts and shows; each employee receives a Christmas food basket; and birthday cards are personally signed by the CEO. At Brantford, Ontario-based S. C. Johnson & Son, employees and their families can take holidays at the company's resort in the Muskokas. The company also provides an on-site massage therapist. All of these companies believe that there is more to rewards than just cash.

All of the following traditional and offbeat benefits are currently offered at various Canadian firms. Rank-order them for yourself, putting those that are most likely to motivate you at the top of your list. Now look at your top five choices. How do you think you will rank them in 10 years? Why?

Flextime

Telecommuting

Dental insurance

Tuition refund

Vision insurance

Health club

Life insurance

On-site daycare

Employee assistance program

Laundry/dry cleaning service

Company car

Subsidized cafeteria

Paid vacation

Profit sharing

Stock purchase plan

Ability to keep frequent flier miles

Pets at work

Management program

Daily naptime

Free snacks/candy

Year-end bonus

Clothing allowance

Flexible spending plan

Free lunch

Retirement plan

Paid sick days

Children's college/university tuition

Annual birthday gift

Non-work-related courses

Company-sponsored sports team

Free uniform

Transportation voucher

Family picnics and parties

Child and elder care referral services

Benefits for unmarried domestic partners

MANAGING WORKFORCE DIVERSITY

Developing Employee Potential: The Bottom Line of Diversity

One of a manager's more important goals is helping employees develop their potential.[81] This is particularly important in managing talented employees from a variety of cultures who can bring new perspectives and ideas to the business but who may find that the workplace environment is not as conducive as it could be to accepting and embracing these different perspectives. For instance, managers at AlcatelLucent's distinguished Bell Labs have worked hard to develop an environment in which the ideas of nonwhite employees are encouraged openly.

What can managers do to ensure that employees from different cultures have the opportunity to develop their potential? One thing they can do is to make sure that there are role models of different cultures in leadership positions so that others see that there are opportunities to grow and advance. Having motivated, talented, hard-working, and enthusiastic diverse employees who excel in decision-making roles can

be a powerful motivator to other employees of the same or similar backgrounds to work hard to develop their own potential. A mentoring program in which diverse employees are given the opportunity to work closely with organizational leaders can be a powerful tool. At Silicon Graphics, for instance, new employees become part of a mentoring group called "Horizons." Through this mentoring group, diverse employees have the opportunity to observe and learn from key company decision makers.

Another way for managers to develop the potential of their diverse employees is to offer developmental work assignments that provide a variety of learning experiences in different organizational areas. DaimlerChrysler, for example, started its Corporate University, which offers a comprehensive series of learning opportunities for all employees. The company's director of diversity and work/family says that employees who are provided the opportunity to learn new processes and how to use new technology are more likely to excel at their work and to stay with the company. These types of developmental opportunities are particularly important for diverse employees because they empower employees with tools that are critical to professional development.

Consider organizations for which you have worked. Did any of them have diversity initiatives? What did they do to either recruit employees from various cultures, or to make them feel more welcome? Were the company's policies effective in managing diversity?

Understanding Groups and Teams

What is the best way to create and manage teams?

1 What are the stages of team development?

2 How do individuals become team players?

3 How can groups become effective teams?

When you are putting together the Canadian team for the 2006 Winter Olympics in Turin, do you go with the proven winners of the 2004 World Cup of Hockey and the 2002 Winter Olympics or put together a new team?[1]

That was the challenge facing Wayne Gretzky and management as they prepared to announce the 24-man roster for Team Canada on December 21, 2005.

Gretzky's 2004 World Cup hockey team beat Finland 3 to 2 in Toronto, taking first place. His 2002 Olympic hockey team beat the Americans 5 to 2 in Salt Lake City, winning the gold medal. It was the first time Canada had won Olympic gold since 1952.

When Steve Tambellini, filling in for Gretzky, whose mother's funeral had been earlier that week, announced the new team in December 2005, 20 of the players had played for either the World Cup team, the 2002 Olympic team, or both. Only three new players were added to the team. There were certainly questions about some of the decisions. Was it right to leave off Pittsburgh Penguin Sidney Crosby, who was having a strong debut season in the NHL? Why include contro-

versial Canuck Todd Bertuzzi, after he attacked Colorado Avalanche player Steve Moore, ending his career? Most importantly, what about 2010? Shouldn't there be some younger players getting experience now in preparation for playing for Olympic gold in Vancouver?

Team Canada assistant coach Wayne Fleming defended against those who complained that there were not enough new faces on the team. This would be a team that would have "instant chemistry, with very little preparation time." Better to go with experience, in other words.

THINK ABOUT IT

What is the best way to choose an effective team? Put yourself in Wayne Gretzky's shoes. Are there other players he should have chosen instead? Could he have put together a better team?

Work teams are one of the realities—and challenges—of managing in today's dynamic global environment. Teams are widely used in Canada. In a survey by The Conference Board of Canada, over 80 percent of the 109 companies surveyed stated that they rely on teams.[2] Thousands of organizations have made the move to restructure work around teams rather than individuals. Why? What do these teams look like? What stages of development do teams go through? And, like the challenge Wayne Gretzky faced, how can managers create effective teams? These are a few of the types of questions we answer in this chapter. First, however, let's begin by developing our understanding of group behaviour.

Hockey Canada
www.hockeycanada.ca

UNDERSTANDING GROUPS AND TEAMS

1 What are the stages of team development?

Because most organizational work is done by individuals who are part of a work group, it's important for managers to understand group behaviour. The behaviour of a group is not simply the sum total of the behaviours of all the individuals in the group. Why? Because individuals act differently in groups than they do when they are alone. Therefore, if we want to understand organizational behaviour more fully, we need to study groups.

What Is a Group?

group

Two or more interacting and interdependent individuals who come together to achieve particular goals.

A **group** is defined as two or more interacting and interdependent individuals who come together to achieve particular goals. Groups can be either formal or informal. *Formal groups* are work groups defined by the organization's structure that have designated work assignments and specific tasks. In formal groups, appropriate behaviours are established by and directed toward organizational goals. Exhibit 10-1 provides some examples of different types of formal groups in today's organizations.

In contrast, *informal groups* are social. These groups occur naturally in the workplace in response to the need for social contact. For example, three employees from different departments who regularly eat lunch together are an informal group. Informal groups tend to form around friendships and common interests.

What Is a Team?

work team

A group whose members work intensely on a specific, common goal using their positive synergy, individual and mutual accountability, and complementary skills.

synergy

Combined efforts that are greater than the sum of individual efforts.

Most of you are already familiar with teams, especially if you have watched organized sports events. Although a sports team has many of the same characteristics as a work team, work teams *are* different from work groups and have their own unique traits. Work groups interact primarily to share information and to make decisions to help each member do his or her job more efficiently and effectively. These groups have no need or opportunity to engage in collective work that requires joint effort. On the other hand, **work teams** are groups whose members work intensely on a specific, common goal using their positive **synergy**, individual and mutual accountability, and complementary skills. In a work team, the combined individual efforts of team members result in a level of performance that is greater than the sum of those individual inputs. How? By generating positive synergy through coordinated effort.

Though teams and groups do differ, we sometimes use "groups" and "teams" interchangeably in our theoretical discussions below (conforming to how scholars have written their research). This simply underscores that in some cases the processes for groups and teams are similar, although teams involve more synergy.

Exhibit 10-1

Examples of Formal Groups

Command Groups: Groups that are determined by the organization chart and composed of individuals who report directly to a given manager.

Task Groups: Groups composed of individuals brought together to complete a specific job task; their existence is often temporary because once the task is completed, the group disbands.

Cross-Functional Teams: Groups that bring together the knowledge and skills of individuals from various work areas, or groups whose members have been trained to do one another's jobs.

Self-Managed Teams: Groups that are essentially independent and, in addition to their own tasks, take on traditional managerial responsibilities such as hiring, planning and scheduling, and performance evaluations.

Types of Teams

Teams can do a variety of things. They can design products, provide services, negotiate deals, coordinate projects, offer advice, and make decisions.[3] The four most common types of teams you are likely to find in an organization are problem-solving teams, self-managed teams, cross-functional teams, and virtual teams.

Problem-Solving Teams

If we look back to when work teams were just beginning to gain in popularity, most were what we call **problem-solving teams**, which are teams of 5 to 12 employees from the same department or functional area who are involved in efforts to improve work activities or to solve specific problems. In problem-solving teams, members share ideas or offer suggestions on how work processes and methods can be improved. However, these teams are rarely given the authority to unilaterally implement any of their suggested actions.

Self-Managed Teams

Self-managed teams are formal groups of employees who operate without a manager and are responsible for a complete work process or segment. Unlike a problem-solving team, the self-managed team is responsible for getting the work done *and* for managing itself. This usually includes planning and scheduling work, assigning tasks to members, collectively controlling the pace of work, making operating decisions, and taking action on problems. For instance, at Hamilton, Ontario-based Dofasco, self-managed teams are given improvement goals; teams assume the responsibility for developing plans to reach the goals.

How effective are self-managed teams? Most organizations that use them find them successful and plan to expand their use in the coming years.[4] For instance, the evidence indicates that self-managed work teams often perform better than teams with formally appointed leaders.[5] Leaders can obstruct high performance when they interfere with self-managed teams.[6] However, managers cannot forget to consider cultural differences when deciding whether to use self-managed teams. For instance, evidence suggests that these types of teams have not fared well in Mexico largely due to that culture's low tolerance of ambiguity and uncertainty and employees' strong respect for hierarchical authority.[7]

Cross-Functional Teams

Cross-functional teams, which we introduced in Chapter 5, are a mixture of employees at about the same hierarchical level, who are experts in various specialties and who work together to accomplish tasks. Many organizations use cross-functional teams. For example, Calgary-based Canadian Pacific Railway (CPR) uses cross-functional teams to figure out ways to cut costs. Individuals from all of the functional areas affected by the spending review (such as supply services, operations, and finance) make up the team.[8] Organic organizations, which we discussed in Chapter 5, are generally structured around cross-functional teams.

Virtual Teams

Virtual teams are teams that use computer technology to link physically dispersed members in order to achieve a common goal. For instance, Karim Ladak, associate director for Toronto-based Procter & Gamble Canada, leads a virtual team of 50 people located in Toronto, Cincinnati, Brussels, Manila, Warsaw, Singapore, San Jose, and Geneva.[9] By relying on this virtual team, Ladak is able to put together a network of talent without unnec-

Teams work toward their goal with an intensity and commitment that General Motors (GM) managers understand well. When GM executive Mike DiGiovanni was putting together his Hummer team, the goal was to create a consumer version of the famous military vehicle on a shoestring budget. "I knew Hummer would never get out of the box without a good team," he said. "I needed some cockiness, irreverence, and a belief that you could change the rules. I needed people who would constantly push each other out of their comfort zone."

problem-solving team
A work team of 5 to 12 employees from the same department or functional area who are involved in efforts to improve work activities or to solve specific problems.

self-managed team
A work team that operates without a manager and is responsible for a complete work process or segment.

Dofasco
www.dofasco.ca

cross-functional team
A group of employees at about the same hierarchical level, but from different work areas, who come together to accomplish a task.

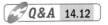
Q&A 14.12

virtual team
A type of work team that uses computer technology to link physically dispersed members in order to achieve a common goal.

essary overhead and complex work arrangements. In a virtual team, members collaborate online with tools such as wide-area networks, videoconferencing, email, fax, or even websites where the team can hold online conferences.[10] Virtual teams can do all the things that other teams can—share information, make decisions, and complete tasks; however, they can suffer from the absence of paraverbal and nonverbal cues and limited social contact. An additional concern about virtual teams is whether members are able to build the same kind of trust that face-to-face teams build.[11]

However, two recent studies examining how virtual teams work on projects indicate that virtual teams can develop close interaction and trust; these qualities simply develop differently than in face-to-face groups.[12] The researchers found that initial electronic messages set the tone and determined the extent to which trust developed on a virtual team. For example, on one team the appointed leader sent an introductory message that had a distrustful tone. This team suffered low morale and poor performance throughout the project. Virtual teams should start with an electronic form of "courtship," with members providing some personal information early on. Teams should assign clear roles to members, so members can identify with each other. By engaging in spontaneous communication with virtual team members, managers can also reduce the likelihood and impact of conflict.[13]

Managing virtual teams effectively has become more important as more employees engage in telecommuting, an alternative work arrangement we discussed in Chapter 9.

Stages of Team Development

Have you ever noticed the stages a team goes through in learning how to work together?

Team development is a dynamic process. Most teams and groups are in a continual state of change, although there is a general pattern that describes how most of them develop. Professor Bruce Tuckman of Ohio State University developed a five-stage model of small group development. His research found that teams pass through a standard sequence of five stages.[14] As shown in Exhibit 10-2, these five stages are *forming, storming, norming, performing,* and *adjourning.*

Exhibit 10-2

Stages of Team Development

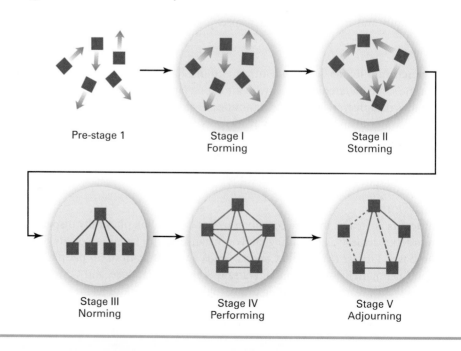

Pre-stage 1

Stage I
Forming

Stage II
Storming

Stage III
Norming

Stage IV
Performing

Stage V
Adjourning

Stage I, **forming**, has two aspects. First, people join the team either because of a work assignment or for some other benefit desired (such as status, self-esteem, affiliation, power, or security).

Once the team's membership is in place, the second part of the forming stage begins: the task of defining the team's purpose, structure, and leadership. This phase is characterized by a great deal of uncertainty. Members are "testing the waters" to determine what types of behaviour are acceptable. This stage is complete when members begin to think of themselves as part of a team.

Stage II, **storming**, is one of intragroup conflict. Members accept the existence of the team but resist the control that the team imposes on individuality. Further, there is conflict over who will control the team. When this stage is complete, there will be a relatively clear hierarchy of leadership within the team and agreement on the team's direction.

Stage III is one in which close relationships develop and the team demonstrates cohesiveness. There is now a strong sense of team identity and camaraderie. This **norming** stage is complete when the team structure solidifies and the team has assimilated a common set of expectations of what defines correct member behaviour.

Stage IV is **performing**. The team structure at this point is fully functional and accepted by team members. Team energy has moved from getting to know and understand each other to performing the task at hand.

Performing is the last stage in the development of permanent work teams. Temporary teams—such as project teams, task forces, and similar groups that have a limited task to perform—have a fifth stage, **adjourning**. In this stage, the team prepares to disband. High levels of task performance are no longer the team's top priority. Instead, attention is directed at wrapping up activities. Responses of team members vary at this stage. Some are upbeat, basking in the team's accomplishments. Others may be saddened by the loss of camaraderie and friendships gained during the work team's life.

Many of you have probably experienced each of these stages in working on a class team project. Team members are selected and then meet for the first time. There is a "feeling out" period to assess what the team is going to do and how it's going to do it. This is usually rapidly followed by a battle for control: Who is going to be in charge? Once this issue is resolved and a "hierarchy" agreed on, the team identifies specific aspects of the task, who is going to do them, and dates by which the assigned work needs to be completed. General expectations are established and agreed upon by each member. These decisions form the foundation for what you hope will be a coordinated team effort culminating in a pro-

forming
The first stage of team development in which people join the group and then define the team's purpose, structure, and leadership.

storming
The second stage of team development, which is characterized by intragroup conflict.

 **Q&A** 14.1

norming
The third stage of team development, which is characterized by close relationships and cohesiveness.

performing
The fourth stage of team development, in which the team structure is fully functional and accepted by team members.

adjourning
The final stage of team development for temporary teams, in which members are concerned with wrapping up activities rather than task performance.

Self-managing teams at Toyo Ink Australia are in the performing stage. There are no more time clocks because team members are responsible for the amount of work they do, and they will soon also be in charge of planning and organizing their own vacation times. Information sharing is more efficient, and communication with management has increased as well.

ject well done. Once the team project is completed and turned in, the team breaks up. Of course, some teams don't get much beyond the first or second stage; these teams typically have serious interpersonal conflicts, turn in disappointing work, and get lower grades.

Should you assume from the preceding discussion that a team becomes more effective as it progresses through the first four stages? Some researchers argue that effectiveness of work teams increases at advanced stages, but that is not always the case.[15] Also, teams don't always proceed clearly from one stage to the next. Sometimes, in fact, several stages may be going on simultaneously, as when teams are storming and performing at the same time. Individuals within a team may also be at different stages, with some performing while others are still in the forming or norming stage. When individuals are shy, it may take them longer to reach the performing stage, and it may be helpful for team members to support and encourage each other through the stages. Teams sometimes regress to previous stages. Therefore, don't always assume that all teams precisely follow this development process or that Stage IV (performing) is always the most preferable. It's better to think of this model as a general framework. It underscores the fact that teams are dynamic entities, and it can help you better understand the problems and issues that are most likely to surface during a team's life.

TURNING INDIVIDUALS INTO TEAM PLAYERS

When Wayne Gretzky put together Team Canada for the 2006 Winter Olympics, he had to balance out many considerations.[16] His 2002 Winter Olympic team and his 2004 World Cup of Hockey team had done a terrific job in representing Canada. Still, having some younger players gain experience for the 2010 Winter Olympics in Vancouver might be a consideration.

Gretzky put together a team that had a lot of experience, particularly international experience. He seemed less concerned with the players' recent performance in the league. Since Mario Lemieux and Steve Yzerman, two veterans whom Gretzky had relied on for leadership roles in the previous Team Canada, were unavailable, Gretzky might have felt experienced players would fill the leadership void. Choosing the players was not the end of the task, however. Gretzky had to get the collection of individuals to play like a team.

THINK ABOUT IT
What does it take to turn an individual into a team player?

---

2 How do individuals become team players?

So far, we have made a strong case for the value and growing popularity of work teams, but not every employee is inherently a team player. Some people prefer to be recognized for their individual achievements. In some organizations, too, work environments are such that only the strong survive. Creating teams in such an environment may meet some resistance. Countries differ in terms of the degree to which individuals are encouraged by societal institutions to be integrated into groups. Teams fit well in countries that score high on collectivism, where working together is encouraged. But what if an organization wants to introduce teams into an individualistic society, like that of Canada? The job becomes more difficult.

The Challenges of Creating Team Players

One substantial barrier to work teams is the individual resistance that may exist. Employees' success, when they are part of teams, is no longer defined in terms of individual performance. Instead, success is a function of how well the team as a whole performs. To perform well as team members, individuals must be able to communicate openly and honestly with one another, to confront differences and resolve conflicts, and to place lower priority on personal goals for the good of the team. For many employees, these are difficult and sometimes impossible assignments. The *Ethical Dilemma Exercise* on page 300 looks at a situation in which an employee does not want to be a team member.

The challenge of creating team players will be greatest when the national culture is highly individualistic and the teams are being introduced into an established organization that has historically valued individual achievement.[17] These organizations prospered by hiring and rewarding corporate stars, and they bred a competitive work climate that encouraged individual achievement and recognition. In this context, employees can experience culture shock caused by a sudden shift in the focus to teamwork.[18]

Team players don't just appear. There is a lot of hard work required to get team members to gel. That is why baseball players, like the Toronto Blue Jays, go to spring training every year—to prepare themselves as a team for the upcoming baseball season.

In contrast, the challenge for management is less demanding when teams are introduced in places in which employees have strong collectivist values—such as Japan or Mexico. The challenge of forming teams will also be less in new organizations that use teams as their initial form of structuring work. For instance, Saturn Corporation (an American organization owned by General Motors) was designed around teams from its start. Everyone at Saturn was hired on the understanding that they would be working in teams, and the ability to be a good team player was a hiring prerequisite. *Managing Workforce Diversity—The Challenge of Managing Diverse Teams* on page 303 considers how you can help team members from different cultures work together more effectively.

What Roles Do Team Members Play?

A **role** refers to a set of expected behaviour patterns attributed to someone who occupies a given position in a social unit. In a group, individuals are expected to perform certain roles because of their positions in the group. **Task-oriented roles** tend to be oriented toward task accomplishment, while **maintenance roles** are oriented toward maintaining group member satisfaction and relationship.[19] Think about groups that you have been in and the roles that you played. Were you continually trying to keep the group focused on getting its work done? If so, you were filling a task accomplishment role. Or were you more concerned that group members had the opportunity to offer ideas and that they were satisfied with the experience? If so, you were performing a maintenance role to preserve the harmony of the group. Both roles are important to the ability of a group to function effectively and efficiently, and some group members are flexible and play both roles.

role
A set of expected behaviour patterns attributed to someone who occupies a given position in a social unit.

task-oriented roles
Roles performed by group members to ensure that the tasks of the group are accomplished.

maintenance roles
Roles performed by group members to maintain good relations within the group.

Shaping Team Behaviour

There are several options available for managers who are trying to turn individuals into team players. The three most popular ways include proper selection, employee training, and rewarding the appropriate team behaviours. Let's look at each of these.

Selection

Some individuals already possess the interpersonal skills to be effective team players. When hiring team members, in addition to checking on the technical skills required to successfully perform the job, the organization should ensure that applicants can fulfill team roles.

As we have mentioned before, some applicants have been socialized around individual contributions and, consequently, lack team skills, as might some current employees whose jobs are being restructured into teams. When faced with such candidates, a manager can do several things. First, and most obvious, if a candidate's team skills are woefully lacking, don't hire that candidate. If successful performance requires interaction, rejecting such a candidate is appropriate. On the other hand, a good candidate who has only some basic team skills can be hired on a probationary basis and required to undergo training to shape him or her into a team player. If the skills are not learned or practised, the individual may have to be let go for failing to achieve the skills necessary for performing successfully on the job.

Training

Performing well in a team involves a set of behaviours. As we discussed in the preceding chapter, new behaviours can be learned. Even a large portion of people who were raised on the importance of individual accomplishment can be trained to become team players. Training specialists can conduct workshops that allow employees to experience the satisfaction that teamwork can provide. The workshops usually cover such topics as team problem solving, communications, negotiations, conflict resolution, and coaching skills. It's not unusual, too, for these employees to be exposed to the five stages of team development that we discussed earlier.[20] At Verizon Communications, for example, trainers focus on how a team goes through various stages before it gels. Employees are reminded of the importance of patience, because teams take longer to do some things—such as make decisions—than do employees acting alone.[21]

Rewards

The organization's reward system needs to encourage cooperative efforts rather than competitive ones. For instance, Lockheed Martin Aeronautics Company has organized its 20 000-plus employees into teams. Rewards are structured to return a percentage increase in the bottom line to the team members on the basis of achievements of the team's performance goals.

Promotions, pay raises, and other forms of recognition should be given to employees who are effective collaborative team members. This does not mean that individual contribution is ignored, but rather that it is balanced with selfless contributions to the team. Examples of behaviours that should be rewarded include training new colleagues, sharing information with teammates, helping resolve team conflicts, and mastering new skills in which the team is deficient.[22] Finally, managers cannot forget the inherent rewards that employees can receive from teamwork. Work teams provide camaraderie. It's exciting and satisfying to be an integral part of a successful team. The opportunity to engage in personal development and to help teammates grow can be a very satisfying and rewarding experience for employees.[23]

TURNING GROUPS INTO EFFECTIVE TEAMS

Wayne Gretzky had many excellent players to choose from for the team that would play in the 2006 Winter Olympics.[24] One strategy for choosing players might have been to pick the absolute best players for each position, examining their records during the previous season. Alternatively, it might have made sense to pick very good players, who also know how to work well with other team members. Gretzky chose the latter strategy, picking 20 players who had been on either the 2004 World Cup of Hockey team or the 2002 Winter Olympic team.

Hockey Canada president Bob Nicholson explained the thinking behind Gretzky's strategy: "We've always stated that we want to have players with experience at the Olympics, world championships and players who have won a Cup. You want players around [the Olympics] who have won."

Clearly Gretzky felt that a team, particularly the Olympic team, was more than just the sum of its parts. Gretzky's choice of team members did not pay off, however. Unlike Team Canada's performance in the 2004 World Cup, going undefeated in the six playoff games and never once trailing in a game, Canada was eliminated in the quarter-finals of the 2006 Winter Olympics, and played three scoreless games on the way to Olympic defeat. Hockey Canada president Bob Nicholson summarized what went wrong: "Seventeen power plays (in the three shutout losses) and zero goals, who would have ever expected that? It wasn't one player, it was a group of individuals that couldn't put the puck in the net."

THINK ABOUT IT

How can managers create effective teams?

---

3 How can groups become effective teams?

Teams are not automatic productivity enhancers. They can also be disappointments. So the challenge is to create effective teams. Effective teams have a number of characteristics, which we review below. In addition, teams need to build group cohesiveness, manage group conflict, and prevent social loafing to perform well. For more insights into creating effective teams, see *Developing Your Interpersonal Skills—Creating Effective Teams* on page 302, at the end of the chapter.

Characteristics of Effective Teams

> *How do you build an effective team? Have you ever done so?*

Research on teams provides insights into the characteristics associated with effective teams.[25] Let's look more closely at these characteristics, which are shown in Exhibit 10-3.

Clear Goals

High-performance teams have a clear understanding of the goals to be achieved. Members are committed to the team's goals; they know what they are expected to accomplish and understand how they will work together to achieve these goals.

Relevant Skills

Effective teams are composed of competent individuals who have the necessary technical and interpersonal skills to achieve the desired goals while working well together. This last point is important since not everyone who is technically competent has the interpersonal skills to work well as a team member.

Mutual Trust

Effective teams are characterized by high mutual trust among members. That is, members believe in each other's ability, character, and integrity. But as you probably know from personal relationships, trust is fragile. For team members to have mutual trust, they must believe that the team is capable of getting the task done and that "the team will not harm the individual or his or her interests."[26] Maintaining this trust requires careful attention by managers.

Unified Commitment

Unified commitment is characterized by dedication to the team's goals and a willingness to expend extraordinary amounts of energy to achieve them. Members of an effective team exhibit intense loyalty and dedication to the team and are willing to do whatever it takes to help their team succeed.

Exhibit 10-3

Characteristics of Effective Teams

Good Communication

Not surprisingly, effective teams are characterized by good communication. Members convey messages, verbally and nonverbally, to each other in ways that are readily and clearly understood. Also, feedback helps to guide team members and to correct misunderstandings. Like a couple who has been together for many years, members on high-performing teams are able to quickly and efficiently share ideas and feelings.

Negotiating Skills

Effective teams are continually making adjustments as to who does what. This flexibility requires team members to possess negotiating skills. Since problems and relationships are regularly changing in teams, members need to be able to confront and reconcile differences.

Appropriate Leadership

Effective leaders can motivate a team to follow them through the most difficult situations. How? By clarifying goals, demonstrating that change is possible by overcoming inertia, increasing the self-confidence of team members, and helping members to more fully realize their potential. Increasingly, effective team leaders act as coaches and facilitators. They help guide and support the team but don't control it. See also *Self-Assessment—How Good Am I at Building and Leading a Team?* on pages 298–299, at the end of the chapter.

Internal and External Support

group cohesiveness
The degree to which group members are attracted to each other and share the group's goals.

The final condition necessary for an effective team is a supportive climate. Internally, the team should have a sound infrastructure, which means having proper training, a clear and reasonable measurement system that team members can use to evaluate their overall performance, an incentive program that recognizes and rewards team activities, and a supportive human resource system. The right infrastructure should support members and reinforce behaviours that lead to high levels of performance. Externally, managers should provide the team with the resources needed to get the job done.

Building Group Cohesiveness

Intuitively, it makes sense that groups in which there is a lot of internal disagreement and lack of cooperation are less effective in completing their tasks than are groups in which members generally agree, cooperate, and like each other. Research in this area has focused on **group cohesiveness**, or the degree to which members are attracted to each other and share the group's goals. Cohesiveness is important because it has been found to be related to a group's productivity.[27]

Research has generally shown that highly cohesive groups are more effective than are less cohesive ones.[28] However, this relationship between cohesiveness and effectiveness is more complex. A key moderating variable is the degree to which the group's attitude aligns with its goals or with the goals of the organization.[29] The more cohesive a group is, the more its members will follow its goals. If the goals are desirable (for instance, high output, quality work, cooperation with individuals outside the group), a cohesive group is more productive than a less cohesive group. But if cohesiveness is high and attitudes are unfavourable, productivity decreases. If cohesiveness is low and goals are supported, productivity increases, but not as much as when both cohesiveness and support are high. When cohesiveness is low and goals are not supported, cohesiveness has no significant effect on productivity. These conclusions are illustrated in Exhibit 10-4.

TIPS FOR MANAGERS

Increasing Group Cohesiveness

Increasing socio-emotional cohesiveness

→ Keep the group relatively **small**.

→ Strive for a **favourable public image** to increase the status and prestige of belonging.

→ Encourage **interaction** and **cooperation**.

→ Emphasize members' **common characteristics** and interests.

→ **Point out environmental threats** (e.g., competitors' achievements) to rally the group.

Increasing instrumental cohesiveness

→ Regularly update and **clarify the group's goal(s)**.

→ Give every group member a **vital "piece of the action."**

→ Channel each group member's special talents toward the **common goal(s)**.

→ **Recognize** and equitably reinforce **every member's contributions**.

→ Frequently remind group members **they need each other** to get the job done.

Source: R. Kreitner and A. Kinicki, *Organizational Behavior*, 6th ed. (New York: McGraw Hill/Irwin, 2004), p. 460. Reprinted by permission of McGraw Hill Education.

Exhibit 10-4

The Relationship Between Cohesiveness and Productivity

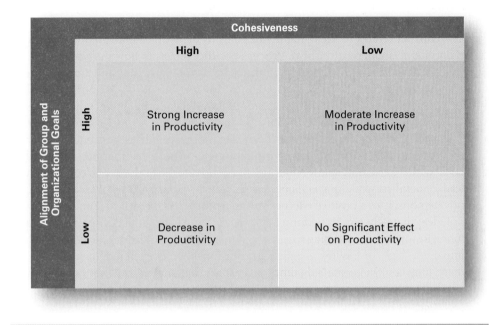

Most studies of cohesiveness focus on *socio-emotional cohesiveness*: the "sense of togetherness that develops when individuals derive emotional satisfaction from group participation."[30] There is also *instrumental cohesiveness*: the "sense of togetherness that develops when group members are mutually dependent on one another because they believe they could not achieve the group's goal by acting separately." Teams need to achieve a balance of these two types of cohesiveness to function well. *Tips for Managers—Increasing Group Cohesiveness* indicates how to increase both socio-emotional and instrumental cohesiveness.

Managing Group Conflict

Another important group process is how a group manages conflict. As a group performs its assigned tasks, disagreements inevitably arise. When we use the term **conflict**, we are referring to *perceived* differences that result in some form of interference or opposition. Whether the differences are real or not is irrelevant. If people in a group perceive that differences exist, then there is conflict. Our definition encompasses the full range of conflict—from subtle or indirect acts to overt acts such as strikes, riots, or wars.

Over the years, three different views have evolved regarding conflict.[31] One view argues that conflict must be avoided—that it indicates a problem within the group. We call this the **traditional view of conflict**. A second view, the **human relations view of conflict**, argues that conflict is a natural and inevitable outcome in any group and need not be negative but, rather, has the potential to be a positive force in contributing to a group's performance. The third and most recent perspective proposes that not only can conflict be a positive force in a group but that some conflict is *absolutely necessary* for a group to perform effectively. This third approach is called the **interactionist view of conflict**.

The interactionist view does not suggest that all conflicts are good. Some conflicts are seen as supporting the goals of the work group and improving its performance; these are **functional conflicts** of a constructive nature. Other conflicts are destructive and prevent a

conflict
Perceived differences that result in some form of interference or opposition.

Q&A 14.8

traditional view of conflict
The view that all conflict is bad and must be avoided.

human relations view of conflict
The view that conflict is a natural and inevitable outcome in any group and has the potential to be a positive force in contributing to a group's performance.

interactionist view of conflict
The view that some conflict is absolutely necessary for a group to perform effectively.

functional conflicts
Conflicts that support the goals of the work group and improve its performance.

dysfunctional conflicts
Conflicts that are destructive and prevent a group from achieving its goals.

 Q&A 14.9

task conflict
Conflict over content and goals of the work.

relationship conflict
Conflict based on interpersonal relationships.

process conflict
Conflict over how the work gets done.

group from achieving its goals. These are **dysfunctional conflicts**. Exhibit 10-5 illustrates the challenge facing managers. They want to create an environment in which there is healthy conflict that will help the group reach a high level of performance.

What differentiates functional from dysfunctional conflict? The evidence indicates that you need to look at the *type* of conflict.[32] Three types have been identified: task, relationship, and process.

Task conflict relates to the content and goals of the work. **Relationship conflict** is based on interpersonal relationships. **Process conflict** relates to how the work gets done. Studies demonstrate that relationship conflicts are almost always dysfunctional. Why? It appears that the friction and interpersonal hostilities inherent in relationship conflicts increase personality clashes and decrease mutual understanding, thereby hindering the completion of organizational tasks. On the other hand, low levels of process conflict and low-to-moderate levels of task conflict are functional. For process conflict to be productive, it must be kept to a minimum. Intense arguments about who should do what become dysfunctional when they create uncertainty about task roles, increase the time taken to complete tasks, and lead to members working at cross-purposes. A low-to-moderate level of task conflict consistently demonstrates a positive effect on group performance because it stimulates discussions of ideas that help groups perform better. Because we have yet to devise a sophisticated measuring instrument for assessing whether a given task, relationship, or process conflict level is optimal, too high, or too low, the manager must make intelligent judgments.

When group conflict becomes dysfunctional, what can managers do? They can select from five conflict-resolution options: avoiding, accommodating, forcing, compromising, and

Exhibit 10-5

Conflict and Group Performance

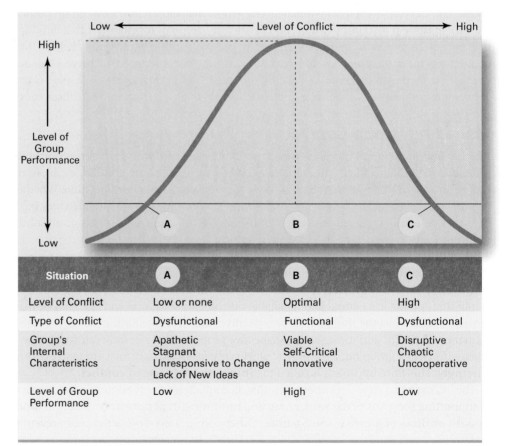

Situation	**A**	**B**	**C**
Level of Conflict	Low or none	Optimal	High
Type of Conflict	Dysfunctional	Functional	Dysfunctional
Group's Internal Characteristics	Apathetic Stagnant Unresponsive to Change Lack of New Ideas	Viable Self-Critical Innovative	Disruptive Chaotic Uncooperative
Level of Group Performance	Low	High	Low

Exhibit 10-6

Conflict-Resolution Techniques

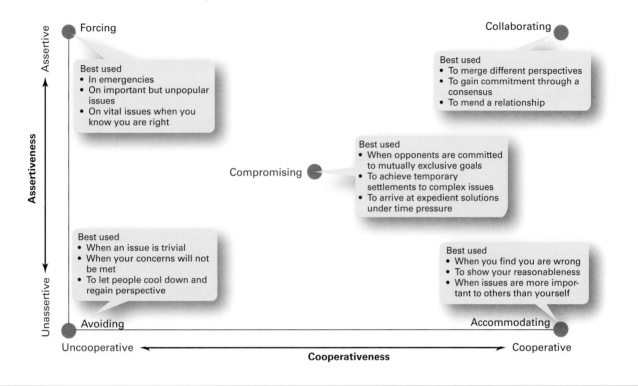

Forcing

Best used
• In emergencies
• On important but unpopular issues
• On vital issues when you know you are right

Collaborating

Best used
• To merge different perspectives
• To gain commitment through a consensus
• To mend a relationship

Compromising

Best used
• When opponents are committed to mutually exclusive goals
• To achieve temporary settlements to complex issues
• To arrive at expedient solutions under time pressure

Best used
• When an issue is trivial
• When your concerns will not be met
• To let people cool down and regain perspective

Avoiding

Best used
• When you find you are wrong
• To show your reasonableness
• When issues are more important to others than yourself

Accommodating

Assertiveness — Assertive / Unassertive

Cooperativeness — Uncooperative ← → Cooperative

Source: Adapted from K. W. Thomas, "Conflict and Negotiation Processes in Organizations," in *Handbook of Industrial and Organizational Psychology,* vol. 3, 2nd ed., ed. M. D. Dunnette and L. M. Hough (Palo Alto, CA: Consulting Psychologists Press, 1992), p. 668; and C. K. W. De Dreu, A. Evers, B. Beersma, E. S. Kluwer, and A. Nauta, "A Theory-Based Measure of Conflict Management Strategies in the Workplace," *Journal of Organizational Behavior* 22, no. 6 (September 2001), pp. 645–668. With permission.

collaborating.[33] (See Exhibit 10-6 for a description of each of these techniques.) Keep in mind that no one option is ideal for every situation. Which approach to use depends on the manager's desire to be more or less cooperative and more or less assertive.

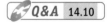 **Q&A** 14.10

Preventing Social Loafing

One of the more important findings related to group size is **social loafing**, which is the tendency of individuals to expend less effort when working with others than when working individually.[34] Social loafing is much more likely to happen in larger groups. This finding directly challenges the logic that the group's productivity should at least equal the sum of the productivity of each group member. What causes social loafing? It may be caused by a belief that others in the group are not doing their fair share. If you see others as lazy or inept, you can reestablish equity by reducing your effort. Another explanation is the dispersion of responsibility. Because the results of the group cannot be attributed to any one person, the relationship between an individual's input and the group's output is clouded. In such situations, individuals may be tempted to become "free riders" and coast on the group's efforts. In other words, there will be a reduction in efficiency when individuals think that their contribution cannot be measured.

The implications of social loafing for managers are significant. When managers use collective work situations to enhance morale and teamwork, they must also have a way to identify individual efforts. If this is not done, they must weigh the potential losses in productivity from using groups against any possible gains in employee satisfaction.[35] However, this con-

social loafing
The tendency of individuals to expend less effort when working collectively than when working individually.

clusion does have a Western bias. It's consistent with individualistic cultures, such as Canada and the United States, that are dominated by self-interest. It's not consistent with collectivist societies, in which individuals are motivated by in-group goals. For instance, in studies comparing employees from the United States with employees from the People's Republic of China and Israel (both collectivist societies), the Chinese and Israelis showed no tendency to engage in social loafing. In fact, they actually performed better in a group than when working alone.[36]

Beware! Teams Are Not Always the Answer

Do you ever find you are tired of working in a team?

Despite considerable success in the use of teams, they are not necessarily appropriate in all situations. Teamwork takes more time and often more resources than individual work; also, it has increased communication demands and the number of conflicts to be managed and meetings to be run. In the rush to enjoy the benefits of teams, some managers have introduced them into situations in which the work is better done by individuals. A 2003 study by Statistics Canada found that the introduction of teamwork lowered job turnover in the service industries, for both high- and low-skilled employees. However, manufacturing companies experienced higher job turnover if they had introduced teamwork and formal teamwork training, compared with not doing so (15.8 percent vs. 10.7 percent).[37]

How do you know if the work of your group would be better done in teams? Three questions can help determine whether a team fits the situation:[38]

- *Can the work be done better by more than one person?* Simple tasks that don't require diverse input are probably better left to individuals.

- *Does the work create a common purpose or set of goals for the people in the group that is more than the sum of individual goals?* For instance, many new-car dealer service departments have introduced teams that link customer service personnel, mechanics, parts specialists, and sales representatives. Such teams can better manage collective responsibility for ensuring that customer needs are properly met.

- *Are the members of the group interdependent?* Teams make sense where there is interdependence between tasks; where the success of the whole depends on the success of each one; and where the success of each one depends on the success of the others. Soccer, for instance, is an obvious *team* sport because of the interdependence of the players. Swim teams, by contrast, are not really teams, but groups of individuals whose total performance is merely the sum of the individual performances.

Researchers have outlined the conditions under which organizations would find teams more useful: "when work processes cut across functional lines; when speed is important (and complex relationships are involved); when the organization mirrors a complex, differentiated, and rapidly changing market environment; when innovation and learning have priority; when the tasks that have to be done require online integration of highly interdependent performers."[39]

SUMMARY AND IMPLICATIONS

1 **What are the stages of team development?** The five stages are forming, storming, norming, performing, and adjourning. These stages describe how teams evolve over time, although teams do not necessarily go through these stages in a completely linear fashion. Some researchers argue that the effectiveness of work teams increases at advanced stages, but it's not that simple. That assumption may be generally true, but what makes a team effective is a complex issue. It's better to think of this model as a general framework of how teams develop. *When Team Canada* *started practising for the 2006 Winter Olympics, individual hockey players knew how to play the game, but team members needed to learn how to work together, even though they were usually opponents.*

2 **How do individuals become team players?** Many individuals resist being team players. To improve the odds that a team will function well, managers can select the right people to be on a team, train individuals in how to work on teams, and make sure that rewards encourage individuals to be cooperative team players. *For the 2006 Winter Olympics, Wayne Gretzky put together a set of players who had international playing experience, hoping this would be enough to create a winning team.*

3 **How can groups become effective teams?** The characteristics associated with effective teams include clear goals, relevant skills, mutual trust, unified commitment, good communication, negotiating skills, appropriate leadership, and internal and external support. Teams also need to build group cohesiveness, manage group conflict, and prevent social loafing to be effective. Teams are not always the answer. It's important for managers to consider whether a team is really necessary to get the work done. *For Team Canada players, perhaps the most important factors in working toward winning the 2004 World Cup of Hockey were learning to trust each other, communicating well, and having the right leadership. The same team chemistry was not apparent in the 2006 Winter Olympics.*

Management @ Work

Reading for Comprehension

1. Contrast (1) self-managed and cross-functional teams and (2) virtual and face-to-face teams.

2. How do virtual teams enhance productivity?

3. What problems might surface in teams during each of the five stages of team development?

4. Describe three ways managers can try to encourage individuals to become team players.

5. Why do you believe mutual trust is important in developing high-performing work teams?

6. Why might a manager want to stimulate conflict in a group or team? How could conflict be stimulated?

Linking Concepts to Practice

1. How do you explain the rapidly increasing popularity of work teams in countries such as Canada and the United States, whose national cultures place a high value on individualism?

2. Think of a team to which you belong (or have belonged). Trace its development through the five stages of team development shown in Exhibit 10-2. How closely did its development parallel the team development model? How might the team development model have been used to improve the team's effectiveness?

3. "All work teams are work groups, but not all work groups are work teams." Do you agree or disagree with the statement? Discuss.

4. Would you prefer to work alone or as part of a team? Why? Support your response with data from your self-assessments.

5. Describe a situation in which individuals, acting independently, outperform teams in an organization.

MANAGEMENT FOR YOU TODAY

One of your professors has just informed your class that you will be working on a new major assignment worth 30 percent of your course mark. The assignment is to be done in teams of 7. Realistically you will need to function as a virtual team, as it turns out that each of you has a different work and class schedule, so that there is almost no time when more than 3 people could meet face to face. As you know, virtual teams have benefits, but they can also face problems. How will you build group cohesiveness in this team? What norms might help the team function, and how should the norms be decided? What will you do to prevent social loafing?

SELF-ASSESSMENT

How Good Am I at Building and Leading a Team?

Use the following rating scale to respond to the 18 statements on building and leading an effective team:[40]

1 = Strongly Disagree	3 = Slightly Disagree	5 = Agree
2 = Disagree	4 = Slightly Agree	6 = Strongly Agree

1. I am knowledgeable about the different stages of development that teams can go through in their life cycles.　　　　　　　　　　　　　　　　1　2　3　4　5　6

2. When a team forms, I make certain that all team members are introduced to one another at the outset.　　　　　　　　　　　　　　　　　　　1　2　3　4　5　6

3. When the team first comes together, I provide directions, answer team members' questions, and clarify goals, expectations, and procedures.   1   2   3   4   5   6

4. I help team members establish a foundation of trust among one another and between themselves and me.   1   2   3   4   5   6

5. I ensure that standards of excellence, not mediocrity or mere acceptability, characterize the team's work.   1   2   3   4   5   6

6. I provide a great deal of feedback to team members regarding their performance.   1   2   3   4   5   6

7. I encourage team members to balance individual autonomy with interdependence among other team members.   1   2   3   4   5   6

8. I help team members become at least as committed to the success of the team as to their own personal success.   1   2   3   4   5   6

9. I help members learn to play roles that assist the team in accomplishing its tasks as well as building strong interpersonal relationships.   1   2   3   4   5   6

10. I articulate a clear, exciting, passionate vision of what the team can achieve.   1   2   3   4   5   6

11. I help team members become committed to the team vision.   1   2   3   4   5   6

12. I encourage a win/win philosophy in the team; that is, when one member wins, every member wins.   1   2   3   4   5   6

13. I help the team avoid groupthink or making the group's survival more important than accomplishing its goal.   1   2   3   4   5   6

14. I use formal process management procedures to help the group become faster, more efficient, and more productive, and to prevent errors.   1   2   3   4   5   6

15. I encourage team members to represent the team's vision, goals, and accomplishments to outsiders.   1   2   3   4   5   6

16. I diagnose and capitalize on the team's core competence.   1   2   3   4   5   6

17. I encourage the team to achieve dramatic breakthrough innovations as well as small continuous improvements.   1   2   3   4   5   6

18. I help the team work toward preventing mistakes, not just correcting them after the fact.   1   2   3   4   5   6

Scoring Key

To calculate your total score, add up your scores on the 18 individual items.

Analysis and Interpretation

The authors of this instrument propose that it assesses team development behaviours in 5 areas: diagnosing team development (statements 1, 16); managing the forming stage (2–4); managing the norming stage (6–9, 13); managing the storming stage (10–12, 14, 15); and managing the performing stage (5, 17, 18). Your score will range between 18 and 108, with higher scores indicating greater ability at building and leading an effective team.

Based on a norm group of 500 business students, the following can help estimate where you are in relation to others:

Total score of 95 or more = You are in the top quartile
72–94 = You are in the second quartile
60–71 = You are in the third quartile
Less than 60 = You are in the bottom quartile

More Self-Assessments

To learn more about your skills, abilities, and interests, take the following self-assessments on your enclosed CD-ROM:

- #28—How Good Are My Listening Skills?
- #32—Do Others See Me as Trustworthy?

WORKING TOGETHER: TEAM-BASED EXERCISE

Puzzle Building

What happens when a group is presented with a task that must be completed within a certain time frame? Does the group exhibit characteristics of the stages of team development? Your instructor will divide the class into groups and give you instructions about building a puzzle or watching others do so.

Note: Instructors can find the instructions for this exercise in the Instructor's Resource Manual.

ETHICAL DILEMMA EXERCISE

Does Everyone Have to Be a Team Player?

You are a production manager at a Saturn plant. One of your newest employees is Barbara Petersen, who has a bachelor's degree in engineering and a recently completed master's degree in business. You hired Barbara for a position in supply chain management.

You have recently been chosen to head up a cross-functional team to look at ways to reduce inventory costs. This team would essentially be a permanent task force. You have decided to have team members come from supplier relations, cost accounting, transportation, and production systems. You have also decided to include Barbara on the team. While she has only been at Saturn for four months, you have been impressed with her energy, intelligence, and industriousness. You think this would be an excellent assignment for her to increase her visibility in the company and expand her understanding of the company's inventory system.

When you called Barbara into your office to give her the good news, you were quite surprised by her response. "I'm not a team player," she said. "I didn't join clubs in high school. I was on the track team and I did well, but track is an individual sport. We were a team only in the sense that we rode together in the same bus to away meets. In university, I avoided the whole sorority thing. Some people may call me a loner. I don't think that's true. I can work well with others, but I hate meetings and committees. To me, they waste so much time. And anything you're working on with a group, you've got all these different personalities that you have to adjust for. I'm an independent operator. Give me a job and I'll get it done. I work harder than anyone I know—and I give my employer 150 percent. But I don't want my performance to be dependent on the other people in my group. They may not work as hard as I will. Someone is sure to shirk some of their responsibilities. I just don't want to be a team player."

What do you do? Should you give Barbara the option of joining the inventory cost reduction team? Is it unethical for you to require someone like Barbara to do his or her job as part of a team?

CASE APPLICATION

BASF

BASF is the world's leading chemical company.[41] In its more than 100 major worldwide manufacturing facilities, the company uses something unusual: something it calls its "Verbund" philosophy—an idea developed by BASF's founder back in 1865. What is *Verbund*? It's the idea of linking each production facility with others so that the products and leftover material from one plant serve as raw materials in the next. For instance, all the facilities at the company's manufacturing complex in Ludwigshafen, Germany, are connected to each other by at least one product or process stage. The goal of *Verbund* is improved global efficiency. This pursuit of global efficiency is important to companies that want to be competitive. For instance, at another of BASF's *Verbund* plants found in Freeport, Texas, teams have played an important role in making the facility more productive and competitive.

Managers at BASF Freeport—like manufacturing managers everywhere—were searching for ways to make the facility's production process more efficient and effective. Rather than tackling the problems themselves from the top down, they created employee project teams, a move that made sense given the fact that these employees worked day in and day out with the production processes. The project teams' assignments were to find specific ways to improve operational efficiency and to implement those ideas.

One of the major responsibilities of the teams was applying statistically designed experiments to gather information and test various production factors. For instance, one team tested 13 production factors using 32 different experiments—a process that took two months to complete. How successful were the project teams? Almost $972 000 was trimmed from annual costs and another $982 500 one-time capital purchase was avoided—a total saving of almost $2 million.

What factors contributed to the employee teams' successes? One factor that the teams said was critical was management commitment and faith in the effort. Many process improvement efforts fail because they lack such support. These teams had their managers' support. Another factor was the training the teams received. In this situation, employee teams were trained to use statistical tools so they could apply them correctly and effectively. Training was provided by outside experts who also assisted the teams throughout the process. Finally, the managers believed that their decision to use a bottom-up approach was valuable because it involved everyone in the search for possible solutions.

Why were the BASF teams successful? What could be done to increase their success?

DEVELOPING YOUR DIAGNOSTIC AND ANALYTICAL SKILLS

Team Ferrari

Imagine working for an organization that employs more than 2000 individuals with each one having the identical focus. Imagine, too, that company management in this organization only wants you to work so hard while still being the best at what you do. If you are employed by Ferrari, these elements are not hard to imagine.[42]

Luca Cordero, president and managing director of Ferrari, believes that his employees truly make a difference in producing one of the world's greatest sports cars. Cordero recognizes that to be the best, he needs employees who understand how to work together and how to achieve common goals. That is because at Ferrari there are no assembly lines. Rather, teams of employees combine their efforts to produce an outstanding automobile that represents one of the highest quality in the automobile industry. You simply will not find traditional assembly lines in the Ferrari factory, nor will you find production quotas. Auto assembly time is not measured in seconds—rather, team tasks often last more than 90 minutes for each portion of a car. Then the team proudly takes its finished work on to the next team so its work can begin. Management of the company wants no more than 4000 Ferraris produced in any one year, even though the company could sell considerably more.

Employees at Ferrari truly enjoy being part of a team. They cite the fact that working toward a common direction is one of the most satisfying elements in their job. They also appreciate what management does for them. They are offered a state-of-the-art fitness centre, annual physicals at the company's on-site clinic, an employee cafeteria, and home-based training for employees to learn English. They feel as if Cordero and his team treat them as associates, not just as cogs in the Ferrari wheel. As one Ferrari employee stated: For many of us, "working for Ferrari is like working in the Vatican."

Is the team concept at Ferrari working? By all accounts it is. The company recently celebrated its first $1-billion year of sales, which resulted in more than $60 million in profits. Profits over the past several years continue to rise, and more importantly for Ferrari's management, there is more than a two-year waiting list for most Ferrari models.

Questions

1. Why do you believe the team concept at Ferrari works so well? Cite specific examples to support your position.

2. Do you believe such a system could be replicated in other automotive manufacturers? If so, in what kind of organizations? If not, why not?

3. Using the characteristics of a high-performing work team (refer to Exhibit 10-3), describe each of the nine elements as they relate to this case. Use examples when appropriate. If a characteristic was not specifically cited in the case, describe how it might have been part of this situation.

Creating Effective Teams

About the Skill

A team is different from a group because its members are committed to a common purpose, have a set of specific performance goals, and hold themselves mutually accountable for the team's results. Teams can produce outputs that are greater than the sum of the individual contributions of its members. The primary force that makes a work group an effective team—that is, a real high-performing team—is its emphasis on performance.

Steps in Developing the Skill

Managers and team leaders have a significant impact on a team's effectiveness. You can be more successful at creating an effective team if you use the following nine suggestions:[43]

1. **Establish a common purpose.** An effective team needs a common purpose to which all members aspire. This purpose is a vision. It's broader than any specific goals. This common purpose provides direction, momentum, and commitment for team members.

2. **Assess team strengths and weaknesses.** Team members will have different strengths and weaknesses. Knowing these strengths and weaknesses can help the team leader build upon the strengths and compensate for the weaknesses.

3. **Develop specific individual goals.** Specific individual goals help lead team members to achieve higher performance. In addition, specific goals facilitate clear communication and help maintain the focus on getting results.

4. **Get agreement on a common approach for achieving goals.** Goals are the ends a team strives to attain. Defining and agreeing on a common approach ensures the team's unity regarding the means for achieving those ends.

5. **Encourage acceptance of responsibility for both individual and team performance.** Successful teams make members individually and jointly accountable for the team's purpose, goals, and approach. Members understand what they are individually responsible for and what they are jointly responsible for.

6. **Build mutual trust among members.** When there is trust, team members believe in the integrity, character, and ability of each other. When trust is lacking, members are unable to depend on each other. Teams that lack trust tend to be short-lived.

7. **Maintain an appropriate mix of team member skills and personalities.** Team members come to the team with different skills and personalities. To perform effectively, teams need three types of skills. First, teams need people with technical expertise. Next, they need people with problem-solving and decision-making skills to identify problems, generate alternatives, evaluate those alternatives, and make competent choices. Finally, teams need people with good interpersonal skills.

8. **Provide needed training and resources.** Team leaders need to make sure that their teams have both the training and the resources they need to accomplish their goals.

9. **Create opportunities for small achievements.** Building an effective team takes time. Team members have to learn to think and work as a team. New teams cannot be expected to hit home runs every time they come to bat, especially at the beginning. Instead, team members should be encouraged to try for small achievements at the beginning.

Practising the Skill

You are the leader of a five-member project team that has been assigned the task of moving your engineering firm into the new booming area of high-speed rail construction. You and your team members have been researching the field, identifying specific business opportunities, negotiating alliances with equipment vendors, and evaluating high-speed rail experts and consultants from around the world. Throughout the process, Tonya, a highly qualified and respected engineer, has challenged everything you say during team meetings and in the workplace. For example, at a meeting two weeks ago, you presented the team with a list of 10 possible high-speed rail projects that had been identified by the team and started evaluating your organization's ability to compete for them. Tonya contradicted virtually all your comments, questioned your statistics, and was quite pessimistic about the possibility of contracts. After this latest display of displeasure, two other group members, Liam and Ahmed, came to you and complained that Tonya's actions were damaging the team's effectiveness. You originally put Tonya on the team for her unique expertise and insight. What should you say to Tonya, and how can you help get the team on the right track to reach its full potential?

The Challenge of Managing Diverse Teams

Understanding and managing teams composed of people who are similar can be difficult! Add in diverse members and managing teams can be even more of a challenge. However, the benefits to be gained from the diverse perspectives, skills, and abilities often more than offset the extra effort.[44] How can you meet the challenge of coordinating a diverse work team? It's important to stress four critical interpersonal behaviours: understanding, empathy, tolerance, and communication.

You know that people are not the same, yet they need to be treated fairly and equitably. And differences (cultural, physical, or other) can cause people to behave in different ways. Team leaders need to understand and accept these differences. Each and every team member should be encouraged to do the same.

Empathy is closely related to understanding. As a team leader, you should try to understand others' perspectives.

Tolerance is another important interpersonal behaviour in managing diverse teams. The fact that you understand that people are different and you empathize with them does not mean that it's any easier to accept different perspectives or behaviours. But it's important to be tolerant in dealing with diverse ages, gender, and cultural backgrounds—to allow team members the freedom to be themselves. Part of being tolerant is being open-minded about different values, attitudes, and behaviours.

Finally, open communication is important to managing a diverse team. Diversity problems may intensify if people are afraid or unwilling to openly discuss issues that concern them. Communication within a diverse team needs to be two-way. If a person wants to know whether a certain behaviour is offensive to someone else, it's best to ask. Likewise, a person who is offended by a certain behaviour of someone else should explain his or her concerns and ask that person to stop. As long as these communication exchanges are handled in a nonthreatening, low-key, and friendly manner, they generally will have positive outcomes. Finally, it helps to have an atmosphere within the team that supports and celebrates diversity.

Put yourself in the place of an Asian woman who has joined a team of Caucasian and Hispanic men. How can you be made to feel more welcome and comfortable with the team? As the Asian woman, what could you do to help the team get along well together and also help your transition to the team?

CoolBrands D: Leadership and Motivation Challenges

Shortly after Michael and Aaron Serruya opened their first Yogen Früz store in the Promenade Mall in Thornhill, Ontario, they realized they had hit upon a great retail idea. Customers were flocking to buy frozen yogurt from them, and suggesting other locations where stores could be opened. "The numbers were three, four times greater than we had anticipated," said Michael.

While the Serruya brothers recognized the opportunities that selling frozen yogurt presented, they also knew that their ages would make it difficult for them to raise the capital they would need to expand. They were also besieged with requests from would-be entrepreneurs, wanting to buy a Yogen Früz franchise. They decided that franchises made the most sense for their company. They also decided they needed another manager, and brother Simon joined the leadership team. Both family ties and managing franchisees present challenges, as the brothers soon found out.

Brothers and Managers

There were three Serruya brothers involved in running CoolBrands, the name the Yogen Früz company took after acquiring US-based Integrated Brands in 1998.

Michael, a co-founder, has been active in the business since its start in 1986. He is the president and CEO of the company. In that role, he develops business plans and supervises the day-to-day operations at head office. He was a 21-year-old graphics arts student at Ryerson in Toronto when he came up with the idea of starting the company.

Aaron, also a co-founder, has been active in the business since its start. He is executive vice-president, and his areas of responsibility include all new franchises and resale, finding new locations, and research and development. He was 19 when the company started.

Simon did not join the company until 1989, at the age of 18. He started as director of operations, and later took on the title of executive vice-president. He oversees company operations, including training, construction, and promotional activities.

The brothers participate in leadership as a team. However, it's now late 2000, and the brothers recognize that one of the challenges of running Yogen Früz is managing the roles of leader/manager with that of brother. The brothers wonder if having an outside "objective" manager to whom they all report might be a better idea for running their business. Currently, Aaron and Simon report to Michael, the oldest brother. All three are fully aware that the McCain brothers ended up not speaking to each other in their later years.

The Challenges of Franchising

There are two definitions of franchising: one legal, one business. From a legal perspective, an entity is a franchise if it licenses a trademark, receives substantial assistance with the business's operations from head office, and pays a franchise fee.

According to Washington, DC, franchise attorney Andrew A. Caffey, "The business definition is, in many ways, a more important and accurate description. The business definition is a continuing, almost symbiotic, relationship between a franchisor, who owns intellectual property and know-how, and a franchisee, who invests money in developing a business using that intellectual property and experience. The franchisee can use a proven program and thereby reduce risk when opening a business. In exchange, the franchisee pays the franchisor a [franchise fee and] royalty."

CoolBrands franchises and licenses retail frozen dessert outlets under the names Yogen Früz, Swensen's, I Can't Believe It's Yogurt, Bresler's, Golden Swirl, and Ice Cream Churn. In 2000, Yogen Früz was the number one frozen yogurt brand in Canada, and had 250 outlets, covering almost every mall and shopping centre in the country. There are also 4900 franchised retail outlets of its different brands in 81 other countries throughout the world.

In order to manage its brand, CoolBrands engages in three types of agreements:

- *Master franchises.* These are sold to individuals who manage specific regions, countries, or other geographical areas. The master franchisee can then sell franchises or grant licences in his or her territory.

- *Retail franchises.* These are sold to individuals who manage larger locations (traditional stores or kiosks) that offer a full range of products.
- *Licensing arrangements.* These are made for smaller locations using mini-counters or carts that are located, generally, on the premises of strategic partners (such as Pizza Hut) and offer a limited selection of products.

Master franchisees and franchisees are chosen because of their financial resources, operational skills, and business experience. Representatives of CoolBrands visit franchise sites from time to time. Master franchisees are required to visit all the sites in their franchise areas on a regular basis.

One of the difficulties with being a franchise owner (for any company) is that the franchise owner invests significant amounts of money (for a Yogen Früz site, the investment is about $100 000), and yet the owner still reports to a company manager, who could terminate the contract if the manager feels that standards are not being met. "Franchising is for the person who wants to be his or her own boss, but at the same time needs to be guided," says Aaron. "If you want to reinvent the wheel, go do that. But if you want to follow what's working, buy a franchise." Still, it is costly for CoolBrands to shut down a store if a franchisee does not work out.

The Decision

What advice would you give to the Serruya brothers about managing their distinct business and family roles? How might the brothers train franchisees and develop relationships with them so that the Yogen Früz brand stays consistent with the brothers' vision? What options should they consider for managing the franchisees?

Sources: CoolBrands International, "Annual Information Form," January 16, 2001; S. Kirshner, "Frozen Yogurt Kings Bask in Their Success," *Canadian Jewish News,* August 2, 2001, p. 40; L. Tiffany, "Breaking the Mold," *Business Start-Ups,* April 1999, http://www.entrepreneur.com/mag/article/0,1539,230062,00.html (accessed November 14, 2004).

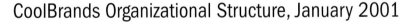

Exhibit 1

CoolBrands Organizational Structure, January 2001

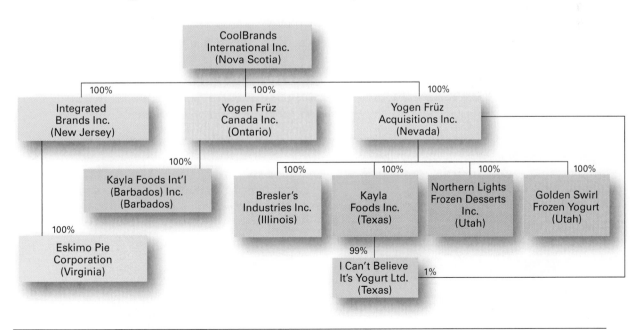

Source: CoolBrands International, "Annual Information Form," January 16, 2001.

Foundations of Control

How do I evaluate the effectiveness of my plans?

1 What is control?

2 How does organizational culture provide control?

3 How do managers engage in control?

4 What tools can be used to monitor and measure performance?

5 What are some current issues in control?

When Li Ka-shing first invested in Calgary-based Husky Oil (now Husky Energy) in 1986, buying 52 percent of its shares, the company had just posted its first year-end loss in the company's history.[1]

The company had no cash on hand, shares had dropped to half of their 1981 value, and the company's debt was growing. Bob Blair, then the CEO at Husky, turned to Li. "We required a lot of capital, more than Husky could generate from its own cash flow," says Blair, in explaining why he approached his friend Li, a wealthy Hong Kong businessman, to invest in the company. In 1991, Li and his holding company bought 43 percent more of the company.

After the 1991 investment, Li immediately sent John Chin-Sung Lau (at right) to Calgary to turn the company around. Li wanted to halt the company's large losses and the "wild expansions" of Husky's previous management. Appointed vice-president at the time, Lau had difficulty working with Husky president Art Price. Lau found Price "a hopeless free-spender," just trying to maintain his position as president.

Lau had a difficult task in front of him to make Husky profitable.

THINK ABOUT IT

What is organizational control? Put yourself in John Lau's shoes. How can he use control to make Husky successful? What did he need to do to turn Husky Energy into one of Canada's largest oil and gas enterprises?

In today's competitive global marketplace, managers want their organizations to achieve high levels of performance, and one way they can do that is by searching out the best practices successful organizations are using. By comparing themselves with the best, managers look for specific performance gaps and areas for improvement—areas where better controls over the work being done are needed. Managers can monitor performance throughout the duration of an activity, or use tools such as financial measures or information controls to evaluate performance after an activity is done.

As we will see in this chapter, John Lau understands the importance of management controls. No matter how thorough the planning, a decision still may be poorly implemented without a satisfactory control system in place. This chapter describes controls for monitoring and measuring performance. It also looks at how to create a well-designed organizational control system.

Husky Energy
www.huskyenergy.ca

WHAT IS CONTROL?

1 What is control?

Both the viewing public and NASA officials were devastated by the tragic *Columbia* space shuttle disaster in February 2003. Investigations of the tragedy suggest that organizational safety controls may not have been as thorough as they should have been.[2] When problems were spotted, managers might have been too quick to dismiss them as non-life-threatening, and in this situation that choice might have led to disastrous consequences. Although most managers won't face such tragic consequences if they ignore signs that something may be wrong, this example does point out the importance of control.

control
The process of monitoring activities to ensure that they are being accomplished as planned, and correcting any significant deviations.

What is **control**? It's the process of monitoring activities to ensure that they are being accomplished as planned, and correcting any significant deviations. All managers should be involved in the control function even if their units are performing as planned. Managers cannot really know whether their units are performing properly until they have evaluated what activities have been done and have compared the actual performance with the desired standard.[3] An effective control system ensures that activities are completed in ways that lead to the attainment of the organization's goals. The criterion that determines the effectiveness of a control system is how well it facilitates goal achievement. The more it helps managers achieve their organization's goals, the better the control system.[4]

Concord, Ontario-based Coldmatic Products International manufactures some of the world's biggest brands in refrigerators. To achieve this success, CEO George Zafir focuses on control: "Control your costs, control your quality, control your service. The result should be substantial control of the market." Controlling costs has been a particular emphasis for Zafir, which explains why he owns all of his manufacturing facilities. "If you rent, you are in the hands of your landlord," he says. "If we own our real estate, we have a much better control of this major area of cost."[5]

Why Is Control Important?

Planning can be done, an organizational structure can be created to efficiently facilitate the achievement of goals, and employees can be motivated through effective leadership. Still, there is no assurance that activities are going as planned and that the goals managers are seeking are, in fact, being attained. Control is important, therefore, because it's the final link in the four management functions. It's the only way managers know whether organizational goals are being met and, if not, the reasons why. The value of the control function lies in its relation to planning, empowering employees, and protecting the organization and workplace.

How can control help a team perform better on a course project?

In Chapter 3, we described goals as the foundation of planning. Goals give specific direction to managers. However, just stating goals or having employees accept your goals is no guarantee that the necessary actions to accomplish those goals have been taken. As the old saying goes, "The best-laid plans often go awry." The effective manager needs to follow up to ensure that what others are supposed to do is, in fact, being done and that their goals are in fact being achieved. In reality, managing is an ongoing process, and controlling provides the critical link to planning (see Exhibit 11-1). If managers did not control, they would have no way of knowing whether their goals and plans were on target and what future actions to take.

Another reason control is important is employee empowerment. Many managers are reluctant to empower their employees because they fear employees will do something wrong for which the manager will be held responsible. Thus, many managers are tempted to do things themselves and avoid empowering. This reluctance, however, can be reduced if managers develop an effective control system that provides information and feedback on employee performance.

The final reason that managers control is to protect the organization and the physical workplace.[6] Given today's environment with heightened security alerts and surprise financial scandals, managers must have plans in place to protect the organization's employees, data, and infrastructure.

Exhibit 11-1

The Planning-Controlling Link

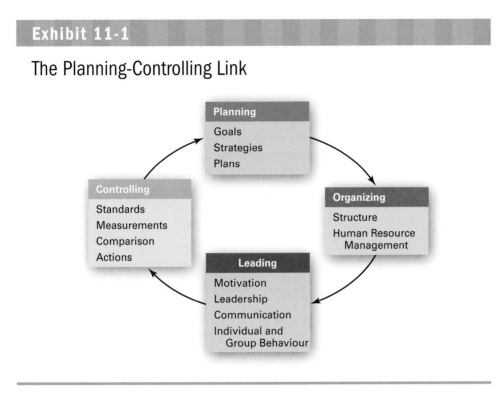

Types of Control Systems

Ideally, every organization would like to efficiently and effectively reach its goals. Does this mean that the control systems organizations use are identical? In other words, would Matsushita, Husky Energy, and WestJet Airlines have the same types of control systems? Probably not. There are generally three approaches to designing control systems: market, bureaucratic, and clan controls.[7] (See Exhibit 11-2.)

Market control is an approach to control that emphasizes the use of external market mechanisms, such as price competition and relative market share, to establish the standards used in the control system. Organizations that use the market control approach often have divisions that are set up as profit centres and evaluated according to the percentage of total corporate profits contributed. For instance, at Japan's Matsushita, which supplies a wide range of products throughout the world, the various divisions (audiovisual and communication networks, components and devices, home appliances, and industrial equipment) are evaluated according to the profits each generates.

market control
An approach to control that emphasizes the use of external market mechanisms, such as price competition and relative market share, to establish the standards used in the control system.

Exhibit 11-2

Characteristics of Three Approaches to Designing Control Systems

Type of Control	Characteristics
Market	Uses external market mechanisms, such as price competition and relative market share, to establish standards used in system. Typically used by organizations whose products or services are clearly specified and distinct and that face considerable marketplace competition.
Bureaucratic	Emphasizes organizational authority. Relies on administrative and hierarchical mechanisms, such as rules, regulations, procedures, policies, standardization of activities, well-defined job descriptions, and budgets to ensure that employees exhibit appropriate behaviours and meet performance standards.
Clan	Regulates employee behaviour by the shared values, norms, traditions, rituals, beliefs, and other aspects of the organization's culture. Often used by organizations in which teams are common and technology is changing rapidly.

bureaucratic control
An approach to control that emphasizes organizational authority and relies on administrative rules, regulations, procedures, and policies.

clan control
An approach to control in which employee behaviour is regulated by the shared values, norms, traditions, rituals, beliefs, and other aspects of the organization's culture.

Another approach to control is **bureaucratic control**, which emphasizes organizational authority and relies on administrative rules, regulations, procedures, and policies. Husky Energy provides a good example of bureaucratic control. Although managers at Husky's various divisions are allowed some freedom to run their units as they see fit, they are expected to adhere closely to their budgets and stay within corporate guidelines.

Clan control is an approach to control in which employee behaviours are regulated by the shared values, norms, traditions, rituals, beliefs, and other aspects of the organization's culture. While market control relies on external standards and bureaucratic control is based on strict hierarchical mechanisms, clan control is dependent on the individuals and the groups in the organization (the clan) to identify appropriate and expected behaviours and performance measures. For instance, at Calgary-based WestJet Airlines, individuals are well aware of the expectations regarding appropriate work behaviour and performance standards, as the following *Management Reflection* shows.

MANAGEMENT REFLECTION

WestJet Airlines' Employees Control Costs

Can employees be encouraged to think just like owners?   WestJet Airlines' CEO, Clive Beddoe, encourages his employees to keep costs low.[8] The airline has a much better profit margin than Air Canada and its other rivals. Beddoe introduced a generous profit-sharing plan to ensure that employees felt personally responsible for the profitability of the airline. The company's accountants insist that profit-sharing turns employees into "cost cops" looking for waste and savings. "We are one of the few companies that has to justify [to employees] its Christmas party every year," Derek Payne, vice-president of finance and corporate services, boasts ruefully.

WestJet encourages teamwork and gives employees a lot of freedom to determine and carry out their day-to-day duties. There are no rigid job descriptions for positions, and employees are required to help with all tasks. Sometimes pilots are recruited to load baggage. When a plane reaches its destination, all employees onboard, even those not working the flight, are expected to prepare the plane for its next takeoff. The company saves $2.5 million annually in cleaning costs by having everyone work together. Planes get turned around much more quickly as well, usually within about a half-hour. When necessary, though, the employees have been able to do it in as little as six minutes. WestJet's profit-sharing program encourages employees to do their best because they see a clear link between their performance, the profits of the company, and their rewards. Not all companies that have profit-sharing programs provide employees with such clear links between behaviour and performance. ■

Most organizations don't rely totally on just one of these approaches to design an appropriate control system. Instead, they choose to emphasize either bureaucratic or clan control, and then add some market control measures. The key is to design an appropriate control system that helps the organization efficiently and effectively reach its goals. Below we discuss how the development of a strong organizational culture leads to more effective clan control.

CLAN CONTROL: UNDERSTANDING HOW ORGANIZATIONAL CULTURE WORKS

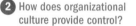 **How does organizational culture provide control?**

We consider clan culture in more detail than the other types of control systems because it provides control that is both more flexible and more enduring than either market or bureaucratic control. As we mentioned earlier, clan control is regulated by organizational culture. When employees are guided by a strong set of organizational values and norms, they can be empowered to make decisions that will benefit the organization in the long run.

Organizational culture is a system of shared meaning and beliefs held by organizational members that determines, in large degree, how they act toward each other and outsiders. It represents a common perception held by an organization's members that influences how they behave. In every organization, there are values, symbols, rituals, myths, and practices that have evolved over time.[9] These shared values and experiences determine, in large degree, what employees perceive and how they respond to their world.[10] When faced with problems or issues, the organizational culture—the "way we do things around here"—influences what employees can do and how they conceptualize, define, analyze, and resolve issues.

Our definition of organizational culture implies three things:

> *How does the culture of your college or university differ from that of your high school?*

- Culture is a *perception*. Individuals perceive the organizational culture on the basis of what they see, hear, or experience within the organization.

- Culture is *shared*. Even though individuals may have different backgrounds or work at different organizational levels, they tend to describe the organization's culture in similar terms.

- Culture is a *descriptive* term. It's concerned with how members perceive the organization, not with whether they like it. It describes rather than evaluates.

Research suggests that there are seven dimensions that capture the essence of an organization's culture.[11] These dimensions are described in Exhibit 11-3. Each dimension ranges from low (it's not very typical of the culture) to high (it's very typical of the culture). Appraising an organization on these seven dimensions gives a composite picture of the organization's culture. In many organizations, one of these cultural dimensions often is

organizational culture
A system of shared meaning and beliefs held by organizational members that determines, in large degree, how employees act.

Exhibit 11-3

Dimensions of Organizational Culture

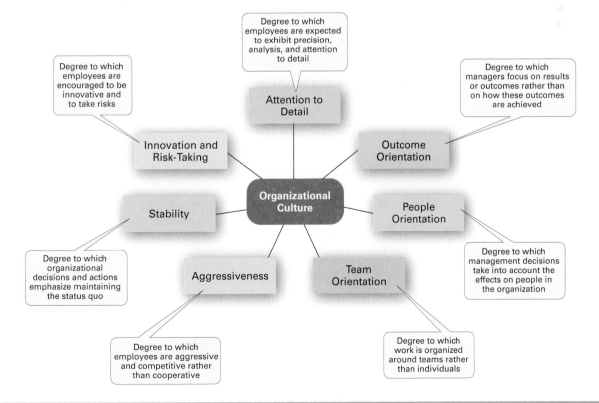

emphasized more than the others and essentially shapes the organization's personality and the way organizational members work. For instance, at Sony Corporation the focus is on product innovation. The company "lives and breathes" new-product development (outcome orientation), and employees' work decisions, behaviours, and actions support that goal. In contrast, WestJet Airlines has made its employees a central part of its culture (people orientation). However, its recent admission of engaging in corporate espionage against Air Canada may cause employees to question WestJet's corporate values.

Strong vs. Weak Cultures

strong cultures
Organizations in which the key values are deeply held and widely shared.

Although all organizations have cultures, not all cultures have an equal impact on employees' behaviours and actions. **Strong cultures**—cultures in which the key values are deeply held and widely shared—have a greater influence on employees than do weak cultures. The more employees accept the organization's key values and the greater their commitment to those values, the stronger the culture is.

Whether an organization's culture is strong, weak, or somewhere in between depends on factors such as the size of the organization, how long it has been around, how much turnover there has been among employees, and the intensity with which the culture started.

Some organizations do not make clear what is important and what is not, and this lack of clarity is a characteristic of weak cultures. In such organizations, culture is unlikely to greatly influence managers. Most organizations, however, have moderate to strong cultures. There is relatively high agreement on what is important, what defines "good" employee behaviour, what it takes to get ahead, and so forth. *Tips for Managers—Creating a More Ethical Culture* provides some suggestions for managers who want to build and maintain a more ethical culture in the workplace.

A growing body of evidence suggests that strong cultures are associated with high organizational performance.[12] It's easy to understand why a strong culture enhances performance. After all, when values are clear and widely accepted, employees know what they are supposed to do and what is expected of them, so they can act quickly to take care of problems, thus preventing any potential performance decline. However, the drawback is that the same strong culture also might prevent employees from trying new approaches, especially during periods of rapid change.[13] Strong cultures do not always yield *positive* results, however.[14] Enron had a very strong, and unethical, culture. This enabled employees and top management to engage in unethical behaviour that was concealed from public scrutiny.

Developing an Organization's Culture

Exhibit 11-4 summarizes how an organization's culture is established and maintained. The original culture is derived from the founders' philosophy. This, in turn, strongly influences the selection criteria used to hire new employees. The actions of the current top

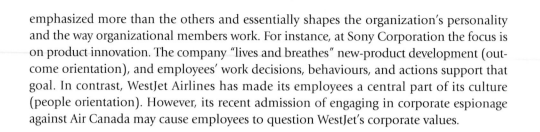

Exhibit 11-4

How an Organization's Culture Is Established and Maintained

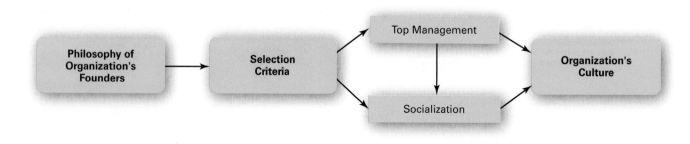

Taking its cue from the television show *Survivor*, Osaka, Japan-based noodle-maker Nissin Foods sent new managers on a wilderness survival trip recently. On a remote island, "managers had to dig toilets, make fire from dry leaves, catch fish ... make their own chopsticks out of bamboo." Company spokesman Masanaga Oguchi noted that the managers "would appreciate our product in a situation where they have to go through a lot of trouble just to make hot water." The socialization into management through the survival trip taught the new managers to work together as a team and introduced them to customers' needs.[15]

managers set the general expectations as to what is acceptable behaviour and what is not. Through the socialization process, new employees learn the organization's way of doing things. If socialization is successful, new employees will learn the values of the organization and behave accordingly, and the organization's culture will be preserved.

How Employees Learn Culture

Culture is transmitted to employees in a number of ways. The most significant are stories, rituals, material symbols, and language.

Stories

An organization's "stories" typically are related to significant people or events, such as the organization's founders, rule breaking, reactions to past mistakes, and so forth.[16] They help employees learn the culture by anchoring the present in the past, providing explanations and legitimacy for current practices, and showing what is important to the organization.[17]

Rituals

An organization's rituals are repetitive sequences of activities that express and reinforce the values of the organization, the goals that are most important, and the people who are most important.[18] One well-known ritual is Wal-Mart's company chant that employees say at the beginning of each workday.

Material Symbols

An organization's material symbols convey to employees who is important, the degree of equality desired by top management, and the kinds of behaviour (for example, risk-taking, conservative, authoritarian, participative, individualistic, and so forth) that are expected and appropriate. The layout of an organization's facilities, how employees dress, the types of automobiles provided to top executives, and the availability of corporate aircraft are examples of material symbols.

TIPS FOR MANAGERS

Creating a More Ethical Culture

→ Be a **visible role model**.

→ Communicate **ethical expectations**.

→ Provide **ethics training**.

→ Visibly **reward ethical acts and punish unethical ones**.

→ Provide **protective mechanisms** so employees can discuss ethical dilemmas and report unethical behaviour without fear.

Exhibit 11-5

Managerial Decisions Affected by Organizational Culture

Planning
- The degree of risk that plans should contain
- Whether plans should be developed by individuals or teams
- The degree of environmental scanning in which management will engage

Organizing
- How much autonomy should be designed into employees' jobs
- Whether tasks should be done by individuals or in teams
- The degree to which department managers interact with each other

Leading
- The degree to which managers are concerned with increasing employee job satisfaction
- What leadership styles are appropriate
- Whether all disagreements—even constructive ones—should be eliminated

Controlling
- Whether to impose external controls or to allow employees to control their own actions
- What criteria should be emphasized in employee performance evaluations
- What repercussions will result from exceeding one's budget

Language

Many organizations and units within organizations use language as a way to identify members of a culture. By learning this language, members attest to their acceptance of the culture and their willingness to help preserve it. New employees are frequently overwhelmed with acronyms and jargon that, after a short period of time, become a natural part of their language. Once learned, this language acts as a common denominator that unites members of a given culture. *Managing Workforce Diversity—Diversity Success Stories* on page 340 discusses companies that have integrated employees from different cultures into the workplace.

How Culture Affects Managers

Q&A 2.8

An organization's culture does more than influence employee behaviour; it also constrains a manager's decision-making options in all management functions. Exhibit 11-5 shows the major areas of a manager's job that are affected by the culture in which he or she operates.

THE CONTROL PROCESS

Everyone seems to agree that John Lau, now president and CEO of Husky Energy, is a difficult and demanding boss. He represents the Li family's interests in the company, and the Li family "favours a top-down, autocratic environment, crammed with checks and balances."[19] As one former executive of the company noted, "If you want to learn manufacturing cost control, unit cost measurement, they are great at it." Lau, trained as an accountant, brought to Husky the financial models that Li uses with his own companies to control costs and improve performance. Husky gets top shareholder returns as a result, but the company is viewed as tough on its employees.

THINK ABOUT IT

How do managers introduce controls? What impact might controls have on employees?

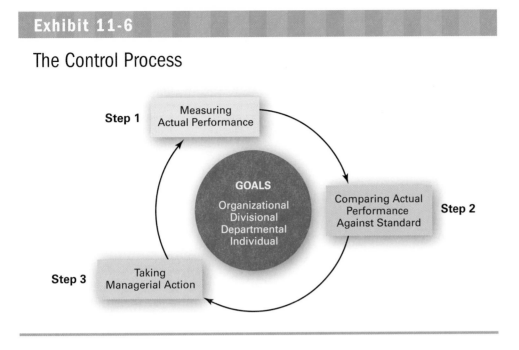

Exhibit 11-6

The Control Process

The **control process** is a three-step process: measuring actual performance, comparing actual performance against a standard, and taking managerial action to correct deviations or inadequate standards (see Exhibit 11-6). The control process assumes that performance standards already exist. These standards are the specific goals created during the planning process against which performance progress is measured. The control process for managers is similar to what you might do as a student at the beginning of the term: set goals for yourself for studying and marks, and then evaluate your performance after midterms, determining whether you have studied enough or need to study more in order to meet whatever goals you set for your marks. To learn more about how proactive you are, see *Self-Assessment—How Proactive Am I?* on page 336, at the end of the chapter.

3 How do managers engage in control?

control process
A three-step process that includes measuring actual performance, comparing actual performance against a standard, and taking managerial action to correct deviations or inadequate standards.

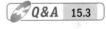 *Q&A* 15.3

Measuring Actual Performance

To determine what actual performance is, a manager must acquire information about it. The first step in control, then, is measuring. Let's consider how we measure and what we measure.

How We Measure

Four sources of information frequently used by managers to measure actual performance are personal observations, statistical reports, oral reports, and written reports. Exhibit 11-7 on page 316 summarizes the advantages and drawbacks of each approach. For most managers, using a combination of approaches increases both the number of input sources and the probability of getting reliable information.

What We Measure

What we measure is probably more critical to the control process than *how* we measure. Why? The selection of the wrong criteria can result in serious dysfunctional consequences. Besides, what we measure determines, to a great extent, what people in the organization will attempt to excel at.[20] For instance, if employees are evaluated by the number of big-ticket items they sell, they may not help customers who are looking for less expensive items.

Some control criteria are applicable to any management situation. For instance, because all managers, by definition, coordinate the work of others, criteria such as employee satisfaction or turnover and absenteeism rates can be measured. Most managers also have

 *Q&A* 15.4

Exhibit 11-7

Common Sources of Information for Measuring Performance

	Advantages	Drawbacks
Personal Observations (Management by Walking Around)	• Get firsthand knowledge • Information isn't filtered • Intensive coverage of work activities	• Subject to personal biases • Time-consuming • Can distract employees
Statistical Reports	• Easy to visualize • Effective for showing relationships	• Provide limited information • Ignore subjective factors
Oral Reports	• Fast way to get information • Allow for verbal and nonverbal feedback	• Information is filtered • Information cannot be documented
Written Reports	• Comprehensive • Formal • Easy to file and retrieve	• Take more time to prepare

budgets set in dollar costs for their areas of responsibility. Keeping costs within budget is, therefore, a fairly common control measure. However, any comprehensive control system needs to recognize the diversity of activities that managers do. For instance, a production manager at a paper-tablet manufacturer might use measures such as quantity of paper tablets produced per day and per labour-hour, scrap rate, and/or percentage of rejects returned by customers. On the other hand, the manager of an administrative unit in a government agency might use number of document pages typed per day, number of client requests processed per hour, and/or average time required to process paperwork. Marketing managers often use measures such as percentage of market held, average dollars per sale, number of customer visits per salesperson, and/or number of customer impressions per advertising medium.

Most jobs and activities can be expressed in tangible and measurable terms. However, when a performance indicator cannot be stated in quantifiable terms, managers should use subjective measures. Although subjective measures have significant limitations, they are better than having no standards at all and ignoring the control function. If an activity is important, the excuse that it's difficult to measure is unacceptable.

Comparing Actual Performance Against Standard

The comparing step determines the degree of variation between actual performance and the standard. Although some variation in performance can be expected in all activities, it's critical to determine the acceptable **range of variation** (see Exhibit 11-8). Deviations that exceed this range become significant and need the manager's attention. In the comparison stage, managers are particularly concerned with the size and direction of the variation. An example can help make this concept clearer.

range of variation
The acceptable degree of variation between actual performance and the standard.

Chris Tanner is sales manager for Beer Unlimited, a distributor of specialty beers in the Prairies. Chris prepares a report during the first week of each month that describes sales for the previous month, classified by brand name. Exhibit 11-9 displays both the sales goal (standard) and the actual sales figures for the month of July.

Should Chris be concerned about July's sales performance? Sales were a bit higher than originally targeted, but does that mean there were no significant deviations? Even though overall performance was generally quite favourable, several brands might need to be examined more closely by Chris. However, the number of brands that deserve attention depends

Exhibit 11-8

Defining the Acceptable Range of Variation

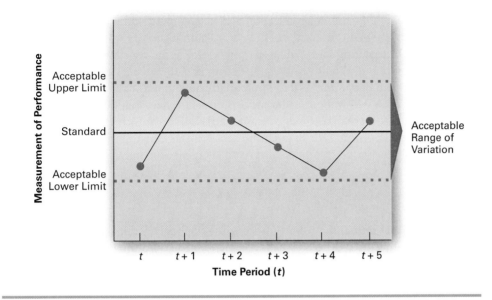

on what Chris believes to be *significant.* How much variation should Chris allow before taking corrective action?

The deviation on two brands (Maple Brown Ale and Full Moon) is very small and probably does not need special attention. On the other hand, are the shortages for Premium Lager, Blanche de Chambly, and Black Cat Lager brands significant? That's a judgment Chris

Exhibit 11-9

Sales Performance Figures for July, Beer Unlimited

Brand	Standard	(hundreds of cases) Actual	Over (Under)
Premium Lager (Okanagan Spring, Vernon, BC)	1075	913	(162)
India Pale Ale (Alexander Keith's, Halifax)	800	912	112
Maple Brown Ale (Upper Canada Brewery, Toronto)	620	622	2
Blanche de Chambly (Brasseries Unibroue, Quebec)	160	110	(50)
Full Moon (Alley Kat, Edmonton)	225	220	(5)
Black Cat Lager (Paddock Wood Brewing, Saskatoon, Saskatchewan)	80	65	(15)
Bison Blonde Lager (Agassiz, Winnipeg)	170	286	116
Total cases	**3130**	**3128**	**(2)**

must make. Premium Lager sales were 15 percent below Chris' goal. This deviation is significant and needs attention. Chris should look for a cause. In this instance, Chris attributes the decrease to aggressive advertising and promotion programs by the big domestic producers, Molson and Labatt's. Because Premium Lager is his company's number-one selling beer, it's most vulnerable to the promotion clout of the big domestic producers. If the decline in sales of Premium Lager is more than a temporary slump (that is, if it happens again next month), then Chris will need to cut back on inventory stock.

An error in understating sales can be as troublesome as an overstatement. For instance, is the surprising popularity of Bison Blonde Lager (up 68 percent) a one-month anomaly, or is this brand becoming more popular with customers? If the brand is increasing in popularity, Chris will want to order more product to meet that demand, so as not to run short and risk losing customers. Again, Chris will have to interpret the information and make a decision. Our Beer Unlimited example illustrates that both overvariance and undervariance in any comparison of measures may require managerial attention.

 **Q&A** 15.5

Taking Managerial Action

The third and final step in the control process is taking managerial action. Managers can choose among three possible courses of action: They can do nothing; they can correct the actual performance; or they can revise the standard. Because "doing nothing" is fairly self-explanatory, let's look more closely at the other two options.

Correcting Actual Performance

If the source of the performance variation is unsatisfactory work, the manager will want to take corrective action. Examples of such corrective action might include changing strategy, structure, compensation practices, or training programs; redesigning jobs; or firing employees.

A manager who decides to correct actual performance has to make another decision: Should immediate or basic corrective action be taken? **Immediate corrective action** corrects problems at once to get performance back on track. **Basic corrective action** looks at how and why performance has deviated and then proceeds to correct the source of deviation. It's not unusual for managers to rationalize that they don't have the time to take basic corrective action and therefore must be content to perpetually "put out fires" with immediate corrective action. Effective managers, however, analyze deviations and, when the benefits justify it, take the time to pinpoint and correct the causes of variance.

immediate corrective action
Corrective action that corrects problems at once to get performance back on track.

basic corrective action
Corrective action that looks at how and why performance deviated and then proceeds to correct the source of deviation.

To return to our Beer Unlimited example, taking immediate corrective action on the negative variance for Premium Lager, Chris might contact the company's retailers and have them immediately drop the price on Premium Lager by 5 percent. However, taking basic corrective action would require more in-depth analysis by Chris. After assessing how and why sales deviated, Chris might choose to increase in-store promotional efforts, increase the advertising budget for this brand, or reduce future purchases from the breweries. The action Chris takes will depend on the assessment of each brand's potential profitability.

Q&A 15.6

Revising the Standard

It's possible that the variance is the result of an unrealistic standard; that is, the goal may have been too high or too low. In such instances, it's the standard that needs corrective attention, not the performance. In our example, Chris might need to raise the sales goal (standard) for Bison Blonde Lager to reflect its growing popularity.

The more troublesome problem is revising a performance standard downward. If an employee, work team, or work unit falls significantly short of reaching its goal, their natural response is to shift the blame for the variance to the goal. For instance, students who make a low grade on a test often attack the grade cut-off standards as too high. Rather than accept the fact that their performance was inadequate, students argue that the standards are unreasonable. Similarly, salespeople who fail to meet their monthly quotas may attribute the failures to unrealistic quotas. It may be true that when a standard is too high, it can result in a significant variation and may even contribute to demotivating those employees being measured. But keep in mind that if employees or managers don't meet the standard, the first thing they are likely to attack is the standard. If you believe that the standard is realistic, fair, and achievable, hold your ground. Explain your position, reaffirm to the employee, team, or unit that you expect future performance to improve, and then take the necessary corrective action to turn that expectation into reality.

Summary of Managerial Decisions in the Control Process

Exhibit 11-10 summarizes the manager's decisions in the control process. Standards evolve out of goals that are developed during the planning process. These goals then provide the basis for the control process, which is essentially a continuous flow between measuring, comparing, and taking managerial action. Depending on the results of comparing, a manager's decision about what course of action to take might be to do nothing, revise the standard, or correct the performance.

Corrective action can take many forms. On the selling floor of Home Depot stores, where one contractor spent 20 minutes waiting for a Home Depot fork-lift operator to arrive so he could load some purchased drywall, the need to improve customer service led to changes in the composition of the workforce. CEO Bob Nardelli realized he had allowed stores to hire too many part-time employees, whose commitment to the job and knowledge about the do-it-yourself business sometimes lagged behind those of full-timers. So he scaled back from a 50-50 mix to a new balance of 40 percent part-time and 60 percent full-time employees and says customer service has since improved.

Exhibit 11-10

Managerial Decisions in the Control Process

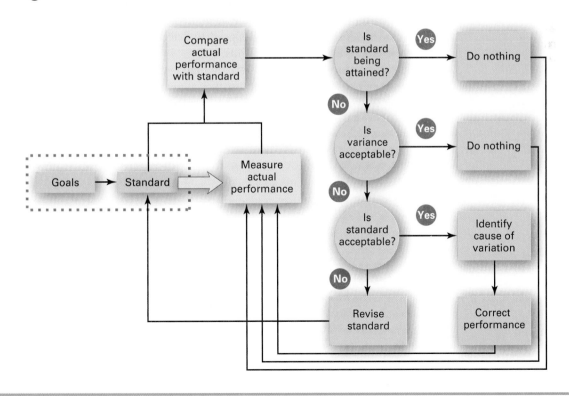

TOOLS FOR CONTROLLING ORGANIZATIONAL PERFORMANCE

④ What tools can be used to monitor and measure performance?

At Murata Manufacturing Company of Kyoto, Japan, managers know that performance will be measured against a challenging goal set by Yasutaka Murata, the company's president. That goal? Thirty percent of annual sales should come from new products. Since Murata manufactures components for information-age devices such as cellphones, personal digital assistants, and so forth, measures of new-product innovation are key indicators.[21]

As this example illustrates, managers need appropriate tools to monitor and measure organizational performance. Before we describe a few performance-specific monitoring and measuring tools managers might use, let's look at the control concepts of feedforward, concurrent, and feedback controls.

Feedforward, Concurrent, and Feedback Controls

Managers can implement controls *before* an activity begins, *during* the time the activity is going on, and *after* the activity has been completed. The first type is called *feedforward control*, the second is *concurrent control*, and the last is *feedback control* (see Exhibit 11-11).

Feedforward Control

feedforward control

A type of control that focuses on preventing anticipated problems, since it takes place before the actual activity.

The most desirable type of control—**feedforward control**—prevents anticipated problems since it takes place before the actual activity.[22] Let's look at some examples of feedforward control.

> *When working on a project, do you anticipate problems ahead of time or wait until they occur?*

When McDonald's Canada opened its first restaurant in Moscow, it sent company quality-control experts to help Russian farmers learn techniques for growing high-quality potatoes and bakers to learn processes for baking high-quality breads. Why? Because McDonald's strongly emphasizes product quality, no matter what the geographic location. It wants a cheeseburger in Moscow to taste like one in Winnipeg. Still another example of feedforward control is the scheduled preventive maintenance programs on aircraft done by airlines. These are designed to detect and, it is hoped, to prevent structural damage that might lead to accidents.

The key to feedforward control is taking managerial action *before* a problem occurs. Feedforward controls are desirable because they allow managers to prevent problems rather than having to correct them later after the damage (such as poor-quality products, lost

Exhibit 11-11

Types of Control

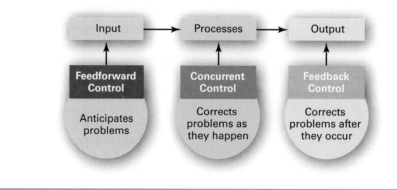

customers, and lost revenue) has already been done. Unfortunately, these controls require timely and accurate information that often is difficult to get. As a result, managers frequently end up using one of the other two types of controls.

Concurrent Control

Concurrent control, as its name implies, takes place while an activity is in progress. When control is enacted while the work is being performed, management can correct problems before they become too costly.

The best-known form of concurrent control is direct supervision. When managers use **management by walking around**, which is a term used to describe a manager being out in the work area, interacting directly with employees, they are using concurrent control. When a manager directly oversees the actions of employees, he or she can monitor their actions and correct problems as they occur. Although, obviously, there is some delay between the activity and the manager's corrective response, the delay is minimal. Problems usually can be addressed before much resource waste or damage has been done. Also, technical equipment (computers, computerized machine controls, and so forth) can be programmed for concurrent controls. For instance, you may have experienced concurrent control when using a computer program such as word-processing software that alerts you to misspelled words or incorrect grammatical usage as you type. In addition, many organizational quality programs rely on concurrent controls to inform employees if their work output is of sufficient quality to meet standards.

concurrent control
A type of control that takes place while an activity is in progress.

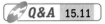 **Q&A 15.11**

management by walking around
A term used to describe a manager being out in the work area, interacting directly with employees.

Feedback Control

> *Have you used feedback with team members after completing a team project?*

The most popular type of control relies on feedback. In **feedback control**, the control takes place *after* the activity is done. For instance, when McDonald's executives learned that a suspected criminal ring had allegedly stolen millions of dollars in top prizes in their customer games, it was discovered through feedback control.[23] Even though the company took corrective action once it was discovered, the damage had already occurred.

feedback control
A type of control that takes place after a work activity is done.

As the McDonald's example shows, the major drawback of this type of control is that by the time the manager has the information, the problems have already occurred—leading to waste or damage. But for many activities, feedback is the only viable type of control available. For instance, financial statements are an example of feedback controls. If, for example, the income statement shows that sales revenues are declining, the decline has already occurred. So at this point, the manager's only option is to try to determine why sales have decreased and to correct the situation.

Feedback controls do have two advantages.[24] First, feedback provides managers with meaningful information on how effective their planning efforts were. Feedback that indicates little variance between standard and actual performance is evidence that the planning was generally on target. If the deviation is significant, a manager can use that information when formulating new plans to make them more effective. Second, feedback control can enhance employee motivation. People want information on how well they have performed and feedback control provides that information. However, managers should be aware that recent research suggests that while individuals raise their goals when they receive positive feedback, they lower their goals when they receive negative feedback.[25] To learn how to give feedback effectively, see *Developing Your Interpersonal Skills—Providing Feedback* on pages 339–340.

Financial Controls

One of the primary purposes of every business firm is to earn a profit. To achieve this goal, managers need financial controls. Managers might, for instance, carefully analyze quarterly income statements for excessive expenses. They might also perform several financial ratio tests to ensure that sufficient cash is available to pay ongoing expenses, that debt levels have not risen too high, or that assets are being used productively. Or they might look at some newer financial control tools such as EVA (economic value added) to see if the company is creating economic value.

Traditional Financial Control Measures

Q&A 15.12

Traditional financial control measures include ratio analysis and budget analysis. Exhibit 11-12 summarizes some of the most popular financial ratios used in organizations. Liquidity ratios measure an organization's ability to meet its current debt obligations. Leverage ratios examine the organization's use of debt to finance its assets and whether it's able to meet the interest payments on the debt. Activity ratios assess how efficiently the firm is using its assets. Finally, profitability ratios measure how efficiently and effectively the firm is using its assets to generate profits.

These ratios are calculated using information from the organization's two primary financial statements (the balance sheet and the income statement); they compare two figures and express them as a percentage or ratio. Because you have undoubtedly discussed these ratios in introductory accounting and finance courses, or you will in the near future, we are not going to elaborate on how they are calculated. Instead, we mention these ratios only briefly here to remind you that managers use such ratios as internal control devices for monitoring how efficiently and profitably the organization uses its assets, debt, inventories, and the like. One Husky Energy executive suggested that the Li family uses such strict financial controls that Husky is known to "peel beavers off nickels."[26]

Exhibit 11-12

Popular Financial Ratios

Objective	Ratio	Calculation	Meaning
Liquidity	Current ratio	$\dfrac{\text{Current assets}}{\text{Current liabilities}}$	Tests the organization's ability to meet short-term obligations
	Acid test	$\dfrac{\text{Current assets less inventories}}{\text{Current liabilities}}$	Tests liquidity more accurately when inventories turn over slowly or are difficult to sell
Leverage	Debt to assets	$\dfrac{\text{Total debt}}{\text{Total assets}}$	The higher the ratio, the more leveraged the organization
	Times interest earned	$\dfrac{\text{Profits before interest and taxes}}{\text{Total interest charges}}$	Measures how far profits can decline before the organization is unable to meet its interest expenses
Activity	Inventory turnover	$\dfrac{\text{Sales}}{\text{Inventory}}$	The higher the ratio, the more efficiently inventory assets are being used
	Total asset turnover	$\dfrac{\text{Sales}}{\text{Total assets}}$	The fewer assets used to achieve a given level of sales, the more efficiently management is using the organization's total assets
Profitability	Profit margin on sales	$\dfrac{\text{Net profit after taxes}}{\text{Total sales}}$	Identifies the profits that various products are generating
	Return on investment	$\dfrac{\text{Net profit after taxes}}{\text{Total assets}}$	Measures the efficiency of assets to generate profits

A budget is a planning tool because it gives direction to work activities. It indicates what activities are important and how much in resources should be allocated to each activity. But budgets are also used for controlling.

Budgets provide managers with quantitative standards against which to measure and compare resource consumption. By pointing out deviations between standard and actual consumption, they become control tools. If the deviations are judged significant enough to require action, the manager will want to examine what has happened and try to uncover the reasons behind the deviations. With this information, he or she can take whatever action is necessary. For example, if you use a personal budget for monitoring and controlling your monthly expenses, you might find one month that your miscellaneous expenses were higher than you had budgeted for. At that point, you might cut back spending in another area or work extra hours to try to get more income. The former BC NDP government did not consider the budget when it launched the building of three fast ferries during the 1990s, as the following *Management Reflection* shows.

MANAGEMENT REFLECTION

BC Ferries Go Seriously Overbudget

What happens when you don't create a budget? In 1994, when the BC NDP government set out to build three new fast ferries for travel between Vancouver and Vancouver Island, they did not put appropriate controls in place.[27] An independent audit done for the provincial government by accountant Hugh Gordon found that the project was "doomed from the start by unrealistic budgets and construction timetables and later hampered by efforts to pretend the ships were on schedule."

The project started without a final business plan, the designs for the ferries were not complete, and there was no final contract controlling costs with one of the primary builders. In addition, the project never stayed on deadline. In 1997, part of the first ferry was put together hurriedly to impress visiting Asia-Pacific Economic Cooperation (APEC) leaders. A year later, it was launched before it was ready.

The original board of directors for the project raised a number of serious questions about the project, even before it was started. Eventually, the directors, who had considerable business experience, were fired, and replaced by board members of BC Ferries.

When the fast-ferry project began, the three ferries were expected to cost $210 million. The final cost of the project was about $450 million, and only the first of the three ferries did much sailing between Vancouver and Vancouver Island. The third ferry was never used. Eventually all three ferries were auctioned off, for about one-third of their total cost. ∎

Other Financial Control Measures

In addition to the traditional financial tools, managers use measures such as EVA (economic value added) and MVA (market value added). The fundamental concept behind these financial tools is that companies are supposed to take in capital from investors and make it worth more. When managers do that, they have created wealth. When they take in capital and make it worth less, they have destroyed wealth.

Economic value added (EVA) is a tool that measures corporate and divisional performance. It's calculated by taking after-tax operating profit minus the total annual cost of capital.[28] EVA is a measure of how much economic value is being created by what a company does with its assets, less any capital investments the company has made in its assets. As a performance control tool, EVA focuses managers' attention on earning a rate of return over and above the cost of capital. About 30 percent of Canadian companies use EVA, including Montreal-based Alcan, Montreal-based Domtar, Markham, Ontario-based Robin Hood Multifoods, and Montreal-based cable company Cogeco.[29] When EVA is used as a performance

economic value added (EVA)
A financial tool that measures corporate and divisional performance, calculated by taking after-tax operating profit minus the total annual cost of capital.

measure, employees soon learn that they can improve their organization's or business unit's EVA by either using less capital (that is, figuring out how to spend less) or by investing capital in high-return projects (that is, projects that will bring in more money, with fewer expenses). Former Molson CEO Daniel O'Neill was well rewarded for EVA improvement to the company in 2002. He "closed several breweries, laid off hundreds of staff and slashed overhead costs, using the savings to modernize remaining breweries," all of which sent Molson shares soaring. O'Neill received a $2.4-million bonus for his efforts.[30]

market value added (MVA)
A financial tool that measures the stock market's estimate of the value of a firm's past and expected capital investment projects.

Market value added (MVA) adds a market dimension, since it is a tool that measures the stock market's estimate of the value of a firm's past and expected capital investment projects. If the company's market value (value of all outstanding stock plus company's debt) is greater than all the capital invested in it (from shareholders, bondholders, and retained earnings), it has a positive MVA, indicating that managers have created wealth. If the company's market value is less than all the capital invested in it, the MVA will be negative, indicating that managers have destroyed wealth. Studies have shown that EVA is a predictor of MVA and that consecutive years of positive EVA generally lead to a high MVA.[31]

Q&A 15.13

To understand that EVA and MVA measure different things, let's consider three companies that had the highest MVA in 2003 and the amount of wealth they created for their shareholders: General Electric ($292 billion), Microsoft ($277 billion), and Wal-Mart ($271 billion). While these three companies had relatively similar MVA, they had very different real profits (measured by EVA). General Electric had the highest EVA ($7.9 billion), followed by Wal-Mart ($3.8 billion), and then Microsoft ($2.9 billion). Wal-Mart, with a lower MVA than Microsoft, delivered a higher EVA.[32]

Balanced Scorecard

The balanced scorecard approach to performance measurement was introduced as a way to evaluate organizational performance from more than just the financial perspective.[33] The **balanced scorecard** is a performance measurement tool that looks at four areas—financial, customer, internal processes, and people/innovation/growth assets—that contribute to a company's performance. According to this approach, managers should develop goals in each of the four areas and measures to determine if these goals are being met. For instance, a company might include cash flow, quarterly sales growth, and return on investment (ROI) as measures of success in the financial area. Or it might include percentage of sales coming from new products as a measure of customer goals. The intent of the balanced scorecard is to emphasize that all of these areas are important to an organization's success and that there should be a balance among them.

balanced scorecard
A performance measurement tool that looks at four areas—financial, customer, internal processes, and people/innovation/growth assets—that contribute to a company's performance.

Although a balanced scorecard makes sense, unfortunately managers still tend to focus on areas that drive their organizations' success.[34] Their scorecards reflect their strategies. If those strategies centre on the customer, for example, then the customer area is likely to get more attention than the other three areas. Yet managers need to recognize that you really cannot focus on one performance area without considering the others. For instance, the Ontario Hospital Association developed a scorecard for 89 hospitals designed to evaluate four main areas: clinical use and outcomes, financial performance and financial condition of the hospital, patient satisfaction, and how the hospital was investing for the future. The scorecard was purposefully designed to recognize the synergies among each of these measures. After hospitals were evaluated on the scorecard measures, the results of the scorecard evaluations were made available to patients, giving them an objective basis for choosing a hospital.[35]

Q&A 15.14

 Ontario Hospital Association
www.oha.com

Information Controls

Information is critical to monitoring and measuring an organization's performance. Managers need the right information at the right time and in the right amount. Inaccurate, incomplete, excessive, or delayed information will seriously impede performance. How can managers use information for control?

Management Information Systems

Although there is no universally agreed-upon definition of a **management information system (MIS)**, we will define it as a system used to provide management with needed information on a regular basis. In theory, this system can be manual or computer-based, although all current discussions focus on computer-supported applications. The term *system* in MIS implies order, arrangement, and purpose. Further, an MIS focuses specifically on providing managers with *information*, not merely *data*. These two points are important and require elaboration.

A library provides a good analogy. Although it can contain millions of volumes, a library does not do users much good if they cannot find what they want quickly. That is why librarians spend a great deal of time cataloguing a library's collections and ensuring that materials are returned to their proper locations. Organizations today are like well-stocked libraries. There is no lack of data. There is, however, an inability to process that data so that the right information is available to the right person when he or she needs it. Likewise, a library is almost useless if it has the book you need immediately, but either you cannot find it or the library takes a week to retrieve it from storage. An MIS, on the other hand, has organized data in some meaningful way and can access the information in a reasonable amount of time. **Data** are raw, unanalyzed facts, such as numbers, names, or quantities. Raw unanalyzed facts are relatively useless to managers. When data are processed and analyzed, they become **information**. An MIS collects data and turns them into relevant information for managers to use.

DST Output prints and mails over 175 million customized billing statements a month for its corporate clients, so in addition to operating a vast array of high-speed printing and insertion equipment it must also manage a tidal wave of information. At the Data Control Center in El Dorado Hills (California), staff members rely on management information systems not only to monitor plant operations but also to receive massive streams of client data in virtually every format. Adding to the complexity of its operations, DST Output also allows its clients to split their data streams and send some customer statements through the mail and others over the Internet. "It is a finely orchestrated symphony of people, processes, and technology," says director of business operations Bob Logue.

management information system (MIS)
A system used to provide management with needed information on a regular basis.

data
Raw, unanalyzed facts.

information
Processed and analyzed data.

How Is Information Used in Controlling?

Managers need information to monitor organizational performance and to control organizational activities. Without information, they would find it difficult to measure, compare, and take action as part of the controlling process. For instance, to measure actual performance, managers need information about what is, in fact, happening within their area of responsibility and about what the standards are to be able to compare actual performance with the standards. Such information helps managers determine acceptable ranges of variation within these comparisons. Managers also rely on information to help them develop appropriate courses of action if there are or are not significant deviations between actual performance and the standards. Information can also be used to control costs, as the following *Management Reflection* shows.

MANAGEMENT REFLECTION

Air Canada Improves Maintenance Procedures

How can wireless technology make maintenance more efficient? Air Canada's former vice-president of IT and CIO Alice Keung found that maintenance costs at Air Canada were skyrocketing because line maintenance (unscheduled repairs to a plane's equipment, instruments, or body) was not handled very effectively.[36] In particular, pilots or mechanics would send a note to the Toronto maintenance facility by teletype or fax or put a note in the plane's log, noting a repair issue. Mechanics often would not get these notes, or the plane would arrive but the mechanic would not have the necessary parts to perform a quick maintenance procedure.

Keung realized that maintenance procedures could be significantly streamlined if mechanics had easy and immediate access to information about repairs that needed to be made, as well as maintenance manuals and diagrams. Mechanics were given tablet-sized display screens mounted on their trucks and connected to a wireless local area network. This made the information easily available, and the display was large enough to show maintenance diagrams when needed.

The technology significantly improved maintenance productivity. Mechanics spent less time travelling back and forth to the hangar to get additional parts, since they could determine what they needed more quickly. Mechanics could also make sure that parts were waiting when planes landed, so simple repairs could be performed without delaying flights. "That all has a bottom-line impact," Keung says. ■

Benchmarking of Best Practices

Managers in diverse industries from medical and educational to financial services and information technology are discovering the benefits of benchmarking. For instance, when the first Chrysler Sebring convertible rolled off the assembly line at DaimlerChrysler's assembly plant, the company was able to avoid $130 million in production costs because it was built using manufacturing best practices shared by Mercedes-Benz, Chrysler's German owner.[37]

We first introduced the concept of benchmarking in Chapter 3. Remember that **benchmarking** is the search for the best practices among competitors or noncompetitors that lead to their superior performance. The **benchmark** is the standard of excellence against which to measure and compare.[38] At its most fundamental level, benchmarking means learning from others.[39] As a tool for monitoring and measuring organizational performance, benchmarking can be used to help identify specific performance gaps and potential areas of improvement.[40] But managers should not look just at external organizations for best practices. It's also important for them to look inside their own organizations for best practices that can be shared.

benchmarking
The search for the best practices among competitors or non-competitors that lead to their superior performance.

benchmark
The standard of excellence against which to measure and compare.

 Q&A 15.15

To ensure the company is on track, Montreal-based BouClair, a home-decorating store, benchmarks everything against past performance and also against what other leading retailers are doing. "If a particular department or category is up 40 percent in sales over last year but we said we expected it to grow at 60 percent, then we are going to investigate and find out why," Gerry Goldberg, president and CEO, says.[41] "Then we look at our own same-store sales increases and compare them to the best companies out there. That's how we measure our efficiency and our productivity."

Did you ever work somewhere that had an employee suggestion box on a wall in an office or in the plant? When an employee had an idea about a new way of doing something—such as reducing costs, improving delivery time, and so forth—it went into the suggestion box where it usually sat until someone decided to empty the box. Businesspeople frequently joked about the suggestion box and cartoons have noted the futility of putting ideas in the employee suggestion box.

Unfortunately, this attitude about suggestion boxes still persists in many organizations, and it should not. Frequently research shows that best practices already exist within an organization but usually go unidentified

SYSCO is a food-services firm headquartered in Houston, Texas, that operates more than 161 subsidiary companies. A recent innovation developed by its human resource department is the Innovation Key Metrics Benchmark System, which provides executives at all SYSCO's regional offices with scorecards showing how well their company has performed against others in the SYSCO family. A database of its business practices also lets SYSCO executives look up subsidiary companies of similar size and learn about what has made them strong in particular areas. Visits to these benchmark firms are encouraged.

Exhibit 11-13

Steps to Successfully Implement an Internal Benchmarking Best-Practices Program

1. *Connect best practices to strategies and goals.* The organization's strategies and goals should dictate what types of best practices might be most valuable to others in the organization.

2. *Identify best practices throughout the organization.* Organizations must have a way to find out what practices have been successful in different work areas and units.

3. *Develop best-practices reward and recognition systems.* Individuals must be given an incentive to share their knowledge. The reward system should be built into the organization's culture.

4. *Communicate best practices throughout the organization.* Once best practices have been identified, that information needs to be shared with others in the organization.

5. *Create a best-practices knowledge-sharing system.* There needs to be a formal mechanism for organizational members to continue sharing their ideas and best practices.

6. *Nurture best practices on an ongoing basis.* Create an organizational culture that reinforces a "we can learn from everyone" attitude and emphasizes sharing information.

Source: Based on T. Leahy, "Extracting Diamonds in the Rough," *Business Finance*, August 2000, pp. 33–37.

and unused.[42] In today's environment, organizations striving for high performance levels cannot afford to ignore such potentially valuable information.

Some companies already have recognized the potential of internally benchmarking best practices as a tool for monitoring and measuring performance. For example, to improve diversity within the company, Saskatoon, Saskatchewan-based Yanke Group, a trucking company, is committed to hiring Aboriginal peoples and people with disabilities. Yanke reviews its employment equity benchmarks quarterly.[43] Toyota Motor Corporation developed a suggestion-screening system to prioritize best practices based on potential impact, benefits, and difficulty of implementation. General Motors sends employees—from upper management to line employees—to different plants where they learn about internal and external best practices.[44] Exhibit 11-13 provides a summary of what managers must do to implement an internal benchmarking best-practices program.

Yanke Group
www.yanke.ca

CURRENT ISSUES IN CONTROL

Husky Energy, like all public organizations, has a board of directors that looks after the interests of shareholders. In recent years, corporate governance has come under scrutiny because of corporate scandals. Many boards were not overseeing management as well as they might have.

Husky has strengthened its board policies on corporate governance in recent years. A major duty of Husky's board is to "approve, monitor and provide guidance on the strategic planning process." While the president and CEO and senior management team create the strategic plan, the board has to review and approve it. The board's role also includes identifying the principal risks of Husky's business and managing and monitoring these risks; and approving Husky's strategic plans, annual budget, and financial plans.[45]

THINK ABOUT IT

Why has corporate governance become so important in recent years? What are the advantages of having a strong board of directors? Would there be any disadvantages?

5 What are some current
issues in control?

The employees of Tempe, Arizona-based Integrated Information Systems thought there was nothing wrong with exchanging copyrighted digital music over a dedicated office server they had set up. Like office betting on college basketball games, it was technically illegal, but harmless, or so they thought. But after the company had to pay a $1.3-million (US) settlement to the Recording Industry Association of America, managers wished they had controlled the situation better.[46]

Control is an important managerial function. What types of control issues do today's managers face? We look at three: cross-cultural differences, workplace concerns, and corporate governance.

Cross-Cultural Differences

The concepts of control that we have discussed so far are appropriate for an organization whose units are not geographically separated or culturally distinct. But what about global organizations? Will control systems be different, and what should managers know about adjusting controls for cross-cultural differences?

Methods of controlling employees and work can be quite different in different countries. The differences we see in control systems of global organizations are primarily in the measurement and corrective action steps of the control process. In a global company, managers of foreign operations tend to be less directly controlled by the home office, if for no other reason than that distance keeps managers from being able to observe work directly. Because distance creates a tendency to formalize controls, the home office of a global company often relies on extensive formal reports for control. The global company also may use the power of information technology to control work activities. For instance, Japan-based Seven & i Holdings, which owns the 7-Eleven convenience store chain, uses automated cash registers not only to record sales and monitor inventory, but also to schedule tasks for store managers and to track managers' use of the built-in analytical graphs and forecasts. If managers don't use them enough, they are told to increase their activities.[47]

Technology's impact on control is most evident in comparisons of technologically advanced nations with those that are less technologically advanced. In countries such as Canada, the United States, Japan, Great Britain, Germany, and Australia, global managers use indirect control devices—especially computer-generated reports and analyses—in addition to standardized rules and direct supervision to ensure that work activities are going as planned. In less technologically advanced countries, managers tend to rely more on direct supervision and highly centralized decision making as means of control.

Also, constraints on what corrective actions managers can take may affect managers in foreign countries because laws in some countries do not allow managers the option of closing facilities, laying off employees, taking money out of the country, or bringing in a new management team from outside the country.

Finally, another challenge for global companies in collecting data is comparability. For instance, a company's manufacturing facility in Mexico might produce the same products as a facility in Scotland. However, the Mexican facility might be much more labour intensive than its Scottish counterpart (to take strategic advantage of lower labour costs in Mexico). If the top-level executives were to control costs by, for example, calculating labour costs per unit or output per employee, the figures would not be comparable. Global managers must address these types of control challenges.

Workplace Concerns

Today's workplace presents considerable control challenges for managers. From monitoring employees' computer use at work to protecting the workplace from disgruntled employees, managers must control the workplace to ensure that the organization's work can be carried out efficiently and effectively as planned. In this section we look at three main workplace concerns: workplace privacy, employee theft, and workplace violence.

Workplace Privacy

Do you think it is right for your employer to monitor your email and web surfing at work?

If you work, do you think you have a right to privacy at your workplace? What can your employer find out about you and your work? You might be surprised by the answers! Employers can (and do), among other things, read your email (even those marked "personal" or "confidential"), tap your telephone, monitor your work by computer, store and review computer files, and monitor you in an employee washroom or dressing room. And these actions are not all that uncommon. Nearly 57 percent of Canadian companies have Internet-use policies restricting employees' personal use of the Internet.[48] Employees for the City of Vancouver are warned that their computer use is monitored, and a desktop agent icon of a spinning head reminds them that they are being watched. Exhibit 11-14 summarizes the percentage of employers engaging in different forms of workplace monitoring.

Why do managers feel they must monitor what employees are doing? A big reason is that employees are hired to work, not to surf the web checking stock prices, placing bets at online casinos, or shopping for presents for family or friends. A 2003 Ipsos Reid poll found that Canadians spend 1.6 billion hours a year online at work for personal reasons, an average of 4.5 hours a week per employee. The amount of personal time has doubled from 2000.[49] That is a significant cost to businesses.

Another reason that managers monitor employee email and computer use is that they don't want to risk being sued for creating a hostile workplace environment because of offensive messages or an inappropriate image displayed on a co-worker's computer screen. Concern about racial or sexual harassment is one of the reasons why companies might want to monitor or keep backup copies of all email. This electronic record can help establish what actually happened and can help managers react quickly.[50] Finally, managers want to ensure that company secrets are not being leaked.[51] Although protecting intellectual property is important for all businesses, it's especially important in high-tech industries. Managers need to be certain that employees are not, even inadvertently, passing information on to others who could use that information to harm the company.

Even with the workplace monitoring that managers can do, Canadian employees do have some protection through the Criminal Code, which prohibits unauthorized interception of electronic communication. The Personal Information Protection and Electronic Documents Act, which went fully into effect in early 2004, gives employees some privacy protection, but it does not make workplace electronic monitoring illegal. Under existing laws, if an indi-

---

Exhibit 11-14

Types of Workplace Monitoring by Employers

Internet use	54.7%
Telephone use	44.0%
Email messages	38.1%
Computer files	30.8%
Job performance using video cameras	14.6%
Phone conversations	11.5%
Voice mail messages	6.8%

Source: Based on S. McElvoy, "E-Mail and Internet Monitoring and the Workplace: Do Employees Have a Right to Privacy?" *Communications and the Law,* June 2002, p. 69.

vidual is aware of a corporate policy of surveillance and does not formally object, or remains at the job, the monitoring is acceptable.[52] Unionized employees may have a bit more privacy with respect to their computers. The Canada Labour Code requires employers operating under a collective agreement to disclose information about plans for technological change. This might provide unions with an opportunity to bargain over electronic surveillance.

Law professor Avner Levin from Toronto's Ryerson University recently conducted a study with several colleagues on the extent of workplace surveillance. He found that employers used "closed-circuit television cameras, listened to recorded phone calls, monitored e-mails and scanned magnetic information from security passes" but did not always report this to employees.[53]

What can managers do to maintain control but do so in a way that is not demeaning to employees? They should develop an unambiguous and viable workplace monitoring policy and communicate it to employees. For instance, managers should tell employees up front that their computer use may be monitored at any time and provide clear and specific guidelines as to what constitutes acceptable use of company email systems and the web. As one example, the Bank of Montreal blocks access to "some of the dubious sites that are high risk," such as Playboy.com and other pornographic sites. The bank has developed policies about appropriate and inappropriate use of the Internet, and these are emailed to all employees several times a year.[54]

Employee Theft

Would you be surprised to find out that up to 75 percent of Canadian organizations have reported employee theft and fraud?[55] It's a costly problem—Air Canada, which has run a campaign against employee theft, noted that the airline "is right in line with industry standards for employee theft, and that means as much as 9 percent of stock such as office supplies and on-board products is taken each year."[56] Employee theft cost Canadian retail businesses more than $2 million a day in 1999, the most recent data available.[57]

employee theft
Any unauthorized taking of company property by employees for their personal use.

Employee theft is defined as any unauthorized taking of company property by employees for their personal use.[58] It can range from embezzlement to fraudulent filing of expense reports to removing equipment, parts, software, and office supplies from company premises. While retail businesses have long faced serious potential losses from employee theft, loose financial controls at start-ups and small companies and the ready availability of information technology have made employee stealing an escalating problem in all kinds and sizes of organizations. It's a control issue that managers need to educate themselves about and with which they must be prepared to deal.[59]

Why do employees steal? The answer depends on whom you ask.[60] Experts in various fields—industrial security, criminology, clinical psychology—all have different perspectives. Industrial security people propose that people steal because the opportunity presents itself through lax controls and favourable circumstances. Criminologists say that it's because people have financial pressures (such as personal financial problems) or vice-based pressures (such as gambling debts). Clinical psychologists suggest that people steal because they can rationalize whatever they are doing as correct and appropriate behaviour ("everyone does it," "they had it coming," "this company makes enough money and they'll never miss anything this small," "I deserve this for all that I put up with," and so forth).[61] Although each of these approaches provides compelling insights into employee theft and has been instrumental in program designs to deter it, unfortunately employees continue to steal.

What can managers do to deter or reduce employee theft or fraud? We can use the concepts of feedforward, concurrent, and feedback controls to identify actions managers can take.[62] Exhibit 11-15 summarizes several possible control measures.

Workplace Violence

Is workplace violence really an issue with which managers might have to deal? Yes. In 2001, 60 murders occurred at Canadian workplaces, 10 percent of all murders for the year.[63] Most of these workplace incidents were carried out by male spouses and partners of female employees. Surprisingly, Canada scores higher than the United States on work-

Exhibit 11-15

Control Measures for Deterring or Reducing Employee Theft or Fraud

Feedforward	Concurrent	Feedback
Use careful prehiring screening.	Treat employees with respect and dignity.	Make sure employees know when theft or fraud has occurred—not naming names but letting people know this is not acceptable.
Establish specific policies defining theft and fraud and discipline procedures.	Openly communicate the costs of stealing.	
Involve employees in writing policies.	Let employees know on a regular basis about their successes in preventing theft and fraud.	Use the services of professional investigators.
Educate and train employees about the policies.	Use video surveillance equipment if conditions warrant.	Redesign control measures.
Have professionals review your internal security controls.	Install "lock-out" options on computers, telephones, and email.	Evaluate your organization's culture and the relationships of managers and employees.
	Use corporate hot lines for reporting incidences.	
	Set a good example.	

Sources: Based on A. H. Bell and D. M. Smith, "Protecting the Company Against Theft and Fraud," *Workforce Online,* December 3, 2000, http://www.workforce.com; J. D. Hansen, "To Catch a Thief," *Journal of Accountancy,* March 2000, pp. 43–46; and J. Greenberg, "The Cognitive Geometry of Employee Theft," in *Dysfunctional Behavior in Organizations: Nonviolent and Deviant Behavior,* ed. S. B. Bacharach, A. O'Leary-Kelly, J. M. Collins, and R. W. Griffin (Stamford, CT: JAI Press, 1998), pp. 147–193.

place violence. In a recent International Labour Organization (ILO) study involving 130 000 employees in 32 countries, Argentina was ranked the most violent. Romania was second, France third, and Canada fourth. The United States placed ninth.[64] Sixty-four percent of union representatives who were surveyed recently reported an increase in workplace aggression, based on their review of incident reports, grievance files, and other solid evidence.[65] The ILO, in a separate 1998 study, found that, per capita, the rate of assault at work for Canadian women was four times that of American women.[66] Anger, rage, and violence in the workplace are intimidating to co-workers and adversely affect their productivity. No detailed Canadian statistics on anger at work are available.[67] However, Toronto-based WarrenShepell Research Group reports that during 2001–2003, nearly 3 percent of public sector employees who went to employee assistance programs did so because of anger management issues.[68] In a separate study, WarrenShepell found that anger rates in the manufacturing sector have been increasing in recent years.[69] A 1996 Gallup poll conducted in the United States found that 25 percent of the working adults surveyed reported being "generally at least somewhat angry at work."[70]

What factors are believed to contribute to workplace violence? Undoubtedly, employee stress caused by rising layoffs, declining value of retirement accounts, long hours, information overload, other daily interruptions, unrealistic deadlines, and uncaring managers play a role. Even office layout designs with small cubicles where employees work amidst the noise and commotion of those around them have been cited as contributing to the problem.[71] Experts have described dangerously dysfunctional work environments that include employee work driven by TNC (time, numbers, and crises), excessively aggressive and/or authoritarian managers, and unsolved grievances.[72] The competitive demands of succeeding in a 24/7 global economy put pressure on organizations and employees in many ways.

What can managers do to deter or reduce workplace violence? We can use the concepts of feedforward, concurrent, and feedback controls to identify actions that managers can take.[73] Exhibit 11-16 on page 332 summarizes several possible control measures.

Exhibit 11-16

Control Measures for Deterring or Reducing Workplace Violence

Feedforward	Concurrent	Feedback
Seek management commitment to functional, not dysfunctional, work environments.	Use MBWA (managing by walking around) to identify potential problems; observe how employees treat and interact with each other.	Communicate openly about incidents and what's being done.
Have employee assistance programs (EAP) to help with serious behavioural problems.	Allow employees or work groups to "grieve" during periods of major organizational change.	Investigate incidents and take appropriate action.
Have organizational policy that any workplace rage, aggression, or violence will not be tolerated.	Be a good role model in how you treat others.	Review company policies and change them, if necessary.
Use careful prehiring screening.	Use corporate hot lines or some mechanism for reporting and investigating incidences.	
Never ignore threats.	Use quick and decisive intervention.	
Train employees in how to avoid danger if situation arises.	Get expert professional assistance if violence erupts.	
Clearly communicate policies to employees.	Provide necessary equipment or procedures for dealing with violent situations (cellphones, alarm systems, code names or phrases, and so forth).	

Sources: Based on M. Gorkin, "Five Strategies and Structures for Reducing Workplace Violence," *Workforce Online,* December 3, 2000, http://www.workforce.com; "Investigating Workplace Violence: Where Do You Start?" *Workforce Online,* December 3, 2000, http://www.workforce.com; "Ten Tips on Recognizing and Minimizing Violence," *Workforce Online,* December 3, 2000, http://www.workforce.com; and "Points to Cover in a Workplace Violence Policy," *Workforce Online,* December 3, 2000, http://www.workforce.com.

Corporate Governance

Although Andrew Fastow, Enron's former chief financial officer, had an engaging and persuasive personality, that still does not explain why Enron's board of directors failed to raise even minimal concerns about management's questionable accounting practices. The board even allowed Fastow to set up off-balance-sheet partnerships for his own profit at the expense of Enron's shareholders.

corporate governance
The system used to govern a corporation so that the interests of shareholders are protected.

Corporate governance, the system used to govern a corporation so that the interests of shareholders are protected, failed abysmally at Enron, as it did at many of the other companies caught in recent financial scandals. In the aftermath of these scandals, there have been increased calls for better corporate governance. Two areas in which corporate governance is being reformed are the role of the board of directors and financial reporting. The concern over corporate governance exists in Canada and globally.[74] For example, 75 percent of senior executives at US and Western European corporations expect their boards of directors to take a more active role in improving corporate governance.[75]

The Role of the Board of Directors

The original purpose of a board of directors was to have a group, independent from management, looking out for the interests of shareholders who, because of the corporate structure, were not involved in the day-to-day management of the organization. However, it has not always worked that way in practice. Board members often enjoy a cozy relationship with managers in which board members "take care" of the CEO and the CEO "takes care" of the board members.

This quid pro quo arrangement is changing. In the United States, since the passage of the Sarbanes-Oxley Act in 2002, demands on board members of publicly traded companies have increased considerably.[76] In Canada, the new Canadian Securities Administrators rules, which came into effect in March 2004, strive to tighten board responsibility somewhat, but these rules are not as stringent as those developed in the United States.

Financial Reporting

In addition to expanding the role of the board of directors, the Canadian Securities Administrators rules require more financial disclosure by organizations but, unlike the Sarbanes-Oxley Act of the United States, do not require senior managers to provide a description and assessment of a company's internal compliance control. Still, these types of changes should lead to somewhat better information—that is, information that is more accurate and reflective of the firm's financial condition.

SUMMARY AND IMPLICATIONS

1 **What is control?** Control is the process of monitoring activities to ensure that they are being accomplished as planned, and correcting any significant deviations. There are generally three approaches to designing control systems: market, bureaucratic, and clan controls. Market control emphasizes the use of external market mechanisms, such as price competition and relative market share, to establish the standards used in the control system. Bureaucratic control emphasizes organizational authority and relies on administrative rules, regulations, procedures, and policies. Under clan control, employee behaviours are regulated by the shared values, norms, traditions, rituals, beliefs, and other aspects of the organization's culture. *Control is often needed to improve organizational performance, as President and CEO John Lau found when he took over Husky Energy and had to halt the company's large losses and the "wild expansions" of the company's previous management.*

2 **How does organizational culture provide control?** Organizational culture influences how people within an organization act, and can provide strong guidelines about what is important. A strong culture where everyone supports the goals of the organization makes it easier for managers to achieve goals. A weak culture, where people do not feel connected to the organization, can make things more difficult for managers; in such a culture, employees are less likely to devote themselves to the organization's goals. Managers can also influence culture, and affect culture's ability to control, through how it is conveyed to employees, what employees are hired, and how rewards occur in organizations. *At Husky Energy, John Lau uses checks and balances to make sure his company is performing well. The company relies on financial models to control costs and improve performance, and takes actions when the performance does not meet the goals set by management.*

3 **How do managers engage in control?** The control process is a three-step process: measuring actual performance, comparing actual performance against a standard, and taking managerial action to correct deviations or inadequate standards.

4 **What tools can be used to monitor and measure performance?** Managers can implement controls before an activity begins (feedforward control), during the time the activity is going on (concurrent control), and after the activity has been completed (feedback control). Managers can use financial controls (as John Lau does at Husky Energy), a balanced scorecard (looking at financial, customer, internal processes, and people/innovation/growth assets), information controls, and benchmarking of best practices.

5 **What are some current issues in control?** Some important contemporary issues in control include cross-cultural differences; workplace privacy, employee theft, and workplace violence; and corporate governance. *Husky Energy has strengthened its board of directors' policies on corporate governance in recent years, putting in place practices that require the board to oversee senior management and ensure that managers make appropriate decisions for the company. While the senior management team creates the strategic plan, the board must review and approve it. The board must also approve Husky's annual budget and financial plans.*

CHAPTER 11

Management @ Work

Reading for Comprehension

1. What is the role of control in management?

2. What are three approaches to designing control systems?

3. Explain the source of an organization's culture and how that culture is maintained.

4. Describe how culture is transmitted to employees.

5. Name four methods managers can use to acquire information about actual organizational performance.

6. Contrast immediate and basic corrective action.

7. What are the advantages and disadvantages of feedforward control?

8. Describe the financial control measures managers can use.

9. What can management do to implement a benchmarking best-practices program?

10. What challenges do managers of global organizations face with their control systems?

Linking Concepts to Practice

1. How are planning and control linked? Is the control function linked to the organizing and leading functions of management? Explain.

2. Why do you think feedback control is the most popular type of control? Justify your response.

3. How could you use the concept of control in your own personal life? Be specific. (Think in terms of feedforward, concurrent, and feedback controls as well as controls for the different areas of your life.)

4. Why is it that what is measured probably is more critical to the control process than how it is measured?

5. When do electronic surveillance devices such as computers, video cameras, and telephone monitoring step over the line from "effective management controls" to "intrusions on employee rights"?

6. What would an organization have to do to change its dominant control approach from bureaucratic to clan? From clan to bureaucratic?

7. "Every individual employee in the organization plays a role in controlling work activities." Do you agree or do you think control is something that only managers are responsible for? Explain.

MANAGEMENT FOR YOU TODAY

Your parents have let you know that they are expecting a big party for their 25th wedding anniversary, and that you are in charge of planning it. Develop a timeline for carrying out the project, and then identify ways to monitor progress toward getting the party planned. How will you know that your plans have been successful? At what critical points do you need to examine your plans to make sure that everything is on track?

SELF-ASSESSMENT

How Proactive Am I?

For each of the following statements, circle the level of agreement or disagreement that you personally feel:[77]

> 1 = Strongly Disagree
> 4 = Neither Agree nor Disagree
> 7 = Strongly Agree

1. I am constantly on the lookout for new ways to improve my life.   1 2 3 4 5 6 7

2. I feel driven to make a difference in my community, and maybe the world.   1 2 3 4 5 6 7

3. I tend to let others take the initiative to start new projects.   1 2 3 4 5 6 7

4. Wherever I have been, I have been a powerful force for constructive change.   1 2 3 4 5 6 7

5. I enjoy facing and overcoming obstacles to my ideas.   1 2 3 4 5 6 7

6. Nothing is more exciting than seeing my ideas turn into reality.   1 2 3 4 5 6 7

7. If I see something I don't like, I fix it.   1 2 3 4 5 6 7

8. No matter what the odds, if I believe in something I will make it happen.   1 2 3 4 5 6 7

9. I love being a champion for my ideas, even against others' opposition.   1 2 3 4 5 6 7

10. I excel at identifying opportunities.   1 2 3 4 5 6 7

11. I am always looking for better ways to do things.   1 2 3 4 5 6 7

12. If I believe in an idea, no obstacle will prevent me from making it happen.   1 2 3 4 5 6 7

13. I love to challenge the status quo.   1 2 3 4 5 6 7

14. When I have a problem, I tackle it head-on.   1 2 3 4 5 6 7

15. I am great at turning problems into opportunities.   1 2 3 4 5 6 7

16. I can spot a good opportunity long before others can.   1 2 3 4 5 6 7

17. If I see someone in trouble, I help out in any way I can.   1 2 3 4 5 6 7

Scoring Key

Add up the numbers for each of your responses to get your total score.

Analysis and Interpretation

This instrument assesses proactive personality. Research finds that the proactive personality is positively associated with entrepreneurial intentions.

Your proactive personality score will range between 17 and 149. The higher your score, the stronger your proactive personality. High scores on this questionnaire suggest you have a strong inclination toward becoming an entrepreneur.

More Self-Assessment

To learn more about your skills, abilities, and interests, take the following self-assessment on your enclosed CD-ROM:
- #24—What Time of Day Am I Most Productive?

Applying Feedforward, Concurrent, and Feedback Controls

You will be assigned one or more of the following tasks:

1. You are a consultant to a manager of a small retail clothing store. Over the past six months the manager has noticed that a significant amount of inventory has gone missing. The manager is not sure whether it is employees or customers who are taking things from the store. The manager has a somewhat limited budget, but wants to know what possibilities there are for controlling inventory. You have agreed to present a set of recommendations, identifying feedforward, concurrent, and feedback mechanisms that the manager might use.

2. You are a student in a business program at a local college or university. Several of your professors have expressed an interest in developing some specific controls to min-

imize opportunities for students to cheat on homework assignments and exams. Because you find cheating offensive, you and some other students have volunteered to write a report outlining some suggestions that might be used to control possible cheating (1) before it happens, (2) while in-class exams or assignments are being completed, and (3) after it has happened.

3. Devise control measures for each of the tasks involved in delivering a beverage to a Starbucks customer. Determine whether the measure is a feedforward, concurrent, or a feedback control.

Be prepared to present your suggestions before the rest of the class.

Pornography and Offensive Email in the Workplace

Pornography and offensive email are two major reasons why many companies establish strict policies and monitor their employees' use of the Internet. Citing legal and ethical concerns, managers are determined to keep inappropriate images and messages out of the workplace. "As a company, if we don't make some effort to keep offensive material off our network, we could end up on the wrong end of a sexual harassment lawsuit or other legal action that could cost the company hundreds of thousands of dollars," says the technology manager at one small business. "To a company our size, that would be devastating." Another reason is cost. Unauthorized Internet activity not only wastes valuable work time but it ties up network resources. Thus, many companies have installed electronic systems to screen email messages and monitor what employees do online. In some companies, one person is designated to review incoming emails and delete offensive messages.

Having a clear policy and a monitoring system are only first steps. Management must be sure that employees are aware of the rules—and understand that the company is seri-

ous about cleaning up any ethics violations. British Telecom (BT), for example, twice sent emails to remind all its employees that looking at online pornography was grounds for dismissal. Despite the warnings, management had to fire 200 employees in an 18-month period. Going further, the company told police about 10 employees' activities, and one has already been sentenced to prison. "We took this decision for the good of BT," explained a spokesperson, "and since we have taken this action the problem has reduced dramatically."[78]

Imagine that you are the administrative assistant for a high-ranking executive at BT. One afternoon you receive an urgent phone call for your manager. You knock on his office door but get no answer, so you open the door, thinking you will leave a note on his desk. Then you notice that your manager is absorbed in watching a very graphic adult website on his personal laptop. As you quietly back out of the office, you wonder how to handle this situation. Review this chapter's discussion of "Workplace Privacy" on pages 329–330 as you consider this ethical challenge.

Air Canada and WestJet Airlines

Without information, managers cannot make good decisions.[79] In order to make good decisions, then, companies need to protect their information. Executives at Air Canada thought they had. However, managers were shocked when they discovered that outsiders had penetrated their website to steal data. Their experience raises some troubling questions about the security of company information in the Internet age.

One of Air Canada's former employees, Jeffrey Lafond, had a password for an Air Canada employee travel website that listed all of the company's flights and passenger loads. The password had been given to him as part of a severance package in 2000. It was meant to enable Lafond to book two free flights of his choice a year through 2005.

Lafond subsequently became a financial analyst at WestJet Airlines, and Mark Hill, WestJet co-founder and vice-president of strategic planning, learned of Lafond's ability to access the Air Canada website. Hill asked for Lafond's password, so that he could access the website himself.

Hill used the password to count Air Canada's load factors, spending about 90 minutes an evening doing so. Because it was so time-consuming to do this by hand, Don Bell,

WestJet's vice-president of customer service and another airline co-founder, asked a WestJet IT staff member to create a program to automatically download and analyze Air Canada's load factors. Air Canada claims that WestJet entered Air Canada's website 240 000 times between May 2003 and March 2004, using Lafond's password.

Air Canada filed a lawsuit against WestJet. In a countersuit, WestJet accused Air Canada of collecting garbage from Hill's house in an effort to determine exactly how he was using Air Canada's data.

In May 2006, to put an end to the lawsuits, WestJet admitted that senior executives stole confidential information and apologized to Air Canada. They agreed to pay Air Canada $5.5 million for its legal fees and donate $10 million to children's charities.

Should Lafond have given Hill his password? What other ethical issues do you see in this case? What should Air Canada's chief information officer do to ensure that information is available to those who need it, but not available to outsiders who may use the information for competitive advantage?

A Control Concern at the FBI

Since the terrorist attacks at both the World Trade Center in New York City and at the Pentagon outside Washington, DC, on September 11, 2001, US officials have been diligently working to take corrective measures. From the establishment of the new Homeland Security Agency to congressional hearings regarding why and how the attacks could have occurred on US soil, officials have been attempting to ensure that such a tragedy does not happen again—ever.

One means of reaching this goal was to beef up security at airports, at the borders, and in major cities. The Federal Bureau of Investigation (FBI) has responsibility for investigating terrorist movements in the United States and for apprehending potential terrorists before a tragedy occurs. But there is something problematic in this plan. Many FBI agents who are critical to ensuring the safety of the citizens of the United States are finding themselves facing a dilemma that they never envisioned—financial difficulties.[80]

For example, one FBI agent, a 34-year-old law school graduate and former Marine captain assigned to the New York City Bureau must live more than 60 kilometres from his office. He simply cannot afford to live near New York City on a salary of $48 000 (US). In another case, an agent left his job in Miami to join the FBI after the September 11, 2001, attacks. He simply wanted to serve his country and believed that becoming an FBI agent was something he could do. Although he knew he would take a cut from his $80 000 (US)-a-year job, he was willing to do so. Shortly after graduating from the FBI academy, he was assigned to San Diego. With his $57 000 (US) salary, he must travel nearly two hours from work to find affordable housing. In serious debt, he is getting to the point that he may not be able to afford to be an FBI agent much longer.

Whereas he and others took an oath to protect and serve the American public, that oath, to some, was a vow of poverty.

For many of these agents—in Los Angeles, San Francisco, Boston, San Diego, and New York City—they handle some of the most sensitive government intelligence in the country. As a result, there is a concern that because of their growing debt, some of these agents may become vulnerable to corruption, which could ultimately threaten national security.

At the heart of the problem is the fact that a new FBI agent starts out with a base salary of $39 000 (US). After five years of service, an agent could make over $70 000 (US) with extensive overtime. Although there is some salary adjustment made for those serving in high-cost areas, it is not enough. That same agent living in Richmond, Virginia, for example, can find housing that is nearly 50 percent less than a comparable house in these high-cost areas. Given that many of the agents have families, the low salaries are adding to financial distress.

A survey conducted by the FBI Agents Association revealed that more than 7700 agents indicate their financial situation is "dangerously unstable." Many have had to cash out parts of their retirement accounts. Needless to say, these financial woes are not healthy for anyone.

Questions

1. Describe the type(s) of control issues that are portrayed in the case. Give specific examples.

2. Assume you are the director of the FBI. This information has just been given to you. What would you do? Explain your reasoning.

DEVELOPING YOUR INTERPERSONAL SKILLS

Providing Feedback

About the Skill

In this chapter, we introduced several suggestions for providing feedback. One of the more critical feedback sessions will occur when you, as a manager, are using feedback control to address performance issues.

Steps in Developing the Skill

You can be more effective at providing feedback if you use the following 10 suggestions:[81]

1. **Schedule the feedback session in advance and be prepared.** One of the biggest mistakes you can make is to treat feedback control lightly. Simply calling in an employee and giving feedback that is not well organized serves little purpose for you and your employee. For feedback to be effective, you must plan ahead. Identify the issues you wish to address and cite specific examples to reinforce what you are saying. Furthermore, set aside the time for the meeting with the employee. Make sure that what you do is done in private and can be completed without interruptions. That may mean closing your office door (if you have one), holding phone calls, and the like.

2. **Put the employee at ease.** Regardless of how you feel about the feedback, you must create a supportive climate for the employee. Recognize that giving and getting this feedback can be an emotional event even when the feedback is positive. By putting your employee at ease, you begin to establish a supportive environment in which understanding can take place.

3. **Make sure the employee knows the purpose of this feedback session.** What is the purpose of the meeting? That is something any employee will wonder. Clarifying what you are going to do sets the appropriate stage for what is to come.

4. **Focus on specific rather than general work behaviours.** Feedback should be specific rather than general. General statements are vague and provide little useful information—especially if you are attempting to correct a problem.

5. **Keep comments impersonal and job-related.** Feedback should be descriptive rather than judgmental or evaluative, especially when you are giving negative feedback. No matter how upset you are, keep the feedback job-related and never criticize someone personally because of an inappropriate action. You are censuring job-related behaviour, not the person.

6. **Support feedback with hard data.** Tell your employee how you came to your conclusion about his or her performance. Hard data help your employees identify with specific behaviours. Identify the "things" that were done correctly and provide a detailed critique. If you do need to criticize, state the basis of your conclusion that a good job was not completed.

7. **Direct the negative feedback toward work-related behaviour that the employee controls.** Negative feedback should be directed toward work-related behaviour that the employee can do something about. Suggest what

he or she can do to improve the situation. This practice helps take the sting out of the criticism and offers guidance to an individual who understands the problem but does not know how to resolve it.

8. **Let the employee speak.** Get the employee's perceptions of what you are saying, especially if you are addressing a problem. Of course, you are not looking for excuses, but you need to be empathetic to the employee. Get his or her side. Maybe there is something that has contributed to the issue. Letting the employee speak involves your employee and just might provide information you were unaware of.

9. **Ensure that the employee has a clear and full understanding of the feedback.** Feedback must be concise and complete enough that your employee clearly and fully understands what you have said. Consistent with active listening techniques, have your employee rephrase the content of your feedback to check whether it fully captures your meaning.

10. **Detail a future plan of action.** Performing does not stop simply because feedback occurred. Good performance must be reinforced and new performance goals set.

However, when there are performance deficiencies, time must be devoted to helping your employee develop a detailed, step-by-step plan to correct the situation. This plan includes what has to be done, when, and how you will monitor the activities. Offer whatever assistance you can to help the employee, but make it clear that it is the employee, not you, who has to make the corrections.

Practising the Skill

This exercise can help you learn how managers might use feedback control when starting a project. Think of a skill you would like to acquire or improve, or a habit you would like to break. Perhaps you would like to learn a foreign language, start exercising, quit smoking, ski better, or spend less. For the purpose of this exercise, assume you have three months to make a start on your project and all the necessary funds. Draft a plan of action that outlines what you need to do, when you need to do it, and how you will know that you have successfully completed each step of your plan. Be realistic, but don't set your sights too low either. Review your plan. What outside help or resources will you require? How will you get them? Add these to your plan. Ask someone to follow the steps in your plan. What modifications did the person suggest you make, if any?

MANAGING WORKFORCE DIVERSITY

Diversity Success Stories

Canadian companies are making progress in their diversity programs.[82] Although many still have a long way to go, some companies are doing their best to make employees of all races full and active participants in their businesses. *Canadian Business* and Rogers OMNI TV recently identified top places for visible minorities and Aboriginal peoples to work. Each of the companies on this list has made a strong commitment to diversity at every organizational level and in every aspect—from new hires to suppliers, and even to the charitable causes supported. Who are some of these diversity champions? The top 10 are Call-Net Enterprises (now part of Rogers), Canadian Imperial Bank of Commerce, TD Bank Financial Group, Bank of Nova Scotia, Bank of Montreal, HSBC Bank Canada, TELUS Mobility, Canadian Western Bank, Citizens Bank of Canada, and Westcoast Energy (now Duke Energy Gas Transmission Canada).

At Vancouver-based HSBC Bank Canada, 43.3 percent of the employees are from visible minorities. "Diversity is core to our business," says Executive Vice-President Sarah Morgan-Silvester.

Canadian Business recently recognized Ottawa-based Nasittuq Corporation, which monitors 47 radar stations that protect Canadian skies from threats, as one of Canada's most inclusive workplaces for Aboriginal peoples.[83] Nasittuq runs a training program that introduces Inuit to the North Warning System. Graduates are then hired by Nasittuq or find jobs with other companies because of the skills they have acquired.

How can companies use control mechanisms to make sure that they have a diverse workforce? Do you think companies should make special efforts to recruit employees with diverse characteristics? Why or why not? What would be the business advantages of doing so?

How can I manage and encourage change?

1 What factors create the need for change?

2 Is change ongoing or episodic?

3 How do organizations manage change and resistance to change?

4 What are current issues in managing change?

Steve Ballmer (pictured), CEO of Microsoft, is facing some tough choices in changing his organization.[1]

This Seattle-based company has dominated PC software for many years, and has been extremely profitable. However, it is facing a serious growth challenge. Although the company grew by about 30 percent per year during the late 1990s, current forecasts for growth are closer to 10 percent per year or less.

Microsoft's big challenges in the 1990s were the rise of the Internet and the Netscape browser. Since then, although the company faced a lengthy antitrust case brought on by the US government, it has dominated the software industry. The popularity of the Linux operating system represents Microsoft's newest challenge. Throughout the 1990s, Microsoft claimed its competitive advantage came from the fact that it offered the lowest-priced software that was also "good enough." Linux, however, is much less expensive, and has become a favourite among many dedicated computer users.

In the technology business, companies tend to have difficulties maintaining growth and profitability once their annual sales reach $30 billion (US). Microsoft reached that in 2002. Professor David Yoffie of Harvard Business School says, "There are very

few companies the size of Microsoft that have been able to keep growing, sustain their profitability and raise their market value over a prolonged period."

THINK ABOUT IT

Put yourself in Steve Ballmer's shoes. You are now faced with your first major competitor in years, and Microsoft has grown so large that it's difficult to act rapidly. How would you go about making Microsoft respond more quickly?

Big companies and small businesses, universities and colleges, and governments at all levels are being forced to significantly change the way they do things. Although change has always been a part of the manager's job, it has become even more important in recent years. In this chapter, we describe the forces that lead to change and how managers can manage change. We conclude by looking at the critical concerns managers face when managing change today.

Microsoft
www.microsoft.com

FORCES FOR CHANGE

1 What factors create the need for change?

organizational change
Any alterations in people, structure, or technology.

If it were not for **organizational change**—that is, any alterations in people, structure, or technology—the manager's job would be relatively easy. Planning would be simple because tomorrow would be no different from today. The issue of effective organizational design would also be solved because the environment would be free from uncertainty and there would be no need to adapt. Similarly, decision making would be dramatically streamlined because the outcome of each alternative could be predicted with almost certain accuracy. It would, indeed, simplify the manager's job if, for example, competitors did not introduce new products or services, if customers did not demand new and improved products, if government regulations were never modified, or if employees' needs never changed. But that is not the way it is. Change is an organizational reality.[2] And managing change is an integral part of every manager's job. In Chapter 2, we pointed out the external and internal forces that constrain managers. These same forces also bring about the need for change. Let's look briefly at these forces.

External Forces

Are there external forces that might suggest to you that your college or university might think about doing things differently?

The external forces that create the need for change come from various sources. In recent years, the *marketplace* has affected companies such as Yahoo! as competition from Google, LookSmart, and Ask Jeeves intensified. These companies constantly adapt to changing consumer desires as they develop new search capabilities.

Government laws and regulations are a frequent impetus for change. For example, the Canadian Securities Administrators rules, which came into effect in 2004, require Canadian companies to change the way they disclose financial information and enact corporate governance.

Technology also creates the need for change. For example, technological improvements in diagnostic equipment have created significant economies of scale for hospitals. Assembly-line technology in other industries is changing dramatically as organizations replace human labour with robots. In the greeting card industry, email and the Internet have changed the way people exchange greeting cards. Technological change from analog to digital recording has meant the shift from records to CDs, videotapes to DVDs, and film to digital cameras. In just seven years, DVD players went from the test stage to being owned by 64 percent of Canadians in 2004, making videotape rentals fall to about 10 percent of the home movie market.[3] The companies that produce videotapes and the companies that rent them have had to develop new strategies or go out of business.

The fluctuation in *labour markets* also forces managers to change. Organizations that need certain kinds of employees must change their human resource management activities to attract and retain skilled employees in the areas of greatest need. For instance, health care organizations facing severe nursing shortages have had to change the way they schedule work hours.

Economic changes, of course, affect almost all organizations. For instance, global recessionary pressures force organizations to become more cost-efficient. But even in a strong economy, uncertainties about interest rates, federal budget deficits, and currency exchange rates create conditions that may force organizations to change.

Internal Forces

In addition to the external forces just described, internal forces also create the need for change. These internal forces tend to originate primarily from the internal operations of the organization or from the impact of external changes.

A redefinition or modification of an organization's *strategy* often introduces a variety of changes. For instance, when Steve Bennett took over as president and CEO of Intuit (Quicken, QuickBooks, and QuickTax are its best-known products), the company was losing money. By orchestrating a series of well-planned and dramatic strategic changes, he turned Intuit into a profitable company with extremely committed employees, as the following *Management Reflection* shows.

MANAGEMENT REFLECTION

Steve Bennett Transforms Intuit

Can a company stay entrepreneurial and become more structured? When Steve Bennett was hired as Intuit's president and CEO in 2000, he had never worked for a high-tech firm.[4] He had spent all of his career with General Electric. Intuit's founder, Scott Cook, was looking for someone who could take Intuit to the next level. The company was struggling to break through the $1 billion (US) revenue wall, and Cook wanted the company to reach $10 billion (US) in revenue.

After he was hired, Bennett spent five weeks interviewing employees at more than 12 of Intuit's locations. He found a company still being run as haphazardly as a start-up venture. "The operation was a mess. It was losing money. Its technology was outdated. Execution was grindingly slow, and nothing was documented."[5] He discovered the organization had a democratic culture that nurtured employees to make sure they felt good. Managers chose whatever brand of PC they wanted to use, the employees were always holding meetings, and different units were responsible for the same product's development and sales support. Bennett felt the employees had to change how they viewed their work: "I wanted them to know that a company can be focused on high performance and still be a good place to work," he says.

Bennett introduced a number of changes, including putting business units in charge of development and customer service, introducing zero-based budgeting, and ordering the same computers for everyone to manage costs. He also flattened the organization, taking on 18 direct reports, rather than 8, so that he could drive change faster. "If you have that many direct reports, you don't have time to meddle in their business. My job is to conduct the orchestra, not to play all the instruments." He also introduced a new motto: "Mind your minutes." Employees were not to be involved in endless meetings, and they were to focus on the things that were really important. ■

In addition, an organization's *workforce* is rarely static. Its composition changes in terms of age, education, ethnic background, sex, and so forth. Take, for instance, an organization in which a large number of older executives, for financial reasons, decide to continue working instead of retiring. There might be a need to restructure jobs in order to retain and motivate younger managers. Also, the compensation and benefits system might need to be adapted to reflect the needs of this older workforce.

The introduction of new *equipment* represents another internal force for change. Employees may have their jobs redesigned, need to undergo training on how to operate the new equipment, or be required to establish new interaction patterns within their work groups.

Finally, *employee attitudes* such as job dissatisfaction may lead to increased absenteeism, more voluntary resignations, and even labour strikes. Such events often lead to changes in management policies and practices.

This chapter's *Managing Workforce Diversity—The Paradox of Diversity*, on page 365, notes the challenge managers face when they are balancing competing goals under change: to encourage employees to accept the organization's dominant values and to encourage employees to accept differences.

The Manager as Change Agent

Organizational changes need a champion. People who assume the responsibility for managing the change process are called **change agents**. Who can be change agents?

We assume that changes are initiated and coordinated by a manager within the organization. However, the change agent could be a nonmanager—for example, a change specialist from the human resource department or even an outside consultant whose expertise is in change implementation. For major system-wide changes, an organization often hires outside consultants to provide advice and assistance. Because they are from the outside, they can offer an objective perspective that insiders may lack. However, outside consultants are

change agents
People who assume the responsibility for managing the change process.

usually at a disadvantage because they have an extremely limited understanding of the organization's history, culture, operating procedures, and people. Outside consultants are also prone to initiate more drastic change than insiders would (which can be either a benefit or a disadvantage) because they don't have to live with the repercussions after the change is implemented. In contrast, internal managers who act as change agents may be more thoughtful, and possibly overcautious, because they must live with the consequences of their decisions.

TWO VIEWS OF THE CHANGE PROCESS

For years Microsoft has been able to dominate the software market, buying up competitors whenever they posed a challenge.[6] Until recently, its response to Linux was mostly to ignore it. Microsoft executives could see no advantage to Linux's open-source software. They believed that "loose teams of volunteer software developers could never produce anything to rival a company with the technical and financial resources of Microsoft." Because Microsoft delayed its response to Linux, it faces a bigger challenge: Linux is expected to grow faster than Windows in the server market through 2007. As a result, Microsoft has started making its software more compatible with Linux.

THINK ABOUT IT

How does change happen in organizations? Is change a constant process, or can organizations take breaks from worrying about change, as Microsoft did with its early response to Linux?

2 Is change ongoing or episodic?

We can use two very different metaphors to describe the change process.[7] One metaphor envisions the organization as a large ship crossing calm waters. The ship's captain and crew know exactly where they are going because they have made the trip many times before. Change comes in the form of an occasional storm, a brief distraction in an otherwise calm and predictable trip. In the other metaphor, the organization is seen as a small raft navigating a raging river with uninterrupted white-water rapids. Aboard the raft are half-a-dozen people who have never worked together before, who are totally unfamiliar with the river, who are unsure of their eventual destination, and who, as if things were not bad enough, are travelling at night. In the white-water rapids metaphor, change is an expected and natural state, and managing change is a continuous process. These two metaphors present very different approaches to understanding and responding to change. Let's take a closer look at each one.

The Calm Waters Metaphor

Up until the late 1980s, the calm waters metaphor pretty much described the situation that managers faced. It's best illustrated by Kurt Lewin's three-step description of the change process.[8] (See Exhibit 12-1.)

Exhibit 12-1

The Change Process

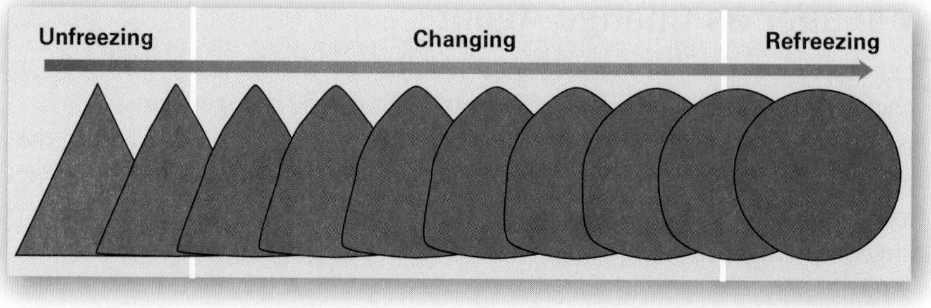

According to Lewin, successful change can be planned and requires *unfreezing* the status quo, *changing* to a new state, and *refreezing* to make the change permanent. The status quo can be considered an equilibrium state. To move from this equilibrium, unfreezing is necessary. Unfreezing can be thought of as preparing for the needed change. It can be achieved by increasing the *driving forces,* which are forces that drive change and direct behaviour away from the status quo; decreasing the *restraining forces,* which are forces that resist change and push behaviour toward the status quo; or combining the two approaches.

Once unfreezing is done, the change itself can be implemented. However, merely introducing change does not ensure that the change will take hold. The new situation needs to be *refrozen* so that it can be sustained over time. Unless this last step is taken, there is a strong chance that the change will be short-lived as employees revert back to the old equilibrium state—that is, the old ways of doing things. The objective of refreezing, then, is to stabilize the new situation by reinforcing the new behaviours.

Note how Lewin's three-step process treats change simply as a break in the organization's equilibrium state. The status quo has been disturbed and change is necessary to establish a new equilibrium state. However, a calm waters environment is not what most managers face today.[9]

Q&A 16.1

The White-Water Rapids Metaphor

The white-water rapids metaphor is consistent with our discussion of uncertain and dynamic environments in Chapters 2 and 3. It's also consistent with a world that is increasingly dominated by information, ideas, and knowledge.[10] We can see how the metaphor applies to Microsoft, which is currently facing an uncertain and dynamic environment after dominating the software industry for many years.

To get a feeling of what managing change might be like when you have to continuously manoeuvre in uninterrupted and uncertain rapids, consider attending a college or university that has the following rules: Courses vary in length. Unfortunately, when you sign up, you don't know how long a course will run. It might go for two weeks or 30 weeks. Furthermore, the instructor can end a course any time he or she wants, with no prior warning. If that is not bad enough, the length of the class changes each time it meets: Sometimes the class lasts 20 minutes; other times it runs for three hours. The time of the next class meeting is set by the instructor during this class. There is one more thing. All exams are unannounced, so you have to be ready for a test at any time. To succeed in this type of environment, you would have to be incredibly flexible and able to respond quickly to changing conditions. Students who are overly structured, "slow" to respond, or uncomfortable with change would not survive.

Growing numbers of managers are coming to accept that their jobs are very much like what students would face in such a college or university. The stability and predictability of the calm waters metaphor do not exist. Disruptions in the status quo are not occasional and temporary, and they are not followed by a return to calm waters. Many managers never get out of the rapids. They face constant change, bordering on chaos.

Is the white-water rapids metaphor an exaggeration? No! Although you would expect this type of chaotic and dynamic environment in high-tech industries, even organizations in non-high-tech industries are faced with constant change.

To learn about your response to working in a changing workplace, see *Self-Assessment—How Well Do I Respond to Turbulent Change?* on pages 360–362, at the end of the chapter.

Putting the Two Views in Perspective

Does *every* manager face a world of constant and chaotic change? No, but the number who don't is dwindling. Managers in such businesses as telecommunications, computer software, and women's clothing have long confronted a world of white-water rapids. These managers used to envy their counterparts in industries such as banking, utilities, oil exploration, publishing, and air transportation, where the environment was historically more stable and predictable. However, those days of stability and predictability are long gone!

Today, any organization that treats change as the occasional disturbance in an otherwise calm and stable world runs a great risk. Too much is changing too fast for an organization or its managers to be complacent. It's no longer business as usual. Managers must be ready to efficiently and effectively manage the changes facing their organizations or their work areas. Nevertheless, managers have to be certain that change is the right thing to do at any given time. Law firm Brobeck, Phleger & Harrison had a disastrous strategy for change, as the following *Management Reflection* shows.

MANAGEMENT REFLECTION

To Change or Not to Change?

How important is a company's strategy for change? Brobeck, Phleger & Harrison had been a prominent San Francisco law firm for 70 years when the technology boom happened in the late 1990s.[11] Located in the heart of California's Silicon Valley, the firm saw great opportunity to engage in dot-com and venture capital deals. At first the strategy paid off, with the company handling 74 initial public offers (IPOs) in 1999. Many new lawyers were added to the firm, and they were offered huge salaries. Average compensation increased more than 50 percent. The company expanded the number of offices it had throughout the United States, and signed very expensive leases for very large buildings to house the offices. Two years later, the firm handled just three IPOs, but Brobeck continued to increase expenses dramatically. By 2003 Brobeck had lost many of its best performing partners and was in debt to Citibank for $120 million (US).

Why did everything go so wrong? When Brobeck developed its plan for the technology boom, the firm decided that it would handle only the corporate side of business: "buying and selling shares, taking options in companies." Brobeck refused any business on the commercial side, which might have balanced things when the technology bubble burst. ■

 Q&A 16.2

As Brobeck's experience shows, companies need to carefully consider change strategies, as change can lead to failure. If change is the appropriate course of action, how should it be managed? That is what we discuss next.

MANAGING CHANGE

Steve Ballmer, Microsoft's CEO, needs to convince both his managers and Wall Street that the company can manage the transition from rapid growth to much slower growth.[12] Microsoft has a great deal of cash on hand, but the company will suffer if it wastes it. Therefore, Ballmer has brought in outside executives to bring more financial discipline to the various business divisions.

THINK ABOUT IT

What advantages might come from bringing in outside executives to help with the changes needed at Microsoft or any other organization?

---

❸ How do organizations manage change and resistance to change?

As change agents, managers should be motivated to initiate change because they are committed to improving their organizations' performance. Initiating change involves identifying what organizational areas might need to be changed and putting the change process in motion. But that is not all there is to managing change. Managers must manage employee resistance to change. What we want to look at now are the types of change that managers can make, how they can make change happen successfully, and how they can deal with resistance to change.

Types of Change

What *can* a manager change? The manager's options fall into three categories: structure, technology, and people (see Exhibit 12-2). Changing *structure* includes any alteration in author-

Exhibit 12-2

Three Categories of Change

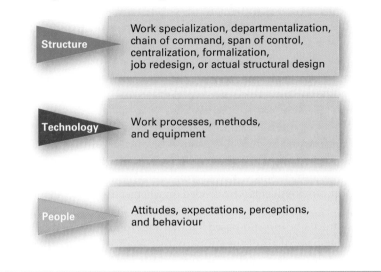

ity relations, coordination mechanisms, employee empowerment, job redesign, or similar structural variables. Changing *technology* encompasses modifications in the way work is performed or the methods and equipment that are used. Changing *people* refers to changes in employee attitudes, expectations, perceptions, and behaviour.

Changing Structure

We discussed organizational structure issues in Chapter 5. Managers' organizing responsibilities include such activities as choosing the organization's formal design, allocating authority, and determining the degree of formalization. Once those structural decisions have been made, however, they are not final. Changing conditions or changing strategies brings about the need to make structural changes.

What options does the manager have for changing structure? The manager has the same ones we introduced in our discussion of organizational structure and design. A few examples should make this clearer. Recall from Chapter 5 that an organization's structure is defined in terms of work specialization, departmentalization, chain of command, span of control, centralization and decentralization, and formalization. Managers can alter one or more of these *structural elements*.

Another option would be to make major changes in the actual *structural design*. For instance, this might involve a shift from a functional to a product structure or the creation of a project structure design. Hamilton, Ontario-based Dofasco became a more profitable steel producer after changing its traditional functional structure to a new design that arranges work around cross-functional teams. Some government agencies and private organizations are looking to new organizational ventures, forming public–private partnerships to deal with change, as the following *Management Reflection* shows.

MANAGEMENT REFLECTION

New Ways for Government to Get Jobs Done

Can public–private partnerships work?   Federal and provincial governments are trying to come up with new ways to get much needed projects completed.[13] Tony Fell, chair of Toronto-based RBC Capital Markets, notes that governments need help financing transportation, water, health care, and education systems, which are "deteriorating at an alarming rate." There is much talk about an innovative way of handling these projects: public–private partnerships (P3s), by which the government and the private sector form companies to get things done. Unfortunately, to date most have not been successful. Almost four out of five P3s fail.

Whether they fail because the idea is unworkable or they suffer from an inability of the public sector and the private sector to figure out appropriate ways to work together is not entirely clear. Gordon Campbell, premier of British Columbia, has been trying to find a successful model to make P3s work. Despite trying to get P3s started that would help with the "$2 billion in public capital projects built annually across the province," only one project has been signed. The private sector seems unwilling to take on risks that the government also does not want to assume.

BC's Canada Line, a rail-based rapid transit line to be built between Vancouver International Airport and downtown Vancouver before the 2010 Olympic Winter Games, was the first BC P3 project to launch, but gaining acceptance for the project was not easy. The provincial government was seen as pushing the project through, while labour unions fought it and Vancouver residents were divided on whether the project should be given a go-ahead.

One successful P3 is Toronto-based Teranet Enterprises, formed in 1995 to create an electronic database of all of the property title records in Ontario, so that lawyers could research and transfer titles in property deals from their office computers. The company has been profitable from the beginning. "The trouble was if government tried it alone, it would probably take 30 to 40 years to get done and cost tens of millions of dollars," says Bonnie Foster, vice-president of corporate affairs and an original member of the Teranet management team.

The difficulties governments face in raising money for and managing large projects suggest that innovative ways to build public infrastructure need to be found. Teranet is one example of how to create a joint public-private venture that works. ■

Changing Technology

Managers can also change the technology used to convert inputs into outputs. This generally involves the introduction of new equipment, tools, or methods; automation (replacing certain tasks done by people with machines); or computerization.

Changing People

organizational development (OD) Techniques or programs meant to change people and the nature and quality of interpersonal work relationships.

Changing people—that is, changing their attitudes, expectations, perceptions, and behaviours—is not easy. Yet, for over 30 years now, academic researchers and actual managers have been interested in finding ways for individuals and groups within organizations to work together more effectively. The term **organizational development (OD)**, although occasionally used to refer to all types of change in an organization, essentially describes techniques or programs that are meant to change people and the nature and quality of interpersonal work relationships.[14] The most popular OD techniques are described in Exhibit 12-3. The common thread in these techniques is that each seeks to bring about changes in the organization's people. For example, executives at Scotiabank, Canada's second-largest bank, knew that the success of a new customer sales and service strategy depended on changing employee attitudes and behaviours. Managers used different OD techniques during the strategic change including team building, survey feedback, and intergroup development. One indicator of how well these techniques worked in getting people to change was that every branch in Canada implemented the new strategy on or ahead of schedule.[15]

Making Change Happen Successfully

When changes are needed, who makes them happen? Who manages them? Although you may think that it's the responsibility of top managers, actually managers at *all* organizational levels are involved in the change process.

Even with the involvement of all levels of managers in change efforts, change processes don't always work the way they should. In fact, a global study of organizational change

Exhibit 12-3

Organizational Development Techniques

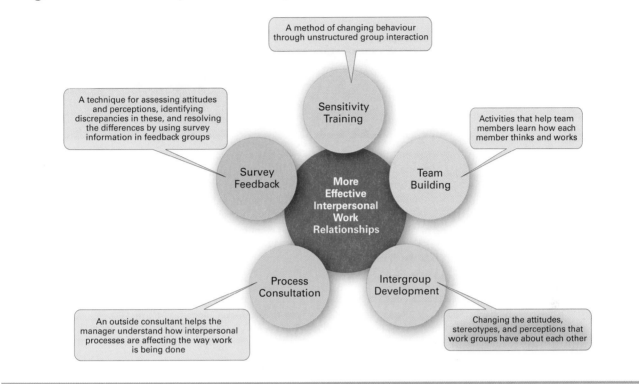

A method of changing behaviour through unstructured group interaction

A technique for assessing attitudes and perceptions, identifying discrepancies in these, and resolving the differences by using survey information in feedback groups

Activities that help team members learn how each member thinks and works

Sensitivity Training

Survey Feedback

Team Building

More Effective Interpersonal Work Relationships

Process Consultation

Intergroup Development

An outside consultant helps the manager understand how interpersonal processes are affecting the way work is being done

Changing the attitudes, stereotypes, and perceptions that work groups have about each other

concludes that "Hundreds of managers from scores of U.S. and European companies [are] satisfied with their operating prowess…[but] dissatisfied with their ability to implement change."[16] One of the reasons that change fails is that managers do not really know how to introduce change in organizations. Professor John Kotter of Harvard Business School identifies a number of places where managers make mistakes when leading change. These are illustrated in Exhibit 12-4 on page 352. We should also note that recent research emphasizes the need in change processes to manage the "hard stuff" as well as the "soft" or people issues in order to be successful.[17]

How can managers make change happen successfully? Managers can increase the likelihood of making change happen successfully in three ways. First, they should focus on making the organization ready for change. Exhibit 12-5 on page 353 summarizes the characteristics of organizations that are ready for change.

Second, managers need to understand their own role in the change process. They do this by creating a simple, compelling statement of the need for change; communicating constantly and honestly throughout the process; getting as much employee participation as possible; respecting employees' apprehension about the change but encouraging them to be flexible; removing those who resist but only after all possible attempts have

Computerization has been the engine for all kinds of changes in the business environment, including employee training. Cisco's Internet Learning Solutions Group is charged with developing electronic training programs both for Cisco's own sales force and channel partners and for the company's hundreds of thousands of customers. The team, whose leaders are pictured here, has developed tools ranging from virtual classrooms to video server technology and content development templates. "We really believe that our e-learning programs are a more effective way to grow skills in high volume in a shorter time than in the past," says the group's director.

Exhibit 12-4

Mistakes Managers Make When Leading Change

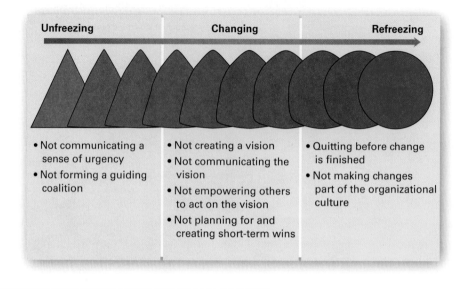

Unfreezing	Changing	Refreezing
• Not communicating a sense of urgency • Not forming a guiding coalition	• Not creating a vision • Not communicating the vision • Not empowering others to act on the vision • Not planning for and creating short-term wins	• Quitting before change is finished • Not making changes part of the organizational culture

Sources: J. P. Kotter, "Leading Change: Why Transformation Efforts Fail," *Harvard Business Review,* March–April 1995, pp. 59–67; and C. Williams, A. Z. Kondra, and C. Vibert, *Management* (Toronto: Nelson Canada, 2004), p. 315.

been made to get their commitment to the change; aiming for short-term change successes since large-scale change can take a long time; and setting a positive example.[18]

Third, managers need to encourage employees to be change agents—to look for those day-to-day improvements and changes that individuals and teams can make. For instance, a recent study of organizational change found that 77 percent of changes at the work-group level were reactions to a specific, current problem or to a suggestion from someone outside the work group; and 68 percent of those changes occurred in the course of employees' day-to-day work.[19]

Communicating Effectively When Undergoing Change

One study examined employee communications programs in 10 leading companies that had successfully undertaken major restructuring programs.[20] Eight factors were found to be related to the effectiveness of employee communications in these companies during times of change: (1) CEOs were committed to communication; (2) management matched their actions to their words; (3) two-way communication between managers and employees was encouraged; (4) the organization emphasized face-to-face communication; (5) managers shared responsibility for employee communication; (6) positive ways were found to deal with bad news; (7) messages were shaped for their intended audience; and (8) communication was treated as an ongoing process. Because the companies studied came from a variety of industries and organizational settings, the authors propose that these eight factors should apply to many types of organizations.

Perhaps the most important lesson from this research is that employees facing change need to be told what is happening and why, in very direct language, in order to reduce their fears. Good communication makes the process of change go more smoothly.

Exhibit 12-5

Characteristics of Change-Capable Organizations

- *Link the present and the future.* Think of work as more than an extension of the past; think about future opportunities and issues and factor them into today's decisions.

- *Make learning a way of life.* Change-friendly organizations excel at knowledge sharing and management.

- *Actively support and encourage day-to-day improvements and changes.* Successful change can come from the small changes as well as the big ones.

- *Ensure diverse teams.* Diversity ensures that things won't be done the way they are always done.

- *Encourage mavericks.* Since their ideas and approaches are outside the mainstream, mavericks can help bring about radical change.

- *Shelter breakthroughs.* Change-friendly organizations have found ways to protect those breakthrough ideas.

- *Integrate technology.* Use technology to implement changes.

- *Build and deepen trust.* People are more likely to support changes when the organization's culture is trusting and managers have credibility and integrity.

Source: Based on P. A. McLagan, "The Change Capable Organization," *Training & Development*, January 2003, pp. 50–58.

Managing Resistance to Change

Change can be a threat to people in an organization. Organizations can build up inertia that motivates people to resist changing their status quo, even though change might be beneficial. Why do people resist change and what can be done to minimize their resistance?

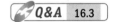

Why People Resist Change

> *How would you feel if your company, two years after you started there, changed the software you used to enter your contact and sales information?*

Resistance to change is well documented.[21] Why *do* people resist change? An individual is likely to resist change for the following reasons: uncertainty, habit, concern over personal loss, and the belief that the change is not in the organization's best interest.[22]

Change replaces the known with ambiguity and uncertainty. When you finish school, you will be leaving an environment where you know what is expected of you to join an organization where things are uncertain. Employees in organizations are faced with similar uncertainty. For example, when quality control methods based on sophisticated statistical models are introduced into manufacturing plants, many quality control inspectors have to learn the new methods. Some inspectors may fear that they will be unable to do so and may, therefore, develop a negative attitude toward the change or behave poorly if required to use the methods.

Another cause of resistance is that we do things out of habit. Every day, when you go to school or work you probably go the same way. If you are like most people, you find a single route and use it regularly. Human beings are creatures of habit. Life is complex enough—we don't want to have to consider the full range of options for the hundreds of decisions we make every day. To cope with this complexity, we rely on habits or programmed responses. But when confronted with change, this tendency to respond in our accustomed ways becomes a source of resistance.

The third cause of resistance is the fear of losing something already possessed. Change threatens the investment you have already made in the status quo. The more that people have invested in the current system, the more they resist change. Why? They fear the loss of status, money, authority, friendships, personal convenience, or other economic benefits that they value. This helps explain why older employees tend to resist change more than

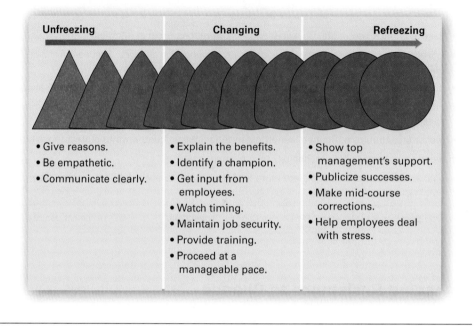

Exhibit 12-6

Helping Employees Accept Change

Unfreezing	Changing	Refreezing
• Give reasons. • Be empathetic. • Communicate clearly.	• Explain the benefits. • Identify a champion. • Get input from employees. • Watch timing. • Maintain job security. • Provide training. • Proceed at a manageable pace.	• Show top management's support. • Publicize successes. • Make mid-course corrections. • Help employees deal with stress.

Source: G. J. Iskat, "What to Do When Employees Resist Change," *Supervision* 57, no. 8 (August 1996), pp. 3–5.

younger employees. Older employees have generally invested more in the current system and thus have more to lose by changing.

A final cause of resistance is a person's belief that the change is incompatible with the goals and interests of the organization. For instance, an employee who believes that a proposed new job procedure will reduce product quality or productivity can be expected to resist the change.

Techniques for Reducing Resistance

When managers see resistance to change as dysfunctional, they can use a variety of actions to deal with it.[23] Exhibit 12-6 shows how to manage resistance at the unfreezing, changing, and refreezing stages. Actions include communicating the reasons for change, getting input from employees, choosing the timing of change carefully, and showing management support for the change process. Providing support to employees to deal with the stress of the change is also important. The actions a manager chooses depend on the type and source of the resistance. In general, resistance is likely to be lower if managers involve people in the change, offer training where needed, and are open to revisions once the change has been implemented. For more suggestions on reducing resistance, see *Developing Your Interpersonal Skills—Managing Resistance to Change* on pages 364–365.

CURRENT ISSUES IN MANAGING CHANGE

One of the most difficult challenges Steve Ballmer faces in moving Microsoft forward is to change the organization's culture.[24] The culture is aggressive, ambitious, and cutthroat. Microsoft's policy has been to "hire the brightest and the best, then let them fight it out for dominance." This worked well when the dominant focus of the company was to write computer code. But now the company needs more teamwork if it is to continue its innovative past. Even founder Bill Gates acknowledges the problem: Because of the aggressive culture, "the information was more in silos than [customers] had expected." The result is that IT systems do not always talk to each other. Now Microsoft needs to get its software products to work together, which means it needs its people to work together better.

THINK ABOUT IT

Is it possible to change from an aggressive, individualistic culture to a more team-oriented culture?

Today's change issues—changing organizational culture and handling employee stress— are critical concerns for managers. What can managers do to change an organization's culture when that culture no longer supports the organization's mission? What can managers do to handle the stress created by today's dynamic and uncertain environment? These are the topics we look at in this section.

4 What are current issues in managing change?

Changing Organizational Culture

When W. James McNerney Jr. took over as CEO of 3M Company, he brought with him managerial approaches from his old employer, General Electric. He soon discovered that what was routine at General Electric was unheard of at 3M. For instance, he was the only one who showed up at meetings without a tie. His blunt, matter-of-fact, and probing style of asking questions caught many 3M managers off guard. McNerney soon realized that he would need to address the cultural issues before tackling any needed organizational changes.[25]

The fact that an organization's culture is made up of relatively stable and permanent characteristics (see Chapter 11) tends to make that culture very resistant to change.[26] A culture takes a long time to form, and once established it tends to become entrenched. Strong cultures are particularly resistant to change because employees have become so committed to them.

The explosion of the space shuttle *Columbia* in 2003 highlights how difficult changing an organization's culture can be. An investigation of the explosion found that the causes were remarkably similar to the reasons given for the *Challenger* disaster 20 years earlier.[27] Although foam striking the shuttle was the technical cause, NASA's organizational culture

To save Air Canada, President and CEO Robert Milton will have to change a corporate culture that has been characterized in the past by friction between management and the unions, by disagreements among the employees, and by resistance to change. Milton hopes to introduce flexibility, cooperation, teamwork, and commitment, along with cost savings and reorganization. The stakes are high; not everyone is sure the airline can survive.

was the real problem. Joseph Grenny, a NASA engineer, noted that "The NASA culture does not accept being wrong." The culture does not accept that "there's no such thing as a stupid question." Instead, "the humiliation factor always runs high."[28] Consequently, people do not speak up. As this example shows, if, over time, a certain culture becomes inappropriate to an organization and a handicap to management, there might be little a manager can do to change it, especially in the short run. Even under favourable conditions, cultural changes have to be viewed in years, not weeks or even months.

Understanding the Situational Factors

Q&A 16.6

What "favourable conditions" might facilitate cultural change? The evidence suggests that cultural change is most likely to take place when most or all of the following conditions exist:

- *A dramatic crisis occurs.* This can be the shock that weakens the status quo and makes people start thinking about the relevance of the current culture. Examples are a surprising financial setback, the loss of a major customer, or a dramatic technological innovation by a competitor.

- *Leadership changes hands.* New top leadership, who can provide an alternative set of key values, may be perceived as more capable of responding to the crisis than the old leaders were. Top leadership includes the organization's chief executive but might include all senior managers.

- *The organization is young and small.* The younger the organization, the less entrenched its culture. Similarly, it's easier for managers to communicate new values in a small organization than in a large one.

- *The culture is weak.* The more widely held the values and the higher the agreement among members on those values, the more difficult it will be to change. Conversely, weak cultures are more receptive to change than are strong ones.[29]

These situational factors help explain why a company such as Microsoft faces challenges in reshaping its culture. For the most part, employees like the old ways of doing things and don't always see the company's problems as critical.

How Can Cultural Change Be Accomplished?

Now we ask the question: If conditions are right, how do managers go about changing culture? The challenge is to unfreeze the current culture, implement the new "ways of doing things," and reinforce those new values. No single action is likely to have the impact necessary to change something that is widely accepted and highly valued. Thus, there needs to be a comprehensive and coordinated strategy for managing cultural change, as shown in *Tips for Managers—Strategies for Managing Cultural Change.*

As you can see, these suggestions focus on specific actions that managers can take to change the ineffective culture. Following these suggestions, however, is no guarantee that a manager's change efforts will succeed. Organizational members don't quickly let go of values that they understand and that have worked well for them in the past. Managers must, therefore, be patient. Change, if it comes, will be slow. And managers must stay constantly alert to protect against any return to old familiar practices and traditions.

Handling Employee Stress

As a student, you have probably experienced stress when finishing class assignments and projects, taking exams, or finding ways to pay rising tuition costs, which may mean juggling a job and school. Then, there is the stress associated with getting a decent job after graduation. Even after you have landed that job, your stress is not likely to stop. For many employees, organizational change creates stress. A dynamic and uncertain environment characterized by mergers, restructurings, forced retirements, and downsizing has created a large number of employees who are overworked and stressed out.[30] In fact, Ipsos Reid recently did a survey of 1500 Canadians with employer-sponsored health care plans.

It found that 62 percent reported experiencing "a great deal of stress on the job." Workplace stress was bad enough to cause 34 percent of those surveyed to say that it had made them physically ill.[31] In this section, we review what stress is, what causes it, how to identify its symptoms, and what managers can do to reduce it.

What Is Stress?

Stress is the physical and psychological tension an individual feels when he or she is facing or experiencing extraordinary demands, constraints, or opportunities, and for which the outcome is perceived to be both uncertain and important.[32] Let's look more closely at what stress is.

Stress is not necessarily bad. Although it's often discussed in a negative context, stress does have a positive value, particularly when it offers a potential gain. Functional stress enables an athlete, stage performer, or employee to perform at his or her highest level in crucial situations.

What are the things that cause you stress?

However, stress is more often associated with fear of loss. When you take a test at school or have your annual performance review at work, you feel stress because you know that there can be either positive or negative outcomes. A good performance review may lead to a promotion, greater responsibilities, and a higher salary. But a poor review may keep you from getting the promotion. An extremely poor review might lead to your being fired.

Just because the conditions are right for stress to surface does not always mean it will. Stress is highest for individuals who are uncertain whether they will win or lose and lowest for individuals who think that winning or losing is a certainty. In addition, if winning or losing is unimportant, there is no stress. An employee who believes that keeping a job or earning a promotion is unimportant will experience no stress before a performance review.

Causes of Stress

As shown in Exhibit 12-7, the causes of stress can be found in issues related to the organization or in personal factors that evolve out of the employee's private life. Clearly, change of any kind has the potential to cause stress. It can present opportunities, constraints, or demands. Moreover, changes are frequently created in a climate of uncertainty and around issues that are important to employees. It's not surprising, then, that change is a major stressor.

TIPS FOR MANAGERS

Strategies for Managing Cultural Change

→ Set the tone through management behaviour. Managers, particularly top management, need to be **positive role models**.

→ Create **new stories, symbols, and rituals** to replace those currently in vogue.

→ Select, promote, and support employees who **adopt the new values** that are sought.

→ **Redesign socialization processes** to align with the new values.

→ Change the reward system to **encourage acceptance** of a new set of values.

→ Replace unwritten norms with **formal rules and regulations** that are tightly enforced.

→ **Shake up current subcultures** through transfers, job rotation, and/or terminations.

→ Work to get peer-group consensus through **employee participation** and creation of a climate with a high level of trust.

stress
The physical and psychological tension an individual feels when he or she is facing or experiencing extraordinary demands, constraints, or opportunities, and for which the outcome is perceived to be both uncertain and important.

 **Q&A** 16.7

Exhibit 12-7

Causes of Stress

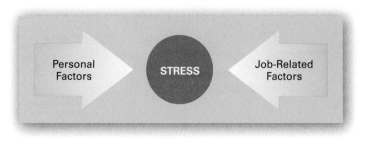

Personal Factors → STRESS ← Job-Related Factors

Symptoms of Stress

What signs indicate that an employee's stress level might be too high? Stress shows itself in a number of ways. For instance, an employee who is experiencing high stress may become depressed, accident prone, or argumentative; may have difficulty making routine decisions; may be easily distracted, and so on. As Exhibit 12-8 shows, stress symptoms can be grouped under three general categories: physical, psychological, and behavioural. Of these, the physical symptoms are least relevant to managers. Of greater importance are the psychological and behavioural symptoms since these directly affect an employee's work.

Reducing Stress

As we mentioned earlier, not all stress is dysfunctional. Since stress can never be totally eliminated from a person's life, either off the job or on, managers are concerned with reducing the stress that leads to dysfunctional work behaviour. How? Through controlling certain organizational factors to reduce organizational stress, and to a more limited extent, offering help for personal stress.

Things that managers can do in terms of organizational factors begin with employee selection. Managers need to make sure that an employee's abilities match the job requirements. When employees are in over their heads, their stress levels typically will be high. A realistic job preview during the selection process can minimize stress by reducing ambiguity about job expectations. Improved organizational communications will keep ambiguity-induced stress to a minimum. Similarly, a performance planning program such as management by objectives (see Chapter 3) will clarify job responsibilities, provide clear performance goals, and reduce ambiguity through feedback. Job redesign is also a way to reduce stress. If stress can be traced to boredom or to work overload, jobs should be redesigned to increase challenge or to reduce the workload. Redesigns that increase opportunities for employees to participate in decisions and to gain social support have also been found to reduce stress.[33] Stress from an employee's personal life raises two problems. First, it's difficult for the manager to control directly. Second, there are ethical considerations. Specifically, does the manager have the right to intrude—even in the subtlest ways—in an employee's personal life? If the manager believes it's ethical and the employee is receptive, there are a few approaches the manager can consider. Employee *counselling* can provide stress relief. Employees often want to talk to someone about their problems, and the organization—through its managers, in-house human resource counsellors, or free or low-cost outside professional help—can meet that need. Companies such as BC Hydro and the

Exhibit 12-8

Symptoms of Stress

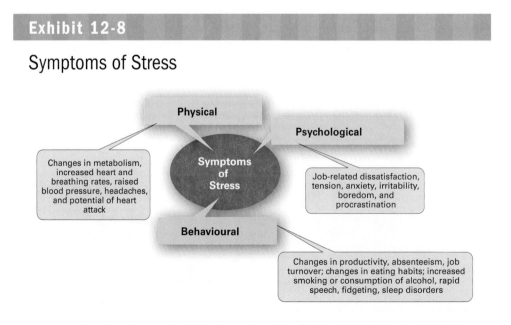

University of British Columbia are just two of many organizations that provide extensive counselling services for their employees. A *time management program* can help employees whose personal lives suffer from a lack of planning that, in turn, creates stress sort out their priorities.[34] Still another approach is organizationally sponsored *wellness programs.* For example, Montreal-based Ericsson Canada, a telecommunications firm, insists that all employees take two weeks of holidays a year, in week-long increments. Peter Buddo, vice-president of human resources, explains his company's policy: "One day off a week is not going to do anyone any good." Hamilton, Ontario-based Dofasco's employees have access to three gyms, one at the plant, and the other two a 15-minute drive from the plant. There are 4000 visits a month to the three gyms combined. Montreal-based Hewlett-Packard Canada gives all of its employees ergonomics training so that they will sit properly at their computer screens and avoid neck, shoulder, and arm injuries from keyboarding. The company also has four subsidized on-site fitness centres for staff in the Toronto area. Employees pay $20 a month for use of the centres at any time of the day, to take breaks and reduce stress.[35]

SUMMARY AND IMPLICATIONS

1 **What factors create the need for change?** Organizations are confronted with the need for change from both external and internal forces. Externally, the marketplace, government laws and regulations, technology, labour markets, and economic changes all put pressure on organizations to change. Internally, organizations may decide to change strategies. The introduction of new equipment can also lead to change. The workforce, both in terms of composition and attitudes, can also lead to demands for change. *Microsoft faces changes because it is a large organization having difficulty achieving the growth targets of its earlier years.*

2 **Is change ongoing or episodic?** Up until the late 1980s, change was viewed as episodic, something that could be planned and managed readily. In between periods of change, organizations "stayed the course." In more recent years, environments have become more uncertain and dynamic, and this has led to more continuous demands for change. *Microsoft has had to respond to various technological changes (even as it introduces technological changes itself), as well as a legal environment that has tried to alter the way Microsoft operates.*

3 **How do organizations manage change and resistance to change?** Managers can change an organization's structure, technology, and people. People tend to resist change, and there are a variety of reasons why they do so. The main reason is that change replaces the known with ambiguity and uncertainty. As well, people do not necessarily like their habits changed; they may fear losing something already possessed (e.g., status, money, friendships); and they may believe that the change could actually reduce product quality or productivity. *One of the challenges that Microsoft needs to manage is that employees have been used to working as stars, and they will likely resist working in teams initially because their own individual work will not be as obvious.*

4 **What are current issues in managing change?** One main consideration in managing change is determining how to introduce change in an existing organizational culture. An organization's culture can make it difficult to introduce change because employees are sometimes committed to old ways of doing things. The other major consideration is how to deal with employee stress while undergoing change. *Microsoft's culture has been one of silos, and now it needs more teamwork from employees. This creates difficulties for CEO Steve Ballmer, who has to figure out how to reward team activities rather than individual actions.*

SNAPSHOT *SUMMARY*

1 **Forces for Change**
External Forces
Internal Forces
The Manager as Change Agent

2 **Two Views of the Change Process**
The Calm Waters Metaphor
The White-Water Rapids Metaphor
Putting the Two Views in Perspective

3 **Managing Change**
Types of Change
Making Change Happen Successfully
Managing Resistance to Change

4 **Current Issues in Managing Change**
Changing Organizational Culture
Handling Employee Stress

CHAPTER 12

Management @ Work

Reading for Comprehension

1. Define *organizational change*.

2. Discuss the external and internal forces for change.

3. Why is handling change an integral part of every manager's job?

4. Describe Lewin's three-step change process. How is it different from the change process needed in the whitewater rapids metaphor of change?

5. Discuss what it takes to make change happen successfully.

6. Explain why people resist change and how resistance might be managed.

Linking Concepts to Practice

1. Who are change agents? Do you think that a low-level employee could act as a change agent? Explain.

2. Why is organization development planned change? Explain how planned change is important for organizations in today's dynamic environment.

3. Which organization—DaimlerChrysler or Apple—do you believe would have more difficulty changing its culture? Explain your position.

4. "Managers have a responsibility to their employees who are suffering serious ill effects from work-related stress." Do you agree or disagree with the statement? Support your position.

5. Do you think changes can occur in an organization without a champion to foster new and innovative ways of doing things? Explain.

6. Organizations typically have limits to how much change they can absorb. As a manager, what signs would you look for that might suggest that your organization has exceeded its capacity to change?

MANAGEMENT FOR YOU TODAY

Think of something that you would like to change in your personal life. It could be your study habits, your fitness and nutrition, the way you interact with others, or anything else that is of interest to you. What values and assumptions have encouraged the behaviour that currently exists (that is, the one you want to change)?

What driving and restraining forces can you address in order to make the desired change?

SELF-ASSESSMENT

How Well Do I Respond to Turbulent Change?

Listed below are a set of statements describing the characteristics of a managerial job.[36] If your job had these features, how would you react to them?

Use the following rating scale for your answers:

1 = This feature would be very unpleasant for me.

2 = This feature would be somewhat unpleasant for me.

3 = I would have no reaction to this feature one way or another; or it would be about equally enjoyable and unpleasant.

4 = This feature would be enjoyable and acceptable most of the time.

5 = I would enjoy this feature very much; it's completely acceptable.

1. I regularly spend 30 to 40 percent of my time in meetings.　　　　　1　2　3　4　5

2. A year and a half ago, my job did not exist, and I have been essentially inventing it as I go along.　　　　　1　2　3　4　5

3. The responsibilities I either assume or am assigned consistently exceed the authority I have for discharging them.　　　　　1　2　3　4　5

4. I am a member of a team and I have no more authority than anyone else on the team.　　　　　1　2　3　4　5

5. At any given moment in my job, I have on the average about a dozen phone calls or emails to be returned.　　　　　1　2　3　4　5

6. My job performance is evaluated by not only my boss but also by my peers and subordinates.　　　　　1　2　3　4　5

7. About three weeks a year of formal management training is needed in my job just to stay current.　　　　　1　2　3　4　5

8. My job consistently brings me into close working contact at a professional level with people of many races, ethnic groups, and nationalities, and of both sexes.　　　　　1　2　3　4　5

9. For many of my work colleagues, English is their second language.　　　　　1　2　3　4　5

10. My boss is from another country and has only been in this country for six months.　　　　　1　2　3　4　5

11. There is no objective way to measure my effectiveness.　　　　　1　2　3　4　5

12. I report to three different bosses for different aspects of my job, and each has an equal say in my performance appraisal.　　　　　1　2　3　4　5

13. On average, about a third of my time is spent dealing with unexpected emergencies that force all scheduled work to be postponed.　　　　　1　2　3　4　5

14. On average, I spend about a week every month out of town on business.　　　　　1　2　3　4　5

15. I frequently have to work until 8 p.m. to get my day's work completed.　　　　　1　2　3　4　5

16. When I have a meeting with the people who report to me, at least one or two will participate by phone or electronic conferencing.　　　　　1　2　3　4　5

17. The degree I earned in preparation for this type of work is now obsolete, and I probably should go back for another degree.　　　　　1　2　3　4　5

18. My job requires me to read 100 to 200 pages per week of technical materials.　　　　　1　2　3　4　5

19. My department is so interdependent with several other departments in the organization that all distinctions about which departments are responsible for which tasks are quite arbitrary.　　　　　1　2　3　4　5

20. I am unlikely to get a promotion anytime in the near future.　　　　　1　2　3　4　5

21. There is no clear career path for me in this job and organization.　　　　　1　2　3　4　5

22. During the period of my employment here, either the entire organization or the division I worked in has been reorganized every year or so.　　　　　1　2　3　4　5

23. While I have many ideas about how to make things work better, I have no direct influence on either the business policies or the personnel policies that govern my division.　　　　　1　2　3　4　5

24. My organization is a defendant in an antitrust suit, and if the case comes to trial I will probably have to testify about some decisions that were made a few years ago.　　　　　1　2　3　4　5

25. Sophisticated new technological equipment and software are continually being introduced into my division, necessitating constant learning on my part.　　　　　1　2　3　4　5

26. The computer I have in my office can be monitored by my bosses without my knowledge.　　　　　1　2　3　4　5

Scoring Key

To calculate your tolerance of change score, add up your responses to all 26 items.

Analysis and Interpretation

This instrument describes a number of characteristics of the changing workplace. The higher your score, the more comfortable you are with change.

The author of this instrument suggests an "average" score is around 78. If you scored over 100, you seem to be accepting the "new" workplace fairly well. If your score was below 70, you are likely to find the manager's job in the twenty-first century unpleasant, if not overwhelming.

More Self-Assessments

To learn more about your skills, abilities, and interests, take the following self-assessments on your enclosed CD-ROM:

- #4—How Well Do I Handle Ambiguity?
- #5—How Creative Am I?
- #50—How Stressful Is My Life?
- #51—Am I Burned Out?

WORKING TOGETHER: TEAM-BASED EXERCISE

The Celestial Aerospace Company

Objectives

1. To illustrate how forces for change and stability must be managed in organizations.
2. To illustrate the effects of alternative change techniques on the relative strength of forces for change and forces for stability.

The Situation

The marketing division of the Celestial Aerospace Company (CAP) has gone through two major reorganizations in the past seven years. Initially, the structure changed from a functional to a matrix form (see Chapter 5), which did not satisfy some functional managers nor did it lead to organizational improvements. The managers complained that the structure confused the authority and responsibility relationships. In reaction to these complaints, senior management returned to the functional form, which maintained market and project teams that were managed by project managers with a few general staff personnel. No functional specialists were assigned to these groups. After the change, some problems began to surface. Project managers complained that they could not obtain the necessary assistance from functional staff. It not only took more time to obtain necessary assistance but also created problems in establishing stable relationships with functional staff members. Because these problems affected customer service, project managers demanded a change in the organizational structure.

Faced with these complaints and demands from project managers, senior management is pondering yet another reorganization for the division. They have requested an outside consultant (you) to help them in their reorganization plan—one that will provide some stability to the structure, address their issues, and help the organization achieve its strategic goals.

Procedure

1. Divide into groups of 5 to 7 and take the role of consultants.
2. Each group should identify the forces necessitating the change and the resistance to that change in the company.
3. Each group should develop a set of strategies for dealing with the resistance to change and for implementing those strategies.
4. Reassemble the class and hear each group's recommendations and explanations.
5. After each group has presented, the other consulting groups should pose probing questions about the presenting group's recommendations.

ETHICAL DILEMMA EXERCISE

The OD Intervention

Organizational development (OD) interventions often produce positive change results. Interventions that rely on the participation of organization members can create openness and trust among co-workers and respect for others. Interventions can also help employees understand that the organization wants to promote risk taking and empowerment. "Living" these characteristics can lead to better organizational performance.

However, a change agent involved in an OD effort imposes his or her value system on those involved in the intervention, especially when the cause for that intervention is co-worker mistrust. To deal with this problem, the change agent may bring all affected parties together to openly discuss their perceptions of the dilemma.

Although many change agents are well versed in OD practices, sometimes they walk a fine line between success and failure. To resolve personal problems in the workplace, participants must disclose private, and often sensitive, information. Even though an individual can refuse to divulge such information, doing so may carry negative ramifications. For example, it could lead to lower performance appraisals, fewer pay increases, or the perception that the employee is not a team player.

On the other hand, active participation can cause employees to speak their minds, but that, too, carries some risks. For instance, imagine in such a setting that an employee questions a manager's competence. This employee fully believes that the manager's behaviour is detrimental to the work unit, but his or her reward for being open and honest could be retaliation from the boss. Although, at the time, the manager might appear to be receptive to the feedback, he or she could retaliate later. In either case—participation or not—employees could be hurt. Even though the intent is to help overcome co-worker mistrust, the result may be more back-stabbing, more hurt feelings, and more mistrust.

Do you think that co-workers can be too open and honest under this type of OD intervention? What do you think a change agent can do to ensure that employees' rights will be protected?

CASE APPLICATION

Electronic Arts

The video game industry is serious business in the United States, with computer and video game revenues surpassing domestic movie box-office receipts.[37] In this industry, where customers are fickle and demanding and competition is intense, one company, Electronic Arts (EA), has prospered. As the number-one video game publisher in the United States, EA lives and dies by its innovations. Its product lineup includes over 100 popular titles including The Sims, Need for Speed, Medal of Honor, FIFA Soccer, The Lord of the Rings, and Madden NFL. The company has created over 50 bestsellers (each with more than 1 million copies sold) since 1998. Fiscal year 2004 was its best year ever. Revenues were $3.9 billion (19 percent higher than 2003) and net income was up by 82 percent. In 2002, EA was ninety-first on *Fortune*'s list of best companies to work for. "EA is more than a successful company in a glamorous industry. It's a model of successful management for companies in any industry."

With its record of accomplishments, you would not think there would be much anxiety or stress at EA. Yet the reality is that paranoia is critical to its success. A top game title takes anywhere from 12 to 36 months to produce and costs between $6.5 million and $13 million. That is a significant investment risk riding on the company's ability to be innovative. John Riccitiello, former president and chief operating officer, says, "The forgotten aspect of creativity is discipline." The hard part, and the part that EA pursues relentlessly, he adds, "is identifying the right idea, assembling the best development team, solving the inevitable technical problems, creating a game that people want to play, getting all of the work done on schedule, getting it to market at the right time, and knowing how to generate buzz about it in an increasingly crowded market." How does EA get this done?

It starts with the discipline of understanding ideas. Game designers try to identify the creative centre of a game—what they call "the creative x"—so they understand what the game is about. Then it's the discipline of understanding the customers by using focus groups to pinpoint desires and likes and dislikes. Also, it's the discipline of sharing best practices and technologies through the company's intranet library. As one employee says, "If somebody develops a better blade of grass in one game, that grass will be in somebody else's game the next day." Then there is the discipline of developing the next generation of creative leaders. The company's "emerging leaders" program gives participants firsthand experience in departments outside their own. And there is the discipline of studying the competition. Employees are encouraged to know the features of competitors' products. Then it's disciplined project management. Riccitiello says, "If you're working on a game and you miss your deadlines, you won't be working here very long." Although the discipline of creativity is important at EA, you cannot overlook the passion of the company's game designers. Nearly everyone at EA grew up playing games. They love what they do and are inspired to look for new and creative challenges not only for the hardcore gamers, but for the casual gamers as well.

The pressure of creating constant hits can be an incredible strain on employees. Larry Probst has recently taken over the position of CEO of EA and wants the devotion, discipline, and innovation that his employees showed under the leadership of John Riccitiello to continue. He knows that if employees don't remain innovative, EA could lose its edge. What should Probst do to ensure EA employees continue to be innovative, and how can he help employees manage stress while doing so?

DEVELOPING YOUR DIAGNOSTIC AND ANALYTICAL SKILLS

Changes in the Health Care Industry

When you think about the significant changes that have occurred in people's lives over the past five decades, clearly the advances in medical science would be at the top of such a list. Diseases have been eradicated and medical procedures and devices have helped save thousands of lives. But don't be too quick to conclude that the health care industry is a model of innovation and efficiency.[38]

Hospitals, in general, have one of the most archaic and costly operating systems of any group of large organizations.

Nearly 95 percent of all hospitals currently use procedures and record-keeping systems that were implemented more than 50 years ago. It's the way it's always been done, and that is how most doctors and technicians prefer it. Individuals in this industry have been highly reluctant to accept and use new technologies.

Doctors and hospital administrators at Prairie General Hospital, however, refuse to be part of "the old guard." Consider the following that happened in the emergency room at Prairie General. A middle-aged patient was brought in by his wife to the emergency room. The patient, who was very overweight, was complaining of shortness of breath and dizziness. Although the patient claimed he was okay, his wife made him go to the hospital. Immediately the staff at Prairie General went to work. While nurses hooked the patient up to heart monitoring equipment and checked his vital signs, a resident wheeled over an emergency room cart, which contained a laptop computer. Logging in the patient's identification number, the ER doctor noticed that the patient had had an EKG in the past year. Immediately reviewing the past EKG records and comparing it with current heart monitoring results, the doctor determined the patient was in the middle of a heart attack. Within 10 minutes of seeing the patient, doctors had determined that he was suffering from a blocked artery. Clot-busting drugs were swiftly administered, and the patient was immediately taken to the cardiac lab where an emergency angioplasty was performed to open up the clogged artery. Within a day, the patient was back on his feet and ready to go home. In most other hospitals, the patient might not have been so lucky!

Prairie General is unusual in the health care industry. This hospital is investing money in technology that enables it to provide better service at a lower cost. Through its system called *CareWeb,* more than 1 million patient records are available. In each of these records are all previous medical orders, such as lab test results and prescriptions, for each patient. When a patient comes to the hospital, that individual's health history is easily retrievable and can be used to assist in the current diagnosis.

What has been the effect of this technology change on Prairie General? The system is saving the hospital more than $1 million each year. It has reduced errors in patient care by more than 90 percent and reduced prescription errors and potential drug interactions by more than 50 percent. Patient charts are now available in moments rather than hours or days. And patients are now discharged more than 30 minutes faster than they had been before CareWeb was implemented.

Cost savings, time savings, increased patient care, and saved lives—all this makes you wonder why every hospital is not making such changes!

Questions

1. Describe the types of changes that have occurred at Prairie General in terms of structure, technology, and people. Cite examples.

2. Why do you believe there is resistance by the medical profession to systems such as CareWeb? Explain.

3. Assume you were going to make a presentation to a group of hospital staff (doctors and administrators) on why they should invest in technology such as CareWeb. How would you attempt to overcome their resistance to change and their attitude about continuing to do what they have always done? Discuss.

DEVELOPING YOUR INTERPERSONAL SKILLS

Managing Resistance to Change

About the Skill

Managers play an important role in organizational change—that is, they often serve as change agents. However, managers may find that change is resisted by employees. After all, change represents ambiguity and uncertainty, or it threatens the status quo. How can this resistance to change be effectively managed?[39]

Steps in Developing the Skill

You can be more effective at managing resistance to change if you use the following three suggestions:[40]

1. **Assess the climate for change.** One major factor why some changes succeed and others fail is the readiness for change. Assessing the climate for change involves asking several questions. The more affirmative answers you get, the more likely it is that change efforts will succeed.

- Is the sponsor of the change high enough in the hierarchy to have power to effectively deal with resistance?

- Is senior management supportive of the change and committed to it?

- Is there a strong sense of urgency from senior managers about the need for change, and is this feeling shared by others in the organization?

- Do managers have a clear vision of how the future will look after the change?

- Are there objective measures in place to evaluate the change effort, and have reward systems been explicitly designed to reinforce them?

- Is the specific change effort consistent with other changes going on in the organization?

- Are managers willing to sacrifice their personal self-interests for the good of the organization as a whole?
- Do managers pride themselves on closely monitoring changes and actions by competitors?
- Are managers and employees rewarded for taking risks, being innovative, and looking for new and better solutions?
- Is the organizational structure flexible?
- Does communication flow both down and up in the organization?
- Has the organization successfully implemented changes in the recent past?
- Are employee satisfaction with and trust in management high?
- Is there a high degree of interaction and cooperation between organizational work units?
- Are decisions made quickly, and do decisions take into account a wide variety of suggestions?

2. **Choose an appropriate approach for managing the resistance to change.** There are five tactics that have been suggested for dealing with resistance to change. Each is designed to be appropriate for different conditions of resistance. These include *education and communication* (used when resistance comes from lack of information or inaccurate information); *participation* (used when resistance stems from people not having all the information they need or when they have the power to resist); *facilitation and support* (used when those with power will lose out in a change); *manipulation and cooptation* (used when any other tactic will not work or is too expensive); and *coercion* (used when speed is essential and change agents possess considerable power). Which one of these tactics will be most effective

depends on the source of the resistance to the change.

3. **During the time the change is being implemented and after the change is completed, communicate with employees regarding what support you may be able to provide.** Your employees need to know that you are there to support them during change efforts. Be prepared to offer the assistance that may be necessary to help your employees enact the change.

Practising the Skill

You are the nursing supervisor at a local hospital that employs both emergency room and floor nurses. Each of these teams of nurses tends to work almost exclusively with others doing the same job. In your professional reading, you have come across the concept of cross-training nursing teams and giving them more varied responsibilities, which in turn has been shown to improve patient care while lowering costs. You call the two team leaders, Sue and Scott, into your office to explain that you want the nursing teams to move to this approach. To your surprise, they are both opposed to the idea. Sue says she and the other emergency room nurses feel they are needed in the ER, where they fill the most vital role in the hospital. They work special hours when needed, do whatever tasks are required, and often work in difficult and stressful circumstances. They think the floor nurses have relatively easy jobs for the pay they receive. Scott, the leader of the floor nurse team, tells you that his group believes the ER nurses lack the special training and extra experience that the floor nurses bring to the hospital. The floor nurses claim they have the heaviest responsibilities and do the most exacting work. Because they have ongoing contact with patients and families, they believe they should not be called away from vital floor duties to help the ER nurses complete their tasks. What should you do about your idea to introduce more cross-training for the nursing teams?

MANAGING WORKFORCE DIVERSITY

The Paradox of Diversity

When organizations bring diverse individuals in and socialize them into the culture, a paradox is created.[41] Managers want these new employees to accept the organization's core cultural values. Otherwise, the employees may have a difficult time fitting in or being accepted. At the same time, managers want to openly acknowledge, embrace, and support the diverse perspectives and ideas that these employees bring to the workplace.

Strong organizational cultures put considerable pressure on employees to conform, and the range of acceptable values and behaviours is limited. Therein lies the paradox. Organizations hire diverse individuals because of their unique strengths, yet

their diverse behaviours and strengths are likely to diminish in strong cultures as people attempt to fit in.

A manager's challenge in this paradox of diversity is to balance two conflicting goals: to encourage employees to accept the organization's dominant values and to encourage employees to accept differences. When changes are made in the organization's culture, managers need to remember the importance of keeping diversity alive.

How difficult do you think it is for managers to encourage employees to accept differences while also trying to get them to all be part of the same organizational culture?

CoolBrands E: Managing Control and Innovation

CoolBrands' co-chair Michael Serruya wonders what it will take to continue being successful, now that CoolBrands has lost its licensing arrangement with Weight Watchers. He studies the company's strategic plan to get a sense of the areas that he might consider when trying to replace the income that came from the Weight Watchers business. Exhibit 1 shows selected financial information for CoolBrands in 2003.

Commitment to Innovation

One factor that Serruya considers is CoolBrands' commitment to innovation throughout the organization. There are many areas to innovate, including developing new production methods, coming up with exciting new products, developing new formulations of existing products, and figuring out ways to make sure that hot-selling products don't lose momentum because of demographic or dietary changes. He wonders how he might encourage innovative ideas from his employees. He also tries to come up with some innovative answers himself. Without new products to power continuing growth, he knows the company will not be able to reach its full potential.

The Strategic Plan

A company's strategic plan informs both managers and shareholders about the direction in which a company is headed. The plan also helps managers evaluate potential new projects by giving them guidelines against which new plans can be compared.

CoolBrands has a five-point strategic plan:

- Control a portfolio of powerful brands that command leading market shares in key high-growth segments.
- Control risk and maximize growth through diversification across every major product category and distribution channel.
- Control quality and costs through vertical integration while capturing additional revenue and profit from related operations.
- Control unique production capacity that will enable us to manufacture the innovative, value-added products that drive our brands.
- Control the downstream distribution of our products.

Exhibit 2 indicates the steps CoolBrands took to achieve the points of its strategic plan in 2003.

The Decision

Michael Serruya knows that strategic plans need to be evaluated. He wonders what control measures he can put in place over the next few years so that he can evaluate whether CoolBrands' strategic plan is still on track or needs to be adjusted. He must identify innovative production methods, products, and changes to existing products to help sustain and grow the business. He also wants to find ways to encourage his employees and franchisees to help contribute to innovative change.

Source: CoolBrands International, *Annual Report*, 2003.

Exhibit 1

Selected Financial Data

Year Ending	August 31/03	August 31/02	% Change
Revenues	357 273	242 222	48
Net Earnings	31 704	20 984	51
Earnings per Share—Basic	0.61	0.44	39
Earnings per Share—Diluted	0.59	0.42	40
EBITDA	58 575	40 064	46
Return on Average Shareholders' Equity	17.7%	13.8%	28
Price/Earnings (P/E) Ratio	29.7	17.6	69
Weighted Average Number of Shares Outstanding	51 746	48 050	8
Working Capital	85 734	57 354	49
Total Assets (In thousands of dollars, except share data)	313 850	283 662	11

Source: CoolBrands International, *Annual Report*, 2003.

Exhibit 2

CoolBrands Strategic Plan Outcomes, 2003

Control portfolio	• Continued growth of Weight Watchers®
	• Acquisition of Dreamery® and Whole Fruit™ and the licence for Godiva® Ice Cream
	• Licenced Atkins® Endulge™ for low-carbohydrate frozen desserts
Control risk	• Extended Weight Watchers into the foodservice channel
	• Launched Tropicana in the franchising segment
	• Finalized plans to introduce Yoplait in the frozen breakfast category
Control quality and costs	• Acquisitions of Americana Foods and Nestlé's DSD distribution system
Control production capacity	• Dramatically enhanced R&D capabilities
	• Developed innovative manufacturing technologies to improve quality and efficiency
	• Expanded total production capacity to facilitate growth
Control distribution	• Marketwide coverage of all distribution channels in US major markets

Source: CoolBrands International, *Annual Report*, 2003.

MANAGEMENT CASES

MC-1 Excel's Tavern

As the end of the fourth quarter of 2003 approached, Sharon Tomay arranged a meeting with the board of directors of CPS Inc. to submit her resignation as general manager. "I have spent my life taking calculated risks and winning," recalled Tomay, "and now with my successes at Excel's Tavern the time is right to find a new challenge." Over the past two years, Excel's Tavern has emerged as the most profitable fine dining venture in the area. Unfortunately, there is no one to assume the general manager position. Proud of her accomplishments, Tomay summarized the key strategies that she used to bring Excel's to its present position. These strategies need to be evaluated to determine their effectiveness and to determine the "right" leader to assume the general manager position and continue the financial success of Excel's Tavern.

Background

Excel's Tavern began as an investment opportunity. CPS Inc., an investment firm specializing in restaurants, jumped at the chance to develop Excel's Tavern into the area's premier dining experience. Originally an estate with large rooms, high ceilings, and incredible views, there was fantastic potential for the right business investment. The immediate area was under-serviced for fine dining restaurants. Everything about this property indicated that it was the ideal location for a charming restaurant. The estate would provide an elegant atmosphere specializing in quality regional cuisine. In addition to the location and operational potential, the property met the key criteria for a long-term investment and was available at an affordable price.

On January 1, 1999, Mark Jacobs became the first general manager for Excel's Tavern. Jacobs was happily married with two young children and was ready for something new. His previous experience was primarily in bar and pub management, not fine dining. He believed that restaurant service was a skill that was transferable, whether it was bars or fine dining restaurants. His philosophy was simple: If you provide people with a product they want, they will buy it.

During the first year, business was brisk (see Exhibit 1). Intensive media marketing efforts attracted many new guests. The restaurant appeared reasonably successful; however, there were some problems. The restaurant was not generating many repeat customers and it was struggling to control the continually high food and labour costs. Guest complaints were increasing and staff morale was declining. Comment cards indicated that the staff appeared careless in their execution of the ser-

vice standards, and verbal confrontations between kitchen staff and servers were soon commonplace.

At the end of the second year, CPS Inc. arranged a meeting with Jacobs to determine what was causing the declining financial results. Specifically, the owners were concerned with the high variable costs the Tavern was reporting (see Exhibit 1). Jacobs was not overly concerned and explained to them that he relied completely on the assistant general manager (AGM) and his executive chef for most of the day-to-day operations. He was rarely on the floor to observe front-line operations. He had done some reading about leadership and had adopted a "hands off" philosophy. He believed in letting people do their work and not getting in their way.

Jacobs said that he had little contact with the purchasing and staffing decisions. He preferred to leave those duties to his AGM and executive chef. He spent most of his day on the phone or at the golf course with advertisers and publicity organizations, trying to attract new customers. His concern was with the "big picture," the long-term success of the restaurant, and determining growth potential, not with the everyday food and labour costs.

In 2001, all performance areas continued to slide (see Exhibit 1). It appeared that the restaurant was about to "go under." Business levels were dropping and guest satisfaction was at an all-time low. Suppliers demanded cash on delivery for each order because of overextended accounts. Employees became increasingly careless in their service delivery. Basic service standards were not met. CPS Inc. was now convinced that Jacobs must go.

Sharon Tomay: General Manager

CPS Inc. decided that a new general manager should be given six months to show some positive results. Effective July 1, 2001, the new general manager was Sharon Tomay. Tomay was a self-made woman in her forties who had been "born into restaurants." She grew up in the kitchen of her parents' business, but left after university to pursue a corporate management career. She soon tired of corporate politics and missed the interaction with people that comes from working at a restaurant. Her stated plans at Excel's Tavern were to "improve the operation through change to the organizational structure and reduce costs through an increase in employee motivation."

Tomay did not make any changes in the first month. She spent time observing each department and interacting with

This case was written by Stephen Lynch. Copyright © 2005 Stephen Lynch, PhD, University of Guelph, Guelph, Ontario. This case is not to be reproduced in whole or in part by any means without the express written consent of the author. Reprinted with permission.

Case modelled on an earlier version of Multi-Products, copyright © 1959 by the President and Fellows of Harvard College. (HBS 9-378-04, 1977)

Exhibit 1

Excel's Tavern (FY 1999–2003)

(07/01/01 Sharon Tomay starts)

Sales	FY 1999	FY 2000	FY 2001	FY 2002	FY 2003	Budget FY03
Quarter 1	525 095	625 095	597 000	599 250	709 250	705 250
Quarter 2	547 000	647 000	607 000	601 150	695 900	685 000
Quarter 3	534 000	634 000	598 500	617 150	686 650	675 000
Quarter 4	601 250	655 250	595 500	621 500		698 500
Year to Date	2 207 345	2 561 345	2 398 000	2 439 050	2 091 800	2 763 750

* Guest Count	FY 1999	FY 2000	FY 2001	FY 2002	FY 2003	Budget FY03
Quarter 1	1 975	2 149	2 055	2 275	2 488	2 445
Quarter 2	2 075	2 274	2 185	2 091	2 324	2 306
Quarter 3	2 149	2 150	2 173	2 129	2 222	2 228
Quarter 4	1 974	2 150	2 230	2 075		2 333
Year to Date	2 043	2 180	2 161	2 143	2 345	2 329

* Guest count is a weekly average per quarter.

*Avg. Cheque	FY 1999	FY 2000	FY 2001	FY 2002	FY 2003	Budget FY03
Quarter 1	$22.15	$24.23	$24.20	$21.95	$23.75	$24.05
Quarter 2	$21.96	$23.70	$23.15	$23.95	$24.95	$24.75
Quarter 3	$22.70	$24.57	$22.95	$24.15	$25.75	$25.25
Quarter 4	$25.37	$25.39	$22.25	$24.95		$24.95
Year to Date	$23.05	$24.47	$23.14	$23.75	$24.82	$24.75

*Average all day cheque per guest per visit (including lunch and dinner).

Net Income	FY 1999	FY 2000	FY 2001	FY 2002	FY 2003	Budget FY03
Quarter 1	(10 500)	25 002	3 550	(5 250)	24 000	23 750
Quarter 2	5 500	26 530	(8 300)	11 500	28 450	26 750
Quarter 3	15 050	27 899	(15 000)	12 800	28 650	26 500
Quarter 4	20 150	28 347	(16 725)	16 250		28 500
Year to Date	$30 200	$107 778	$(36 475)	$35 300	$81 110	$105 500

*Turnover	FY 1999	FY 2000	FY 2001	FY 2002	FY 2003	Budget FY03
Quarter 1	70 %	60 %	150 %	125 %	85 %	75%
Quarter 2	50 %	55 %	110 %	105 %	64 %	75%
Quarter 3	55 %	110 %	185 %	65 %	95 %	75%
Quarter 4	75 %	80 %	150 %	95 %		75%
Year to Date	62.5%	76.25%	148.75%	97.50%	81.3%	75%

*Industry average is approximately 110%.

(Continued)

Exhibit 1 (continued)

*Controllable Costs	FY 1999	FY 2000	FY 2001	FY 2002	FY 2003	Budget FY 2003
Q1 Food %	38.95	37.1	36.95	36.95	35.95	35.5
Beverage %	31.65	33.05	32.85	32.5	32.05	32
Labour %	35.75	29.95	33.25	32.4	30.4	31
Q2 Food %	36.01	35.85	38.1	36.75	35.75	35.5
Beverage %	33.15	31.7	33.5	33.3	31.95	32.1
Labour %	33.3	30.05	34.75	32.15	31.15	31.5
Q3 Food %	36.35	35.45	37.25	35.5	35.1	35.5
Beverage %	32.35	33.75	31.75	31.5	31.5	31.95
Labour %	32.05	28.85	34.41	32	31	30.5
Q4 Food %	35.95	36.15	37.35	34.55		35.5
Beverage %	32.15	32	32.5	31		32
Labour %	31.05	27.2	34.25	29.15		32.5
YTD Food %	**36.82**	**36.14**	**37.41**	**35.94**	**35.6**	**35.5**
Beverage %	**32.33**	**32.63**	**32.65**	**32.08**	**31.83**	**32.01**
Labour %	**33.04**	**29.01**	**34.17**	**31.43**	**30.85**	**31.38**

*Numbers relate to the controllable costs of food, beverage, and labour as a percentage of cost of sales. Food percentage is then calculated as a percentage of the cost of food, and beverage percentage is calculated as a percentage of the cost of total beverage sales (alcohol: wine, beer, spirits). Labour percentage is based on total sales; it includes pay and benefits (exclusive of gratuities).

the staff and guests, while watching the operation in order to get a "feel" for the informal organization. The service staff remarked to each other that this was the first time they could remember seeing a GM outside their office wandering around the restaurant, interacting with customers and staff.

During the second month, Tomay went to work on her structural plans. First, she called in the service manager and informed him that the staff change room would be relocated to an area downstairs. The service manager protested that the new area would only accommodate half of the 40 service staff. Tomay replied, "That's right, by tomorrow I want a list of who is staying." She also called in the executive chef and informed him that his staff was to be reduced by one-third. The chef protested that such a reduction was impossible and that he would need to cover the lost labour himself by getting "behind the line." Tomay replied, "I'll be here after service tonight, I want you to come in and tell me either that you're the one for the job and that you have a plan, or that you're resigning."

Management Practices into Action

About two months after her arrival, Tomay took the managers and supervisors out for dinner. She told them what she was trying to accomplish. She displayed profit and sales charts and laid out the service standards that were to be implemented. She then made the following announcement: "We are imple-

menting a new policy. The management shifts begin at 10 a.m. or 3 p.m. We are all going to be at work and on the floor at these times. Not fifteen or twenty minutes after or whenever people feel like traipsing in." The assistant general manager interrupted, "How about voting on it?" Tomay said, "Fine, but if anyone votes no, I will accept their resignation." Nobody voted. After the meeting, the assistant general manager said to Tomay, "You certainly got off easy." Tomay replied, "No, I had to deal with your suggestion; that's enough anguish for one evening. Your laissez-faire behaviour is unacceptable."

A major problem that Tomay faced at Excel's Tavern was trying to turn the management people into a cost-and-profit conscious team. They were all able to relate to the guests and the staff, but their attention to the bottom line was lacking. At every opportunity, Tomay underscored the need for all managers to examine costs within their departments.

Food costs continued above 37 percent (see Exhibit 1). The sous chef in charge of purchasing bought a few cases of inferior quality chicken. Instead of organizing its return or obtaining an adjustment in price, he put it in the refrigerator and ended up throwing most of the product out. Although Tomay was furious, she did not fire the man. It was disclosed a short time later that following a severe tongue-lashing, she told the sous chef that she was "putting him on notice," while at the same time assuring him that if he resigned, he would receive a very poor business reference. "You appear to be worth challenging, so I am keeping you, but the food costs must be reduced and food quality maintained."

Tomay's bar manager, who was purchasing vast quantities of alcohol every week, was very indignant when Tomay called her to the office to discuss the matter. "I thought that we were still following Jacobs's policy of standing orders, where we get the same product each week." Tomay countered with, "You have two weeks to get bar stock to the appropriate level, and I don't have any room in this organization for screw-ups. Your focus must be to stock the bar with the items that will sell, without adding extra inventory to the shelves. Remember the goal: Reduce the costs in every department."

Tomay learned that one of the senior cooks was planning to open up a restaurant and was negotiating the funding. The cook had a number of unexplained absences and often came in late and left early. When Tomay questioned her, she complained that she had not been told that when the chef was out of town she would be required to work evenings and weekends in addition to her regular morning prep. Tomay replied, "No, I didn't say anything about that, but the work needs to be done, and that's why we pay you a good salary. When are you leaving?" "When do you want me to?" the cook asked. "Tomorrow," said Tomay. "I'd hoped you'd let me stay around until I get my planning complete," the cook said, "and anyway, my time ought to be my own." Tomay said, "OK, fine. I'll give you a cheque tomorrow and you'll have all the free time you want."

On another occasion, a supervisor complained, "It's been a year and a half since the last raise." Tomay barely glanced at her, replying, "The length of time has no bearing on whether you get a raise or not. Anyway, you were reviewed a few months ago; all you talked about was how much the staff liked you and how you enjoy working here. You didn't mention anything about how you've devised methods to increase employee productivity or about how many measures to reduce costs you have initiated. Are you working with your staff to encourage them to exceed our service standards?" The supervisor replied, "I've always been a hard worker." Tomay said, "I don't know that. We have rules that say you start work at ten or three. You arrive in the building exactly on the hour and aren't on the floor for another ten or fifteen minutes. There have been more than a few occasions where you leave work in the middle of a shift to run personal errands when there is no other manager on duty. These behaviours do not provide your staff with a strong role model. Come back four weeks from today with ideas to improve the operation and whether you're earning the salary you're already being paid. Prove to me that you're improving the operation and there will be a significant raise."

Tomay considered in-house promotions and "comps"† as problem areas. She felt the ability to void a meal for a service error was used too often as a quick fix to a problem. Tomay felt that simply removing a meal from a bill was not always an efficient approach to service recovery. Tomay regarded this practice as a way for the management team to "hide" behind a blanket solution and not deal with the issue themselves. Often, the guest could be satisfied with a simple apology and correction of the error, without providing the meal for free. On one occasion, Tomay noticed a server returning a steak to the kitchen,

as it apparently had not been properly cooked. When she asked the server the problem, the server replied, "The man at table eight just wants this cooked a bit more." Tomay was furious when she later found out that one of the supervisors heard the mistake and removed the thirty-two-dollar meal from the bill, without ever speaking to the guest. Had the supervisor taken time to determine the severity of the situation, such a costly decision could have been avoided with a simple apology for the error and fixing the problem right away. Incidents such as these were part of Tomay's claim that a lack of "cost consciousness" could be found at each level of the restaurant.

Another major issue that confronted Tomay was unscheduled cigarette breaks. She felt that this privilege was being abused. She sent out the following memo:

To all employees,

It has come to my attention that cigarette-smoking breaks have become a serious issue at Excel's Tavern because of:

- the increasing number of accumulated cigarette butts in and around the building;
- the unauthorized increase in the number of cigarette breaks beyond those allocated to all staff during their shifts; and
- the resulting image to guests who arrive at the restaurant and see our staff smoking outside the back door.

Effective immediately, smoking is prohibited while in uniform and is confined to the designated restricted areas at the rear of the restaurant. Management understands that this may be a major concern for some people. We are willing to cover up to 50 percent of the costs of a smoking cessation program for all staff who successfully complete the program.

A couple of weeks after the directive was posted, Tomay passed Tim, one of the supervisors, and asked to speak with him, to which he responded, "Sure, I am just on my way outside. Can we walk and talk?" Tomay replied, "Wasn't your scheduled break an hour ago?" Tim said, "Yes, you're right, I was just going out for a quick smoke." Tomay said, "Discussions of issues need to be addressed here and now. The restaurant cannot afford the time for additional breaks." The next day, the supervisor was notified that Tomay had ordered a pay reduction for that day. His co-workers supported his protests, but when he approached Tomay she said, "I am not running a charity here, I am running a business, and I can't allow any individual, particularly a member of the management team, to undermine it."

Once her reorganization was completed, Tomay set up a schedule of performance reviews for every employee. Front-line staff, including the kitchen staff and servers, were reviewed on a three-month basis. Management level employees were reviewed on a six-month schedule. If performance was deemed satisfactory, the employee received a raise. If not, the employee had three months to improve performance. If there was no improvement, the person was demoted or dismissed. Tomay found that although her management and supervisors would complain when any of their staff were released, the appraisals began to reveal generally improved performance. Sometimes

---

† "Comps" is the short-form for complementary items that may be given to guests for a variety of reasons.

Tomay would review individual personnel files at random. She would then walk around the restaurant and observe the employee just before quitting time. "I can get an idea of how good people are by watching them at the end of their shifts. My comments to supervisors often hit the nail right on the head." At other times, Tomay would just call in a supervisor and discuss an employee's performance. She would require the manager to be able to discuss the individualized employee growth plan and the progress made toward agreed goals. She wanted her management team to really know what each employee actually did on the job instead of just making out a blanket report that the person was doing a good job.

Sharon Tomay Takes Excel's in a New Direction

Within a couple of years, the restaurant grew and prospered; they were soon selling out at least four nights a week and were generating good lunch revenue from those who could not get a reservation at night. Business was good and the operation was running smoothly. Employee turnover was at a record low and guest satisfaction was at an all-time high. Tomay reflected on what she could do to capitalize on the huge demand that was continuing to grow. The impact of a food culture was developing from the immense popularity of food programs on television. With this phenomenon, the home cook wanted to learn how to create dishes that had the complexity and quality found at high-end restaurants. The requests for recipes from Excel's Tavern were increasing daily. Tomay decided to capitalize on this developing market. Instead of opening another restaurant that would compete with her directly, she decided to open a cooking school operation that would cater to groups and individuals from outside the industry. This concept would afford emerging "home cooks" an opportunity to come in and learn the tricks of the trade from top-quality chefs. She looked to her staff for people who were interested in attempting a new venture in the high-pressure environment of teaching people some of the dishes from the restaurant. As well, Tomay believed that committed and progressive organizations could use this "cooking experience" to engage in an activity that could create effective intact work teams.

Soon, both the restaurant and the cooking school were doing well. Business levels were good at the restaurant and the cooking school drew customers from a variety of local establishments.

Tomay's whole philosophy boiled down to getting a satisfactory return on investment, whether in labour or equipment. She did not believe in expansion for its own sake. Tomay had dinner with several of the largest original investors from CPS Inc., at which they discussed the way the operation of Excel's Tavern had grown and what the future held. Tomay's most important point was how the operation had grown from a business that was in "the toilet" to one that continued to provide a top-of-the-line product and had successfully expanded into new markets. "You know, I have really worked myself out of a job here, I don't do a thing except sit around and read the *Financial Post* and look for emerging markets. Unfortunately, I wish I felt more confident about my management group; I don't see a successor in their ranks. The younger managers around me, or in the country at large, apparently have not learned any critical lessons. It is really not their fault, I guess; they just haven't been trained to accept responsibility and to be held accountable. It irritates me that they come to Excel's Tavern, develop some skills as managers, and then leave, supposedly for greener pastures. I go to other restaurants and I see the way the young managers stand watching their staffs work, providing no guidance or structure to the way they are doing their jobs. They just stand at the front in expensive suits to look important, not producing. With the competitive nature of the industry, and new restaurants opening all the time, the way that these businesses waste money, how are they ever going to survive? There is no one to take over for me as general manager at Excel's Tavern."

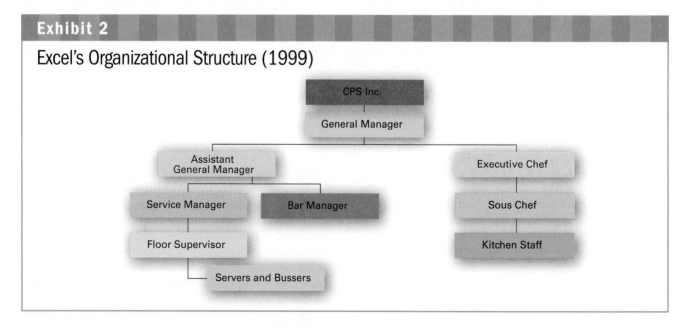

Exhibit 2

Excel's Organizational Structure (1999)

Exhibit 3

Excel's Organizational Structure (2003)

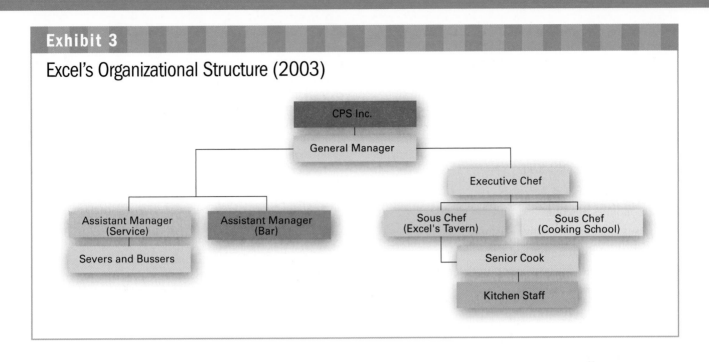

MC-2 Atlantic Health Centre

It was January 2004, and Jim Cormier was reviewing the last year's results of his business concern. Cormier, 35, had extensive experience in various small- and medium-size businesses, both as an employee and as an entrepreneur. While working full-time, he had studied on a part-time basis and earned a bachelor's degree in business administration. The Atlantic Health Centre, his latest venture, had undergone a major expansion over the last five years. Cormier was worried: Was the business moving in the right direction or did he need to make significant operational or strategic modifications to ensure its viability in the long run?

Starting the Health Centre

After working for various companies for about 15 years, Cormier had opened a small health club in 1999 in Barnes, Nova Scotia, a town of some 40 000 people. Over the following three-year period, he gradually expanded the business from three employees to five as revenues, memberships, assets, and profitability increased. As a hands-on owner/operator of a small business, he identified and rectified quickly any issues as they arose. The employees wore many "hats," and assisted with each other's responsibilities. Cormier maintained the leadership role and looked after the behind-the-scenes management of the business, but he also helped the employees with any task as needed, from front desk recep-

tion, personal training, marketing material, and administration to cleaning the washrooms. Duties and responsibilities were defined on a daily, weekly, and monthly basis. Employees worked on a two-shifts-a-day schedule—from 6 a.m. to 2 p.m. or from 2 p.m. to 10 p.m.

In 2002, an opportunity had come up for a major expansion. His three-year lease was expiring when the landlord offered him a much larger space nearby that had become available due to the previous tenant's having built and moved into its own new location. The landscape of the Canadian health, fitness, and recreation industry was changing rapidly, and Cormier knew that in order to survive in this changing environment, health and fitness providers had to deal with numerous challenges. (Appendix 3 gives some information about trends in the industry based on reports collected by the industry association.)

Until about 2000, health clubs typically offered just the basic exercise facilities. But the focus had begun to shift towards health clubs becoming health "centres," expanding their service offerings to better accommodate the growing demands of an increasingly sophisticated market. Cormier saw some similarities to what had happened in the grocery industry with one-stop supermarkets replacing the traditional corner grocery stores. The bigger health clubs began doing the same thing—they did not wish to restrict themselves to exercise equipment, but began to offer members a complete lifestyle and wellness centre. Cormier believed that the future success of health clubs would not come from focusing all their efforts on recruiting new

This case was written by Shripad Pendse and Kevin Doucette. Copyright © 2005 Shripad Pendse and Kevin Doucette, Saint Mary's University, Halifax, NS B3H 3C3. This case is not to be reproduced in whole or in part by any means without the express written consent of the author. Reprinted by permission of Shripad Pendse and Kevin Doucette. This case describes real events, but some details have been changed.

members, but from increasing the revenue per member from sources other than the monthly or annual dues.

The main components of a total health–oriented lifestyle are physical, mental, and social well-being. The expansion strategy Cormier decided on was to continue with the health club for physical well-being; to add a full-service day spa (including a hair salon) for mental well-being and relaxation; and a restaurant/lounge for social well-being. Cormier saw various advantages to his expansion plans. He felt that with the broadening of the facilities he could obtain

- economies of scale;
- economies of scope;
- a sustainable competitive advantage;
- increased client loyalty and retention;
- increased promotional opportunities; and
- complementary cash flows.

Mission Statement

With the expansion strategy, Cormier felt it necessary to create a new mission statement. For the first three years of operation in the smaller location, the mission statement was posted near the entrance of the facility, and it read as follows:

- To be the best health and fitness facility provider in the community based on our commitment to service
- To never lose a great member
- To never lose a great employee
- To be the best in all that we do

With his decision to offer a day spa/hair salon and a restaurant/lounge in addition to the improved exercise equipment, Cormier prepared a new mission statement, as follows:

- To provide the best services and products at reasonable rates
- To ensure the future growth of our business based on our reputation for greater service
- To ensure high retention of our clients by reinvesting in the business to adhere to market changes and by providing great service
- To promote excellence in our employees by providing the necessary tools to perform at the highest level of service

Expansion Strategy

Over an 18-month period starting in 2002, Cormier negotiated a $250 000 small business loan from his bank; a $250 000 forgivable grant from a government economic development agency to create 25 new full-time positions; and a $500 000 leasehold improvement investment to be financed by the landlord over the term of a 10-year lease. A mentor had once told him that the secret to success was using other people's money. So Cormier focused on the growth of his business with $1 000 000 of other people's money.

With his strategy of expansion, Cormier gave some thought to the internal relationships among the three aspects of the new health centre. From a financial perspective, each of the three business units was to be responsible for contributing revenues, while common area expenses were allocated on a square-metre basis. In essence, there were three profit centres—the health club, the day spa, and the restaurant/lounge.

Exhibit 1 outlines the overall management structure as well as the organizational structures of the three business units.

To take advantage of opportunities for synergy, the health club's promotion was tied to the two new units in various ways:

- All health club members were given promotional booklets with gift certificates for nutritional counselling, personal training, spa services, and restaurant meals.
- Daily "Healthy Xpress Lunch Specials" were offered to members when they checked in at the health club. Members would check the appropriate lunch special, the time required, and whether they preferred to eat in or take out.
- Spa packages also included complimentary healthy choice menu items from the restaurant to be provided between services in the day spa.
- Membership packages and spa packages were also promoted in the restaurant for non–health club members.

To capitalize on economies of scope, the customer service staffs for the health club and the day spa were integrated. Both of these strategic business units (SBUs) shared the same reception area. However, the health club manager was responsible for assignment of duties and responsibilities. If the spa manager had an issue with any of the customer service representatives, the problem was to be directed to the health club manager first. (This policy was implemented after customer service representatives felt that they were being pulled in two directions since they were supervised by both the health club and day spa managers.)

Operational Issues

With the addition of the spa and the restaurant segments, the number of staff had increased rapidly from five to 40, and this had created some difficulties as illustrated by the customer service representatives being supervised by two different managers. Cormier was not satisfied with the current structure and was searching for new approaches to deal with the challenges facing him as the owner-manager.

For a year and a half, the expansion was planned from a financial and equipment utilization perspective by conducting extensive research into the industries. Cormier attended trade shows, seminars, conferences, and even contracted for the services of industry-specific design consultants. Utilizing industry journals on profiles of success, he was able to determine the appropriate financial measurements and appropriate ratios in measuring financial performance. For example, he discovered that attrition rates in the health club industry average between 30 and 35 percent, food costs should be no more

Exhibit 1

Management Structures

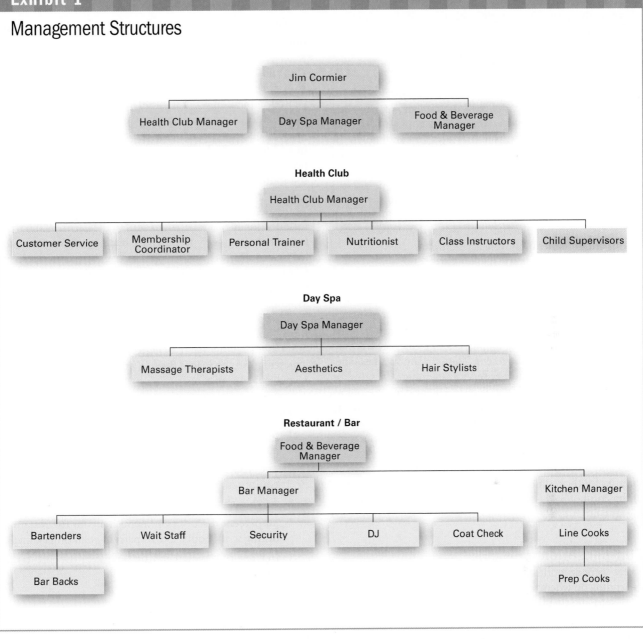

than 32 percent of revenue, and spa services should be operating at an 80 percent utilization rate before expanding.

The day spa had limiting factors based on service providers and room availability. Specific rooms were equipped to perform specialized services. An example would be a person's booking a "spa package." A spa package usually entailed a minimum of two treatments that coincided sequentially. The customer service representative would have to book the treatment (room and therapist); then the spa treatments would have to be scheduled around that time slot. Scheduling rooms, therapists, and treatments became difficult at the best of times, but Cormier had resolved this challenge creatively. The day spa was designed with a lounge area and a private steam bath.

If delays or a scheduling mistake occurred, the client would relax in the quiet lounge area and be given a complimentary snack and beverage from the menu, or have a complimentary steam bath until the logistics problem had been corrected. Fortunately, when this did occur, clients usually perceived it as value-added service and not a scheduling mistake on the health centre's part. The customer received better service while at the same time the solution alleviated stress among the employees by creating a "buffer zone."

Management of Employees

With the exception of the registered massage therapists, licensed aestheticians, the kinesiologist (personal trainer), and the nutritionist, the bulk of the employees required neither formal training nor education to carry out their assigned jobs. This was the case, for example, with most of the restaurant employees. These employees were low wage earners who were there for paycheques and not for careers—the restaurant industry is seen as providing low paying wages and experiences high turnover.

All the employees requiring technical qualifications were hired based on their experience in the industry and/or their certifications. Each employee was given a copy of his or her responsibilities and duties, as well as a policy handbook to be read and signed-off on upon employment. This served as a summary of job duties. As for skills, effort, and competencies, these were addressed in the interview process. Cormier looked after the hiring for the health club and the day spa, while the food and beverage manager was responsible for the hiring of all the restaurant/lounge staff. During the interviews, expectations and remuneration were agreed upon.

Training

As a member of the International Health, Racquet and Sportsclub Association (IHRSA), Cormier was able to purchase industry-specific training videos and guides. These were used when training health club employees in a one-day training session upon their employment. The training was task-specific, whether it be customer service, membership sales, or developing a personal training clientele. For the day spa employees and customer service representatives, a one-week on-site training program was established. The vendor of the day spa equipment flew in a representative from Toronto for one week to train all the relevant staff in the correct use of all the equipment and products to be used during the services and for retail sales. As for the restaurant, the training was limited to the use of the Point of Sale (POS) system, its capabilities, and reporting structure.

Compensation

There were several different compensation schemes used depending on where the employees worked (restaurant, health club, spa) and their level in the organization.

The Restaurant

The restaurant/lounge employees (with the exception of the food and beverage manager) were paid an hourly wage and kept any tips for themselves.

The food and beverage manager received a salary and a profit-share bonus. The profit-sharing plan was based on meeting defined financial objectives, which revolved around controlling costs. These objectives were established because controlling costs is the key to success in the food and beverage industry. The profit-sharing scheme for the food and beverage manager was structured as follows:

- must maintain monthly beverage costs below 35 percent
- must maintain monthly food costs below 32 percent
- monthly payroll must not exceed 25 percent of monthly sales

- to receive a monthly bonus, actual monthly results must meet budgets and the previous three targets.

If the above criteria were met, then the monthly profit share would be 15 percent of EBIT (earnings before interest and taxes).

The Spa

The day spa employees also worked under a quantifiable compensation plan. In order to build an established clientele in a new business, Cormier agreed to pay a base hourly wage of $10 to the spa employees, whether the services were booked or not. In addition to the base wage, the spa employees received 15 percent of the fee charged to the client. This was the norm in the spa industry. Thus at the breakeven point, 85 percent of the revenue from services would contribute to the bottom line.

In addition to the above, a 15 percent commission was included for all spa retail items sold to the client. When a customer came in solely to purchase retail items, however, this led to a conflict as to who would receive the commission. The front-end computer system was used to alleviate this issue. When a client received a service, the service provider was assigned as the sales person for that customer. Any future purchases by that client would be credited to the therapist and show on a sales summary report. If there was no record of the purchaser's having been a client, then the customer service representative who logged the sale would be given credit for the 15 percent commission.

The day spa employees also received the following additional benefits:

- 50 percent co-pay on insurance plan after six months of employment
- one week training seminar on spa services, products, and equipment use prior to opening
- free health club membership
- 50 percent discount on menu items in the restaurant during work hours and 20 percent at all other times
- free use of the baby-sitting service in the health club when required
- two free spa services per month

The Health Club

In the health club industry, monitoring and controlling retention rates is critical to profitable operation. The performance of personal trainers and the membership coordinator were measured strictly on achieving the quantifiable objectives. The performance standards of these positions were written down and signed by the employees and Cormier as the agreed upon terms for the compensation structure. The signed forms were then maintained in the employee files.

Personal Trainers The personal trainers were paid an hourly wage for complimentary training sessions for all new members. This provided a value-added service for all new members and gave the personal trainers the opportunity to sell personal training packages. Other than the wage for the complimentary sessions, personal trainers were compensated on the following scale during each two-week pay period.

- 0–$750 revenue (fees charged to the clients)—40 percent of revenue
- $751–$1499 revenue—50 percent of revenue
- $1500+ in revenue—60 percent of revenue

Cormier saw this as a good compensation system because the objectives were quantifiable, measurable, understood by all parties involved, and required little, if any, effort other than the administrative time necessary to keep track of all the quantifiable items.

The Membership Coordinator The membership coordinator was paid

- a base salary
- 35 percent of the registration fees for new members
- 4 percent of clients' monthly dues if those dues met or exceeded the previous month's results
- 2 percent of clients' monthly dues if those dues were below the previous month's results

Other Staff The customer service representatives and other health club staff received a base wage and 15 percent commission on retail sales. The nutritionist was compensated based on biweekly revenue volume (higher percentage commission for higher volume sales per pay period).

Non-Monetary Rewards

A part of Cormier's mission statement was "To promote excellence in our employees." Cormier believed that non-monetary and intrinsic rewards were just as important to achieve this as monetary rewards. Thus he introduced the following features:

Social Rewards

- Every Sunday, after closing at 9 pm, there was a movie night for all staff from each of the three business units, as well as their family members. The movie was shown on a 12 × 10 foot projection screen with free finger food and "Happy Hour" prices for drinks.
- Staff had the opportunity to participate in team events during charity functions.
- Every employee received a birthday cake on his or her birthday with an informal gathering in the restaurant, usually during downtime in the afternoon.

Intrinsic Job Rewards

- The spa staff had considerable job autonomy because they could arrange their own schedule to a great extent.
- The jobs of the spa employees were further enriched by allowing one of the staff to be responsible for scheduling, one to be responsible for inventory management, and another to be responsible for monitoring services and retail sales and allocating the credits to the appropriate personnel.
- Staff received quarterly reviews and feedback.

Overall Assessment of the Business and Conclusion

Cormier assessed the overall performance of each unit every month based on income statements, inventory levels, and attainment of cost control objectives. The performance of the restaurant was reviewed by Cormier and the food and beverage manager, and they micromanaged any problems that needed to be addressed. The remainder of the restaurant staff was involved in monthly meetings on the first Monday of every month. As for the health club, the membership coordinator, the health club manager and Cormier sat down on the first Tuesday of every month and reviewed the membership revenues from new members and the attrition proportions of members who did not renew their memberships. Similarly, Cormier met each month with the day spa manager to review revenues and expenses generated by the spa, and the rest of the spa/salon staff was given the opportunity to offer their suggestions and comments in a monthly staff meeting.

There were several things that Cormier was concerned about regarding the results achieved in the first year after the expansion. He had created the fixed-wage-plus-commission structure for the trainers and spa employees so that employees could depend on getting some income even when the business was slow. This worked fine when the utilization rate was around 20 percent in the first three months and the staff were not doing a lot of work. But when the utilization rate increased to 80 percent in some months, staff complained that they were "only" getting $19 from the $60 fee charged to each client ($10 base wage plus 15 percent of $60, or $9), although they were getting 31.67 percent of the fee collected. As mentioned earlier, there had also been conflicts over who was to get the commission when a client walked in and purchased something from the spa or when the client had both a massage and a facial. The staff also seemed to abuse the flextime system put in for their benefit.

Cormier expressed his overall feeling of frustration in these words: "In short, I tried to create a non-intimidating and pleasant work environment for all employees, hoping that it would be effective in encouraging good performance. Within a year, I had a 100 percent turnover in staff! Two of the staff left and opened a small business of their own. The hair stylist also opened his own hair salon. The staff repeatedly complained about how hard they had been working, the perceived unfairness of the amounts earned by employees in each of the three units in comparison to each other, and especially about who got how much commission for which kind of sales. At the same time, I was working seven days a week, often 12 or more hours each day, and yet the income I derived from the business seemed very small in relation to that of the employees, in spite of the fact that I was the only one taking all the financial risks as the owner."

Balance Sheet as of March 31, 2003

Assets	Item Details	Totals
Current Assets		
Petty Cash	2 000	
Bank–Operating	–9 556	
Total Cash		–7 556
Accounts Receivable		8 281
Health Club Inventory	4 906	
Day Spa Inventory	3 149	
Restaurant/Lounge Inventory		
Food	7 320	
Beverage	6 436	
Total Inventory		21 811
Total Current Assets		22 536
Equipment & Leaseholds		
Equipment	683 485	
Accumulated Depreciation	–159 685	
Equipment: Net		523 800
Leaseholds*	329 777	
Accumulated Depreciation	–24 485	
Leaseholds: Net		305 292
Total Assets		**874 164**
Liabilities		
Current Portion		
Small Business Loan #1		11 390
Small Business Loan #2		15 661
Lease #1		9 191
Lease #2		1 898
Lease #3		6 278
Lease #4		18 203
Lease #5		953
Deferred Revenue		2 668
Accounts Payable		223 547
EI Payable	4 327	
CPP Payable	3 939	
Income Tax Payable	8 053	
Receiver General Payable		16 319
Vacation Payable		5 377
WCB Payable		2 156
HST (Harmonized Sales Tax) Collected on Sales	253 262	
HST Paid on Purchases	–244 884	
ITC Adjustments	–3 686	
HST Owing (Refund)		4 692
Total Current Liabilities		318 333

(Continued)

Appendix 1 (continued)

Assets	Item Details	Totals
Long-Term Portion		
Small Business Loan #1		36 070
Small Business Loan #2		129 203
Lease #1		14 866
Lease #2		2 375
Lease #3		9 417
Lease #4		27 305
Lease #5		1 588
Angel Money		45 000
Total Long-Term Liabilities		265 824
Total Liabilities		584 157
Equity/Share Capital		
Government Grant	250 000	
Retained Earnings	27 546	
Current Earnings	12 461	
Total Equity		290 007
Total Liabilities & Equity		**874 164**

* Leaseholds—does not include the $500 000 in leaseholds financed by the landlord in the term of the lease.

Appendix 2

Consolidated Income Statement for the month ending March 31, 2003

REVENUES	Item Details	Totals
Health Club Revenue		
Monthly Membership Dues	21 322.39	
Membership in Full	2 957.56	
Supplements	2 879.67	
Accessories	358.31	
Personal Training	2 100.00	
Nutrition Counselling	1 600.00	
Tanning	2 550.73	
Total Health Club Revenue		33 768.77
Day Spa Revenue		
Massage Therapy	4 705.50	
Aesthetic Services	3 882.90	
Hair Services	3 689.50	
Spa Retail	1 347.58	
Total Day Spa Revenue		13 625.48
Restaurant/Bar Revenue		
Beverage Sales	41 788.63	
Food Sales	22 131.34	
Total Restaurant/Bar Revenue		63 919.97
Total Revenue		**111 314.11**

(Continued)

EXPENSES	Item Details	Totals
Health Club COGS		
Supplements	1 180.39	
Accessories	175.43	
Tanning	127.86	
Total Health Club COGS		1 483.68
Day Spa COGS		
Spa Back Bar	119.07	
Spa Retail	558.07	
Total Spa COGS		677.14
Restaurant/Bar COGS		
Restaurant COGS	14 312.62	
Food COGS	7 614.63	
Total Restaurant/Bar COGS		21 927.25
Freight	546.05	
Total COGS		24 088.07
Payroll Expenses		
Wages Health Club	15 837.27	
Wages Day Spa	8 231.10	
Wages Restaurant/Bar	22 925.53	
EI Expense	1 575.53	
CPP Expense	1 406.76	
WCB Expense	384.35	
Vacation Pay Expense	857.22	
Benefits	127.16	
Total Payroll Expense		51 344.92
Advertising & Promotion Expenses		
Radio	2 250.00	
Newspaper	1 250.00	
Yellow Pages	125.00	
Direct Mail	197.56	
Promotion	500.00	
Total Advertising & Promotion Expense		4 322.56
General Administration		
Professional Fees	125.00	
EFT Fees	356.00	
Business Occupancy Tax	146.52	

(Continued)

EXPENSES	Item Details	Totals
General Administration		
POS Interact/Visa Discount Fees	987.56	
Travel	249.65	
Meals & Entertainment	137.56	
Vehicle	543.14	
Vehicle Insurance	207.72	
Vehicle Maintenance	162.99	
Courier & Transport Costs	147.81	
Insurance	642.17	
Bank Interest	1 857.06	
Bank Charges	657.42	
Interest Expense	1 204.01*	
Rent	12 500.00**	
Repairs & Maintenance	432.56	
Cleaning & Supplies	681.56	
Garbage Removal	150.00	
Telephone	1 454.33	
Satellite	189.25	
Power	3 867.71	
Propane	1 873.97	
Total General Administration Expenses		28 573.99
Total Expenses		108 329.54
Net Income		2 984.57

* Includes Interest Expense from Payable and Equipment Leases.
** Rent includes $500 000 investment for leaseholds from the landlord financed over the 10-year term of the lease.

Appendix 3

Expansion Plans

The following information represents a sample of findings from research reports from the International Health, Racquet, and Sportsclub Association (IHRSA). The column titled "2000" indicates percentage of clubs that added the listed facility in 2000. The last column indicates the percentage of clubs planning to add a given facility in the next 24 months.

Club Facilities	2000	Next 24 months
	%	%
Cardiovascular Equipment	26.5	24.9
Resistance Equipment	21.0	23.8
Aerobics/Dance Studio	19.3	16.0
Free Weight Area	18.8	23.8
Office Space	15.5	14.4
Locker Rooms	13.8	19.3
Pro Shop	12.2	8.8
Child Care Area	11.6	13.8
Front Desk	11.6	8.3
Food & Beverage	11.0	8.3
Day Spa/Rehabilitation	8.8	15.5
Meeting Rooms	8.3	7.2
Children's Recreation Area	6.1	9.4
Indoor Pool	4.4	5.0
Lounges	3.9	7.2
Gymnasium	3.9	5.0

Part 1: Defining the Manager's Terrain

CBC | **CBC Video Case Incident**

The Counterfeiting Crusader

Counterfeiting is a big drain on a country's economy. In the United Kingdom, trade in counterfeit and pirated goods cost the economy an estimated £9 billion in 2004. The United States estimates the cost of counterfeiting to its economy at more than $200 billion (US) annually and 750 000 jobs. The annual cost of counterfeit and unlicensed software to Microsoft alone is estimated at $467 million (US) per year.

Lorne M. Lipkus is "the Counterfeiting Crusader." He is a founding partner in the Toronto, Ontario, law firm of Kestenberg Siegal Lipkus LLP, and practises throughout Canada in the area of intellectual property litigation with a principal focus on anticounterfeiting enforcement. He assists law enforcers in executing criminal search warrants and dealing with all aspects of border enforcement.

Counterfeit products are typically of inferior quality and do not meet industry safety standards—stuffed animals filled with anything off a factory floor in Asia; fake brand-name blankets for children without fire retardant protection; toys for children that can be hazardous due to design flaws.

For the manufacturers of legitimate products, counterfeiting has two key effects: loss of revenue and a negative impact on reputation. David Davenport of Hasbro Toys points out that there are significant investment costs in the design, safety tests, and promotion of products that cannot be recovered when counterfeiters sell fakes at greatly reduced prices. As well, unsuspecting purchasers of "brand name" products will presume the company is compromising quality when the product falls apart or fails. In the case of Hasbro, counterfeits of the company's Blizzard Bowl toys always lose the game.

Counterfeiters invest mostly in packaging and have evolved sophisticated ways to "copy" the packaging of real products. However, Lipkus says packaging without copyright notices and with spelling errors can indicate a fake product.

According to Lipkus, Canadian legal penalties for counterfeiting "are laughable." Canada is considered soft on counterfeiters and often serves as a conduit through which counterfeit goods find their way to the United States. Unsurprisingly, Canada's lack of border controls on counterfeit goods and slack laws are seen as a problem by our main trading partner, the United States.

In addition to the US government, some major corporations are critical of Canada's efforts to combat counterfeiting. Members of the International AntiCounterfeiting Coalition, which includes firms such as Nike, General Motors, and Microsoft, expect more from Canada, but the Canada Border Services Agency and the RCMP say they are doing the best they can with their resources and in light of their other priorities.

QUESTIONS

1. *For analysis:* How much control does a manager have over the potential counterfeiting of his/her company's products? Does globalization enhance or diminish a manager's control of counterfeit activities?

2. *For analysis:* Any company is affected by both its *specific* and *external* environment. What is the influence of counterfeiting on both of these environments, and how does this affect the company?

3. *For application:* Counterfeiting is clearly unethical, but a customer can easily be fooled into buying a counterfeit product he or she believes is made by the real company. The customer's reaction may well be to accuse the company of unethical behaviour in selling products that are of inferior quality. How can a manager respond to this erroneous perception?

4. *For debate:* In some people's opinion, a name-brand product indicates status, shows prestige, and creates particular impressions. With a few exceptions, only a well-trained eye can differentiate between a fake product and the real thing. If someone wishes only to make an impression and is willing to do so by knowingly investing in a fake, they should not be denied access to fake products that are typically available at a fraction of the cost of the real thing. Do you agree or disagree with this?

Sources: Based on "Counterfeit Business—'The Counterfeiting Crusader,'" *CBC Venture*, December 21, 2003, VA-2050C; "The Real Rip Off: Counterfeiting Costs Britain an Annual £9.2 Billion," Alliance Against IP Theft, http://www.allianceagainstiptheft.co.uk/cost/index.html (accessed November 16, 2006); "CSIS Project on Corruption, Counterfeiting, and Cyber-Fraud," Center for Strategic & International Studies, http://www.csis.org/schollchair/corruption/ (accessed November 16, 2006); A. Donoghue, "Counting the Cost of Counterfeiting," *CNET News.com*, http://news.com.com/Counting+the+cost+of+counterfeiting/2100-7348_3-6074831.html (accessed November 16, 2006); and http://www.csa.ca/news/LL.html.

Candy

The Life Savers plant in Holland, Michigan, has moved to Montreal, Canada. The move wiped out 600 union jobs in Michigan that paid an average of $15.50 per hour. For 35 years, the Life Savers plant symbolized stability and financial security for 155 000 Michigan residents and produced 200 million rolls a year. Why did Wrigley move its Life Savers production to Canada? The reason has a lot to do with the price of sugar.

United States candy makers pay between three and five times the world price for sugar. Since 1789 the United States has protected its sugar growers by slapping tariffs on imported sugar. The tariff has had the effect of making cheaper, imported sugar more expensive than domestic sugar, guaranteeing US farmers a good price. According to some American sugar beet farmers, without this protectionism they would go bankrupt.

In contrast, the National Confectioners Association, composed of 700 candy manufacturers, is lobbying the government to abandon the prevailing sugar policy, eliminate tariffs on imported sugar, and let sugar into the American market at world prices.

Canada's sugar industry operates under a free-market sugar policy in which tariffs on imported raw sugar are zero and tariffs on refined sugar are minimal. Most of Canada's trading partners maintain high tariffs on imports of both raw and refined sugar. About 90 percent of Canada's refined sugar is produced from raw cane sugar imported from tropical regions such as Australia, the Caribbean, and South and Central America. Canada's sugar policy makes sugar available for high volume users at much less cost than in other countries, providing producers of sugar-containing products with a significant competitive advantage.

In the United States, sugar is responsible for contributing $26.2 billion (US) and 420 000 jobs to the US economy. Chicago-based Ferrara Pan Candy, maker of Atomic Fireball candy, uses 2 million pounds of sugar per week in its operations. The company's sugar costs are 29 cents per pound—in Canada they would be 12 cents per pound. Life Savers uses 113 tons of sugar every day, and each Life Savers candy is 95 percent sugar. As a result, Life Savers, like many candy makers, has moved to Canada.

Opponents of relocating candy operations to Canada contend that the move has little to do with the cost of sugar and more to do with favourable exchange rates and cheaper labour. Supporters of this move argue that it makes good business sense because the greatest expense of producing candy is the cost of sugar. The savings make the move an easy decision.

QUESTIONS

1. *For analysis:* How does the move of Life Savers from Michigan to Montreal demonstrate the effect on Life Savers of its general environment?

2. *For analysis:* Who are some of the stakeholders affected by Life Savers' move?

3. *For application:* How does this case demonstrate the effect of globalization on operating a business?

4. *For debate:* Among other things, globalization means that firms will locate wherever they perceive they have the capacity to either create or to sustain a competitive advantage. This means that no business will necessarily be located in a country or community indefinitely. As such, businesses should invest in only short-term socially responsible initiatives and in those short-term activities that can be discontinued without creating undue hardship on stakeholders. Would you agree or disagree with this statement?

Sources: "Candy," *CBC Venture*, May 5, 2002, VA-2032C; R. Frammolino, "Workers Feel Like Suckers," *Los Angeles Times*, March 20, 2002, http://www.commondreams.org/headlines02/0320-02.htm (accessed November 16, 2006); "Administering Sugar Imports," United States Department of Agriculture, http://www.fas.usda.gov/itp/imports/ussugar.asp (accessed November 16, 2006); and Canadian Sugar Institute website, http://www.sugar.ca/index.htm (accessed November 16, 2006).

Part 2: Planning

Montreal Sandwich

Frederick Haneuse is a Montrealer with a taste for the finer things in life. When he discovered Lina's Café, a successful luxury sandwich franchise, he thought it would work well in the business district of Montreal.

Haneuse decided to open a Lina's Café in Place Ville Marie; many of the 25 000 people who work in the area are affluent brokers, lawyers, and businesspeople. Haneuse soon found out that planning a restaurant, even when it is a franchise, is not simple. In addition to finding money for the start-up costs, he needed to scout the competition, find an appropriate location, as well as hire and locate architects, construction contractors, food suppliers, and staff.

Founded in Paris in 1989, Lina's Café was built around the idea of the *luxury sandwich,* which costs about twice the price of the competition's. The concept is an up-market restaurant offering very high quality products, first choice ingredients, strict hygiene control, recipes developed around freshness, and highly trained staff. Franchise contracts for Lina's Cafés typically run for five years and require an average initial entry fee of 35 000 euros (approximately CDN$50 000). Franchisees are typically required to pay 7 percent of gross revenue to cover brand royalties and company advertising. The average investment for the franchisee is approximately 1000 to 1200 euros per square metre of restaurant space, and the average surface area of a typical Lina's is 200 square metres—representing an investment of approximately 200 000 to 240 000 euros, or CDN$285 000 to $340 000.

With financial support from family and friends, as well as bank loans, Haneuse embarked on his dream. He experienced difficulty in getting support from banks, as well as construction issues and costs that soon soared $80 000 over budget. To try to reduce the deficit, he opted for less expensive air conditioning, furniture, and lighting, but even with these compromises he was still short $40 000 to $50 000.

With these financial challenges came other problems—including construction delays and a winter storm—which pushed back opening day several times. Opening day finally arrived on January 6, well after the busy Christmas shopping crowds that Haneuse had hoped to feed had gone. At the end of his first day, Haneuse had sold 50 sandwiches, at about $10 each. But with initial equipment costs of more than $50 000, architectural and construction set-up costs of more than $200 000, and a total initial investment of almost $400 000,

Haneuse would need to sell around 250 sandwiches per day to become profitable.

How is he doing? Haneuse is still in business. He has added a catering service, and while he has lowered the price of sandwiches somewhat, they are still more expensive than those offered by the local competition. He is selling approximately 200 sandwiches per day—enough to pay the bills.

QUESTIONS

1. *For analysis:* Run through the steps of the decision-making process that Frederick Haneuse might have followed in deciding on Lina's Café as the appropriate restaurant for his start-up.

2. *For analysis:* Strategic management is defined as that set of managerial decisions and actions that determines the long-run performance of an organization. How did Frederick Haneuse demonstrate each step in the six-step strategic management process?

3. *For analysis:* Which corporate-level strategy do you think Lina's Café is pursuing?

4. *For application:* If you were Frederick Haneuse, which techniques would you use to assess the environment to ensure a continuation of the success of Lina's Café in Place Ville Marie?

5. *For debate:* Scenario planning involves planning for contingencies. If Frederick Haneuse has planned properly, he has planned for the arrival of a competitor in the food market in Place Ville Marie. This would be the most important serious threat to his business. Would you agree or disagree?

Sources: "Montreal Sandwich," *CBC Venture,* August 17, 2003, VA-2050A; and Lina's Café website, http://www.linascafe.fr/english.htm (accessed November 16, 2006).

CBC ⬤ CBC Video Case Incident

Seeds of Dreams

Daniel Bouchard wants to help his community, which has been hit hard by heavy job losses as farmers give up on farming. Bouchard is from Falher, Alberta, a town of 1000. As general manager of the Falher Co-operative Seed Cleaning Plant, he was asked by his board of directors to find ways to help the co-op expand and diversify. Bouchard recommends the purchase of a local grain elevator that could be converted into an oat-processing plant.

Bouchard needs to convince the local townspeople to invest in the oat-processing plant. He estimates it will take $6 million to build the plant; he needs to raise more than $2 million more. His goal is to convince 500 people to buy shares in the new plant, at $5000 a share. He meets with much skepticism from the townspeople, even though he projects that the facility will handle 1.5 million bushels of oats in its first year, thereby ensuring its success. Demand for oats is increasing in North America. "We

have a reliable supply of quality oats and can expect consistently good inventory, year in and year out," he says.

Bouchard failed in his attempt to get half of the town of Falher to support him, but he was able to raise nearly 60 percent of the capital he needed through a variety of other sources. With the money, he started Peace Country Oats Processors as a division of the co-op, operating it with three full-time staff, including himself.

As Bouchard has discovered, it is not easy to raise money. Now he needs to develop a Plan B. "One of the options we're considering is setting up a partnership with outside investors for the rest of the capital," says Bouchard. However, he is not completely comfortable with this idea. "We were hoping to remain more independent of larger corporations, but that's hard," he says. He's also willing to cut down the scope of the project and build the business in stages, if necessary.

1. *For analysis:* Evaluate the pros and cons of Bouchard's forming a partnership with outside investors to raise additional capital. Instead, should he stay small, relying on the capital he already has?

2. *For analysis:* Bouchard was not successful in convincing local farmers to invest in his business. How could he have used planning to develop more support for his business?

3. *For application:* Using the steps of the decision-making process, how would you evaluate whether to continue to stay small or develop a larger business by finding some partners who will invest in the business?

4. *For application:* Show how a SWOT analysis could be used to help Bouchard make plans for his company's growth over the next five years.

5. *For debate:* One of the options for the board of directors of Peace Country Oats Processors is to find a partner who would own half of the company. What are the advantages and disadvantages of doing this? Should Bouchard bring a partner into his business?

Sources: "Falher, Alberta," *CBC Venture,* May 4, 2003, VA2051H, 878; "Oat Processing Facility a Regional Effort," *Peace Region Economic Development Alliance,* May 2003, http://www.peacecountrycanada.com/files/may2003.pdf (accessed November 17, 2006); R. Froese, "Peace Country Oats Falls Short of Target for Shares," *Smoky River Express,* March 10, 2004, http://www.smokyriverexpress.com/newsroom/ volume38/040310/news2.html (accessed November 17, 2006); and R. Cairney, "A Feeling for Alberta," *Folio,* March 5, 2004, http://www.ualberta.ca/~publicas/folio/ 41/12/08.html (accessed November 17, 2006).

Part 3: Organizing

CBC | **CBC Video Case Incident**

Email Alert

Every day in North America, 500 million email messages are sent or forwarded and, while the volume of messages is impressive, the level of candour and the absence of discretion in the content of many messages are shocking.

It appears that people will say anything in email messages, frequently sharing employers' secrets, and this lack of judgment can cause havoc for a company when lawyers are called in. The smart lawyers typically subpoena volumes of records, including emails downloaded from hard drives. Just because a person deletes an email doesn't mean that it's gone forever. In fact, email continues to live on in hard drives until the memory is exhausted and the space occupied by "deleted" data is replaced by more current files. Considering the memory capacity of most hard drives, these deleted emails can live for quite some time.

KPMG Forensics' mandate is "to assist in resolving issues when corporate behaviour [violates] ethical standards, and to help create clarity when information, organizations or individuals disagree." The company's services include investigating electronic records in an effort to help assemble facts in a coherent manner. Using some of the latest technology, KPMG recovers almost 1 million pages per day as evidence for legal cases!

In 1999, in light of the rise in companies offering secure email systems, ZDNet.com asked the question "Can secure email help sidestep suits?" ZDNet.com cited an emerging nightmare: subpoena-empowered lawyers searching computer networks for email conversations that stick around. In one case, American Home Products Corporation, a pharmaceutical company, had to pay $3.75 billion in damages as a result of information discovered by a team of cyber-savvy lawyers that searched over 33 million emails and documents on the company's servers. According to cryptographer and security specialist Bruce Schneier, "The [secure email] system works as long as the employee cooperates . . . . Employees who want to can certainly bypass the policy."

Managers face enormous information management challenges in the information age. In the midst of globalization, the growing number of virtual offices located both next door and around the world, and the emerging culture of instant information expectations, what can be done to protect company secrets?

Protecting and securing information is a growing industry, with more and more companies offering approaches to digital security. One example of such a company is Entrust, which secures an organization's "digital life" by providing software solutions that protect an organization's digital identity, enforce policy through content scanning, and protect information assets through encryption.

According to the 2006 Entrust Mobile Workforce Survey of 114 enterprises, more than 90 percent of the respondents said that they rely on employees to comply with security policies. Although information security policies and the use of technology can help protect sensitive data, the key message remains: Think before you hit "Send."

1. *For analysis:* How have advances in information and communications technology affected communications in organizations?

2. *For analysis:* How has email both simplified and complicated management?

3. *For debate:* Advances in information and communications technology can be both a blessing and a curse to managers. In particular, email has strong benefits, but for each benefit there is also a strong challenge. For large bureaucratic organizations, the challenges frequently outweigh the benefits. Do you agree or disagree with this?

Sources: "eMail Alert," *CBC Venture,* October 27, 2002, VA-2040A; "Forensic," KPMG Canada, http://www.kpmg.ca/en/services/advisory/forensic/ (accessed November 16, 2006); "Can Secure E-mail Help Sidestep Suits?" ZDNet.com, October 8, 1999, http://listserv.muohio.edu/scripts/wa.exe?A2=ind9910b&L=archives&P=23958 (accessed November 16, 2006); Entrust website, http://www.entrust.com/corporate/index.htm (accessed November 16, 2006); and Entrust, "Organizations Cite Data Encryption as Best Strategy in New Entrust Survey," news release, November 7, 2006, http://www.cnw.ca/fr/releases/archive/November2006/07/c9330.html (accessed November 16, 2006).

CBC | **CBC Video Case Incident**

Caribbean Beer

Successfully running a microbrewery is tough business, particularly when big brewers own 90 percent of the market. So, when Peter Harrison bought Hart Breweries of Carleton Place in 2001, he knew it would be a gamble whether his $1 million investment in this microbrewery would pay off.

Hart Brewery was founded by Lorne Hart in Carleton Place, Ontario. The company's first batch was brewed in 1991. Later, Hart merged with Robinson Brewing Company to become the Hart/Robinson Brewing Co., with locations in Carleton Place and Mississauga, Ontario. The brewery was famous for cask-conditioned ale ("real ale").

Harrison believed that a possible niche market might exist in the production of Caribbean beer through a licencing agreement with Banks Beer of Barbados. Banks Beer, known as "the beer of Barbados," was first produced in 1961. The premium lager is brewed from British and Australian malted barleys. It is Barbados' water, along with a special strain of yeast, that makes Banks Beer distinct. Hart Brewery began producing Hart Beer, Banks Beer, and an energy drink called Malta.

Hart was hampered by a variety of problems: continuous equipment failures, machinery problems, higher-than-expected production costs, and high alcohol taxes. There were also changes in personnel—more specifically, brewmasters: in some cases inexperienced brewmasters, in others "brewmasters" who were not professionally trained.

Notwithstanding these challenges, a big break came with an expression of interest to purchase Banks Beer from Grace Foods, a big distributor of Caribbean foods. But Hart's request for 50 percent of the contract value up front and a two-year deal was rejected by Grace Foods, who preferred a series of 90-day deals instead.

Initiatives to cut costs resulted in a 10 percent savings on the cost of bottles by contracting with a new bottle supplier. Despite Hart products being carried in 350 beer stores in Ontario, the microbrewery was just breaking even.

QUESTIONS

1. *For analysis:* How important is human resource management to the success of a small company, such as a microbrewery, and what are the key challenges?

2. *For analysis:* Using the Internet as a basis for your research, is Hart/Robinson still in operation? Comment on your findings.

3. *For application:* How would you organize a microbrewery? What factors would affect your choice of organizational structure?

4. *For debate:* Developing a successful small business, such as the Hart/Robinson breweries, is a very difficult and risky undertaking. Having the right people with the right skills, ambitions, and attitudes is often more important for small businesses than for large businesses. In large businesses, marginal performers can be sometimes "lost" somewhere in the bureaucracy. Would you agree with this statement?

Sources: "Caribbean Beer," *CBC Venture,* July 20, 2003, VA-2042A; "Brewing in Canada," Draft Horse Brewery, http://www.drafthorsebrewery.ca/brewingincanada.html (accessed November 16, 2006); and Banks Beer website, http://www.banksbeer.com (accessed November 16, 2006).

Part 4: Leading

Leading With Integrity

Founded in January 2000, Quova, a small Mountain View, California, start-up is one of the highly profitable survivors of the information technology bust. Quova is "the world's leading provider and developer of web geography services and technologies." Quova's GeoPoint service can determine the geographic location of website visitors, including their countries, regions, cities, and postal codes. One application of this software is to identify web fraud by determining whether an online buyer who claims a Canadian billing and mailing address is actually placing an order from Canada, or whether the order is coming from countries known to have a high rate of credit card fraud. Geo-location can also be used by bookmakers, casinos, and lottery operators for fraud detection. Using Quova's geo-location software, clients can target marketing campaigns by pinpointing a user's location, all without violating any privacy rights.

CEO Marie Alexander attributes Quova's success to its front-runner software solutions and to her "hands-under" leadership style. She believes in catching people if they fall, encouraging her staff to stretch themselves, learning from conflict, and taking sole responsibility for tough decisions when circumstances require her to do so.

QUESTIONS

1. *For analysis:* How might the path-goal contingency-based theory be used to analyze Marie Alexander's leadership style?

2. *For analysis:* From a leadership perspective, what are the advantages and disadvantages of Quova's relatively small size?

3. *For application:* Quova also maintains European headquarters in Amsterdam. As the company grows, what additional skills will Alexander need in order to provide online leadership to employees in various locations?

4. *For application:* What are some of the ethical or moral challenges that Alexander might prepare herself for, as the use of geo-location software becomes more prevalent?

5. *For debate:* After a colleague gave her a backhanded compliment referring to her gender, Alexander simply replied, "I didn't feel I was lacking any body parts while we were having those discussions." Do you think this was a good response? Support your position.

Sources: Based on "Leading with Integrity and Compassion: Quova," Introduction to Business Video Library, © 2003 Prentice Hall, produced in conjunction with *Business NOW*; and http://www.quova.com (accessed November 22, 2006).

Millionaire on a Mission

Bill Young is a millionaire with a heart. After making millions leading high-growth entrepreneurial organizations, he decided to invest in helping others. He founded Toronto-based Social Capital Partners (SCP) in 2001. SCP provides support to businesses that hire people who often have difficulties finding employment: youths, single mothers, Aboriginals, new immigrants, people with disabilities, and those with substance abuse issues.

SCP provides start-up capital to business ventures that it thinks will be able to grow and turn a profit within about three years. The business owners must commit to helping improve the lives of their employees by making them financially self-sufficient while providing training and other support as necessary.

The types of businesses supported by SCP are known as "social enterprises." They look like typical businesses, except most of their employees come from groups that rely heavily on government assistance to live and have found it nearly impossible to get full-time jobs for a variety of reasons. These businesses have a "double bottom line": "a financial bottom line like traditional businesses but also a social bottom line—getting people who have traditionally faced significant employment barriers back into the economic mainstream."

SCP funds a number of social enterprises, including Winnipeg-based Inner City Renovation (ICR). ICR, founded in August 2002, is a construction and renovation company that works mainly on nonprofit housing projects. The company's work helps address the lack of affordable housing in Winnipeg, and also provides employment to Aboriginal peoples who live in the inner city. Employees often work on houses in their own neighbourhoods, which means that their work is also improving their local environment. ICR's employees earn a steady income, and also learn a skilled trade that they can use in the future. An Aboriginal social worker on staff helps employees address personal problems, including alcohol and chemical dependency.

By mid-2004, SCP and Winnipeg-based Community Ownership Solutions had invested $100 000 in ICR. The company generated almost $1 million in revenue after its first year, but also suffered a $350 000 loss. By the end of 2005, however, the company generated more than $1 million in revenue, with a loss of only $3000. Young acknowledges that ICR is a "wonderful learning experience. It's not like it's gone smoothly. It's such an exciting model, this notion of combining housing and employment. It's taking a radically different approach to structural social problems in a lot of urban areas. There are exciting implications, if we can make this work."

QUESTIONS

1. *For analysis:* What leadership style(s) might be effective when dealing with employees who have personal challenges, such as those who are employed by Inner City Renovation?

2. *For analysis:* From a leadership perspective, what are the advantages and disadvantages of leading a company identified as a social enterprise?

3. *For application:* Inner City Renovation would like to reduce the absenteeism and turnover rates of its employees. How should it go about doing this?

4. *For application:* What are some of the challenges that Bill Young faces in trying to identify social enterprises to invest in?

5. *For debate:* "Only money motivates employees. Inner City Renovation should pay its employees more in order to solve its turnover problems." Do you agree or disagree with these statements? Explain.

Sources: "Social Capitalist," *CBC Venture*, February 29, 2004, 916; http://www.socialcapitalpartners.ca/index.html (accessed January 23, 2005); M. Cook, "Chasing the Double Bottom Line: Series: The Charity Industry," *Ottawa Citizen*, March 1, 2004, p. D7; and http://www.socialcapitalpartners.ca/articles/ICRReport%20Card%202005.ppt.

Part 5: Controlling

Video Case Incident

Creative Age Publications

Founded in 1971 by president and CEO Deborah Carver, Creative Age Publications has single-handedly revolutionized the trade magazine industry. Careful planning and a management style that "shows heart" to both customers and employees, along with a quality product, have more than quadrupled the company's growth in the past eight years. By promoting from within, emphasizing coordination between departments, and setting realistic goals to prevent "burnout," the company maintains an organizational culture that fosters creativity and teamwork.

Carver is particularly open to promoting alternative work arrangements for her employees. When Creative Age decided to publish *Launchpad* in 2002, Carver's choice for executive editor was Marianne Dougherty. Dougherty was living in Pittsburgh, Pennsylvania, and caring for her aging parents. Carver was determined that Dougherty was right for the job, and agreed to let her work from Pittsburgh, rather than require her to move to the company's head office in Van Nuys, California. "Out of hundreds of magazines, probably only one would be willing to do something like this," Carver said. "It works because Marianne is a consummate professional, truly."

The magazine titles published by Creative Age today—*Nailpro, DAYSPA, Launchpad, Beauty Store Business, Medesthetics, Inspire,* and *Sunless*—serve the needs of the beauty industry. These titles represent a significant change from Carver's original goals for Creative Age. When the company was founded, its focus was on medical journals (it published *Dialysis & Transplantation*, the world's largest renal care journal, until 2005). Although it had been a leading publisher of medical journals for two decades, it shifted its focus in the late 1980s by moving into professional beauty publishing. Today, the company has a European office and a Japanese edition and is working on franchising throughout the world.

QUESTIONS

1. *For analysis:* Based on what you know about the management structure of Creative Age, why is it critical that managers possess not only excellent technical skills but interpersonal and conceptual skills as well?

2. *For analysis:* What are some of the challenges that managers should anticipate when a company expands into foreign markets?

3. *For application:* What are some steps that Creative Age Publications might take in order to ensure that growth of its existing business operations does not threaten the company's long-term success?

4. *For application:* What might Creative Age Publications do to make sure its foreign offices and franchises have the same spirit of innovation and teamwork that exists in its California office?

5. *For debate:* To help bring change to the organization, Deborah Carver advocates hiring talented people who have learned their skills in industries other than publishing. Do you agree with her opinion that hiring someone from another field benefits the individual as well as the organizational culture at Creative Age Publications? Support your position.

Sources: Based on "Creative Age Publications," Introduction to Business Video Library, Prentice Hall Business News Network; http://www.creativeage.com (accessed November 16, 2006); and T. Schooley, "Fashion Journalist Returns to Her Roots to Head Beauty, Salon Magazine," *Pittsburgh Business Times*, September 5, 2003, p. 4.

CBC Video Case Incident

TELUS Troubles

Burnaby, BC-based TELUS is Canada's second largest phone company, formed in 1999 by a merger of BC TEL and the Alberta-only version of TELUS. Shortly thereafter, the company faced a bitter labour dispute with the Telecommunications Workers Union (TWU) when its contract expired at the end of 2000.

In 2002, the company eliminated 6000 employees and reduced the number of call centres for customer service from 56 to 10. These changes had a considerable impact on customer service. Customers often complained of being put on hold for two hours when they called for service and about repair people not showing up for appointments. Judy Zerr, whose phone was out of service for a month, elaborated: "At one time, our local pay phone was actually broken as well so we had to hop in the car and drive a little bit farther just to make a phone call to say the phone wasn't working."

One TELUS repairman said, "I just want people to know that the guys out here, we're just doin' the best job that we can do." Even so, operators record the mood of customers who call for service on a scale of one to five. Customers have become frustrated. One manager wrote a memo to employees noting that some customers could be violent. According to an employee, "We used to get emails about how to fend off vicious dogs. Now we're getting emails about how to fend off mad customers!"

The Canadian Radio-television and Telecommunications Commission (CRTC) got involved in the situation after receiving hundreds of complaints from customers. CRTC rules state that customer calls are supposed to be answered within 20 seconds and out-of-service phones are supposed to be fixed within 24 hours in most cases.

TELUS improved its performance in 2003 and 2004. In 2003, 1275 complaints were received in June and this dropped to 702 in December. In 2004, there were 150 service complaints in June and July, and 202 in October. But Sid Shniad, a research director for the TWU, offers another possibility: "I would suggest to you [that] complaints may be down, but that's not because there are no problems—that's because people are giving up in frustration. They're not getting any kind of responsiveness."

After nearly five years of not being able to negotiate a new contract with the TWU, TELUS made its last offer on April 12, 2005. Picket lines were set up on July 12, and the two parties finally signed a new contract in November 2005. Despite the labour problems, the number of customer complaints to the CRTC showed only a small increase from 2004, with 6968 complaints in 2005 versus 6887 in 2004. However, the third quarter of 2006 showed that the company performed below standard in access to the repair bureau, access to the business office, and clearing out-of-service trouble reports within 24 hours in rural areas.

QUESTIONS

1. *For analysis:* What control measures can TELUS put into place to reduce customer complaints?

2. *For analysis:* How might TELUS transform itself into a more customer-responsive organization?

3. *For application:* You're the manager of a large corporation with 18 000 employees, and the company is just about to lay off one third of them. What can you do to lessen the impact of downsizing on the remaining employees?

4. *For application:* How might a manager introduce new control measures to encourage employees to quickly change their customer service behaviour?

5. *For debate:* "Control measures make employees more accountable for their work, and this could ultimately demoralize them and decrease their performance." Do you agree with this statement? Why or why not?

Sources: "Telus Complaints," *CBC Marketplace*, December 2, 2003; http://www.cbc.ca/consumers/market/files/services/telus/ (accessed January 23, 2005); N. O'Connor, "Phone Problems Rampant—Union: 80-Year-Old's Story No Anomaly Say Workers," *Vancouver Courier*, December 15, 2004, p. 17; N. O'Connor, "Woman Questions Telus Service," *Maple Ridge, Pitt Meadows Times*, December 24, 2004, p. 26; http://about.telus.com/community/social_responsibility/en/commitment/stakeholders.html (accessed November 19, 2006); and http://www.crtc.gc.ca/eng/publications/reports/8660/Telus.htm (accessed November 19, 2006).

ENDNOTES

Chapter 1

1. Based on "A Promise to Be Broken," *Ottawa Citizen,* January 21, 2004, p. B4; T. Murray, "Independence Key for Ontario's New MOH," *Medical Post,* February 10, 2004, p. 47; L. Krugel, "City's Voice of Calm and Reason in a Crisis," *National Post,* March 6, 2004, p. SR06; K. Palmer and B. Demara, "Big Ideas and a Down-to-Earth Style," *Toronto Star,* January 20, 2004, p. A15; and R. Mackie, "Ontario Names New Chief Medical Officer," *Globe and Mail,* January 19, 2004, p. A9.

2. T. Schwartz, "The Greatest Sources of Satisfaction in the Workplace Are Internal and Emotional," *Fast Company,* November 2000, pp. 398–402; K. Dobbs, "Plagued by Turnover? Train Your Managers," *Training,* August 2000, pp. 62–65.

3. KPMG/Ipsos Reid, *Eleventh Annual Survey of Canada's Most Respected Corporations,* http://www.mostrespected.ca/en/documents/CMRC2005En.pdf (accessed August 1, 2006).

4. K. Palmer and B. Demara, "Big Ideas and a Down-to-Earth Style," *Toronto Star,* January 20, 2004, p. A15.

5. D. J. Campbell, "The Proactive Employee: Managing Workplace Initiative," *Academy of Management Executive,* August 2000, pp. 52–66.

6. See http://www.health.gov.on.ca/english/public/ministry/bios/basrur.html; and "Significant Progress Made, but Work Remains to Be Done to Renew Public Health Says Chief Medical Officer of Health," *Canada NewsWire,* January 17, 2006, p. 1.

7. K. Leslie, "Ontario Won't Compensate Bars, Restaurants for Smoking Rooms That Will Be Banned," *Canadian Press NewsWire,* March 1, 2006; and L. Krugel, "City's Voice of Calm and Reason in a Crisis," *National Post,* March 6, 2004, p. SR06.

8. R. Mackie, "Ontario Names New Chief Medical Officer," *Globe and Mail,* January 19, 2004, p. A9.

9. P. Drucker, *Management: Tasks, Responsibilities, Practices* (New York: Harper & Row, 1974).

10. H. Fayol, *Industrial and General Administration* (Paris: Dunod, 1916).

11. For a comprehensive review of this question, see C.P. Hales, "What Do Managers Do? A Critical Review of the Evidence," *Journal of Management,* January 1986, pp. 88–115.

12. H. Mintzberg, *The Nature of Managerial Work* (New York: Harper & Row, 1973); and J. T. Straub, "Put on Your Manager's Hat," *USA Today,* October 29, 2002, http://www.usatoday.com.

13. S. J. Carroll and D. A. Gillen, "Are the Classical Management Functions Useful in Describing Managerial Work?" *Academy of Management Review,* January 1987, p. 48.

14. H. Koontz, "Commentary on the Management Theory Jungle—Nearly Two Decades Later," in *Management: A Book of Readings,* 6th ed., ed. H. Koontz, C. O'Donnell, and H. Weihrich (New York: McGraw-Hill, 1984); S. J. Carroll and D. A. Gillen, "Are the Classical Management Functions Useful in Describing Managerial Work?" *Academy of Management Review,* January 1987, p. 48; and P. Allan, "Managers at Work: A Large-Scale Study of the Managerial Job in New York City Government," *Academy of Management Journal,* September 1981, pp. 613–619.

15. R. L. Katz, "Skills of an Effective Administrator," *Harvard Business Review,* September–October 1974, pp. 90–102.

16. D. Nebenzahl, "People Skills Matter Most," *Gazette* (Montreal), September 20, 2004, p. B1.

17. H. G. Barkema, J. A. C. Baum, and E. A. Mannix, "Management Challenges in a New Time," *Academy of Management Journal,* October 2002, pp. 916–930; M. A. Hitt, "Transformation of Management for the New Millennium," *Organizational Dynamics,* Winter 2000, pp. 7–17; T. Aeppel, "Power Generation," *Wall Street Journal,* April 7, 2000, p. A11; "Rethinking Work," *Fast Company,* April 2000, p. 253; "Workplace Trends Shifting over Time," *Springfield News Leader,* January 2, 2000, p. 7B1; "Expectations: The State of the New Economy," *Fast Company,* September 1999, pp. 251–264; T. J. Tetenbaum, "Shifting Paradigms: From Newton to Chaos," *Organizational Dynamics,* Spring 1998, pp. 21–33; T. A. Stewart, "Brain Power: Who Owns It ... How They Profit from It," *Fortune,* March 17, 1997, pp. 105–110; G. P. Zachary, "The Right Mix," *Wall Street Journal,* March 13, 1997, p. A11; W. H. Miller, "Leadership at a Crossroads," *IndustryWeek,* August 19, 1996, pp. 42–56; M. Scott, "Interview with Dee Hock," *Business Ethics,* May–June 1996, pp. 37–41; J. O. C. Hamilton, S. Baker, and B. Vlasic, "The New Workplace," *BusinessWeek,* April 29, 1996, pp. 106–117.

18. Industry Canada, "Establishments by Employment Size Category and Region," http://strategis.ic.gc.ca/sc_ecnmy/sio/ciseste.html.

19. C. Harris, "Prime Numbers: A Statistical Look at the Trends and Issues That Will Dominate Our Future," *Financial Post,* November 15/17, 1997, p. P13.

20. Industry Canada, "Key Small Business Statistics," July 2005, http://strategis.gc.ca/sbstatistics.

21. Industry Canada, "Key Small Business Statistics," July 2005, http://strategis.gc.ca/sbstatistics.

22. These figures are from August 2006 and based on information in Statistics Canada, "Latest Release from the Labour Force Survey," September 8, 2006, http://www.statcan.ca/english/Subjects/Labour/LFS/lfs-en.htm.

23. Canada Post, *Annual Report, 2005,* http://www.canadapost.ca/corporate/about/annual_report/contents_EN/introduction-e.html (accessed September 24, 2006); and "50 Biggest Employers (2005)," *Report on Business,* http://www.theglobeandmail.com/v5/content/tp1000/index.php?view=top_50_employers (accessed September 24, 2006).

24. K. Palmer, "MDs Fear It's Headed for 'Back Burner'; 'Irons in the Fire' but Little Happening," *Toronto Star,* March 8, 2004, p. A9.

25. K. Davis and W. C. Frederick, *Business and Society: Management, Public Policy, Ethics,* 5th ed. (New York: McGraw-Hill, 1984), pp. 28–41, 76.

26. See, for example, R. A. Buccholz, *Essentials of Public Policy for Management,* 2nd ed. (Upper Saddle River, NJ: Prentice Hall, 1990).

27. M. Friedman, *Capitalism and Freedom* (Chicago: University of Chicago Press, 1962); and M. Friedman, "The Social Responsibility of Business Is to Increase Profits," *New York Times Magazine,* September 13, 1970, p. 33.

28. J. Bakan, *The Corporation* (Toronto: Big Picture Media Corporation, 2003).

29. Information from Avon's website, http://www.avoncompany.com/women/avoncrusade/ (accessed August 3, 2006).

30. E. P. Lima, "Seeding a World of Transformation," *IndustryWeek*, September 6, 1999, pp. 30–31.

31. E. White, "PR Firms Advise Corporations on Social Responsibility Issues," *Wall Street Journal*, November 13, 2002, p. B10.

32. The Triple Bottom Line was first introduced in J. Elkington, *Cannibals with Forks: The Triple Bottom Line of 21st Century Business* (Stony Creek, CT: New Society Publishers, 1998).

33. See, for example, A. B. Carroll, "The Pyramid of Corporate Social Responsibility: Toward the Moral Management of Organizational Stakeholders," *Business Horizons*, July–August 1991, pp. 39–48.

34. This section has been influenced by E. Gatewood and A. B. Carroll, "The Anatomy of Corporate Social Response," *Business Horizons*, September–October 1981, pp. 9–16.

35. See, for instance, P. Cochran and R. A. Wood, "Corporate Social Responsibility and Financial Performance," *Academy of Management Journal*, March 1984, pp. 42–56; K. Aupperle, A. B. Carroll, and J. D. Hatfield, "An Empirical Examination of the Relationship Between Corporate Social Responsibility and Profitability," *Academy of Management Journal*, June 1985, pp. 446–463; J. B. McGuire, A. Sundgren, and T. Schneeweis, "Corporate Social Responsibility and Firm Financial Performance," *Academy of Management Journal*, December 1988, pp. 854–872; D. M. Georgoff and J. Ross, "Corporate Social Responsibility and Management Performance" (paper presented at the National Academy of Management Conference, Miami, Florida, August 1991); S. A. Zahra, B. M. Oviatt, and K. Minyard, "Effects of Corporate Ownership and Board Structure on Corporate Social Responsibility and Financial Performance" (paper presented at the National Academy of Management Conference, Atlanta, Georgia, August 1993); "Social Responsibility and the Bottom Line," *Business Ethics*, July–August 1994, p. 11; D. B. Turban and D. W. Greening, "Corporate Social Performance and Organizational Attractiveness to Prospective Employees," *Academy of Management Journal*, June 1996, pp. 658–672; S. A. Waddock and S. B. Graves, "The Corporate Social Performance–Financial Performance Link," *Strategic Management Journal*, April 1997, pp. 303–319; S. L. Berman, A. C. Wicks, S. Kotha, and T. M. Jones, "Does Stakeholder Orientation Matter? The Relationship Between Stakeholder Management Models and Firm Financial Performance," *Academy of Management Journal*, October 1999, pp. 488–506.

36. D. J. Wood and R. E. Jones, "Stakeholder Mismatching: A Theoretical Problem in Empirical Research on Corporate Social Performance," *International Journal of Organizational Analysis* 3, no. 3 (1995), pp. 229–267.

37. See A. A. Ullmann, "Data in Search of a Theory: A Critical Examination of the Relationships Among Social Performance, Social Disclosure, and Economic Performance of U.S. Firms," *Academy of Management Review*, July 1985, pp. 540–557; R. E. Wokutch and B. A. Spencer, "Corporate Saints and Sinners: The Effects of Philanthropic and Illegal Activity on Organizational Performance," *California Management Review*, Winter 1987, pp. 62–77; R. Wolfe and K. Aupperle, "Introduction to Corporate Social Performance: Methods for Evaluating an Elusive Construct," ed. J. E. Post, *Research in Corporate Social Performance and Policy* 13 (1991), pp. 265–268; and D. J. Wood and R. E. Jones, "Stakeholder Mismatching: A Theoretical Problem in Empirical Research on Corporate Social Performance," *International Journal of Organizational Analysis* 3 (1995), pp. 229–267.

38. D. Macfarlane, "Why Now?" *Report on Business Magazine*, March 2004, pp. 45–46.

39. "Hispanics Now Top Minority," *Hispanic Business*, March 2003, p. 16.

40. Information for this paragraph was based on Statistics Canada, "Canada's Ethnocultural Portrait: The Changing Mosaic," January 2003, http://www12.statcan.ca/english/census01/products/analytic/companion/etoimm/provs.cfm (accessed May 16, 2003).

41. J. E. Garten, "Globalism Without Tears," *Strategy & Business*, Fourth Quarter 2002, pp. 36–45; L. L. Bierema, J. W. Bing, and T. J. Carter, "The Global Pendulum," *Training & Development*, May 2002, pp. 70–78; C. Taylor, "Whatever Happened to Globalization?" *Fast Company*, September 1999, pp. 228–236; and S. Zahra, "The Changing Rules of Global Competitiveness in the 21st Century," *Academy of Management Executive*, February 1999, pp. 36–42.

42. See http://money.cnn.com/magazines/fortune/global500/2006/countries/C.html.

43. A. Shama, "Management Under Fire: The Transformation of Management in the Soviet Union and Eastern Europe," *Academy of Management Executive* 7, no. 1 (1993), pp. 22–35.

44. L. Krugel, "City's Voice of Calm and Reason in a Crisis," *National Post*, March 6, 2004, p. SR06.

45. Based on J. B. Miner and N. R. Smith, "Decline and Stabilization of Managerial Motivation Over a 20-Year Period," *Journal of Applied Psychology*, June 1982, pp. 297–305; and J. B. Miner, B. Ebrahimi, and J. M. Wachtel, "How Deficiencies in Motivation to Manage Contribute to the United States' Competitiveness Problem (and What Can Be Done About It)," *Human Resource Management*, Fall 1995, pp. 363–386.

46. E. Church, "Market Recovery Delivers Executive Payout Bonanza," *Globe and Mail*, May 4, 2005, p. B1; and http://www.theglobeandmail.com/servlet/story/RTGAM.20060508.wexec-comp-main0509/BNStory/Business/home.

47. See, for example, "Executive Hires and Compensations: Performance Rules," *HRfocus*, July 2003, p. 1; and H. B. Herring, "At the Top, Pay and Performance Are Often Far Apart," *New York Times*, August 17, 2003, p. B9.

48. L. Lavelle, "CEO Pay: Nothing Succeeds Like Failure," *BusinessWeek*, September 11, 2000, p. 48.

49. D. Dias, "Bang for the Buck: CEO Scorecard," *National Post Business*, November 2005, p. 79.

50. Information from company website, http://www.thethinkers.com (accessed March 15, 2003); and N. K. Austin, "Tear Down the Walls," *Inc.*, April 1999, pp. 66–76.

51. Based on H. Rothman, "The Boss as Mentor," *Nation's Business*, April 1993, pp. 66–67; J. B. Cunningham and T. Eberle, "Characteristics of the Mentoring Experience: A Qualitative Study," *Personnel Review*, June 1993, pp. 54–66; S. Crandell, "The Joys of Mentoring," *Executive Female*, March–April 1994, pp. 38–42; and W. Heery, "Corporate Mentoring Can Break the Glass Ceiling," *HRfocus*, May 1994, pp. 17–18.

Supplement 1

1. Opening vignette based on "Coffee Crisis Prompts Action from Aid Groups," *CTV News*, September 19, 2002; http://www.java-jazz.ca/about_us.htm (accessed August 21, 2004); G. Shaw, "No Turning Back Once the Money Rolls In: $30,000 Loan from a Friend Puts Jazzed-Up Coffee Van on the Road with Espresso Machine at the Ready," *Vancouver Sun*, August 21, 2004, p. J1.

2. F. W. Taylor, *The Principles of Scientific Management* (New York: Harper, 1911), p. 44. For other information on F. W. Taylor, see M. Banta, *Taylored Lives: Narrative Productions in the Age of Taylor, Veblen, and Ford* (Chicago: University of Chicago Press, 1993); R. Kanigel, *The One Best Way: Frederick Winslow Taylor and the Enigma of Efficiency* (New York: Viking, 1997).

3. See, for example, F. B. Gilbreth, *Motion Study* (New York: Van Nostrand, 1911); and F. B. Gilbreth and L. M. Gilbreth, *Fatigue Study* (New York: Sturgis and Walton, 1916).

4. G. Colvin, "Managing in the Info Era," *Fortune,* March 6, 2000, pp. F6–F9; and A. Harrington, "The Big Ideas," *Fortune,* November 22, 1999, pp. 152–153.

5. H. Fayol, *Industrial and General Administration* (Paris: Dunod, 1916).

6. M. Weber, *The Theory of Social and Economic Organizations,* ed. T. Parsons, trans. A. M. Henderson and T. Parsons (New York: Free Press, 1947).

7. E. Mayo, *The Human Problems of an Industrial Civilization* (New York: Macmillan, 1933); F. J. Roethlisberger and W. J. Dickson, *Management and the Worker* (Cambridge, MA: Harvard University Press, 1939).

8. See, for example, A. Carey, "The Hawthorne Studies: A Radical Criticism," *American Sociological Review,* June 1967, pp. 403–416; R. H. Franke and J. Kaul, "The Hawthorne Experiments: First Statistical Interpretations," *American Sociological Review,* October 1978, pp. 623–643; B. Rice, "The Hawthorne Defect: Persistence of a Flawed Theory," *Psychology Today,* February 1982, pp. 70–74; J. A. Sonnenfeld, "Shedding Light on the Hawthorne Studies," *Journal of Occupational Behavior,* April 1985, pp. 111–130; and S. R. G. Jones, "Worker Interdependence and Output: The Hawthorne Studies Reevaluated," *American Sociological Review,* April 1990, pp. 176–190; S. R. Jones, "Was There a Hawthorne Effect?" *American Sociological Review,* November 1992, pp. 451–468; G. W. Yunker, "An Explanation of Positive and Negative Hawthorne Effects: Evidence from the Relay Assembly Test Room and Bank Wiring Observation Room Studies" (paper presented at Academy of Management annual meeting, August 1993, Atlanta, Georgia).

9. With thanks to a reviewer who provided this example.

10. K. B. DeGreene, *Sociotechnical Systems: Factors in Analysis, Design, and Management* (Englewood Cliffs, NJ: Prentice Hall, 1973), p. 13.

Chapter 2

1. C. Alphonso, "A Coast-to-Coast Cover-Up," *Globe and Mail,* April 3, 2004, p. F2.

2. G. Richards, "School Dress Codes Cross Cultures," *Calgary Herald,* March 26, 2004, p. A12.

3. J. Colebourn and L. Sin, "Richmond Seeks to Curb 'Extreme' Dress in Schools," *Province* (Vancouver), March 26, 2004, p. A3.

4. T. M. Hout, "Are Managers Obsolete?" *Harvard Business Review,* March–April 1999, pp. 161–168; and J. Pfeffer, "Management as Symbolic Action: The Creation and Maintenance of Organizational Paradigms," in *Research in Organizational Behavior,* vol. 3, ed. L. L. Cummings and B. M. Staw (Greenwich, CT: JAI Press, 1981), pp. 1–52.

5. G. Richards, "School Dress Codes Cross Cultures," *Calgary Herald,* March 26, 2004, p. A12.

6. J. Greenwood, "Home Depot Runs into Vancouver Red Tape," *Financial Post* (*National Post*), May 10, 2004, pp. FP1, FP11.

7. D. Calleja, "Equity or Else," *Canadian Business,* March 19, 2001, p. 31.

8. R. Annan, "Merger Remedies in Canada," Competition Bureau, June 20, 2006, http://www.competitionbureau.gc.ca/internet/index.cfm?itemID=2134&lg=e#25 (accessed September 24, 2006).

9. T. S. Mescon and G. S. Vozikis, "Federal Regulation—What Are the Costs?" *Business,* January–March 1982, pp. 33–39.

10. J. Thorpe, "Inter-Provincial Trade Barriers Still a Concern for Executives 'Handicapping Country Economically,'" *Financial Post* (*National Post*), September 13, 2004, p. FP2.

11. See http://www.canada.com/nationalpost/entrepreneur/savoie.html (accessed August 10, 2006).

12. See http://www.fritolay.ca/nutrition/press.html.

13. See http://www.ctv.ca/servlet/ArticleNews/story/CTVNews/_1069789271153_26/?hub=Health.

14. G. Bonnell, "Food Industry Rushes to Drop Trans Fats," *Calgary Herald,* March 11, 2004, p. D1.

15. "WTO Policy Issues for Parliamentarians," World Trade Organization, http://www.wto.org/english/res_e/booksp_e/parliamentarians_e.pdf (accessed September 3, 2004), p. 1.

16. Data for 2004. http://europa.eu.int/abc/keyfigures/index_en.htm (accessed May 7, 2006).

17. See http://www.eurunion.org/profile/EUUSStats.htm (accessed September 24, 2006).

18. D. T. Griswold and W. R. Hawkins, "Symposium: Free Trade Agreement, 1991, United States–Canada–Mexico," *Insight on the News,* January 21, 2003, pp. 46–49.

19. See http://www.statcan.ca/english/Pgdb/gblec02a.htm.

20. This section is based on materials from the World Trade Organization website, http://www.wto.org.

21. G. Abramovich, "Google's China Syndrome," *DM News,* June 20, 2006, http://www.dmnews.com/cms/dm-news/search-marketing/37089.html (accessed August 11, 2006).

22. G. Hofstede, *Culture's Consequences: International Differences in Work-Related Values,* 2nd ed. (Thousand Oaks, CA: Sage, 2001), pp. 9–15; and G. Hofstede, "The Cultural Relativity of Organizational Practices and Theories," *Journal of International Business Studies,* Fall 1983, pp. 75–89.

23. G. Hofstede, *Culture's Consequences: International Differences in Work-Related Values* (Beverly Hills, CA: Sage, 1980); G. Hofstede, *Cultures and Organizations: Software of the Mind* (London: McGraw-Hill, 1991); and G. Hofstede, "Cultural Constraints in Management Theories," *Academy of Management Executive,* February 1993, pp. 81–94.

24. Hofstede called this dimension *masculinity versus femininity* [italics added], but we have changed his terms because of their strong sexist connotation.

25. The five usual criticisms and Hofstede's responses (in parentheses) are: 1. Surveys are not a suitable way to measure cultural differences (answer: they should not be the only way); 2. Nations are not the proper units for studying cultures (answer: they are usually the only kind of units available for comparison); 3. A study of the subsidiaries of one company cannot provide information about entire national cultures (answer: what was measured were differences among national cultures. Any set of functionally equivalent samples can supply information about such differences); 4. The IBM data are old and therefore obsolete (answer: the dimensions found are assumed to have centuries-old roots; they have been validated against all kinds of external measurements; recent replications show no loss of validity); 5. Four or five dimensions are not enough (answer: additional dimensions should be statistically independent of the dimensions defined earlier; they should be valid on the basis of correlations with external measures; candidates are welcome to apply). See A. Harzing and G. Hofstede, "Planned Change in Organizations: The Influence of National Culture," in *Research in the Sociology of Organizations,* 14: *Cross Cultural Analysis of Organizations,* ed. P. A. Bamberger, M. Erez, and S. B. Bacharach (Greenwich, CT: JAI Press, 1996), pp. 297–340.

26. G. Hofstede, *Culture's Consequences: Comparative Values, Behaviors, Institutions and Organizations Across Nations*, 2nd ed. (Thousand Oaks, CA: Sage), 2001.

27. Based on "BCTF Tackle Foreign Students," *Richmond News,* March 19, 2005, p. 6; E. Edmonds, "District Battles $700,000 Shortfall, Declining Enrolment," *Richmond News,* April 21, 2006, p. 5; and E. Edmonds, "Extra School Money Is Less Than Hoped," *Richmond News,* March 19, 2005. p. 3.

28. D. A. Aaker, *Developing Business Strategies*, 5th ed. (New York: John Wiley & Sons, 1998); and J. A. Byrne, "Borderless Management," *BusinessWeek,* May 23, 1994, pp. 24–26.

29. "Mega Bloks Builds Global Brand," *Financial Post* (*National Post*), October 17, 2003, p. FP07.

30. International Trade Canada, http://www.dfait-maeci.gc.ca/eet/cimt/2005/pfact_annual_trade_2006-04-en.asp#1 (accessed May 8, 2006).

31. International Trade Canada, http://www.dfait-maeci.gc.ca/eet/cimt/2005/pfact_annual_trade_2006-04-en.asp#1 (accessed May 8, 2006).

32. L. Frost, "Starbucks Lures French Café Society," *Associated Press,* January 16, 2004.

33. Based on "BCTF Tackle Foreign Students," *Richmond News,* March 19, 2005, p. 6; and J. Steffenhagen, "B.C. Schools Screen Young Foreign Pupils," *Vancouver Sun,* January 22, 2004, p. B6.

34. T. Donaldson and L. E. Preston, "The Stakeholder Theory of the Corporation: Concepts, Evidence, and Implications," *Academy of Management Review,* January 1995, pp. 65–91.

35. J. S. Harrison and C. H. St. John, "Managing and Partnering With External Stakeholders," *Academy of Management Executive,* May 1996, pp. 46–60.

36. A. J. Hillman and G. D. Keim, "Shareholder Value, Stakeholder Management, and Social Issues: What's the Bottom Line?" *Strategic Management Journal,* March 2001, pp. 125–139; J. Kotter and J. Heskett, *Corporate Culture and Performance* (New York: Free Press, 1992).

37. J. S. Harrison and C. H. St. John, "Managing and Partnering With External Stakeholders," *Academy of Management Executive,* May 1996, pp. 46–60.

38. O. Ward, "Pop Goes Globalization," *Toronto Star,* March 13, 2004, http://www.thestar.com (accessed March 21, 2004).

39. "Measuring Globalization: Economic Reversals, Forward Momentum," *Foreign Policy,* March–April 2004, http://www.foreignpolicy.com/story/cms.php?story_id=2493 (accessed March 28, 2004).

40. A. Kreamer, "America's Yang Has a Yen for Asia's Yin," *Fast Company,* July 2003, p. 58; D. Yergin, "Globalization Opens Door to New Dangers," *USA Today,* May 28, 2003, p. 11A; K. Lowrey Miller, "Is It Globaloney?" *Newsweek,* December 16, 2002, pp. E4–E8; L. Gomes, "Globalization Is Now a Two-Way Street—Good News for the U.S.," *Wall Street Journal,* December 9, 2002, p. B1; J. Kurlantzick and J. T. Allen, "The Trouble With Globalism," *U.S. News & World Report,* February 11, 2002, pp. 38–41; J. Guyon, "The American Way," *Fortune,* November 26, 2001, pp. 114–120.

41. J. Guyon, "The American Way," *Fortune,* November 26, 2001, pp. 114–120.

42. Adapted from G. M. Spreitzer, M. W. McCall Jr., and J. D. Mahoney, "Early Identification of International Executive Potential," *Journal of Applied Psychology,* February 1997, pp. 6–29.

43. Information from company website, http://www.inditex.com (accessed January 5, 2003); and M. Helft, "Fashion Fast-Forward," *Business 2.0,* May 2002, pp. 60–66.

44. Based on M. R. Cohn, "Indian Villagers Set to Battle Alcan," *Toronto Star,* July 3, 2004, pp. A1, A10–A12; A. Swift, "Alcan to Do Well in 2004, Says CEO," *Trail Times,* April 23, 2004, p. 14; and L. Moore, "Alcan Sees Bright Year Ahead," *Gazette* (Montreal), April 23, 2004, p. B1.

45. Based on http://www.nba.com/canada/Canadians_in_the_NBA-Canada_Generic_Article-18022.html; D. Eisenberg, "The NBA's Global Game Plan," *Time,* March 17, 2003, pp. 59–63; J. Tyrangiel, "The Center of Attention," *Time,* February 10, 2003, pp. 56–60; "Spin Master Stern," *Latin Trade,* July 2000, p. 32; Information from NBA website, http://www.nba.com (accessed July 1, 2004); J. Tagliabue, "Hoop Dreams, Fiscal Realities," *New York Times,* March 4, 2000, p. B11; D. Roth, "The NBA's Next Shot," *Fortune,* February 21, 2000, pp. 207–216; A. Bianco, "Now It's NBA All-the-Time TV," *BusinessWeek,* November 15, 1999, pp. 241–242; and D. McGraw and M. Tharp, "Going Out on Top," *U.S. News & World Report,* January 25, 1999, p. 55.

46. See http://www.nba.com/schedules/international_nba_tv_schedule.html (accessed September 24, 2006).

47. C. Harvey and M. J. Allard, *Understanding and Managing Diversity: Readings, Cases, and Exercises,* 2nd ed. (Upper Saddle River, NJ: Prentice Hall, 2002); P. L. Hunsaker, *Training in Management Skills* (Upper Saddle River, NJ: Prentice Hall, 2001); and J. Greenberg, *Managing Behavior in Organizations: Science in Service to Practice,* 2nd ed. (Upper Saddle River, NJ: Prentice Hall, 1999).

CoolBrands A

1. This information is from Yogen Früz World-Wide, *Prospectus,* June 11, 1997, with limited modification.

2. This information is from Yogen Früz World-Wide, *Prospectus,* June 11, 1997, with limited modification.

Chapter 3

1. Based on S. Sperounes, "A Sensation Rises from Out of the Blue," *Edmonton Journal,* September 30, 2003, p. C1; and "Masters of Splatter May Turn Your Mood Indigo," *People Weekly,* June 8, 1992, pp. 108–110.

2. V. Pilieci, "The Lost Generation of Business Talent," *Vancouver Sun,* May 2, 2001, pp. D1, D9.

3. See, for example, J. A. Pearce II, K. K. Robbins, and R. B. Robinson Jr., "The Impact of Grand Strategy and Planning Formality on Financial Performance," *Strategic Management Journal,* March–April 1987, pp. 125–134; L. C. Rhyne, "Contrasting Planning Systems in High,

Medium, and Low Performance Companies," *Journal of Management Studies,* July 1987, pp. 363–385; J. A. Pearce II, E. B. Freeman, and R. B. Robinson Jr., "The Tenuous Link Between Formal Strategic Planning and Financial Performance," *Academy of Management Review,* October 1987, pp. 658–675; D. K. Sinha, "The Contribution of Formal Planning to Decisions," *Strategic Management Journal,* October 1990, pp. 479–492; N. Capon, J. U. Farley, and J. M. Hulbert, "Strategic Planning and Financial Performance: More Evidence," *Journal of Management Studies,* January 1994, pp. 22–38; C. C. Miller and L. B. Cardinal, "Strategic Planning and Firm Performance: A Synthesis of More Than Two Decades of Research," *Academy of Management Journal,* March 1994, pp. 1649–1685; P. J. Brews and M. R. Hunt, "Learning to Plan and Planning to Learn: Resolving the Planning School/Learning School Debate," *Strategic Management Journal,* December 1999, pp. 889–913.

4. S. Sperounes, "A Sensation Rises from Out of the Blue," *Edmonton Journal,* September 30, 2003, p. C1; K. Powers, "Blue Coup," *Forbes,* March 19, 2001, p. 136; and S. Hampson, "Blue Cogs in a Corporate Wheel," *Globe and Mail,* July 12, 2003, p. R3.

5. R. Molz, "How Leaders Use Goals," *Long Range Planning,* October 1987, p. 91.

6. P. N. Romani, "MBO by Any Other Name Is Still MBO," *Supervision,* December 1997, pp. 6–8; and A. W. Schrader and G. T. Seward, "MBO Makes Dollar Sense," *Personnel Journal,* July 1989, pp. 32–37.

7. P. N. Romani, "MBO by Any Other Name Is Still MBO," *Supervision,* December 1997, pp. 6–8; and R. Rodgers and J. E. Hunter, "Impact of Management by Objectives on Organizational Productivity," *Journal of Applied Psychology,* April 1991, pp. 322–336.

8. For additional information on goals, see, for instance, P. Drucker, *The Executive in Action* (New York: HarperCollins Books, 1996), pp. 207–214; and E. A. Locke and G. P. Latham, *A Theory of Goal Setting and Task Performance* (Upper Saddle River, NJ: Prentice Hall, 1990).

9. See http://www.canada.com/nationalpost/entrepreneur/transat.html.

10. J. D. Hunger and T. L. Wheelen, *Strategic Management,* 7th ed. (Upper Saddle River, NJ: Prentice Hall, 2000).

11. Several of these factors were suggested by J. S. Armstrong, "The Value of Formal Planning for Strategic Decisions: Review of Empirical Research," *Strategic Management Journal,* July–September 1982, pp. 197–211; and R. K. Bresser and R. C. Bishop, "Dysfunctional Effects of Formal Planning: Two Theoretical Explanations," *Academy of Management Review,* October 1983, pp. 588–599.

12. P. J. Brews and M. R. Hunt, "Learning to Plan and Planning to Learn: Resolving the Planning School/Learning School Debate," *Strategic Management Journal,* December 1999, pp. 889–913.

13. P. J. Brews and M. R. Hunt, "Learning to Plan and Planning to Learn: Resolving the Planning School/Learning School Debate," *Strategic Management Journal,* December 1999, pp. 889–913.

14. H. Mintzberg, *The Rise and Fall of Strategic Planning* (New York: Free Press, 1994).

15. H. Mintzberg, *The Rise and Fall of Strategic Planning* (New York: Free Press, 1994).

16. H. Mintzberg, *The Rise and Fall of Strategic Planning* (New York: Free Press, 1994).

17. G. Hamel and C. K. Prahalad, *Competing for the Future* (Boston: Harvard Business School Press, 1994).

18. D. Miller, "The Architecture of Simplicity," *Academy of Management Review,* January 1993, pp. 116–138.

19. Based on "Blue Brand Group," http://robwalker.net/html_docs/bluemen.html (accessed September 24, 2006).

20. J. W. Dean Jr. and M. P. Sharfman, "Does Decision Process Matter? A Study of Strategic Decision-Making Effectiveness," *Academy of Management Journal,* April 1996, pp. 368–396.

21. T. L. Wheelen and J. D. Hunger, *Strategic Management and Business Policy,* 7th ed. (Upper Saddle River, NJ: Prentice Hall, 2000), p. 3.

22. See http://www.worksafebc.com/corporate/about/goals/_default.asp.

23. C. K. Prahalad and G. Hamel, "The Core Competence of the Corporation," *Harvard Business Review,* May–June 1990, pp. 79–91.

24. See http://www.canada.com/nationalpost/entrepreneur/cpl.html.

25. Based on G. Pitts, "Tide Turns for P&G Canada President," *Globe and Mail,* October 14, 2002, p. B3; and S. Heinrich, "P&G Still the Best Step Up," *National Post,* April 14, 2003, p. FP4.

26. H. Mintzberg, "The Strategy Concept I: Five Ps for Strategy," *California Management Review,* Fall 1987, pp. 11–24.

27. Based on M. Knelman, "Blue Man Takes a Pounding," *Toronto Star,* September 28, 2006, http://www.thestar.com (accessed September 28, 2006).

28. P. Marck, "Tim Hortons Brews Up Record Sales: No Holes in Doughnut Business in Canada," *Edmonton Journal,* January 7, 2004, p. A1; and http://www.timhortons.com/en/about/faq.html.

29. G. Pitts, "Small Is Beautiful, Conglomerates Signal," *Globe and Mail,* April 1, 2002, pp. B1, B4; and http://www.brascancorp.com/index.html.

30. V. Ramanujam and P. Varadarajan, "Research on Corporate Diversification: A Synthesis," *Strategic Management Journal* 10 (1989), pp. 523–551. Also see A. Shleifer and R. W. Vishny, "Takeovers in the 1960s and 1980s: Evidence and Implications," in *Fundamental Issues in Strategy,* ed. R. P. Rumelt, D. E. Schendel, and D. J. Teece (Boston: Harvard Business School Press, 1994).

31. J. A. Pearce, II, "Retrenchment Remains the Foundation of Business Turnaround," *Strategic Management Journal* 15 (1994), pp. 407–417.

32. "Jif, Crisco Find a New Home With Smucker," *USA Today,* June 3, 2002, p. 7B.

33. See, for example, M. E. Porter, *Competitive Strategy: Techniques for Analyzing Industries and Competitors* (New York: Free Press, 1980); M. E. Porter, *Competitive Advantage: Creating and Sustaining Superior Performance* (New York: Free Press, 1985); G. G. Dess and P. S. Davis, "Porter's (1980) Generic Strategies as Determinants of Strategic Group Membership and Organizational Performance," *Academy of Management Journal,* September 1984, pp. 467–488; G. G. Dess and P. S. Davis, "Porter's (1980) Generic Strategies and Performance: An Empirical Examination With American Data—Part I: Testing Porter," *Organization Studies* 7, no. 1 (1986), pp. 37–55; G. G. Dess and P. S. Davis, "Porter's (1980) Generic Strategies and Performance: An Empirical Examination With American Data—Part II: Performance Implications," *Organization Studies* 7, no. 3 (1986), pp. 255–261; M. E. Porter, "From Competitive Advantage to Corporate Strategy," *Harvard Business Review,* May–June 1987, pp. 43–59; A. I. Murray, "A Contingency View of Porter's 'Generic Strategies,'" *Academy of Management Review,* July 1988, pp. 390–400; C. W. L. Hill,

"Differentiation Versus Low Cost or Differentiation and Low Cost: A Contingency Framework," *Academy of Management Review,* July 1988, pp. 401–412; I. Bamberger, "Developing Competitive Advantage in Small and Medium-Sized Firms," *Long Range Planning,* October 1989, pp. 80–88; D. F. Jennings and J. R. Lumpkin, "Insights Between Environmental Scanning Activities and Porter's Generic Strategies: An Empirical Analysis," *Strategic Management Journal* 18, no. 4 (1992), pp. 791–803; N. Argyres and A. M. McGahan, "An Interview with Michael Porter," *Academy of Management Executive,* May 2002, pp. 43–52; and A. Brandenburger, "Porter's Added Value: High Indeed!" *Academy of Management Executive,* May 2002, pp. 58–60.

34. G. Pitts, "Ganong Boss Aims for Sweet Spot," *Globe and Mail,* March 3, 2003, p. B4.

35. Vignette based on W. Hanley, "Mowat's Lefty Ways Pay Big Dividends," *National Post,* February 28, 2004, p. IN01; and "Pigeon Park Savings Partners With VanCity to Help Marginalized Residents," https://www.vancity.com/MyCommunity/CommunityInvestment/ AccesstoFinancialServices/PigeonParkSavings/ (accessed September 24, 2006).

36. See http://www.vancity.com/MyMoney/Tools/FindBranchATM/ ?region=VancouverEastSide&service=all&showTag=FindBranchTag (accessed September 25, 2006).

37. D. Miller and J. Toulouse, "Strategy, Structure, CEO Personality, and Performance in Small Firms," *American Journal of Small Business,* Winter 1986, pp. 47–62.

38. C. W. L. Hill, "Differentiation versus Low Cost or Differentiation and Low Cost: A Contingency Framework," *Academy of Management Review,* July 1988, pp. 401–412; R. E. White, "Organizing to Make Business Unit Strategies Work," in *Handbook of Business Strategy,* 2nd ed., ed. H. E. Glass (Boston: Warren Gorham and Lamont, 1991), pp. 24.1–24.14; D. Miller, "The Generic Strategy Trap," *Journal of Business Strategy,* January–February 1991, pp. 37–41; S. Cappel, P. Wright, M. Kroll, and D. Wyld, "Competitive Strategies and Business Performance: An Empirical Study of Select Service Businesses," *International Journal of Management,* March 1992, pp. 1–11; and J. W. Bachmann, "Competitive Strategy: It's O.K. to Be Different," *Academy of Management Executive,* May 2002, pp. 61–65.

39. S. Sperounes, "A Sensation Rises from Out of the Blue," *Edmonton Journal,* September 30, 2003, p. C1; K. Powers, "Blue Coup," *Forbes,* March 19, 2001, p. 136; and S. Hampson, "Blue Cogs in a Corporate Wheel," *Globe and Mail,* July 12, 2003, p. R3.

40. See, for example, B. Krone, "Total Quality Management: An American Odyssey," *The Bureaucrat,* Fall 1990, pp. 35–38; A. Gabor, *The Man Who Discovered Quality* (New York: Random House, 1990); J. W. Dean Jr. and D. E. Bowen, "Management Theory and Total Quality: Improving Research and Practice through Theory Development," *Academy of Management Review,* July 1994, pp. 392–418; C. A. Reeves and D. A. Bednar, "Defining Quality: Alternatives and Implications," *Academy of Management Review,* July 1994, pp. 419–445; R. K. Reger, L. T. Gustafson, S. M. Demarie, and J. V. Mullane, "Reframing the Organization: Why Implementing Total Quality Is Easier Said Than Done," *Academy of Management Review,* July 1994, pp. 565–584; T. C. Powell, "Total Quality Management as Competitive Advantage: A Review and Empirical Study," *Strategic Management Journal,* January 1995, pp. 15–37; J. R. Hackman and R. Wageman, "Total Quality Management: Empirical, Conceptual, and Practical Issues," *Administrative Science Quarterly,* June 1995, pp. 309–342; T. A. Stewart, "A Conversation With Joseph Juran," *Fortune,* January 11, 1999, pp. 168–170; and J. Jusko, "Tried and True," *IW,* December 6, 1999, pp. 78–84.

41. T. C. Powell, "Total Quality Management as Competitive Advantage: A Review and Empirical Study," *Strategic Management Journal,* January 1995, pp. 15–37.

42. See R. J. Schonenberger, "Is Strategy Strategic? Impact of Total Quality Management on Strategy," *Academy of Management Executive,* August 1992, pp. 80–87; C. A. Barclay, "Quality Strategy and TQM Policies: Empirical Evidence," *Management International Review,* Special Issue (1993), pp. 87–98; T. E. Benson, "A Business Strategy Comes of Age," *IndustryWeek,* May 3, 1993, pp. 40–44; R. Jacob, "TQM: More Than a Dying Fad?" *Fortune,* October 18, 1993, pp. 66–72; R. Krishnan, A. B. Shani, R. M. Grant, and R. Baer, "In Search of Quality Improvement Problems of Design and Implementation," *Academy of Management Executive,* November 1993, pp. 7–20; B. Voss, "Quality's Second Coming," *Journal of Business Strategy,* March–April 1994, pp. 42–46; M. Barrier, "Raising TQM Consciousness," *Nation's Business,* April 1994, pp. 62–64; and a special issue of *Academy of Management Review* devoted to TQM, July 1994, pp. 390–584.

43. F. Jossi, "Take a Peek Inside," *HR Magazine,* June 2002, pp. 46–52; and R. A. Martins, "Continuous Improvement Strategies and Production Competitive Criteria: Some Findings in Brazilian Industries," *Total Quality Management,* May 2001, pp. 281–291.

44. Ford Motor Company, "New Range Rover Debuts at North American International Auto Show," news release, January 7, 2002, http://media.ford.com/article_display.cfm?article_id=10686 (accessed August 16, 2006).

45. See, for example, J. P. Wilson, M. A. T. Walsh, and K. L. Needy, "An Examination of the Economic Benefits of ISO 9000 and the Baldrige Award to Manufacturing Firms," *Engineering Management Journal,* December 2003, pp. 3–5; and International Organization for Standardization, "ISO 9000 and ISO 14000," International Organization for Standardization, http://www.iso.org/iso/ en/iso9000-14000/index.html (accessed August 16, 2006).

46. T. B. Schoenrock, "ISO 9000: 2000 Gives Competitive Edge," *Quality Progress,* May 2002, p. 107.

47. See, for instance, L. P. Dodd Jr., "The Team Approach to ISO 9000: 2000 at Standard Aero Alliance," *Journal for Quality and Participation,* Spring 2002, pp. 41–44; and S. Smith, "The Cutting Edge of Environmental Management," *Occupational Hazards,* February 2002, pp. 33–37.

48. C. Mitman, "Get ISO Certified on Time and Within Budget," *Quality,* November 2001, pp. 46–48.

49. "Green Belt Training Starts February 4; Other Courses On-Line," *Quality Progress,* February 2002, p. 13; J. M. Lucas, "The Essential Six Sigma," *Quality Progress,* January 2002, pp. 27–31, and D. Treichler, R. Carmichael, A. Kusmanoff, J. Lewis, and G. Berthiez, "Design for Six Sigma: 15 Lessons Learned," *Quality Progress,* January 2002, p. 33.

50. T. Aeppel, "Career Journal: Nicknamed 'Nag,' She's Just Doing Her Job," *Wall Street Journal,* May 14, 2002, p. B1.

51. L. Heuring, "Six Sigma in Sight," *HR Magazine,* March 2004, pp. 76–80; G. Eckes, "Making Six Sigma Last (and Work)," *Ivey Business Journal,* January–February 2002, pp. 77–81.

52. "Six Sigma Gets Its Day," *Quality,* January 2002, p. 48.

53. "Is 99.9% Good Enough?" *Training,* March 1991, p. 38. See also J. Petty, "When Near Enough Is Not Good Enough," *Australian CPA,* May 2000, pp. 34–35.

54. M. Arndt, "Quality Isn't Just for Widgets," *BusinessWeek,* July 22, 2002, pp. 72–74.

55. R. E. Quinn, S. R. Faerman, M. P. Thompson, and M. R. McGrath, *Becoming a Master Manager: A Competency Framework* (New York: Wiley, 1990), pp. 33–34.

56. Situation adapted from information in S. Leith, "Coke Faces Damage Control," *Atlanta Journal-Constitution,* June 19, 2003, p. C1; C. Terhume, "Coke Employees Acted Improperly in Marketing Test," *Wall Street Journal,* June 18, 2003, pp. A3, A6; and T. Howard, "Burger King, Coke May Face Off in Frozen Coke Suit," *USA Today,* June 6, 2003, http://www.usatoday.com/money/industries/food/_2003-06-04.bk_x.htm.

57. Information on Lend Lease comes from Hoover's Online, http://www.hoovers.com (accessed November 8, 2004); the Lend Lease website, http://www.lendlease.com (accessed November 8, 2004, and August 16, 2006); P. LaBarre, "A Company Without Limits," *Fast Company,* September 1999, pp. 160–186; and "Lend Lease Building on Its Success," *Business Asia,* March 15, 1999, p. 11.

58. B. Horovitz, "By Year's End, Regular Size Will Have to Do," *USA Today,* March 3, 2004, http://www.usatoday.com; and J. Woestendiek and A. Hirsch, "McDonald's to Trim Super Size," *Baltimore Sun,* March 4, 2004, http://www.baltimoresun.com.

Chapter 4

1. Based on B. Constantineau, "Canaccord Reluctantly Considers Going Public," *Vancouver Sun,* March 25, 2004, p. D3; and T. Tedesco and W. Dabrowski, "Canaccord Readies for Summer IPO," *National Post,* March 24, 2004, p. FP1.

2. Based on B. Constantineau, "Canaccord Reluctantly Considers Going Public," *Vancouver Sun,* March 25, 2004, p. D3.

3. Based on B. Constantineau, "Canaccord Reluctantly Considers Going Public," *Vancouver Sun,* March 25, 2004, p. D3.

4. I. Wylie, "Who Runs This Team Anyway?" *Fast Company,* April 2002, pp. 32–33.

5. D. A. Garvin and M. A. Roberto, "What You Don't Know About Making Decisions," *Harvard Business Review,* September 2001, pp. 108–116.

6. W. Pounds, "The Process of Problem Finding," *Industrial Management Review,* Fall 1969, pp. 1–19.

7. P. C. Nutt, *Why Decisions Fail: Avoiding the Blunders and Traps That Lead to Debacles* (San Francisco, CA: Berrett-Koehler Publishers, 2002).

8. B. Constantineau, "Canaccord Reluctantly Considers Going Public," *Vancouver Sun,* March 25, 2004, p. D3.

9. See H. A. Simon, "Rationality in Psychology and Economics," *Journal of Business,* October 1986, pp. 209–224; A. Langley, "In Search of Rationality: The Purposes Behind the Use of Formal Analysis in Organizations," *Administrative Science Quarterly,* December 1989, pp. 598–631.

10. See, for example, J. G. March, *A Primer on Decision Making* (New York: Free Press, 1994), pp. 8–25; and A. Langley, H. Mintzberg, P. Pitcher, E. Posada, and J. Saint-Macary, "Opening Up Decision Making: The View from the Black Stool," *Organization Science,* May–June 1995, pp. 260–279.

11. See N. McK. Agnew and J. L. Brown, "Bounded Rationality: Fallible Decisions in Unbounded Decision Space," *Behavioral Science,* July 1986, pp. 148–161; B. E. Kaufman, "A New Theory of Satisficing," *Journal of Behavioral Economics,* Spring 1990, pp. 35–51; and D. R. A. Skidd, "Revisiting Bounded Rationality," *Journal of Management Inquiry,* December 1992, pp. 343–347.

12. T. A. Stewart, "How to Think With Your Gut," *Business 2.0,* November 2002, p. 102.

13. See K. R. Hammond, R. M. Hamm, J. Grassia, and T. Pearson, "Direct Comparison of the Efficacy of Intuitive and Analytical Cognition in Expert Judgment," in *IEEE Transactions on Systems, Man, and Cybernetics* SMC-17, no. 5 (1987), pp. 753–770; W. H. Agor, ed., *Intuition in Organizations* (Newbury Park, CA: Sage Publications, 1989); O. Behling and N. L. Eckel, "Making Sense Out of Intuition," *The Executive,* February 1991, pp. 46–47; L. A. Burke and M. K. Miller, "Taking the Mystery Out of Intuitive Decision Making," *Academy of Management Executive,* October 1999, pp. 91–99; A. L. Tesolin, "How to Develop the Habit of Intuition," *Training & Development,* March 2000, p. 76; and T. A. Stewart, "How to Think With Your Gut," *Business 2.0,* November 2002, pp. 98–104.

14. V. Pospisil, "Gut Feeling or Skilled Reasoning?" *IndustryWeek,* March 3, 1997, p. 12.

15. S. Maich, "Promises, Promises but Tax Bill Grows," *Financial Post (National Post),* June 1, 2004, p. FP1.

16. A. J. Rowe, J. D. Boulgarides, and M. R. McGrath, *Managerial Decision Making, Modules in Management Series* (Chicago: SRA, 1984), pp. 18–22.

17. C. Shaffran, "Mind Your Meeting: How to Become the Catalyst for Culture Change," *Communication World,* February–March 2003, pp. 26–29.

18. I. L. Janis, *Victims of Groupthink* (Boston: Houghton Mifflin, 1972); R. J. Aldag and S. Riggs Fuller, "Beyond Fiasco: A Reappraisal of the Groupthink Phenomenon and a New Model of Group Decision Processes," *Psychological Bulletin,* May 1993, pp. 533–552; T. Kameda and S. Sugimori, "Psychological Entrapment in Group Decision Making: An Assigned Decision Rule and a Groupthink Phenomenon," *Journal of Personality and Social Psychology,* August 1993, pp. 282–292.

19. R. G. Vleeming, "Machiavellianism: A Preliminary Review," *Psychology Reports,* February 1979, pp. 295–310.

20. Based on J. Brockner, *Self Esteem at Work* (Lexington, MA: Lexington Books, 1988), chapters 1–4.

21. See, for example, L. K. Michaelson, W. E. Watson, and R. H. Black, "A Realistic Test of Individual vs. Group Consensus Decision Making," *Journal of Applied Psychology* 74, no. 5 (1989), pp. 834–839; R. A. Henry, "Group Judgment Accuracy: Reliability and Validity of Postdiscussion Confidence Judgments," *Organizational Behavior and Human Decision Processes,* October 1993, pp. 11–27; P. W. Paese, M. Bieser, and M. E. Tubbs, "Framing Effects and Choice Shifts in Group Decision Making," *Organizational Behavior and Human Decision Processes,* October 1993, pp. 149–165; N. J. Castellan Jr., ed., *Individual and Group Decision Making* (Hillsdale, NJ: Lawrence Erlbaum Associates, 1993); and S. G. Straus and J. E. McGrath, "Does the Medium Matter? The Interaction of Task Type and Technology on Group Performance and Member Reactions," *Journal of Applied Psychology,* February 1994, pp. 87–97.

22. E. J. Thomas and C. F. Fink, "Effects of Group Size," *Psychological Bulletin,* July 1963, pp. 371–384; F. A. Shull, A. L. Delbecq, and L. L. Cummings, *Organizational Decision Making* (New York: McGraw-Hill, 1970), p. 151; A. P. Hare, *Handbook of Small Group Research* (New York: Free Press, 1976); M. E. Shaw, *Group Dynamics: The Psychology of Small Group Behavior,* 3rd ed. (New York: McGraw-Hill, 1981); P. Yetton and P. Bottger, "The Relationships Among Group Size, Member Ability, Social Decision Schemes, and Performance," *Organizational Behavior and Human Performance,* October 1983, pp. 145–159.

23. D. Kahneman and A. Tversky, "Judgment Under Uncertainty: Heuristics and Biases," *Science* 185 (1974), pp. 1124–1131.

24. Information for this section is taken from S. P. Robbins, *Decide & Conquer* (Upper Saddle River, NJ: Financial Times/Prentice Hall, 2004).

25. See, for example, B. M. Staw, "The Escalation of Commitment to a Course of Action," *Academy of Management Review,* October 1981, pp. 577–587; D. R. Bobocel and J. P. Meyer, "Escalating Commitment to a Failing Course of Action: Separating the Roles of Choice and Justification," *Journal of Applied Psychology,* June 1994, pp. 360–363; C. F. Camerer and R. A. Weber, "The Econometrics and Behavioral Economics of Escalation of Commitment: A Re-examination of Staw's Theory," *Journal of Economic Behavior and Organization,* May 1999, pp. 59–82; V. S. Rao and A. Monk, "The Effects of Individual Differences and Anonymity on Commitment to Decisions," *Journal of Social Psychology,* August 1999, pp. 496–515; and G. McNamara, H. Moon, and P. Bromiley, "Banking on Commitment: Intended and Unintended Consequences of an Organization's Attempt to Attenuate Escalation of Commitment," *Academy of Management Journal,* April 2002, pp. 443–452.

26. Canaccord Annual Report, 2006, and Canaccord Capital Inc., Code of Business Conduct and Ethics, May 19, 2006.

27. K. Davis and W. C. Frederick, *Business and Society: Management, Public Policy, Ethics,* 5th ed. (New York: McGraw-Hill, 1984), pp. 28–41, 76.

28. G. F. Cavanagh, D. J. Moberg, and M. Valasquez, "The Ethics of Organizational Politics," *Academy of Management Journal,* June 1981, pp. 363–374. See also F. N. Brady, "Rules for Making Exceptions to Rules," *Academy of Management Review,* July 1987, pp. 436–444, for an argument that the theory of justice is redundant with the prior two theories. See also T. Donaldson and T. W. Dunfee, "Toward a Unified Conception of Business Ethics: Integrative Social Contracts Theory," *Academy of Management Review,* April 1994, pp. 252–284; M. Douglas, "Integrative Social Contracts Theory: Hype Over Hypernorms," *Journal of Business Ethics,* July 2000, pp. 101–110; and E. Soule, "Managerial Moral Strategies—In Search of a Few Good Principles," *Academy of Management Review,* January 2002, pp. 114–124, for discussions of integrative social contracts theory.

29. E. Soule, "Managerial Moral Strategies—In Search of a Few Good Principles," *Academy of Management Review,* January 2002, p. 117.

30. F. D. Sturdivant, *Business and Society: A Managerial Approach,* 3rd ed. (Homewood, IL: Richard D. Irwin, 1985), p. 128.

31. D. J. Fritzsche and H. Becker, "Linking Management Behavior to Ethical Philosophy—An Empirical Investigation," *Academy of Management Journal,* March 1984, pp. 166–175.

32. Sears example taken from series of posters called "Sears Ethics and Business Practices: A Century of Tradition," in *Business Ethics,* May–June 1999, pp. 12–13; and B. J. Feder, "The Harder Side of Sears," *New York Times,* July 20, 1997, p. BU11; Enron example taken from P. M. Lencioni, "Make Your Values Mean Something," *Harvard Business Review,* July 2002, p. 113.

33. L. Bogomolny, "Good Housekeeping," *Canadian Business,* March 1, 2004, pp. 87–88.

34. See http://www.csa-acvm.ca/html_CSA/about.html.

35. W. Dabrowski, "Tighter Guidelines Issued on Disclosure: Canada's 'Sarbanes,'" *Financial Post* (*National Post*), March 30, 2004, p. FP1.

36. L. Bogomolny, "Good Housekeeping," *Canadian Business,* March 1, 2004, pp. 87–88.

37. "Global Ethics Codes Gain Importance as a Tool to Avoid Litigation and Fines," *Wall Street Journal,* August 19, 1999, p. A1; and J. Alexander, "On the Right Side," *World Business,* January–February 1997, pp. 38–41.

38. P. Richter, "Big Business Puts Ethics in Spotlight," *Los Angeles Times,* June 19, 1986, p. 29.

39. F. R. David, "An Empirical Study of Codes of Business Ethics: A Strategic Perspective" (paper presented at the 48th Annual Academy of Management Conference, Anaheim, California, August 1988).

40. "Ethics Programs Aren't Stemming Employee Misconduct," *Wall Street Journal,* May 11, 2000, p. A1.

41. L. Bogomolny, "Good Housekeeping," *Canadian Business,* March 1, 2004, pp. 87–88.

42. A. K. Reichert and M. S. Webb, "Corporate Support for Ethical and Environmental Policies: A Financial Management Perspective," *Journal of Business Ethics,* May 2000; G. R. Weaver, L. K. Trevino, and P. L. Cochran, "Corporate Ethics Programs as Control Systems: Influences of Executive Commitment and Environmental Factors," *Academy of Management Journal,* February 1999, pp. 41–57; G. R. Weaver, L. K. Trevino, and P. L. Cochran, "Integrated and Decoupled Corporate Social Performance: Management Commitments, External Pressures, and Corporate Ethics Practices," *Academy of Management Journal,* October 1999, pp. 539–552; and B. Z. Posner and W. H. Schmidt, "Values and the American Manager: An Update," *California Management Review,* Spring 1984, pp. 202–216.

43. L. Nash, "Ethics Without the Sermon," *Harvard Business Review,* November–December 1981, p. 81.

44. Adapted from W. H. Agor, *AIM Survey* (El Paso, TX: ENP Enterprises, 1989), Part I. With permission.

45. A. Regalado, "Experiments in Controversy—Ethicists, Bodyguards Monitor Scientists' Effort to Create Copy of Human Embryo," *Wall Street Journal* (July 13, 2001), p. B1; and G. Naik, "Stem-Cell Research Is Forging Ahead in Europe," *Wall Street Journal,* July 13, 2001, p. B6.

46. Information from C. F. Martin's website, http://www.cfmartin. com (accessed April 24, 2003); D. Lieberman, "Guitar Sales Jam Despite Music Woes," *USA Today,* December 16, 2002, p. 2B; and S. Fitch, "Stringing Them Along," *Forbes,* July 26, 1999, pp. 90–91.

47. A. Deslongchamps, "'Hard' to Raise Wages at Air Canada, ACE's Milton Warns," *National Post,* March 30, 2006, p. FP4; "ACE Aviation to Pay Shareholders $266M in Aeroplan Units," *National Post,* February 17, 2006, p. FP6.

48. J. V. Anderson, "Mind Mapping: A Tool for Creative Thinking," *Business Horizons,* January–February 1993, pp. 42–46; M. Loeb, "Ten Commandments for Managing Creative People," *Fortune,* January 16, 1995, pp. 135–136; M. Henricks, "Good Thinking," *Entrepreneur,* May 1996, pp. 70–73; H.-S.Choi and L. Thompson, "Old Wine in a New Bottle: Impact of Membership Change on Group Creativity," *Organizational Behavior and Human Decision Processes* 98, no. 2 (2005), pp. 121–132; R. Florida and J. Goodnight, "Managing for Creativity," *Harvard Business Review* 83, no. 7 (2005), pp. 124+; L. L. Gilson, J. E. Mathieu, C. E. Shalley, T. M. Ruddy, "Creativity and Standardization: Complementary or Conflicting Drivers of Team Effectiveness?" *Academy of Management Journal* 48, no. 3 (2005), pp. 521–531; and K. G. Smith, C. J. Collins, and K. D. Clark, "Existing Knowledge, Knowledge Creation Capability, and the Rate of New Product Introduction in High-Technology Firms," *Academy of Management Journal* 48, no. 2 (2005), pp. 346–357.

49. Information for this box comes from B. C. McDonald and D. Hutcheson, "Dealing With Diversity Is Key to Tapping Talent,"

Atlanta Business Chronicle, December 18, 1998, p. 45A1; P. M. Elsass and L. M. Graves, "Demographic Diversity in Decision-Making Groups: The Experience of Women and People of Color," *Academy of Management Review*, October 1997, pp. 946–973; and N. J. Adler, ed., *International Dimensions of Organizational Behavior*, 4th ed. (Cincinnati: South-Western College Publishing, 2001).

Chapter 5

1. See http://www.theaircanadacentre.com/bios/peddie.html (accessed August 24, 2006).

2. See, for example, R. L. Daft, *Organization Theory and Design*, 6th ed. (St. Paul, MN: West Publishing, 1998).

3. S. Melamed, I. Ben-Avi, and M. S. Green, "Objective and Subjective Work Monotony: Effects on Job Satisfaction, Psychological Distress, and Absenteeism in Blue-Collar Workers," *Journal of Applied Psychology*, February 1995, pp. 29–42.

4. This section is based on B. Critchley, "Royal Bank/DS Now Restructured," *Financial Post* (*National Post*), February 10, 2000, p. D2.

5. D. Drickhamer, "Moving Man," *IndustryWeek*, December 2002, pp. 44–46.

6. For a discussion of authority, see W. A. Kahn and K. E. Kram, "Authority at Work: Internal Models and Their Organizational Consequences," *Academy of Management Review*, January 1994, pp. 17–50.

7. B. Arthur, "Peddie Gives New GM 'Autonomy' for Change," *National Post*, June 8, 2004, p. S2.

8. See http://www.fan590.com/columnists/columnist1article.jsp?content=20060327_113940_4056 (accessed September 24, 2006).

9. D. Van Fleet, "Span of Management Research and Issues," *Academy of Management Journal*, September 1983, pp. 546–552.

10. *Management Reflection* based on L. Millan, "Who's Scoffing Now? The Lemaire Brothers Started Out Using Recycled Fibre in One Small Paper Mill in Rural Quebec," *Canadian Business*, March 27, 1998, pp. 74–77; and http://www.cascades.com (accessed August 23, 2006).

11. See, for example, H. Mintzberg, *Power in and Around Organizations* (Upper Saddle River, NJ: Prentice Hall, 1983); and J. Child, *Organization: A Guide to Problems and Practices* (London: Kaiser & Row, 1984).

12. T. Burns and G. M. Stalker, *The Management of Innovation* (London: Tavistock, 1961); D. A. Morand, "The Role of Behavioral Formality and Informality in the Enactment of Bureaucratic Versus Organic Organizations," *Academy of Management Review*, October 1995, pp. 831–872.

13. See, for instance, R. E. Miles and C. C. Snow, *Organizational Strategy, Structure, and Process* (New York: McGraw-Hill, 1978); D. Miller, "The Structural and Environmental Correlates of Business Strategy," *Strategic Management Journal*, January–February 1987, pp. 55–76; H. L. Boschken, "Strategy and Structure: Reconceiving the Relationship," *Journal of Management*, March 1990, pp. 135–150; H. A. Simon, "Strategy and Organizational Evolution," *Strategic Management Journal*, January 1993, pp. 131–142; R. Parthasarthy and S. P. Sethi, "Relating Strategy and Structure to Flexible Automation: A Test of Fit and Performance Implications," *Strategic Management Journal* 14, no. 6 (1993), pp. 529–549; D. C. Galunic and K. M. Eisenhardt, "Renewing the Strategy-Structure-Performance Paradigm," in *Research in Organizational Behavior*, vol. 16, ed.

B. M. Staw and L. L. Cummings (Greenwich, CT: JAI Press, 1994), pp. 215–255; and D. Jennings and S. Seaman, "High and Low Levels of Organizational Adaptation: An Empirical Analysis of Strategy, Structure, and Performance," *Strategic Management Journal*, July 1994, pp. 459–475.

14. See, for instance, P. M. Blau and R. A. Schoenherr, *The Structure of Organizations* (New York: Basic Books, 1971); D. S. Pugh, "The Aston Program of Research: Retrospect and Prospect," in *Perspectives on Organization Design and Behavior*, ed. A. H. Van de Ven and W. F. Joyce, pp. 135–166 (New York: John Wiley, 1981); R. Z. Gooding and J. A. Wagner III, "A Meta-Analytic Review of the Relationship between Size and Performance: The Productivity and Efficiency of Organizations and Their Subunits," *Administrative Science Quarterly*, December 1985, pp. 462–481.

15. J. Woodward, *Industrial Organization: Theory and Practice* (London: Oxford University Press, 1965).

16. See, for instance, C. Perrow, "A Framework for the Comparative Analysis of Organizations," *American Sociological Review*, April 1967, pp. 194–208; J. D. Thompson, *Organizations in Action* (New York: McGraw-Hill, 1967); J. Hage and M. Aiken, "Routine Technology, Social Structure, and Organizational Goals," *Administrative Science Quarterly*, September 1969, pp. 366–377; C. C. Miller, W. H. Glick, Y. D. Wang, and G. P. Huber, "Understanding Technology-Structure Relationships: Theory Development and Meta-Analytic Theory Testing," *Academy of Management Journal*, June 1991, pp. 370–399.

17. D. Gerwin, "Relationships Between Structure and Technology," in *Handbook of Organizational Design*, vol. 2, ed. P. C. Nystrom and W. H. Starbuck (New York: Oxford University Press, 1981), pp. 3–38; D. M. Rousseau and R. A. Cooke, "Technology and Structure: The Concrete, Abstract, and Activity Systems of Organizations," *Journal of Management*, Fall–Winter 1984, pp. 345–361.

18. F. E. Emery and E. Trist, "The Causal Texture of Organizational Environments," *Human Relations*, February 1965, pp. 21–32; P. Lawrence and J. W. Lorsch, *Organization and Environment: Managing Differentiation and Integration* (Boston: Harvard Business School, Division of Research, 1967); M. Yasai-Ardekani, "Structural Adaptations to Environments," *Academy of Management Review*, January 1986, pp. 9–21.

19. L. A. Perlow, G. A. Okhuysen, and N. P. Repenning, "The Speed Trap: Exploring the Relationship Between Decision Making and Temporal Context," *Academy of Management Journal* 45, 2002, pp. 931–995.

20. H. Mintzberg, *Structure in Fives: Designing Effective Organizations* (Upper Saddle River, NJ: Prentice Hall, 1983), p. 157.

21. R. J. Williams, J. J. Hoffman, and B. T. Lamont, "The Influence of Top Management Team Characteristics on M-Form Implementation Time," *Journal of Managerial Issues*, Winter 1995, pp. 466–480.

22. See, for example, R. E. Hoskisson, C. W. L. Hill, and H. Kim, "The Multidivisional Structure: Organizational Fossil or Source of Value?" *Journal of Management* 19, no. 2 (1993), pp. 269–298; I. I. Mitroff, R. O. Mason, and C. M. Pearson, "Radical Surgery: What Will Tomorrow's Organizations Look Like?" *Academy of Management Executive*, February 1994, pp. 11–21; T. Clancy, "Radical Surgery: A View from the Operating Theater," *Academy of Management Executive*, February 1994, pp. 73–78; M. Hammer, "Processed Change: Michael Hammer Sees Process as 'the Clark Kent of Business Ideas'—A Concept That Has the Power to Change a Company's Organizational Design," *Journal of Business Strategy*, November–December 2001, pp. 11–15; D. F. Twomey, "Leadership, Organizational Design, and Competitiveness for the 21st Century," *Global Competitiveness*, Annual 2002, pp. S31–S40; G. J. Castrogiovanni, "Organization Task Environments: Have They

Changed Fundamentally over Time?" *Journal of Management* 28, no. 2 (2002), pp. 129–150.

23. T. Starner, "Room for Improvement," *IQ Magazine,* March–April 2003, pp. 36–37.

24. See, for example, H. Rothman, "The Power of Empowerment," *Nation's Business,* June 1993, pp. 49–52; B. Dumaine, "Payoff from the New Management," *Fortune,* December 13, 1993, pp. 103–110; J. A. Byrne, "The Horizontal Corporation," *BusinessWeek,* December 20, 1993, pp. 76–81; J. R. Katzenbach and D. K. Smith, *The Wisdom of Teams* (Boston: Harvard Business School Press, 1993); L. Grant, "New Jewel in the Crown," *U.S. News & World Report,* February 28, 1994, pp. 55–57; D. Ray and H. Bronstein, *Teaming Up: Making the Transition to a Self-Directed Team-Based Organization* (New York: McGraw Hill, 1995); and D. R. Denison, S. L. Hart, and J. A. Kahn, "From Chimneys to Cross-Functional Teams: Developing and Validating a Diagnostic Model," *Academy of Management Journal,* December 1996, pp. 1005–1023.

25. C. Fishman, "Whole Foods Is All Teams," *Fast Company,* Greatest Hits, vol. 1, 1997, pp. 102–113.

26. W. Hillier, "BC Forest Fires: A Time of Need," *Canadian Underwriter,* January 2004, pp. 22–23.

27. P. LaBarre, "This Organization Is Dis-Organization," *Fast Company,* http://www.fastcompany.com (accessed April 16, 1997).

28. See, for example, G. G. Dess, A. Rasheed, K. J. McLaughlin, and R. L. Priem, "The New Corporate Architecture," *Academy of Management Executive,* August 1995, pp. 7–20.

29. For additional readings on boundaryless organizations, see M. Hammer and S. Stanton, "How Process Enterprises Really Work," *Harvard Business Review,* November–December 1999, pp. 108–118; T. Zenger and W. Hesterly, "The Disaggregation of Corporations: Selective Intervention, High-Powered Incentives, and Modular Units," *Organization Science* 8 (1997), pp. 209–222; R. Ashkenas, D. Ulrich, T. Jick, and S. Kerr, *The Boundaryless Organization: Breaking the Chains of Organizational Structure* (San Francisco: Jossey-Bass, 1997); R. M. Hodgetts, "A Conversation With Steve Kerr," *Organizational Dynamics,* Spring 1996, pp. 68–79; and J. Gebhardt, "The Boundaryless Organization," *Sloan Management Review,* Winter 1996, pp. 117–119. For another view of boundaryless organizations, see B. Victor, "The Dark Side of the New Organizational Forms: An Editorial Essay," *Organization Science,* November 1994, pp. 479–482.

30. See, for instance, W. H. Davidow and M. S. Malone, *The Virtual Corporation* (New York: HarperCollins, 1992); H. Chesbrough and D. Teece, "When Is Virtual Virtuous? Organizing for Innovation," *Harvard Business Review,* January–February 1996, pp. 65–73; G. G. Dess, A. Rasheed, K. J. McLaughlin, and R. L. Priem, "The New Corporate Architecture," *Academy of Management Executive,* August 1995, pp. 7–20; M. Sawhney and D. Parikh, "Break Your Boundaries," *Business 2.0,* May 2000, pp. 198–207; D. Pescovitz, "The Company Where Everybody's a Temp," *New York Times Magazine,* June 11, 2000, pp. 94–96; W. F. Cascio, "Managing a Virtual Workplace," *Academy of Management Executive,* August 2000, pp. 81–90; D. Lyons, "Smart and Smarter," *Forbes,* March 18, 2002, pp. 40–41; and B. Hedberg, G. Dahlgren, J. Hansson, and N. Goran Olve, *Virtual Organizations and Beyond: Discovering Imaginary Systems* (New York: John Wiley, 2001).

31. R. E. Miles and C. C. Snow, "Causes of Failures in Network Organizations," *California Management Review* 34, no. 4 (1992), pp. 53–72; R. E. Miles and C. C. Snow, "The New Network Firm: A Spherical Structure Built on Human Investment Philosophy," *Organizational Dynamics,* Spring 1995, pp. 5–18; C. Jones, W. Hesterly, and S. Borgatti, "A General Theory of Network

Governance: Exchange Conditions and Social Mechanisms," *Academy of Management Review,* October 1997, pp. 911–945; and R. E. Miles, C. C. Snow, J. A. Mathews, G. Miles, and H. J. Coleman, "Organizing in the Knowledge Age: Anticipating the Cellular Form," *Academy of Management Executive,* November 1997, pp. 7–24.

32. S. Reed, A. Reinhardt, and A. Sains, "Saving Ericsson," *BusinessWeek,* November 11, 2002, pp. 64–68.

33. J. Barthelemy and D. Adsit, "The Seven Deadly Sins of Outsourcing," *Academy of Management Executive* 17, no. 2 (2003), pp. 87–100.

34. K. Restivo, "Most Canadian Tech Firms Prefer Not to Outsource, Study Shows," *Financial Post* (*National Post*), June 11, 2004, p. FP5.

35. D. A. Ketchen Jr. and G. T. M. Hult, "To Be Modular or Not to Be? Some Answers to the Question," *Academy of Management Executive,* May 2002, pp. 166–167; M. A. Schilling, "The Use of Modular Organizational Forms: An Industry-Level Analysis," *Academy of Management Journal,* December 2001, pp. 1149–1168; D. Lei, M. A. Hitt, and J. D. Goldhar, "Advanced Manufacturing Technology: Organizational Design and Strategic Flexibility," *Organization Studies* 17, no. 3 (1996), pp. 501–523; R. Sanchez and J. Mahoney, "Modularity, Flexibility and Knowledge Management in Product and Organization Design," *Strategic Management Journal* 17 (1996), pp. 63–76; and R. Sanchez, "Strategic Flexibility in Product Competition," *Strategic Management Journal* 16 (1995), pp. 135–159.

36. D. A. Ketchen Jr. and G. T. M. Hult, "To Be Modular or Not to Be? Some Answers to the Question," *Academy of Management Executive,* May 2002, pp. 166–167.

37. K. Kerwin, "GM: Modular Plants Won't Be a Snap," *BusinessWeek,* November 9, 1998, pp. 168–169.

38. P. M. Senge, *The Fifth Discipline: The Art and Practice of Learning Organizations* (New York: Doubleday, 1990).

39. J. M. Liedtka, "Collaborating Across Lines of Business for Competitive Advantage," *Academy of Management Executive,* April 1996, pp. 20–37; G. Szulanski, "Exploring Internal Stickiness: Impediments to the Transfer of Best Practice within the Firm," *Strategic Management Journal,* Winter Special Issue 1996, pp. 27–43; D. Zell, "Overcoming Barriers to Work Innovations: Lessons Learned at Hewlett-Packard," *Organizational Dynamics,* Summer 2001, pp. 77–86; M. Schulz, "The Uncertain Relevance of Newness: Organizational Learning and Knowledge Flows," *Academy of Management Journal,* August 2001, pp. 661–681; R. Cross, A. Parker, L. Prusak, and S. Borgatti, "Supporting Knowledge Creation and Sharing in Social Networks," *Organizational Dynamics,* Fall 2001, pp. 100–120; and B. Marr, "How to Knowledge Management," *Financial Management,* February 2003, pp. 26–27.

40. Based on J. F. Veiga and J. N. Yanouzas, *The Dynamics of Organization Theory: Gaining a Macro Perspective* (St. Paul, MN: West, 1979), pp. 158–160.

41. Situation adapted from information in "HR Pressured to Breach Ethics Policies, Says Survey," *HR Briefing,* June 1, 2003, p. 1; S. Pulliam, "A Staffer Ordered to Commit Fraud Balked, Then Caved," *Wall Street Journal,* June 23, 2003, pp. A1, A6; and J. Gilbert, "A Matter of Trust," *Sales & Marketing Management,* March 2003, pp. 30–31.

42. Information on company from Indigo Books & Music website, http://www.chapters.indigo.ca (accessed October 2, 2004); and Hoover's Online, http://www.hoovers.com (accessed October 2, 2004); and H. Shaw, "Montreal's Steel Magnolia Won Canada's Book Battle," *Financial Post,* March 31, 2001, p. F3.

43. Case based on N. George, "The Virtues of Being Local," *Financial Times,* October 8, 2003, pp. 4–5; "Svenska Handelsbanken Branches

Out in the UK," *European Banker,* November 2003, p. 6; the company's website, http://www.handelsbanken.se (accessed 2004); and N. George, "Counting on the Spirit of Independent Branches," *Financial Times,* November 5, 2001, p. 10.

44. Based on P. L. Hunsaker, *Training in Management Skills* (Upper Saddle River, NJ: Prentice Hall, 2001), pp. 135–136 and 430–432; R. T. Noel, "What You Say to Your Employees When You Delegate," *Supervisory Management,* December 1993, p. 13; and S. Caudron, "Delegate for Results," *IndustryWeek,* February 6, 1995, pp. 27–30.

Chapter 6

1. T. Dixon, *Communication, Organization, and Performance* (Norwood, NJ: Ablex Publishing Corporation, 1996), p. 281; P. G. Clampitt, *Communicating for Managerial Effectiveness* (Newbury Park, CA: Sage Publications, 1991); L. E. Penley, E. R. Alexander, I. E. Jernigan, and C. I. Henwood, "Communication Abilities of Managers: The Relationship to Performance," *Journal of Management,* March 1991, pp. 57–76.

2. "Electronic Invective Backfires," *Workforce,* June 2001, p. 20; and E. Wong, "A Stinging Office Memo Boomerangs," *New York Times,* April 5, 2001, p. C11.

3. C. O. Kursh, "The Benefits of Poor Communication," *Psychoanalytic Review,* Summer–Fall 1971, pp. 189–208.

4. W. G. Scott and T. R. Mitchell, *Organization Theory: A Structural and Behavioral Analysis* (Homewood, IL: Richard D. Irwin, 1976).

5. D. K. Berlo, *The Process of Communication* (New York: Holt, Rinehart & Winston, 1960), pp. 30–32.

6. T. R. Kurtzberg, C. E. Naquin, and L. Y. Belkin, "Electronic Performance Appraisals: The Effects of E-Mail Communication on Peer Ratings in Actual and Simulated Environments," *Organizational Behavior and Human Decision Processes* 98, no. 2 (2005), pp. 216–226.

7. J. Kruger, N. Epley, J. Parker, and Z.-W. Ng, "Egocentrism Over E-Mail: Can We Communicate as Well as We Think?" *Journal of Personality and Social Psychology* 89, no. 6 (2005), pp. 925–936.

8. Thanks to an anonymous reviewer for providing this elaboration.

9. P. G. Clampitt, *Communicating for Managerial Effectiveness* (Newbury Park, CA: Sage Publications, 1991).

10. A. Warfield, "Do You Speak Body Language?" *Training & Development,* April 2001, pp. 60–61; D. Zielinski, "Body Language Myths," *Presentations,* April 2001, pp. 36–42; and "Visual Cues Speak Loudly in Workplace," *Springfield News-Leader,* January 21, 2001, p. 8B.

11. C. Cavanagh, *Managing Your E-Mail: Thinking Outside the Inbox* (Hoboken, NJ: John Wiley & Sons, 2003).

12. K. Macklem, "You've Got Too Much Mail," *Maclean's,* January 30, 2006, pp. 20–21.

13. K. Macklem, "You've Got Too Much Mail," *Maclean's,* January 30, 2006, pp. 20–21.

14. D. K. Berlo, *The Process of Communication* (New York: Holt, Rinehart & Winston, 1960), p. 103.

15. A. Mehrabian, "Communication Without Words," *Psychology Today,* September 1968, pp. 53–55.

16. See, for instance, S. P. Robbins and P. L. Hunsaker, *Training in Interpersonal Skills,* 3rd ed. (Upper Saddle River, NJ: Prentice Hall, 2003); M. Young and J. E. Post, "Managing to Communicate, Communicating to Manage: How Leading Companies Communicate

with Employees," *Organizational Dynamics,* Summer 1993, pp. 31–43; J. A. DeVito, *The Interpersonal Communication Book,* 6th ed. (New York: HarperCollins, 1992); and A. G. Athos and J. J. Gabarro, *Interpersonal Behavior* (Upper Saddle River, NJ: Prentice Hall, 1978).

17. V. Galt, "Top-Down Feedback," *Vancouver Sun,* February 15, 2003, pp. E1, E2.

18. Cited in "Heard It Through the Grapevine," *Forbes,* February 10, 1997, p. 22.

19. See, for instance, A. Bruzzese, "What to Do About Toxic Gossip," *USA Today,* March 14, 2001, http://www.usatoday.com; N. B. Kurland and L. H. Pelled, "Passing the Word: Toward a Model of Gossip and Power in the Workplace," *Academy of Management Review,* April 2000, pp. 428–438; N. DiFonzo, P. Bordia, and R. L. Rosnow, "Reining in Rumors," *Organizational Dynamics,* Summer 1994, pp. 47–62; M. Noon and R. Delbridge, "News from Behind My Hand: Gossip in Organizations," *Organization Studies* 14, no. 1 (1993), pp. 23–26; and J. G. March and G. Sevon, "Gossip, Information and Decision Making," in *Decisions and Organizations,* ed. G. March (Oxford: Blackwell, 1988), pp. 429–442.

20. "Human Capital Index: 2001/2002 Survey Report," Watson Wyatt Worldwide, Washington, DC.

21. G. Buckler, "Instant Messaging Replacing Pagers in the Enterprise," *Computing Canada,* March 26, 2004, p. 18.

22. J. Rohwer, "Today, Tokyo: Tomorrow, the World," *Fortune,* September 18, 2000, pp. 140–152; J. McCullam and L. Torres, "Instant Enterprising," *Forbes,* September 11, 2000, p. 28; J. Guyon, "The World Is Your Office," *Fortune,* June 12, 2000, pp. 227–234; S. Baker, N. Gross, and I. M. Kunii, "The Wireless Internet," *BusinessWeek,* May 29, 2000, pp. 136–144; R. Lieber, "Information Is Everything . . ." *Fast Company,* November 1999, pp. 246–254.

23. M. Vallis, "Nasty E-mail from the Boss May Mean More Sick Days," *National Post,* January 9, 2004, pp. A1, A9. Study was done by George Fieldman, a psychologist at Buckinghamshire Chilterns University College, and presented at the 2004 Annual Occupational Psychology Conference of the British Psychological Society.

24. Derived from P. Kuitenbrouwer, "Office E-Mail Runs Amok," *Financial Post,* October 18, 2001, p. FP11.

25. See http://findarticles.com/p/articles/mi_qn4200/is_ 20060529/ai_n16432818 (accessed September 25, 2006).

26. G. Hilson, "Simplicity Takes Top Billing for Business Users at BMO," *Computing Canada,* June 6, 2003, p. 3.

27. G. Hilson, "Sklar Peppler Gets Comfy With Web Tools," *Computing Canada,* June 6, 2003, p. 24.

28. J. Karaian, "Where Wireless Works," *CFO,* May 2003, pp. 81–83.

29. Statistics on "Worldwide Number of Mobile Users and Consumers, 2001," available on http://epaynews.com/statistics (accessed May 28, 2003).

30. M. Blanchard, "Johnson Inc. Relies on IP Telephony," *Globe and Mail,* May 13, 2004.

31. K. Hafner, "For the Well Connected, All the World's an Office," *New York Times,* March 30, 2000, p. D11.

32. Reprinted from *Supervisory Management,* January 1989. American Management Association, New York. http://www.amanet.org. All rights reserved.

33. Information for one incident comes from "Martha Stewart Could Be Charged as 'Tippee,' Court Papers in Guilty Plea by a Merrill Employee Say She Based Sales on Inside Information," *Wall Street*

Journal, October 3, 2002, p. C1; and M. Roman, "A Fresh Stew for Martha," *BusinessWeek,* September 23, 2002, p. 50.

34. Information on company from Hoover's Online, http://www.hoovers.com (accessed May 29, 2003); and S. Clifford, "How to Get the Geeks and the Suits to Play Nice," *Business 2.0,* May 2002, pp. 92–93.

35. E. Anderssen and M. Valpy, "Face the Nation: Canada Remade," *Globe and Mail,* June 7, 2003, pp. A10–A11.

36. G. Schellenberg, *Immigrants in Canada's Census Metropolitan Areas,* Catalogue no. 89-613-MIE—No. 003 (Ottawa: Statistics Canada, August 2004).

37. Statistics Canada, "2001 Census: Census of Population: Language, Mobility and Migration," *The Daily,* December 10, 2002.

38. Case based on D. D. Hatch, J. E. Hall, and M. T. Miklave, "New EEOC Guidance on National-Origin Discrimination," *Workforce,* April 2003, p. 76; and A. Piech, "Going Global: Speaking in Tongues," *Inc.,* June 2003, p. 50.

39. Based on C. R. Rogers and R. E. Farson, *Active Listening* (Chicago: Industrial Relations Center of the University of Chicago, 1976); and P. L. Hunsaker, *Training in Management Skills* (Upper Saddle River, NJ: Prentice Hall, 2001), pp. 61–62.

40. J. Langdon, "Differences Between Males and Females at Work," *USA Today,* February 5, 2001, http://www.usatoday.com; J. Manion, "He Said, She Said," *Materials Management in Health Care,* November 1998, pp. 52–62; G. Franzwa and C. Lockhart, "The Social Origins and Maintenance of Gender Communication Styles, Personality Types, and Grid-Group Theory," *Sociological Perspectives* 41, no. 1 (1998), pp. 185–208; D. Tannen, *Talking from 9 to 5: Women and Men in the Workplace* (New York: Avon Books, 1995).

Chapter 7

1. Information from Hoover's Online, http://www.hoovers.com; R. Waugh, "Getting More Leaders Is Hard Enough, but the Job Skills Needed Are Changing, Too," *Canadian HR Reporter,* January 26, 2004, p. 18; J. Kirby, "In the Vault," *Canadian Business,* March 1–14, 2004, pp. 68–72; S. Greengard, "Brett Ellison," *IQ Magazine,* November–December 2002, p. 52; http://www.scotiabank.com/cda/content/0,1608,CID821_LIDen,00.html (accessed September 30, 2006); and http://www.scotiabank.com/cda/content/0,1608,CID7148_LIDen,00.html# (accessed September 30, 2006).

2. P. M. Wright and G. C. McMahan, "Theoretical Perspectives for Strategic Human Resource Management," *Journal of Management* 18, no. 1 (1992), pp. 295–320; A. A. Lado and M. C. Wilson, "Human Resource Systems and Sustained Competitive Advantage," *Academy of Management Review,* October 1994, pp. 699–727; J. Pfeffer, *Competitive Advantage Through People* (Boston: Harvard Business School Press, 1994); and J. Pfeffer, *The Human Equation* (Boston: Harvard Business School Press, 1998).

3. "Human Capital Index," Watson Wyatt Worldwide website, http://www.watsonwyatt.com/research/_resrender.asp?id=W-488&page=1 (accessed September 21, 2004).

4. Statistics Canada, "Fact-sheet on Unionization in Canada," *The Daily,* August 28, 2003.

5. S. Premack and J. E. Hunter, "Individual Unionization Decisions," *Psychological Bulletin* 103, no. 2 (1988), pp. 223–234.

6. Based on M. King, "Union at Indigo," *Gazette* (Montreal), February 11, 2003, p. B3.

7. S. Armour, "Lawsuits Pin Target on Managers," *USA Today,* October 1, 2002, http://www.usatoday.com.

8. R. Waugh, "Getting More Leaders Is Hard Enough, but the Job Skills Needed Are Changing, Too," *Canadian HR Reporter,* January 26, 2004, p. 18.

9. E. Beauchesne, "Skills Training Rebounds: But Labour Shortage May Still Be Looming," *Telegram,* November 21, 2003, p. D1.

10. J. Sullivan, "Workforce Planning: Why to Start Now," *Workforce,* September 2002, pp. 46–50.

11. Based on A. Tomlinson, "The Many Benefits of Online Job Boards," *Canadian HR Reporter,* July 15, 2002, pp. 17–18. The Career webpage is at http://www.scotiabank.com/cda/content/0,1608,CID9031_LIDen,00.html (accessed September 25, 2006).

12. T. J. Bergmann and M. S. Taylor, "College Recruitment: What Attracts Students to Organizations?" *Personnel,* May–June 1984, pp. 34–46; and A. S. Bargerstock and G. Swanson, "Four Ways to Build Cooperative Recruitment Alliances," *HR Magazine,* March 1991, p. 49.

13. J. R. Gordon, *Human Resource Management: A Practical Approach* (Boston: Allyn and Bacon, 1986), p. 170.

14. F. Loyie, "Police in a Rush to Lure New Recruits," *Edmonton Journal,* April 24, 2004, p. B3.

15. S. Burton and D. Warner, "The Future of Hiring—Top 5 Sources for Recruitment Today," *Workforce Vendor Directory,* 2002, p. 75.

16. "FlipDog Flips Online Recruiting on End," *Workforce,* December 2002, p. 60.

17. G. Shaw, "An Offer That's Hard to Refuse," *Vancouver Sun,* November 12, 2003, p. D5.

18. See, for example, J. P. Kirnan, J. E. Farley, and K. F. Geisinger, "The Relationship Between Recruiting Source, Applicant Quality, and Hire Performance: An Analysis by Sex, Ethnicity, and Age," *Personnel Psychology,* Summer 1989, pp. 293–308; and R. W. Griffeth, P. Hom, L. Fink, and D. Cohen, "Comparative Tests of Multivariate Models of Recruiting Sources Effects," *Journal of Management* 23, no. 1 (1997), pp. 19–36.

19. K. Harley, "Zero Churn," *Progress,* May 2001, pp. 30–33.

20. G. W. England, *Development and Use of Weighted Application Blanks,* rev. ed. (Minneapolis: Industrial Relations Center, University of Minnesota, 1971); J. J. Asher, "The Biographical Item: Can It Be Improved?" *Personnel Psychology,* Summer 1972, p. 266; G. Grimsley and H. F. Jarrett, "The Relation of Managerial Achievement to Test Measures Obtained in the Employment Situation: Methodology and Results," *Personnel Psychology,* Spring 1973, pp. 31–48; E. E. Ghiselli, "The Validity of Aptitude Tests in Personnel Selection," *Personnel Psychology,* Winter 1973, p. 475; I. T. Robertson and R. S. Kandola, "Work Sample Tests: Validity, Adverse Impact, and Applicant Reaction," *Journal of Occupational Psychology* 55, no. 3 (1982), pp. 171–183; A. K. Korman, "The Prediction of Managerial Performance: A Review," *Personnel Psychology,* Summer 1986, pp. 295–322; G. C. Thornton, *Assessment Centers in Human Resource Management* (Reading, MA: Addison-Wesley, 1992); C. Fernandez-Araoz, "Hiring Without Firing," *Harvard Business Review,* July–August, 1999, pp. 108–120; and A. M. Ryan and R. E. Ployhart, "Applicants' Perceptions of Selection Procedures and Decisions: A Critical Review and Agenda for the Future," *Journal of Management* 26, no. 3 (2000), pp. 565–606.

21. See, for instance, R. D. Arvey and J. E. Campion, "The Employment Interview: A Summary and Review of Recent Research," *Personnel Psychology,* Summer 1982, pp. 281–322; and M. M. Harris, "Reconsidering the Employment Interview: A Review of Recent

Literature and Suggestions for Future Research," *Personnel Psychology,* Winter 1989, pp. 691–726; J. H. Prager, "Nasty or Nice: 56-Question Quiz," *Wall Street Journal,* February 22, 2000, p. A4; and M. K. Zachary, "Labor Law for Supervisors," *Supervision,* March 2001, pp. 23–26.

22. See, for instance, G. Nicholsen, "Screen and Glean: Good Screening and Background Checks Help Make the Right Match for Every Open Position," *Workforce,* October 2000, p. 70.

23. R. L. Dipboye, *Selection Interviews: Process Perspectives* (Cincinnati: South-Western Publishing, 1992), p. 6.

24. See, for instance, R. D. Arveny and J. E. Campion, "The Employment Interview: A Summary and Review of Recent Research," *Personnel Psychology,* Summer 1982, pp. 281–322; and M. M. Harris, "Reconsidering the Employment Interview: A Review of Recent Literature and Suggestions for Future Research," *Personnel Psychology,* Winter 1989, pp. 691–726.

25. J. Merritt, "Improv at the Interview," *BusinessWeek,* February 3, 2003, p. 63.

26. S. Caudron, "Who Are You Really Hiring?" *Workforce,* November 2002, pp. 28–32.

27. P. Johnson, "Fibbing Applicants Filtered Out," *Springfield News Leader,* August 4, 2002, p. 6E.

28. See, for example, S. L. Premack and J. P. Wanous, "A Meta-Analysis of Realistic Job Preview Experiments," *Journal of Applied Psychology,* November 1985, pp. 706–720; J. A. Breaugh and M. Starke, "Research on Employee Recruitment: So Many Studies, So Many Remaining Questions," *Journal of Management* 26, no. 3 (2000), pp. 405–434; B. M. Meglino, E. C. Ravlin, and A. S. DeNisi, "A Meta-Analytic Examination of Realistic Job Preview Effectiveness: A Test of Three Counterintuitive Propositions," *Human Resource Management Review* 10, no. 4 (2000), pp. 407–434; and Y. Ganzach, A. Pazy, Y. Ohayun, and E. Brainin, "Social Exchange and Organizational Commitment: Decision-Making Training for Job Choice as an Alternative to the Realistic Job Preview," *Personnel Psychology,* Autumn 2002, pp. 613–637.

29. A. Wahl, "People Power," *Canadian Business,* March 29–April 11, 2004, p. 58.

30. C. L. Cooper, "The Changing Psychological Contract at Work: Revisiting the Job Demands–Control Model," *Occupational and Environmental Medicine,* June 2002, p. 355; D. M. Rousseau and S. A. Tijoriwala, "Assessing Psychological Contracts: Issues, Alternatives and Measures," *Journal of Organizational Behavior* 19, S1 (1998), pp. 679–695; and S. L. Robinson, M. S. Kraatz, and D. M. Rousseau, "Changing Obligations and the Psychological Contract: A Longitudinal Study," *Academy of Management Journal,* February 1994, pp. 137–152.

31. T. Galvin, "2002 Industry Report," *Training,* October 2002, pp. 24–33.

32. R. Ferguson, "Brewery's Baccalaureates of Beer," *Toronto Star,* July 19, 2003, pp. D1, D10; and http://www.conferenceboard.ca/press/2005/LearnDev_Outlook.asp (accessed September 30, 2006).

33. B. Hall, "The Top Training Priorities for 2003," *Training,* February 2003, p. 40; and T. Galvin, "2002 Industry Report," *Training,* October 2002, pp. 24–33.

34. B. Hall, "The Top Training Priorities for 2003," *Training,* February 2003, p. 40.

35. Based on K. Harding, "Once and Future Kings," *Globe and Mail,* April 9, 2003, pp. C1, C6.

36. V. Galt, "Training on Tap," *Globe and Mail,* November 20, 2002, pp. C1, C8.

37. U. Boser, "Gaming the System, One Click at a Time," *U.S. News & World Report,* October 28, 2002, p. 60.

38. L. Fowlie, "Online Training Takes the Slow Train: 'Next Big Thing' Fails to Live Up to Initial Hype," *Daily Townsman,* March 5, 2004, p. 11.

39. S. Purba, "When Reviews Deserve a Failing Grade," *Globe and Mail,* June 11, 2004, p. C1.

40. K. Clark, "Judgment Day," *U.S. News & World Report,* January 13, 2003, pp. 31–32; E. E. Lawler III, "The Folly of Forced Ranking," *Strategy & Business,* Third Quarter 2002, pp. 28–32; K. Cross, "The Weakest Links," *Business 2.0,* June 26, 2001, pp. 36–37; J. Greenwald, "Rank and Fire," *Time,* June 18, 2001, pp. 38–39; D. Jones, "More Firms Cut Workers Ranked at Bottom to Make Way for Talent," *USA Today,* May 30, 2001, p. B11; and M. Boyle, "Performance Reviews: Perilous Curves Ahead," *Fortune,* May 28, 2001, pp. 187–188.

41. K. Clark, "Judgment Day," *U.S. News & World Report,* January 13, 2003, pp. 31–32.

42. R. D. Bretz Jr., G. T. Milkovich, and W. Read, "The Current State of Performance Appraisal Research and Practice: Concerns, Directions, and Implications," *Journal of Management,* June 1992, p. 331.

43. M. Debrayen and S. Brutus, "Learning from Others' 360-Degree Experiences," *Canadian HR Reporter,* February 10, 2003, pp. 18–19.

44. M. Johne, "It's Good PR to Keep Employees Loyal," *Globe and Mail,* September 20, 2002, p. C1.

45. M. A. Peiperl, "Getting 360° Feedback Right," *Harvard Business Review,* January 2001, 142–147.

46. This section based on R. I. Henderson, *Compensation Management in a Knowledge-Based World,* 9th ed. (Upper Saddle River, NJ: Prentice Hall, 2003).

47. L. R. Gomez-Mejia, "Structure and Process of Diversification, Compensation Strategy, and Firm Performance," *Strategic Management Journal* 13 no. 5 (1992), pp. 381–397; and E. Montemayor, "Congruence Between Pay Policy and Competitive Strategy in High-Performing Firms," *Journal of Management* 22, no. 6 (1996), pp. 889–908.

48. E. E. Lawler III, G. E. Ledford Jr., and L. Chang, "Who Uses Skill-Based Pay and Why," *Compensation & Benefits Review,* March–April 1993, p. 22; G. E. Ledford, "Paying for the Skills, Knowledge and Competencies of Knowledge Workers," *Compensation & Benefits Review,* July–August 1995, pp. 55–62; C. Lee, K. S. Law, and P. Bobko, "The Importance of Justice Perceptions on Pay Effectiveness: A Two-Year Study of a Skill-Based Pay Plan," *Journal of Management* 26, no. 6 (1999), pp. 851–873.

49. M. Rowland, "It's What You Can Do That Counts," *New York Times,* June 6, 1993, p. F17.

50. D. E. Super and D. T. Hall, "Career Development: Exploration and Planning," in *Annual Review of Psychology,* vol. 29, ed. M. R. Rosenzweig and L. W. Porter (Palo Alto, CA: Annual Reviews, 1978), p. 334.

51. M. Cianni and D. Wnuck, "Individual Growth and Team Enhancement: Moving Toward a New Model of Career Development," *Academy of Management Executive,* February 1997, pp. 105–115.

52. D. E. Super, "A Life-Span Life Space Approach to Career Development," *Journal of Vocational Behavior,* Spring 1980, pp. 282–298. See also E. P. Cook, and M. Arthur, *Career Theory Handbook* (Upper

Saddle River, NJ: Prentice Hall, 1991), pp. 99–131; and L. S. Richman, "The New Worker Elite," *Fortune,* August 22, 1994, pp. 56–66.

53. R. Henkoff, "Winning the New Career Game," *Fortune,* July 12, 1993, pp. 46–49; "10 Tips for Managing Your Career," *Personnel,* October 1995, p. 106; A. Fisher, "Six Ways to Supercharge Your Career," *Fortune,* January 13, 1997, pp. 46–48; A. K. Smith, "Charting Your Own Course," *U.S. News & World Report,* November 6, 2000, pp. 56–65; and D. D. Dubois, "The 7 Stages of One's Career," *Training & Development,* December 2000, pp. 45–50.

54. Based on C. Petten, "Progressive Aboriginal Relations Important to Scotiabank," *Windspeaker,* March 2002, p. B7.

55. L. Crawford, "Motivation, Not a Degree Key at Ikea," *Financial Post* (*National Post*), February 24, 2004, p. FP12.

56. A. Wahl, "Opening Doors," *Canadian Business,* March 29–April 11, 2004, p. 45.

57. J. Hickman, "America's 50 Best Companies for Minorities," *Fortune,* July 8, 2002, pp. 110–120; J. Kahn, "Diversity Trumps the Downturn," *Fortune,* July 9, 2001, pp. 114–116; and http://www.dennys.com/en/cms/Diversity/36.html (accessed August 29, 2006).

58. "Employers Underestimate Extent of Sexual Harassment, Report Says," *Vancouver Sun,* March 8, 2001, p. D6.

59. J. Monchuk, "Female Mounties Allege Sex Harassment Not Investigated to Protect RCMP," *Canadian Press Newswire,* September 26, 2003.

60. "Employers Underestimate Extent of Sexual Harassment, Report Says," *Vancouver Sun,* March 8, 2001, p. D6.

61. A. B. Fisher, "Sexual Harassment: What to Do," *Fortune,* August 23, 1993, pp. 84–88.

62. "U.S. Leads Way in Sex Harassment Laws, Study Says," *Evening Sun,* November 30, 1992, p. A11; and W. Hardman and J. Heidelberg, "When Sexual Harassment Is a Foreign Affair," *Personnel,* April 1996, pp. 91–97.

63. *Janzen* v. *Platy Enterprises Ltd.* (1989), 10 C.H.R.R. D/6205 (S.C.C.).

64. "Facts About Sexual Harassment," *U.S. Equal Employment Opportunity Commission,* http://www.eeoc.gov (accessed June 1, 2003).

65. A. Fisher, "After All This Time, Why Don't People Know What Sexual Harassment Means?" *Fortune,* January 12, 1998, p. 68; and A. R. Karr, "Companies Crack Down on the Increasing Sexual Harassment by E-Mail," *Wall Street Journal,* September 21, 1999, p. A1.

66. See T. S. Bland and S. S. Stalcup, "Managing Harassment," *Human Resource Management,* Spring 2001, pp. 51–61; K. A. Hess and D. R. M. Ehrens, "Sexual Harassment—Affirmative Defense to Employer Liability," *Benefits Quarterly,* Second Quarter 1999, p. 57; J. A. Segal, "The Catch-22s of Remedying Sexual Harassment Complaints," *HR Magazine,* October 1997, pp. 111–117; S. C. Bahls and J. E. Bahls, "Hands-Off Policy," *Entrepreneur,* July 1997, pp. 74–76; J. A. Segal, "Where Are We Now?" *HR Magazine,* October 1996, pp. 69–73; B. McAfee and D. L. Deadrick, "Teach Employees to Just Say No," *HR Magazine,* February 1996, pp. 86–89; G. D. Block, "Avoiding Liability for Sexual Harassment," *HR Magazine,* April 1995, pp. 91–97; and J. A. Segal, "Stop Making Plaintiffs' Lawyers Rich," *HR Magazine,* April 1995, pp. 31–35.

67. C. Oglesby, "More Options for Moms Seeking Work–Family Balance," *CNN.com,* May 10, 2001, http://www.cnn.com.

68. F. Hansen, "Truths and Myths About Work/Life Balance," *Workforce,* December 2002, pp. 34–39.

69. L. Duxbury, C Higgins, and D. Coghill, "Voices of Canadians: Seeking Work–Life Balance," *Human Resources and Social Development Canada,* January 2003, http://www.hrsdc.gc.ca; and S. D. Friedman and J. H. Greenhaus, *Work and Family—Allies or Enemies?* (New York: Oxford University Press, 2000).

70. N. P. Rothbard, T. L. Dumas, and K. W. Phillips, "The Long Arm of the Organization: Work–Family Policies and Employee Preferences for Segmentation" (paper presented at the 61st Annual Academy of Management meeting, Washington, DC, August 2001).

71. L. T. Cullen, "Where Did Everyone Go?" *Time,* November 18, 2002, pp. 64–66.

72. S. Alleyne, "Stiff Upper Lips," *Black Enterprise,* April 2002, p. 59; C. Hymowitz, "Getting a Lean Staff to Do 'Ghost Work' of Departed Colleagues," *Wall Street Journal,* October 22, 2002, p. B1; E. Krell, "Defusing Downsizing," *Business Finance,* December 2002, pp. 55–57.

73. P. P. Shah, "Network Destruction: The Structural Implications of Downsizing," *Academy of Management Journal,* February 2000, pp. 101–112.

74. See, for instance, K. A. Mollica and B. Gray, "When Layoff Survivors Become Layoff Victims: Propensity to Litigate," *Human Resource Planning,* January 2001, pp. 22–32.

75. S. Koudsi, "You're Stuck," *Fortune,* December 10, 2001, pp. 271–274.

76. L. A. Mainiero and C. L. Tromley, *Developing Managerial Skills in Organizational Behavior* (Upper Saddle River, NJ: Prentice-Hall, 1994). Adapted by permission of Prentice-Hall, Inc.

77. Situation adapted from information in J. Russell, "Older Goodyear Workers Who Say Age Played into Evaluations Get Day in Court," *Akron Beacon Journal,* July 3, 2003, http://www.ohio.com/bj; and K. Clark, "Judgment Day," *U.S. News & World Report,* January 13, 2003, pp. 31–32.

78. Information on company from Mitsubishi Motors North America website, http://www.mitsubishicars.com (accessed June 1, 2004); "Mitsubishi Plans Big Boost to U.S. Production," *IndustryWeek,* March 18, 2003, http://www.industryweek.com; D. Kiley, "Workplace Woes Almost Eclipse Mitsubishi Plant," *USA Today,* October 21, 2002, p. B11; "EEOC Responds to Final Report of Mitsubishi Consent Decree Monitors," *Equal Employment Opportunity Commission,* http://www.eeoc.gov (accessed May 23, 2001); and S. Greengard, "Zero Tolerance: Making It Work," *Workforce,* May 1999, pp. 28–34.

79. Based on S. P. Robbins and D. A. DeCenzo, *Fundamentals of Management,* 4th ed. (Upper Saddle River, NJ: Prentice Hall, 2004), p. 194.

Chapter 8

1. Information from Hoover's Online, http://www.hoovers.com (accessed May 16, 2004); L. Pratt, "Success Fuelled by Ambition: Proving Women Could Do Men's Work Was a Key to Her Success," *National Post,* March 6, 2004, p. SR02; and S. Haggett, "Shell CEO Steps on the Gas," *Calgary Herald,* October 11, 2003, p. D1.

2. R. N. Kanungo, "Leadership in Organizations: Looking Ahead to the 21st Century," *Canadian Psychology* 39, nos. 1–2 (1998), p. 77. For more evidence of this consensus, see N. Adler, *International Dimensions of Organizational Behavior,* 3rd ed. (Cincinnati, OH: South

Western College Publishing, 1997); R. J. House, "Leadership in the Twenty-First Century," in *The Changing Nature of Work*, ed. A. Howard (San Francisco: Jossey-Bass, 1995), pp. 411–450; R. N. Kanungo and M. Mendonca, *Ethical Dimensions of Leadership* (Thousand Oaks, CA: Sage Publications, 1996); and A. Zaleznik, "The Leadership Gap," *Academy of Management Executive* 4, no. 1 (1990), pp. 7–22.

3. Based on "Alumna Continues Her Success as New Shell CEO," *KU Connection*, http://www.kuconnection.org/2003feb/people_2.asp; and C. Cattaneo, "Shell Anoints the Queen of Oilpatch: Linda Cook Becomes the Most Powerful Woman in Canada," *National Post*, June 27, 2003, p. FP1.

4. See S. A. Kirkpatrick and E. A. Locke, "Leadership: Do Traits Matter?" *Academy of Management Executive*, May 1991, pp. 48–60; and T. A. Judge, J. E. Bono, R. Ilies, and M. Werner, "Personality and Leadership: A Qualitative and Quantitative Review," *Journal of Applied Psychology*, August 2002, pp. 765–780.

5. See T. A. Judge, J. E. Bono, R. Ilies, and M. Werner, "Personality and Leadership: A Review" (paper presented at the 15th Annual Conference of the Society for Industrial and Organizational Psychology, New Orleans, 2000); T. A. Judge, J. E. Bono, R. Ilies, and M. W. Gerhardt, "Personality and Leadership: A Qualitative and Quantitative Review," *Journal of Applied Psychology*, August 2002, pp. 765–780; and D. A. Hofmann and L. M. Jones, "Leadership, Collective Personality, and Performance," *Journal of Applied Psychology* 90, no. 3 (2005), pp. 509–522.

6. J. Kirby, "In the Vault," *Canadian Business*, March 1–March 14, 2004, pp. 68–72.

7. J. Kirby, "In the Vault," *Canadian Business*, March 1–March 14, 2004, pp. 68–72.

8. K. Lewin and R. Lippitt, "An Experimental Approach to the Study of Autocracy and Democracy: A Preliminary Note," *Sociometry* 1 (1938), pp. 292–300; K. Lewin, "Field Theory and Experiment in Social Psychology: Concepts and Methods," *American Journal of Sociology* 44 (1939), pp. 868–896; K. Lewin, R. Lippitt, and R. K. White, "Patterns of Aggressive Behavior in Experimentally Created Social Climates," *Journal of Social Psychology* 10 (1939), pp. 271–301; R. Lippitt, "An Experimental Study of the Effect of Democratic and Authoritarian Group Atmospheres," *University of Iowa Studies in Child Welfare* 16 (1940), pp. 43–95.

9. B. M. Bass, *Stogdill's Handbook of Leadership* (New York: Free Press, 1981), pp. 289–299.

10. R. M. Stogdill and A. E. Coons, eds., *Leader Behavior: Its Description and Measurement*, Research Monograph No. 88 (Columbus: Ohio State University, Bureau of Business Research, 1951). For an updated literature review of Ohio State research, see S. Kerr, C. A. Schriesheirn, C. I. Murphy, and R. M. Stogdill, "Toward a Contingency Theory of Leadership Based upon the Consideration and Initiating Structure Literature," *Organizational Behavior and Human Performance*, August 1974, pp. 62–82; and B. M. Fisher, "Consideration and Initiating Structure and Their Relationships with Leader Effectiveness: A Meta-Analysis," in *Proceedings of the 48th Annual Academy of Management Conference*, ed. F. Hoy (Anaheim, California, 1988), pp. 201–205.

11. R. Kahn and D. Katz, "Leadership Practices in Relation to Productivity and Morale," in *Group Dynamics: Research and Theory*, 2nd ed., ed. D. Cartwright and A. Zander (Elmsford, NY: Row, Paterson, 1960).

12. R. R. Blake and J. S. Mouton, *The Managerial Grid III* (Houston, TX: Gulf Publishing, 1984).

13. L. L. Larson, J. G. Hunt, and R. N. Osborn, "The Great Hi-Hi Leader Behavior Myth: A Lesson from Occam's Razor," *Academy*

of Management Journal, December 1976, pp. 628–641; and P. C. Nystrom, "Managers and the Hi-Hi Leader Myth," *Academy of Management Journal*, June 1978, pp. 325–331.

14. T. A. Judge, R. F. Piccolo, and R. Ilies, "The Forgotten Ones? The Validity of Consideration and Initiating Structure in Leadership Research," *Journal of Applied Psychology*, 89, no. 1 (February 2004), pp. 36–51; and R. T. Keller, "Transformational Leadership, Initiating Structure, and Substitutes for Leadership: A Longitudinal Study of Research and Development Project Team Performance," *Journal of Applied Psychology* 91, no. 1 (2006), pp. 202–210.

15. R. McQueen, "The Long Shadow of Tom Stephens: He Branded MacBlo's Crew as Losers, Then Made Them into Winners," *Financial Post* (*National Post*), June 22, 1999, pp. C1, C5.

16. A. J. Mayo and N. Nohria, "Zeitgeist Leadership," *Harvard Business Review* 83, no. 10 (2005), pp. 45–60.

17. H. Wang, K. S. Law, R. D. Hackett, D. Wang, and Z. X. Chen, "Leader–Member Exchange as a Mediator of the Relationship Between Transformational Leadership and Followers' Performance and Organizational Citizenship Behavior," *Academy of Management Journal* 48, no. 3 (June 2005), pp. 420–432.

18. F. E. Fiedler, *A Theory of Leadership Effectiveness* (New York: McGraw-Hill, 1967).

19. G. Johns and A. M. Saks, *Organizational Behaviour*, 5th ed. (Toronto: Pearson Education Canada, 2001), pp. 278–279.

20. L. H. Peters, D. D. Hartke, and J. T. Pholmann, "Fiedler's Contingency Theory of Leadership: An Application of the Meta-Analysis Procedures of Schmidt and Hunter," *Psychological Bulletin*, March 1985, pp. 274–285; C. A. Schriesheim, B. J. Tepper, and L. A. Tetrault, "Lease Preferred Co-Worker Score, Situational Control, and Leadership Effectiveness: A Meta-Analysis of Contingency Model Performance Predictions," *Journal of Applied Psychology*, August 1994, pp. 561–573; and R. Ayman, M. M. Chemers, and F. Fiedler, "The Contingency Model of Leadership Effectiveness: Its Levels of Analysis," *Leadership Quarterly*, Summer 1995, pp. 147–167.

21. See E. H. Schein, *Organizational Psychology*, 3rd ed. (Upper Saddle River, NJ: Prentice Hall, 1980), pp. 116–117; and B. Kabanoff, "A Critique of Leader Match and Its Implications for Leadership Research," *Personnel Psychology*, Winter 1981, pp. 749–764.

22. P. Hersey and K. Blanchard, "So You Want to Know Your Leadership Style?" *Training & Development*, February 1974, pp. 1–15; P. Hersey and K. Blanchard, *Management of Organizational Behavior: Leading Human Resources*, 8th ed. (Englewood Cliffs, NJ: Prentice Hall, 2001).

23. See, for instance, C. F. Fernandez and R. P. Vecchio, "Situational Leadership Theory Revisited: A Test of an Across-Jobs Perspective," *Leadership Quarterly* 8, no. 1 (1997), pp. 67–84; and C. L. Graeff, "Evolution of Situational Leadership Theory: A Critical Review," *Leadership Quarterly* 8, no. 2 (1997), pp. 153–170.

24. V. H. Vroom and P. W. Yetton, *Leadership and Decision-Making* (Pittsburgh, PA: University of Pittsburgh Press, 1973).

25. V. H. Vroom and A. G. Jago, *The New Leadership: Managing Participation in Organizations* (Upper Saddle River, NJ: Prentice Hall, 1988). See especially Chapter 8.

26. Based on V. H. Vroom, "Leadership and the Decision-Making Process," *Organizational Dynamics* 28, no. 4 (2000), p. 84.

27. V. H. Vroom, "Leadership and the Decision-Making Process," *Organizational Dynamics* 28, no. 4 (2000), pp. 82–94.

28. R. J. House, "A Path-Goal Theory of Leader Effectiveness," *Administrative Science Quarterly*, September 1971, pp. 321–338; R. J. House and T. R. Mitchell, "Path-Goal Theory of Leadership,"

Journal of Contemporary Business, Autumn 1974, p. 86; R. J. House, "Path-Goal Theory of Leadership: Lessons, Legacy, and a Reformulated Theory," *Leadership Quarterly,* Fall 1996, pp. 323–352.

29. J. C. Wofford and L. Z. Liska, "Path-Goal Theories of Leadership: A Meta-Analysis," *Journal of Management,* Winter 1993, pp. 857–876; M. G. Evans, "R. J. House's 'A Path-Goal Theory of Leader Effectiveness,'" *Leadership Quarterly,* Fall 1996, pp. 305–309; C. A. Schriesheim and L. L. Neider, "Path-Goal Leadership Theory: The Long and Winding Road," *Leadership Quarterly,* Fall 1996, pp. 317–321; A. Somech, "The Effects of Leadership Style and Team Process on Performance and Innovation in Functionally Heterogeneous Teams," *Journal of Management* 32, no. 1 (2006), pp. 132–157; and S. Yun, S. Faraj, and H. P. Sims, "Contingent Leadership and Effectiveness of Trauma Resuscitation Teams," *Journal of Applied Psychology* 90, no. 6 (2005), pp. 1288–1296.

30. J. M. Howell and B. Shamir, "The Role of Followers in the Charismatic Leadership Process: Relationships and Their Consequences," *Academy of Management Review* 30, no. 1 (2005), pp. 96–112.

31. B. M. Bass, "Leadership: Good, Better, Best," *Organizational Dynamics,* Winter 1985, pp. 26–40; J. Seltzer and B. M. Bass, "Transformational Leadership: Beyond Initiation and Consideration," *Journal of Management,* December 1990, pp. 693–703.

32. B. J. Avolio and B. M. Bass, "Transformational Leadership, Charisma, and Beyond" (working paper, School of Management, State University of New York, Binghamton, 1985), p. 14.

33. J. J. Hater and B. M. Bass, "Supervisors' Evaluation and Subordinates' Perceptions of Transformational and Transactional Leadership," *Journal of Applied Psychology,* November 1988, pp. 695–702; and B. M. Bass and B. J. Avolio, "Developing Transformational Leadership: 1992 and Beyond," *Journal of European Industrial Training,* January 1990, p. 23.

34. B. M. Bass and B. J. Avolio, "Developing Transformational Leadership: 1992 and Beyond," *Journal of European Industrial Training,* January 1990, p. 23; R. T. Keller, "Transformational Leadership and the Performance of Research and Development Project Groups," *Journal of Management,* September 1992, pp. 489–501; J. M. Howell and B. J. Avolio, "Transformational Leadership, Transactional Leadership, Locus of Control, and Support for Innovation: Key Predictors of Consolidated-Business-Unit Performance," *Journal of Applied Psychology,* December 1993, pp. 891–911; T. A. Judge and J. E. Bono, "Five-Factor Model of Personality and Transformational Leadership," *Journal of Applied Psychology,* October 2000, pp. 751–765; N. Sivasubramaniam, W. D. Murry, B. J. Avolio, and D. I. Jung, "A Longitudinal Model of the Effects of Team Leadership and Group Potency on Group Performance," *Group and Organization Management,* March 2002, pp. 66–96; T. Dvir, D. Eden, B. J. Avolio, and B. Shamir, "Impact of Transformational Leadership on Follower Development and Performance: A Field Experiment," *Academy of Management Journal,* August 2002, pp. 735–744.

35. R. Pillai, C. A. Schriesheim, and E. S. Williams, "Fairness Perceptions and Trust as Mediators of Transformational and Transactional Leadership: A Two-Sample Study," *Journal of Management* 25, 1999, pp. 897–933.

36. H. Wang, K. S. Law, R. D. Hackett, D. Wang, and Z. X. Chen, "Leader–Member Exchange as a Mediator of the Relationship Between Transformational Leadership and Followers' Performance and Organizational Citizenship Behavior," *Academy of Management Journal* 48, no. 3 (June 2005), pp. 420–432; T. Dvir, D. Eden, B. J. Avolio, and B. Shamir, "Impact of Transformational Leadership on Follower Development and Performance: A Field Experiment," *Academy of Management Journal* 45, no. 4 (2002), pp. 735–744; R. J. House, J. Woycke, and E. M. Fodor, "Charismatic and

Noncharismatic Leaders: Differences in Behavior and Effectiveness," in *Charismatic Leadership in Organizations,* ed. J. A. Conger and R. N. Kanungo (Thousand Oaks, CA: Sage, 1998), pp. 103–104; and S. A. Kirkpatrick and E. A. Locke, "Direct and Indirect Effects of Three Core Charismatic Leadership Components on Performance and Attitudes," *Journal of Applied Psychology,* February 1996, pp. 36–51.

37. F. Vogelstein, "Mighty Amazon," *Fortune,* May 26, 2003, pp. 60–74.

38. J. A. Conger and R. N. Kanungo, "Behavioral Dimensions of Charismatic Leadership," in *Charismatic Leadership,* ed. J. A. Conger and R. N. Kanungo (San Francisco: Jossey-Bass, 1988), pp. 78–97; G. Yukl and J. M. Howell, "Organizational and Contextual Influences on the Emergence and Effectiveness of Charismatic Leadership," *Leadership Quarterly,* Summer 1999, pp. 257–283; and J. M. Crant and T. S. Bateman, "Charismatic Leadership Viewed from Above: The Impact of Proactive Personality," *Journal of Organizational Behavior,* February 2000, pp. 63–75.

39. J. A. Conger and R. N. Kanungo, *Charismatic Leadership in Organizations* (Thousand Oaks, CA: Sage, 1998).

40. R. J. House, J. Woycke, and E. M. Fodor, "Charismatic and Noncharismatic Leaders: Differences in Behavior and Effectiveness," in *Charismatic Leadership,* ed. J. A. Conger and R. N. Kanungo (San Francisco: Jossey-Bass, 1988), pp. 103–104; D. A. Waldman, B. M. Bass, and F. J. Yammarino, "Adding to Contingent-Reward Behavior: The Augmenting Effect of Charismatic Leadership," *Group & Organization Studies,* December 1990, pp. 381–394; S. A. Kirkpatrick and E. A. Locke, "Direct and Indirect Effects of Three Core Charismatic Leadership Components on Performance and Attitudes," *Journal of Applied Psychology,* February 1996, pp. 36–51; G. P. Shea and C. M. Howell, "Charismatic Leadership and Task Feedback: A Laboratory Study of Their Effects on Self-Efficacy," *Leadership Quarterly,* Fall 1999, pp. 375–396; R. W. Rowden, "The Relationship Between Charismatic Leadership Behaviors and Organizational Commitment," *Leadership & Organization Development Journal,* January 2000, pp. 30–35; J. A. Conger, R. N. Kanungo, and S. T. Menon, "Charismatic Leadership and Follower Effects," *Journal of Organizational Behavior* 21 (2000), pp. 747–767; J. Paul, D. Costley, J. Howell, P. Dorfman, and D. Trafimow, "The Effects of Charismatic Leadership on Followers' Self-Concept Accessibility," *Journal of Applied Social Psychology,* September 2001, pp. 1821–1844.

41. T. Dvir, D. Eden, B. J. Avolio, and B. Shamir, "Impact of Transformational Leadership on Follower Development and Performance: A Field Experiment," *Academy of Management Journal* 45, no. 4 (2002), pp. 735–744; R. J. House, J. Woycke, and E. M. Fodor, "Charismatic and Noncharismatic Leaders: Differences in Behavior and Effectiveness," in *Charismatic Leadership in Organizations,* ed. J. A. Conger and R. N. Kanungo (Thousand Oaks, CA: Sage, 1998), pp. 103–104; D. A. Waldman, B. M. Bass, and F. J. Yammarino, "Adding to Contingent-Reward Behavior: The Augmenting Effect of Charismatic Leadership," *Group & Organization Studies,* December 1990, pp. 381–394; S. A. Kirkpatrick and E. A. Locke, "Direct and Indirect Effects of Three Core Charismatic Leadership Components on Performance and Attitudes," *Journal of Applied Psychology,* February 1996, pp. 36–51; and J. A. Conger, R. N. Kanungo, and S. T. Menon, "Charismatic Leadership and Follower Outcome Effects" (paper presented at the 58th Annual Academy of Management Meetings, San Diego, CA, August 1998).

42. J. M. Howell and P. J. Frost, "A Laboratory Study of Charismatic Leadership," *Organizational Behavior & Human Decision Processes* 43, no. 2 (April 1989), pp. 243–269.

43. "Building a Better Boss," *Maclean's,* September 30, 1996, p. 41.

44. "Building a Better Boss," *Maclean's,* September 30, 1996, p. 41.

45. A. Elsner, "The Era of CEO as Superhero Ends Amid Corporate Scandals," *Globe and Mail,* July 10, 2002, http://www.globeandmail.com.

46. J. A. Conger and R. N. Kanungo, "Training Charismatic Leadership: A Risky and Critical Task," in *Charismatic Leadership,* ed. J. A. Conger and R. N. Kanungo (San Francisco: Jossey-Bass, 1988), pp. 309–323; S. Caudron, "Growing Charisma," *IndustryWeek,* May 4, 1998, pp. 54–55; and R. Birchfield, "Creating Charismatic Leaders," *Management,* June 2000, pp. 30–31.

47. R. J. House, "A 1976 Theory of Charismatic Leadership" in *Leadership: The Cutting Edge,* ed. J. G. Hunt and L. L. Larson (Carbondale, IL: Southern Illinois University Press); R. J. House and R. N. Aditya, "The Social Scientific Study of Leadership: Quo Vadis?" *Journal of Management* 23, no. 3 (1997), pp. 316–323; and J. G. Hunt, K. B. Boal, and G. E. Dodge, "The Effects of Visionary and Crisis-Responsive Charisma on Followers: An Experimental Examination," *Leadership Quarterly,* Fall 1999, pp. 423–448.

48. G. M. Spreitzer, K. H. Perttula, and K. Xin, "Traditionality Matters: An Examination of the Effectiveness of Transformational Leadership in the United States and Taiwan," *Journal of Organizational Behavior* 26, no. 3 (2005), pp. 205–227.

49. This definition is based on M. Sashkin, "The Visionary Leader," in *Charismatic Leadership,* ed. J. A. Conger and R. N. Kanungo (San Francisco: Jossey-Bass, 1988), pp. 124–125; B. Nanus, *Visionary Leadership* (New York: Free Press, 1992), p. 8; N. H. Snyder and M. Graves, "Leadership and Vision," *Business Horizons,* January–February 1994, p. 1; and J. R. Lucas, "Anatomy of a Vision Statement," *Management Review,* February 1998, pp. 22–26.

50. B. Nanus, *Visionary Leadership* (New York: Free Press, 1992), p. 8.

51. Based on M. Sashkin, "The Visionary Leader," in *Charismatic Leadership,* ed. J. A. Conger and R. N. Kanungo (San Francisco: Jossey-Bass, 1988), pp. 128–130; and J. R. Baum, E. A. Locke, and S. A. Kirkpatrick, "A Longitudinal Study of the Relation of Vision and Vision Communication to Venture Growth in Entrepreneurial Firms," *Journal of Applied Psychology,* February 1998, pp. 43–54.

52. S. Caminiti, "What Team Leaders Need to Know," *Fortune,* February 20, 1995, p. 93.

53. S. Caminiti, "What Team Leaders Need to Know," *Fortune,* February 20, 1995, p. 100.

54. N. Steckler and N. Fondas, "Building Team Leader Effectiveness: A Diagnostic Tool," *Organizational Dynamics,* Winter 1995, p. 20.

55. R. S. Wellins, W. C. Byham, and G. R. Dixon, *Inside Teams* (San Francisco: Jossey-Bass, 1994), p. 318.

56. N. Steckler and N. Fondas, "Building Team Leader Effectiveness: A Diagnostic Tool," *Organizational Dynamics,* Winter 1995, p. 21.

57. T. Kepner, "Jeter Shows Once Again Why He's the Captain," *New York Times,* July 3, 2004, http://www.nytimes.com (accessed July 3, 2004).

58. Based on L. Pratt, "Success Fuelled by Ambition: Proving Women Could Do Men's Work Was a Key to Her Success," *National Post,* March 6, 2004, p. SR02; C. Cattaneo, "Shell Anoints the Queen of Oilpatch: Linda Cook Becomes the Most Powerful Woman in Canada," *National Post,* June 27, 2003, p. FP1; M. DaCruz, "Women Have 'Bigger' Choice Outside Canada," *National Post,* June 5, 2004, p. FP5; J. Stevenson, "Shell Canada's CEO Back to Europe," *Gazette* (Montreal), May 19, 2004, p. B1; and information at the company website, http://www.shell.com (accessed October 3, 2006).

59. See J. R. P. French Jr. and B. Raven, "The Bases of Social Power," in *Group Dynamics: Research and Theory,* ed. D. Cartwright and

A. F. Zander (New York: Harper & Row, 1960), pp. 607–623; P. M. Podsakoff and C. A. Schriesheim, "Field Studies of French and Raven's Bases of Power: Critique, Reanalysis, and Suggestions for Future Research," *Psychological Bulletin,* May 1985, pp. 387–411; R. K. Shukla, "Influence of Power Bases in Organizational Decision Making: A Contingency Model," *Decision Sciences,* July 1982, pp. 450–470; D. E. Frost and A. J. Stahelski, "The Systematic Measurement of French and Raven's Bases of Social Power in Workgroups," *Journal of Applied Social Psychology,* April 1988, pp. 375–389; and T. R. Hinkin and C. A. Schriesheim, "Development and Application of New Scales to Measure the French and Raven (1959) Bases of Social Power," *Journal of Applied Psychology,* August 1989, pp. 561–567.

60. See the Royal Australian Navy website, http://www.navy.gov.au.

61. J. Partridge and J. Saunders, "Milton's Right-Hand Man Quits Air Canada," *Globe and Mail,* April 7, 2004, p. A1.

62. J. M. Kouzes and B. Z. Posner, *Credibility: How Leaders Gain and Lose It, and Why People Demand It* (San Francisco: Jossey-Bass, 1993), p. 14.

63. Based on L. T. Hosmer, "Trust: The Connecting Link Between Organizational Theory and Philosophical Ethics," *Academy of Management Review,* April 1995, p. 393; R. C. Mayer, J. H. Davis, and F. D. Schoorman, "An Integrative Model of Organizational Trust," *Academy of Management Review,* July 1995, p. 712; and G. M. Spreitzer and A. K. Mishra, "Giving Up Control Without Losing Control," *Group & Organization Management,* June 1999, pp. 155–187.

64. P. L. Schindler and C. C. Thomas, "The Structure of Interpersonal Trust in the Workplace," *Psychological Reports,* October 1993, pp. 563–573.

65. H. H. Tan and C. S. F. Tan, "Toward the Differentiation of Trust in Supervisor and Trust in Organization," *Genetic, Social, and General Psychology Monographs,* May 2000, pp. 241–260.

66. K. T. Dirks and D. L. Ferrin, "Trust in Leadership: Meta-Analytic Findings and Implications for Research and Practice," *Journal of Applied Psychology,* August 2002, pp. 611–628.

67. This section is based on F. Bartolome, "Nobody Trusts the Boss Completely—Now What?" *Harvard Business Review,* March–April 1989, pp. 135–142; J. K. Butler Jr., "Toward Understanding and Measuring Conditions of Trust: Evolution of a Conditions of Trust Inventory," *Journal of Management,* September 1991, pp. 643–663; and K. T. Dirks and D. L. Ferrin, "Trust in Leadership: Meta-Analytic Findings and Implications for Research and Practice," *Journal of Applied Psychology,* August 2002, pp. 611–628.

68. This section is based on R. B. Morgan, "Self- and Co-Worker Perceptions of Ethics and Their Relationships to Leadership and Salary," *Academy of Management Journal,* February 1993, pp. 200–214; E. P. Hollander, "Ethical Challenges in the Leader–Follower Relationship," *Business Ethics Quarterly,* January 1995, pp. 55–65; J. C. Rost, "Leadership: A Discussion About Ethics," *Business Ethics Quarterly,* January 1995, pp. 129–142; R. N. Kanungo and M. Mendonca, *Ethical Dimensions of Leadership* (Thousand Oaks, CA: Sage Publications, 1996); J. B. Ciulla, ed., *Ethics: The Heart of Leadership* (New York: Praeger Publications, 1998); J. D. Costa, *The Ethical Imperative: Why Moral Leadership Is Good Business* (Cambridge, MA: Perseus Press, 1999); and N. M. Tichy and A. McGill, eds., *The Ethical Challenge: How to Build Honest Business Leaders* (New York: John Wiley & Sons, 2003).

69. J. M. Burns, *Leadership* (New York: Harper & Row, 1978).

70. J. M. Avolio, S. Kahai, and G. E. Dodge, "The Ethics of Charismatic Leadership: Submission or Liberation?" *Academy of Management Executive,* May 1992, pp. 43–55.

71. L. K. Trevino, M. Brown, and L. P. Hartman, "A Qualitative Investigation of Perceived Executive Ethical Leadership: Perceptions From Inside and Outside the Executive Suite," *Human Relations,* January 2003, pp. 5–37.

72. Based on information from J. Stevenson, "Shell Canada CEO Leaves After a Year: Will Head Royal Dutch Petroleum," *Telegram,* May 19, 2004, p. D3.

73. C. Kleiman, "Virtual Teams Make Loyalty More Realistic," *Chicago Tribune,* January 23, 2001, p. B1.

74. B. J. Alge, C. Wiethoff, and H. J. Klein, "When Does the Medium Matter? Knowledge-Building Experiences and Opportunities in Decision-Making Teams," *Organizational Behavior and Human Decision Processes* 91, no. 1 (2003), pp. 26–37; C. O. Grosse, "Managing Communication Within Virtual Intercultural Teams," *Business Communication Quarterly,* December 2002, pp. 22–38; M. M. Montoya-Weiss, A. P. Massey, and M. Song, "Getting It Together: Temporal Coordination and Conflict Management in Global Virtual Teams," *Academy of Management Journal,* December 2001, pp. 1251–1262; M. L. Maznevski and K. M. Chudoba, "Bridging Space Over Time: Global Virtual-Team Dynamics and Effectiveness," *Organization Science* 11 (2000), pp. 473–492; W. F. Cascio, "Managing a Virtual Workplace," *Academy of Management Executive,* August 2000, pp. 81–90; A. M. Townsend, S. M. DeMarie, and A. R. Hendrickson, "'Virtual Teams' Technology and the Workplace of the Future," *Academy of Management Executive,* August 1998, pp. 17–29.

75. W. F. Cascio, "Managing a Virtual Workplace," *Academy of Management Executive,* August 2000, pp. 88–89.

76. N. Desmond, "The CEO Dashboard," *Business 2.0,* August 2002, p. 34.

77. J. McFarland, "Women Still Find Slow Rise to Power Positions," *Globe and Mail,* March 13, 2003, pp. B1, B7.

78. L. Ramsay, "A League of Their Own," *Globe and Mail,* November 23, 2002, p. B11.

79. L. Ramsay, "A League of Their Own," *Globe and Mail,* November 23, 2002, p. B11.

80. S. Armour, "More Women Cruise to the Top," *USA Today,* June 25, 2003, http://www.usatoday.com; and "The World's Women 2000: Trends and Statistics: Table 5F," *United Nations Statistics Division,* http://unstats.un.org/unsd/demographic/products/indwm/.

81. G. N. Powell, D. A. Butterfield, and J. D. Parent, "Gender and Managerial Stereotypes: Have the Times Changed?" *Journal of Management* 28, no. 2 (2002), pp. 177–193.

82. A. H. Eagly and B. T. Johnson, "Gender and Leadership Style: A Meta-Analysis," *Psychological Bulletin,* September 1990, pp. 233–256; A. H. Eagly and S. J. Karau, "Gender and the Emergence of Leaders: A Meta-Analysis," *Journal of Personality and Social Psychology,* May 1991, pp. 685–710; J. B. Rosener, "Ways Women Lead," *Harvard Business Review,* November–December 1990, pp. 119–125; A. H. Eagly, M. G. Makhijani, and B. G. Klonsky, "Gender and the Evaluation of Leaders: A Meta-Analysis," *Psychological Bulletin,* January 1992, pp. 3–22; A. H. Eagly, S. J. Karau, and B. T. Johnson, "Gender and Leadership Style Among School Principals: A Meta-Analysis," *Educational Administration Quarterly,* February 1992, pp. 76–102; L. R. Offermann and C. Beil, "Achievement Styles of Women Leaders and Their Peers," *Psychology of Women Quarterly,* March 1992, pp. 37–56; R. L. Kent and S. E. Moss, "Effects of Size and Gender Role on Leader Emergence," *Academy of Management Journal,* October 1994, pp. 1335–1346;

C. Lee, "The Feminization of Management," *Training,* November 1994, pp. 25–31; H. Collingwood, "Women as Managers: Not Just Different: Better," *Working Woman,* November 1995, p. 14; J. B. Rosener, *America's Competitive Secret: Women Managers* (New York: Oxford University Press, 1995); and J. Cliff, N. Langton, and H. Aldrich, "Walking the Talk? Gendered Rhetoric vs. Action in Small Firms," *Organizational Studies* 26, no. 1 (2005), pp. 63–91.

83. See F. J. Yammarino, A. J. Dubinsky, L. B. Comer, and M. A. Jolson, "Women and Transformational and Contingent Reward Leadership: A Multiple-Levels-of-Analysis Perspective," *Academy of Management Journal,* February 1997, pp. 205–222; M. Gardiner and M. Tiggemann, "Gender Differences in Leadership Style, Job Stress and Mental Health in Male- and Female-Dominated Industries," *Journal of Occupational and Organizational Psychology,* September 1999, pp. 301–315; C. L. Ridgeway, "Gender, Status, and Leadership," *Journal of Social Issues,* Winter 2001, pp. 637–655; W. H. Decker and D. M. Rotondo, "Relationships Among Gender, Type of Humor, and Perceived Leader Effectiveness," *Journal of Managerial Issues,* Winter 2001, pp. 450–465; J. M. Norvilitis and H. M. Reid, "Evidence for an Association Between Gender-Role Identity and a Measure of Executive Function," *Psychological Reports,* February 2002, pp. 35–45; N. Z. Selter, "Gender Differences in Leadership: Current Social Issues and Future Organizational Implications," *Journal of Leadership Studies,* Spring 2002, pp. 88–99; J. Becker, R. A. Ayman, and K. Korabik, "Discrepancies in Self/Subordinates' Perceptions of Leadership Behavior: Leader's Gender, Organizational Context, and Leader's Self-Monitoring," *Group & Organization Management,* June 2002, pp. 226–244; A. H. Eagly and S. J. Karau, "Role Congruity Theory of Prejudice Toward Female Leaders," *Psychological Review,* July 2002, pp. 573–598; and K. M. Bartol, D. C. Martin, and J. A. Kromkowski, "Leadership and the Glass Ceiling: Gender and Ethnic Influences on Leader Behaviors at Middle and Executive Managerial Levels," *Journal of Leadership & Organizational Studies,* Winter 2003, pp. 8–19.

84. M. Gardiner and M. Tiggemann, "Gender Differences in Leadership Style, Job Stress and Mental Health in Male- and Female-Dominated Industries," *Journal of Occupational and Organizational Psychology,* September 1999, pp. 301–315.

85. J. M. Norvilitis and H. M. Reid, "Evidence for an Association Between Gender-Role Identity and a Measure of Executive Function," *Psychological Reports,* February 2002, pp. 35–45; W. H. Decker and D. M. Rotondo, "Relationships Among Gender, Type of Humor, and Perceived Leader Effectiveness," *Journal of Managerial Issues,* Winter 2001, pp. 450–465; H. Aguinis and S. K. R. Adams, "Social-Role Versus Structural Models of Gender and Influence Use in Organizations: A Strong Inference Approach," *Group & Organization Management,* December 1998, pp. 414–446; A. H. Eagly, S. J. Karau, and M. G. Makhijani, "Gender and the Effectiveness of Leaders: A Meta-Analysis," *Psychological Bulletin* 117 (1995), pp. 125–145.

86. A. H. Eagly, M. C. Johannesen-Schmidt, and M. L. van Engen, "Transformational, Transactional, and Laissez-Faire Leadership Styles: A Meta-Analysis Comparing Women and Men," *Psychological Bulletin* 129, no. 4 (July 2003), pp. 569–591; K. M. Bartol, D. C. Martin, and J. A. Kromkowski, "Leadership and the Glass Ceiling: Gender and Ethnic Influences on Leader Behaviors at Middle and Executive Managerial Levels," *Journal of Leadership & Organizational Studies,* Winter 2003, pp. 8–19; R. Sharpe, "As Leaders, Women Rule," *BusinessWeek,* November 20, 2000, pp. 74–84.

87. K. M. Bartol, D. C. Martin, and J. A. Kromkowski, "Leadership and the Glass Ceiling: Gender and Ethnic Influences on Leader Behaviors at Middle and Executive Managerial Levels," *Journal of Leadership & Organizational Studies,* Winter 2003, pp. 8–19.

88. Adapted with permission from T. Sergiovanni, R. Metzcus, and L. Burden, "Toward a Particularistic Approach to Leadership Style:

Some Findings," *American Educational Research Journal* 6, no. 1 (January 1969), American Educational Research Association, Washington, D.C.

89. Situation adapted from information in J. Menn, "Ellison Talks Tough on Bid for PeopleSoft," *Los Angeles Times,* July 10, 2003, p. C11; M. Mangalindan, D. Clark, and R. Sidel, "Hostile Move Augurs High-Tech Consolidation," *Wall Street Journal,* June 9, 2003, p. A11; A. Pham, "Oracle's Merger Hurdles Get Higher," *Los Angeles Times,* June 30, 2003, p. C11; S. Pannill, "Smashmouth PR Meets High Tech," *Forbes,* May 28, 2001, p. 9; and F. Vogelstein, "Oracle's Ellison Turns Hostile," *Fortune,* June 23, 2003, p. 28.

90. Based on C. Jenkins, "Teresa Earnhardt Keeps Team on Track," *USA Today,* June 23, 2003, http://www.usatoday.com; D. Newton, "Teresa Earnhardt: Driving Force Behind a Racing Empire," *State,* March 18, 2003, http://www.charlotte.com; and "Owner's Profile" at NASCAR website, http://www.nascar.com.

91. M. Henricks, "Kids These Days," *Entrepreneur,* May 2002, pp. 71–72.

92. Based on H. Mintzberg, *Power In and Around Organizations* (Upper Saddle River, NJ: Prentice Hall, 1983), p. 24; and P. L. Hunsaker, *Training in Management Skills* (Upper Saddle River, NJ: Prentice Hall, 2001), pp. 339–364.

Chapter 9

1. Based on Hoover's Online, http://www.hoover.com; S. Butcher, "Relentless Rise in Pleasure Seekers," *Financial Times,* July 6, 2003, http://news.ft.com (accessed July 7, 2003); C. Blackhurst, "The Chris Blackhurst Interview: Sir Terry Leahy," *Management Today,* February 2004, pp. 32–34; and http://www.tescocorporate.com/page.aspx?pointerid=A8E0E60508F94A8DBA909E2ABB5F2CC7 (accessed September 26, 2006).

2. G. P. Latham and C. C. Pinder, "Work Motivation Theory and Research at the Dawn of the Twenty-First Century,"*Annual Review of Psychology* 56, no. 1 (2005), pp. 485–516; and C. C. Pinder, *Work Motivation in Organizational Behavior* (Upper Saddle River, NJ: Prentice Hall, 1998), p. 11. See also E. A. Locke and G. P. Latham, "What Should We Do About Motivation Theory? Six Recommendations For the Twenty-First Century," *Academy of Management Review* 29, no. 3 (July 1, 2004), pp. 388–403.

3. See, for instance, T. R. Mitchell, "Matching Motivational Strategies With Organizational Contexts," in *Research in Organizational Behavior,* vol. 19, ed. B. M. Staw and L. L. Cummings (Greenwich, CT: JAI Press, 1997), pp. 60–62; and R. Katerberg and G. J. Blau, "An Examination of Level and Direction of Effort and Job Performance," *Academy of Management Journal,* June 1983, pp. 249–257.

4. G. Shaw, "Canada Lags World on Job Quality," *Vancouver Sun,* September 18, 2004, p. F5.

5. Based on S. Butcher, "Relentless Rise in Pleasure Seekers," *Financial Times,* July 6, 2003, http://news.ft.com (accessed July 7, 2003).

6. A. Maslow, *Motivation and Personality* (New York: McGraw-Hill, 1954); A. Maslow, D. C. Stephens, and G. Heil, *Maslow on Management* (New York: John Wiley & Sons, 1998); M. L. Ambrose and C. T. Kulik, "Old Friends, New Faces: Motivation Research in the 1990s," *Journal of Management* 25, no. 3 (1999), pp. 231–292; "Dialogue," *Academy of Management Review,* October 2000, pp. 696–701.

7. G. P. Latham and C. C. Pinder, "Work Motivation Theory and Research at the Dawn of the Twenty-First Century," *Annual Review of Psychology* 56, no. 1 (2005), pp. 485–516.

8. See, for example, D. T. Hall and K. E. Nongaim, "An Examination of Maslow's Need Hierarchy in an Organizational Setting," *Organizational Behavior and Human Performance,* February 1968, pp. 12–35; E. E. Lawler III and J. L. Suttle, "A Causal Correlational Test of the Need Hierarchy Concept," *Organizational Behavior and Human Performance,* April 1972, pp. 265–287; R. M. Creech, "Employee Motivation," *Management Quarterly,* Summer 1995, pp. 33–39; J. Rowan, "Maslow Amended," *Journal of Humanistic Psychology,* Winter 1998, pp. 81–92; J. Rowan, "Ascent and Descent in Maslow's Theory," *Journal of Humanistic Psychology,* Summer 1999, pp. 125–133; and M. L. Ambrose and C. T. Kulik, "Old Friends, New Faces: Motivation Research in the 1990s," *Journal of Management* 25, no. 3 (1999), pp. 231–292.

9. D. McGregor, *The Human Side of Enterprise* (New York: McGraw-Hill, 1960). For an updated analysis of Theories X and Y, see R. J. Summers and S. F. Conshaw, "A Study of McGregor's Theory X, Theory Y and the Influence of Theory X, Theory Y Assumptions on Causal Attributions for Instances of Worker Poor Performance," in *Organizational Behavior, ASAC 1988 Conference Proceedings,* vol. 9, part 5, ed. S. L. McShaneed (Halifax, NS: ASAC, 1988), pp. 115–123.

10. K. W. Thomas, *Intrinsic Motivation at Work* (San Francisco: Berrett-Koehler, 2000); and K. W. Thomas, "Intrinsic Motivation and How It Works," *Training,* October 2000, pp. 130–135.

11. F. Herzberg, B. Mausner, and B. Snyderman, *The Motivation to Work* (New York: John Wiley, 1959); F. Herzberg, *The Managerial Choice: To Be Effective or to Be Human,* rev. ed. (Salt Lake City: Olympus, 1982); R. M. Creech, "Employee Motivation," *Management Quarterly,* Summer 1995, pp. 33–39; M. L. Ambrose and C. T. Kulik, "Old Friends, New Faces: Motivation Research in the 1990s," *Journal of Management* 25, no. 3 (1999), pp. 231–292.

12. G. Bellett, "Firm's Secret to Success Lies in Treating Workers Right," *Vancouver Sun,* March 21, 2001, pp. D7, D11; V. Galt, "Getting Fit on the Job," *Globe and Mail,* November 6, 2002, p. C1.

13. C. Lochhead, "Healthy Workplace Programs at Pazmac Enterprises Ltd.," *Canadian Labour and Business Centre,* March 2002.

14. D. C. McClelland, *The Achieving Society* (New York: Van Nostrand Reinhold, 1961); J. W. Atkinson and J. O. Raynor, *Motivation and Achievement* (Washington, DC: Winston, 1974); D. C. McClelland, *Power: The Inner Experience* (New York: Irvington, 1975); and M. J. Stahl, *Managerial and Technical Motivation: Assessing Needs for Achievement, Power, and Affiliation* (New York: Praeger, 1986).

15. D. C. McClelland, *The Achieving Society* (New York: Van Nostrand Reinhold, 1961).

16. R. A. Clay, "Green Is Good for You," *Monitor on Psychology,* April 2001, pp. 40–42.

17. Based on S. Butcher, "Relentless Rise in Pleasure Seekers," *Financial Times,* July 6, 2003, http://news.ft.com (accessed July 7, 2003); A. Nottage, "Tesco," *Human Resources,* May 2003, p. 10; and C. Blackhurst, "The Chris Blackhurst Interview: Sir Terry Leahy," *Management Today,* February 2004, pp. 32–34.

18. M. L. Ambrose and C. T. Kulik, "Old Friends, New Faces: Motivation Research in the 1990s," *Journal of Management* 25, no. 3 (1999), pp. 231–292.

19. B. F. Skinner, *Science and Human Behavior* (New York: Free Press, 1953); and B. F. Skinner, *Beyond Freedom and Dignity* (New York: Knopf, 1972).

20. The same data, for instance, can be interpreted in either goal-setting or reinforcement terms, as shown in E. A. Locke, "Latham vs. Komaki: A Tale of Two Paradigms," *Journal of Applied Psychology,* February 1980, pp. 16–23. Also, see M. L. Ambrose and C. T. Kulik,

"Old Friends, New Faces: Motivation Research in the 1990s," *Journal of Management* 25, no. 3 (1999), pp. 231–292.

21. J. R. Hackman and G. R. Oldham, "Development of the Job Diagnostic Survey," *Journal of Applied Psychology,* April 1975, pp. 159–170; J. R. Hackman and G. R. Oldham, "Motivation Through the Design of Work: Test of a Theory," *Organizational Behavior and Human Performance,* August 1976, pp. 250–279.

22. J. R. Hackman, "Work Design," in *Improving Life at Work,* ed. J. R. Hackman and J. L. Suttle (Glenview, IL: Scott, Foresman, 1977), p. 129; M. L. Ambrose and C. T. Kulik, "Old Friends, New Faces: Motivation Research in the 1990s," *Journal of Management* 25, no. 3 (1999), pp. 231–292.

23. See http://www.canada.com/nationalpost/ entrepreneur/ail.html (accessed September 6, 2006).

24. J. S. Adams, "Inequity in Social Exchanges," in *Advances in Experimental Social Psychology,* vol. 2, ed. L. Berkowitz (New York: Academic Press, 1965), pp. 267–300; M. L. Ambrose and C. T. Kulik, "Old Friends, New Faces: Motivation Research in the 1990s," *Journal of Management* 25, no. 3 (1999), pp. 231–292.

25. See, for example, P. S. Goodman and A. Friedman, "An Examination of Adams' Theory of Inequity," *Administrative Science Quarterly,* September 1971, pp. 271–288; E. Walster, G. W. Walster, and W. G. Scott, *Equity: Theory and Research* (Boston: Allyn & Bacon, 1978); J. Greenberg, "Cognitive Reevaluation of Outcomes in Response to Underpayment Inequity," *Academy of Management Journal,* March 1989, pp. 174–184.

26. See, for example, M. R. Carrell, "A Longitudinal Field Assessment of Employee Perceptions of Equitable Treatment," *Organizational Behavior and Human Performance,* February 1978, pp. 108–118; R. G. Lord and J. A. Hohenfeld, "Longitudinal Field Assessment of Equity Effects on the Performance of Major League Baseball Players," *Journal of Applied Psychology,* February 1979, pp. 19–26; and J. E. Dittrich and M. R. Carrell, "Organizational Equity Perceptions, Employee Job Satisfaction, and Departmental Absence and Turnover Rates," *Organizational Behavior and Human Performance,* August 1979, pp. 29–40.

27. Some of the data in this vignette is based on http://www.parl.gc.ca/information/about/process/info/.

28. P. S. Goodman, "An Examination of Referents Used in the Evaluation of Pay," *Organizational Behavior and Human Performance,* October 1974, pp. 170–195; S. Ronen, "Equity Perception in Multiple Comparisons: A Field Study," *Human Relations,* April 1986, pp. 333–346; R. W. Scholl, E. A. Cooper, and J. F. McKenna, "Referent Selection in Determining Equity Perception: Differential Effects on Behavioral and Attitudinal Outcomes," *Personnel Psychology,* Spring 1987, pp. 113–127; C. T. Kulik and M. L. Ambrose, "Personal and Situational Determinants of Referent Choice," *Academy of Management Review,* April 1992, pp. 212–237.

29. P. S. Goodman, "Social Comparison Process in Organizations," in *New Directions in Organizational Behavior,* ed. B. M. Staw and G. R. Salancik (Chicago: St. Clair, 1977), pp. 97–132; J. Greenberg, "A Taxonomy of Organizational Justice Theories," *Academy of Management Review,* January 1987, pp. 9–22.

30. V. H. Vroom, *Work and Motivation* (New York: John Wiley, 1964).

31. See, for example, H. G. Heneman III and D. P. Schwab, "Evaluation of Research on Expectancy Theory Prediction of Employee Performance," *Psychological Bulletin,* July 1972, pp. 1–9; and L. Reinharth and M. Wahba, "Expectancy Theory as a Predictor of Work Motivation, Effort Expenditure, and Job Performance," *Academy of Management Journal,* September 1975, pp. 502–537.

32. See, for example, V. H. Vroom, "Organizational Choice: A Study of Pre- and Postdecision Processes," *Organizational Behavior and Human Performance,* April 1966, pp. 212–225; L. W. Porter and E. E. Lawler III, *Managerial Attitudes and Performance* (Homewood, IL: Richard D. Irwin, 1968); W. Van Eerde and H. Thierry, "Vroom's Expectancy Models and Work-Related Criteria: A Meta-Analysis," *Journal of Applied Psychology,* October 1996, pp. 575–586; and M. L. Ambrose and C. T. Kulik, "Old Friends, New Faces: Motivation Research in the 1990s," *Journal of Management* 25, no. 3 (1999), pp. 231–292.

33. See, for instance, M. Siegall, "The Simplistic Five: An Integrative Framework for Teaching Motivation," *Organizational Behavior Teaching Review* 12, no. 4 (1987–1988), pp. 141–143.

34. S. Butcher, "Relentless Rise in Pleasure Seekers," *Financial Times,* July 6, 2003, http://news.ft.com (accessed July 7, 2003); and "Tesco Pilots Student Benefits," *Employee Benefits,* November 7, 2003, p. P12.

35. R. Bernard, D. Cosgrave, and J. Welsh, *Chips and Pop: Decoding the Nexus Generation* (Toronto: Malcolm Lester Books, 1998).

36. J. R. Billings and D. L. Sharpe, "Factors Influencing Flextime Usage Among Employed Married Women," *Consumer Interests Annual,* vol. 45 (Ames, IA: American Council on Consumer Interests, 1999), pp. 89–94; and I. Harpaz, "The Importance of Work Goals: An International Perspective," *Journal of International Business Studies,* First Quarter 1990, pp. 75–93.

37. N. J. Adler, *International Dimensions of Organizational Behavior,* 4th ed. (Cincinnati: South-Western, 2002), p. 174.

38. G. Hofstede, "Motivation, Leadership and Organization: Do American Theories Apply Abroad?" *Organizational Dynamics,* Summer 1980, p. 55.

39. J. K. Giacobbe-Miller, D. J. Miller, and V. I. Victorov, "A Comparison of Russian and U.S. Pay Allocation Decisions, Distributive Justice Judgments and Productivity Under Different Payment Conditions," *Personnel Psychology,* Spring 1998, pp. 137–163.

40. S. L. Mueller and L. D. Clarke, "Political–Economic Context and Sensitivity to Equity: Differences Between the United States and the Transition Economies of Central and Eastern Europe," *Academy of Management Journal,* June 1998, pp. 319–329.

41. I. Harpaz, "The Importance of Work Goals: An International Perspective," *Journal of International Business Studies,* First Quarter 1990, pp. 75–93.

42. G. E. Popp, H. J. Davis, and T. T. Herbert, "An International Study of Intrinsic Motivation Composition," *Management International Review,* January 1986, pp. 28–35.

43. P. Falcone, "Motivating Staff Without Money," *HR Magazine,* August 2002, pp. 105–108.

44. P. Falcone, "Motivating Staff Without Money," *HR Magazine,* August 2002, pp. 105–108.

45. See, for instance, M. Alpert, "The Care and Feeding of Engineers," *Fortune,* September 21, 1992, pp. 86–95; G. Poole, "How to Manage Your Nerds," *Forbes ASAP,* December 1994, pp. 132–136; and T. J. Allen and R. Katz, "Managing Technical Professionals and Organizations: Improving and Sustaining the Performance of Organizations, Project Teams, and Individual Contributors," *Sloan Management Review,* Summer 2002, pp. S4–S5.

46. "One CEO's Perspective on the Power of Recognition," *Workforce Management,* March 2, 2004, http://www.workforce.com; and R. Fournier, "Teamwork Is the Key to Remote Development—Inspiring Trust and Maintaining Motivation Are Critical for a Distributive Development Team," *InfoWorld,* March 5, 2001, p. 48.

47. D. W. Krueger, "Money, Success, and Success Phobia," in *The Last Taboo: Money as a Symbol and Reality in Psychotherapy and Psychoanalysis,* ed. D. W. Krueger (New York: Brunner/Mazel, 1986), pp. 3–16.

48. T. R. Mitchell and A. E. Mickel, "The Meaning of Money: An Individual-Difference Perspective," *Academy of Management,* July 1999, pp. 568–578.

49. Information in this paragraph based on D. Grigg and J. Newman, "Labour Researchers Define Job Satisfaction," *Vancouver Sun,* February 16, 2002, p. E2.

50. This paragraph is based on T. R. Mitchell and A. E. Mickel, "The Meaning of Money: An Individual-Difference Perspective," *Academy of Management,* July 1999, pp. 568–578. The reader may want to refer to the myriad references cited in the article.

51. F. Luthans and A. D. Stajkovic, "Provide Recognition for Performance Improvement," in *Principles of Organizational Behavior,* ed. E. A. Locke (Oxford, UK: Blackwell, 2000), pp. 166–180.

52. Hewitt Associates, "Employers Willing to Pay for High Performance," news release, September 8, 2004, http://was4.hewitt.com/hewitt/resource/newsroom/pressrel/2004/09-08-04eng.htm (accessed October 9, 2004); and http://www.newswire.ca/en/releases/archive/September2006/05/c2519.html (accessed August 30, 2006).

53. "Secrets of Their Success (and Failure)," *Report on Business,* January 2006, pp. 54–55.

54. S. L. Rynes, B. Gerhart, and L. Parks, "Personnel Psychology: Performance Evaluation and Pay for Performance," *Annual Review of Psychology* 56, no. 1 (2005), p. 572; and A. M. Dickinson, "Are We Motivated by Money? Some Results from the Laboratory," *Performance Improvement* 44, no. 3 (March 2005), pp. 18–24.

55. R. K. Abbott, "Performance-Based Flex: A Tool for Managing Total Compensation Costs," *Compensation and Benefits Review,* March–April 1993, pp. 18–21; J. R. Schuster and P. K. Zingheim, "The New Variable Pay: Key Design Issues," *Compensation and Benefits Review,* March–April 1993, pp. 27–34; C. R. Williams and L. P. Livingstone, "Another Look at the Relationship Between Performance and Voluntary Turnover," *Academy of Management Journal,* April 1994, pp. 269–298; A. M. Dickinson and K. L. Gillette, "A Comparison of the Effects of Two Individual Monetary Incentive Systems on Productivity: Piece Rate Pay Versus Base Pay Plus Incentives," *Journal of Organizational Behavior Management,* Spring 1994, pp. 3–82.

56. Hewitt Associates, "Employers Willing to Pay for High Performance," news release, September 8, 2004, http://was4.hewitt.com/hewitt/resource/newsroom/pressrel/2004/09-08-04eng.htm (accessed October 9, 2004); Hewitt Associates, "Hewitt Study Shows Pay-for-Performance Plans Replacing Holiday Bonuses," news release, December 6, 2005, http://was4.hewitt.com/hewitt/resource/newsroom/pressrel/2005/12-06-05eng.pdf (accessed April 29, 2006); P. Brieger, "Variable Pay Packages Gain Favour: Signing Bonuses, Profit Sharing Taking Place of Salary Hikes," *Financial Post (National Post),* September 13, 2002, p. FP5; and http://www.newswire.ca/en/releases/archive/September2006/05/c2519.html (accessed August 30, 2006).

57. E. Beauchesne, "Pay Bonuses Improve Productivity, Study Shows," *Vancouver Sun,* September 13, 2002, p. D5; and The Conference Board of Canada, "Variable Pay Offers a Bonus for Unionized Workplaces," news release, September 12, 2002, http://www.conferenceboard.ca/press/2002/variable_pay.asp (accessed April 29, 2006).

58. "Hope for Higher Pay: The Squeeze on Incomes Is Gradually Easing Up," *Maclean's,* November 25, 1996, pp. 100–101.

59. G. D. Jenkins Jr., N. Gupta, A. Mitra, and J. D. Shaw, "Are Financial Incentives Related to Performance? A Meta-Analytic Review of Empirical Research," *Journal of Applied Psychology,* October 1998, pp. 777–787.

60. T. Coupé, V. Smeets, and F. Warzynski, "Incentives, Sorting and Productivity Along the Career: Evidence from a Sample of Top Economists," *Journal of Law Economics & Organization* 22, no. 1 (April 2006), pp. 137–167.

61. A. Kauhanen and H. Piekkola, "What Makes Performance-Related Pay Schemes Work? Finnish Evidence," *Journal of Management and Governance* 10, no. 2 (2006), pp. 149–177.

62. E. Beauchesne, "Pay Bonuses Improve Productivity, Study Shows," *Vancouver Sun,* September 13, 2002, p. D5.

63. P. A. Siegel and D. C. Hambrick, "Pay Disparities Within Top Management Groups: Evidence of Harmful Effects on Performance of High-Technology Firms," *Organization Science* 16, no. 3 (May–June 2005), pp. 259–276; S. Kerr, "Practical, Cost-Neutral Alternatives That You May Know, but Don't Practice," *Organizational Dynamics* 28, no. 1 (1999), pp. 61–70; E. E. Lawler, *Strategic Pay* (San Francisco: Jossey Bass, 1990); and J. Pfeffer, *The Human Equation: Building Profits by Putting People First* (Boston: Harvard Business School Press, 1998).

64. T. Reason, "Why Bonus Plans Fail," *CFO,* January 2003, p. 53; and "Has Pay for Performance Had Its Day?" *McKinsey Quarterly,* no. 4 (2002), accessed on Forbes website, http://www.forbes.com.

65. V. Sanderson, "Sweetening Their Slice: More Hardware and Lumberyard Dealers Are Investing in Profit-Sharing Programs as a Way to Promote Employee Loyalty," *Hardware Merchandising,* May–June 2003, p. 66.

66. J. Gray, "A Tale of Two CEOs," *Canadian Business,* April 26–May 9, 2004, pp. 35–36.

67. J. McFarland, "Missing Link: CEO Pay and Results," *Globe and Mail,* June 1, 2006, p. B1.

68. W. J. Duncan, "Stock Ownership and Work Motivation," *Organizational Dynamics,* Summer 2001, pp. 1–11.

69. P. Brandes, R. Dharwadkar, and G. V. Lemesis, "Effective Employee Stock Option Design: Reconciling Stakeholder, Strategic, and Motivational Factors," *Academy of Management Executive,* February 2003, pp. 77–95; J. Blasi, D. Kruse, and A. Bernstein, *In the Company of Owners: The Truth About Stock Options* (New York: Basic Books, 2003).

70. G. Shaw, "Top Gamers Kept on the Job With Array of Sweet Deals," *Vancouver Sun,* March 25, 2004, p. D1.

71. "Health Club Membership, Flextime Are Most Desired Perks," *Business West,* September 1999, p. 75.

72. A. Geller, "Employers Trim Job Flexibility Schemes: Seen as Easy Way to Reduce Costs," *Ottawa Citizen,* October 25, 2003, p. K5.

73. This paragraph is based on "Paying Workers Well Is Not Enough, Survey Finds," *Financial Post (National Post),* May 16, 2001, p. C10.

74. "What Employees Want," *CMA Management* 75, no. 7 (October 2001), p. 8.

75. Information in this paragraph is based on D. Grigg and J. Newman, "Labour Researchers Define Job Satisfaction," *Vancouver Sun,* February 16, 2002, p. E2.

76. J. Greenberg and R. Baron, *Behavior in Organizations,* 6th ed. (Upper Saddle River, NJ: Prentice-Hall, 1995). Reprinted by permission of Prentice-Hall, Inc., Upper Saddle River, NJ.

77. Situation adapted from information in W. Zellner, "They Took More Than They Needed from Us," *BusinessWeek,* June 2, 2003, p. 58; "Coffee, Tea, or Bile?" *BusinessWeek,* June 2, 2003, p. 56; "US Airways Pilots' Stand on Management," *New York Times,* May 24, 2003, p. C2; and "US Airways Flight Attendants Delay Concession Talks," *New York Times,* December 4, 2002, p. C4.

78. Information on company from Motive website, http://www. motive.com, and Hoover's Online, http://www.hoovers.com (accessed June 21, 2004); A. E. Lemen, "Motivated to Grow," *Austin Business Journal,* May 30, 2003, http://www. bizjournals.com/ austin/stories/2003/06/02/smallb1.html (accessed June 21, 2004); and J. Gordon, "Management by Black Belt," *Forbes,* February 17, 2003, p. 54.

79. Based on A. C. Poe, "Keeping Hotel Workers," *HR Magazine,* February 2003, pp. 91–93.

80. K. Clark, "Perking Up the Office," *U.S. News & World Report,* November 22, 1999, p. 73: L. Brenner, "Perks That Work," *BusinessWeek Frontier,* October 11, 1999, pp. F22–F40.

81. Based on D. Jones, "Ford, Fannie Mae Tops in Diversity," *USA Today,* May 7, 2003, http://www.usatoday.com; S. N. Mehta, "What Minority Employees Really Want," *Fortune,* July 10, 2000, pp. 180–186; K. H. Hammonds, "Difference Is Power," *Fast Company,* July 2000, pp. 258–266; "Building a Competitive Workforce: Diversity, the Bottom Line," *Forbes,* April 3, 2000, pp. 181–194; and "Diversity: Developing Tomorrow's Leadership Talent Today," *BusinessWeek,* December 20, 1999, pp. 85–100.

Chapter 10

1. Based on D. Cox, "Team Canada Has It All: Depth, Experience and, Oh Yes, Talent," *Toronto Star,* December 22, 2005, p. 1; M. MacDonald, "Teamwork Key to Gold—On and Off the Ice," *Nanaimo Daily News,* January 27, 2003, p. A9; S. Burnside and B. Beacon, "Lafleur Says Team Canada Well Chosen, Even if There's No Canadiens," *Canadian Press,* May 18, 2004; and "Primeau Looks Like Conn Man," *StarPhoenix,* May 17, 2004. p. C2.

2. P. Booth, *Challenge and Change: Embracing the Team Concept,* Report 123-94 (Ottawa: The Conference Board of Canada, 1994).

3. See, for instance, E. Sunstrom, K. DeMeuse, and D. Futrell, "Work Teams: Applications and Effectiveness," *American Psychologist,* February 1990, pp. 120–133.

4. G. M. Spreitzer, S. G. Cohen, and G. E. Ledford Jr., "Developing Effective Self-Managing Work Teams in Service Organizations," *Group & Organization Management,* September 1999, pp. 340–366.

5. R. I. Beekun, "Assessing the Effectiveness of Sociotechnical Interventions: Antidote or Fad?" *Human Relations,* October 1989, pp. 877–897.

6. S. G. Cohen, G. E. Ledford, and G. M. Spreitzer, "A Predictive Model of Self-Managing Work Team Effectiveness," *Human Relations,* May 1996, pp. 643–676.

7. C. E. Nicholls, H. W. Lane, and M. Brehm Brechu, "Taking Self-Managed Teams to Mexico," *Academy of Management Executive,* August 1999, pp. 15–27.

8. R. Lepine and K. Rawson, "Strategic Savings on the Right Track: How Canadian Pacific Railway Has Saved Millions of Dollars in the Past Four Years Through Strategic Sourcing," *CMA Management,* February 2003, pp. 20–23.

9. S. Prashad, "Building Trust Tricky for 'Virtual' Teams," *Toronto Star,* October 23, 2003, p. K06.

10. F. Keenan and S. E. Ante, "The New Teamwork," *BusinessWeek e.biz,* February 18, 2002, pp. EB12–EB16; G. Imperato, "Real Tools for Virtual Teams" *Fast Company,* July 2000, pp. 378–387.

11. See, for example, C. M. Fiol and E. J. O'Connor, "Identification in Face-to-Face, Hybrid, and Pure Virtual Teams: Untangling the Contradictions," *Organization Science* 16, no. 1 (January–February 2005), pp. 19–32; and L. L. Martins, L. L. Gilson, and M. T. Maynard, "Virtual Teams: What Do We Know and Where Do We Go from Here?" *Journal of Management* 30, no. 6 (December 2004), pp. 805–835.

12. J. M. Wilson, S. G. Straus, and B. McEvily. "All in Due Time: The Development of Trust in Computer-Mediated and Face-To-Face Teams," *Organizational Behavior and Human Decision Processes* 99, no. 1 (2006), pp. 16–33; and S. L. Jarvenpaa, K. Knoll, and D. E. Leidner, "Is Anybody Out There? Antecedents of Trust in Global Virtual Teams," *Journal of Management Information Systems,* Spring 1998, pp. 29–64.

13. P. J. Hinds and M. Mortensen, "Understanding Conflict in Geographically Distributed Teams: The Moderating Effects of Shared Identity, Shared Context, and Spontaneous Communication," *Organization Science* 16, no. 3 (2005), pp. 290–307.

14. B. W. Tuckman and M. C. Jensen, "Stages of Small-Group Development Revisited," *Group and Organizational Studies,* December 1977, pp. 419–427; M. F. Maples, "Group Development: Extending Tuckman's Theory," *Journal for Specialists in Group Work,* Fall 1988, pp. 17–23.

15. L. N. Jewell and H. J. Reitz, *Group Effectiveness in Organizations* (Glenview, IL: Scott, Foresman, 1981); and M. Kaeter, "Repotting Mature Work Teams," *Training,* April 1994, pp. 54–56.

16. Based on B. Beacon, "Continuity Rules on Squad," *Leader-Post,* December 22, 2005, p. C2.

17. See, for instance, J. E. Salk and M. Y. Brannien, "National Culture, Networks, and Individual Influence in a Multinational Management Team," *Academy of Management Journal,* April 2000, p. 191; B. L. Kirkman, C. B. Gibson, and D. L. Shapiro, "Enhancing the Implementation and Effectiveness of Work Teams in Global Affiliates," *Organizational Dynamics,* Summer 2001, pp. 12–30; and B. L. Kirkman and D. L. Shapiro, "The Impact of Cultural Values on Employee Resistance to Teams: Towards a Model of Globalized Self-Managing Work Team Effectiveness," *Academy of Management Review,* July 1997, pp. 730–757.

18. S. Stern, "Teams That Work," *Management Today,* June 2001, p. 48.

19. G. Prince, "Recognizing Genuine Teamwork," *Supervisory Management,* April 1989, pp. 25–36; R. F. Bales, *SYMOLOG Case Study Kit* (New York: Free Press, 1980); K. D. Benne and P. Sheats, "Functional Roles of Group Members," *Journal of Social Issues* 4, no. 2 (1948), pp. 41–49.

20. R. M. Yandrick, "A Team Effort," *HR Magazine,* June 2001, pp. 136–141.

21. R. M. Yandrick, "A Team Effort," *HR Magazine,* June 2001, pp. 136–141.

22. M. A. Marks, C. S. Burke, M. J. Sabella, and S. J. Zaccaro, "The Impact of Cross-Training on Team Effectiveness," *Journal of Applied Psychology,* February 2002, pp. 3–14; and M. A. Marks, S. J. Zaccaro, and J. E. Mathieu, "Performance Implications of

Leader Briefings and Team Interaction for Team Adaptation to Novel Environments," *Journal of Applied Psychology,* December 2000, p. 971.

23. C. Garvey, "Steer Teams with the Right Pay: Team-Based Pay Is a Success When It Fits Corporate Goals and Culture, and Rewards the Right Behavior," *HR Magazine,* May 2002, pp. 71–77.

24. Based on "Canada Lacked Cohesion, Chemistry," *Edmonton Journal,* February 24, 2006, p. C3; and E. Duhatschek, "Under Pressure, Gretzky Scores in Balancing Act," *Globe and Mail,* May 17, 2004, p. S1.

25. G. R. Jones and G. M. George, "The Experience and Evolution of Trust: Implications for Cooperation and Teamwork," *Academy of Management Review,* July 1998, pp. 531–546; A. R. Jassawalla and H. C. Sashittal, "Building Collaborative Cross-Functional New Product Teams," *Academy of Management Executive,* August 1999, pp. 50–63; R. Forrester and A. B. Drexler, "A Model for Team-Based Organization Performance," *Academy of Management Executive,* August 1999, pp. 36–49; V. U. Druskat and S. B. Wolff, "The Link Between Emotions and Team Effectiveness: How Teams Engage Members and Build Effective Task Processes," *Academy of Management Proceedings,* CD-ROM, 1999; M. Mattson, T. Mumford, and G. S. Sintay, "Taking Teams to Task: A Normative Model for Designing or Recalibrating Work Teams," *Academy of Management Proceedings,* CD-ROM, 1999; J. D. Shaw, M. K. Duffy, and E. M. Stark, "Interdependence and Preference for Group Work: Main and Congruence Effects on the Satisfaction and Performance of Group Members," *Journal of Management* 26, no. 2 (2000), pp. 259–279; G. L. Stewart and M. R. Barrick, "Team Structure and Performance: Assessing the Mediating Role of Intrateam Process and the Moderating Role of Task Type," *Academy of Management Journal,* April 2000, pp. 135–148; J. E. Mathieu, T. S. Heffner, G. F. Goodwin, E. Salas, and J. A. Cannon-Bowers, "The Influence of Shared Mental Models on Team Process and Performance," *Journal of Applied Psychology,* April 2000, pp. 273–283; J. M. Phillips and E. A. Douthitt, "The Role of Justice in Team Member Satisfaction With the Leader and Attachment to the Team," *Journal of Applied Psychology,* April 2001, pp. 316–325; J. A. Colquitt, R. A. Noe, and C. L. Jackson, "Justice in Teams: Antecedents and Consequences of Procedural Justice Climate," *Personnel Psychology* 55 (2002), pp. 83–100; M. A. Marks, M. J. Sabella, C. S. Burke, and S. J. Zaccaro, "The Impact of Cross-Training on Team Effectiveness," *Journal of Applied Psychology,* February 2002, pp. 3–13; S. W. Lester, B. W. Meglino, and M. A. Korsgaard, "The Antecedents and Consequences of Group Potency: A Longitudinal Investigation of Newly Formed Work Groups," *Academy of Management Journal,* April 2002, pp. 352–368.

26. D. R. Ilgen, J. R. Hollenbeck, M. Johnson, and D. Jundt, "Teams in Organizations: From Input-Process-Output Models to IMOI Models," *Annual Review of Psychology* 56, no. 1 (2005), pp. 517–543.

27. C. R. Evans and K. L. Dion, "Group Cohesion and Performance: A Meta-Analysis," *Small Group Research,* May 1991, pp. 175–186; B. Mullen and C. Copper, "The Relation Between Group Cohesiveness and Performance: An Integration," *Psychological Bulletin,* March 1994, pp. 210–227; P. M. Podsakoff, S. B. MacKenzie, and M. Ahearne, "Moderating Effects of Goal Acceptance on the Relationship Between Group Cohesiveness and Productivity," *Journal of Applied Psychology,* December 1997, pp. 974–983.

28. See, for example, L. Berkowitz, "Group Standards, Cohesiveness, and Productivity," *Human Relations,* November 1954, pp. 509–519; and B. Mullen and C. Copper, "The Relation Between Group Cohesiveness and Performance: An Integration," *Psychological Bulletin,* March 1994, pp. 210–227.

29. S. E. Seashore, *Group Cohesiveness in the Industrial Work Group* (Ann Arbor: University of Michigan, Survey Research Center, 1954).

30. Paragraph based on R. Kreitner and A. Kinicki, *Organizational Behavior,* 6th ed. (New York: Irwin, 2004), pp. 459–461.

31. This section is adapted from S. P. Robbins, *Managing Organizational Conflict: A Nontraditional Approach* (Upper Saddle River, NJ: Prentice Hall, 1974), pp. 11–14. Also, see D. Wagner-Johnson, "Managing Work Team Conflict: Assessment and Preventative Strategies," Center for the Study of Work Teams, University of North Texas, http://www.workteams.unt.edu/reports/wagner.html (accessed November 3, 2000); and M. Kennedy, "Managing Conflict in Work Teams," Center for the Study of Work Teams, University of North Texas, http://www.workteams.unt.edu/reports/kennedy-m.html (accessed November 3, 2000).

32. See K. A. Jehn, "A Multimethod Examination of the Benefits and Detriments of Intragroup Conflict," *Administrative Science Quarterly,* June 1995, pp. 256–282; K. A. Jehn, "A Qualitative Analysis of Conflict Type and Dimensions in Organizational Groups," *Administrative Science Quarterly,* September 1997, pp. 530–557; K. A. Jehn, "Affective and Cognitive Conflict in Work Groups: Increasing Performance Through Value-Based Intragroup Conflict," in *Using Conflict in Organizations,* ed. C. K. W. DeDreu and E. Van deVliert (London: Sage, 1997), pp. 87–100; K. A. Jehn and E. A. Mannix, "The Dynamic Nature of Conflict: A Longitudinal Study of Intragroup Conflict and Group Performance," *Academy of Management Journal,* April 2001, pp. 238–251; and C. K. W. DeDreu and A. E. M. Van Vianen, "Managing Relationship Conflict and the Effectiveness of Organizational Teams," *Journal of Organizational Behavior,* May 2001, pp. 309–328.

33. K. W. Thomas, "Conflict and Negotiation Processes in Organizations," in *Handbook of Industrial and Organizational Psychology,* vol. 3, 2nd ed., ed. M. D. Dunnette and L. M. Hough (Palo Alto, CA: Consulting Psychologists Press, 1992), pp. 651–717.

34. See D. R. Comer, "A Model of Social Loafing in Real Work Groups," *Human Relations,* June 1995, pp. 647–667.

35. S. G. Harkins and K. Szymanski, "Social Loafing and Group Evaluation," *Journal of Personality and Social Psychology,* December 1989, pp. 934–941.

36. See P. C. Earley, "Social Loafing and Collectivism: A Comparison of the United States and the People's Republic of China," *Administrative Science Quarterly,* December 1989, pp. 565–581; and P. C. Earley, "East Meets West Meets Mideast: Further Explorations of Collectivistic and Individualistic Work Groups," *Academy of Management Journal,* April 1993, pp. 319–348.

37. D. Brown, "Innovative HR Ineffective in Manufacturing Firms," *Canadian HR Reporter,* April 7, 2003, pp. 1–2.

38. A. B. Drexler and R. Forrester, "Teamwork—Not Necessarily the Answer," *HR Magazine,* January 1998, pp. 55–58.

39. R. Forrester and A. B. Drexler, "A Model for Team-Based Organization Performance," *Academy of Management Executive,* August 1999, p. 47. See also S. A. Mohrman, with S. G. Cohen and A. M. Mohrman Jr., *Designing Team-Based Organizations* (San Francisco: Jossey-Bass, 1995); and J. H. Shonk, *Team-Based Organizations* (Homewood, IL: Business One Irwin, 1992).

40. Adapted from D. A. Whetten and K. S. Cameron, *Developing Management Skills,* 3rd ed. (New York: HarperCollins, 1995), pp. 534–535.

41. Information on company from BASF website, http://www.basf.com, and Hoover's Online, http://www.hoovers.com (accessed June 19, 2003); and D. Drickhamer, "BASF Breaks Through with Statistics," *IndustryWeek,* June 2002, pp. 81–82.

42. Based on M. Moskowitz and R. Levering, "100 Best Companies to Work For: 10 Great Companies to Work for in Europe: Ferrari Good Food, Good People, Lots of Fun—Sounds Like a European Holiday? No, It's a Great Job," *Fortune,* January 7, 2003, http://www.fortune.com and http://www.ferrari.com (accessed 2004).

43. Based on P. L. Hunsaker, *Training in Management Skills* (Upper Saddle River, NJ: Prentice Hall, 2001), chapter 12.

44. Based on L. Copeland, "Making the Most of Cultural Differences at the Workplace," *Personnel,* June 1988, pp. 52–60; C. R. Bantz, "Cultural Diversity and Group Cross-Cultural Team Research," *Journal of Applied Communication Research,* February 1993, pp. 1–19; L. Strach and L. Wicander, "Fitting In: Issues of Tokenism and Conformity for Minority Women," *SAM Advanced Management Journal,* Summer 1993, pp. 22–25; M. L. Maznevski, "Understanding Our Differences: Performance in Decision-Making Groups With Diverse Members," *Human Relations,* May 1994, pp. 531–552; F. Rice, "How to Make Diversity Pay," *Fortune,* August 8, 1994, pp. 78–86; J. Jusko, "Diversity Enhances Decision Making," *IndustryWeek,* April 2, 2001, p. 9; and K. Lovelace, D. L. Shapiro, and L. R. Weingart, "Maximizing Cross-Functional New Product Teams' Innovativeness and Constraint Adherence: A Conflict Communications Perspective," *Academy of Management Journal,* August 2002, pp. 779–793.

Chapter 11

1. Based on "Energy Roughneck," *Canadian Business,* August 1996, pp. 20+, and Hoover's Online, http://www.hoovers.com; C. Cattaneo, "Husky CEO Lau Reveals Intention to Retire," *National Post (Financial Post),* April 23, 2004, p. FP4.

2. J. Kluger and B. Liston, "A Columbia Culprit?" *Time,* February 24, 2003, p. 13.

3. K. A. Merchant, "The Control Function of Management," *Sloan Management Review,* Summer 1982, pp. 43–55.

4. E. Flamholtz, "Organizational Control Systems as a Managerial Tool," *California Management Review,* Winter 1979, p. 55.

5. See http://www.canada.com/nationalpost/entrepreneur/coldmatic.html.

6. P. Magnusson, "Your Jitters Are Their Lifeblood," *BusinessWeek,* April 14, 2003, p. 41; S. Williams, "Company Crisis: CEO Under Fire," *Hispanic Business,* March 2003, pp. 54–56; T. Purdum, "Preparing for the Worst," *IndustryWeek,* January 2003, pp. 53–55; S. Leibs, "Lesson from 9/11: It's Not About Data," *CFO,* September 2002, pp. 31–32.

7. W. G. Ouchi, "A Conceptual Framework for the Design of Organizational Control Mechanisms," *Management Science,* August 1979, pp. 833–838; W. G. Ouchi, "Markets, Bureaucracies, and Clans," *Administrative Science Quarterly,* March 1980, pp. 129–141.

8. *Management Reflection* based on P. Fitzpatrick, "Wacky WestJet's Winning Ways: Passengers Respond to Stunts That Include Races to Determine Who Leaves the Airplane First," *National Post,* October 16, 2000, p. C1.

9. L. Smircich, "Concepts of Culture and Organizational Analysis," *Administrative Science Quarterly,* September 1983, p. 339; D. R. Denison, "What Is the Difference between Organizational Culture and Organizational Climate? A Native's Point of View on a Decade of Paradigm Wars" (paper presented at Academy of Management Annual Meeting, Atlanta, Georgia, 1993); M. J. Hatch, "The Dynamics of Organizational Culture," *Academy of Management Review,* October 1993, pp. 657–693.

10. K. Shadur and M. A. Kienzle, "The Relationship Between Organizational Climate and Employee Perceptions of Involvement," *Group & Organization Management,* December 1999, pp. 479–503; A. M. Sapienza, "Believing Is Seeing: How Culture Influences the Decisions Top Managers Make," in *Gaining Control of the Corporate Culture,* ed. R. H. Kilmann, M. J. Saxton, and R. Serpa (San Francisco: Jossey-Bass, 1985), p. 68.

11. C. A. O'Reilly III, J. Chatman, and D. F. Caldwell, "People and Organizational Culture: A Profile Comparison Approach to Assessing Person–Organization Fit," *Academy of Management Journal,* September 1991, pp. 487–516; J. A. Chatman and K. A. Jehn, "Assessing the Relationship Between Industry Characteristics and Organizational Culture: How Different Can You Be?" *Academy of Management Journal,* June 1994, pp. 522–553.

12. See, for example, D. R. Denison, *Corporate Culture and Organizational Effectiveness* (New York: Wiley, 1990); G. G. Gordon and N. DiTomaso, "Predicting Corporate Performance from Organizational Culture," *Journal of Management Studies,* November 1992, pp. 793–798; J. P. Kotter and J. L. Heskett, *Corporate Culture and Performance* (New York: Free Press, 1992), pp. 15–27; J. C. Collins and J. I. Porras, *Built to Last* (New York: HarperBusiness, 1994); J. C. Collins and J. I. Porras, "Building Your Company's Vision," *Harvard Business Review,* September–October 1996, pp. 65–77; R. Goffee and G. Jones, "What Holds the Modern Company Together?" *Harvard Business Review,* November–December 1996, pp. 133–148; and J. B. Sorensen, "The Strength of Corporate Culture and the Reliability of Firm Performance," *Administrative Science Quarterly* 47, no. 1 (2002), pp. 70–91.

13. J. B. Sorensen, "The Strength of Corporate Culture and the Reliability of Firm Performance," *Administrative Science Quarterly* 47, no. 1 (2002), pp. 70–91.

14. G. Probst and S. Raisch, "Organizational Crisis: The Logic of Failure," *Academy of Management Executive* 19, no. 1 (February 2005), pp. 90–105.

15. Caption based on information in H. Dolezalek, "Outwit, Outlast, Outlearn," *Training,* January 2004, p. 18.

16. J. Forman, "When Stories Create an Organization's Future," *Strategy & Business,* Second Quarter 1999, pp. 6–9; D. M. Boje, "The Storytelling Organization: A Study of Story Performance in an Office-Supply Firm," *Administrative Science Quarterly,* March 1991, pp. 106–126; C. H. Deutsch, "The Parables of Corporate Culture," *New York Times,* October 13, 1991, p. F25; and T. Terez, "The Business of Storytelling," *Workforce,* May 2002, pp. 22–24.

17. A. M. Pettigrew, "On Studying Organizational Cultures," *Administrative Science Quarterly,* December 1979, p. 576.

18. A. M. Pettigrew, "On Studying Organizational Cultures," *Administrative Science Quarterly,* December 1979, p. 576.

19. Based on C. Cattaneo, "Li May Usher in Sea Change at Air Canada," *National Post (Financial Post),* November 24, 2003, p. FP03.

20. S. Kerr, "On the Folly of Rewarding A, While Hoping for B," *Academy of Management Journal,* December 1975, pp. 769–783.

21. P. Landers, "Japan Tech Star Sticks to Manufacturing," *Wall Street Journal,* April 24, 2000, p. A22.

22. H. Koontz and R. W. Bradspies, "Managing Through Feedforward Control," *Business Horizons,* June 1972, pp. 25–36.

23. "An Open Letter to McDonald's Customers," *Wall Street Journal,* August 22, 2001, p. A5.

24. W. H. Newman, *Constructive Control: Design and Use of Control Systems* (Upper Saddle River, NJ: Prentice Hall, 1975), p. 33.

25. R. Ilies and T. A. Judge, "Goal Regulation Across Time: The Effects of Feedback and Affect," *Journal of Applied Psychology* 90, no. 3 (May 2005), pp. 453–467.

26. C. Cattaneo and J. Harding, "Husky Sheds Its 'Dog' Tag," *National Post (Financial Post)*, August 14, 2006, p. FP1.

27. C. McInnes, J. Beatty, and J. Hunte, "Fast Ferry Directors Resign as Projected Cost Hits $450 Million: A Scathing Audit Finds Senior BC Ferries Managers Misled Their Board and the Minister Responsible for the Project," *Vancouver Sun,* February 25, 1999, p. A1.

28. F. Hansen, "The Value-Based Management Commitment," *Business Finance,* September 2001, pp. 2–5.

29. M. Acharya and T. Yew, "A New Kind of Top 10," *Toronto Star,* June 30, 2002, p. C01.

30. M. Acharya and T. Yew, "A New Kind of Top 10," *Toronto Star,* June 30, 2002, p. C01.

31. K. Lehn and A. K. Makhija, "EVA and MVA as Performance Measures and Signals for Strategic Change," *Strategy & Leadership,* May–June 1996, pp. 34–38.

32. S. Taub, "MVPs of MVA: Which Companies Created the Most Wealth for Shareholders Last Year?" *CFO,* July 1, 2003, http://www.cfo.com (accessed June 22, 2004). All figures are in US dollars.

33. *Balanced Scorecard Collaborative,* http://www.bscol.com (accessed June 29, 2003); K. Graham, "Balanced Scorecard," *New Zealand Management,* March 2003, pp. 32–34; K. Ellis, "A Ticket to Ride: Balanced Scorecard," *Training,* April 2001, p. 50; and T. Leahy, "Tailoring the Balanced Scorecard," *Business Finance,* August 2000, pp. 53–56.

34. T. Leahy, "Tailoring the Balanced Scorecard," *Business Finance,* August 2000, pp. 53–56.

35. T. Leahy, "Tailoring the Balanced Scorecard," *Business Finance,* August 2000, pp. 53–56.

36. "When Wireless Works," *CIO,* February 12, 2002, http://www.cio.de (accessed July 2, 2004).

37. "Mercedes-Benz Benchmarking Saves DaimlerChrysler $100 Million," *IndustryWeek,* October 27, 2000, http://www.industryweek.com.

38. Y. F. Jarrar and M. Zairi, "Future Trends in Benchmarking for Competitive Advantage: A Global Survey," *Total Quality Management,* December 2001, pp. 906–912.

39. M. Simpson and D. Kondouli, "A Practical Approach to Benchmarking in Three Service Industries," *Total Quality Management,* July 2000, pp. S623–S630.

40. K. N. Dervitsiotis, "Benchmarking and Paradigm Shifts," *Total Quality Management,* July 2000, pp. S641–S646.

41. See http://www.canada.com/nationalpost/entrepreneur/bouclair.html.

42. T. Leahy, "Extracting Diamonds in the Rough," *Business Finance,* August 2000, pp. 33–37.

43. "Recognizing Commitment to Diversity," *Canadian HR Reporter,* November 3, 2003, p. 12.

44. B. Bruzina, B. Jessop, R. Plourde, B. Whitlock, and L. Rubin, "Ameren Embraces Benchmarking as a Core Business Strategy,"

Power Engineering, November 2002, pp. 121–124; T. Leahy, "Extracting Diamonds in the Rough," *Business Finance,* August 2000, pp. 33–37.

45. See http://www.huskyenergy.ca/abouthusky/corporategovernance/ for Husky Energy's corporate governance policy.

46. J. Yaukey and C. L. Romero, "Arizona Firm Pays Big for Workers' Digital Downloads," *Springfield News-Leader,* May 6, 2002, p. 6B.

47. N. Shirouzu and J. Bigness, "7-Eleven Operators Resist System to Monitor Managers," *Wall Street Journal,* June 16, 1997, p. B1.

48. E. O'Connor, "Pulling the Plug on Cyberslackers," *StarPhoenix,* May 24, 2003, p. F22.

49. E. O'Connor, "Pulling the Plug on Cyberslackers," *StarPhoenix,* May 24, 2003, p. F22.

50. D. Hawkins, "Lawsuits Spur Rise in Employee Monitoring," *U.S. News & World Report,* August 13, 2001, p. 53; L. Guernsey, "You've Got Inappropriate Mail," *New York Times,* April 5, 2000, p. C11; and R. Karaim, "Setting E-Privacy Rules," *Cnnfn Online,* December 15, 1999, http://www.cnnfn.com.

51. E. Bott, "Are You Safe? Privacy Special Report," *PC Computing,* March 2000, pp. 87–88.

52. E. O'Connor, "Pulling the Plug on Cyberslackers," *StarPhoenix,* May 24, 2003, p. F22.

53. "Employers Spying on Canadian Workers, Study Suggests," *CBC News* (online), July 10, 2006, http://www.cbc.ca/canada/story/2006/07/10/privacy-workplace.html. The report can be found at http://www.ryerson.ca/faculties/business/news/archive/UnderTheRadar.pdf.

54. A. Tomlinson, "Heavy-Handed Net Policies Push Privacy Boundaries," *Canadian HR Reporter,* December 2, 2002, pp. 1–2.

55. C. Sorensen, "Canada Ranks High in Employee Theft: Global Survey Findings," *National Post,* May 28, 2004, p. FP9.

56. A. Perry, "Back-to-School Brings Pilfering: Some Employees Raid Office for Kids," *Toronto Star,* August 30, 2003, p. B01.

57. "Employee Theft Reaches $2 Million a Day in 1999," *Times Colonist,* September 19, 2001, p. C3.

58. J. Greenberg, "The STEAL Motive: Managing the Social Determinants of Employee Theft," in *Antisocial Behavior in Organizations,* ed. R. Giacalone and J. Greenberg (Newbury Park, CA: Sage, 1997), pp. 85–108.

59. "Crime Spree," *BusinessWeek,* September 9, 2002, p. 8; B. P. Niehoff and R. J. Paul, "Causes of Employee Theft and Strategies That HR Managers Can Use for Prevention," *Human Resource Management,* Spring 2000, pp. 51–64; and G. Winter, "Taking at the Office Reaches New Heights: Employee Larceny Is Bigger and Bolder," *New York Times,* July 12, 2000, p. C11.

60. This section is based on J. Greenberg, *Behavior in Organizations: Understanding and Managing the Human Side of Work,* 8th ed. (Upper Saddle River, NJ: Prentice Hall, 2003), pp. 329–330.

61. A. H. Bell and D. M. Smith, "Why Some Employees Bite the Hand That Feeds Them," *Workforce,* May 16, 2000, http://www.workforce.com (accessed December 3, 2000).

62. A. H. Bell and D. M. Smith, "Protecting the Company Against Theft and Fraud," *Workforce,* May 18, 2000, http://www.workforce.com (accessed December 3, 2000); J. D. Hansen, "To Catch a Thief," *Journal of Accountancy,* March 2000, pp. 43–46; J. Greenberg, "The Cognitive Geometry of Employee Theft," in *Dysfunctional Behavior in Organizations: Nonviolent and Deviant Behavior,* ed. S. B. Bacharach,

A. O'Leary-Kelly, J. M. Collins, and R. W. Griffin (Stamford, CT: JAI Press, 1998), pp. 147–193.

63. S. Boyes, "Workplace Violence: Coping in a Dangerous World," *Canadian Consulting Engineer,* January–February 2002, pp. 51–52.

64. W. M. Glenn, "An Employee's Survival Guide: An ILO Survey of Workplaces in 32 Countries Ranked Argentina the Most Violent, Followed by Romania, France and Then, Surprisingly, Canada," *Occupational Health & Safety,* April–May 2002, p. 28+.

65. W. M. Glenn, "An Employee's Survival Guide: An ILO Survey of Workplaces in 32 Countries Ranked Argentina the Most Violent, Followed by Romania, France and Then, Surprisingly, Canada," *Occupational Health & Safety,* April–May 2002, p. 28+.

66. "Work Rage," *BCBusiness Magazine,* January 2001, p. 23.

67. D. Flavelle, "Managers Cited for Increase in 'Work Rage,'" *Vancouver Sun,* April 11, 2000, pp. D1, D11.

68. WarrenShepell, "Public Sector Workers' Rates of Anger and Depression Reaching Critical Levels," news release, July 12, 2004.

69. WarrenShepell, "Reports Anger and Addiction Trend in Manufacturing Sector," news release, March 5, 2003.

70. E. Girardet, "Office Rage Is on the Boil," *National Post,* August 11, 1999, p. B1.

71. R. McNatt, "Desk Rage," *BusinessWeek,* November 27, 2000, p. 12.

72. M. Gorkin, "Key Components of a Dangerously Dysfunctional Work Environment," *Workforce,* November 1, 1999, http://www.workforce.com (accessed December 3, 2000).

73. "Ten Tips on Recognizing and Minimizing Violence"; M. Gorkin, "Five Strategies and Structures for Reducing Workplace Violence"; "Investigating Workplace Violence: Where Do You Start?"; and "Points to Cover in a Workplace Violence Policy": all articles from *Workforce,* http://www.workforce.com (accessed December 3, 2000).

74. "A Revolution Where Everyone Wins: Worldwide Movement to Improve Corporate-Governance Standards," *BusinessWeek,* May 19, 2003, p. 72.

75. J. S. McClenahen, "Executives Expect More Board Input," *IndustryWeek,* October 2002, p. 12.

76. D. Salierno, "Boards Face Increased Responsibility," *Internal Auditor,* June 2003, pp. 14–15.

77. T. S. Bateman and J. M. Crant, "The Proactive Component of Organizational Behavior: A Measure and Correlates," *Journal of Organizational Behavior,* March 1993, p. 112; and J. M. Crant, "Proactive Behavior in Organizations," *Journal of Management* 26, no. 3 (2000), pp. 435–462.

78. Situation adapted from information in K. Cushing, "E-Mail Policy," *Computer Weekly,* June 24, 2003, p. 8; "Spam Leads to Lawsuit Fears, Lost Time," *InternetWeek,* June 23, 2003, http://www.internetweek.com.

79. Case based on P. Vieira, "The Airline, the Analyst and the Secret Password," *Financial Post,* June 30, 2004, p. FP1; C. Wong, "WestJet Disputes Air Canada Allegations of Corporate Espionage," *Canadian Press,* July 1, 2004; and T. Gignac, "WestJet Settles Air Canada Corporate-Espionage Suit," *Vancouver Sun,* May 30, 2006, p. D2.

80. Case based on K. Johnson and T. Locy, "Low Pay Squeezes FBI Agents—and Perhaps U.S. Security," *USA Today,* April 5, 2004, pp. A-1, A-2; and D. E. Sanger, "In Testimony to 9/11 Panel, Rice Sticks to the Script," *New York Times,* April 9, 2004, p. A-1.

81. Based on P. L. Hunsaker, *Training in Management Skills* (Upper Saddle River, NJ: Prentice Hall, 2001), pp. 60–61.

82. Based on J. Hickman, C. Tkaczyk, E. Florian, J. Stemple, and D. Vazquez, "50 Best Companies for Minorities," *Fortune,* July 7, 2003, pp. 103–120; and S. M. Mehta, "What Minority Employees Really Want," *Fortune,* July 10, 2000, pp. 180–186; and "Why Diversity Pays," *Canadian Business,* March 29–April 11, 2004, cover story.

83. "Why Diversity Pays," *Canadian Business,* March 29–April 11, 2004, cover story.

Chapter 12

1. Based on R. Waters, "Microsoft Reaches Middle Age," *Financial Times,* July 27, 2003, http://www.ft.com.

2. C. R. Leana and B. Barry, "Stability and Change as Simultaneous Experiences in Organizational Life," *Academy of Management Review,* October 2000, pp. 753–759.

3. K. Griffin, "New DVDs Spell Demise of VHS," *Vancouver Sun,* April 3, 2004, p. D4.

4. Based on L. Tischler, "Sudden Impact," *Fast Company,* September 2002, pp. 106–113.

5. E. Nee, "The Hottest CEO in Tech," *Business 2.0,* June 2003, p. 86.

6. Based on R. Waters, "Microsoft Reaches Middle Age," *Financial Times,* July 27, 2003, http://www.ft.com; and "AT&T Tests Linux to Replace Microsoft's Windows on 70,000 PCs," *Bloomberg.com,* October 5, 2004, http://quote.bloomberg.com/apps/ (accessed October 27, 2004); and http://www.microsoft.com/presspass/features/2005/aug05/08-100penSourceLab.mspx (accessed September 26, 2006).

7. The idea for these metaphors came from J. E. Dutton, S. J. Ashford, R. M. O'Neill, and K. A. Lawrence, "Moves That Matter: Issue Selling and Organizational Change," *Academy of Management Journal,* August 2001, pp. 716–736; B. H. Kemelgor, S. D. Johnson, and S. Srinivasan, "Forces Driving Organizational Change: A Business School Perspective," *Journal of Education for Business,* January–February 2000, pp. 133–137; G. Colvin, "When It Comes to Turbulence, CEOs Could Learn a Lot from Sailors," *Fortune,* March 29, 1999, pp. 194–196; and P. B. Vaill, *Managing as a Performing Art: New Ideas for a World of Chaotic Change* (San Francisco: Jossey-Bass, 1989).

8. K. Lewin, *Field Theory in Social Science* (New York: Harper & Row, 1951).

9. For contrasting views on episodic and continuous change, see K. E. Weick and R. E. Quinn, "Organizational Change and Development," in *Annual Review of Psychology,* vol. 50, ed. J. T. Spence, J. M. Darley, and D. J. Foss (Palo Alto, CA: Annual Reviews, 1999), pp. 361–386.

10. G. Hamel, "Take It Higher," *Fortune,* February 5, 2001, pp. 169–170.

11. Based on S. Rubin, "Blinded by the Dazzle of the Deal," *Financial Post (National Post),* February 12, 2004, pp. FP8–FP9.

12. Based on R. Waters, "Microsoft Reaches Middle Age," *Financial Times,* July 27, 2003, http://www.ft.com.

13. Based on T. Belford, "Half Public, Half Private, It Beats Odds," *Financial Post (National Post),* June 9, 2003, p. BE4; S. Tafler, "BC + X = P3: BC Struggles With the Partnering Numbers," *Summit: Canada's Magazine for Public Sector Purchasing,* September 2002, pp. 16–18; P. Vieira, "RBC Pushes Public–Private Partnerships," *Financial Post (National Post),* November 26, 2002, p. FP10.

14. See, for example, T. C. Head and P. F. Sorensen, "Cultural Values and Organizational Development: A Seven-Country Study," *Leadership & Organization Development Journal,* March 1993, pp. 3–7; A. H. Church, W. W. Burke, and D. F. Van Eynde, "Values, Motives, and Interventions of Organization Development Practitioners," *Group & Organization Management,* March 1994, pp. 5–50; W. L. French and C. H. Bell Jr., *Organization Development: Behavioral Science Interventions for Organization Improvement,* 6th ed. (Upper Saddle River, NJ: Prentice Hall, 1998); N. A. Worren, K. Ruddle, and K. Moore, "From Organizational Development to Change Management," *Journal of Applied Behavioral Science,* September 1999, pp. 273–286; G. Farias, "Organizational Development and Change Management," *Journal of Applied Behavioral Science,* September 2000, pp. 376–379; W. Nicolay, "Response to Farias and Johnson's Commentary," *Journal of Applied Behavioral Science,* September 2000, pp. 380–381; S. Hicks, "What Is Organization Development?" *Training & Development,* August 2000, p. 65.

15. T. White, "Supporting Change: How Communicators at Scotiabank Turned Ideas into Action," *Communication World,* April 2002, pp. 22–24.

16. P. A. McLagan, "Change Leadership Today," *Training & Development,* November 2002, p. 29.

17. H. L. Sirkin, P. Keenan, and A. Jackson, "The Hard Side Of Change Management," *Harvard Business Review* 83, no. 10 (October 1, 2005), pp. 108–118.

18. W. Pietersen, "The Mark Twain Dilemma: The Theory and Practice for Change Leadership," *Journal of Business Strategy,* September–October 2002, pp. 32–37; C. Hymowitz, "To Maintain Success, Managers Must Learn How to Direct Change," *Wall Street Journal,* August 13, 2002, p. B1; J. E. Dutton, S. J. Ashford, R. M. O'Neill, and K. A. Lawrence, "Moves That Matter: Issue Selling and Organizational Change," *Academy of Management Journal,* August 2001, pp. 716–736.

19. P. A. McLagan, "The Change-Capable Organization," *Training & Development,* January 2003, pp. 50–58.

20. M. Young and J. E. Post, "Managing to Communicate, Communicating to Manage: How Leading Companies Communicate With Employees," *Organizational Dynamics,* Summer 1993, pp. 31–43.

21. See, for example, B. M. Staw, "Counterforces to Change," in *Change in Organizations,* ed. P. S. Goodman and Associates (San Francisco: Jossey-Bass, 1982), pp. 87–121; A. A. Armenakis and A. G. Bedeian, "Organizational Change: A Review of Theory and Research in the 1990s," *Journal of Management* 25, no. 3 (1999), pp. 293–315; C. R. Wanberg and J. T. Banas, "Predictors and Outcomes of Openness to Changes in a Reorganizing Workplace," *Journal of Applied Psychology,* February 2000, pp. 132–142; S. K. Piderit, "Rethinking Resistance and Recognizing Ambivalence: A Multidimensional View of Attitudes Toward an Organizational Change," *Academy of Management Review,* October 2000, pp. 783–794; R. Kegan and L. L. Lahey, "The Real Reason People Won't Change," *Harvard Business Review,* November 2001, pp. 85–92; M. A. Korsgaard, H. J. Sapienza, and D. M. Schweiger, "Beaten Before Begun: The Role of Procedural Justice in Planning Change," *Journal of Management* 28, no. 4 (2002), pp. 497–516; C. E. Cunningham, "Readiness for Organizational Change: A Longitudinal Study of Workplace, Psychological and Behavioral Correlates," *Journal*

of Occupational and Organizational Psychology, December 2002, pp. 377–392.

22. J. P. Kotter and L. A. Schlesinger, "Choosing Strategies for Change," *Harvard Business Review,* March–April 1979, pp. 107–109; P. Strebel, "Why Do Employees Resist Change?" *Harvard Business Review,* May–June 1996, pp. 86–92; J. Mariotti, "Troubled by Resistance to Change," *IndustryWeek,* October 7, 1996, p. 30; and A. Reichers, J. P. Wanous, and J. T. Austin, "Understanding and Managing Cynicism About Organizational Change," *Academy of Management Executive,* February 1997, pp. 48–57.

23. J. P. Kotter and L. A. Schlesinger, "Choosing Strategies for Change," *Harvard Business Review,* March–April 1979, pp. 106–111; K. Matejka and R. Julian, "Resistance to Change Is Natural," *Supervisory Management,* October 1993, p. 10; C. O'Connor, "Resistance: The Repercussions of Change," *Leadership & Organization Development Journal,* October 1993, pp. 30–36; J. Landau, "Organizational Change and Barriers to Innovation: A Case Study in the Italian Public Sector," *Human Relations,* December 1993, pp. 1411–1429; A. Sagie and M. Koslowsky, "Organizational Attitudes and Behaviors as a Function of Participation in Strategic and Tactical Change Decisions: An Application of Path-Goal Theory," *Journal of Organizational Behavior,* January 1994, pp. 37–47; V. D. Miller, J. R. Johnson, and J. Grau, "Antecedents to Willingness to Participate in a Planned Organizational Change," *Journal of Applied Communication Research,* February 1994, pp. 59–80; P. Pritchett and R. Pound, *The Employee Handbook for Organizational Change* (Dallas: Pritchett Publishing, 1994); R. Maurer, *Beyond the Wall of Resistance: Unconventional Strategies That Build Support for Change* (Austin, TX: Bard Books, 1996); D. Harrison, "Assess and Remove Barriers to Change," *HRfocus,* July 1999, pp. 9–10; L. K. Lewis, "Disseminating Information and Soliciting Input During Planned Organizational Change," *Management Communication Quarterly,* August 1999, pp. 43–75; J. P. Wanous, A. E. Reichers, and J. T. Austin, "Cynicism About Organizational Change," *Group & Organization Management,* June 2000, pp. 132–153; K. W. Mossholder, R. P. Settoon, and A. A. Armenakis, "Emotion During Organizational Transformations," *Group & Organization Management,* September 2000, pp. 220–243; S. K. Piderit, "Rethinking Resistance and Recognizing Ambivalence: A Multidimensional View of Attitudes Toward an Organizational Change," *Academy of Management Review,* October 2000, pp. 783–794.

24. Based on R. Waters, "Microsoft Reaches Middle Age," *Financial Times,* July 27, 2003, http://www.ft.com.

25. C. Hymowitz, "How Leader at 3M Got His Employees to Back Big Changes," *Wall Street Journal,* April 23, 2002, p. B1; and J. Useem, "Jim McNerney Thinks He Can Turn 3M from a Good Company into a Great One—With a Little Help from His Former Employer: General Electric," *Fortune,* August 12, 2002, pp. 127–132.

26. See T. H. Fitzgerald, "Can Change in Organizational Culture Really Be Managed?" *Organizational Dynamics,* Autumn 1988, pp. 5–15; B. Dumaine, "Creating a New Company Culture," *Fortune,* January 15, 1990, pp. 127–131; P. F. Drucker, "Don't Change Corporate Culture—Use It!" *Wall Street Journal,* March 28, 1991, p. A14; J. Martin, *Cultures in Organizations: Three Perspectives* (New York: Oxford University Press, 1992); D. C. Pheysey, *Organizational Cultures: Types and Transformations* (London: Routledge, 1993); C. G. Smith and R. P. Vecchio, "Organizational Culture and Strategic Management: Issues in the Strategic Management of Change," *Journal of Managerial Issues,* Spring 1993, pp. 53–70; P. Bate, *Strategies for Cultural Change* (Boston: Butterworth-Heinemann, 1994); and P. Anthony, *Managing Culture* (Philadelphia: Open University Press, 1994).

27. M. L. Wald and J. Schwartz, "Shuttle Inquiry Uncovers Flaws in Communication," *New York Times,* August 4, 2003, http://nytimes.com.

28. M. L. Wald and J. Schwartz, "Shuttle Inquiry Uncovers Flaws in Communication," *New York Times,* August 4, 2003, http://nytimes.com.

29. See, for example, R. H. Kilmann, M. J. Saxton, and R. Serpa, eds., *Gaining Control of the Corporate Culture* (San Francisco: Jossey-Bass, 1985); and D. C. Hambrick and S. Finkelstein, "Managerial Discretion: A Bridge Between Polar Views of Organizational Outcomes," in *Research in Organizational Behavior,* vol. 9, ed. B. M. Staw and L. L. Cummings (Greenwich, CT: JAI Press, 1987), p. 384.

30. M. A. Cavanaugh, W. R. Boswell, M. V. Roehling, and J. W. Boudreau, "An Empirical Examination of Self-Reported Work Stress Among U.S. Managers," *Journal of Applied Psychology,* February 2000, pp. 65–74; M. A. Verespej, "Stressed Out," *IndustryWeek,* February 21, 2000, pp. 30–34; J. Laabs, "Time-Starved Workers Rebel," *Workforce,* October 2000, pp. 26–28; and C. Daniels, "The Last Taboo," *Fortune,* October 28, 2002, pp. 137–144.

31. I. Phaneuf, "Drug Company Study Finds Rise in Work-Related Stress," *Vancouver Sun,* May 5, 2001, p. D15.

32. Adapted from R. S. Schuler, "Definition and Conceptualization of Stress in Organizations," *Organizational Behavior and Human Performance,* April 1980, p. 189. For an updated review of definitions, see R. L. Kahn and P. Byosiere, "Stress in Organizations," in *Handbook of Industrial and Organizational Psychology,* vol. 3, 2nd ed., ed. M. D. Dunnette and L. J. Hough (Palo Alto, CA: Consulting Psychologists Press, 1992), pp. 573–580.

33. S. E. Jackson, "Participation in Decision Making as a Strategy for Reducing Job-Related Strain," *Journal of Applied Psychology,* February 1983, pp. 3–19; C. D. Fisher, "Boredom at Work: A Neglected Concept," *Human Relations,* March 1993, pp. 395–417; C. A. Heaney, B. A. Israel, S. J. Schurman, E. A. Baker, J. S. House, and M. Hugentobler, "Industrial Relations, Worksite Stress Reduction and Employee Well-Being: A Participatory Action Research Investigation," *Journal of Organizational Behavior,* September 1993, pp. 495–510; P. Froiland, "What Cures Job Stress?" *Training,* December 1993, pp. 32–36; C. L. Cooper and S. Cartwright, "Healthy Mind, Healthy Organization—A Proactive Approach to Occupational Stress," *Human Relations,* April 1994, pp. 455–471; A. A. Brott, "New Approaches to Job Stress," *Nation's Business,* May 1994, pp. 81–82; C. Daniels, "The Last Taboo," *Fortune,* October 28, 2002, pp. 137–144.

34. See R. S. Schuler, "Time Management: A Stress Management Technique," *Personnel Journal,* December 1979, pp. 851–855; and M. E. Haynes, *Practical Time Management: How to Make the Most of Your Most Perishable Resource* (Tulsa, OK: Penn Well Books, 1985).

35. "Employee Wellness," *Canadian HR Reporter,* February 23, 2004, pp. 9–12.

36. Adapted from P. B. Vaill, *Managing as a Performing Art: New Ideas for a World of Chaotic Change* (San Francisco: Jossey-Bass, 1989), pp. 8, 9.

37. Information on company from Electronic Arts website, http://www.ea.com, and Hoover's Online, http://www.hoovers.com (accessed October 27, 2004); C. Salter, "Playing to Win," *Fast Company,* December 2002, pp. 80–91; G. L. Cooper and E. K. Brown, "Video Game Industry Update," Bank of America Securities Equity Research Brief, *Leisure,* June 7, 2002; and M. Athitakis, "Steve Rechtschaffner, Game Wizard," *Business 2.0,* May 2002, p. 82.

38. Based on M. Warner, "Under the Knife," *Business 2.0,* February 2004, http://www.business20.com.

39. See also T. Pollock, "Mind Your Own Business: The Gentle Art of Selling Change," *Supervision,* December 2000, p. 11; and R. M. Kanter, "The Enduring Skills of Change Leaders," *Ivey Business Journal,* May 2000, p. 31.

40. Based on J. P. Kotter and L. A. Schlesinger, "Choosing Strategies for Change," *Harvard Business Review,* March–April 1979, pp. 106–114; and T. A. Stewart, "Rate Your Readiness to Change," *Fortune,* February 7, 1994, pp. 106–110.

41. Based on C. Lindsay, "Paradoxes of Organizational Diversity: Living Within the Paradoxes," in *Proceedings of the 50th Academy of Management Conference,* ed. L. R. Jauch and J. L. Wall (San Francisco, 1990), pp. 374–378.

GLOSSARY/SUBJECT INDEX

Note: Pages in bold refer to pages on which key terms are defined.

A

Acceptable range of variation, 316, 317*f*

Accommodative approach. Managers make choices that try to balance the interests of shareholders with those of other stakeholders. **16–17**

Accountability. The need to report and justify work to a manager's superiors. **134**

Achievement-oriented leader, 232

Acquisition. When a larger company buys a smaller company and integrates it into the larger company. **83**

Active listening. Listening for full meaning without making premature judgments or interpretations. **167**, 168*f*, 183

Actual performance
  common sources of information for measuring, 316*f*
  correction of, 318–319
  measurement of, 315–316
  vs. standard, 316–318

Adjourning. The final stage of team development for temporary teams, in which members are concerned with wrapping up activities rather than task performance. **287**

All-channel network, 171

Alternatives
  analysis of, 102–103, 103*f*, 104*f*
  development of, 102
  implementation of, 103–104
  selection of, 103

Analytic style. A decision-making style characterized by a rational way of thinking and a high tolerance for ambiguity. **110**

Analytical skills, 97, 123–124, 153, 182

Anti-discrimination legislation, 190

Application forms, 195

Assessment centres. Places in which job candidates undergo performance-simulation tests to evaluate managerial potential. **189**

Association of Southeast Asian Nations (ASEAN). A trading alliance of 10 Southeast Asian countries. **45**

Assumptions of rationality, 105, 106*f*

Authority. The rights inherent in a managerial position to tell people what to do and to expect them to do it. **134**

Autocratic style. A leadership style where the leader tends to centralize authority, dictate work methods, make unilateral decisions, and limit employee participation. **224**

Autonomy. The degree to which the job provides substantial freedom, independence, and discretion to the individual in scheduling the work and determining the procedures to be used in carrying it out. **260**

B

Baby Boomers, 266

Background investigations, 197

Balanced scorecard. A performance measurement tool that looks at four areas—financial, customer, internal processes, and people/innovation/growth assets—that contribute to a company's performance. **324**

Bargaining power, 85

Basic corrective action. Corrective action that looks at how and why performance deviated and then proceeds to correct the source of deviation. **318**

Behavioural style. A decision-making style characterized by an intuitive way of thinking and a low tolerance for ambiguity. **111**

Behavioural theories. Leadership theories that identify behaviours that differentiate effective leaders from ineffective leaders. **224**, 225*f*

Behaviourally anchored rating scales (BARS). A performance appraisal method in which the evaluator rates an employee on examples of actual job behaviours. **203**

Benchmark. The standard of excellence against which to measure and compare. **326**

Benchmarking. The search for the best practices among competitors or noncompetitors that lead to their superior performance. **90–91**, **326**–327, 327*f*

Benefits, 204, 205*f*, 209, 216

Biases
  confirmation bias, 114
  in decision making, 113–115, 114*f*
  hindsight bias, 115
  overconfidence bias, 114
  selective perception bias, 114
  self-serving bias, 115

Board of directors, 332

Body language. Gestures, facial expressions, and other body movements that convey meaning. **164**

Borderless organization. A type of global organization in which artificial geographical barriers are eliminated. **49**

Boundaryless organization. An organization that is not defined by a chain of command, places no limits on spans of control, and replaces departments with empowered teams. **145**
  described, 145
  modular organization, 147
  network organization, 146–147
  virtual organization, 146

Bounded rationality. Limitations on a person's ability to interpret, process, and act on information. **106**

Budget, 322–323

Bureaucratic control. An approach to control that emphasizes organizational authority and relies on administrative rules, regulations, procedures, and policies. **310**

Business-level strategy
  competitive advantage, 84
  competitive strategies, 87*f*
  cost leadership strategy, 86
  differentiation strategy, 86–88
  focus strategy, 89
  stuck in the middle, 89

Buyers, 85

C

Calm waters metaphor, 346–347, 346*f*

Canada
  diversity, 17–18
  and global challenges, 18

Canada Labour Code, 189–190

Canadian Human Rights Act, 190

Canadian Securities Administrators rules, 333

Career. A sequence of positions held by a person during his or her lifetime. **205**

Career development, 205–207

Centralization. The degree to which decision making is concentrated at a single point in the organization. **135**–137, 137*f*

Certainty. A condition in which a decision maker can make accurate decisions because the outcome of every alternative is known. **109**

Chain network, 170–171

Chain of command. The continuous line of authority that extends from the top of the organization to the lowest level and clarifies who reports to whom. **133**–134

Change. *See* organizational change

Change agents. People who assume the responsibility for managing the change process. **345**–346

Change-capable organizations, 353*f*

Change management
  changing people, 350, 351*f*
  cultural change, 355–356
  current issues, 354–359
  effective communication, 352
  employee stress, 356–359
  mistakes in leading change, 351–352*f*
  organizational culture, change in, 355–356
  organizational structure, change in, 349–350
  resistance to change, 353–354, 354*f*, 364–365
  successful change, 350–352
  technology, change in, 350–351
  types of change, 348–350, 349*f*

Changing organization, 11, 12*f*

Channel. The medium a message travels along. **160**, 161, 162–164

Charismatic leader. An enthusiastic, self-confident leader whose personality and actions influence people to behave in certain ways. **234**–235

Charter of Rights and Freedoms, 190

China, 46

Civil servant. A person who works in a local, provincial, or federal government department. **12**

Clan control. An approach to control in which employee behaviour is regulated by the shared values, norms, traditions, rituals, beliefs, and other aspects of the organization's culture. 310–314, **316**
see also organizational culture

Classical view. The view that management's only social responsibility is to maximize profits. **14**–15

Code of ethics. A formal statement of an organization's primary values and the ethical rules it expects its employees to follow. **117**–118

Coercive power. The power a leader has through his or her ability to punish or control. **238**

Collectivism, 47

Combination strategy. The simultaneous pursuit by an organization of two or more of growth, stability, and retrenchment strategies. **84**

Command economy. An economic system in which all economic decisions are planned by a central government. **46**

Commitment, 291

Communication. The transfer and understanding of meaning. **158**
and change management, 352
diagonal communication, 170
downward communication, 169–170
formal communication, 169
functions of, 159
good communication, meaning of, 158
importance of effective communication, 158
informal communication, 169
information technology, effect of, 172–175
interpersonal communication. *See* interpersonal communication
lateral communication, 170
meaning of, 158
online leadership, 241
organizational communication, 158, 168–172
teams and, 292
understanding communication, 157–159
upward communication, 169–170
Communication barriers
defensiveness, 166
emotions, 165
filtering, 165
information overload, 165
language, 166
national culture, 166
overcoming, 166–168
selective perception, 166
Communication channels. *See* channel
Communication flow, 169–170

Communication networks. The variety of patterns of vertical and horizontal flows of organizational communication. **170**–172, 171f

Communication process. The seven elements involved in transferring meaning from one person to another. **160**, 160f

Compensation, 204, 205f

Competence, 239

Competition Act, 42

Competition Bureau, 42

Competitive advantage. What sets an organization apart: its distinct edge. **84**, 89–91

Competitive forces, 85, 86f

Competitive strategies, 84–89, 87f

Competitors, 41

Complexity, 53

Compressed workweek. A workweek in which employees work longer hours per day but fewer days per week. **272**

Concentration, 82–83

Conceptual skills. The mental ability to analyze and generate ideas about abstract and complex situations. **9**

Conceptual style. A decision-making style characterized by an intuitive way of thinking and a high tolerance for ambiguity. **111**

Concurrent control. A type of control that takes place while an activity is in progress. **321**

Confirmation bias, 114

Conflict. Perceived differences that result in some form of interference or opposition. **293**
dysfunctional conflicts, 294
functional conflicts, 293–294
and group performance, 294f
human relations view of conflict, 293
interactionist view of conflict, 293
process conflict, 294
relationship conflict, 294
task conflict, 294
traditional view of conflict, 293
Conflict-resolution techniques, 295f

Consideration. The extent to which a leader has job relationships characterized by mutual trust and respect for group members' ideas and feelings. **225**

Consistency, 239

Contemporary organizational design
boundaryless organization, 145–147
described, 142, 143f
matrix structure, 144–145
project structure, 144–145
team structure, 142–143
Contemporary theories of motivation, 258–265

Contingency approach, 34–35, 35f

Contingency factors, 75
described, 139
environmental uncertainty, 140–141
size, 139
strategy, 139
technology, 140, 140f
Contingency theories, 226–233

Control. The process of monitoring activities to ensure that they are being accomplished as planned, and correcting any significant deviations. **308**

benchmarking, 326–327, 327f
board of directors, role of, 332
bureaucratic control, 310
clan control, 310–314, 316
see also organizational culture
and communication, 159
concurrent control, 321
corporate governance, 332–333
cross-cultural differences, 328
current issues, 327–333
employee theft, 330, 331f
feedback control, 321
feedforward control, 320
financial controls, 321–324
financial reporting, 333
importance of, 308
information controls, 324–325
management by walking around, 321
market control, 309
types of control, 320f
types of control systems, 309–310, 309f
workplace concerns, 328–331
workplace privacy, 329–330
workplace violence, 330–331, 332f

Control process. A three-step process that includes measuring actual performance, comparing actual performance against a standard, and taking managerial action to correct deviations or inadequate standards. **315**
actual performance *vs.* standard, 316–318
illustration of, 315f
managerial action, 318–319
managerial decisions, summary of, 319, 319f
measurement of actual performance, 315–316
range of variation, 316, 317f
revising the standard, 318–319

Controlling. A management function that involves monitoring actual performance, comparing actual to standard, and taking corrective action when necessary. **8**

Core competencies. The organization's major value-creating skills, capabilities, and resources that determine its competitive advantage. **79**

Corporate governance. The system used to govern a corporation so that the interests of shareholders are protected. **332**
board of directors, role of, 332
financial reporting, 333

Corporate-level strategy
combination strategy, 84
grand strategies, 82–84
growth strategy, 82–83
retrenchment strategy, 84
stability strategy, 84

Corporate social responsibility. A business's obligation, beyond that required by law and economics, to pursue long-term goals that are good for society. **14**
accommodative approach, 16
approaches to, 16f
classical view, 14–15
comparison of views, 16
defensive approach, 16

and economic performance, 17
obstructionist approach, 16
proactive approach, 17
socio-economic view, 15–16

Corrective action, 318

Cost leadership strategy. A business-level strategy in which the organization sets out to be the lowest-cost producer in its industry. **86**

Creative problem solving, 124–125

Creativity, 76, 124

Credibility. The degree to which someone is perceived as honest, competent, and able to inspire. **239**

Critical incidents. A performance appraisal method in which the evaluator focuses on the critical behaviours that separate effective from ineffective job performance. **203**

Cross-cultural differences. See national culture

Cross-functional teams. A group of employees at about the same hierarchical level, but from different work areas, who come together to accomplish a task. **133, 285**

Crown corporations. A commercial company owned by the government but independently managed. **12**

Cultural awareness, 61

Cultural change, 355–356

Cultural environment, 46–48

Culture. See national culture; organizational culture

Customer departmentalization. Groups jobs on the basis of customers who have common needs or problems. **131, 133**

Customer service, 175–176

Customers, 40

D

Data. Raw, unanalyzed facts. **325**

Decentralization. The degree to which lower-level employees provide input or actually make decisions. **135–137, 137f**

Decision. A choice from two or more alternatives. **100**
evaluation of effectiveness of, 104
nonprogrammed decisions, 108
organizational design, 138–141
programmed decision, 107–108
types of, 107–108

Decision criteria. Criteria that define what is relevant in making a decision. **100, 101–102, 102f**

Decision making
analytic style, 111–110
behavioural style, 111
biases, 113–115, 114f
bounded rationality, 106
codes of ethics, and decision rules, 117–118
conceptual style, 111
conditions, 109–110
directive style, 110
errors, 113–115, 114f
and ethics, 115–118, 118f
group decision making, 111–113
group vs. individual, 113, 113f

intuitive decision making, 106–107, 107f
in the management functions, 105f
nonprogrammed decisions, 108
policy, 108
procedure, 108
programmed decision, 107–108
rational decision making, 105
rule, 108
structured problems, 107–108
styles of, 110–111, 111f
types of problems and decisions, 107–108
unstructured problems, 108
and workforce diversity, 125

Decision-making conditions
certainty, 109
risk, 109
uncertainty, 110

Decision-making process. A set of eight steps that includes identifying a problem, selecting an alternative, and evaluating the decision's effectiveness. **100**
allocation of weights to criteria, 101–102, 102f
analysis of alternatives, 102–103, 103f, 104f
decision criteria, identification of, 100
development of alternatives, 102
evaluation of decision effectiveness, 104
illustration of, 101f
implementation of alternative, 103–104
problem, identification of, 100
selection of alternative, 103

Decision-making styles, 110–111, 111f

Decisional roles. Management roles that revolve around making choices. **8**

Decoding. A receiver's translation of a sender's message. **160**

Decruitment. Techniques for reducing the organization's workforce. **191**, 192, 193f

Defensive approach. Managers rely only on legally established rules to take the minimal position toward corporate social responsibility. **16**

Defensiveness, 166

Delegating style, 230

Delegation. The assignment of authority to another person to carry out specific duties, allowing the employee to make some of the decisions. **134, 153–154**

Deliberate structure, 11

Democratic style. A leadership style where the leader tends to involve employees in decision making, delegate authority, encourage participation in deciding work methods and goals, and use feedback as an opportunity for coaching employees. **224**

Demographic conditions, 44

Departmentalization. The basis on which jobs are grouped together. **131–133, 132f**

Diagnostic skills, 97, 123–124, 153, 182, 216

Diagonal communication. Communication that cuts across both work areas and organizational levels. **170**

Differentiation strategy. A business-level strategy in which a company seeks to offer unique products that are widely valued by customers. **86–88**

Directional plans. Plans that are flexible and that set out general guidelines. **74**, 75f

Directive leader, 232

Directive style. A decision-making style characterized by a rational way of thinking and a low tolerance for ambiguity. **110**

Discipline. Actions taken by a manager to enforce an organization's standards and regulations. **204**

Distinct purpose, 10

Diversification, 83

Diversity. See workforce diversity

Divisional structure. An organizational structure that consists of separate business units or divisions. **142**

Downsizing. The planned elimination of jobs in an organization. **210**

Downward communication. Communication that flows downward from managers to employees. **169**–170

Driving forces, 347

Dynamic environment, 52, 76

Dysfunctional conflicts. Conflicts that are destructive and prevent a group from achieving its goals. **293**–**294**

E

Economic changes, 344

Economic conditions, 42, 189

Economic environment, 46

Economic performance, and corporate social responsibility, 17

Economic value added (EVA). A financial tool that measures corporate and divisional performance, calculated by taking after-tax operating profit minus the total annual cost of capital. **323**–324

Effective teams, 290–292, 291f, 302

Effectiveness. Completing activities so that organizational goals are achieved; referred to as "doing the right things." **6**

Efficiency. Getting the most output from the least amount of inputs; referred to as "doing things right." **6**

Electronic data interchange (EDI). A way for organizations to exchange standard business transaction documents using direct computer-to-computer networks. **174**

Email, 173, 337

Emotional expression, 159

Emotions
as communication barriers, 165
constraining, 168

Employee benefits, 204, 205f, 209, 216

Employee counselling. A process designed to help employees overcome performance-related problems. **204**, 358

Employee empowerment. Giving employees responsibility for what they do. **137**

Employee motivation. See motivation

Employee recognition programs. Reward programs that provide managers with opportunities to give employees personal attention

gender differences, understanding, 242–243

initiating structure, 225

laissez-faire-style style, 224

moral leadership, 240

online leadership, 240–242

participating style, 230

power, management of, 238

selling style, 229

seven traits associated with, 223, 223f

team leadership, 235–237, 236f, 292

telling style, 229

transformational-transactional leadership, 233

trust, development of, 239

visionary leadership, 235

vs. managership, 222, 222f

Leadership theories

behavioural theories, 224, 225f

contingency theories, 226–233

early theories, 222–226

Fiedler contingency model, 227–229, 228f

leader participation model, 231

managerial grid, 226, 227f

Ohio State studies, 225–226

path-goal theory, 232–233, 232f

Situational Leadership, 229–231, 230f

trait theories, 223

University of Iowa studies, 224–225

University of Michigan studies, 226

Leading. A management function that involves motivating subordinates, directing the work of individuals or teams, selecting the most effective communication channels, and resolving employee conflicts. **7**

Learning organization. An organization that has developed the capacity to continuously learn, adapt, and change. **147**–148, 147f

Least-preferred co-worker (LPC) questionnaire. A questionnaire that measures whether a leader is task oriented or relationship oriented. **228**

Legal-political conditions, 42–43

Legal-political environment, 46

Legitimate power. The power a leader has as a result of his or her position in the organization. **238**

Licensing. An approach to going global in which a manufacturer gives another organization the right to use its brand name, technology, or product specifications. **50**

Line authority, 134

Long-term orientation, 47

Long-term plans. Plans with a time frame beyond three years. **74**

Loyalty, 239

M

Maintenance roles. Roles performed by group members to maintain good relations within the group. **289**

Management. Coordinating work activities so that they are completed efficiently and effectively with and through other people. **6**

see also manager

career suggestions, 207

global management challenges, 55–56

omnipotent view of management, 38

and reality of work, 20

and self-employment, 20

skills, 8–10, 10f

strategic management. See strategic management

study of, 18–20

symbolic view of management, 38

universality of management, 19, 19f

vs. leadership, 222, 222f

Management by objectives (MBO). An approach to goal setting in which specific measurable goals are jointly set by managers and employees, progress on goals is periodically reviewed, and rewards are allocated on the basis of this progress. **71**, 71f, 203

Management by walking around. A term used to describe a manager being out in the work area, interacting directly with employees. **321**

Management challenges

corporate social responsibility, 14–17

ethics, 13–14

globalization, 18

workforce diversity, 17–18

Management functions. Planning, organizing, leading, controlling. **7**

controlling, 8

decision making in, 105f

described, 7f

leading, 7

organizing, 7

planning, 7

vs. management roles, 8

Management information system (MIS). A system used to provide management with needed information on a regular basis. **325**

Management roles. Specific categories of managerial behaviour. **8**

decisional roles, 8

described, 9

informational roles, 8

interpersonal roles, 8

vs. management functions, 8

Management science, 30–31

Management theories

contingency approach, 34–35, 35f

development of major theories, 28f

emphases of major theories, 35f

general administrative theory, 29–30

history of, 27–35

organizational behaviour, 32–33

quantitative approach, 30–31

scientific management, 28–29

summary of, 35

systems approach, 33–34, 34f

Manager. Someone who works with and through other people by coordinating their work activities in order to accomplish organizational goals. **4**

see also management

challenges. See management challenges

as change agent, 345–346

control, amount of, 38

as decision maker, 105f

effectiveness, 6

efficiency, 6

external environment, effect of, 51–56

first-line managers, 4

line managers, 134

middle managers, 4–5

organizational culture, effect of, 314, 314f

parameters of managerial discretion, 39f

staff managers, 134

top managers, 5

types of, 4–5

women as managers, 242–243, 243f

Managerial action, 318–319

Managerial discretion, 39f

Managerial grid. A two-dimensional view of leadership style that is based on concern for people vs. concern for production. **226**, 227f

Managerial levels, 5f

Market control. An approach to control that emphasizes the use of external market mechanisms, such as price competition and relative market share, to establish the standards used in the control system. **309**

Market economy. An economic system in which resources are primarily owned and controlled by the private sector. **46**

Market value added (MVA). A financial tool that measures the stock market's estimate of the value of a firm's past and expected capital investment projects. **324**

Marketing boards, 42

Marketplace, 344

Masculinity, 47

Maslow's hierarchy of needs theory, 255–255f

Mass production. The production of items in large batches. **140**

Material symbols, 313

Matrix structure. An organizational structure that assigns specialists from different functional departments to work on one or more projects. **142**–144

McClelland's theory of needs, 258

McGregor's Theory X and Theory Y, 256

Mechanistic organizations. An organizational design that is rigid and tightly controlled. **138**–139, 138f

Mentoring, 25–26

Merger. When two companies of relatively similar size combine resources to form a new company. **83**

Message. A purpose to be conveyed. **160**, 161

Middle managers. Managers between the first-line level and the top level of the organization who manage the work of first-line managers. **5**

Minimum-wage employees, 267–268

Mission. The purpose of an organization. **72**

components of mission statement, 78f

identification of, 78–79

Modular organization. A manufacturing organization that uses outside suppliers to provide product components or modules that are then assembled into final products. **147**

Money, 268–269, 273

Moral leadership, 240

Motivation. An individual's willingness to exert high levels of effort to reach organizational goals, conditioned by the degree to which that effort satisfies some individual need. **254**
- and communication, 159
- cultural diversity, 266–267
- current issues in, 265–272
- diverse workforce, 265–268
- effective rewards programs, 268–271
- extrinsic motivation, 256
- intrinsic motivation, 256
- maximization of employee effort, 279–280
- minimum-wage employees, 267–268
- process, 222f
- professional employees, 268
- suggestions, 272–273
- technical employees, 268
- theories. See motivation theories
- work-life balance, 271–272

Motivation-hygiene theory. Herzberg's theory that intrinsic factors are related to job satisfaction and motivation, whereas extrinsic factors are related to job dissatisfaction. **256**–257, 257f

Motivation theories
- contemporary theories, 258–265
- early theories, 254–258
- equity theory, 262–263, 262f
- expectancy theory, 263–264, 264f
- hierarchy of needs theory, 255–255f
- job characteristics model (JCM), 259–261, 260f
- motivation-hygiene theory, 256–257, 257f
- reinforcement theory, 259
- theory of needs, 258
- Theory X, 256
- Theory Y, 256

Motivators. Factors that increase job satisfaction and motivation. **257**

Multinational corporations (MNCs). A company that maintains significant operations in multiple countries but manages them from a base in the home country. **49**

Multiperson comparisons. A performance appraisal method by which one individual's performance is compared with that of others. **203**

N

National culture. The values and attitudes shared by individuals from a specific country that shape their behaviour and beliefs about what is important. **47**
- collectivism, 47
- as communication barrier, 166
- and control, 328
- femininity, 47
- individualism, 47
- long-term vs. short-term orientation, 47
- masculinity, 47
- and motivation, 266–267

- power distance, 47
- uncertainty avoidance, 47
- values, 47, 48f

Need. An internal state that makes certain outcomes appear attractive. **222**
- esteem needs, 255
- physiological needs, 255
- safety needs, 255
- self-actualization needs, 255
- social needs, 255

Need for achievement (nAch). The drive to excel, to achieve in relation to a set of standards, and to strive to succeed. **258**

Need for affiliation (nAff). The desire for friendly and close interpersonal relationships. **258**

Need for power (nPow). The need to make others behave in a way that they would not have behaved otherwise. **258**

Negotiating skills, 292

Network organization. A small core organization that outsources major business functions. **146**

Networked computer systems, 173–174

New entrants, 85

Noise. Disturbances that interfere with the transmission, receipt, or feedback of a message. **160**

Nonprofit sector. The part of the economy that is run by organizations which operate for purposes other than making a profit (that is, providing charity or services). **12**

Nonprogrammed decisions. Decisions that are unique and nonrecurring and require custom-made solutions. **108**

Nonverbal communication. Communication transmitted without words. **164**

Nonverbal cues, 168

Norming. The third stage of team development, which is characterized by close relationships and cohesiveness. **287**

North American Free Trade Agreement (NAFTA). An agreement among the Canadian, American, and Mexican governments in which barriers to free trade were reduced. **45**

O

Obstructionist approach. The avoidance of corporate social responsibility; managers engage in unethical and illegal behaviour that they try to hide from organizational stakeholders and society. **16**

Occupational health and safety legislation, 189

Offensive email in the workplace, 337

Ohio State studies (leadership), 225–226

Omnipotent view of management. The view that managers are directly responsible for an organization's success or failure. **38**

Online leadership
- communication, 241
- performance management, 241
- trust, 242

Openness, 239

Operational plans. Plans that specify the details of how the overall goals are to be achieved. **73**

Operations research, 30–31

Opportunities. Positive trends in external environmental factors. **79**–80, 80f

Organic organization. An organizational design that is highly adaptive and flexible. 138f, **138**–139

Organization. A deliberate arrangement of people who act together to accomplish some specific purpose. **10**
- boundaryless organization, 145–147
- changing organization, 11, 12f
- characteristics of, 10–11, 11f
- Crown corporations, 12
- global organizations, 49
- information technology, effect of, 175–176
- material symbols, 313
- modular organization, 147
- network organization, 146–147
- nonprofit sector, 12
- private sector, 12
- privately held organizations, 12
- public sector, 12
- publicly held, 12
- rituals, 313
- size of organizations, 11
- stories, 313
- types of organizations, 12–13
- virtual organization, 146

Organizational behaviour, 32–33

Organizational change. Any alterations in people, structure, or technology. **344**
- calm waters metaphor, 346–347, 346f
- change-capable organizations, 353f
- change management. See change management
- change process, views of, 346–348
- degree of, 52
- and environmental uncertainty, 52
- external forces, 344
- internal forces, 344–345
- organizational structure, change in, 349–350
- successful change, 350–352
- technology, change in, 350–351
- types of change, 348–350, 349f
- white-water rapids metaphor, 347

Organizational communication. All the patterns, networks, and systems of communication within an organization. **158**
- communication networks, 170–172, 171f
- diagonal communication, 170
- direction of communication flow, 169–170
- downward communication, 169–170
- formal vs. informal communication, 169
- lateral communication, 170
- upward communication, 169–170

Organizational culture. A system of shared meaning and beliefs held by organizational members that determines, in large degree, how employees act. **311**
- change in, 355–356
- development of, 312–313
- dimensions of, 311f, 311–312
- establishment of, 312f
- ethical culture, 313
- implications of definition, 311
- and language, 314

NAME AND ORGANIZATION INDEX

Note: Page references in bold refer to pages on which weblinks appear.

LIST OF CANADIAN COMPANIES, BY PROVINCE

LIST OF INTERNATIONAL COMPANIES, BY COUNTRY

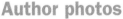

PHOTO CREDITS

Author photos
Page TBC, courtesy of Stephen P. Robbins (top); courtesy of Mary Coulter (centre); courtesy of Gary Schwartz (bottom).

Chapter 1
Page 3, Andrew Stawicki/CP Photo Archive; page 5, Michael Quan/The New York Times; page 14, Tom Mihalek/EPA/Landov; page 15, Photo: Heather Taweel; page 18, AP/Wide World Photos.

Supplement 1
Page 27, PhotoDisc.

Chapter 2
Page 37, Courtesy of Dr. J.A.B. Beairsto; page 38, Don Healy/Leader Post; page 43, Yvonne Berg; page 47, Bloomberg News; page 51, Munshi Ahmed Photography; page 54, Reforma-ENRED/Newscom.

Chapter 3
Page 67, AP/Wide World Photos; page 69, Meredith Heuer, J Group Photo; page 70, Don Hogan Charles/The New York Times; page 74, Peter Battistoni/The Vancouver Sun; page 76, Blake Little Photography; page 80, Reprinted with permission from The Globe and Mail; page 83, Jim Ross; page 85, Photo by Colin O'Connor; page 88, Glenn Lowson.

Chapter 4
Page 99, Courtesy of Canaccord; page 102, Thor Swift Photography; page 108, Gerard Burkhart/The New York Times; page 109, Beige Jones/Ripple Resort Media; page 112, © 2002 Brian Smith.

Chapter 5
Page 129, J.P. Moczulski/CP Photo Archive; page 131, Michuel Mendez Photography; page 136, Xerox Canada Limited; page 139, AP/Wide World Photos; page 144, Acxiom Corporation; page 146, Reuters/Shannon Stapleton/Corbis.

Chapter 6
Page 157, Nancy Langton; page 159, Frederic Jorez/Getty Images; page 161, Jenny Schulder; page 165, Ann States; page 170, David Deal; page 175, Kim Christensen Photography.

Chapter 7
Page 187, Marianne Helm/CP Photo Archive; page 193, Dick Loek/Toronto Star; page 199, Lucas Oleniuk/The Toronto Star; page 209, Bill Keay/Vancouver Sun; page 210, Dauphin Friendship Centre.

Chapter 8
Page 221, Dave Olecko/Bloomberg News/Landov; page 224, Mike Aporius/CP Photo Archive; page 231, Mark Van Manen/The Vancouver Sun; page 236, Jim Young/CP Photo Archive; page 241, Randall Scott.

Chapter 9
Page 253, Andy Shaw/Bloomberg News/Landov; page 260, Burkhart Schittney; page 266, © John Garrett/Corbis; page 267, Ian Lindsay/Vancouver Sun; page 269, Nichols Food Ltd.; page 273, Joel Page/The New York Times.

Chapter 10
Page 283, Paul Chiasson/CP Photo Archive; page 285, AP/Wide World Photos; page 287, courtesy of Toyo Inc.

Chapter 11
Page 307, Adrian Wyld/CP Photo Archive; page 313, Chiaki Tsukumo/AP; page 319, Reuters/Win McNamee/Landov; page 325, DST Output; page 326, SYSCO Corporation.

Chapter 12
Page 343, Jeff Christensen/Reuters/Landov; page 351, © 2002 Robert Houser (roberthouser.com); page 355, Ryan Remiorz/CP Photo Archive.

"AS IS" LICENSE AGREEMENT AND LIMITED WARRANTY

READ THIS LICENSE CAREFULLY BEFORE OPENING THIS PACKAGE. BY OPENING THIS PACKAGE, YOU ARE AGREEING TO THE TERMS AND CONDITIONS OF THIS LICENSE. IF YOU DO NOT AGREE, DO NOT OPEN THE PACKAGE. PROMPTLY RETURN THE UNOPENED PACKAGE AND ALL ACCOMPANYING ITEMS TO THE PLACE YOU OBTAINED THEM. *THESE TERMS APPLY TO ALL LICENSED SOFTWARE ON THE DISK EXCEPT THAT THE TERMS FOR USE OF ANY SHAREWARE OR FREEWARE ON THE DISKETTES ARE AS SET FORTH IN THE ELECTRONIC LICENSE LOCATED ON THE DISK:*

1. **GRANT OF LICENSE and OWNERSHIP:** The enclosed computer programs and any data ("Software") are licensed, not sold, to you by Pearson Canada Inc. ("We" or the "Company") in consideration of your adoption of the accompanying Company textbooks and/or other materials, and your agreement to these terms. You own only the disk(s) but we and/or our licensors own the Software itself. This license allows instructors and students enrolled in the course using the Company textbook that accompanies this Software (the "Course") to use and display the enclosed copy of the Software for academic use only, so long as you comply with the terms of this Agreement. You may make one copy for back up only. We reserve any rights not granted to you.

2. **USE RESTRICTIONS:** You may not sell or license copies of the Software or the Documentation to others. You may not transfer, distribute or make available the Software or the Documentation, except to instructors and students in your school who are users of the adopted Company textbook that accompanies this Software in connection with the course for which the textbook was adopted. You may not reverse engineer, disassemble, decompile, modify, adapt, translate or create derivative works based on the Software or the Documentation. You may be held legally responsible for any copying or copyright infringement that is caused by your failure to abide by the terms of these restrictions.

3. **TERMINATION:** This license is effective until terminated. This license will terminate automatically without notice from the Company if you fail to comply with any provisions or limitations of this license. Upon termination, you shall destroy the Documentation and all copies of the Software. All provisions of this Agreement as to limitation and disclaimer of warranties, limitation of liability, remedies or damages, and our ownership rights shall survive termination.

4. **DISCLAIMER OF WARRANTY: THE COMPANY AND ITS LICENSORS MAKE NO WARRANTIES ABOUT THE SOFTWARE, WHICH IS PROVIDED "AS-IS." IF THE DISK IS DEFECTIVE IN MATERIALS OR WORKMANSHIP, YOUR ONLY REMEDY IS TO RETURN IT TO THE COMPANY WITHIN 30 DAYS FOR REPLACEMENT UNLESS THE COMPANY DETERMINES IN GOOD FAITH THAT THE DISK HAS BEEN MISUSED OR IMPROPERLY INSTALLED, REPAIRED, ALTERED OR DAMAGED. THE COMPANY DISCLAIMS ALL WARRANTIES, EXPRESS OR IMPLIED, INCLUDING WITHOUT LIMITATION, THE IMPLIED WARRANTIES OF MERCHANTABILITY AND FITNESS FOR A PARTICULAR PURPOSE. THE COMPANY DOES NOT WARRANT, GUARANTEE OR MAKE ANY REPRESENTATION REGARDING THE ACCURACY, RELIABILITY, CURRENTNESS, USE, OR RESULTS OF USE, OF THE SOFTWARE.**

5. **LIMITATION OF REMEDIES AND DAMAGES: IN NO EVENT, SHALL THE COMPANY OR ITS EMPLOYEES, AGENTS, LICENSORS OR CONTRACTORS BE LIABLE FOR ANY INCIDENTAL, INDIRECT, SPECIAL OR CONSEQUENTIAL DAMAGES ARISING OUT OF OR IN CONNECTION WITH THIS LICENSE OR THE SOFTWARE, INCLUDING, WITHOUT LIMITATION, LOSS OF USE, LOSS OF DATA, LOSS OF INCOME OR PROFIT, OR OTHER LOSSES SUSTAINED AS A RESULT OF INJURY TO ANY PERSON, OR LOSS OF OR DAMAGE TO PROPERTY, OR CLAIMS OF THIRD PARTIES, EVEN IF THE COMPANY OR AN AUTHORIZED REPRESENTATIVE OF THE COMPANY HAS BEEN ADVISED OF THE POSSIBILITY OF SUCH DAMAGES.** SOME JURISDICTIONS DO NOT ALLOW THE LIMITATION OF DAMAGES IN CERTAIN CIRCUMSTANCES, SO THE ABOVE LIMITATIONS MAY NOT ALWAYS APPLY.

6. **GENERAL:** THIS AGREEMENT SHALL BE CONSTRUED AND INTERPRETED ACCORDING TO THE LAWS OF THE PROVINCE OF ONTARIO. This Agreement is the complete and exclusive statement of the agreement between you and the Company and supersedes all proposals, prior agreements, oral or written, and any other communications between you and the company or any of its representatives relating to the subject matter.

Should you have any questions concerning this agreement or if you wish to contact the Company for any reason, please contact in writing: Permissions, Pearson Education Canada, a division of Pearson Canada Inc., 26 Prince Andrew Place, Toronto, Ontario M3C 2T8.